C0-BKJ-342

This book is for the memory
of M. Aldrich and Major Richard Collum,
who first reported the deeds

For Abbot, Boyd, Gibbons, Scanlon,
John Thomason
and the Publicity Bureau.
Their writing made the deeds a legend.

For Fegan, McClellan, Metcalf and Webb
who kept the legend alive

And for Hersey, Sherrod, Tregaskis,
Denig, the Combat Correspondents
and the Historical Branch.
They made the legend flourish.

For Robert Heinl and Robert Leckie
who told it like it was about Marines,
always

And for all the others who tried.

CREATING A LEGEND

The Complete Record of Writing about the United States Marine Corps

. . . by Capt. John B. Moran, USMCR (Ret.)

Publishing Division
Moran / Andrews, Inc.
Chicago

International Standard Book Number:
0-912286-00-8

Library of Congress Catalog Card Number:
79-139570

Published by Moran/Andrews, Inc.
535 North Michigan Avenue
Chicago, Illinois 60611

Printed in the United States of America

First edition 1973

Designed by Barbara Callaway

FOREWORD

It has been said, often by rival services, that every Marine goes into combat with a correspondent on one side and a photographer on the other. Although the Marine Corps has repeatedly denied this allegation, evidence persists that more has been written about the Corps than any other military force in history. The attraction of the Corps' tradition, valor and glory to writers may be accountable for this phenomenon.

But, the histories of the Corps' accomplishments form only a small segment of the voluminous printed matter about Marines. The men who made the Corps, the weapons it used, the places it served, its peacetime mission, its role in aviation and the development of the Amphibious Doctrine, followed by the latest technique of Vertical Assault, all have inherited their generous share of recognition in print.

With this wealth of material in existence—some hidden in musty archives, some available in magazine articles or in book form—it was inevitable that someone would, one day, attempt to bibliograph the vast chronicles of the Corps. Painstaking, time-consuming, sometimes frustrating, the task has been accomplished; this remarkable volume is the result.

It is fortunate that the author is neither a professional bibliographer or a career Marine. He is an advertising man who is a former Marine officer. *Creating A Legend* is written in the clear, succinct style of consumer advertising rather than the musty, obscure style of most bibliographies.

Perhaps even more important, the book is subject-indexed. You don't have to be a serious student of Marine Corps history, or a librarian, to find what you are looking for fast. Instead of listing the entries in order by the mindless coincidence of the spelling of the author's last name, entries in *Creating A Legend* are listed by content.

The need for this book, too long unfulfilled, will be immediately recognized by historians and scholars, but Marines, both enlisted and officer, will find it an invaluable reference aid while pursuing their particular fields in the Corps.

Reservists, too, will find their separate category interesting. Articles on Reserve units listed contain the location of the unit and the type of duty—Infantry, Communications, Supply, Engineer, Motor Transport, Artillery and all the others. Combined Reserve maneuvers are also included.

Nor have the Women Marines been overlooked; from the button-shoed, long-skirted Marinettes of World War I to the smartly uniformed Lady Marines of today, their history and valuable service can be found in the articles and books listed here.

Historic accounts, from the authorization of the Continental Marines, through the Tripoli affair, the Civil War, the Banana Wars, World Wars I and II, Korea and Vietnam, are listed by title with brief but complete annotations on each.

The growth of aviation in the Corps, from the "Noisy Nan," the first Marine plane piloted not too successfully by Alfred Cunningham, the Corps' first aviator, to the vertical takeoff Harrier first flown by Marines in 1971, can be thoroughly researched from the works covered in this book.

Articles on weapons, from the old Gatling gun to the modern M-60 machine gun, and from the cannon aboard Old Ironsides to the 175mm self-propelled "Big Mama" used to discourage the North Vietnamese, are to be found under their individual categories.

For the Marine who is probing for material on any one of the Corps' old stamping grounds, there are lists with notes on Samar, Nicaragua, Tripoli, Corregidor, Chosin Reservoir, the Yalu, Khe Sanh, Chu Lai and Da Nang, and every other hot spot where the Corps has served. The posts and stations where Marines provide security and train, both Stateside and abroad, are also listed with complete information on the type of duty and the location.

The fighting men of the Corps and those who directed its destinies occupy their deserved places in this work. The names of Presley O'Bannon, Archie Henderson, Chesty Puller, Lou Diamond, Dan Daly, "Manila John" Basilone, "Old Gimlet Eye" Smedley Butler and the many others whose illustrious careers in the Corps left indelible brands on its history are listed, along with where to find the volumes of biographical material written about them.

All writing about Marines—books, articles from general and military magazines, plays, poems, short stories, youth books; even movies, is included. In-print books are so indicated as are paperback editions. You are given specific instructions on how to obtain out-of-print books about Marines so that you can build your own Marine Corps Library. Information on obtaining any of the more than 7,000 magazine articles is included, and a complete author's index permits you to find all the writing of a favorite Marine author.

Here, then, is the masterkey to the history, the weapons, the aviation, the wars, the places and the men who have given the United States Marine Corps its luster, fame and glory. If you're interested in writing about Marines, this book will chart your way to where it is hidden. And tell you how to get it.

Karl A. Schuon

Quantico,
June, 1973

CONTENTS

INTRODUCTION: HOW TO BUILD YOUR OWN MARINE CORPS LIBRARY

All of the information you'll need to build your personal Marine Corps library is included in this book. You can work at your own pace, set your own budget, and enjoy the results of your work for the rest of your life. And you won't even have to leave home to get the job done!

These step-by-step instructions assume that you know as much about "Want Lists," "Book Finders" and "Out-Of-Print Titles" as the author did three years ago . . .

"What the hell do those things mean?"

The first thing a Marine does before setting forth is . . . "Determine the objective." It can be to collect every book ever written about Marines and the Corps, or it can be less ambitious. Perhaps you'll want to get underway by limiting your selections to Marine books about Korea, or World War 2, or Vietnam.

If you decide on World War 2, for example, turn to Part 3 of this book and make a list of the book titles that interest you. Books are listed in boldface type and they're all there—every book ever written about Marines in World War 2. Paperbacks, if published, are indicated in the right hand column below the publisher of the regular hard cover edition. You may want to collect paperbacks until you can replace them with the more scarce and more expensive hard cover editions.

WANT LIST

The list you are making is called a "Want List." It is your key to obtaining the out-of-print books you'll want later, so do it properly now.

On an 8½" x 11" sheet of paper, type or write (or have someone with good handwriting write) this heading, followed by your address and list:

SEND ASKING PRICE AND CONDITION OF THESE BOOKS

TO:	John B. Moran 535 North Michigan Avenue Chicago, Illinois 60611
ASPREY, R.	Semper Fidelis: The U.S. Marines in World War 2
CRUMP, I.	Our Marines
FOSTER, J.	Hell in the Heavens
HERBER, W.	Tomorrow To Live
HEINL, R.	Marines At Midway

It is not necessary to include the publisher's name, date published, or a description of the book, but set up your list so that the author's last name is first and the entries are in alphabetical order by author. Include any special conditions under which you will do business on the first page under the heading. These might include, "Do not quote paperbacks," or "Indicate availability of dust jacket with response."

If you can't tell whether or not you want the book from the annotation (brief description), see if your library has the book. Chances are, it won't. Marine books disappear from libraries fast. But, it's worth a try.

OBTAINING IN-PRINT BOOKS

Your first target should be to obtain in-print books on your list. They are indicated by (IP) after the date. These books were in-print in January of 1973. Books remain in-print for only a short time—usually less than one year—so don't be disappointed if they are no longer in-print. Paperbacks disappear even faster, and when a book goes out-of-print, it's usually forever.

If you want an in-print title from Headquarters, Marine Corps, (designated HQMC), write:

Historical Branch,
U.S. Marine Corps
Headquarters, U.S. Marine Corps
Washington, D.C. 20380

You can order only three titles at a time, and it is a good idea to include a reason why you want the publication with your request. It can be as simple as, "I collect Marine Corps books."

For in-print titles from the U.S. Naval Institute, write:

United States Naval Institute
Annapolis, Maryland 21402

For titles from the United States Government Printing Office (USGPO) write:

Superintendent of Documents
Government Printing Office
Washington, D.C. 20402

Be sure to include the order number and a check for the exact amount (included in the annotation), and allow eight weeks for delivery.

The best way to obtain other in-print titles is from the Marine Corps Gazette's Bookservice. This includes any in-print title: not just the ones featured in the *Professional Bookshop* column of the magazine. Write Box 1775, Quantico, Virginia 22134. If you enclose a check with your order, you'll save the shipping and handling charge. In addition, you receive a 10 percent discount if you are a member of the Marine Corps Association (a subscriber to the Gazette). Remember, this service is for in-print titles only.

If you want to save more than 10 percent on in-print books, other companies offer larger discounts:

NATIONAL BOOK SERVICE
328 Pennsylvania Avenue, S.E.
Washington, D.C. 20003
15 percent discount

NEW YORK BOOK AND RECORD CLUB
4 West 43rd Street
New York, N.Y. 10036
20-25 percent discount

There are many companies like these which provide in-print books by mail at a discount. Frequently, they advertise in the Sunday newspaper in major metropolitan cities. With all such companies, beware of the shipping charges. Sometimes they more than cancel out the advertised savings. And if something goes wrong, it will take forever for them to straighten it out.

Another obvious source of in-print titles is a bookstore. Any in-print book you want will be ordered for you if the store doesn't stock it.

In addition to bookstores, you can order directly from the publisher. You will find publishers' addresses at your library in a book called *Writer's Market, 1973.* Or, you can call information in the publisher's city and get his address with the phone number. Call the local area code, then 555-1212. There is no charge for this call, but you may or may not get the address. It depends on the mood of the long distance operator when you have the encounter with her. Most publishers are in New York; Area Code 212, or Chicago, 312.

To keep up to date on new titles as they are announced, read *Leatherneck* and the *Marine Corps Gazette.* You can also check the *Books-In-Print Catalog* at your local library or bookstore. Get the catalog that's subject-indexed and look under "Marines, United States."

An even easier way to keep up-to-date is to get on the mailing list of bookstores which specialize in military books. The two best ones are:

THE BEACHCOMBER BOOKSHOP
Route 1
Blaine, Washington 98230

THE SOLDIER SHOP
1013 Madison Avenue
New York, N.Y. 10021

Write, and get on the mailing list. Their catalogs are very interesting. As an additional benefit, you might find that they stock some of the Marine books you want.

OUT-OF-PRINT BOOKS

Most of the Marine books you'll want for your library will be out-of-print. Obtaining them involves executing a more complicated plan, but the satisfaction of owning these scarce books makes it worth the effort. There are five ways to obtain out-of-print books. You can use any combination of them simultaneously. They are:

1. Companies which sell used books by mail
2. Used bookstores
3. Used book sales
4. Book finders
5. Advertising for out-of-print books

USED BOOKS BY MAIL

Companies in this business send you lists of titles periodically. These lists can be professionally printed, or handwritten on cheap paper. You have to scan the lists to find the books you want, and you have to act fast when you find them. Frequently, the titles you want are gone by the time your order arrives.

The advantage of using these companies is economy. You have to do the work of scanning the lists and it's a tedious job. They are always arranged by author rather than subject. For your persistence, however, you are able to "steal" Marine books at prices so low you'll think the seller made a mistake.

Here are some of these companies:

ANTHEIL BOOKSELLERS
2177 Isabelle Court
No. Bellmore, N.Y. 11710

CONRADS BOOKS
Box 338
Farmington, Michigan 48024

EDITIONS
Boiceville, N.Y. 12412

HARCO
Box 52
Carmel, Indiana 46032

MARBORO BOOKS
205 Moonachie Road
Moonachie, N.J. 07074

NEW ENGLANDIA
Box 787
North Adams, Mass. 01247

WILLIAM H. POWERS
R.F.D. 3
Export, Pa. 15632

STRAND BOOK STORE
828 Broadway
New York, N.Y. 10003

TARTAN BOOK SALES
P.O. Box 914
Williamsport, Pa. 17701

Write and ask to be added to the mailing list. When the first list comes, you're bound to find something you want. As your library grows, the chances diminish because the books you need get more scarce.

USED BOOKSTORES

If you are in an area which has used bookstores, try them. But, don't expect too much. Every city has some, but you may not be aware of their existence because usually they are located in the low rent district. Call first, because the odds on them having the particular Marine book you want from the millions of titles available are remote. If it sounds as though it's worth a trip, pay a visit. Dress in old clothes. Your appearance will help your bargaining position, and you'll save on a cleaning bill. Most of these stores are offshoots of junk dealers. That's what the stores are like. Used book stores do business on a Persian Bazaar basis. That means that the marked price or first verbal price isn't necessarily the price you have to pay. If you are a good bargainer, you can walk out with some real values.

SALES OF USED BOOKS

Every library has a sale of used books from time to time. Chances of Marine books being included are small, but it may be worth a try. In some cities, organizations raise funds by collecting used books from their members and selling them at an Auction or a Fair. In the Chicago area, for example, the Brandeis Book Fair is an Annual Event looked forward to by book collectors from all over the country. Values are unbelievable. Marine books that sell for $10.00 and $15.00 through other channels go for 50¢, but you have to get there early and have very sharp elbows. It's a real bargain basement hassle. Bring your wife and children, and brief them properly in advance. The more elbows on your side, the better.

BOOK FINDERS

The easiest but most expensive way to obtain out-of-print Marine books is from Book Finders. These companies have book scouts all over the country who look for particular books wanted by customers. All you have to do is send a copy of your Want List.

They will notify you when they have found a book on the list, and tell you how much it is and in what condition. You do not have to buy the book when they notify you that it is available. Pass it, if you think it's too expensive. Once you say "yes," however, you'll have a difficult time getting your money back since the Book Finder must pay the scout whether he sells the book or not.

The best Book Finder for Marine books is:

INTERNATIONAL BOOK FINDERS
P.O. Box 3003
Olympic Station
Beverly Hills, California 90212

Three others worth trying are:

AEROPHILIA
29A Grove Street
Boston, Mass. 02114

BOOKPORT WORLDWIDE SEARCH
1464 Neptune
Leucadia, California 92024

BOOKS-ON-FILE
Union City, New Jersey 07087

Remember, this is the luxury way to build your library. You have to pay accordingly. Unless money is no object, use Book Finders only when you have exhausted the other methods of obtaining out-of-print Marine books.

BACK ISSUE MAGAZINES

Getting the old magazine articles you want is more difficult, but it can be done in two ways:

1. Obtaining copies from the publisher or from a library
2. Purchasing copies of the magazine from used magazine dealers.

Most publishers maintain files of back issues. Some will make copies of the articles you want for a small charge; some will not. You'll just have to try your luck. Big city libraries may have the back issues of the magazines you want, and there are always self-service copy machines in libraries.

A few reliable dealers for back issues of magazines are:

ABRAHAM'S MAGAZINE SERVICE
56 East 13th Street
New York, New York 10003

P. AND H. BLISS
Middletown, Connecticut 06457

MIDTOWN MAGAZINES, INC.
Box 917
Maywood, New Jersey 07607

ADVERTISING FOR BOOKS

Perhaps the least-used but most efficient way to obtain out-of-print books is to advertise for them in a publication read by out-of-print dealers throughout the country. It is called

BOOKMAN'S WEEKLY
Box 1100
Newark, N.J. 10701

The cost of a full-page advertisement is $40.00. That size ad has room for about 120 authors and titles.

All you have to do is send your Want List and they will bill you. You can estimate the cost of the ad if it's to include fewer or more titles than 120.

A few days after the ad appears, you will begin to receive postcards and letters from dealers all over the world. The prices the books are offered at are low . . . so low that you soon pay for the ad from the money you save per book. Wait at least four weeks after the ad has run to make sure you have received all the responses. Then, select the best offer, and send a check (to eliminate shipping charges) along with your order.

In ten days or less, the book will arrive, wrapped in newspaper or brown wrapping paper, but always in the exact condition described in the response to your ad. Books like the scarce World War 2 Marine Corps Monographs, which sell for $15-$25 each from Book Finders, are sometimes available for $2 or $3 when obtained this way.

Three other publications can be used for your "Books Wanted" advertising. They are:

THE ANTIQUE TRADER
Kewanee, Illinois 61443

COLLECTOR'S NEWS
Box 156
Grundy Center, Iowa 50638

EASTERN ANTIQUITY
1 Dogwood Drive
Washington, N.J. 07882

Prices for display ads in these publications are ridiculously low; around $2.50 per column inch, but they are not as effective as *Bookman's Weekly.* That's because they cover the whole field of collecting rather than just books. For the price, it is worth it to run this ad:

WANTED: U.S. MARINE CORPS BOOKS
Check with order by return mail.
Send title, author, asking price
and condition to:
Your Name
Address
City, State and Zip

The cost of acquiring the author's 350-volume Marine Corps Library was around $800. The average price is so low (less than $2.50 per book) because some of the titles are available free. Acquiring the remaining 115 books on the Want List will cost another $200 or so. This price includes the purchase price of the books as well as postage, advertising, etc.

Marine Corps books are sure to appreciate in value as the demand for the limited supply increases, so the money spent is really an investment. It's an investment that will pay dividends in pleasure for the rest of your life, and be a part of your estate.

If you are a career Marine, the dividends will be more than pleasure.

HOW TO USE THIS BOOK

Creating A Legend is organized by subject rather than by the way the author spells his last name, or some other convenient but mindless device. Subject organized means that you can find what you are looking for without being an expert. Everything written about every Marine Corps subject is in one place.

SELECTION CRITERIA

To be included, a book or article had only to pass this test:

Is it about the United States Marine Corps?

All Marine Corps books are included. All publications of the Historical Branch (HQMC), Marine Corps Schools and the U.S. Government Printing Office are included. All articles from general magazines and United States Naval Institute Proceedings are included. Articles from the two major Marine magazines are included from 1940 through 1972. Before 1940, *Gazette* and *Leatherneck* included information about the comings and goings of Marines, births of offspring, marriages, deaths, etc. They were more like "house organs" than the significant journals of today.

CONTENT AND ORGANIZATION

Reviewing a few details about the content and organization will make it easy for you to use this book efficiently:

1. Subject organized means *totally* subject organized. Even fiction is entered by subject rather than by the author's last name wherever possible, (but it is always clearly identified as fiction).
2. The "Contents" page lists only the ten major Parts. Turn to the page indicated in the Contents Page for a complete description of what is in each Part.
3. Use the "Finder Words" in the margins and the "Running heads" at the top of each page as signposts.
4. Paperback editions of hard cover books are listed separately. If a book is available only in paperback, it is so indicated. Many pamphlets, such as all of the publications of the Historical Branch (HQMC), also have soft covers. These are not indicated.
5. Rank shown for authors is the rank at time of authorship. Service is USMC or USMCR, unless indicated otherwise.
6. When the author's name is missing, the article or book was unsigned (staff written). When other information is missing, such as the date published or the publisher, the information was not available.
7. Publishers are in New York, unless otherwise indicated.
8. (IP) means that the publication was in-print in January of 1973.
9. All books and many articles are annotated (described). If an article is not annotated, it does not necessarily mean that the article is insignificant.
10. There are no Roman numerals in *Creating A Legend.* (Quick now, what does MCMLXXIII mean?*)
11. There are no other Latin words either, such as passim, ibid, op. cit., loc. cit. This book was written for Marines; not scholars (although it is correct and complete from the scholarly point-of-view).

*1973

1. MARINES AND THE CORPS

General Histories of the Corps. Histories of related subjects including Marine Aviation, Bases and Histories of Units. Collections of stories about Notable Marines.

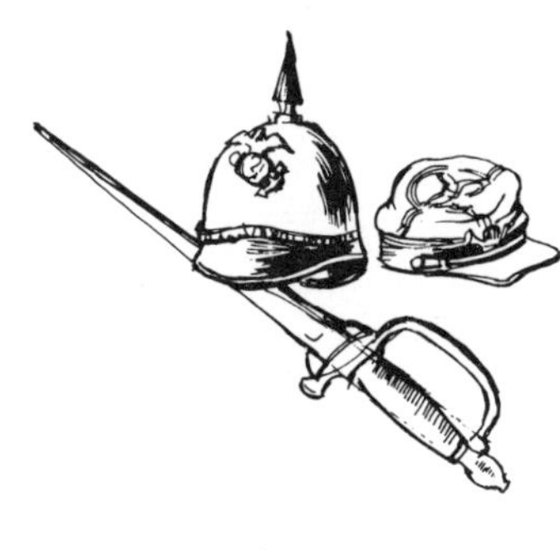

CONTENTS: PART 1

ASSOCIATIONS

FLEET RESERVE ASSN. Marines and sailors welfare comes first with this national 20-year-old association	Cushman, GySgt G. *Leatherneck*	May 63	FRA
THE ASSOCIATION SWORD	*Gazette*	Jan 56	MCA
FOUNDERS AND ORIGINAL MEMBERS OF THE MARINE CORPS ASSOCIATION	*Gazette*	Jun 57	
THE MARINE CORPS ASSOCIATION	*Gazette*	Jun 55	
MARINE CORPS ASSOCIATION NEWS	*Gazette*	Oct 59	
THE MARINE CORPS ASSOCIATION, ITS FORMATION AND OBJECTS	*Gazette*	Mar 60	
IT'S 40 YEARS LATER	*Gazette*	Apr 53	
WHAT IS THE MCA?	Shaw, BGen S. *Gazette*	Jan 59	
THEY GET INVOLVED Marine Corps Father's Association	Evans, GySgt E. *Leatherneck*	Jan 71	MCFA
MARINE CORPS LEAGUE One of its missions is to preserve Corps' traditions	Kester, SSgt C. *Leatherneck*	Aug 63	MCL
THE MARINE CORPS LEAGUE "Once a Marine, Always a Marine" is its motto.	Barnum, MSgt E. *Leatherneck*	Jul 55	
MCROA: A BRIEF HISTORY OF THE MARINE CORPS RESERVE OFFICERS ASSOCIATION	MCROA, Washington	1961	MCROA
EVERGREEN CHAPTER Seattle Chapter of Women Marines' Association is two	Evans, GySgt E. *Leatherneck*	Mar 70	WMA

AVIATION

AN HISTORICAL ANALYSIS OF THE REQUIREMENTS PLACED UPON FIGHTER AVIATION From Nicaragua through Nam	Silver, Capt S. *Gazette*	Feb 72
AVIATION IN THE NAVY Reprint of earlier story by first Marine aviator	Cunningham, Lt A. *Gazette*	May 60
BEYOND DUTY'S CALL List of 14 Marine aviators who won the Medal of Honor between 1918-1944	Spieler, Sgt C. *Gazette*	May 53
BIKE WHEELS TO JETS Pictorial history	Evans, GySgt E. *Leatherneck*	May 70
A BRIEF HISTORY OF MARINE CORPS AVIATION Excellent history that should remain in-print (but doesn't).	Tierney, E., and R. Gill HQMC	1969
THE EVOLUTION OF MARINE AVIATION Concise history by the CO of the 1ST MAW in Korea and later, Asst. Commandant	Megee, Gen V. *Gazette*	Aug-Oct 65
EVOLUTION OF SPEED From Cunningham's "Noisy Nan" to the first pre-Korea jets.	*Gazette*	Jul 48
FROM JENNIES TO JETS	DeChant, J. *Leatherneck*	Nov 53
GOLDEN WINGS: A PICTORIAL HISTORY OF THE UNITED STATES NAVY AND MARINE CORPS IN THE AIR Scarce out-of-print book. Excellent photos	Caiden, M. Random House, Inc.	1960
MARINE AVIATION A not too serious look at the history of Marine aviation	*Leatherneck*	Nov 57
MARINE AVIATION'S OLD CORPS Back to 1912	*Leatherneck*	Nov 54

MARINE AVIATION: ORIGIN AND GROWTH Another excellent history	Boggs, Capt C. *Gazette*	Nov 50, May 56
MARINE AVIATION, A RECORD OF ACHIEVEMENT	*Gazette*	Nov 30
MARINE CORPS AIRCRAFT, 1913-1965 Chronological listing of aircraft assigned to the Corps	HQMC	1967 (IP)
MARINE CORPS AVIATION—CUNNINGHAM TO CHU LAI One of the most up-to-date general histories which includes early Nam activities	Bradshaw, Maj H. *Proceedings*	Nov 66
MARINE CORPS AVIATION: THE EARLY DAYS Cunningham & Company	Sherrod, R. *Gazette*	May, Jun 52
MISSION: HELICOPTERS History from 1947-72	Marks, Capt W. *Gazette*	May 72
PYLON DERBY Historic role of Marines in the Cleveland Air Races of the 30's	Gould, Cpl M. *Leatherneck*	Jul 48
60 YEARS OF MARINE AIR: 1912-1972	Hill, MajGen H. *Gazette*	May 72
THE STORY OF MARINE AVIATION	*Navy*	Jul 65
STRUTS AND GUTS Early Marine pilots and planes	Leahy, M. *Leatherneck*	May 65
A TEXT ON THE EMPLOYMENT OF MARINE CORPS AVIATION	MCS, Quantico	1935
U. S. MARINE CORPS AIRCRAFT, 1914-1959 A pictorial history with brief commentary	Larkins, W. Aviation History Publications, Concord, Cal.	1959(IP)
UNITED STATES NAVY AND MARINE CORPS FIGHTERS, 1918-1962 Illustrated account of the development and combat employment of Marine aircraft	Robertson, B. Aero Publishers, Inc., Fallbrook Cal.	1962 (IP)

WHAT'S UP? Anniversary, Marine aviation	Berger, P. *Leatherneck*	May 64

CORPS

ALMANAC OF THE MARINE CORPS Most items are included in later Historical Branch Chronologies.	*Gazette*	Nov 41, Mar, Jun, Sep, Nov 42
AN ANNOTATED READING LIST OF UNITED STATES MARINE CORPS HISTORY Brief descriptions of 174 books, 54 Historical Branch publications 100 *Gazette* articles and significant articles from other publications. Subject index.	Hilliard, J. HQMC	1971 (IP)
BACK IN THE OLD CORPS	Frew, J. *Gazette*	Nov 63
BATTLES BEFORE WORLD WAR 2	Hoffman, Capt C. *Gazette*	Nov 50
BIBLIOGRAPHY OF THE UNITED STATES MARINE CORPS List of books and magazine articles. No annotations. Mostly articles from the *Gazette* and *Leatherneck.* Many errors.	Dollen, Fr. C. The Scarecrow Press	1963
BIBLIOGRAPHY—UNITED STATES MARINE CORPS HISTORY List of 57 books, 104 *Leatherneck* articles, 227 *Gazette* articles, etc. Usefully arranged in chronological order by subject. No annotations.	MCS, Quantico	
A BRIEF HISTORY OF THE U.S. MARINE CORPS All Commandants were authors.	Lejeune, MajGen J. *Gazette*	Mar 23
A BRIEF HISTORY OF THE UNITED STATES MARINE CORPS Fifty page general history about the same as you get in Boot Camp. Ends with Lebanon.	Hicks, Maj N. HQMC	1964

CALENDAR OF IMPORTANT EVENTS IN THE HISTORY OF THE UNITED STATES MARINE CORPS	Ellsworth, Capt H. *Gazette*	 Nov 35
THE CAT WITH MORE THAN NINE LIVES Excellent article which summarizes all the attempts to abolish the Corps since 1775. (There were many).	Heinl, LtCol R. *Proceedings*	 Jun 54
CHRONOLOGY OF OUTSTANDING EVENTS OF AMERICAN MARINES	Jenkins, J. *Gazette*	 Nov 40
THE COMPACT HISTORY OF THE UNITED STATES MARINE CORPS Taut, well-written history which hides nothing* and still manages to be Gung-Ho. Through Korean War. Lots of anecdotes; some you may not have heard before. * The adventures of Commandant Gale, and Marines participation in BullRun, for example.	Pierce, LtCol P., and LtCol F. Hough Hawthorn Books, Inc.	 1960 (IP)
A CONCISE HISTORY OF THE UNITED STATES MARINE CORPS: 1775-1969 Compact history with good organizational charts, list of Commandants, Medal of Honor winners. Cat No D214, 13M 34/2775-969 S/N 0855-0050 $1.25	Parker, Capt W., USGPO	 1971 (IP)
CORPS ALBUM Photos of the "Old Corps"	Dryden, D. *Leatherneck*	 Nov 62
THE CORPS IN HISTORY	*Gazette*	Nov 30
THE CORPS SINCE 1775 Four famous authors divide the history of the Corps into parts for this Anniversary issue story	*Leatherneck*	Nov 62
1775-1825	Leckie, R.	
1825-1875	Pierce, Capt P.	
1875-1925	Ludwig, Maj V.	
1925-1962	Asprey, R.	

CREATING A LEGEND: THE COMPLETE RECORD OF WRITING ABOUT THE UNITED STATES MARINE CORPS — Moran, Capt J. Moran/Andrews, Inc., Chicago 1973 (IP)

ENGAGEMENT MAP — *Gazette* Nov 50
Shows location of all Marine engagements to that date.

A FORCE IN READINESS — Edwards, LtCol H. *Gazette* Apr 54
Historical concept of the role of Marines

FOUR STREAMERS ADDED TO CORPS BATTLE STANDARD — *Gazette* Dec 72
They are for:
Quasi-War with France
Barbary States Wars
African Slave Trade Patrol
West Indian Pirate Ops

GREAT DATES IN APRIL — Evans, GySgt E. *Leatherneck* Apr 70
April seemed to be the month of destiny for the Corps

HISTORY AND TRADITIONS OF THE UNITED STATES MARINE CORPS — MCS, Quantico 1944

HISTORY OF THE UNITED STATES MARINE CORPS — Aldrich, M. Henry L. Shepard and Co., Boston 1875
Official reports and narrative history through 1875. Covers Marines' roles in John Brown raid, Corean Expedition of 1871, War of 1812, Barrier Forts, China and Brooklyn Whiskey Rebellion. Includes list of all Marine officers on duty from 1798 through 1875. This is the first history of the Corps. Extremely valuable.

HISTORY OF THE UNITED STATES MARINE CORPS — Collum, R. L. R. Hamersly & Co. Philadelphia 1903
Follow-up to History above.

HISTORY OF THE UNITED STATES MARINE CORPS — McClellan, Maj E. HQMC 1925
This unpublished manuscript is the most-quoted and the most used history. It was furnished to a few libraries when McClellan ended his tour as first head of the Historical Division in 1925. It did more to "Create The Legend" than any other publication.

A HISTORY OF THE UNITED STATES MARINE CORPS	Metcalf, LtCol C. G. P. Putnam's Sons	1939

From 1775 through 1938. Crisp, concise and professionally written by the Corps' Chief Historian.

HISTORY, TRADITIONS, CUSTOMS AND COURTESIES MANUAL	HQMC	1959
INCIDENTS AND ANECDOTES FROM U. S. MARINE CORPS HISTORY	MCS, Quantico	
INTRODUCTION TO MARINE CORPS HISTORY	Hittinger, Maj F. MCS, Quantico	
THE LEATHERNECKS: AN INFORMAL HISTORY OF THE U. S. MARINE CORPS	Schuon, K. Franklin Watts, Inc.	1963

Smedley Butler, Presley O'Bannon and Lt Gillespie lead this parade of salty Marines from the pages of *Leatherneck.* Forty-four vignettes of Marines in historically significant situations.

MARINE CORPS ENGAGEMENTS	*Gazette*	Nov 50
MARINE CORPS GLOSSARY	*Gazette*	Nov 52
MARINE CORPS HISTORY	MCS, Quantico	1968
MARINE CORPS HISTORY	*Leatherneck*	Nov 57

Once again, four talented authors split the history of the Corps in four parts for an Anniversary issue of *Leatherneck.*

1917-1927	Montross, L.
1927-1937	Stolley, F.
1937-1947	Tallent, SSgt R.
1947-1957	Mainard, TSgt A.

MARINE CORPS . . . HISTORY OF THE MARINE CORPS	Burrows, J. USGPO	1909
THE MARINE CORPS READER	Metcalf, Col C. G. P. Putnam's Sons	1944

A collection of fact and fiction about Marines from 1775 through Bougainville. Reads like a good novel. Chapters on "The Story of the Regiments, Customs of the Early Marine Corps, Flying Marines," and others.

MARINES: ARE THEY FULL OF IT . . . OR WHAT? "X, Writer" Vantage Press, Inc. 1967 (IP)
The conclusion is "They aren't full of it," by former Marine who had to get something off his chest.

THE MARINES MARCH PAST Williams, BGen D. *Gazette* Nov 31

MEMORIES OF THE OLD CORPS Ostermann, E. *Gazette* Nov 64

PRELIMINARY INVENTORY OF THE CARTOGRAPHIC RECORDS OF THE UNITED STATES MARINE CORPS: RECORD GROUP 127 Ashby, C. U.S. National Archives, Washington 1954

THE PRESIDENTS AND THE MARINES *Gazette* Feb 33
Role of the Corps for different presidents.

THE PRE-WAR ERA Greenwood, Col J. *Gazette* Sep 72
About the calm before the storm. Any pre-war era is when the Corps prepares for the next war.

RECORDS OF THE UNITED STATES MARINE CORPS; RECORD GROUP 127 Johnson, M. U.S. National Archives, Washington 1970
Inventory of Marine Corps records in the National Archives on Dec 7, 1968

A SELECTED BIBLIOGRAPHY OF MARINE CORPS HISTORY (UNOFFICIAL) AND FICTION HQMC 1959
Listings with brief annotations of books and articles about Marine Corps history, famous Marines, Wars and Campaigns, Banana Wars and WW-2.

SEMPER FIDELIS Leatherneck Association, Washington 1942
Early WW-2 propaganda

SEMPER FIDELIS Maurois, A. Marine Corps League, Washington 1948
Historical booklet by a famous French author on commission from the League

SEMPER FIDELIS — *Leatherneck* Nov 50
Listing of wars and battles in which Marines participated from 1775 to 1950

1775-1965 — Beardsley, F. *Leatherneck* Nov 65
A page history for each of these years: 1775, 1836, 1859, 1900, 1918, 1942, 1950 and 1965

SINCE '17 — Dickson, D. *Leatherneck* Nov 67
Anniversary piece for *Leatherneck* reviews the past 50 years

SINCE 1775 — *Leatherneck* Nov 61

SOLDIERS OF THE SEA: THE STORY OF THE UNITED STATES MARINE CORPS — Abbot, W. Dodd, Mead & Co., Inc. 1919
Narrative history until World War 1 with many illustrations.

SOLDIERS OF THE SEA: THE UNITED STATES MARINE CORPS, 1775-1962 — Heinl, Col R. U.S. Naval Institute, Annapolis 1962 (IP)
Nearly 700 pages of history written the way it should be. Exciting, Fast Moving. The illustrations (20 pages) and maps are worth the price. This is the "class" history of the Marine Corps written by an officer who obviously loved his job.

SOME HISTORICAL EXAMPLES — Peck, LtCol D. *Gazette* Nov 37
How historical landings influence training

THE STORY OF THE UNITED STATES MARINES: COMPILED FROM AUTHENTIC RECORDS, 1740-1919 — Leonard, J., and F. Chitty U.S. Marine Corps Publicity Bureau Philadelphia 1920
WW-1 oriented history. Heady, in keeping with the spirit of the times. List of Marines who won significant decorations in "The War To End All Wars."

TELL IT TO THE MARINES? — Pierce, Maj P. *Gazette* May 52

U.S. MARINE CORPS MONTHLY CALENDAR OF HISTORICAL EVENTS HQMC
An internal publication of the Historical Branch, not for public release

U. S. MARINES IN ACTION Fehrenbach, T.
Good little paperback history told in terms of significant Marine actions. Fourteen episodes including Belleau Wood, Nicaragua, Guadalcanal, Okinawa and four from Korea
Paperback edition only, Monarch Books, Inc., Derby, Conn. 1962

THE UNITED STATES MARINES Manchester, W.
By the author who gained fame later from his book about the Kennedy assassination.
Holiday Nov 57

THE UNITED STATES MARINE CORPS Donovan, Col J.
Frederick A. Praeger 1967
More an explanation of how the Corps "got that way" than a history. Explains such things as amphibious doctrine, joint operations and strategy in a detailed and somewhat stuffy way.

THE UNITED STATES MARINE CORPS Jenkins, J.
Gazette Nov 40

THE UNITED STATES MARINE CORPS Paperback edition only, Osprey Men-At-Arms Series London, Eng., 1972 (IP)
Forty pages including eight pages of color plates and drawings.

THE UNITED STATES MARINES: A PICTORIAL HISTORY Montross, L.
Bramhall House 1959
There isn't a better way to tell an action story than with pictures and captions. All the famous pictures are here along with little-known ones that shed new light on obscure Corps history.

THE UNITED STATES MARINES: A PICTORIAL HISTORY OF THE MARINES Crane, J.
Paperback edition only, Army & Navy Publishing Co., Baton Rouge 1952
Published under the auspices of the Marine Corps War Memorial Foundation.

WE BLOW OUR TOP IN APRIL Pearl Harbor and Korea are the only significant historical dates that happened to the Corps in a month other than April	*Leatherneck*	Apr 57
WHY MARINES? Who needs them? (Then he answers the question.)	Hargreaves, R. *Gazette*	May 49
WHY THE MARINES?	Heinl, Col R. *Navy*	Jun 65
YE OLD CORPS Cartoons by Lasswell	Lasswell, F. *Leatherneck*	Sep 44
YESTERDAY'S FAIRS Marines at the World's Fairs: Paris Exposition, 1889; San Diego Exposition, 1915; Sesquicentennial, 1926, etc.	Frank, B. *Leatherneck*	Jul 64
YULETIDE INVASIONS New Britain, and others	Langille, Sgt V. *Leatherneck*	Dec 47, Dec 72

LOGISTICS

A BRIEF HISTORY OF RATIONS	Tompkins, LtCol R. *Gazette*	Feb 46
CHOW DOWN History of chow from 1794 through Korea	Fugate, MSgt R. *Leatherneck*	Jul 54

MARINES

GENERAL

THE BOLD CORPS Tall tales develop characters	Stolley, WO F. *Leatherneck*	Nov 54
FAMOUS AMERICAN MARINES: AN ACCOUNT OF THE CORPS, THE EXPLOITS OF OFFICERS AND MEN ON LAND, BY AIR AND SEA, FROM THE DECKS OF THE BONHOMME RICHARD TO THE SUMMIT OF MOUNT SURIBACHI With a title like that, who needs an annotation!	Lewis, C. L. S. Page & Co., Boston	1950

FIGHTING MARINES — Hirsch, P.
Twelve vignettes of famous Marines in the situations that made them famous — Paperback edition only, Pyramid Books 1964

GUTS, NOBILITY AND A HEART — Clark, RAdm R., USN
Courage of Marines in certain situations. Nam, Korea and 1955 flood rescue in Mexico — *Gazette* Dec 72

HAZARD: MARINES ON MISSION — Parrott, M.
Very well done historical vignettes of famous Marines becoming famous — Doubleday & Company, Inc., Garden City, N.Y. 1962

HEROES, U.S. MARINE CORPS, 1861-1955, ARMED FORCES AWARDS, FLAGS. — Blakeney, J.
Guthrie Lithograph Co., Washington 1957
Fantastic "Bible-like" manual which includes write-ups of *every* Marine who won the Silver Star or above for every war through Korea. Many charts and color photos. There'll never be another book like this one.

THE NATION'S HIGHEST — Polete, Sgt H.
All the Marines who won the Medal of Honor — *Leatherneck* Oct 46

PERSONALITIES—MEN WHO DIFFERED — Hough, Maj F.
The Corps had its share of them, and many were proven right in retrospect — *Gazette* Nov 50

U.S. MARINE CORPS BIOGRAPHICAL DICTIONARY: THE CORPS FIGHTING MEN, WHAT THEY DID, WHERE THEY SERVED — Schuon, K.
Franklin Watts, Inc. 1963
Biogs of famous and not so famous combat Marines from the beginning through Korea

ATHLETES

BOONDOCKERS TO SPIKES — Hull, D.
Famous ball players who were Marines, like Hank Bauer, Sam Mele, Hal Naragon, Alvin Dark, Gil Hodges, Ted Williams, Roberto Clemente and others — *Leatherneck* Oct 64

CORPS SPORTS Marine athletes through 1957	Jones, MSgt W. *Leatherneck*	Nov 57	
MARINE ATHLETES Top Marine athletes through the years, including Frank Goettge, "Harry, the Horse" Liversedge, Joe Bartos, "Swede" Larson, Johnny Beckett, Gene Tunney.	Papurca, J. *Leatherneck*	Nov 50	
COMMANDANTS OF THE MARINE CORPS	Metcalf, LtCol C. *Gazette*	May 37	**COMMANDANTS**
COMMANDANTS OF THE MARINE CORPS	Gayle, LtCol G. *Gazette*	Nov 50	
WHEN THEY WEREN'T COMMANDANT What Commandants from Gale through Shoup did after they retired.	Hull, D. *Leatherneck*	Jun 64	
ACADEMY GRADUATES COMMISSIONED IN THE MARINE CORPS: 1887-1968 Unpublished manuscript	HQMC	1968	**NAVAL ACADEMY**
SEVENTY-FIVE YEARS OF ACADEMY MARINES Annapolis grads who chose the Corps are discussed and listed	Greenwood, Capt J., USN *Shipmate*	Nov 57	

MARINES/NAVY

THE BELL FROM "OLD ONE" USS Henderson bell now, appropriately enough, at Henderson Hall	Suhosky, TSgt R. *Leatherneck*	Mar 55
FLOATING NAMESAKES Navy ships named after Marines	Sims, SSgt R. *Leatherneck*	May 53
FLOATING NAMESAKES	Bowen, B. *Leatherneck*	Oct 66
GUNBOATS ON CHINA'S YANGTZE Boat-by-boat review including role of Marines	Willinger, I. *Covers*	Feb 66

NAVY-MARINE CORPS TEAM Historical rundown of the Navy and Marines working together since 1775. Emphasis on Amphibious Ops.	Bowen, B. *Leatherneck*	Oct 66
"OL' NO. I" The USS Henderson	O'Brien, Maj R. *Leatherneck*	Nov 69
U.S.S. FRIGATE CONSTELLATION After serving in seven major wars, the oldest fighting ship in the Navy is restored in Baltimore	Jones, AGySgt M. *Leatherneck*	Jun 60
USS RALPH TALBOT Destroyer named after Marine Medal of Honor winner of WW-1	*Gazette*	Nov 36

MARKMANSHIP

THE HISTORY OF MARINE CORPS COMPETITIVE MARKSMANSHIP Hard-cover history from the beginning through 1960. Many lists and charts. Not much biographical information.	Barde, Maj R. HQMC	1961
THE LAUCHHEIMER TROPHY History of the Corps' most prestigious marksmanship trophy	O'Quinlivan, M., and B. Frank HQMC	1960
MARINE MARKSMEN Corps sharpshooters from 1900. Thomas J. Jones, Percy Howes, H. L. Smith, Morris Fisher and others.	Abribat, M., and R. Tallent *Leatherneck*	Nov 50

PERSONNEL

GENERAL	**A BRIEF HISTORY OF CERTAIN ASPECTS OF MANPOWER UTILIZATION IN THE MARINE CORPS** How the Marines used blacks as servants and other off-beat uses of man-power is discussed in detail	Nalty, B. HQMC	1957

A BRIEF HISTORY OF HEADQUARTERS MARINE CORPS STAFF ORGANIZATION Concise account of the evolution of HQMC and Staff organization.	Condit, K., Maj J. Johnstone and E. Nargele HQMC	1970 (IP)	
INSPECTION IN THE U.S. MARINE CORPS, 1775-1957; HISTORICAL BACKGROUND	Nalty, B. HQMC	1960	
THE WAGE FOR THE JOB Pay scales do not an Army make, (or a Marine Corps?)	Hargreaves, Maj R. *Gazette*	Oct 52	
WITHOUT PREJUDICE OR PARTIALITY Fitness reports, back to 1877.	Nalty, B. *Leatherneck*	Sep 58	
THE BREVET IN THE MARINE CORPS	Magruder, Col J. *Gazette*	Nov 55	**RANKS AND GRADES**
UNITED STATES MARINE CORPS RANKS AND GRADES, 1775-1969	Nalty, B. HQMC	1970 (IP)	

Historical survey of the development of officer and enlisted ranks and grades. Includes annotated list of Commandants showing the progressive changes in rank.

WHAT'S YOUR RANK?	*Gazette*	Nov 52	

POSTS/PLACES

POST OF THE CORPS Used by *Leatherneck* as a subscription premium. This book was never sold.	Paperback edition only, The Leatherneck Association, Washington	1963 (IP)	**GENERAL**
CAMP LEJEUNE History from 1940 to 1955	Fugate, MSgt R. *Leatherneck*	Apr 55	**CAMP LEJEUNE**
LAST ROUND History of Camp Matthews Rifle Ranges from 1918 to deactivation in 1964	Bradshow, J. *Leatherneck*	Nov 64	**CAMP MATTHEWS**
MARINES OF THE MARGARITA Beautifully illustrated and bound history of Pendleton. This oversized book is a must for your Marine Corps library.	Witty, R., and N. Morgan Frye & Smith, Ltd., San Diego, Cal.	1970 (IP)	**CAMP PENDLETON**

CHERRY POINT	**UNITED STATES MARINE CORPS AIR STATION—CUNNINGHAM FIELD, CHERRY POINT, NORTH CAROLINA**	Carraway, G. Published by the author	1946
COMMANDANT'S HOME	THE COMMANDANT'S HOUSE	*Gazette*	May 54
	HOME OF THE COMMANDANTS 150th Anniversary of Henderson's Home	*Leatherneck*	Nov 55
	HOME OF THE COMMANDANTS Pictures of the home through the years with biographies of each resident	Schuon, K. The Leatherneck Association, Washington	1956
PARRIS ISLAND	AFTER THREE HUNDRED AND FIFTY YEARS History	Osterhout, Maj G. *Gazette*	Jun 23
	THE CRADLE OF THE CORPS	Phillips, Sgt J. *Leatherneck*	Mar 46
	A BRIEF HISTORY OF THE MARINE CORPS RECRUIT DEPOT, PARRIS ISLAND, S.C. 1891-1962	Champie, E. HQMC	1962
	MARINE CORPS RECRUIT DEPOT, PARRIS ISLAND, S.C. "Cruise Books" sold to recruits at Parris Island and San Diego. Pictures of their platoons, DI's, etc. ("You'd better buy one, lad")	Albert Love Enterprises, Inc., Atlanta	
	P.I. 400 YEARS AGO If you think it's unhospitable today, you should have seen it then.	Dickson, D. *Leatherneck*	May 62
	THE ROMANCE OF PARRIS ISLAND What romance?	Willett, N. *Leatherneck*	Oct 31
QUANTICO	**. . . ABOUT QUANTICO**	MCS, Quantico	
	COLLEGE OF THE CORPS The schools of Quantico and history, back to 1917. Many old pictures	Thompson, J. *Leatherneck*	Nov 50
	THE DEVELOPMENT OF MCS Marine officer training, from 1891	Croizat, LtCol V. *Gazette*	Sep 54

HISTORY OF THE MARINE CORPS SCHOOLS History of the various officer training schools from 1891 to 1945 with chronology of events, list of Commandants and list of Commandants of Marine Corps Schools	Frances, A. MCS, Quantico	1945	
A BRIEF HISTORY OF THE MARINE CORPS BASE AND RECRUIT DEPOT, SAN DIEGO, CALIFORNIA, 1914-1962	Champie, E. HQMC	1967 (IP)	**SAN DIEGO**
THE MARINE CORPS BASE AT SAN DIEGO	*Leatherneck*	Apr 29	
MARINE CORPS RECRUIT DEPOT, SAN DIEGO, CALIFORNIA	Albert Love Enterprises, Inc., Atlanta		
THE MARINES IN SAN DIEGO COUNTY	*Union Title Trust Topics*	May, Jun 53	
RECRUIT DEPOT, MARINE CORPS BASE, SAN DIEGO, CAL.	Moses, LtCol E. *Leatherneck*	Jun 32	
THE SAN DIEGO MARINE BASE	Williams, Col A. *Gazette*	Jun 26	
THE STORY OF SAN DIEGO	*Leatherneck*	Jun 32	
THE UNITED STATES NAVY AND THE U.S. MARINE CORPS AT SAN DIEGO: AN AUTHENTIC RECORD OF THE ESTABLISHMENT OF THE U.S. NAVY AND MARINE CORPS FACILITIES IN AND ADJACENT TO SAN DIEGO, CALIF. The title is longer than the book	Davis, E. Paperback edition only, Published by the author San Diego	1955	
HIGHLIGHTS OF U.S. MARINE CORPS ACTIVITIES IN THE DISTRICT OF COLUMBIA Based on records of the Society	Thacker, J. Columbia Historical Society, Washington	1952	**WASHINGTON, D.C.**

RECRUITING

A BRIEF HISTORY OF MARINE CORPS OFFICER PROCUREMENT: 1775-1969 General history of the subject	Nalty, B., and LtCol R. Moody HQMC	1970 (IP)

from 1775-1969 with special sections on Marine aviation and Women Marine officers

FLYING WITH THE MARINE CORPS An early recruiting pamphlet	Ceck Engraving Co., Washington	
THE GAZETTE TAKES A LOOK AT MARINE RECRUITING POSTERS Back to 1775, believe it or not.	*Gazette*	Jan 50
LEATHERNECK SALESMEN Recruiting through the years	Snoddy, LtCol L. *Gazette*	Aug 55
PHILADELPHIA MARINE RECRUITER Posters of Early WW-2	U.S. Marine Corps Publicity Bureau, Philadelphia	Jul, Aug 41, Sep 43
RECRUITING—PAST AND PRESENT	Proctor, SgtMaj C. *Leatherneck*	Feb 32
REFERENCES ON MARINE CORPS RECRUITING POSTERS	HQMC	1963
U.S. MARINES: DUTIES, EXPERIENCES, OPPORTUNITIES, PAY Recruiting pamphlet which was up-dated many times	Recruiting Publicity Bureau, New York	1912

RESERVE

BEYOND TOMORROW: A PRESENTATION OF THE MARINE AIR RESERVE 72-page pamphlet	Marine Air Reserve Training Command, Glenview, Ill.	1955
HISTORY OF THE MARINE CORPS RESERVE	*Gazette*	Mar 47
MARINE CORPS RESERVE—A HISTORY Excellent publication with many illustrations. D214:13 R31/2 S/N 0855-0039 311 pages. $3.50	USGPO	1966 (IP)

THE MARINE RESERVE READY History with lists of Organized Units both Ground and Air.	Lyons, R. *Leatherneck*	Nov 50
MCR'S FIRST 50 YEARS Historical rundown with lists of units	Hall, H. *Leatherneck*	Aug 66

ROLES AND MISSIONS

AND BY MAINTENANCE IN READINESS OF EXPEDITIONARY FORCES	McClellan, Maj E. *Gazette*	Nov 32
DEPLOYMENTS OF U.S. MARINE CORPS BRIGADES FOR EXPEDITIONARY DUTY Brief, chronological list from Apr-1885 through July-1958. Annotated.	MCS, Quantico	1962
EXPEDITIONS AND RELATED ACTIONS	Rentz, Maj J. *Gazette*	Nov 50
A HISTORY OF MARINE CORPS ROLES AND MISSIONS 1775-1962	Roe, Col T. HQMC	1962 (IP)
ONE HUNDRED EIGHTY LANDINGS OF UNITED STATES MARINES, 1880-1934 1—Abyssina to Fiji Islands 2—Formosa to Uruguay	Ellsworth, Capt H. HQMC	1934
PER MARE, PER TERRAM On land and sea	Rankin, LtCol R. *Gazette*	Apr 53
SUMMARY OF OPERATIONS, DEPLOYMENTS AND SHOWS OF FORCE BY U.S. MARINES OUTSIDE CONTINENTAL LIMITS OF U.S. IN PEACE-TIME, 1800-1958	HQMC	1959

SUPPORTING ARMS

ARTILLERY

ARTILLERY IN MARINE CORPS HISTORY Especially at Trenton and Princeton	McClellan, Maj E. *Gazette*	Aug 31

	TIME ON TARGET—177 YEARS History of artillery in the Corps	Evans, MSgt E. *Gazette*	Feb 54
CLOSE AIR SUPPORT	A FRAGILE PAIR OF WINGS Brief history from WW-1 to 1972	Bartlett, T. *Leatherneck*	May 72
NAVAL GUNFIRE	THE DEVELOPMENT OF NAVAL GUNFIRE SUPPORT OF AMPHIBIOUS OPERATIONS From the 1920's to 1948	McMillian, Capt I., USN *Proceedings*	Jan 48
	NAVAL GUNFIRE TRAINING IN THE PACIFIC Complete history of Naval Gunfire Section, Fleet Marine Force, Pacific	Heinl, LtCol R. *Gazette*	Jun 48

TRADITIONS

THE BATTLE STANDARD OF THE U.S. MARINE CORPS Listing of the streamers on the U.S. Marine Corps Battle Standard, with the texts of all citations earned through the years. Not for public distribution.	HQMC	1970 (IP)
THE CAKE AND THE SLICE	Phillips, LtCol C. *Gazette*	Jan 50
THE DEVICE OF THE MARINE CORPS The Globe and Anchor	*Gazette*	Nov 30
THE EAGLE, GLOBE AND ANCHOR	Magruder, Col J. *Gazette*	Nov 68
GENTLEMEN . . . DINNER IS SERVED Mess Night history	Fraser, Col A. *Gazette*	Mar 57
HOW TO RESPECT AND DISPLAY OUR FLAG Webb's classic is still the Bible on this subject	Webb, MTSgt P. USGPO	
"I AM OLD GLORY" One of his early poems	Webb, MTSgt P. Recruiting Publicity Bureau, Philadelphia	

THE INVISIBLE ASSET Tradition	*Gazette*	Dec 49
LOOKING AT ORIGINS	*Gazette*	May 49
THE MARINE AND HIS TRADITIONS	Heinl, Col R. *Gazette*	Nov 64
THE MARINE CORPS EMBLEM "THE FIRST HUNDRED YEARS" A Board appointed by Gen J. Zeilin designed the emblem.	Long, R., and Col D. Wyckoff *Proceedings*	Nov 69
MARINE CORPS LORE	HQMC	1960
THE MARINE TRADITION Excellent illustrated article by the famous Civil War author	Catton, B. *American Heritage*	Feb 59
THE MARINES' HYMN How it started	*Gazette*	Jan 47
"THE MARINES' HYMN"	*Gazette*	Sep 42
THE MARINES' PRAYER	*Gazette*	Mar 67
MESS NIGHT	Sarokin, MSgt P. *Leatherneck*	Apr 58
MESS NIGHT	Williams, Col R. *Gazette*	Dec 55
MESS NIGHT BRIEF	Bestwick, SgtMaj W., and SgtMaj J. Zim *Leatherneck*	Jun 59
THE NCO SWORD History of the sword	Rankin, R. *Leatherneck*	Nov 68
NOR BY SWORD ALONE Examples of peace-time efforts of Marines overseas	Baylis, Lt C. *Gazette*	Feb 31
THE OFFICERS' SWORD	Magruder, Col J. *Gazette*	Mar 55
THE OLD SLOUCH HAT	Heinl, Col R. *Gazette*	Jun 52
THE REAL TRADITIONS	Tompkins, MajGen R. *Gazette*	Apr 65

SWORD MANUAL Illustrated story includes execution of the Sword Manual	*Leatherneck*	Nov 68
THIS IS MY RIFLE	Merrill, Capt W. *Gazette*	Dec 60
WHAT MAKES A MARINE A MARINE Tradition, says MSgt Crumb	Crumb, MSgt C. *Gazette*	Oct 49

UNIFORMS

THE CHEVRON	Magruder, Maj J. *Gazette*	Nov 54
THE EAGLE, GLOBE AND ANCHOR Technical Monograph #1	Driscoll, Col J. Marine Corps Museum Quantico	1971 (IP)
MARINE UNIFORMS: FROM 1775 TO 1950	Hoffman, Maj C., and J. Thacker *Gazette*	Nov 50
REGULATIONS FOR THE UNIFORM AND DRESS OF THE NAVY AND MARINE CORPS OF THE UNITED STATES	U.S. Navy Department, Philadelphia	1859
REGULATIONS FOR THE UNIFORM AND DRESS OF THE NAVY AND MARINE CORPS OF THE UNITED STATES	Collins, T. and P. U.S. Navy Department, Philadelphia	1852
UNIFORM REGULATIONS: UNITED STATES MARINE CORPS, 1912 Illustrations of uniforms the Corps should have worn during WW-1 but didn't because it was supplied from Army stores	HQMC	1912
UNIFORMS OF THE AMERICAN MARINES	McClellan, Maj E. HQMC	1932
UNIFORMS OF THE MARINES Beautifully illustrated in color book with narrative history	Rankin, Col R. G. P. Putnam's Sons	1970 (IP)
WHERE DID YOU GET THAT HAT? History of Marine hats through the years. Some were unbelievable.	Dickson, D. *Leatherneck*	Apr 71

UNITS

Title	Author / Source	Date	Subject
THE MARINES' AMPHIBIAN Amphibious Tractor developments, 1924-1953	Croizat, LtCol V. *Gazette*	Jun 53	**AMTRACS**
WHALEBOATS TO AMTRAC	Schreier, K. *Gazette*	Feb 69	
. . . AND 60 FIFERS Marine Band, from 1861	Young, G. *Leatherneck*	Nov 72	**BAND**
THE MARINE BAND	*Gazette*	Nov 30	
MARINE BAND HISTORY AND ITS LEADERS	Proctor, J. The Washington Sunday Star,	May 8, 1932	
THE PRESIDENT'S OWN	Lautenbacher, C. *Gazette*	Nov 68	
THE SOUSA BAND, A DISCOGRAPHY A Discography is a catalog of phonograph records. This one is 123 pp.	Smart, J. Library of Congress, Washington	1970	
THE UNITED STATES MARINE BAND: ITS HISTORY AND ACHIEVEMENTS, A MESSAGE FOR MUSICIANS Twenty-page pamphlet	USGPO	1941	
DENIG'S DEMONS AND HOW THEY GREW: THE STORY OF MARINE COMBAT CORRESPONDENTS, PHOTOGRAPHERS, AND ARTISTS 80-page history included with Silver Anniversary Program of the Association	Frank, B. Paperback edition only, Marine Corps Combat Correspondents Assn., Washington	1967	**COMBAT CORRESPONDENTS**
THE BIRTH OF THE FLEET MARINE FORCE Scholarly treatment by the famous Marine scholar	Russell, MajGen J. *Proceedings*	Oct 36 Jan 46	**FMF**
THE GENESIS OF FMF DOCTRINE; 1879-1899	Russell, W. *Gazette*	Apr-Jul 51 Nov 55	

Subject	Title	Author / Source	Date
HISTORICAL BRANCH	THE CORPS FILM ARCHIVES Where all the history is kept	*Gazette*	Apr 51
	EVERY MARINE AN HISTORIAN By the head of the Historical Branch	Caldwell, Col F. *Gazette*	Mar 66
	LIVING HISTORY Oral History Program of Historical Branch where Corps leaders are interviewed on tape	Frank, B. *Gazette*	Nov 70
INFANTRY	THE MAN WITH THE RIFLE History of the infantry	Montross, L. *Gazette*	Nov, Dec 53, Jan 54
LEATHERNECK	LEATHERNECK IS 50 Anniversary history	Schuon, K. *Leatherneck*	Nov 67
PUBINFO	**THIS HIGH NAME: PUBLIC RELATIONS AND THE U.S. MARINE CORPS** A documented history of Marine Corps public relations from 1900-1955. Only treatment of its kind about men who "Created A Legend."	Lindsay, R. Paperback edition only, University of Wisconsin Press, Madison, Wis.	1956 (IP)
PO	USMC POSTAL HISTORY Interesting treatment of an off-beat subject	Jersey, S. *Bulletin of the War Covers Club*	Oct, Dec 62
RAIDERS	SUPER SOLDIERS History of Raiders, Recon men, Commandos. Author's conclusion is, "Who needs them?" Regular Marines can handle the special jobs with ease	Wyckoff, LtCol D. *Gazette*	Nov 63
REGIMENTS	REGIMENTS OF THE CORPS Includes lineage chart for all 29 regiments of the Corps	Santelli, J., and G. Neufeld *Gazette*	Nov 72
	A BRIEF HISTORY OF THE 1ST MARINES All of these histories include lists of Commanding Officers, Medal of Honor winners, and Chronology.	Johnstone, Maj J. HQMC	1968 (IP)

A BRIEF HISTORY OF THE 2D MARINES	Kane, Capt R. HQMC	1969 (IP)
A BRIEF HISTORY OF THE 3D MARINES	Frank, B. HQMC	1969 (IP)
A BRIEF HISTORY OF THE 4TH MARINES	Santelli, J. HQMC	1970 (IP)
HOLD HIGH THE TORCH: A HISTORY OF THE 4TH MARINES The only hard cover Marine regimental history. Scarce.	Condit, K., and E. Turnbladh HQMC	1960
A BRIEF HISTORY OF THE 5TH MARINES	Yingling, Maj J. HQMC	1968 (IP)
A BRIEF HISTORY OF THE 9TH MARINES	Strobridge, T. HQMC	1968 (IP)
A BRIEF HISTORY OF THE 11TH MARINES	Emmet, Lt R. HQMC	1968 (IP)
HISTORY OF THE ELEVENTH REGIMENT, U.S. MARINES	*Gazette*	Jun 42
A BRIEF HISTORY OF THE 12TH MARINES	HQMC	1972 (IP)

SEAGOING

SEAGOING MARINES Pictorial essay	*Proceedings*	Nov 71

WM'S

HIGH BUTTON SHOES History of WM's	*Gazette*	Oct 49
WOMEN MARINES	Milhon, W. *Leatherneck*	Nov 50
WOMEN MARINES	Pickel, TSgt V. *Gazette*	Nov 57

WEAPONS

HAND GRENADE: 1775-1963	Driver, MSgt J. *Gazette*	Mar 63
MARINE WEAPONS: FROM MUSKET TO M-1	Johnson, LtCol M. *Gazette*	Nov 50
SHOULDER ARMS History of rifles	Evans, Sgt E. *Leatherneck*	Aug 48

2.
TUN'S TAVERN TO WORLD WAR 2

The Chronological Roll of writing about the role of the United States Marines in particular wars, battles and events from 1740 to 1940.

CONTENTS: PART 2

THE AMERICAN MARINES, 1740-1742 Marines in Adm Vernon's expedition against Cartigana	McClellan, Maj E. *Gazette* Dec 29	**1740-1742**

REVOLUTION

AN ANNOTATED BIBLIOGRAPHY OF MARINES IN THE AMERICAN REVOLUTION	Tyson, C., and R. Gill HQMC 1972 (IP)	**GENERAL, 1775-1783**
AMERICAN MARINES IN THE REVOLUTION	McClellan, Maj E. *Proceedings* Jun 23	
CAPTAIN ROBERT MULLAN'S COMPANY, CONTINENTAL MARINES, 1779 Plate No. 2 in the "Military Uniforms of America" series.	*Military Collector & Historian* Jan 49	
A CHRONOLOGY OF THE UNITED STATES MARINE CORPS, VOLUME 1—1775-1934 1775-1785 American Marines in the Revolution 1786-1819 Early Days of the Marine Corps 1820-1859 The Marine Corps At Sea and on the Shore 1860-1903 American Marines from the Civil War to the Era of Caribbean Interventions 1904-1934 American Marines in the Era of Expanding Responsibilities	Miller, Col W., and Maj J. Johnstone HQMC 1965 (IP)	
THE CONTINENTAL MARINES: A BRIEF BIBLIOGRAPHY	O'Quinlivan, M. HQMC 1958	
THE CORPS IN THE DAYS OF THE REVOLUTION	Heavey, Maj J. *Military Engineer* Nov-Dec 40	
MARINE OFFICERS OF THE AMERICAN REVOLUTION It names them.	McClellan, E. *DAR Magazine* Jun 21, Jul 23	

Date	Title	Source	Date
	THE MARINE REGIMENT OF MARBLEHEAD FISHERMEN	Aldridge, Maj F. *Gazette*	Jan 50
	OUT-LETTERS OF THE CONTINENTAL MARINE COMMITTEE AND BOARD OF ADMIRALTY, AUGUST 1776-SEPT 1780 Two volumes of priceless history	Paullin, C.	1914
	REVOLUTIONARY WAR	*Gazette*	Nov 65
	WILLIAM JENNISON: CONTINENTAL MARINE At the age of 19, he was in the 13th Massachusetts Regiment.	Nalty, B., and T. Strobridge *Leatherneck*	Aug 63
MAY 25, 1775	MONEY BY THE CARTLOAD Marines guard money for the Revolution, May 25, 1775, on a trip from Albany to Fort Ticonderoga	Montross, L. *Leatherneck*	Aug 56
NOV 10, 1775	THE COMMITTEE ON NOVA SCOTIA At Philadelphia Nov 10, 1775, John Hancock presided at a session of the Continental Congress which adopted a resolution to raise two battalions of Marines	Turnbladh, E. *Leatherneck*	Nov 60
	GREAT DATES OF THE CORPS: NOV. 10, 1775	Thacker, J. *Leatherneck*	Nov 53
	RESOLUTION TO RAISE A BATTALION TO BE CALLED THE MARINE CORPS	American State Papers, Naval Affairs Washington	1834
NEW PROVIDENCE, MAR 2, 1776	THE AMERICAN INVASION OF NASSAU IN THE BAHAMAS Feb and Mar, 1776. The Continental Marines under Capt Sam Nicholas	McCusker, J. *American Neptune*	Jul 65
	A CRUISE FOR GUNPOWDER New Providence	Hanks, C. *Proceedings*	Mar 59
	GREAT DATES IN THE MARINE CORPS: MARCH 2, 1776—THE FIRST LANDING—FORT NASSAU	*Leatherneck*	Mar 48

Title	Author / Publication	Date	Event
THE CANNONEERS HAVE HAIRY EARS . . . CHRONICLES OF THE CORPS Battle of Fort Sullivan at Charleston, S.C., Jun 4, 1776	Montross, L. *Leatherneck*	Jul 57, Dec 71	**FORT SULLIVAN, JUN 4, 1776**
THE BATTLE OF VALCOUR BAY: A VICTORIOUS DEFEAT Oct 11, 1776	Greathouse, Lt R. *Gazette*	Nov 58	**VALCOUR BAY, OCT 11, 1776**
THE NAVY AT THE BATTLES OF TRENTON AND PRINCETON Marines from ships serve ashore in these battles	McClellan, Maj E. *Proceedings*	Nov 23	**TRENTON/ PRINCETON, JAN 2, 1777**
HELL'S HALF ACRE Marines, commanded by Maj Nicholas, lose Fort Mifflin on Oct 1, 1777	Montross, L. *Leatherneck*	Nov 56, Nov 71	**FORT MIFFLIN, OCT 1, 1777**
FIRST AMERICAN FLAG TO FLY OVER FOREIGN SOIL At New Providence, 1778	McClellan, Maj E. *Gazette*	May 33	**NEW PROVIDENCE, JAN 27, 1778**
THREE HISTORIC WITHDRAWALS FROM OVERSEAS OPERATIONS New Providence is one	McClellan, Maj E. *Gazette*	Feb 31	
ANATOMY OF DEFEAT Penobscot Expedition and Court Martial of Paul Revere	Pierce, P. *Gazette*	Nov 68	**PENOBSCOT BAY, JUL 28, 1779**
PENOBSCOT ASSAULT 1779	Shaw, H. *Military Affairs*	Summer 53	
THE UNITED STATES MARINES IN THE PENOBSCOT BAY EXPEDITION: 1779	Chester, RAdm D., USN *Gazette*	Dec 18	
FROM 1783 TO 1798	McClellan, Maj E. *Gazette*	Sep 22	**1783**
THE EARLY YEARS OF THE MARINE CORPS	Metcalf, LtCol C. *Gazette*	Nov 36	
THE EARLY YEARS OF THE MARINE CORPS	*Gazette*	Sep 19	

FRENCH NAVAL WAR

1789-1800	THE AMERICAN MARINES OF "OLD IRONSIDES"	*Gazette*	May 31
	AN AFFAIR OF HONOR—1800 A dual between Marines	*Gazette*	Sep 47
	NAVAL DOCUMENTS RELATED TO THE QUASI-WAR BETWEEN THE UNITED STATES AND FRANCE Many references to the role of Marines	USGPO	1935-38
	THE NAVAL WAR WITH FRANCE 1789-1800	McClellan, Maj E. *Gazette*	Dec 22
	THE NAVY AND MARINE CORPS AT CURACAO Twenty Marines take Curacao from the French, Sep 23, 1800	O'Quinlivan, M. *Navy*	May 59
	OLD IRONSIDES—LUCKIEST SHIP Went to sea Jul 2, 1798. Won four battles against overwhelming odds.	Smith, E. (Karl Schuon) *Leatherneck*	Nov 60, Oct 72
	REFERENCES ON THE U.S. MARINES IN THE FRENCH NAVAL WAR	HQMC	1963
	U.S. MARINE CORPS, 1797-1804 Pictures and description of Marine uniforms of this era (plate no. 113)	*Military Collector & Historian*	Spring 56
	THE U.S. NAVY'S FIRST SEAGOING MARINE OFFICER Capt John Cormick, 1798-1816	Dunn, Capt L., USN (Ret.) *Proceedings*	Aug 49

TRIPOLI

1801-1805	ASSAULT LANDING, EGYPT O'Bannon & Company	*Gazette*	Sep 52
	CLOSING EVENTS OF THE WAR WITH TRIPOLI	Rodgers, R. *Proceedings*	Sep 08

O'BANNON IN LIBYA Marines march "To the Shores of Tripoli"	Cooke, F. *Leatherneck*	Aug 42	
REFERENCES ON THE U.S. MARINES IN THE BARBARY WARS	HQMC	1963	
TO THE SHORES . . .	Geer, A. *Leatherneck*	Nov 52, Nov 71	
TO THE SHORES OF TRIPOLI History of O'Bannon	Lanier, W. *Proceedings*	Jan 42	
TO THE SHORES OF TRIPOLI	Rentfrow, F. *Leatherneck*	Dec 29	
TO THE SHORES OF TRIPOLI	Eller, Lt E., USN *Proceedings*	Mar 33	
TRIPOLI	*Gazette*	Nov 65	
TRIPOLITAN BACKGROUND OF THE WAR OF 1801-1805	Howland, F. *Gazette*	Mar 38	
THE UNITED STATES MARINES IN THE TRIPOLITAN WAR: A BRIEF BIBLIOGRAPHY	HQMC	1957	
U.S. MARINE CORPS, CIRCA, 1805-1818 Pictures and description of Marine uniforms of this era (plate no. 24)	*Military Collector & Historian*	Jun 50	**1805**

PATRIOT'S WAR

CAPTAIN JOHN WILLIAMS, U.S. MARINE CORPS, A TRADITION Free blacks and Indians kill Williams in Florida, 1812	Richards, BGen G. *Gazette*	Aug 32	**1807-1813**
MARINE CORPS HISTORY 1807-1812 Marines role in Patriot's War in Georgia	McClellan, Maj E. *Gazette*	Mar 23	

WAR OF 1812

1812-1814	AMPHIBIOUS DOUBLEHEADER Marines assault Fort George and British take Sackett's Harbor on the same day in May	Montross, L. *Gazette*	Apr 58
	AN AMPHIBIOUS OPERATION THAT FAILED: THE BATTLE OF NEW ORLEANS Why it failed	Ainsworth, Adm W., USN *Proceedings*	Feb 45
	THE BATTLE OF NEW ORLEANS	Jahncke, E. *Proceedings*	Mar 31
	BETSY ROSS, MARINE WIFE? Marine uniforms are found in her home	Nicholson, D. *Leatherneck*	Jun 56
	BLADENSBURG	*Gazette*	Nov 65
	THE CAPTURE OF NEW ORLEANS	McClellan, Maj E. *Gazette*	Dec 20
	THE CAPTURE OF WASHINGTON	Davis, Capt M., USN *Proceedings*	Jun 37
	THE CORPS ONE HUNDRED YEARS AGO	Evans, Capt F. *Gazette*	Mar 16
	THE DARKEST DAY—THE WASHINGTON BALTIMORE CAMPAIGN And particularly the Battle of Bladensburg	Muller, C. J. B. Lippincott Company, Philadelphia	1963
	ECHOES OF THE WAR OF 1812	*Gazette*	Sep 17
	ESPIRIT DE CORPS—1812	Dulacki, L. *Gazette*	Nov 67
	GREAT DATES OF THE MARINE CORPS: AUGUST 19, 1812 "AS ON THE SEA" Lt William Bush, USMC, is killed as Marines from the Constitution board the Guerriere	*Leatherneck*	Aug 47
	GREAT DATES IN THE MARINE CORPS: AUGUST 24, 1814 BATTLE OF BLADENSBURG	*Leatherneck*	Aug 48

LEGENDARY LADY MARINE, LUCY BREWER	Poling, J. *Coronet*	Mar 61
LUCY BREWER EXPOSED There "ain't no such person," says Zimmerman.	Zimmerman, J. *Leatherneck*	Aug 48
MARINE CORPS HISTORY: 1815-1817 Featuring the New Orleans Campaign of Dec 1814-Jan 1815	McClellan, Maj E. *Gazette*	Dec 23
MARINES AND SAILORS DEFEND WASHINGTON, D.C.	Aldridge, Maj F. *Gazette*	Mar 50
THE NAVY AT THE BATTLE OF NEW ORLEANS	McClellan, Maj E. *Proceedings*	Dec 24
POST FOR A DAY Fort Henry, Canada	Barnum, MSgt E. *Leatherneck*	Nov 54
REFERENCES ON THE UNITED STATES MARINES IN THE WAR OF 1812	HQMC	1963
A TOUCH OF TRADITION About Lt Bush of Constitution	Magruder, J. *Gazette*	Nov 58

JOHN GAMBLE

Gamble, Lt John

AN OLD FASHIONED FIGHTING MARINE The only Marine officer ever to command a Navy ship-of-the-line. He did it in 1814	*Gazette*	Jun 28
JOHN GAMBLE: U.S. MARINE	Hanks, C. *Proceedings*	Jan 42
MOST UNLUCKY MARINE Captured in 1812	Pole, J. *Leatherneck*	Mar 60, Sep 72
A SEAMAN FOR ALL SEASONS	Monroe, Lt A., USNR *Proceedings*	Feb 71

1817

MARINE CORPS HISTORY, 1817-1821 Detailed summary for those years as only McClellan could compile it	McClellan, Maj E. *Gazette*	Mar 24

1824	THE MASSACHUSETTS MUTINY—1824	*Gazette*	Jun 47
1826	U.S. MARINE CORPS, 1826 Picture and story about Marine uniform of that time (plate no. 130)	*Military Collector & Historian*	Spring 57
1829	LINEAL LIST 1829	*Gazette*	May 59

QUALLA BATTOO

1832	**AMERICAN VOYAGES TO THE ORIENT, 1690-1865** Fascinating stories of these trips. Marines played an important part in them. Includes Qualla Battoo and the opening of China and then Japan	Paullin, C. U.S. Naval Institute, Annapolis	1971 (IP)
	AN EARLY GLOBE CIRCLING CRUISE Diary kept by anonymous Marine aboard the USS Potomac describes the Qualla Battoo action of 1832	Maclay, E. *Proceedings*	Jun 10
	GREAT DATES IN THE MARINE CORPS . . . FEBRUARY 7, 1832 QUALLAH BATTOO	*Leatherneck*	Feb 48
	THE OCCUPATION OF THE VIRGIN ISLANDS OF THE UNITED STATES OF AMERICA	Salladay, LtCol J. *Gazette*	Sep 18
	PEPPER PIRATES AND GRAPE SHOT	Campbell, J. *American Neptune*	Oct 61
	PIRATES AND PEPPER	Nalty, B. *Leatherneck*	Nov 60

FLORIDA WAR

1835-1842	FLAMES OVER THE LIGHTHOUSE Marines save the lighthouse after the Dade Massacre of 1836 in Florida	Caygill, H. *Leatherneck*	Mar 55
	THE FLORIDA WAR	*Gazette*	Dec 44

HISTORY OF THE SECOND SEMINOLE WAR, 1835-1842 A modern account utilizing material not available to earlier historians like Sprague	Mahon, J. University of Florida Press, Gainsville, Fla. 1967 (IP)	
THE ORIGIN, PROGRESS AND CONCLUSION OF THE FLORIDA WAR	Sprague, J. D. Appleton-Century Company, Inc. 1848	
THE SEVEN YEARS WAR Henderson's role is featured	Pierce, Capt P., and Capt L. Meyers *Gazette* Sep 48	
THE UNFINISHED WAR Indian Wars, 1836-52, with Henderson	Hilliard, J. *Gazette* Nov 65	
WAR WITH THE SEMINOLES	Montross, L. *Leatherneck* Nov 60, Nov 71	
WHEN OUR COMMANDANT TOOK THE FIELD Henderson	Metcalf, Maj C. *Gazette* Feb 36	
FIRST MARINES IN SOUTH PACIFIC Marines with the Wilkes Exploring Expedition from 1839-1842	*Leatherneck* Oct 42	**1839**

MEXICAN WAR

A CONCLUSIVE EXCULPATION OF THE MARINE CORPS IN MEXICO FROM THE SLANDEROUS ALLEGATIONS OF ONE OF ITS FORMER OFFICERS WITH A FULL OFFICIAL COPY OF THE RECORD OF THE GENERAL COURT MARSHALL HELD AT BROOKLYN, N.Y. 1852; BY WHICH HE WAS FOUND GUILTY AND DISMISSED FROM THE SERVICE: AND COLLATERAL DOCUMENTS Any questions?	Reynolds, Bvt Maj J. Frank Taylor, Washington 1853	**1846-1848**

THE CONQUEST OF CALIFORNIA	McClellan, Maj E. *Gazette*	Sep 23
EL PUCHERO; OR A MIXED DISH FROM MEXICO A Naval Surgeon's account of the march of Watson's Marine Battalion from Vera Cruz to Mexico City	McSherry, R. J. B. Lippincott Co., Philadelphia	1850
"FROM THE HALLS OF MONTEZUMA"	*Gazette*	Mar 41
GREAT DATES OF THE MARINE CORPS: SEPTEMBER 14, 1847 "FROM THE HALLS OF MONTEZUMA" Marines storm Chapultepec	*Leatherneck*	Sep 47
LEVI TWIGGS, 1834-1850 Interesting account of life of Marine officer who served in Mexico written from his letters and memorabilia.	Davis, D. Marine Corps Museum, Quantico	1968 (IP)
THE HALLS OF MONTEZUMA	*Gazette*	Nov 65
THE MARINE CORPS IN MEXICO: SETTING FORTH ITS CONDUCT AS ESTABLISHED BEFORE A GENERAL COURT MARTIAL CONVENED AT BROOKLYN, N. Y. SEPT., 1852, FOR THE TRIAL OF FIRST LT. JOHN S. DEVLIN, USMC	Towers, L. Washington	1852
THE NAVY'S PART IN THE ACQUISITION OF CALIFORNIA, 1846-1848 And the Marines' part.	Neeser, R. *Proceedings*	Mar 08
REFERENCES ON THE MARINES IN THE WAR WITH MEXICO	HQMC	1963
SURFBOATS AND HORSE MARINES: U.S. NAVAL OPERATIONS IN THE MEXICAN WAR, 1846-48 Beautifully-done book with reproductions of old illustrations and documents.	Bauer, K. U.S. Naval Institute	1969 (IP)

Title	Author / Source	Date	Subject
COMEDY AND TRAGEDY IN OUR OCCUPATION OF CALIFORNIA	*Gazette*	Mar 51	**GILLESPIE**
FORGOTTEN MAN Archibald Gillespie	Allen, Sgt L. *Leatherneck*	Jul 48	
GREAT DATES OF THE MARINE CORPS: JULY 8, 1846 "ONE HUNDRED AND ONE YEARS AGO" ARCHIBALD GILLESPIE	*Leatherneck*	Jul 47	
THE HALLS OF MONTEZUMA Gillespie carries dispatches 12,000 miles to Fremont in California. They play a large role in making California American	Lanier, W. *Proceedings*	Oct 41	
MESSENGER OF DESTINY: THE CALIFORNIA ADVENTURES, 1846-1847, OF ARCHIBALD H. GILLESPIE, U.S. MARINE CORPS	Marti, W. John Howell Books San Francisco	1960	
THE SECRET MISSION OF ARCHIBALD GILLESPIE	Simmons, E. *Gazette*	Nov 68	
TO THE HALLS OF MONTEZUMA	*Gazette*	Sep 59	
AMPHIBIOUS OPERATIONS IN THE GULF OF CALIFORNIA, 1847-1848	Craven, T. *American Neptune*	Apr 45	**VERA CRUZ, 1847**
CALIFORNIA BEACHHEADS—1847	*Gazette*	Jan 47	
THE CAPTURE OF VERA CRUZ	*Knickerbocker*	Jul 1847	
THE LANDING OF THE EXPEDITION AGAINST VERA CRUZ	*Military Service Institution of the United States*	May 1899	
THE VERA CRUZ EXPEDITION OF 1847	Bauer, K. *Military Affairs*	Fall 56	
MARINES READY TO INVADE JAPAN IN 1849	*Gazette*	Dec 44	**1849**

PERRY'S EXPEDITION

Year	Title	Author / Source	Date
1853	GREAT DATES OF THE MARINE CORPS, MAY 26, 1853, FIRST MARINES ON OKINAWA From Perry's expedition	*Leatherneck*	May 48
	FIRST MARINE BURIAL IN JAPAN Pvt Robert Williams from the USS Mississippi has the honor. (Honor?)	Drury, Cdr C., USNR *Leatherneck*	Jul 45
	ONE FAR CORNER	Wendt, W. *Leatherneck*	Dec 53
	OUR FIRST LANDING AT OKINAWA	*Leatherneck*	Jun 45
1854	**CHINA AND JAPAN AND A VOYAGE THITHER**	Case, J. Lockwood & Brainard, Hartford, Conn.	1870
	EARLY VOYAGES OF AMERICAN NAVAL VESSELS TO THE ORIENT	Paullin, C. *Proceedings*	Jun 11
	U.S. MARINES ENTER THE SOUTH SEAS	Kirk, Cdr N., USN *Proceedings*	Mar 55

BARRIER FORTS

Year	Title	Author / Source	Date
1856	**THE BARRIER FORTS: A BATTLE, A MONUMENT AND A MYTHICAL MARINE** Canton, China, in 1856, during the British-Chinese War	Nalty, B. HQMC	1962 (IP)
	THE CAPTURE OF THE BARRIER FORTS IN THE CANTON RIVER, CHINA	McClellan, Maj E. *Gazette*	Sep 20
	STORMING THE BARRIER FORTS	*Gazette*	Jul 48
1857	FORMOSA SPY Capt John Sims on mission in Formosa in 1857	Donnelly, R. *Gazette*	Nov 68
	THE WASHINGTON RIOT—1857	*Gazette*	Jul 47

Title	Source	Year
FIJIAN ADVENTURE Marines from USS Vandalia land at Waya, Fiji Islands	Ammon, Lt W., USN *Proceedings* Feb 37	**1858**
REGULATIONS FOR THE UNIFORM AND DRESS OF THE MARINE CORPS OF THE UNITED STATES, 1859 Reprinted from authentic publication	West, C. *Military Collector & Historian* Spring, Summer 1965	**1859**
U.S. MARINE CORPS, FIELD SERVICE, 1859-1868 Pictures and description of Marine uniforms of this period (plate no. 71)	*Military Collector & Historian* Jun 53	
U.S. MARINE CORPS, 1859-1875 Plate no. 13	*Military Collector & Historian* Dec 49	

HARPER'S FERRY

Title	Source	Year
THE ANNALS OF HARPER'S FERRY	Josephus, Jr. (Joseph Barry) Dechert & Co., Hagerstown, Md. 1872	**1859**
AT ALL TIMES READY—THE MARINES AT HARPER'S FERRY	Nalty, B. *Gazette* Oct 59	
THE CAPTURE OF JOHN BROWN	Green, I. *North American Review* Dec 1885	
THE CAPTURE OF JOHN BROWN	Thomason, J. *Gazette* Sep 29	
COLONEL LEE AND THE MARINES AT HARPER'S FERRY	Bubeck, A. *Gazette* Dec 49	
ECHOES OF HARPER'S FERRY	Redpath, J. Thayer & Eldridge, Boston 1860	
INCIDENT AT HARPER'S FERRY	Stone, E. Prentice-Hall, Inc. Englewood Cliffs, N.J. 1956	
JOHN BROWN AT HARPER'S FERRY	Daingerfield, J. *Century* Jun 1885	

	THE LIFE AND LETTERS OF JOHN BROWN	Sanborn, F. Roberts Bros., Boston	1885
	THE PUBLIC LIFE OF CAPTAIN JOHN BROWN	Redpath, J. Thayer & Eldridge, Boston	1860
	RETURN TO HARPER'S FERRY During the Centennial Observance at Harper's Ferry, Marines helped "recapture" John Brown	Ellis, ASSgt T. *Leatherneck*	Dec 59
	THUNDER AT HARPER'S FERRY "You are there" technique is used effectively in this book	Keller, A. Prentice-Hall, Inc., Englewood Cliffs, N.J.	1958
	WHAT A SCHOOLGIRL SAW OF JOHN BROWN'S RAID	Chambers, J. *Harper's*	Jan 02
1861	A FORGOTTEN FIGHT IN FLORIDA Expedition to destroy Negro Fort at Apalachecola River, Ala., Jul 1861	Knox, Capt D., USN *Proceedings*	Apr 36

CIVIL WAR

GENERAL, 1861-1865	**AN ANNOTATED BIBLIOGRAPHY OF THE UNITED STATES MARINES IN THE CIVIL WAR**	O'Quinlivan, M., and R. Gill HQMC	1968 (IP)
	BLUE AND GRAY Marines on both sides fought bravely	Nalty, B. *Leatherneck*	Nov 60, Nov 71
	CIVIL WAR LETTERS AND DOCUMENTS OF FREDERICK TOMLINSON PEET	Peet, F. Published by the author Newport, R.I.	1917
	ELLET'S HORSE MARINES	Day, Lt H. *Gazette*	Mar 39
	FIELD SERVICE IN THE CIVIL WAR; SQUADRON MARINES IN COMBINED OPERATIONS	Cassidy, Sgt J. *Gazette*	Sep 16

A JOURNAL OF THE CRUISE OF THE U.S. SHIP SUSQUEHANNA DURING THE YEARS 1860, 1861, 1862 AND 1863 By a Marine on board her. One of the few "first person" accounts of Marines in this war	Burton, A. Edward O. Jenkins 1863
LANDING STUDIES	Kenyon, Capt H. *Gazette* Mar 38
LETTERS FROM NAVAL OFFICERS IN REFERENCE TO THE UNITED STATES MARINE CORPS	Harris, Col J. Published by the author Washington 1864
THE MARINE CORPS IN THE AMERICAN CIVIL WAR	Hayes, RAdm J., USN *Shipmate* Nov 60, Nov 69
PERSONAL EXPERIENCES IN THE CIVIL WAR Memoirs of a Marine Lt who served in the Marine battalion assigned to the Charleston operation	Peet, F. Published by the author Newport, R.I. 1905
PRIVATES FOR GENERAL SERVICE	Thomas, Capt T. *Gazette* Feb 58
REGISTER OF THE COMMISSIONED, WARRANT AND VOLUNTEER OFFICERS OF THE NAVY OF THE UNITED STATES, INCLUDING OFFICERS OF THE MARINE CORPS AND OTHERS, 1861-1865	USGPO 1866
SEND ME THIRTY MARINES Adm Porter wrote to Commandant Harris "Send me thirty Marines and I shall forever be your debtor."	Long, R. *Leatherneck* Apr, May 61
SERGEANT'S SWORD: A SYMBOL SHEATHED IN HONOR History of this sword which was first worn in the Civil War	Magruder, Maj J. *Gazette* Nov 54

	SERVICES OF THE MARINES DURING THE CIVIL WAR Pamphlet	Collum, Capt R. L. R. Hamersly & Co.	1886
	SOLDIERS OF THE SEA IN CIVIL WAR TIMES	*Marines*	Apr 16
	THE UNITED STATES MARINES AT HARPER'S FERRY AND IN THE CIVIL WAR	Nalty, B. HQMC	1966 (IP)
GOSPORT, APR 20, 1861	GREAT DATES IN THE MARINE CORPS: APRIL 20, 1861 GOSPORT (VIRGINIA) Marines destroy Naval Base there so Confederates can't use it	*Leatherneck*	Apr 48
JUDAH, SEP 14, 1861	GREAT DATES IN THE MARINE CORPS: SEPTEMBER 14, 1861, DESTRUCTION OF THE JUDAH Confederate ship Judah is destroyed by Marines from USS Colorado	*Leatherneck*	Sep 48
HILTON HEAD/ PORT ROYAL NOV 8, 1861	HILTON HEAD MARINES Port Royal operation	*Gazette*	Mar 40
	HILTON HEAD AND PORT ROYAL, 1861	Heinl, R. *Gazette*	Mar 41
	THE WRECK OF THE GOVERNOR It foundered on Nov 2, 1861, as it was carrying a Battalion of Marines to the Port Royal operation	Magruder, LtCol J. *Leatherneck*	Nov 55
NEW BERN, MAR 17, 1862	AN AMPHIBIOUS PRIMER: BATTLE FOR NEW BERN	Ward, R. *Gazette*	Aug 52
	NEW RIVER LANDING—1862	*Gazette*	Jun 48
	YEMASSEE	*Gazette*	Nov 65
DREWREY'S BLUFF, MAY 18, 1862	BATTLE OF DREWREY'S BLUFF Battle produces first Marine Medal of Honor winner of Civil War, Cpl John F. Mackie	*Gazette*	Nov 70
	ON TO RICHMOND Drewrey's Bluff, May 18, 1862	Rentfrow, F. *Leatherneck*	Jan 39

Title	Author / Source	Date	Subject
TWO NAVAL JOURNALS: 1864 (AT THE BATTLE OF MOBILE BAY) THE JOURNAL OF MR. JOHN C. O'CONNELL, CSN, ON THE C.S.S. TENNESSEE—THE JOURNAL OF PVT CHARLES BROTHER, USMC, ON THE U.S.S. HARTFORD	Smith, C. Wyvern Press of S.F.E., Inc., Chicago	1964	**MOBILE BAY, AUG 5, 1864**
ASSAULT ON FORT FISHER	Asprey, R. *Gazette*	Nov 65	**FORT FISHER, DEC 25, 1864**
THE CAPTURE OF FORT FISHER	McClellan, Maj E. *Gazette*	Mar 20	
THE FEDERALS AND FORT FISHER	Simmons, Maj E. *Gazette*	Jan, Feb 51	
THE FORT FISHER CAMPAIGNS, 1864-1865	King, Capt J., USN *Proceedings*	Aug 51	
GREAT DATES OF THE MARINE CORPS: DECEMBER 25, 1864 THE ASSAULT ON FORT FISHER How can a defeat be a "Great Date?"	Evans, Sgt E. *Leatherneck*	Dec 47	
AN INCIDENT AT FORT FISHER Marine Pvt Henry Wasmuth saves the life of a Mr. Evans	Rentfrow, F. *Leatherneck*	Nov 38	
WE FIGHT OUR COUNTRY'S BATTLES Fort Fisher	Rentfrow, F. *Leatherneck*	Feb 30	
AN ESCORT FOR LINCOLN Lt Cochrane makes the trip to Gettysburg with Lincoln	Nalty, B. *Leatherneck*	Feb 61	**GETTYSBURG, 1865**
THE 1868 MARINE CORPS EMBLEM History of the development of the "Globe and Anchor."	Driscoll, LtCol J. *Military Collector & Historian*	Summer 68	**1868**
MISSION TO PEKING, 1870. CAPTAIN McLANE TILTON'S LETTER DESCRIBING HIS TRIP WITH THE SEWARD PARTY TO PEKING	Strobridge, T., and B. Nalty *American Neptune*	Apr 65	**1870**

	THEY LANDED TO LOWER THE FLAG Marine landing party hits Honolulu in 1870	Nalty, B., and T. Strobridge *Proceedings*	Nov 71
	THE WHISKY WAR IN BROOKLYN If you have to fight a war, this is one of the better reasons	*Gazette*	May 48

KOREA-1

1871	THE AMERICAN NAVY IN THE ORIENT IN RECENT YEARS Emphasis on Korean Expedition of 1871	Paullin, C. *Proceedings*	Dec 11
	CAPT MC LANE TILTON AND THE KOREAN INCIDENT OF 1871	Runyan, Maj C. *Gazette*	Feb, Mar 58
	CAPTURE OF THE COREAN PORTS Korea was first spelled with "C"	McClellan, Maj E. *Marines*	Feb 20
	FORGOTTEN GLORY	Pierce, Capt P. *Gazette*	Jan 48
	GLORY OF THE RIVER Marines are assigned to Kangwha for Garrison protection	Tompkins, R. *Leatherneck*	Nov 55
	GREAT EVENTS IN THE MARINE CORPS: KOREA EXPEDITION OF 1871	*Leatherneck*	Dec 48
	THE KOREAN EXPEDITION OF 1871	Bauer, J. *Proceedings*	Feb 48
	KOREA, FORTS AND BATTERIES	*Gazette*	Jan 48
	THE MARCH FROM CHEMULPO TO SEOUL, KOREA	Reisinger, Col H. *Gazette*	Jun 29
	MARINE AMPHIBIOUS LANDING IN KOREA, 1871	Tyson, C. Naval Historical Foundation, Washington	1966
	MC LANE TILTON, 1861-1914 Collection of papers of Marine officer who led the first Korean expedition	Wood, C., and J. Hilliard Marine Corps Museum, Quantico	1968 (IP)

THE NAVY IN KOREA, 1871	Gosnell, H. *American Neptune* Apr 47	
OUR BRIEF CLASH WITH KOREA	Howell, LtCdr G., USN *Proceedings* Nov 35	
OUR FIRST KOREAN WAR	terHorst, Capt J. *Gazette* Dec 53	
OUR LITTLE WAR WITH THE HEATHEN: FIRST KOREAN WAR IN 1871	Castel, A., and A. Nahm *American Heritage* Apr 68	
REFERENCES ON THE KOREAN EXPEDITION OF 1871	HQMC	
VOYAGE TO KOREA	Bronson, V., and TSgt R. Suhosky *Leatherneck* Nov 54	
WHERE WE COULD TAKE A GUN	Rentfrow, F. *Leatherneck* Jan 31	
INFORMATION IN REGARD TO THE UNITED STATES MARINE CORPS 53 page pamphlet	U.S. Marine Corps J. L. Pearson, printer, Washington 1875	**1875**

LABOR RIOTS

THE LABOR RIOTS—SERVICES OF THE 1ST BATTALION 1877	Cochrane, Capt H. *United Service Magazine*	**1877**
THE LABOR RIOTS—SERVICES OF THE 2D BATTALION SEPARATE DETACHMENTS 1877	Cochrane, Capt H. *United Service Magazine*	
BATTLES OF THE AMERICAN MARINES: ALEXANDRIA, EGYPT IN 1882 Marines preserve order after the British bombard the city	McClellan, Maj E. *Marines* Jul 20	**1882**

PANAMA

THE FIRST EXPEDITION TO PANAMA	Evans, Capt F. *Gazette* Jun 16	**1860-1914**

Year	Title	Author / Source	Date
	MARINES AT MATACHIN Protecting the railroad against insurgents in 1885	Ellicott, Capt J., USN (Ret.) *Gazette*	Sep 50
	ON THE ISTHMUS, 1885	Elliott, MajGen G. as told to Col H. Reisinger *Gazette*	Dec 28
	REFERENCES ON THE U.S. MARINES IN PANAMA, 1860-1914	HQMC	
	REPORT OF COMMANDER (B. H.) McCALLA UPON THE NAVAL EXPEDITION TO THE ISTHMUS OF PANAMA, APRIL 1885	USGPO	1885
	WHEN THE MARINES DID DUTY AT PANAMA One of Percy Webb's first published pieces	Webb, GySgt P. *Marines*	Oct 21
1889	ANOTHER MARINE FIRST George LeBlanche (a former Marine) knocks out Jack Dempsey (another one) on August 27, 1889	Miller, Col H. *Leatherneck*	Oct 46
1890	UNDRESS INSPECTION OF THE MARINES	Kelley, J. *Harper's*	Mar 15, 1890

SPANISH AMERICAN WAR

Year	Title	Author / Source	Date
1898	THE BATTLE OF SANTIAGO	*Leatherneck*	Jul 48
	THE CABLE CUTTERS Marines who cut the cable between Spain and Cuba at Cienfuegos in 1898.	Pierce, P. *Leatherneck*	Feb 65
	HENRY CLAY COCHRANE, 1841-1911 Papers of this Marine officer whose career included service in the Spanish-American War	Coker, Capt C. Marine Corps Museum, Quantico	1968 (IP)
	EARLY DAYS OF THE 1ST MARINES: 1899-1902	Giusti, Maj E. HQMC	1958
	GREAT DATES OF THE MARINE CORPS: JULY 3, 1898 THE BATTLE OF SANTIAGO	*Leatherneck*	Jul 48

Title	Source
THE GUANTANAMO CAMPAIGN OF 1898	McCawley, Col C. *Gazette* Sep 16
HISTORY OF THE PIONEER MARINE BATTALION Colorful, first-hand account of the formation and services of Huntington's Battalion in the War with Spain.	Clifford, J. Published by the author Portsmouth, N.H. 1930
HOW WE GOT GUANTANAMO	Heinl, Col R. *Proceedings* Feb 62
HOW THE NAVY WON GUANTANAMO BAY And the Marine Corps	McNeal, LtCdr H., USN *Proceedings* Jun 53
INCIDENTS OF THE VOYAGE OF THE U.S.S. CHARLESTON TO MANILA IN 1898	Farenholt, Capt A., USN *Proceedings* May 24
THE JOURNAL OF FRANK KEELER Letters and diaries of Keeler are edited and brought up-to-date in this interesting account of the War with Spain by a member of Huntington's Battalion	Tyson, C. Marine Corps Museum, Quantico 1971 (IP)
MARINES AT MANILA BAY	Ellicott, Capt J., USN *Gazette* May 53
MARINES AT PLAYA DEL ESTE Cable Station in Cuba destroyed by Marines on Jun 7, 1898	Hanks, C. *Proceedings* Nov 41
MARINES SIGNALING UNDER FIRE AT GUANTANAMO By the famous author of *The Red Badge of Courage.*	Crane, S. *Gazette* Nov 16, Nov 65, Nov 69
MY MEMORIES OF CUBA	Clifford, J. *Leatherneck* Jun 29
OPERATIONS OF THE NAVY AND MARINE CORPS IN THE PHILIPPINE ARCHIPELAGO, 1898-1902	Niblack, LtCdr A., USN *Proceedings* Dec 04
PAGES OF MARINE CORPS HISTORY: AMERICAN MARINES IN PORT RICO DURING THE SPANISH WAR	McClellan, Maj E. *Marines* Feb 20

Title	Author / Source	Date
RECALL IN CUBA A Cuban recalls the Marblehead Expedition of May 11, 1898	Burks, Maj A. *Leatherneck*	Dec 47
REFERENCES ON THE MARINES IN THE WAR WITH SPAIN	HQMC	1962
THE SERGEANT'S PRIVATE MADHOUSE	Crane, S. *Gazette*	Sep 16
"SIR, I HAVE TO REPORT THAT THE SHIP HAS BEEN BLOWN UP AND IS SINKING" The ship is the Maine	McClellan, Maj E. *Leatherneck*	Jan 26
THIRTY YEARS AGO	Williams, BGen D. *Gazette*	Mar 28
THE UNITED STATES MARINES IN THE WAR WITH SPAIN	Nalty, B. HQMC	1967 (IP)
WAR MEMORIES OF GUANTANAMO	Crane, S. *Gazette*	Dec 16
WHEN A CRUISER CAPTURED AN ISLAND Playa Del Este	Hanks, C. *Proceedings*	Jul 22

SAMAR

Year	Title	Author / Source	Date
1901	AMBUSH IN SAMOA Natives ambush Marines	O'Quinlivan, M., and B. Nalty *Leatherneck*	Nov 59
	ATTACK ON SOHOTON CLIFFS	*Gazette*	Nov 70
	GREAT DATES OF THE MARINE CORPS: OCT, 1901 ". . . HE SERVED ON SAMAR"	*Leatherneck*	Oct 48
	HE SERVED ON SAMAR How the tradition started.	*Leatherneck*	Oct 48
	THE MADNESS OF CRANSTON Fiction. About Phillipine Insurrection	Evans, Capt F. *Gazette*	Nov 69
	THE ORDEAL OF SAMAR Fast moving book which tells the story from the historical point-of-view.	Schott, J. The Bobbs-Merrill Company, Indianapolis	1964

SAMAR	Pierce, P. *Leatherneck*	Aug 64
SAMAR	Fry, J. *Gazette*	Nov 65
SAMAR TODAY AND YESTERDAY	Mackie, Sgt W. *Leatherneck*	Jul 45
STAND, GENTLEMEN "He served on Samar."	*Proceedings*	Mar 19
STAND, GENTLEMEN!	Zimmerman, J. *Proceedings*	May 49
STAND, GENTLEMEN Cpl Walter Patterson, one of four survivors of "F" Co., 2d Marines, recalls the ordeal	Stewart, AMSgt W. *Leatherneck*	Jun 59
"STAND, GENTLEMEN, HE SERVED ON SAMAR" Manuscript history	Thacker, J. HQMC	1945
WALLER OF SAMAR	Asprey, R. *Gazette*	May, Jun 61

CHINA

1900-1940

THE AMERICAN LEGATION GUARD ANNUAL Published annually (this is Volume 2, Number 7.)	Carlson, Lt E. The Yu Lein Press Peking	1933
AMERICAN MARINES IN CHINA	Butler, S. Annals of the American Academy	Jul 29
APPROACH TO PEIPING	Thomason, J. *Geographic*	Feb 36
ARMY AND MARINES ON THE CHINA STATION: A STUDY IN MILITARY AND POLITICAL RIVALRIES	Morton, L. *Pacific Historical Review*	Feb 60
THE CANTON BELL	*Globe and Laurel*	Apr 51
THE CHINA EXPEDITION	Shoup, D. *Gazette*	Nov 65

CHINA MARINE Protecting American lives and property was routine business for the Marines on the "China Station."	Leventhal, R. *Gazette*	Nov 72
A CHINA PATROL RECALLED	Brown, W. *Gazette*	Nov 67
CHINA SIDE, 1927	Burks, LtCol A. *Gazette*	Apr 49
THE FESSENDEN FIFES Part of the 4th Marines Regimental Band in China	Carlson, Capt E. *Leatherneck*	Feb 28
GUNBOATS ON CHINA'S YANGTZE The 4th Marines in China from 1927 until WW-2	Willinger, I. *Covers*	Feb 66
LAST REVIEW: MOUNTED MARINES IN CHINA DISBANDED	*Time*	Mar 7, 1938
LIVING CONDITIONS IN CHINA	*Gazette*	Mar 28
THE MARINE'S HANDBOOK OF PRACTICAL CHINESE Beginner lessons in Mandarin Chinese written by a Marine for Marines.	Aldridge, Sgt D. *The Walla Walla*	1938
THE MARINES IN CHINA 1900-01, 1911-12, 1924-25, 1927-29, 1931-38	Metcalf, LtCol C. *Gazette*	Sep 38
MARINES AS AN AID TO DIPLOMACY IN CHINA	Carlson, Capt E. *Gazette*	Feb 36
THE MYSTERIOUS PEKING MUTINY	McClellan, Maj E. *Gazette*	Feb 36
THE OLD CORPS China Marines including WO E. Deegan, F. Knapp, A. Lamar, Capt Q. Strickland, S. Robinson and C. Bates.	Spalding, A. *Leatherneck*	Mar 45
SHANGHAI, 1937 Tactical control of a formation for riot control which served as a forerunner for the Fire Team	Greene, Gen W. *Gazette*	Nov 65

THE SHANGHAI INCIDENT	Vance, Col R. *Gazette*	Oct 53
SOME EXPERIENCES IN FREE CHINA	*Gazette*	Jun 41
YANGTZE PATROL	*Gazette*	Nov 65

BOXER REBELLION 1900

ACTION IN TIENTSIN Russians and USMC fight side-by-side	*Leatherneck*	Sep 42
AMERICAN MARINES IN THE SEIGE OF PEKING	Fenn, C. *Independent*	Nov 29, 1900
AMERICA IN THE CHINA RELIEF EXPEDITION	Daggett, BGen A. Hudson-Kimberly, Kansas City	1903
AN ANNOTATED BIBLIOGRAPHY OF THE UNITED STATES MARINES IN THE BOXER REBELLION Brief (9 pp.) pamphlet which includes historical perspective.	O'Quinlivan, M. HQMC	1961
BATTLES OF THE AMERICAN MARINES: THE BATTLE OF TIENTSIN	McClellan, Maj E. *Marines*	Jan 20
BILL HORTON AND THE BOXER REBELLION Medal of Honor winner remembers the Rebellion	Jaunal, SgtMaj J. *Gazette*	Nov 71
BOXER WAR	*Gazette*	Nov 65
COMRADES IN ARMS How Marines made friends with Royal Marines in Boxer Rebellion	Hargreaves, R. *Gazette*	Oct 64
EXPERIENCES DURING THE BOXER REBELLION	Taussig, Capt J. *Proceedings*	Apr 27
55 DAYS AT PEKING Fiction. A novel about Americans in the Boxer Rebellion	Edwards, S. Paperback edition only, Bantam Books, Inc.	1963
FROM FILIPINOS TO BOXERS IN 1900	Bevan, J. *Leatherneck*	Apr 35

	HELL IN CHINA	Heinl, Col R. *Gazette*	Nov 59
	"IN MANY A STRIFE, WE FOUGHT FOR LIFE"	Rentfrow, F. *Leatherneck*	Jul 31
	MILITARY OPERATIONS AND DEFENSES OF THE SEIGE OF PEKING	Myers, Capt J. *Proceedings*	Sep 02
	THE MISSION OF MAJOR LEONARD	Rentfrow, F. *Leatherneck*	Feb 39
	OPERATIONS IN NORTH CHINA	Davidson, LtW., USN *Proceedings*	Dec 1900
	THE SEYMOUR RELIEF EXPEDITION	Wurtsbaugh, Lt D., USN *Proceedings*	Jun 02
	"WE WILL DO OUR BEST" Narrative of Marine actions in the defense of the Peking Legation	Smith, Capt O. *Proceedings*	Nov 28
	"WHICH WE ARE PROUD TO SERVE"	Rentfrow, F. *Leatherneck*	Jun 31
	WITH THE MARINES ON THE MARCH TO PEKING, CHINA—1900	Bevan, J. *Leatherneck*	Jun, Jul 35

BANANA WARS

GENERAL, 1850-1935	THE AIR SERVICE IN MINOR WARFARE	Rowell, Maj R. *Proceedings*	Oct 29
	AIRCRAFT IN BUSH WARFARE Marine air in Haiti and Nicaragua	Rowell, Maj R. *Gazette*	Sep 29
	AVIATION IN GUERRILLA WARFARE	Campbell, Capt H. *Gazette*	Feb, May 31
	BANANA GOLD	Beals, C. J. B. Lippincott Co., Philadelphia	1932
	BUSH BRIGADES "Pete" Ellis could write as well as spy	Ellis, E. *Gazette*	Mar 21, Mar 29, Mar 66

CONSTABULARIES FOR CENTRAL AMERICA	Keyser, Maj R. *Gazette*	Jun 26
CRISIS DIPLOMACY: A HISTORY OF INTERVENTION POLICIES AND PRACTICES It hasn't changed much	Graber, D. Public Affairs Press, Washington	1959
THE FIVE REPUBLICS OF CENTRAL AMERICA And the American role in exploiting them.	Munro, D. Oxford University Press	1918
INDOCTRINATION OF LATIN-AMERICAN SERVICE	Davis, LtCol H. *Gazette*	Jun 20
PROTECTION OF AMERICAN INTERESTS Nicaragua and China	*Gazette*	Sep 27
THE PROTECTION OF CITIZENS ABROAD BY THE ARMED FORCES OF THE UNITED STATES Lists the 76 interventions between 1813 and 1927	Offutt, M. Johns Hopkins Press, Baltimore	1928
THE RAMBLING ROCHESTER Famous Banana Wars ship	Rene, Lt J. *Gazette*	Nov 30
RIGHT TO PROTECT CITIZENS IN FOREIGN COUNTRIES	U.S. Department of State, Washington	1934
THEY WERE CALLED "BANANA WARS"	Savage, W. *The State* Columbia, S.C.	Sep 8, 1963
U.S. INTERVENTION IN LATIN AMERICA: 1900-1965	*Scholastic*	Sep 16, 1965
THE UNITED STATES AND THE CARIBBEAN AREA	Munro, D. World Press Foundation, Boston	1934
THE UNITED STATES MARINES IN THE DOMINICAN REPUBLIC, HAITI AND NICARAGUA: A BIBIOLGRAPHY OF PUBLISHED WORKS AND MAGAZINE ARTICLES	HQMC	

NICARAGUA

GENERAL, 1853-1933

AMERICAN MARINES IN NICARAGUA	McClellan, Maj E. *Gazette*	Mar, Jun 21
AMERICAN POLICY IN NICARAGUA	Stimson, H. Charles Scribner's Sons	1927
THE BANANA EMPIRE: A CASE STUDY OF ECONOMIC IMPERIALISM	Kepner, C., and J. Soothill Vanguard Press, Chicago	1935
A BRIEF HISTORY OF THE RELATIONS BETWEEN THE UNITED STATES AND NICARAGUA, 1909-1928	U.S. Department of State, Washington	1928
DOLLARS FOR BULLETS—STORY OF AMERICAN RULE IN NICARAGUA	Denny, H. Dial Press	1929
GUERRILLA LESSONS FROM NICARAGUA	Megee, V. *Gazette*	Jun 65
HIKING AND FIGHTING	Nichols, Sgt J. *Recruiters' Bulletin*	Nov 16
THE KENTUCKY FEUD IN NICARAGUA	Carter, C. *The World's Work*	Jul 27
THE LOOTING OF NICARAGUA	DeNogales, R. Robert M. McBride & Company	1928
NICARAGUA AND THE UNITED STATES	Cox, I. World Peace Foundation, Boston	1927
OUR NEIGHBOR NICARAGUA	Cramer, F. Frederick A. Stokes Co.	1929
THE UNITED STATES MARINES IN NICARAGUA	Nalty, B. HQMC	1962 (IP)

Title	Author / Source	Date	Section
THE WALL BETWEEN Fiction. A novel about Marine Master Sgt John Kendall who falls in love with the Colonel's niece and sees action in Nicaragua	Paine, R. Charles Scribner's Sons	1914	
MARINES SEE THE REVOLUTION: NICARAGUA	Thomason, J. *Scribner's Magazine*	Jul 27	**FIRST INTERVENTIONS, 1853-1925**
THE NAVY AND FILIBUSTERING IN THE FIFTIES The first time in Nicaragua in the 1850's	Feipel, L. *Proceedings*	Jul 18	
ACTION AND PATROL REPORTS, LA PAZ CENTRO, OCOTAL, TELPANECA CHIPOTE	HQMC *Gazette*	1928-29	**SECOND INTERVENTION, 1926-1933**
AMERICAN SUPERVISION OF THE NICARAGUAN ELECTIONS	Dodds, H. *Foreign Affairs*	Apr 29	
BEHIND THE RECORD	Reisinger, Col H. *Gazette*	Aug 33	
BLUEJACKETS Narrative of the Second Nicaraguan Campaign dealing especially with the landings of 1926-27	Pagano, D. Meador Publishing Co., Boston	1932	
COCO PATROL	Stiff, LtCol H. *Gazette*	Feb 57	
THE COCO PATROL—1928 Picture on the back cover	*Gazette*	Dec 47	
THE COCO RIVER PATROL The famous action which established the reputation of Edson as a jungle fighter	Edson, Capt M. *Gazette*	Aug, Nov 36 Feb 37	
COMBAT OPERATIONS IN NICARAGUA The fight at La Paz Centro, May 18, 1927	Fitzgerald, Sgt G. *Gazette*	Dec 28	
COMBAT OPERATIONS IN NICARAGUA Summary of action reports	Hatfield, Capt G. *Gazette*	Jan, Mar, Jun, Sep 29	

Title	Author / Source	Date
DON'T PLAN THESE BATTLES They never go according to the script	Daniels, J. *Gazette*	Sep 41
EVENTS IN NICARAGUA SINCE FEB 28, 1928	*Gazette*	Jun-Sep 28
EXPEDITION TO MATAGALPA	Jenkins, J. *Gazette*	Sep 41
THE FIGHT OF COYOTEPE HILL	*Gazette*	Nov 65
LA FLOR ENGAGEMENT Marines meet Sandino in May of 1928	Bleasdale, Capt V. *Gazette*	Feb 32
THE LAST BANANA WAR Second Nicaraguan Campaign	Heinl, Col R. *Leatherneck*	Oct, Nov 60
LEADING NATIVE TROOPS: COUNTERINSURGENCY CASE STUDY By the author of *The Sandino Affair*	Macaulay, N. *Gazette*	Jun 63
MARINES RETURN FROM NICARAGUA	*Gazette*	Feb 33
MR. COOLIDGE'S JUNGLE WAR	O'Conner, R. *American Heritage*	Dec 67
THE MOUNTED EXPEDITION TO MATAGALPA	*Gazette*	Sep 41
NICARAGUA: IN AGAIN, OUT AGAIN	*Foreign Affairs*	Apr 31
THE NICARAGUAN ELECTIONS IN 1928	McNeill, V. *Gazette*	Sep 66
THE NICARAGUAN SITUATION	Williams, BGen D. *Gazette*	Jun 27, Nov 30
NO SURRENDER For Sandino on Jul 15, 1927	Wright, J. *Leatherneck*	Oct 40
THE NEUVA SEGOVIA EXPEDITION Sandino	McClellan, Maj E. *Gazette*	May, Aug 31

PROFESSIONAL NOTES Air/Ground operations against El Chipote Jul 1, 1927	Rowell, Maj R. *Gazette* Dec 28
QUIJOTE ON A BURRO: SANDINO AND THE MARINES	Cummins, L. University of California Press, Berkeley, Cal. 1958
THE SAGA OF THE COCO Edson's patrol	McClellan, Maj E. *Gazette* Nov 30 *Proceedings* Jan 33
THE SANDINO AFFAIR Excellent study by former Marine officer of what made Sandino tick. Includes maps, illustrations and references to the amazing number of later-famous Marines who fought Sandino.	Macaulay, N. Quadrangle Press, Chicago 1967
SANDINO CALLS OFF HIS GADFLY WAR	*Literary Digest* Feb 18, 1933
SANDINO OF NICARAGUA, BANDIT OR PATRIOT?	*Literary Digest* Feb 4, 1928
SANDINO STRIKES AGAIN April, 1931 raids	Wood, Capt J., and Lt J. Wilmeth *Leatherneck* Feb 39
THE SECOND NICARAGUA CAMPAIGN	Gray, Maj J. *Gazette* Feb 33
THE STRATEGIC DEFENSIVE IN NICARAGUA, 1927-1929 An essay from the point-of-view of Sandino	Weltman, B. U.S. Naval Academy, Annapolis 1956
SUPERVISING NICARAGUAN ELECTIONS, 1928	McClellan, Maj E. *Proceedings* Jan 33
THE SUPPLY SERVICE IN WESTERN NICARAGUA	Sanderson, LtCol C. *Gazette* May 32
TESTIMONY BEFORE SENATE FOREIGN RELATIONS COMMITTEE, 18 FEBRUARY 1928	Lejeune, MajGen J. *Gazette* Mar 28
TIGER OF THE MOUNTAINS "Chesty" Puller	McKenzie, Lt S. *Gazette* Nov 71

Subject	Title	Author / Source	Date
	A TRY AT PEACE AND JUSTICE WITH SANDINO	Sayre, J. *World Tomorrow*	Mar 28
	TYPICAL COMBAT PATROLS IN NICARAGUA The parallels between Nicaragua and Vietnam are amazing	Walraven, Lt J. *Gazette*	Dec 29
	UNITED STATES SUPERVISION OF THE NICARAGUAN ELECTIONS 29 pp pamphlet on Marines' supervision of the elections of 1928, 30 and 32	Jamison, Capt R. University of Maryland Press, College Park, Md.	1961
	THE UNLOVABLE LATIN (AUGUSTINO SANDINO)	Tallent, SSgt R. *Gazette*	Nov 59
	WITH THE HORSE MARINES IN NICARAGUA	Holmes, Capt M. *Leatherneck*	Apr 31
	WITH SANDINO IN NICARAGUA	Beals, C. *Nation*	Mar 28, 1928
AVIATION	AIR ACTION IN NICARAGUA Maj Ross Rowell and squadron dive bomb Sandino	Roper, W. *Gazette*	Nov 72
	AIR SUPPORT TO THE MARINE CORPS EXPEDITIONARY FORCE IN EASTERN NICARAGUA, 1927-1929 Essay which indicates how air support contributed to the overall success of the Second Nicaraguan Campaign. Includes excerpts from reports made then.	Kilday, J. U.S. Naval Academy, Annapolis	1959
	BRINGING "DUCKS" FROM NICARAGUA "Ducks" were the aircraft of the Squadrons on duty in Nicaragua. They were flown from Managua to Quantico in December of 1932	Major, H. *Proceedings*	Dec 33
	CLOSE AIR SUPPORT AS DEVELOPED BY THE UNITED STATES IN NICARAGUA, 1927-1933	Glover, Mid W., USN Midshipman Class Essays of 1954 U.S. Naval Academy, Annapolis	1955

FLIGHT Novel about a Marine Aero Squadron in Nicaragua. A movie was made from this novel later	Franklyn, T.	1929	
FORCED DOWN IN THE JUNGLES OF NICARAGUA	Heritage, SSgt G. *Leatherneck*	May 32	
THE GENESIS OF AIR SUPPORT IN GUERRILLA OPERATIONS	Megee, Gen V. *Proceedings*	Jun 65	
GREAT EVENTS IN THE MARINE CORPS: AIR RESCUE AT QUILALI Schilt wins his Medal of Honor	*Leatherneck*	Nov 48	
HE REMEMBERED HIS MISSION Maj Pierce over Nueva-Segovia, May 31, 1927	McClellan, Maj E. *Gazette*	Nov 30	
THE MARINE AUTOGIRO IN NICARAGUA Forerunner of the Chopper	Montross, L. *Gazette*	Feb 53	
MARINE AVIATORS IN NICARAGUA	*Leatherneck*	Mar 28	
MARINE CORPS AVIATION Lessons learned in Nicaragua	Brainard, Maj E. *Gazette*	Mar 28	
MARINE CORPS AVIATION IN SECOND NICARAGUAN CAMPAIGN	Mulcahy, Capt F., USN *Proceedings*	Aug 33	
QUILALI AIR STRIP	*Gazette*	Nov 70	
THE CONSTABULARY IN THE DOMINICAN REPUBLIC AND NICARAGUA: PROGENY AND LEGACY OF UNITED STATES INTERVENTION	Goldwirt, M. University of Florida Press, Gainsville, Fla.	1962	**GUARDIA DE NACIONAL**
A DISCUSSION OF THE VOLUNTARIO TROOPS IN NICARAGUA By the Marine who killed Charlemagne	Hanneken, Maj H. *Gazette*	Nov 42	
GUARDIA NACIONAL	Smith, J. *Gazette*	Nov 65	

	THE GUARDIA NACIONAL DE NICARAGUA By the famous leader of the 2d Marine Raiders in WW-2	Carlson, Capt E. *Gazette*	Aug 37
	THE GUARDIA AS A POLICE FORCE	Carlson, Capt E. *Leatherneck*	Oct 32
	LA PALABRA DEL GRINTO: LEADERSHIP OF THE NICARAGUAN NATIONAL GUARD	Reisinger, Col H. *Proceedings*	Feb 35
	NATIVE OFFICERS CORPS, GUARDIA NACIONAL DE NICARAGUA One of the first published efforts of the head Combat Correspondent of WW-2	Denig, LtCol R. *Gazette*	Nov 32
	A REVIEW OF THE ORGANIZATION AND OPERATIONS OF THE GUARDIA NACIONAL DE NICARAGUA 1927-1933 Another early writing effort by a WW-2 leader	Smith, Maj J. MCS, Quantico	1937
1902	PALMA TROPHY MATCH Rifle Match	*Shooting and Fishing*	Sep 16, 1902
1903	**GUESTS OF THE CONQUERING LION—THE DIPLOMATIC MISSION TO ABYSSINIA, 1903** Marines visit Africa	Nalty, B. HQMC	1961
1906	MARINES IN SAN FRANCISCO FIRE AND EARTHQUAKE	*Gazette*	Nov 36
	THE "PLATT AMENDMENT" The U.S. makes itself responsible for a stable government in Cuba. Marines enforce the policy	*Gazette*	Nov 65
1908	AN ASSOCIATION WAS FORMED The attempts in 1908-09 to remove the Corps from the Navy	Heinl, Col R. *Gazette*	Apr 63
1911	SITTING ON THE LID	Noble, C. *Harper's*	Jun 24, 1911
1912	RECOLLECTIONS OF THE 1912 CUBAN EXPEDITION	Gray, Maj J. *Gazette*	May 32

SOLDIERS AND SAILORS, TOO Marines are both	Archibald, J., and B. Braley *Collier's* May 16, 1914	**1914**
SOLDIERS OF THE SEA	Lee, F. *Overland* Sep 14	
UNITED STATES MARINE CORPS	Parker, W. *Outlook* Nov 25, 1914	
WALTER GARVIN IN MEXICO Fiction. Marine officer is on a spy mission to Mexico just prior to Vera Cruz Expedition of 1914. Butler's real life adventures inspired the novel	Butler, BGen S., and Lt A. Burks Dorrance & Co., Inc., Philadelphia 1927	
WITH THE LITTLE BROTHER OF THE NAVY Thanks!	Palmer, F. *Everybody's* Jun 14	

VERA CRUZ

GEORGE C. REID, 1898-1960 Papers of an officer whose career included pre-World War 1 service in Vera Cruz	Davis, D., R. Long and Col T. Wilson Marine Corps Museum, Quantico 1967 (IP)	**1914**
THE LANDINGS AT VERA CRUZ: 1914 Typically well done Institute book with authentic documentation and illustrations of the Expedition.	Sweetman, J. U.S. Naval Institute, Annapolis 1968 (IP)	
VERA CRUZ	Osterman, E. *Gazette* Nov 65	
THE VERA CRUZ STORY	Houck, LtCol H. *Gazette* Nov 69	
WITH THE U.S. MARINES IN MEXICO	*Gazette* Sep 16	
MILL FOR MARKSMANSHIP Marine training	Jenks, J. *Harper's* Oct 16, 1915	**1915**

HAITI

	Title	Author / Publisher	Date
1915-1934	**THE AMERICAN INTERVENTION IN HAITI AND THE DOMINICAN REPUBLIC**	Kelsey, C. American Academy of Political and Social Science, Philadelphia	1922
	BLACK BAGDAD Adventures of Craige who served in Haiti during this period	Craige, Capt J. Minton, Balch and Company	1933
	BLACK BANDITS OF HAITI	Bimberg, E. *Leatherneck*	Aug 41
	BLACK DEMOCRACY, THE STORY OF HAITI	Davis, H. Dial Press	1936
	BLACK HAITI	Niles, B. G. P. Putnam's Sons	1926
	BOUCAN CARRE Guard de'Haiti operations against the Cacos Bandits	Gray, Maj J. *Gazette*	Nov 31
	A BRIEF HISTORY OF THE INTERVENTION IN HAITI	Coffey, Cdr R., USN *Proceedings*	Aug 22
	A BRIEF HISTORY OF THE INTERVENTION IN HAITI	Coffey, R. U.S. Naval Institute, Annapolis	1922
	CANNIBAL COUSINS Sequel to *Black Bagdad*	Craige, Capt J. Minton, Balch and Company	1934
	THE CROSS OF BARON SAMEDI Fiction. Marine officer is in the Gendarmerie d'Haiti during Marine involvement	Dohrman, R. Houghton-Mifflin Company, Boston	1958
	THE DEVELOPMENT OF HAITI DURING THE LAST FISCAL YEAR By the Commandant	Russell, BGen J. *Gazette*	Jun 30
	GARDE D'HAITI, 20 YEARS OF ORGANIZATION AND TRAINING BY THE UNITED STATES MARINE CORPS: 1915-1934 Factual report of the futility of trying to train other countries to do it the way we think it should be done	McCrocklin, J. U.S. Naval Institute, Annapolis	1956 (IP)

THE GENDARMERIE D'HAITI	Bride, Capt F. *Gazette*	Dec 18
GREAT DATES OF THE CORPS: OCTOBER 31, 1919 THE DEATH OF CHARLEMAGNE Hannekin shoots him	*Leatherneck*	Oct 47
GUARD D'HAITI	Calixte, Col D. *Gazette*	Feb 36
HAITI	Hanneken, H. *Gazette*	Nov 65
HAITI UNDER AMERICAN CONTROL, 1915-30	Millspaugh, A. World Peace Foundation, Boston	1931
HAITI AND ITS REGENERATION BY THE UNITED STATES	*Geographic*	Dec 20
HAITI AND THE UNITED STATES, 1714-1938	Montague, L. Duke University Press, Durham, N.C.	1940
THE HAITIAN GENDARMERIE	*Gazette*	Jun 26
INQUIRY INTO THE OCCUPATION AND ADMINISTRATION OF HAITI AND SANTO DOMINGO	U.S. Congressional Record	1921-22
KING FAUSTIN—2 Faustin Wirkus was the "White King." He was a Marine NCO feared and respected by the Haitians.	Engle, E. *Gazette*	Nov 68
KING OF LA GONAVE About WO Faustin Wirkus	Pierce, P. *Leatherneck*	Jul 60
KING OF THE BANANA WAR Wirkus	Greathouse, Lt R. *Gazette*	Jun 60
LONG LOVE THE KING!	Mardus, E. *Leatherneck*	Sep 47
THE MAGIC ISLAND	Seabrook, W. Published by the author	1929
THE MARINE "KING"	Myers, R. *Leatherneck*	Jan 44

A MARINE REMEMBERS HAITI	Scott, D. *Leatherneck*	Feb 43
A MEDAL FOR LT OSTERMANN Killed in Haiti in 1916	MacCloskey, M. *Gazette*	Nov 64
MONOGRAPH: REPUBLIC OF HAITI	HQMC	1943
OCCUPIED HAITI	Balch, E. Writers' Publishing Co.	1927
PAPA DOC—THE TRUTH ABOUT HAITI TODAY Includes some references to Marines' futile efforts there	Diederich, B., and A. Burt McGraw-Hill, Inc.	1969 (IP)
THE RAID AT PORT AU PRINCE Jan 16, 1916	Dennison, L. *Recruiters' Bulletin*	Mar 20
SALIENT HAITIAN FACTS	Evans, Col F. *Gazette*	Feb, May 31
THE SEIZURE OF HAITI BY THE UNITED STATES	Bausman, F. Foreign Policy Association	1922
SELF-DETERMINING HAITI	Johnson, J. *Nation*	Aug, Sep 20
SERVICE IN HAITI	Coyle, Capt R. *Gazette*	Dec 16
SMALL WINGS 4th Marine Air Squadron in Haiti in 1919	Hall, Sgt H. *Leatherneck*	Nov 62
THE TAKING OF FORT RIVIERE	Thrasher, Maj T. *Gazette*	Feb 31
WATCHING BANDITS IN HAITI FROM THE AIR	Smith, 1st Sgt N. *Recruiters' Bulletin*	Oct 19
THE WHITE KING OF LA GONAVE Wirkus was the King and La Gonave was his kingdom (small island, part of Haiti)	Wirkus, F., and T. Dudley Doubleday, Doran & Co., Inc., Garden City, N.Y.	1931

THE YEAR IN HAITI	*Gazette* Nov 30	

DOMINICAN REPUBLIC

THE AMERICANS IN SANTO DOMINGO	Knight, M. Vanguard Press, Inc. 1928	**1915-1925**
. . . AND SANTO DOMINGO With VO-1M flying the DH-4B in 1922	Boyden, BGen H. *Gazette* Nov 72	
BAD HOMBRE Fiction. A novel about the Marines in Santo Domingo.	Flewelling, W. Meador Publishing Co., Boston 1931	
CAMPAIGNING IN SANTO DOMINGO	Winans, SgtMaj R. *Recruiters' Bulletin* Mar 17	
DIPLOMATIC SPURS Dominican Republic, 1916-24	Saxon, T. *Gazette* Nov 65	
DIPLOMATIC SPURS: OUR EXPERIENCES IN SANTO DOMINGO	Miller, LtCol C. *Gazette* Feb, May, Aug 35	
DOMINICAN ESCAPADE	Cameron, C. *Recruiters' Bulletin* Jun 17	
DOMINICAN SERVICE	Thorpe, Col G. *Gazette* Dec 19	
INDOCTRINATION IN SANTO DOMINGO	Kilmartin, R. *Gazette* Dec 22	
LA GUARDIA NACIONAL DOMINICANS	Williams, Maj C. *Gazette* Sep 18	
MAPPING ACTIVITIES AND COMPILATION OF HAND-BOOKS BY THE SECOND BRIGADE, USMC, IN THE DOMINICAN REPUBLIC	Wellman, Lt L. *Gazette* Sep 23	
MARINE AVIATORS DEFEAT BANDIT BAND	*Recruiters' Journal* Sep 19	
OPERATIONS ASHORE IN THE DOMINICAN REPUBLIC	McClellan, Maj E. *Proceedings* Feb 21	

	PRIVATE KEMP REPORTS ON OUR WAR IN SANTO DOMINGO Thank you, Private Kemp	*Literary Digest* Feb 22, 1919
	TRAINING NATIVE TROOPS IN SANTO DOMINGO	Fellows, Lt E. *Gazette* Dec 23
	THE UNITED STATES AND THE DOMINICAN REPUBLIC	Calixte, Col D. Hispanic-American Historical Review Feb 27
	THE UNITED STATES OCCUPATION OF THE SANTO DOMINICAN REPUBLIC	Baughman, Cdr C., USN *Proceedings* Dec 25
1916	A PLEA FOR A MISSION AND DOCTRINE Corps soon got one at Belleau Wood	Russell, MajGen J. *Gazette* Jun 16
	WHAT THE MARINES ARE DOING, A MONTHLY SUMMARY OF ACTIVITIES	*Marines* Jan 16
1917	BLOOD IS THICKER THAN WATER: THE U.S. MARINE CORPS' RECOLLECTIONS OF THE ROYAL WELSH FUSELIERS From Boxer Rebellion	Richards, Gen G. *Century* Sep 17
	FIRST TO FIGHT ON LAND OR SEA	Cushing, C. *Independent* May 26, 1917
	THE GROWTH OF A HUNDRED YEARS	Evans, Capt F. *Gazette* Jun 17
	SOMETHING NEW FOR THE MARINES	*Literary Digest* Nov 10, 1917
	UNITED STATES MARINE CORPS	*Science American* Jul 28, 1917

WORLD WAR I

GENERAL 1917-1918	AMERICAN DECORATIONS AND INSIGNIA OF HONOR AND SERVICE	*Geographic* Dec 19
	AMERICAN MARINES	Kauffman, R. *Living Age* Jul 6, 1918

AMERICAN MARINES IN SIBERIA DURING THE WORLD WAR	McClellan, Maj E. *Gazette* Jun 20
AN ANNOTATED BIBLIOGRAPHY OF THE UNITED STATES MARINE CORPS IN THE FIRST WORLD WAR	Hilliard, J. HQMC 1967 (IP)
AND A FEW MARINES Fiction. A selection of short stories about Marines in WW-1, and elsewhere.	Thomason, Col J. Charles Scribner's Sons 1943
AS IT WAS BEFORE	Jenkins, J. *Gazette* Mar 41
THE "BABE" GySgt Herman Tharau, killed in France, August 8, 1918	Nilo, J. *Gazette*
BRAVE DEEDS OF THE MARINE CORPS	Daniels, J. *N.Y. Times Current History Magazine* Jan 19, 1919
CRUISE AMONG THE LEATHER-NECKS ON THE FIRING LINE	*Literary Digest* Sep 28, 1918
DEMOBILIZING THE BRIGADES	Evans, LtCol F. *Gazette* Dec 19
DEVIL DOGS Reprint of a story from *Fix Bayonets.*	Thomason, Col J. *Leatherneck* Nov 50
DEVIL DOGS IN THE MAKING AT RECRUIT DEPOT, U.S. MARINE CORPS, PARRIS ISLAND, S.C.	U.S. Marine Corps Publicity Bureau Brooklyn, N.Y. 1917
THE ETERNAL SPIRIT	Asprey, Capt R. *Gazette* Nov 61
FIGHTING IN FRANCE WITH THE MARINES	Jenkins, N. Scribner's Jan 19
THE FIRST MARINE AVIATION FORCE	Emmons, R. *Cross and Cockade Journal* Summer, Autumn 65
FIRSTS IN FRANCE	*Gazette* May 35

FIX BAYONETS Fiction. The classic about Marines in WW-1. A collection of short stories so real that this book is in the History Department of most libraries (rather than the Fiction Dept.)	Thomason, Capt J. Charles Scribner's Sons	1926
FOURRAGERE OF THE 5TH AND 6TH MARINES How Marines won the Award	Thacker, J. *Gazette*	Mar 44
FRENCH FOURRAGERE	*Leatherneck*	Apr 48
GLORY—AND SOME OF THE HUMOR OF THE MARINES	*Literary Digest*	Jan 11, 1919
HARBORD AND LEJEUNE: A COMMAND PRECEDENT How a Marine and an Army General handled a tricky command relationship problem	Edwards, LtCol H. *Gazette*	Jul 53
THE INSIGNIA OF OUR UNIFORMED FORCES	*Geographic*	Oct 17
LEATHERNECKS AND DOUGHBOYS	Gordon, G. Published by the author, Chicago	1927
LIAISON IN THE WORLD WAR	Ellis, Maj E. *Gazette*	Jun 20
A LIST OF THE OFFICERS AND ENLISTED MEN OF THE UNITED STATES MARINE CORPS WHO LOST THEIR LIVES WHILE SERVING OVERSEAS DURING THE WORLD WAR	HQMC	1918
THE MARINES HAVE LANDED	Evans, Maj F. *Gazette*	Dec 17
THE MEDICAL DEPARTMENT OF THE UNITED STATES NAVY WITH THE ARMY AND MARINE CORPS IN FRANCE IN WORLD WAR 1; ITS FUNCTIONS AND EMPLOYMENT—NAVMED 1197	USGPO	1947

1917	Montross, L. *Leatherneck*	Nov 71
NO NEED FOR DESPAIR	Baldwin, H. *Gazette*	Oct, Nov 62
NOT SINGLE-HANDED Reflections of staying power of Germans as learned by WW-1 Marines	Laughlin, Lt P. *Gazette*	Mar 42
PARRIS ISLAND IN THE WAR	Coyle, W. *Gazette*	Dec 25
POINTS OF HONOR Eleven short stories about Marines in France written by a Marine who also wrote the best Marine novel of World War 1—*Through the Wheat.*	Boyd, T. Charles Scribner's Sons	1925
SUPPLY OF AN INFANTRY DIVISION IN ACTIVE OPERATIONS	Puryear, Maj B. *Gazette*	Jun 20
THROUGH THE WHEAT If you think your War was tough, read this book. One of the three or four best Marine books of all time.	Boyd, T. Charles Scribner's Sons Paperback edition by Award Books	1927 1964
THE UNITED STATES MARINE CORPS IN THE WORLD WAR Complete summary of Marine operations including charts and tables	McClellan, Maj E. HQMC	1920 1968 (IP)
WHEN THE MARINES WENT TO FRANCE: 1917-1918 Operations of the 4th Marine Brigade	*Proceedings*	Nov 67
WHERE THE MARINES FOUGHT IN FRANCE Pictorial guide to places associated with the 4th Brigade in France	Antrim, R. Park and Antrim, Chicago	1919
WITH THE U.S. MARINES AT PARRIS ISLAND TRAINING STATION Pictorial tour of the facilities used to train recruits for duty in France	Culp, Sgt J. Marine Publicity Bureau, Philadelphia	1918

	Title	Source
	YOU WOULDN'T DARE TELL IT TO THE MARINES NOW	*Literary Digest* Jun 29, 1918
BELLEAU WOOD, JUN, 1918	. . . AND BELLEAU WOOD	Johnson, Capt R. *Gazette* Jun 55
	AT BELLEAU WOOD Thoroughly documented book about the battle from all three sides (Marines, French, Germans). Reads like a novel, only better.	Asprey, R. G. P. Putnam's Sons 1965
	THE BATTLE OF BELLEAU WOOD: THE MARINES STAND FAST A readable, well illustrated account of the battle	Suskind, R. The Macmillan Company 1969
	THE BATTLE FOR THE POSSESSION OF BELLEAU WOODS, JUNE, 1918 Fascinating account from the Kraut point-of-view. (He thought Marines were crazy!)	Otto, LtCol E. (German Army) *Proceedings* Nov 28
	THE BATTLES FOR THE POSSESSION OF BELLEAU WOODS JUNE, 1918	Otto, LtCol E. (German Army) U.S. Naval Institute, Annapolis 1928
	BELLEAU WOOD	*Leatherneck* Jun 48
	BELLEAU WOOD	Krulewitch, MajGen M. *Gazette* Nov 71
	BELLEAU WOOD AND THE AMERICAN ARMY, THE 2D AND 26TH DIVISIONS, JUNE AND JULY, 1918 From the French point-of-view	Androit, Capt R. (French Army) Belleau Wood Memorial Association, Washington 1923
	BLOOD AND WHEAT First person description of the action	Barnett, B. *Leatherneck* Dec 42
	BLOODY BELLEAU WOOD Written from experience, by the author of "What Price, Glory?" who lost a leg at Belleau Wood	Stallings, L. *American Heritage* Jun 63

Title	Source
BOIS DE BELLEAU Woods of Belleau	Robertson, Capt J. *Gazette* Nov 62
BOIS DE LA BRIGADE DE MARINE	Wilmeth, Lt J., USA *Gazette* Mar 39
A BRIGADE OF MARINES	Silverthorn, LtGen M. *Gazette* Nov 71
CAPTURE OF BELLEAU WOOD	*N.Y. Times Current History Magazine* Jul 18
CAPTURE OF HILL 142, BATTLE OF BELLEAU WOOD AND CAPTURE OF BOURESCHES	McClellan, Maj E. *Gazette* Sep-Dec 20
DAN DALY The Sgt Maj hero of Belleau Wood who reportedly said, "Come on, you guys, do you want to live forever?"	*Leatherneck* Mar 49
DAN DALY Medal of honor hero of Belleau Wood	*Gazette* Nov 54
DAN DALY: RELUCTANT HERO	Dieckmann, E. *Gazette* Nov 60
DEVIL DOGS How the Marines got the name at Belleau Wood	Mackin, E. *Leatherneck* Nov 72
DO YOU WANT TO LIVE FOREVER! Fictionalized account of Daly and the other Marines at Belleau Wood	Suskind, R. Paperback edition only. Bantam Books, Inc. 1964
ETERNITY IN THREE DAYS: BATTLE OF CHATEAU THIERRY	Frothingham, G. *Independent* Jul 14, 1928
GOD HAVE MERCY ON US; A STORY OF 1918 Prize war novel of WW-1 about Belleau Wood. Very dramatic. Lots of action	Scanlon, W. Houghton-Mifflin Co., Boston 1929

GREAT DATES OF THE MARINE CORPS: JUNE 3, 1918, "RETREAT, HELL, WE JUST GOT HERE" Said by a Marine officer whose name is not known just before the battle	Johnston, Sgt L. *Leatherneck*	Jun 47
GREAT DATES IN THE MARINE CORPS: JUNE 6, 1918, BELLEAU WOOD	*Leatherneck*	Jun 48
THE GREATEST DAY	Mowry, W. *Gazette*	Jul 63
GY SGT LOUIS CUKELA Medal of Honor winner	Dieckmann, E. *Gazette*	Dec 61
HOW DOUGHBOYS AND MARINES BEAT THE HUNS IN AND NEAR CHATEAU THIERRY	*Literary Digest*	May 17, 1919
HELLWOOD 23 pp pamphlet by a survivor	Pattulo, G. Curtis Publishing Co., Philadelphia	1918
INTO BELLEAU WOOD In *Fix Bayonets,* this story is called "Battle Sights."	Thomason, J. Scribner's *Gazette*	 Mar 26 Nov 59
A MONTH IN BELLEAU WOOD IN 1918 Second prize is two months	Harbord, MajGen J., USA *Leatherneck*	Jun 28
THE NEAREST POINT TO PARIS IN 1918	McClellan, E. *Sea Power*	Jun 21
OVER THERE: WITH THE MARINES AT CHATEAU THIERRY	Ralphson, Capt G. M. A. Donohue & Company, Chicago	1919
RETREAT, HELL!	Feland, L. *Gazette*	Jun 21
THE 2D DIVISION IN CHATEAU THIERRY	Bundy, MajGen O. *Everybody's*	Mar 19
2D DIVISION N.W. OF CHATEAU-THIERRY JUNE 1 TO JULY 10, 1918	Thomason, J.	
SOMETHING OF VALUE The cemetery at Belleau Wood where many Marines are buried	Hull, D. *Leatherneck*	Nov 66

THE AISNE-MARNE OFFENSIVE	McClellan, Maj E. *Gazette*	Mar 21	**SOISSONS, JUL, 1918**
THE CHARGE AT SOISSONS	Thomason, J. Scribner's *Gazette*	 Jun 25 Nov 69	
SOISSONS	Thomas, G. *Gazette*	Nov 65	
IN THE MARBACHE SECTOR Aug 8, 1918	McClellan, Maj E. *Gazette*	Sep 21	**ST MIHIEL, AUG, 1918**
THE ST. MIHIEL OFFENSIVE	McClellan, Maj E. *Gazette*	Dec 21	
THE BATTLE OF BLANC MONT, OCTOBER 2-10, 1918	Otto, LtCol E. (German Army) *Proceedings*	Mar-May 30	**BLANC MONT, OCT, 1918**
THE BATTLE OF BLANC MONT RIDGE	McClellan, Maj E. *Gazette*	Mar, Jun, Sep 22	
A CRITICAL ANALYSIS OF FLANK PROTECTION, SECOND DIVISION (AEF FRANCE) 3 OCT TO 9 OCT, 1918	Schubert, Maj R. *Gazette*	Nov 41	
MARINES AT BLANC MONT	Thomason, J. *Scribner's*	Sep 25	
RESUME OF THE OPERATIONS OF THE SECOND AMERICAN DIVISION IN CHAMPAGNE FROM OCT 2 TO 9, 1918	Lejeune, LtGen J. *Gazette*	Sep 42	
THE RAID ON THIELT: AN ACCOUNT OF THE FIRST MARINE AIR COMBAT OPERATION Bombing raid carried out Oct 14, 1918	Emmons, R. Published by the author San Diego	1966	**THIELT, OCT, 1918**
AN ANALYSIS OF THE CROSSING OF THE MEUSE RIVER	Brewster, LtCol D. *Gazette*	Mar 41	**MEUSE ARGONNE, NOV, 1918**
WATCH ON THE RHINE 4th Brigade of 2d Division stayed in Europe after WW-I Armistice	*Gazette*	Nov 65	**1918**

EXPERIENCES

AND THEY THOUGHT WE WOULDN'T FIGHT Flamboyant writing in the style of its author, Floyd Gibbons, who lost an eye at Belleau Wood. In retrospect, this was a propaganda book, but it served the cause well at the time	Gibbons, F. George H. Doran Company	1918
DEAR FOLKS AT HOME—THE GLORIOUS STORY OF THE UNITED STATES MARINES IN FRANCE, AS TOLD BY THEIR LETTERS FROM THE BATTLEFIELD	Cowing, K., and C. Cooper Houghton Mifflin Company, Boston	1919
THE DIARY OF PVT SULLIVAN WW-1 combat with an introduction by General W. C. Neville	Sullivan, J. *Gazette*	Nov 68
DID HE DESERT FROM QUANTICO? GySgt Miles Barrett deserts from Quantico to get overseas. He fought bravely.	*Gazette*	Sep 42
DUEL IN THE SKY Ralph Talbot, the only Marine aviator to win the Medal of Honor in WW-1	*Gazette*	Nov 70
LEAVES FROM A WAR DIARY Personal journal of the Army General who commanded the 2d Division which included the 4th Marine Brigade. (Secretly, he wished he was a Marine)	Harbord, Gen J., USA Dodd, Mead & Co., Inc.	1925
A MARINE AT THE FRONT Diary of an officer with the 6th Marines	Bellamy, D. *American History Illustrated*	Feb 71
A MARINE TELLS IT TO YOU Autobiography of the salty CO of 2/1 who also served with the China Relief Expedition during the Boxer Rebellion. Tells his side of Belleau Wood controversy.	Wise, Col F., as told to M. Frost J. H. Sears & Co., Inc.	1929

MARINES TELL IT TO THEMSELVES	Baily, R. *Sunset*	Apr 18
ONCE A MARINE The experiences of a WW-1 Marine from Boot Camp to a hospital bed in Paris	Hemrick, L. Carlton Press	1968
ONE MAN'S WAR Combat adventures of the Marine author	Rendinell, Cpl J. and G. Pattullo J. H. Sears & Co., Inc.	1928
ONE MAN'S WAR Condensed version of the book	Pattullo, G., and J. Rendinell *Sat Eve Post* Jul 16, Aug 13,	1927
THE TALE OF A DEVIL DOG	Carter, W. The Canteen Press, Washington	1920
THAT QUARTET I CAN'T FORGET Travels of a quartet from Quantico in WW-1	Barnett, B. *Leatherneck*	Oct 42
VALLEY OF THE ONE-LEGGED HEINE	Barnett, B. *Leatherneck*	Apr 43
A WAR DIARY An enlisted Marine's service with the 75th Co., 6th Marines	Bulberg, M. Drake Press, Chicago	1927
WITH THE HELP OF GOD AND A FEW MARINES Autobiography of CO of 6th Marines	Catlin, BGen A. Doubleday, Page & Co., Long Island, N.Y.	1919

UNIT HISTORIES

DIVISION

COMMENDATIONS OF 2ND DIVISION: AMERICAN EXPEDITIONARY FORCES, 1917-1919, FRANCE, GERMANY	Second Division Association, Cologne, Germany	1919
THE 2D DIVISION, AMERICAN EXPEDITIONARY FORCES, 1917-1919	Harraden, Sgt G., and PFC R. Stedman Neuwied, Germany	

	Title	Source
	THE 2D DIVISION, AMERICAN EXPEDITIONARY FORCES IN FRANCE, 1917-1919	Spaulding, O., USA and Col J. Wright, USA Hillman Press 1937
	2D DIVISION SUMMARY OF OPERATIONS IN THE WORLD WAR	USGPO 1944
BRIGADE	A BRIEF HISTORY OF THE 4TH BRIGADE OF MARINES May 29, 1917-Aug 13, 1919	McClellan, Maj E. *Gazette* Dec 19
	THE 4TH BRIGADE OF MARINES IN THE TRAINING AREAS AND THE OPERATIONS IN THE VERDUN SECTOR	McClellan, Maj E. *Gazette* Mar 20
	THE MARINE BRIGADE	Thomason, Capt J. *Proceedings* Nov 28
	OPERATIONS OF THE 4TH BRIGADE OF MARINES IN THE AISNE DEFENSIVE	McClellan, Maj E. *Gazette* Jun 20
REGIMENT	**A BRIEF HISTORY OF THE 6TH REGIMENT, UNITED STATES MARINES**	U.S. Marine Corps
	11TH REGIMENT, U.S. MARINES, 1919 Journal of the Regiment containing many personal sketches of its members	Gievres, France
	THE 13TH REGIMENT—WORLD WAR 1	*Gazette* Nov 42
BATTALION	**HISTORY OF THE 1ST BATTALION, 5TH REGIMENT, U.S. MARINES: JUNE, 1917 TO AUGUST, 1919**	U.S. Marine Corps
	HISTORY OF THE 2D BATTALION, 5TH REGIMENT, U.S. MARINES, JUNE 1, 1917-JAN 1, 1919	
	HISTORY OF THE 3D BATTALION, 6TH REGIMENT, U.S. MARINES From August, 1917 to August, 1919	Akers, H. MacRitchie & Hurlbut, Hillsdale, Mich. 1919

THE 6TH MACHINE GUN BATTALION, 4TH BRIGADE, U.S. MARINES, SECOND DIVISION, AND ITS PARTICIPATION IN THE GREAT WAR	Curtis, Capt T., and Capt L. Long U.S. Marine Corps Neuwied, Germany	1919	
HISTORY OF THE 96TH COMPANY, 2D BATTALION, 6TH MARINE REGIMENT IN WORLD WAR 1	Cates, LtCol C. HQMC	1935	**COMPANY**
MACHINE GUNS OF THE 4TH BRIGADE 6th Machine Gun Company, Aug 1917-Nov 1918	Waller, Maj L. *Gazette*	Mar 20	
OVER THE TOP WITH THE 18TH CO., 5TH REGIMENT, U.S. MARINES: A HISTORY	Field, Cpl H., and Sgt H. James Rodenbach, Germany		
THEN AND NOW: HISTORY OF MARINE AVIATION IN WORLD WAR 1	First Marine Force Veterans' Association		**AVIATION**
CONDUCT AND ADMINISTRATION OF NAVAL AFFAIRS	*Gazette*	Mar 18	**1918**
ROSE BOWL '18 Mare Island Marines win	Furby, S. *Leatherneck*	Jan 53	
STATEMENT OF ESTIMATES FOR MARINE CORPS	*Gazette*	Mar 18	
EXTRACTS FROM THE NAVAL APPROPRIATION BILL AS REPORTED TO THE SENATE BY THE SENATE NAVAL COMMITTEE	*Gazette*	Mar 19	**1919**
HOLDING BACK THE MARINES	Platt, J. *Ladies Home Journal*	Sep 19	
LAST VOYAGE Marine Honor Guard accompanies the unknown soldier on his return to Washington in 1921	Nicholson, D. *Leatherneck*	Jun 58	**1921**
THE MARCH OF EVENTS	*Gazette*	Sep, Dec 21, Mar, Jun, Sep 22	

	MARINES WELL REPRESENTED IN INTERNATIONAL RIFLE AND PISTOL MATCHES	*Leatherneck*	Jul 23, 1921

MAIL GUARD

1921-1927	THE GREAT MAIL CALL Marines guard the mails after armed robberies become the thing to do.	Tallent, MSgt R. *Leatherneck*	Feb 55
	THE MAIL GUARD	*Gazette*	Dec 26
	MARINE CORPS MAIL GUARDS CARRY IMPROVED MACHINE GUNS	*Leatherneck*	Dec 26
	POSTAL POSTS Historical rundown on Marines who guarded the mails	Bowen, B. *Leatherneck*	Mar 66
	PROFESSIONAL NOTES—MAIL GUARD	*Gazette*	Mar 27
	WHERE ARE THE MAIL BANDITS NOW? They disappeared where the Marines took over	*Leatherneck*	Jan 27
	YOU WILL FIND US ALWAYS ON THE JOB Marines guard the Mail Trains in 1921. Not one robbery happened after they took over	Rentfrow, F. *Leatherneck*	Apr 31
1922	DON'T GIVE UP THE SHIP Speech the author made to Marines at Quantico on Jan 19, 1921, in which he predicted that celebrating the Marines' Birthday on November 10 would become a regular event	Richards, G. *Proceedings*	Dec 22
	MARINES SNATCH VICTORY FROM DEFEAT National Rifle Matches at Camp Perry	Scofield, K. *Arms and The Man*	Oct 15, 1922
	THE 1922 RIFLE AND PISTOL TEAM	Keyser, Maj R. *Gazette*	Dec 22

THE U.S. NAVAL AIR FORCE IN ACTION	Edwards, LtCdr W., USN *Proceedings*	Nov 22	
THE MISSION AND DOCTRINE OF THE MARINE CORPS	Lane, R. *Gazette*	Mar 23	1923
THE UNITED STATES MARINE CORPS: DELIVERED AT THE NAVAL WAR COLLEGE, NEWPORT, RHODE ISLAND, DEC. 14, 1923 Introduction of Advanced Base Concept which governed WW-2 strategy	Lejeune, J. *Gazette*	Dec 23	
MARINES ON TEAPOT DOME Scandal affects the Corps.	*Nation*	Mar 12, 1924	1924
THE BROADCAST 4th Marines at Santa Barbara earthquake	*Leatherneck*	Jul, Aug ,1925	1925
THE UNITED STATES MARINE CORPS	Lejeune, MajGen J. *Proceedings*	Oct 25	
MARINES HAVE LANDED, WHY?	Platt, J. *Independent*	Jan9,1926	
DOVER DEVILDOGS Marine heroes at explosion at Naval Powder Depot, Dover, N.J.	Tallent, R. *Leatherneck*	Nov 55	1926
HISTRIONIC MARINES Acting Marines	Cushing, C. *Independent*	Mar 20, 1926	
THE MARINE CORPS, 1926 By the then Commandant	Lejeune, MajGen J. *Proceedings*	Oct 26	
UNCLE SAM'S OLDEST FIGHTING FORCE It ain't the Army or the Navy	*Mentor*	Jul 26	
ANNUAL REPORT OF AIRCRAFT SQUADRONS, 2D BRIGADE, U.S. MARINE CORPS	Rowell, Maj R. *Gazette*	Dec 28	1928
THE 1928 MARINE CORPS RIFLE AND PISTOL TEAM By CO of 2D MAR DIV at Tarawa	Smith, Maj J. *Gazette*	Dec 28	

	TESTIMONY OF THE MAJOR GENERAL COMMANDANT BEFORE THE SENATE COMMITTEE ON FOREIGN RELATIONS	Lejeune, MajGen J. *Gazette*	Mar 28
	WITH UNCLE SAM'S DEVIL DOGS	*Popular Mechanics*	Jul 28
1929	THE UNITED STATES MARINE CORPS The new Commandant reports	Neville, MajGen W. *Proceedings*	Oct 29
1931	MANAGUA DISASTER Marines help Nicaraguans the first time (history *does* repeat itself).	Williams, BGen D. *Gazette*	Aug 31
	THE UNITED STATES MARINE CORPS	*Current History*	1931
	WE LEAVE THE VIRGIN ISLANDS	*Gazette*	May 31
1932	THE MARINE CORPS: ITS MISSION, ORGANIZATION, AND LIMITATION	Miller, Col E. *Gazette*	Nov 32
	WAGES OF CIVIL EMPLOYEES IN FIELD SERVICES OF NAVY DEPARTMENT AND MARINE CORPS, 1932	*Monthly Labor Relations*	May 32
1933	NAVY ABSORBS MARINE CORPS The most interesting title of 8,000 in *Creating A Legend.*	*Newsweek*	Dec 23, 1933
	SEMPER FIDELIS	*Sat Eve Post*	Feb 18, 1933
1934	LEATHERNECK SPORTS Marines vs. Japs in 1934 football game in Tokyo	Harwell, Sgt E. *Leatherneck*	Nov 45
	PROSPECTS IN THE CARIBBEAN	Jones, C. *Gazette*	Nov 34
1935	**A CHRONOLOGY OF THE UNITED STATES MARINE CORPS, VOL. 2—1935-1946** Eleven years of history, mostly about WW-2	Tyson, C. HQMC	1965 (IP)

6TH MARINES BREAK RECORD IN WINNING SAN DIEGO TROPHY Marksmanship	*Leatherneck*	May 35	
FINAL REPORT OF THE CMC Russell checks out as boss	Russell, J. *Gazette*	Nov 36	**1936**
FLYING MARINES OVER FLORIDA PALMS	*Literary Digest*	Dec 12, 1936	
WAGES OF CIVIL EMPLOYEES IN FIELD SERVICES OF NAVY DEPARTMENT AND MARINE CORPS, 1936	*Monthly Labor Relations*	Jul 36	
SHANGHAI EMERGENCY In 1937, during the Chinese-Japanese War	Rothwell, Maj R. *Gazette*	Nov 72	**1937**
MARINE CORPS RESERVE RIFLE TEAM, 1938	Hankins, Capt J. *Gazette*	Sep 38	**1938**
GOOD-BYE TO SQUADS RIGHT Drill is changed	*Gazette*	Mar 39	**1939**
MARINE CORPS RIFLE AND PISTOL TEAMS AND THE NATIONAL MATCHES, 1939	Edson, Maj M. *Gazette*	Sep 39	
POLAR PILOT T/Sgt Pete Petras flew with the Byrd expedition to the Antarctic	Evans, E. *Leatherneck*	Mar 47	
SEA SAFARI A land-based Marine takes his "03" and goes after a sea lion	Pierce, P. *Leatherneck*	May 61	
WITH ADMIRAL BYRD Marines accompany the Admiral	*Leatherneck*	Jan 40	

DUTIES

THE MARINE CORPS BATTALION INTELLIGENCE SERVICE	*Gazette*	Nov 41	**INTELLIGENCE**
MILITARY INTELLIGENCE	Kayser, Maj R. *Gazette*	Dec 20	
THE BUREAU'S OWN PAGE	*Recruiters' Bulletin*	Nov 16	**PUBINFO**

	FIRST MARINE CORPS PUBLICITY BUREAU	Proctor, GySgt C. *Recruiters' Bulletin*	Aug 20
	KEEP YOUR EYE ON THE EDITOR	Webb, GySgt P. *Recruiters' Bulletin*	Apr 20
	LEADING ADVERTISING EXPERTS COMMEND SUCCESS OF MARINES' PUBLICITY CAMPAIGN	Wolff, W. *Recruiters' Bulletin*	Dec 18
	OLD TIME PUBLICITY BUREAU	Smith, Cpl L. *Marines*	Jun 16
	PRESS AGENT IN THE NAVY	Pearson, C. *Technical World*	Oct 14
	PUBLIC RELATIONS	*Gazette*	Nov 36
	TWO ALICES IN WONDERLAND	Williamson, Capt C. *Gazette*	Nov 34
QM	THE QUARTERMASTERS' DEPARTMENT	Sanderson, LtCol C. *Gazette*	Mar 30
ROYAL NAVY	AMERICAN MARINES IN THE BRITISH GRAND FLEET	McClellan, Maj E. *Gazette*	Jun 22
STAFF	THE EXECUTIVE STAFF	Collier, Capt E. *Gazette*	Dec 23

FICTION

Stamper, Lt William James		
BEYOND THE SEAS Sixteen short stories about Marines in foreign countries written by a Marine officer	Published by the author Norfolk, Va.	1935
Thomason, Col John W., Jr.		
MAIL DAY	*Scribner's*	Apr 26
MARINES AND OTHERS A collection of short stories as only Thomason can write them	Charles Scribner's Sons	1929
MONKEY MEAT	*Scribner's*	Nov 25

RED PANTS AND OTHER STORIES Another collection by the "Master Storyteller"	Charles Scribner's Sons	1927
SALT WINDS AND GOBI DUST Thomason's final collection of short stories	Charles Scribner's Sons	1934
SERGEANT BRIDOON OF THE HORSE MARINES	*Sat Eve Post*	Dec 23, 1939
THE SERGEANT AND THE BANDITS The immortal Sgt Houston series	*Sat Eve Post*	Dec 14, 1935
THE SADDLE OF JENGHIZ KHAN	*Sat Eve Post*	Feb 1, 1936
THE SERGEANT RUNS AWAY	*Sat Eve Post*	Aug 15, 1936
THE SERGEANT AND THE SHIP	*Sat Eve Post*	Jul 5, 1941
THE SERGEANT AND THE SIREN	*Sat Eve Post*	Jun 13, 1936
THE SERGEANT AND THE SPY	*Sat Eve Post*	Nov 23, 1935

MARINES

GENERAL

GENERAL REGISTER OF THE UNITED STATES NAVY AND MARINE CORPS—LIST OF OFFICERS OF THE NAVY OF THE UNITED STATES AND OF THE MARINE CORPS—1775-1900	Callahan, E. T.H.S. Hamersly, Washington	
LIST OF OFFICERS OF THE NAVY OF THE UNITED STATES AND OF THE MARINE CORPS	Callahan, E.	1901
THE RECORDS OF LIVING OFFICERS OF U.S. NAVY AND MARINE CORPS: COMPILED FROM OFFICIAL SOURCES There were at least six more editions after this one	Hamersly, L. J. B. Lippincott & Co., Philadelphia	1870

Broome, John Lloyd

JOHN LLOYD BROOME, 1849-1898 — Davis, D. — Marine Corps Museum, Quantico 1972 (IP)
Manuscript Register Series Number 6

Buchanan, Capt Richard Bell

CAPTAIN RICHARD BELL BUCHANAN, U.S. MARINE — Williams, BGen D. — *Gazette* Jun 27

Burrows, William Ward

FIRST COMMANDANT OF THE MARINE CORPS WILLIAM WARD BURROWS — McClellan, E. — *DAR Magazine* Mar 25

Butler, Smedley

THE COURT MARTIAL OF SMEDLEY BUTLER — Asprey, R. — *Gazette* Dec 59
For insulting Mussolini, no less

OLD GIMLET EYE — Polete, Sgt H. — *Leatherneck* Jan 48
Butler role against the Boxers in 1900 and in Haiti in 1915

OLD GIMLET EYE: THE ADVENTURES OF SMEDLEY BUTLER — Thomas, L. — Farrar & Rinehart, Incorporated 1933

THE OTHER SMEDLEY BUTLER — Utter, L. — *Gazette* Nov 64
Statesman

Cunningham, Maj Alfred

THE PILOT OF "NOISY NAN" — Morris, MSgt W. — *Leatherneck* Mar 50

Curtis, Claude H.

A MARINE AMONG THE IDOLS — Curtis, C. — Zondervan Publishing House, Grand Rapids, Mich. 1940
One of the worst books ever written about *anything.* Marine Curtis wanders around China until he finds religion. The plot is as crooked as the Great Wall of China

Ellis, Pete

THE MARINES' FIRST SPY — Zimmerman, Maj J. — *Sat Eve Post* Nov 23, 1946
One of the most interesting Marines of all time, and one of the ones who attracted the most "ink." Was he, or wasn't he? (a spy).

THE MYSTERY OF PETE ELLIS — Montross, L. *Gazette* Jul 54

THE UNSOLVED MYSTERY OF PETE ELLIS — Pierce, LtCol P. *Gazette* Feb 62

Fisher, GySgt Morris

GY SGT MORRIS FISHER IS TENDERED FOR SINGULAR HONOR — *Leatherneck* Jan 31, 1925

Made Life Member of Veterans' Athletes, a very exclusive club. Fisher was Marine's leading marksman of the era between the World Wars (perhaps of any era).

THE RIFLE MASTER — Allen, Sgt L. *Leatherneck* May 48

Freeman, Capt Bill

CAPTAIN BILL FREEMAN— TRADITION MAKER — McClellan, Maj E. *Gazette* Sep 26

Henderson, BGen Archibald

ARCHIBALD HENDERSON: AN ERA — Pierce, LtCol P., and LtCol F. Hough *Gazette* Jul 60

This is chapter 4 of the book *Compact History of the Marine Corps.*

BRIGADIER GENERAL ARCHIBALD HENDERSON, USMC — Jenkins, J. *Gazette* Jun 41

With apologies to Gen Cushman, they just don't make them like Henderson any more.

REFERENCES ON BREVET BRIGADIER GENERAL ARCHIBALD HENDERSON, COLONEL COMMANDANT OF THE MARINE CORPS, 1820-1859 — HQMC 1963

Hunter, Stuart

CAPTAIN STUART HUNTER, USMC — Williams, BGen D. *Gazette* Mar 29

Killed by Guerrilla Giron in 1927. Won the Navy Cross

Jodon, James K.

MY FOUR YEARS IN THE MARINES — Jodon, J. Vantage Press 1971 (IP)

Interesting autobiography by Marine enlisted man who served before World War 1

Krulewitch, MajGen M. L.

SKIRMISH ON THE HUDSON — Krulewitch, MajGen M. *Gazette* Sep 72

The General's adventures with the 303rd Reserve Company during the 1920's and 30's in New York

Larson, Swede

SWEDE LARSON — Voigt, PFC R. *Leatherneck* Apr 46

Coach of the Quantico Marines football team during the WW-1 era. His best team was in 1922.

Lejeune, John A.

JOHN A. LEJEUNE: TRUE SOLDIER — Asprey, Capt R. *Gazette* Apr 62

In terms of lasting impact on the Corps, Lejeune is in a class with Henderson, and few others.

THE REMINISCENCES OF A MARINE — Lejeune, J. Dorrance & Co., Inc. Philadelphia 1930

A thick autobiography with many illustrations. Well written for a first person job by a non-professional writer.

VISION OF JOHN A. LEJEUNE — Dodd, J. *Gazette* Nov 67

Letcher, John Seymour

ONE MARINE'S STORY — Letcher, J. McClure Press Verona, Virginia 1970 (IP)

Autobiography of Marine who served through WW-2.

Miller, Samuel

SAMUEL MILLER, 1814-1856 — Davis, D., and J. Hilliard Marine Corps Museum Quantico 1967 (IP)

Papers of a Marine who served in the War of 1812

Nicholas, Samuel

SAMUEL NICHOLAS, THE FIGHTING QUAKER The first Commandant was a paradox, but there was no question about his ability as a Marine officer	Feldman, L. *Leatherneck*	Nov 27
SAMUEL NICHOLAS, THE FIRST MARINE OFFICER	*Gazette*	Dec 25
SAMUEL NICHOLAS, FIRST OFFICER OF AMERICAN MARINES	Fagan, Maj L. *Gazette*	Nov 33
SAMUEL NICHOLAS: INNKEEPER-MARINE	Stevens, Capt H. *Gazette*	Nov 53

Pendleton, Joe

UNCLE JOE About Pendleton's service in Nicaragua in 1912 and the Dominican Republic in 1916	Allen, TSgt L. *Leatherneck*	Jan 49

Quick, Maj John

ALL BUSINESS: THE SAGA OF SGT MAJ JOHN QUICK The famed signaller of Guantanamo Bay	Dieckmann, E. *Gazette*	Jun 63

Robillard, MajGen Fred S.

AS ROBIE REMEMBERS Autobiographical anecdotes of Marine officer who served from WW-1 through WW-2. He headed the Marine Corps' Division of Motor Transport during the "Big War."	Robillard, MajGen F. Wright Investors' Service, Bridgeport, Conn.	1969 (IP)

Russell, John Henry, Jr.

PATCHWORK CHILD Offbeat autobiography of daughter of the 16th Commandant. Recalls her early life in Panama, China, Haiti and other duty stations with her father. Interesting sidelights on the life of a Corps officer from 1900 until WW-1	Astor, B. Harper & Row	1962

Scala, Francis Maria

FRANCIS MARIA SCALA: A LEADER OF THE BAND, U.S. MARINE CORPS	Clark, A. Columbia Historical Society Records, Washington	1935
FRANCIS SCALA: LEADER OF THE MARINE BAND FROM 1855 TO 1871	Ingalls, D. USGPO	1957

Slade, Maj D.

ONE WAS A MARINE Fiction. A Marine officer's experiences with the Corps from Nicaragua to Korea	New, Maj D. New Greenwich Publishers	1959

Sousa, John Philip

MARCHING ALONG Rather stuffy and grandiose autobiography by a man who lacked nothing in the ego department. This is a valuable book (about $50), if you can find it.	Sousa, J. Hale, Cushman & Flint Boston	1941
SOUSA'S 100TH ANNIVERSARY	McConnell, TSgt J. *Leatherneck*	Nov 54

Thomason, Colonel John W., Jr.

COLONEL JOHN W. THOMASON JR., CHRONICLER OF THE CORPS	Willock, Col R. *Gazette*	May 57
FIGHTING-WRITING MARINE	Tolbert, TSgt F. *Leatherneck*	Apr 44
LONE STAR MARINE: A BIOGRAPHY OF THE LATE COLONEL JOHN W. THOMASON, JR. Too bad Thomason didn't live to write his own autobiography. He wouldn't have cared much for this book.	Willock, Col R. Published by the author Princeton, N.J.	1961
SOMETHING OF RUDYARD KIPLING	*American Mercury*	Jun 37

A THOMASON SKETCHBOOK Priceless record of Thomason's "sketch of a sketch" technique. Includes many little known illustrations of Marines.	Rosenfeld, A. University of Texas Press, Austin, Tex. 1969 (IP)	

POSTS/PLACES

THE MARINE CORPS AND THE CHANGING CARIBBEAN POLICY	Metcalf, LtCol C. *Gazette* Nov 37	**CARIBBEAN**
SERVICE IN GUAM	Picket, Capt H. *Gazette* Dec 17	**GUAM**
MARINES AT MIDWAY	*Gazette* May 35	**MIDWAY**
TO OPEN NEW BARRACKS AT SAN DIEGO	*Leatherneck* Mar 21	**SAN DIEGO**

RECRUITING

POSTERS	*Recruiters' Bulletin* Nov 14, Oct 18, Feb 19, Nov 21
RECRUITING DOCTRINE	Meade, Col J. *Gazette* May 35

RESERVE

HIGH QUALITY OF OUR RESERVE	Reisinger, H. *Proceedings* Nov 34
THE MARINE CORPS RESERVE	Meade, J. *Gazette* Dec 25
FLYING RESERVE OF THE LEATHERNECKS	Reisinger, Col H. *Proceedings* Oct 33
THE UNITED STATES MARINE CORPS RESERVE	Upshur, BGen W. *Proceedings* Apr 39

TACTICS

ADDENDUM TO OPERATIONS OF THE NAVY AND MARINE CORPS	Barry, Cdr E., USN *Proceedings* Jun 05

AN INTRODUCTION TO THE TACTICS OF SMALL WARS	Utley, Maj H. *Gazette*	May 31, Aug, Nov 33
BOATS IN A FORCED LANDING ON ENEMY SHORE	*Gazette*	Aug 31
COUNTERBATTERY IN A LANDING OPERATION	Henderson, Lt F. *Gazette*	Nov 39
FIRST LINE OF DEFENSE By WW-2's leading Marine artillery officer	DelValle, LtCol P. *Gazette*	Nov 35
THE FLEET AND THE MARINES	Broadbent, LtCdr E., USNR *Proceedings*	Mar 31
INFANTRY AIR COMMUNICATION	Pierce, Capt F. *Gazette*	Dec 38
JOINT MILITARY-NAVAL OPERATIONS	Broadbent, E. *Proceedings*	Mar 34
JOINT OVERSEAS OPERATIONS	Cole, E. *Proceedings*	Nov 29
JUNIOR MARINES IN MINOR IRREGULAR WARFARE	Johnson, Capt S. *Gazette*	Jun 21
LIGHT ARTILLERY SUPPORT IN LANDING OPERATIONS	Bowser, Lt A. *Gazette*	Jun 38
MARCH SECURITY IN BUSH WARFARE	Keyser, Maj R. *Gazette*	Mar 29
THE MARINE CORPS IN SUPPORT OF THE FLEET Interesting photo story	Miller, Col E., and LtCdr C. Richardson, USN *Proceedings*	Jun 33
THE MOBILE DEFENSE OF AN ADVANCE BASE	Lejeune, Col J. *Gazette*	Mar 16
NAVAL GUNFIRE IN SUPPORT OF A LANDING	Ansel, Lt W. *Gazette*	May 32
PACK HOWITZER BATTERY IN LANDING ATTACK	LeGette, Maj G. *Gazette*	Mar 36

PRACTICAL EMPLOYMENT OF THE THOMPSON SUB MACHINE GUN	Peard, Capt R. *Gazette*	Jun 30

Throw it at the enemy, and run like hell.

PROPOSED FIVE MAN SQUAD	Butcher, Lt J. *Leatherneck*	Dec 38
A RIFLE SQUAD IN DEFENSE (MUSKETRY PROBLEM)	Wilson, B. *Leatherneck*	May 39
A SEMI-AUTOMATIC RIFLEMAN	Johnson, Lt M. *Gazette*	May 36
SHIP TO SHORE IN AMPHIBIOUS WARFARE	DelValle, Maj P. *Gazette*	Feb 32
SHOULD THE MARINE CORPS USE CHEMICAL AGENTS IN GUERRILLA WARFARE?	Linsert, Lt E. *Gazette*	Aug 33
SPECIAL BOATS FOR LANDING OPERATIONS	Utley, Maj H. *Proceedings*	Apr 31
SQUAD MUSKETRY PROBLEM WHICH CAN BE FIRED ON RIFLE RANGES	Letcher, Capt J. *Gazette*	Mar 39
STREAMLINED FIGHTING TEAMS	Johnson, M. *Gazette*	Jun 38
VALUE OF AVIATION TO THE MARINE CORPS	Cunningham, Maj A. *Gazette*	Sep 20

By the pilot of "Noisy Nan"

TRAINING

GENERAL

TEACHING LANDING OPERATIONS WITH MODELS	Richardson, LtCdr C., USN *Proceedings*	Jun 34
TOWARD A BETTER LANDING FORCE	Henderson, Lt F. *Gazette*	Nov 40
WHY QUANTICO?	Breckenridge, Col J. *Proceedings*	Nov 28

DRILL

A MARINE CORPS DRILL BOOK	Upshur, Maj W. *Gazette*	Jun 19

	A PLEA FOR THE MARINE CORPS DRILL BOOK	Spicer, W. *Gazette*	Dec 18
	A PLEA FOR THE ADOPTION OF THE REVISED INFANTRY DRILL REGULATIONS OF THE ARMY	Low, Capt T. *Proceedings*	Mar 05
	AN ADDITIONAL PLEA FOR A MARINE CORPS DRILL BOOK All right, already.	Karow, Capt G. *Gazette*	Mar 19
	UNIFORMITY IN INFANTRY DRILL It does add a certain something	Hill, Capt W. *Gazette*	Mar 16
MANEUVERS	BLUE MARINE CORPS EXPEDITIONARY FORCE Army-Navy-Marine Amphibious maneuver in Hawaii in 1925	Williams, BGen D. *Gazette*	Sep 25
	NO "CONSTRUCTIVE" WAR Hawaii training maneuver	Hines, MajGen J., USA *Leatherneck*	May 25
	MARINES STAGE FINAL PRACTICE FOR OAHU MANEUVER	*Leatherneck*	Apr 25
	THIS GLORIOUS WAR	*Leatherneck*	May 23, 1925
MARKSMANSHIP	THE MARINE CORPS RIFLE TEAM	Holcomb, Capt T. *Recruiters' Bulletin*	Jul 15
	MARK 44, A SKETCH OF 44 YEARS OF RIFLE SHOOTING	Wheeler, Capt O. *Gazette*	Feb 35
	MARKSMANSHIP IN THE MARINE CORPS	Abribat, M. *Gazette*	Nov 30
	MEMORIES OF FIVE YEARS Of marksmanship	Evans, Col F. *Gazette*	Feb 35
	RIFLE MARKSMANSHIP—MARINE CORPS RESERVE	Staley, LtCol J. *Leatherneck*	Nov 32
	THE TRAINING OF A NATIONAL MATCH TEAM	Smith, Maj W. *Gazette*	Dec 19
	THE TRAINING OF A NATIONAL MATCH RIFLE TEAM	Edson, M. *Gazette*	Feb 37

UNITS

THE FITA-FITA GUARD The native security force at the Naval Station, Samoa, in 1904. It was trained by Marines	Bates, 1stSgt C. *Leatherneck*	Oct 40
FAMOUS MARINE CORPS REGIMENT MAKES SAN DIEGO HOME 4th Marines	Carney, SgtMaj T. *Marines*	May 16
THE NAVAL BRIGADE	Soley, Lt J., USN *Proceedings*	1880
THE NAVAL BRIGADE: ITS ORGANIZATION, EQUIPMENT AND TACTICS	Hutchins, Lt C. *Proceedings*	1887
NOTES ON THE NAVAL BRIGADE	Rogers, W. *Proceedings*	1888
THE RIO GUARD THROUGH BRAZILIAN EYES	*Gazette*	Dec 22
SAN DIEGO WELCOMES THE FOURTH REGIMENT HOME	*Leatherneck*	Sep 24
WITH THE SPECIAL SERVICE SQUADRON	Thomason, Capt J. *Gazette*	Jun 27

3.
WORLD WAR 2

Marines in "The Big War" from Iceland through Okinawa. General histories, battle histories, unit histories. Biographies and autobiographies of Biddle, Boyington, Carlson, Puller, Smith, Vandegrift and the rest.

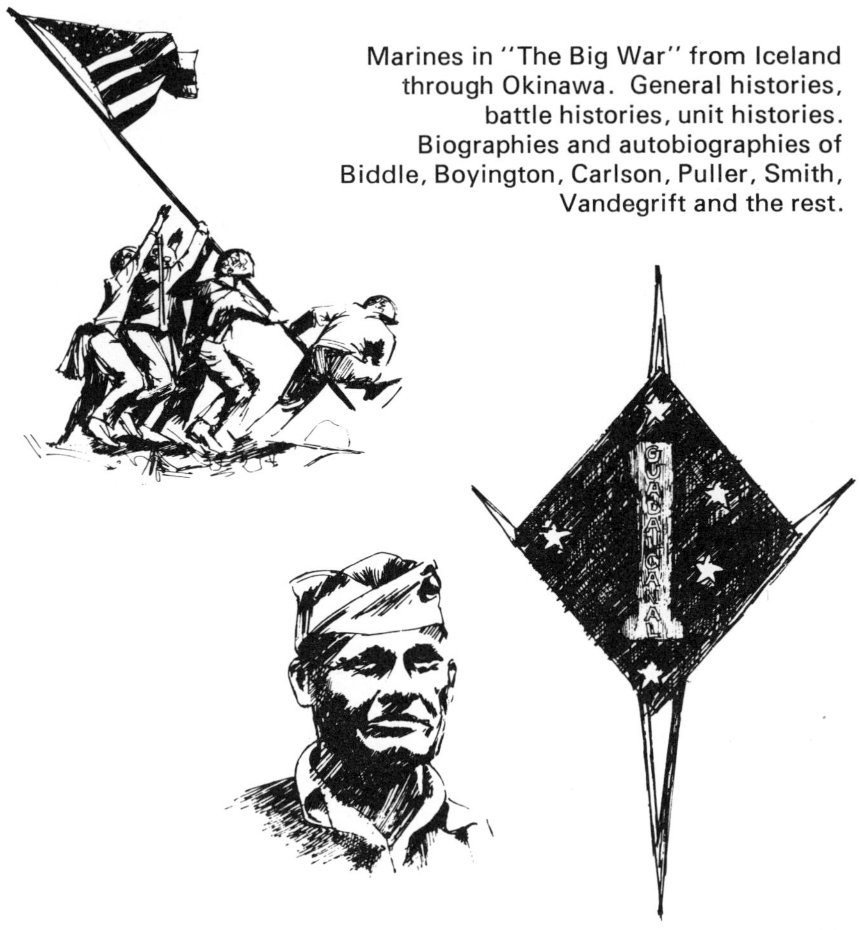

CONTENTS: PART 3

EVENTS/1940-1945

Title	Source	Date	
THE BIG WIND AT PARRIS ISLAND Hurricane destroys the tents	*Gazette*	Sep 40	**1940**
THE BLUE UNIFORM—1940 Picture of pre-war Dress Blues	*Gazette*	Oct 47	
THE COMMANDANT'S MESSAGE "Now hear this," from Gen Holcomb	*Gazette*	Nov 40	
M-DAY FOR THE RESERVES Mobilization Day	*Gazette*	Nov 40	
NEW STYLES IN ORGANIZATION	*Gazette*	Sep 40	
ONE HUNDRED SIXTY-FIVE YEARS OF SERVICE And lots more to come	*Gazette*	Nov 40	
"PARRIS ISLAND HURRICANE"	Morrow, L. *Leatherneck*	Oct 40	
THE UNITED STATES MARINE CORPS	*Gazette*	Nov 40	
AMERICA'S NEW DISASTER FIGHTERS The Corps	*Gazette*	Mar 41	**1941, GENERAL**
ESCAPE FROM SHANGHAI 4th Marines leave China Nov 28, 1941	Jensen, O. *Leatherneck*	Jan 43	
GENERAL SMITH DOES A JOB AT GUANTANAMO, ON THE SOUTHEAST COAST OF CUBA Gen H. M. Smith, that is.	*Time*	May 5, 1941	
MARINES RAPIDLY BOOSTED FOR MODERN FIRST-LINE WARFARE	*Newsweek*	Jun 23, 1941	
MARINE CORPS MARKS 166 YEARS OF SERVICE The last pre-war Birthday	*Gazette*	Nov 41	

	THE MARINES—OLD STYLE	*Gazette*	Sep 41
	NAVY'S ARMY Thanks a lot!	*Life*	Jun 21, 1941
	UNITED STATES MARINES STAND GUARD ON OUR OUTPOSTS IN THE PACIFIC	*Life*	Dec 29, 1941
ICELAND— 7 JUL 41	**THE 1ST MARINE BRIGADE (PROVISIONAL) ICELAND, 1941-1942**	Zimmerman, Maj J. HQMC	1946
	HISTORY OF U.S. MARINE CORPS OPERATIONS IN WORLD WAR 2: VOLUME 1—PEARL HARBOR TO GUADALCANAL First volume in the five-part history begins with an "Introduction to the Marine Corps and its Amphibious Mission," and ends with the end of Guadalcanal. First operation discussed is Iceland. This definitive history of the Corps in WW-2 is fascinating reading.	Hough, LtCol F., Maj V. Ludwig and H. Shaw HQMC	1958
	ICELAND	Tompkins, MajGen R. *Gazette*	Nov 65
	MARINES IN COLD STORAGE In Iceland with their tropical uniforms and summer sleeping bags	Conner, Sgt J. *Leatherneck*	Nov 44
	A NOTE ON THE OCCUPATION OF ICELAND BY AMERICAN FORCES	Zimmerman, LtCol J. *Political Science Quarterly*	Mar 47
	REFERENCES ON THE U.S. MARINES IN THE OCCUPATION OF ICELAND, 1941-1942	HQMC	
	SOME LIKE IT COLD	Hubler, Capt R. *Gazette*	Feb 44
	THE UNDECLARED WAR: 1940-1941 Definitive history of this period with discussion of Iceland	Langer, W., and S. Gleason Harper and Bros.	1953
	THE UNITED STATES MARINES IN ICELAND: 1941-1942 Mostly excerpts from other books. An update of Zimmerman's earlier HQMC publication	Clifford, LtCol J. HQMC	1970 (IP)

ICELAND

PEARL HARBOR— 7 DEC 41

INITIAL DEFEAT . . . ULTIMATE VICTORY — Elliott, GySgt J. — *Leatherneck* Dec 71
Update of the battle in historical perspective

MARINE AVIATION AT PEARL HARBOR — DeChant, Capt J. — *Gazette* Feb 44
Part 1: *Devilbirds: The Story of United States Marine Corps Aviation in World War 2.* This series appeared later as a book published by Harper and Bros. in 1947

PEARL HARBOR — Emmons, Sgt R. — *Gazette* Feb 44

PEARL HARBOR: TWENTY YEARS AGO — Pierce, LtCol P. — *Leatherneck* Dec 61
Another update of the disaster

PHILIPPINES—1 10 DEC 41

ACTION REPORT: BATAAN — Hogaboom, Lt W. — *Gazette* Apr 46

AIR ACTION AT LEYETE — Stick, D. — *Leatherneck* Mar 45
Featuring the enlisted pilots who took on the Japs early in WW-2

CORREGIDOR — Keene, Col J. — *Gazette* Nov 65
4th Marines role

DEATH TO THE INVADERS — Crumbie, F. — *Leatherneck* May 43
Fiction. Marines and natives fight the Japs after the surrender on Corregidor

DESTINATION CORREGIDOR — Underbrink, R. — U.S. Naval Institute Annapolis 1971 (IP)
Too little and too late efforts to supply Bataan and Corregidor in 1942

THE 4TH MARINES AT CORREGIDOR — Baldwin, H. — *Gazette* Nov 46-Feb 47
Excellent four-part history by the renowned historian

THE MARINES IN CHINA AND THE PHILIPPINES — Thacker, J. — *Gazette* Sep 43
4th Marines early in the war

	NAVAL BATTALION AT MARIVELES Of which the 4th Marines was a part	Prickett, LtCol W. *Gazette*	Jun 50
	THE NAVAL BATTALION ON BATAAN Defense of Corregidor/Bataan by the Naval/Marine unit under Cdr F. J. Bridget, USN	Prickett, Col W. *Proceedings*	Nov 60
	OBSERVATIONS DURING THE CAMPAIGN ON LUZON	*Gazette*	Nov 42
	REFERENCES ON U.S. MARINE OPERATIONS IN THE PHILIPPINES, 1941-1945 Coverage of "both times around."	HQMC	1964
	RETREAT, HELL! Fiction. A novel about the 4th Marines on Corregidor complete with early war propaganda of Japs shooting parachuting pilots, killing babies, raping women, etc.	Camp, W. D. Appleton-Century Company, Inc.	1943
	"ROCK" MORALE	Banks, LtCol C. *Gazette*	Feb 46
	SALUTE TO THE MARINES Fiction. Another propaganda novel of early WW-2 about the 4th Marines	White, R. Grosset & Dunlap	1943
PHILIPPINES—1 MARINES	Chamberlain, Cpl Reid Carlos		
	GUERRILLA He fights on after the surrender	James, Lt W. *Leatherneck*	Jan 45
	A MARINE GUERRILLA'S DIARY From May 42-Nov 43	Fink, S. *Leatherneck*	Aug 45
	THE MARINE WHO CAME BACK TO LIFE	*Leatherneck*	Apr 44
	Clement, Col William T.		
	BY SUB FROM CORREGIDOR	*Leatherneck*	Sep 42

With 30 Navy specialists, Clement is rescued from Corregidor just before the surrender. All were experts with special talents needed to plan the war (How do you get to be an expert?)

WAKE ISLAND— 8 DEC 41

THE DEFENSE OF WAKE First of 15 official Monographs published about the Marines' role in WW-2 battles. Excellent reading, but limited historical value because a monograph does not position a particular battle strategically.	Heinl, LtCol R. HQMC	1947
FLAME OF GLORY: WAKE'S HOPELESS, GALLANT FIGHT	*Time*	Jan 19, 1942
LEATHERNECKS TO THE LAST: HEROIC DEFENDERS OF WAKE ISLAND	Furnas, W. *Collier's*	Nov 21, 1942
MARINE AVIATION AT BATTLE OF WAKE ISLAND Part 1: *Devilbirds*	DeChant, Capt J. *Gazette*	Feb 47
PIONEER PARTY—WAKE ISLAND	Deerdorff, Capt R., USN *Proceedings*	Apr 43
RAID ON WAKE ISLAND An air raid after it became Jap territory	*Gazette*	Jan 44
REFERENCES ON THE DEFENSE OF WAKE	HQMC	1962
THE SAGA OF WAKE	Baldwin, H. *Virginia Quarterly Review*	Fall 1942
SAGA OF WAKE ISLAND A poem	Phillips, H. *Leatherneck*	Feb 42
THE SIEGE OF WAKE ISLAND	Burroughs, J. *American Heritage*	Jun 59
THE STORY OF WAKE ISLAND The real story by the commander of Marines there	Devereaux, Col J. J. B. Lippincott Co., Philadelphia	1947

	WAKE ISLAND As one reviewer said, "It's going to be a long war for poetry lovers if this poem is an example of what to expect."	Rukeyser, M. Doubleday, Doran & Co., Inc., Garden City, N.Y.	1942
	WAKE ISLAND	Votaw, H. *Proceedings*	Jan 41
	WAKE ISLAND	*Gazette*	Jun 42
	WAKE ISLAND COMMAND RAdm Cunningham's story of the battle from his viewpoint as Commander of Troops. A bunch of BS, from the viewpoint of Marines who served under him	Cunningham, W., and L. Sims Little, Brown and Co., Boston Paperback by Popular Library	1961 1962
	WAKE ISLAND MEMORIAL	*Gazette*	Dec 60
	THE WAKE STORY The real story is told from information furnished by Marine POW's now returned	Harwell, Sgt E. *Leatherneck*	Nov 45
	WAKE SURRENDER	Bayler, Col W. *Gazette*	Nov 45
	WE'RE HEADED FOR WAKE Story of the abortive rescue mission for Wake in which Heinl participated	Heinl, Col R. *Gazette*	Jun 46
WAKE ISLAND MARINES	Devereux, Maj J. P. S. **"FOUR HUNDRED AGAINST AN EMPIRE"**	Thomas, L. From *These Men Shall Never Die* The John C. Winston Company	1943
	JIMMY DEVEREUX Biography	Hicks, Sgt P., and Sgt L. Allen *Leatherneck*	Nov 48
	McAllister, Lt John, and Lt John Kenney RETURN FROM THE WAKE They return from Jap Prison Camp to tell the tale of Wake	Conner, Sgt J. *Leatherneck*	Oct 45

Putnam, Maj Paul A.
"THE FOUR PLANE AIR FORCE" Thomas, L.
Putnam's aviators in the battle of Wake — From *These Men Shall Never Die* The John C. Winston Company 1943

Tharin, Capt Frank C.
THE WAKE — Bartlett, T. *Leatherneck* Sep 65
Gen Tharin, MGySgt Joe Jamerson and SgtMaj Robert Winslow meet to talk over old times when they were prisoners of war. All were captured on Wake

1942, GENERAL

FROM SNOWS OF ALASKA TO SHORES OF SOLOMONS, MARINES CARRYING ON THEIR 167 YEAR TRADITION — *Newsweek* Nov 9, 1942

HOW DOES THE 1918 MARINE CORPS COMPARE WITH THE 1942? — *Gazette* Nov 42

LT GEN HOLCOMB SENDS MESSAGE TO MARINES IN THE SOLOMONS — *Gazette* Nov 42

THE MAD MONKS — Miller, J. *Gazette* Nov 68
Marines attached to Sino-American Cooperative Organization in 1942

MARINE CORPS RE-ENLISTS CHAMPION RIFLE MARKSMAN — *Gazette* Jun 42

MARINE DEFENDS BLUEJACKET — *Gazette* Nov 42
Court Martial on the USS Oklahoma

MARINES HAVE LANDED: THEY MAKE QUICK WORK OF FORTIFYING OUR PACIFIC BASES. — Morris, F. *Collier's* Jul 4, 1942

SERVICE COMRADSHIP — *Gazette* Sep 42
Camp Elliott Marines presented with trophy by British Marines with whom they served in Iceland

U.S. MARINE CORPS TO CELEBRATE 167TH ANNIVERSARY — *Gazette* Nov 42

SAMOA— 25 JAN 42

BAREFOOT MARINES — Owens, Lt R. *Gazette* Nov 48

BUILDING SAMOA'S DEFENSES — Larsen, MajGen H. *Gazette* Feb 44

COMMAND OF NATIVE TROOPS — Oppenheimer, H. *Gazette* Oct 51
Also includes some experiences in Haiti

GUARDING THE CROSSROADS: THE 7TH DEFENSE BATTALION IN SAMOA — Larsen, MajGen H. *Gazette* Jan 44
Starting with the construction of defenses on Jan 25, 1942

MARCH TO THE SOUND OF DRUMS — Oppenheimer, BGen H. Wabash Press Danville, Ill 1966 (IP)
Collection of short stories and articles which "cover the motives, lives and problems of the professional soldier in different cultures, environments and at different ranks." Whatever that means.

MIDWAY— 8 JUN 42

JAPAN'S NAVY AND THE BATTLE OF MIDWAY — Vogel, B. *Gazette* Dec 47

LIFE ON MIDWAY — *Life* Nov 23, 1942
Picture story

MARINE AVIATION IN THE BATTLE OF MIDWAY — DeChant, Capt J. *Gazette* Feb 47
Part 1: *Devilbirds*

MARINES AT MIDWAY — D'Andrea, T. *Gazette* Nov 64
Role of Corps in this naval battle

MARINES AT MIDWAY — Heinl, LtCol R. HQMC 1948
Monograph featuring Marine participation in this Naval battle

NEVER A BATTLE LIKE MIDWAY — Bryan, J. *Sat Eve Post* Mar 26, 1949
In retrospect, we never should have won it, and wouldn't have, except for pilots who were courageous beyond belief

Bayler, LtCol Walter L. J.	
LAST MAN OFF WAKE ISLAND Misleading title. Bayler *was* the last Marine off Wake, but he obviously left before the battle. This book is about his experiences at Midway and Guadalcanal	Bayler, LtCol W., and C. Carnes The Bobbs-Merrill Co., Indianapolis 1943
LAST MAN OFF WAKE ISLAND Magazine series which preceeded the book	Bayler, LtCol W., and C. Carnes *Sat Eve Post* Apr 3, 10,1943
Fleming, Capt Richard **HEROISM BY CALM DELIBERATION** Medal of Honor winner KIA	Thomas, L. From *These Men Shall Never Die* The John C. Winston Company 1943
Henderson, Maj Lofton R. **THE SUPREME SACRIFICE** Another Marine squadron commander killed at Midway. Guadalcanal Airfield was named after him	Thomas, L. from *These Men Shall Never Die* The John C. Winston Company 1943

THE ART OF WAR IN THE JUNGLES	Walker, G. *Christian Science Monthly* Jun 12, 1944
THE ATTACK OF THE SENDAI: PREPARATION Part 4: *Marines in the Pacific War.* Series later published as a book *The Marines' War.* This chapter deals with the first Jap defeat of WW-2, the Battle of the Tenaru	Pratt, F. *Gazette* Dec 46
THE ATTACK OF THE SENDAI: REALIZATION Part 5: *Marines in the Pacific War*	Pratt, F. *Gazette* Jan 47
THE BATTLE OF BLOODY HILL: HOW HENDERSON FIELD WAS SAVED By Raiders and Paramarines commanded by Merritt Edson, Sep 13 and 14, 1942	Whipple, S., and Maj W. McKennan *Sat Eve Post* Feb 20, 1943

THE BATTLE FOR GUADALCANAL So professionally objective you would never guess that Griffith was there as a 1st Raider officer. Excellent use of Jap documents and interviews. Many maps and pictures. The best of many books about this battle	Griffith, Gen S. J. B. Lippincott Co., Philadelphia 1963 Paperback by Ballantine Books, Inc. 1970
BATTLE OF THE MATANIKAU RIVER: TYPICAL MARINE ENGAGEMENT IN THE MUD AND JUNGLE OF GUADALCANAL The real flavor of Guadalcanal is captured by Hersey	Hersey, J. *Life* Nov 23, 1942 *Digest* Feb 43
BATTLE OF THE TENARU	Cates, BGen C. *Gazette* Oct 43
BATTLE FOR THE SOLOMONS An Army-oriented book which can't help but give Marines some of the credit for Guadalcanal (Thank you, Ira!)	Wolfert, I. Houghton Mifflin Co., Boston 1943
BLOODY RIDGE	Cates, BGen C. *Gazette* Nov 43
BLOODY RIDGE: GUADALCANAL Poem about "Raider's Ridge"	Henri, Maj R. *Harper's* Jun 45
THE CAMPAIGN FOR GUADALCANAL: A BATTLE THAT MADE HISTORY The newest book about Guadalcanal. Oversize (9"x11") with more than 150 illustrations. $9.95	Coggins, J. Doubleday & Company, Inc., Garden City, N.Y. 1972 (IP)
CAMPAIGN FOR THE SOLOMONS Three part series by the famous historian who was quite partial to Marines	Pratt, F. *Harper's* Mar-May 44
CARLSON'S RAIDERS AT GUADALCANAL Part 6: *Marines in the Pacific War.* Detail about the most successful combat patrol of WW-2.	Pratt, F. *Gazette* Feb 47

CHALLENGE FOR THE PACIFIC Leckie weaves the individual experiences of men from both sides into an exciting narrative. All the heroes of "The Canal" come to life. The fact that he was there as a machine gunner helps authenticity	Leckie, R. Doubleday & Company, Inc. 1965
COLONEL ICHIKI ARRIVES Part 2: *Marines in the Pacific War* But he doesn't leave alive	Pratt, F. *Gazette* Oct 46
CRISIS ON GUADALCANAL Which one?	Miller, J. *Military Affairs* Winter 1947
DO NOT GO GENTLE Fiction. Takes a group of Marines through training to their experiences on Guadalcanal. One of the better novels of this kind.	McCuish, D. Doubleday, Doran & Co., Inc., Garden City, N.Y. 1960 Paperback by Crest Books, Inc.
FIGHTING ON GUADALCANAL Lessons learned there grow into "Bible" for the rest of the Pacific War	General Staff, U.S. War Dept 1943
FIRE OVER THE ISLANDS 1ST MAR DIV and the Coast Watchers are featured in this 247-page book written by a veteran of the 1st Raider Bn who fought on Guadalcanal	Horton, D. A. H. & A. W. Reed, Sydney, Australia 1970 (IP)
1ST MARINES IN THE SOUTH PACIFIC Early action reports	*Leatherneck* Oct 42
FLASH FROM RADIO TOKYO: AIRFIELD TAKEN Part 3: *Marines in the Pacific War* It was? (Dewey was elected, too!)	Pratt, F. *Gazette* Nov 46
GUADALCANAL	Barker, A. Paperback edition only, Ballantine Books, Inc. 1971

GUADALCANAL ATTACK REPULSED — *Gazette* — Nov 42
Early reports of Bloody Ridge

THE GUADALCANAL CAMPAIGN — Zimmerman, Maj J. HQMC 1949; Lancaster Books, Chicago 1972 (IP)
This long out-of-print Monograph is now available again for $5.50. Probably the best of the series because the battle lends itself to the Monograph technique (scholarly report on a specific and usually limited subject)

GUADALCANAL: CLOSING OPERATIONS — Pratt, F. *Gazette* — Mar 47
Part 6: *Marines in the Pacific War*

GUADALCANAL COMMUNICATORS UNPERTURBED BY JAP SNIPERS — *Gazette* — Nov 42

GUADALCANAL DIARY — Tregaskis, R. Random House, Inc. — 1943
Day-by-day story of the Guadalcanal Marines starting on shipboard 12 days before the landing. You live (and sometimes die) with them in this simple, straightforward report on the first seven weeks of the battle

GUADALCANAL: THE FIFTH BATTLE OF THE SOLOMONS — Hurlbut, TSgt J. From *Masterpieces of War Reporting* Julian Messner, Inc. — 1962
Eyewitness report of a naval battle off Savo

GUADALCANAL: ISLAND ORDEAL — Kent, G. Paperback edition only, Ballantine Books Inc. — 1971 (IP)
Part of the popular *Illustrated History of World War 2* series at many newsstands now. Good, brief history. Valuable because it was written from a non-American and possibly more objective point-of-view. (Mr. Kent is British)

GUADALCANAL: THE JAP, PAINTINGS BY NAVY LT D. SHEPLER — Hersey, J. *Life* — Dec 27, 1943
Commentary by Hersey and these paintings make this a valuable article

GUADALCANAL: THE LAND SIDE
Report on the nature of the enemy.
Wolfert, I.
From *Masterpieces of War Reporting*
Julian Messner, Inc. 1962

GUADALCANAL NATIVE STORY
Sgt Vouza & Company
Helfer, Sgt H.
Leatherneck May 45

GUADALCANAL: THE PLANNING PHASE
Part 1: *Marines in the Pacific War*
Pratt, F.
Gazette Sep 46

HELMET FOR MY PILLOW
Leckie, R.
Random House, Inc. 1957
Paperback by Bantam Books, Inc. 1958
The night the 1st Marines floated 900 Japs on the Tenaru, Robert Leckie fed a very busy heavy-50. This book tells it like it was, all the way. Best personal experience book of Guadalcanal; maybe of Marines in WW-2 (Includes Leckie's incredible experiences at Peleliu, also.)

HEROES IN THE SOLOMONS
Gazette Mar, Apr 43

INCIDENT AT GUADALCANAL
Picture of Vouza
Gazette Feb 48

INTERLUDE ON GUADALCANAL
Marchant, W.
Gazette May 44

INTO THE VALLEY: A SKIRMISH OF THE MARINES
Hersey, J.
A. A. Knopf 1943
Until the article upon which this book is based appeared in *Life,* home-front Americans' obscure images of Guadalcanal were based on the only jungle they knew. Tarzan's. *Into the Valley* made the Marines' war real. The battle, an insignificant skirmish, was unimportant. So was the fact that we lost. Hersey's low-key description of the sights, sounds, smells and sheer terror of jungle war is what makes this book a classic.

THE ISLAND: A HISTORY OF THE 1ST MARINE DIVISION ON GUADALCANAL, AUG 7 - DEC 9, 1942
Merillat, Capt H.
Houghton Mifflin Co., Boston 1944
Merillat, a combat correspondent, landed when the 1ST MAR DIV landed, and left when it left. His job was to report what the Division gave, and took, during those

four months. *The Island* was written too soon after the campaign for historical perspective, but it is an authentic "log" of who did what on "The Canal."

JAPAN'S LOSING STRUGGLE FOR GUADALCANAL Fascinating view of the enemy side	Tanaka, Vice Admiral R. (IJN), and R. Pineau *Proceedings* Aug 56
THE LEATHERNECKS COME THROUGH A different slant by the Chaplain of the unit which landed first and left last . . . Col J. Arthur's 2d Marines. A Chaplain in combat helps bury the dead, comfort the wounded and give strength to the rest. Willard's six months on Guadalcanal were filled with an abundance of all three duties.	Willard, Lt W., ChC, USNR Fleming H. Revell Company 1944
LETTERS FROM U.S. COMMANDER ON GUADALCANAL	Vandegrift, Gen A. *Life* Nov 16, 1942
LIMEADE ON GUADALCANAL	Hubler, Capt R. *Proceedings* Dec 44
MACHINE GUNS IN THE SOLOMONS Early tactical report	Kennedy, R. *Leatherneck* Oct, Nov 43
MALAITA PATROL Fiction. A patrol action in the Solomons.	Crain, Maj J. *Leatherneck* Aug 50
MARINE ARTILLERY IN GUADALCANAL By the foremost Marine artilleryman of WW-2	delValle, BGen P. *Gazette* Dec 43, Jan, Feb 44
MARINE CORPS EQUIPMENT IN USE ON GUADALCANAL	*Gazette* Mar 43
MARINE, YOU DIE! Report of battle of Oct 15	Smith, Lt E. *Gazette* Oct 43 *Harper's* Sep 43
MARINES ATTACK SOLOMONS First report of the first American offensive of WW-2	*Life* Aug 24, 1942

THE MARINES HAVE LANDED — *Leatherneck* — Sep 42
Sketchy (due to censorship) story and pictures of Marine landings on Guadalcanal and Tulagi

MARINES ON GUADALCANAL — Hersey, J. *Life* Nov 9, 1942

NAVAL GUNFIRE IN THE SOLOMONS — Henderson, Col F. *Gazette* Mar, Jun, Dec 56
The author participated in this first test of the pre-war doctrine and theory of Naval Gunfire support for assault forces. This series was written from the troops' point-of-view, and includes experiences when we were on the receiving end of Naval Gunfire for the only time in WW-2.

PACIFIC GAINS: WEWOK AIRFIELDS DEVASTATED, AMPHIBIANS ATTACK IN SOLOMONS — *Newsweek* Aug 30, 1943

POSTAL HISTORY OF UNITED STATES FORCES IN THE BRITISH SOLOMON ISLANDS PROTECTORATE DURING WORLD WAR 2 — Jersey, S. *Journal of American Philatelic Society* 1965
Interesting story on little-known aspect of military operations

ON VALOR'S SIDE — Gallant, T. Doubleday & Company, Inc., Garden City, N.Y. 1963; Paperback by Avon Books 1966
Autobiography of a Cpl with the 11th Marines. He finally gets to Guadalcanal on page 223. By that time, you don't care. Artillerymen didn't see much action in this campaign, anyway. Gallant doesn't drink, smoke or swear. Neither does his book.

REFERENCES ON THE U.S. MARINES IN THE SOLOMON ISLANDS CAMPAIGN — HQMC 1963

SECOND BATTLE OF THE MATANIKAU — *Gazette* Nov 44

	SOLOMON ISLANDS MAP	*Gazette*	Dec 49
	SOLOMONS ACTION DEVELOPS INTO BATTLE FOR SOUTH PACIFIC Excellent picture story.	Baldwin, H. *Gazette*	Nov 42 Aug 72
	SOLOMONS BATTLE BACK Vague re-cap on the situation in the Solomons gleaned from security-cautious releases	*Leatherneck*	Dec 42
	SOLOMONS LADDER	*Newsweek*	Nov 8, 1943
	SOLOMONS SPEARHEAD First story after censorship off	Cooke, F. *Leatherneck*	Oct 42
	TENARU FRONT	Tregaskis, R. *Gazette*	Jan 45
	THIRTY YEARS AGO Anniversary of Guadalcanal	Young, G. *Leatherneck*	Nov 72
	THE UNITED STATES MARINES IN THE GUADALCANAL CAMPAIGN Brief history (14 pages) based largely on the Zimmerman monograph which preceded it.	Shaw, H. HQMC	1962 (IP)
	A WEEK IN GUADALCANAL	*Gazette*	Nov 42
GUADALCANAL MARINES	Basilone, SSgt John		
	HERO ON THE COVER Picture of Basilone	Bishop, J. *Collier's*	Jun 24, 1944
	HERO'S HOMECOMING	*Life*	Oct 11, 1943
	LIFE AND DEATH OF MANILA JOHN	*Time*	Mar 19, 1945
	MANILA JOHN BASILONE	Dieckmann, E. *Gazette*	Oct 63
	PORTRAIT OF A HERO After he was killed on Iwo	*Newsweek*	Mar 19, 1945
	Casemento, A.		
	HUMAN TARGET BALKS JAPS	Casamento, A., as told to J. Horan and G. Frank *Science Digest*	Dec 43

Dickson, Major Donald

HE TELLS THE BIG-SHOTS — Cooke, F. *Leatherneck* Apr 43
About Maj D. Dickson, artist of Guadalcanal

NO 1. D-DAY — Dickson, D. *Leatherneck* Aug 62, Nov 71
Paintings of Guadalcanal D-Day

Dunn, Pvt Harry

"THE LOYALTY OF A MARINE" — Thomas, L. from *These Men Shall Never Die* The John C. Winston Company 1943
Pvt Harry Dunn, Navy Cross winner

Fordyce, Cpl

MARINES IN ACTION: CPL FORDYCE SPELLS NEMESIS FOR JAPS — *Leatherneck* Apr 44
At Gavutu

Goss, Sgt A., Maj Harry Torgerson and Cpl G. Grady

"BLASTING THE JAPANESE OUT OF THEIR HOLES" — Thomas, L. from *These Men Shall Never Die* The John C. Winston Company 1943
Parachute Marines at Tulagi

Hooker, Hurshall

MARINES IN ACTION: HURSHALL HOOKER TOLL IS EIGHT JAPS — *Leatherneck* Feb 44
Won two Silver Stars on Guadalcanal

Lebendeff, Sgt

"HOW A MARINE KILLED HIS PAL" — Heym, S. from *My Favorite War Story* Wittlesey House 1945
Sgt Lebendeff kills Judd Aubrey accidentally because he didn't say the password on Guadalcanal

Ling, Patty

A CHILD OF MIRACLES — Gehring, Rev R., and M. Abramson Funk & Wagnalls Company, Inc. 1962
About Patty Ling, orphan girl adopted by the Marines on Guadalcanal

Paige, Sgt Mitchell		
MARINES IN ACTION: MITCHELL PAIGE—HE HELD THE LINE	*Leatherneck*	Jan 44
Randy, PFC Red		
LONG COUNT ON TANAMBOGO About PFC Red Randy, a professional fighter, who was adept at tossing grenades	*Leatherneck*	Apr 44
Ross, Cpl Barney		
"BARNEY ROSS'S TOUGHEST ROUND" Another fighter's adventures on "The Canal"	Thomas, L. from *These Men Shall Never Die* The John C. Winston Company	1943
Schmid, Sgt Al		
"THE BATTLE OF TENARU RIVER" About Al Schmid, blinded by Jap grenade	Thomas, L. from *These Men Shall Never Die* The John C. Winston Company	1943
AL SCHMID, MARINE Book on which the John Garfield movie "Pride of the Marines" is based. Actually a biography of Schmid, who won the Navy Cross for stacking up Japs with his machine gun in the first battle of the Tenaru	Butterfield, R. Farrar & Rinehart Incorporated	1944
Stone, Sgt Jim		
BUSY HILLBILLY Silver Star winner Sgt Jim Stone at work in the jungle	Bergman, PFC H. *Leatherneck*	Feb 44
Vouza, SgtMaj		
"THE LOYALTY OF SERGEANT MAJOR VOUZA" Look at the scars, if you don't believe he's loyal	Thomas, L. from *These Men Shall Never Die* The John C. Winston Company	1943

VOUZA AND THE SOLOMON ISLANDS — MacQuarrie, H. The Macmillan Company 1945
A British Colonial Administrator tells pre-war tales about the natives of the Solomons including the famous SgtMaj

"VOUZA, SUPERMAN OF THE SOLOMONS" — Tregaskis, R. from *My Favorite War Story* Wittlesey House 1945
He was good at getting ink, too.

GUADALCANAL AVIATION

AIR BATTLE OVER GUADALCANAL — *Gazette* Nov 42
Early, heavily censored report

AIR POWER IN THE SOLOMONS — Miller, R. *Gazette* Mar, Apr 43

BUILDING THE GUADALCANAL AIR BASE — Fox, Col W. *Gazette* Mar 44

THE CACTUS AIR FORCE — Miller, T. Harper and Row Publishers 1969
On Aug 20, 1942, Marines at Henderson Field welcomed 31 planes from MAG-23. The Cactus Air Force was in business. During the next three months, this rag-tag bunch of Marine, Army and Navy pilots shot down what was left of the good Jap pilots along with the bad ones. They slaughtered enemy reinforcements on the ground and water by the thousands. This book tells their story. How could it be anything but exciting and fast-moving?

FORTY-SIX CAME BACK — McCarty, M. *Leatherneck* Oct 43
From a Squadron of Marine Dive Bombers on Guadalcanal

THE INCREDIBLE CACTUS AIR FORCE — Kirkland, Lt T. *Gazette* May 59

MARINE AIRMEN ON GUADALCANAL — Sydney, R. *Flying* Apr 43

MARINE AVIATION IN THE BATTLE FOR GUADALCANAL — DeChant, Capt J. *Gazette* Mar 47
Part 2: *Devilbirds*

	MARINE AVIATION IN THE SOLOMONS Part 3: *Devilbirds*	DeChant, Capt J. *Gazette* Apr 47
GUADALCANAL AIRMEN	Byrd, Dennis Earl	
	"SCARED" GUNNER Dennis Earl Byrd, the rear-seat gunner for Maj Richard Mangrum	*Leatherneck* Dec 43
	Cram, Lt Col Jack "Mad Jack"	
	INCIDENT OF THE BLUE GOOSE "Mad Jack" Cram torpedoes a Jap ship with his PBY and lives to tell about it.	DeChant, Capt J. *Gazette* Nov 44
	MARINES IN ACTION: LTCOL CRAM TORPEDOES JAPANESE SHIP FROM PBY	*Leatherneck* Mar 44
	Foss, Capt Joe	
	ALL-AMERICAN BENCH WARMER Joe Foss was a bench warmer for three years of college football, but he made the first string on Guadalcanal	Pierce, P. *Leatherneck* Jan 61
	FIRST FLIGHT FOR FOSS His first time in the air was with a barnstormer pilot who was drunk	Scott, Lt J., USNR *Leatherneck* Nov 45
	JOE FOSS, FLYING MARINE Autobiography, surprisingly low-key and not as "apple-pie-and-Mom"—oriented as other hero biographies of the early war.	Foss, Capt J., and W. Simmons E. P. Dutton & Co., Inc. 1943
	JOE FOSS: NO. 1 ACE	Myers, R. *Leatherneck* Jun 43 Field, J. *Life* Jun 7, 1943
	"KILLER JOE FOSS"	Thomas, L. from *These Men Shall Never Die* The John C. Winston Company 1943

MEDAL OF HONOR WINNER ADDS TO SCORE	*Gazette* Jan 44	
NO. 1 ACE	*Time* Dec 21, 1942	
OUR NUMBER ONE ACE COMES HOME	Graham, Capt G. *Sat Eve Post* Feb 27, 1943	
PORTRAIT	*Life* May 31, 1943 *N.Y. Times Magazine* Apr 25, 1943	
Mangrum, LtCol Richard C. JOURNAL OF GUADALCANAL Diary kept on Guadalcanal by Marine Dive Bomber pilot	Mangrum, LtCol R. *American* Feb 43	
"ONE HUNDRED PERCENT MARINE" Was Col Mangrum	Thomas, L. from *These Men Shall Never Die* The John C. Winston Company 1943	
Smith, Maj John L., Maj Robert E. Galer and Capt Marion Carl **"THE FLYING FOOLS"** Marine heroes of the Cactus Air Force	Thomas, L. from *These Men Shall Never Die* The John C. Winston Company 1943	
BACK TO MAKIN With the Army unit that captured it long after Carlson's raid	Graham, Capt G. *Gazette* Feb 44	**MAKIN— 16 AUG 42**
CEMETERY DUEL 2nd Raiders Joe Sebock	*Leatherneck* Apr 44	
THE MAKIN ISLAND RAID Early action report of famous (or infamous) raid by Carlson's Raiders which was not received too kindly by certain high ranking Marine officers (Their names were Holcomb, Vandegrift and Smith)	*Gazette* Mar, Apr 43	
WE MOPPED UP MAKIN ISLAND By Carlson's exec	LeFrancois, Lt W. *Sat Eve Post* Dec 4, 11, 1943	

Subject	Title	Author / Source	Date
1943, GENERAL	AN EPOCHAL YEAR There's never been another year like it	*Gazette*	Nov 43
	FROM THE HALLS OF MONTEZUMA Birthday report	Pratt, W. *Newsweek*	Nov 15, 1943
	HOW TO EARN A STRIPE About Sgt N. H. Baike who participated in Commando Raid on Oran, North Africa	Tolbert, F. *Leatherneck*	Apr 43
	LEATHERNECKS: ENLISTMENT GOAL REACHED	*Time*	Dec 6, 1943
	THE 168TH YEAR	Bergman, H. *Leatherneck*	Nov 43
	THEY TOOK THIRTY MARINES With the Army to North Africa	Cooke, F. *Leatherneck*	Jul 43
	VANDEGRIFT'S BATTLE INSTRUCTIONS	Vandegrift, Gen A. *Gazette*	Oct 43
	U.S. NAVAL GROUP, CHINA A few Marines were members	Miles, RAdm M., USN *Proceedings*	Jul 46
RUSSELLS—21 FEB 43	**HISTORY OF U.S. MARINE CORPS OPERATIONS IN WORLD WAR 2: VOLUME 2—ISOLATION OF RABAUL** The definitive history of the Corps in WW-2 continues with operations from the Russells through Bougainville to Tarawa. Includes New Georgia and New Britain	Shaw, H., and Maj D. Kane HQMC	1963
	THE MARCH TO VERU HARBOR The story of this little-known chapter in Marine history is included in this anthology of war stories by disabled veterans. Marine Raider Coulis was disabled in this operation	Coulis, A. From *Purple Testament,* Doubleday & Company, Inc., Garden City, N.Y.	1946
	OCCUPATION OF THE RUSSELLS Picture story of this operation by the 3rd and 4th Raider Battalions	*Leatherneck*	Aug 43

RUSSELL ISLAND ROUND-UP Cattle are rounded-up by Marines	Frank, Sgt W. *Leatherneck*	Jul 44	
ACTION AT ENOGAI: OPERATIONS OF THE 1ST RAIDER BATTALION IN THE NEW GEORGIA CAMPAIGN Operations from 4-11 Jul by this unit led by the author	Griffith, LtCol S. *Gazette*	Mar 44	**NEW GEORGIA— 28 JUN 43**
BATTLE FOR RENDOVA Picture story	*Leatherneck*	Oct 43	
BATTLE WITHOUT A NAME Minor skirmish on Rendova, but it wasn't minor to the Marines killed and wounded	Blake, Capt R. *Sat Eve Post*	Apr 15, 1944	
THE CAPTURE OF ENOGAI Early action reports	McDevitt, F., and M. Marder *Gazette*	Sep 43	
THE CAPTURE OF MUNDA	Mathieu, C. *Gazette*	Nov 43	
CORRY'S BOYS	Griffith, Col S. *Gazette*	May 49	
THE FIGHTING BELLY ROBBERS Marine cooks turn into sharpshooters with the Raiders on New Georgia	*Leatherneck*	Apr 44	
THE JAPANESE GUESSED WRONG IN NEW GEORGIA	Shaw, Cdr J., USN *Gazette*	Dec 49	
JAPS TRIED TO DRIVE US CRAZY: CAMPAIGN IN NEW GEORGIA ONE OF GRISLIEST IN AMERICAN MILITARY HISTORY Wolfert could make a telephone directory sound sensational	Wolfert, I. *Collier's*	Nov 13, 1943	
LIVERSEDGE'S RAIDERS AT ENOGAI Part 8: *Marines in the Pacific War* "Harry, the Horse," & company	Pratt, F. *Gazette*	Mar 47	
MARINE AVIATION IN THE BATTLE FOR NEW GEORGIA Part 3: *Devilbirds*	DeChant, Capt J. *Gazette*	Apr 47	

	MARINE AVIATION IN THE MUNDA CAMPAIGN	*Gazette*	Oct 43
	MARINES IN THE CENTRAL SOLOMONS Interesting Monograph covering the last small unit operations. After this, the Raiders and Parachute Marines were disbanded and the operations were of Divisions	Rentz, Maj J. HQMC	1952
	MEET THE MARINE RAIDERS WHO TOOK ENOGAI Liversedge's Raiders in picture story	*Leatherneck*	Nov 43
	THE MESSAGE MUST GO THROUGH Work of runners on New Georgia	Helfer, Cpl H. *Leatherneck*	Sep 44
	NEW GEORGIA OFFENSIVE	*Life*	Jul 26, 1943
NEW GEORGIA MARINES	Boyd, Capt Clay Allen ADVANCE MAN Story of Boyd's two pre-invasion trips to New Georgia and Rendova for recon. His exploits paved the way for the Raiders	Tolbert, F. *Leatherneck*	Mar 45
	Ferguson, Maj Phillip C. GENTLEMEN FROM NEW GEORGIA Operations officer of an unidentified Raider Bn there	Tolbert, F. *Leatherneck*	Dec 43
	Linton, Pvt Fred C. PREACHER'S KID Hero of the New Georgia campaign	Tolbert, F. *Leatherneck*	Nov 43
	Powers, Pvt "Jinx" JINX Raider Private on New Georgia	Tolbert, F. *Leatherneck*	Jan 44
NEW BRITAIN—26 DEC 43	AN EPISODE ON CAPE GLOUCESTER Vignette on Hill 660 battle	Donahue, TSgt V., and SSgt A. Mielke *Leatherneck*	May 45

ATTACK AND COUNTER ATTACK ON HILL 660 In the mud of Cape Gloucester	Stavisky, Sgt S., and J. O'Leary *Leatherneck*	Jul 44
THE CAMPAIGN ON NEW BRITAIN The Monograph of this incredible campaign wherein the finest fighting force in the Pacific was loaned to the Army to "keep them busy." Many 1ST MAR DIV Marines were killed by falling trees in the tropical rain forest of Cape Gloucester which nobody wanted anyway.	Hough, LtCol F., and Maj J. Crown HQMC	1952
CANNON, MUD AND JAPS Artillery at the Cape	Luckey, LtCol R. *Gazette*	Oct 44
CAPE GLOUCESTER	*Life*	Jan 31, 1944
THE CAPE GLOUCESTER CAMPAIGN This article preceded the Cape Gloucester Monograph by Hough and Crown	Hough, Capt F. *Gazette*	Apr 44
CAPE GLOUCESTER ENGINEERS They never had lousier working conditions	Hallman, SSgt D. *Gazette*	Sep 44
CAPE GLOUCESTER: MARINES UNDER MAC ARTHUR Part 16: *Marines in the Pacific War*	Pratt, F. *Gazette*	Dec 47
CAPE GLOUCESTER PRELUDE: A DAY IN MAC ARTHUR'S COMMAND POST Second prize is two days.	*Newsweek*	Jan 3, 1944
CAPE HAPPY MACS Cartoons of Marines on the Cape	*Leatherneck*	Oct 44
GENERAL RUPERTUS' IMPROVISED AIR FORCE Bailing wire and tape held it together	Hunt, Capt R. *Gazette*	Jun 49

	THE MARINES LAND AT CAPE GLOUCESTER	*Gazette*	Apr 44
	NEW BRITAIN	*Gazette*	Mar 44
	NIGHT LANDINGS ON NEW BRITAIN: WITH PAINTINGS BY D. FREDENTHAL	*Life*	Aug 21, 1944
	PACIFIC VICTORY: CONQUEST OF CAPE GLOUCESTER But this conquest had little to do with the big Pacific victory	*Newsweek*	Jan 10, 1944
	SCOUTING AT CAPE GLOUCESTER	McMillan, G. *Gazette*	May 46
	SUICIDE CREEK: MARINES AT CAPE GLOUCESTER By combat correspondent who was there	Bordages, TSgt A. *Collier's*	May 26, Jun 2, 1945
	THREE DAYS—FIVE MILES: A VICTORY ON NEW BRITAIN Walt's Ridge, where Lew's boys muscled a 75-mm howitzer into position	Bordages, Sgt A. *Leatherneck*	Jul 44
CAPE GLOUCESTER MARINES	Garrett, Charlie, Frank Newell and Hank Kciuk THEY TOOK THE POINT Point men in the invasion	McVay, Sgt I. *Leatherneck*	Feb 45
	Gross, Capt Seymour Arnold THE MARINE WHO WOULDN'T GIVE UP Booby trapped by Japs, but he lived to tell of it	Gross, Capt S. *Digest*	Jan 45
	Hansen, PFC Paul and Leslie HANSEN TWINS USE 'GATOR FOR ROLLING FORT	*Leatherneck*	Aug 44
	YULETIDE INVASIONS "Merry Christmas" for the Japs as we land on Cape Gloucester on Dec 25. Historical review of other Christmas invasions, including Washington crossing the Delaware, etc.	Langille, Sgt V. *Leatherneck*	Dec 47, Dec 72

WILLAUMEZ: MARINES UNDER MAC ARTHUR Part 17: *Marines in the Pacific War.* Little-known operation of 1ST MAR DIV when it was under command of MacArthur during the Cape Gloucester campaign	Pratt, F. *Gazette*	Jan 48	**WILLAUMEZ PENINSULA— 26 DEC 43**
BRUTE AND COMPANY LtCol Krulak and his battalion of Parachute Marines	*Time*	Nov 22, 1943	**CHOISEUL**
CHOISEUL DIVERSION Part 9: *Marines in the Pacific War.* Krulak's Parachute Marines land on small island and keep the Japs busy while the 1st Marine Amphibious Corps lands at Bougainville	Pratt, F. *Gazette*	May 47	
I'VE GOT MINE Fiction. A novel based on the famous Choiseul Diversion of 1943.	Hubler, Capt R. G. P. Putnam's Sons Paperback edition titled *Walk Into Hell* by Popular Library 1963	1946	
MISSION: TO RAISE HELL Story upon which the book is based	Hubler, Capt R. *Gazette*	Mar 44	
THE PINEAPPLE KID PFC Johnny Geddings wins the Silver Star for grenade exploits on Choiseul	*Leatherneck*	Jul 44	
ARTILLERY IN THE BOUGAINVILLE CAMPAIGN	Guenther, J. *Field Artillery Journal*	Jun 45	**BOUGAINVILLE— 1 NOV 43**
BATTLE OF CIBIK'S RIDGE	Cibik, Capt S., J. Horan and G. Frank *Sat Eve Post*	Nov 18, 1944	
BATTLE OF EMPRESS AUGUSTA BAY Early history by famous WW-2 Navy historian	Karig, W. *Proceedings*	Dec 43	

BATTLE OF EMPRESS AUGUSTA BAY Action report with heavy censorship	*Life*	Nov 29, 1943
THE BATTLE OF PIVA FORKS	Schmuck, Maj D. *Gazette*	Jan 44
BOUGAINVILLE Picture story	*Gazette*	Jan 44
BOUGAINVILLE: BEACHHEAD IN THE JUNGLE Part 10: *Marines in the Pacific War*	Pratt, F. *Gazette*	Jun 47
BOUGAINVILLE BOOGIE Natives perform for the Marines	Lewis, SSgt A. *Leatherneck*	Sep 44
BOUGAINVILLE LANDING	Azine, H. *Harper's*	Mar 44
THE BOUGAINVILLE LANDING AND THE BATTLE OF EMPRESS AUGUSTA BAY, 27 OCTOBER - 2 NOVEMBER 1943 Official Navy version	Office of Naval Intelligence, U.S. Navy Dept	1945
BOUGAINVILLE AND THE NORTHERN SOLOMONS Monograph of 1 MAC operations from pre-D-Day through 15 Dec 43	Rentz, Maj J. HQMC	1948
BOUGAINVILLE PATROL The jungle was never quite as frightening as here (except possibly for Guadalcanal)	Revels, WO C. *Gazette*	Oct 44
BOUGAINVILLE PAY-OFF	Tucker, J. *Infantry Journal*	Mar 45
BOUGAINVILLE PERIMETER: FIERY BATTLE OF CANNON RIDGE REPELS JAP ATTACK	*Newsweek*	Mar 7, 1944
BOUGAINVILLE SCENE: ARTILLERY'S INTERMITTENT BUT FROGS NEVER STOP	Hipple, W. *Newsweek*	Apr 3, 1944
BOUGAINVILLE WATER CO. How the Engineers provided fresh water in the jungle	*Leatherneck*	Jun 44

BOUGAINVILLE'S BEST KNOWN CHARACTER "Chowhound Charlie"	*Science Digest*	Jun 45
CIBIK RIDGE—PRELUDE TO VICTORY	Edwards, Maj H. *Gazette*	Mar 51
COMBAT PATROL With the Parachute Marines	*Leatherneck*	Jun 44
"D" DAY FOR DOGS War Dogs in action for the first time	Marder, TSgt M. *Leatherneck*	May 44
END RUN IN THE SOLOMONS 1 MAC at Bougainville	Bowser, MajGen A. *Gazette*	Nov 47
FIJI PATROL ON BOUGAINVILLE With Duncan and the "best jungle fighters in the world"	Duncan, D. *Geographic*	Jan 45
HOT CIRCUIT Communications in the jungles	*Leatherneck*	Jul 44
HOW WE CAPTURED CAPE TOROKINA	Devine, Sgt F. *Leatherneck*	Apr 44
JUNGLE WAR: BOUGAINVILLE AND NEW CALEDONIA Excellent picture story	Draper, W. *Geographic*	Apr 44
THE LANDING ON BOUGAINVILLE	DeChant, Lt J. *Gazette*	Jan 44
LIFE ON A BULL'S EYE The "Bull's Eye" is Puruata, a small island off Bougainville	O'Sheel, Capt P. *Leatherneck*	Jun 44
MARINE AVIATION IN THE BATTLE FOR BOUGAINVILLE Part 4: *Devilbirds*	DeChant, Capt J. *Gazette*	May 47
MOMENT OF ATTACK: BOUGAINVILLE, PLOESTI A strange combination of offensives, but Allied offensives weren't too plentiful then	Azine, H., and W. Banks *Harper's*	Mar 44
OUR OWN BAEDEKER A baedeker is a guidebook	*New Yorker*	Dec 18, 1943

	A RIBBON AND A STAR: THE 3D MARINES AT BOUGAINVILLE Monks, a Combat Correspondent, joins the 3RD MAR DIV for the Bougainville operation. This gung-ho little book is a report of the battle from his viewpoint. One of the few books about Bougainville.	Monks, J. Henry Holt and Company Paperback by Pyramid Books	 1945 1966
	SAVING LIVES AT BOUGAINVILLE Duties of Corpsmen, Navy medical personnel, etc.	McKenna, Sgt C. *Gazette*	 Mar 44
	SEA BATTLE BOUGAINVILLE Historical article on the battle from the Japanese point-of-view	O'Brien, C. *Leatherneck*	
	THE SECOND BATTLE OF BOUGAINVILLE	Guenther, J. *Infantry Journal*	 Feb 45
	SECOND BATTLE OF BOUGAINVILLE	Jackson, R. *Military Review*	 Apr 45
	THE 3D MARINES AT BOUGAINVILLE History of the Regiment	VanOrden, Lt G. *Gazette*	 May 44
	THREE MONTHS ON BOUGAINVILLE That's long enough	Hains, H. *Field Artillery Journal*	 Jul 44
BOUGAINVILLE MARINES	Gurney, PFC Howard PFC GURNEY: UNSATISFIED WITH 29 JAPS Maybe he learned how in his home town, Chicago.	 *Leatherneck*	 Jul 44
	Henze, Sgt Gilbert H. MARINES IN ACTION: SGT HENZE, RADIO-GUNNER TURNS PILOT	 *Leatherneck*	 Jul 44
	UNSCHEDULED SOLO When the pilot is killed by AA in flight over Bougainville, Henze lands the aircraft from the rear seat	Mahon, J. From *My Favorite War Story* Wittlesey House	 1945

Owens, Sgt Robert G., Jr.
SGT R. OWENS: HIS COURAGEOUS ACTION SAVED THE DAY AT CAPE TOROKINA — *Leatherneck* — Feb 45
Navy Cross winner

Ragland, Sgt Maurice
HOW TO MAKE SERGEANT THE HARD WAY — *Leatherneck* — Aug 44

Watkins, Lt George, USNR
AN EVENING IN BOUGAINVILLE — *Leatherneck* — Jun 44
Naval surgeon operates on wounded Marines

TARAWA—13 NOV 43

ADMIRAL NIMITZ DECORATES TARAWA HEROES — Feldkamp, TSgt F. *Gazette* — Apr 44
But many of them weren't around to decorate

AMPHIBIOUS OPERATION: THE STORY OF TARAWA — *Leatherneck* — Feb 44
Detailed picture story

APAMAMA—A MODEL OPERATION IN MINIATURE — Tolbert, Sgt F. *Leatherneck* — Feb 45
Recon Bn takes a little island a lot easier than the Division takes Tarawa

APPOINTMENT IN TARAWA — Wertenbaker, G. *New Yorker* — Feb 12, 1944

ARTILLERY AT TARAWA — Rixey, LtCol P., and Maj W. Best *Gazette* — Nov 44
What it did, and didn't do

THE ATTACK ON TARAWA — *Gazette* — Jan 44

THE BATTLE FOR TARAWA — Stockman, Capt J. HQMC — 1947
Monograph on the most important battle of the war from the viewpoint of changing Amphibious tactics.

BATTLE OF TARAWA — *Newsweek* — Dec 6, 1943
Action report

BETIO BEACHHEAD: U.S. MARINES' OWN STORY OF THE BATTLE OF TARAWA Diary-style little book (160 pp) with entries for the four days of the battle the Marines came the closest to losing. Typical Combat Correspondent's reporting. Page after page of great pictures	Wilson, Capt E., G. P. Putnam's Sons	1945
BETIO MEMORIAL	*Leatherneck*	Aug 45
DEATH AT CLOSE QUARTERS Close combat on Betio	Tolbert, Sgt F. *Leatherneck*	Jul 44
DIEPPE AND TARAWA Historical comparison makes Tarawa look better than Dieppe	Lowe, B. *Gazette*	Feb 46
THE EPIC OF TARAWA The Gilberts belonged to Great Britain before WW-2. This book tells the story of their recapture for the English reader. More than half the book (75 of 96 pages) is "background." The rest is a filled-with-awe treatment of the battle and the Marines. Some good pictures.	Richardson, W. Odhams Press, London	1945
FIGHT FOR TARAWA Early action story	*Life*	Dec 13, 1943
HISTORY OF U.S. MARINE CORPS OPERATIONS IN WORLD WAR 2: VOLUME 3—CENTRAL PACIFIC DRIVE This volume includes: Launching the Central Pacific Offensive The Gilberts Operation The Marshalls; Quickening the Pace Saipan; the Decisive Battle Assault on Tinian The Return to Guam	Shaw, H., B. Nalty and E. Turnbladh HQMC	1966
LESSONS OF THE TARAWA FIGHTING	Pratt, W. *Newsweek*	Dec 13, 1943

MEN OF TARAWA	*N.Y. Times Magazine* Dec 12, 1943
MY FIRST DAY ON TARAWA	Jonas, C. *Sat Eve Post* Mar 4, 1944
THE REEF Fiction. Capt Nickerson is not equal to his moment of supreme decision. He remains on a reef instead of leading his company onto the beach at Tarawa. This novel is a study of the moral and physical degeneration which results from his own guilt.	Wheeler, K. E. P. Dutton & Co., Inc. 1951
REPORT ON TARAWA	Sherrod, R. *Time* Dec 6, 1943
ROUND ABOUT GRIM TARAWA	Moore, R. *Geographic* Feb 45
SIGNIFICANCE OF OUR SEIZURE OF THE GILBERTS There really wasn't any, in retrospect, except for learning from our mistakes.	Pratt, W. *Newsweek* Dec 6, 1943
TARAWA The good guys win and the sneaky little yellow bast . . . . are annihilated! Sensationalized version of the battle that is sensational enough when you play it straight.	Bailey, T. Paperback edition only, Monarch Books, Inc., Derby, Conn. 1962
TARAWA	Graham, Capt G. *Gazette* Apr 44
TARAWA The other three battles in this book are Stalingrad, Normandy and the Ardennes	Rooney, A. From *The Fortunes of War: Four Great Battles of World War 2* Little, Brown and Company, Boston 1962
TARAWA By the CO of the 2D MAR DIV in the battle	Smith, LtGen J. *Proceedings* Nov 53

TARAWA BOMBARDMENT Battleships, cruisers and destroyers bombard Tarawa while Japs go about their business of getting ready in their coconut log bunkers	Emmons, MSgt R. *Gazette*	Mar 48
TARAWA: A LEGEND IS BORN Most recent Tarawa book. Starts with the old question, "Why Tarawa?" The answer is, "We had to learn the hard way." It's as good an answer as any. Book then shifts to excellent hour-by-hour report of the battle which includes valuable commentary on the enemy side. Good maps, pictures.	Shaw, H. Paperback edition only, Ballantine Books, Inc.	1969 (IP)
TARAWA: MARINES WIN NEW GLORY IN THE GILBERTS AND PROVE THERE IS NO CHEAP WAY TO VICTORY	*Life*	Dec 6, 1943
TARAWA: THE STORY OF A BATTLE Sherrod wrote this book from notes he scribbled as he sat against the seawall of the 20-foot wide beachhead during the first two days of Tarawa. He waded in the 700 yards with the 5th Wave on D-Day. This book is the most authentic chronicle in existence of Hawkins, Bonnyman, Crowe, Shoup and the other 2D MAR DIV Marines. Includes list of all Tarawa casualties	Sherrod, R. Duell, Sloan and Pearce, Inc.	1944
TARAWA: THE TIDE THAT FAILED	McKeernan, P. *Proceedings*	Feb 62
TARAWA: THE TOUGH NUT Part 8: *Marines in the Pacific War*	Pratt, F. *Gazette*	Apr 47
TARAWA: TOUGHEST BATTLE IN MARINE CORPS HISTORY Picture book with commentary by Combat Correspondents	Hannah, SSgt D. Duell, Sloan and Pearce, Inc.	1944
TARAWA: THE TOUGHEST 60 HOURS IN MARINE CORPS HISTORY Eyewitness report from the beach filed with AP on Nov 23, 1943	Johnson, R. From *Masterpieces of War Reporting* Julian Messner, Inc.	1962

THIRD DAY ON RED BEACH Excellent account using the "You are there" technique	Hammel, E., and J. Lane *Gazette*	 Nov 70
THIS WAS TARAWA	*Time*	Dec 13, 1943
TRIBUTE Words inscribed on a plaque on Tarawa honor fallen Marines	*Leatherneck*	Nov 50
TWO FLAGS AT TARAWA Picture story on the back cover	Lucas, J. *Gazette*	 Jan 46
THE UNITED STATES MARINES IN THE GILBERTS CAMPAIGN One of the "Brief History" series. Unfortunately, out-of-print	Nalty, B. HQMC	 1961

TARAWA MARINES

Cowart, Pvt William Franklin		
POSTSCRIPT TO TARAWA Cowart's wife has a beautiful baby daughter shortly after he is killed on Tarawa	Sherrod, R. *Leatherneck*	 Oct 48
Gross, PFC		
PFC GROSS: TARAWA'S HUB OF COMMUNICATIONS	*Leatherneck*	May 44
Hawkins, Lt Dean		
A GUY NAMED HAWKINS Exploits of Hawkins which Sherrod considers to be the most influential in changing outcome of a battle by an individual Marine in all of WW-2. As a correspondent, Sherrod saw a lot of battles and a lot of Marines	Sherrod, R. *Gazette*	 Apr 44 Nov 70
TARAWA AIRFIELD NAMED FOR MARINE Hawkins Field.	*Gazette*	Jan 44
Johnson, Sgt Roy W.		
SGT JOHNSON: HE STOPPED A TANK WITH A DARING ACT Navy Cross winner	*Leatherneck*	Nov 44
Spillane, Sgt John J.		
WINNING PITCHER: SPILLANE Wins Navy Cross for playing grenade catch with the enemy	Tolbert, Sgt F. *Leatherneck*	 Aug 44

	Vanderbeck, Sgt Jack FAMILY REUNION Home on leave after being wounded at Tarawa	*Leatherneck*	Jun 44
	Wallace, Cpl Arlton K. MOP-UP BEYOND BETIO Wallace mops-up stray Japs on other islands shortly after Betio is secured	Tolbert, Sgt F. *Leatherneck*	Jun 44
1944, GENERAL	CHRISTMAS EVE AT MAUI With the new 4th Marines in Hawaii	Landmesser, C. *Leatherneck*	Dec 49
	CHANGE MARINE OCS REQUIREMENTS	*Army & Navy Journal*	Dec 16, 1944
	GENERALS FOR MARINE CORPS List of new ones	*Army & Navy Journal*	Dec 16, 1944
	HISTORIC DEFENSE OF THE CORPS	*Gazette*	Jun 44
	HOLLANDIA Marine Tank Co participates in this Army operation	Stavisky, TSgt S. *Leatherneck*	Aug 44
	THE MARINE CORPS	Vandegrift, LtGen A. *Gazette*	Jun 44
	MARINE CORPS APPOINTMENTS	*Army & Navy Journal*	Sep 23, 1944
	MARINE CORPS CONFIRMATIONS	*Army & Navy Journal*	Jan 22, 1944
	MARINE CORPS HIGH COMMAND	*Army & Navy Journal*	Oct 14, 1944
	MARINE CORPS NOMINATIONS	*Army & Navy Journal*	Jan 15, 1944
	MARINE CORPS PROMOTIONS	*Army & Navy Journal*	Oct 21, Nov 18, 1944
	MARINE CORPS RETIREMENTS	*Army & Navy Journal*	Sep 9, 1944
	MARINE PHYSICAL DISCHARGES	*Army & Navy Journal*	Oct 28, 1944

MARINE UNIFORM CHANGES	*Army & Navy Journal*	Feb 26, 1944
MARINES BEGIN 170TH YEAR	*Army & Navy Journal*	Nov 11, 1944
MARINES LAND: PACIFIC FRONT	Beaufort, J. *Christian Science Monthly*	Dec 16, 1944
MARINES 169TH ANNIVERSARY	*Army & Navy Journal*	Nov 4, 1944
MARINES RETURN ON ROTATION	*Army & Navy Journal*	Oct 14, 1944
NAVY, MARINE COMMISSIONS	*Army & Navy Journal*	Nov 11, 1944
NEW MARINE GENERALS	*Gazette*	Feb 44
PACIFIC '44 Twenty-year-ago anniversary piece. Re-cap of the battles fought in 1944	*Leatherneck*	Nov 64
THREE MARINES AWARDED MEDAL OF HONOR	*Gazette*	Jun 44
TWELVE MONTHS OF MARINE HISTORY: YEAR 169	*Leatherneck*	Nov 44
WELCOME HOME! 1ST MAR DIV vet returns home	*Leatherneck*	Oct 44
WHERE DO WE GO FROM HERE? To Saipan!	Graham, Capt G. *Gazette*	May 44
WOMEN MARINES' FIRST BIRTHDAY	*N.Y. Times Magazine*	Feb 13, 1944
WOMEN'S RESERVE BIRTHDAY	*Time*	Feb 14, 1944
WOMEN'S RESERVES ONE YEAR OLD	*Gazette*	Mar 44
YOUNG MARINES INTO BATTLE	*Army & Navy Journal*	Sep 30, 1944

MARSHALLS—31 JAN 44

AIR BATTLE FOR THE MARSHALLS	Trefethen, Capt E. *Leatherneck*	Sep 44
IN THE BIG LEAGUE PHASE	Metcalf, Col C. *Gazette*	Apr 44

	THE LITTLE ONES COUNT, TOO Majuro, Arno and Erikub atolls are captured	*Leatherneck*	Sep 44
	MARINE AVIATION IN THE BATTLE FOR THE MARSHALLS Part 5: *Devilbirds*	DeChant, Capt J. *Gazette*	Jun 47
	THE MARSHALLS: INCREASING THE TEMPO Monograph of Marine operations from 31 Jan-6 Apr 44	Heinl, LtCol R., and LtCol J. Crown HQMC	1954
	THE MARSHALLS: OFFENSIVE IN HIGH GEAR Part 9: *Marines in the Pacific War*	Pratt, F. *Gazette*	May 47
	THE "RECON BOYS" AT MAJURO In the Marshalls, like everywhere, the "Recon Boys" get the most ink	Tolbert, Sgt F. *Leatherneck*	Jun 45
	SECURING THE MARSHALLS	Morehouse, Capt C. *Gazette*	Apr 44
	SORENSON: HE DESERVED A MIRACLE And got one. PFC Richard K. Sorenson falls on a grenade, and lives.	*Leatherneck*	Dec 44
	THE UNITED STATES MARINES IN THE MARSHALLS CAMPAIGN Another out-of-print "Brief History"	Nalty, B. HQMC	1961
KWAJALEIN—31 JAN 44	DESTRUCTION AT KWAJALEIN	*Gazette*	Mar 44
	FREEDOM ON KWAJELEIN For the natives	Bailey, G. *Asia*	Oct 44
	KWAJALEIN AIRFIELD NAMED FOR MARINE	*Gazette*	Apr 44
ROI-NAMUR—31 JAN 44	THE BATTLE OF THE DRAINS	Bishop, J. *Sat Eve Post*	Jun 3, 1944
	THE EAR-BANGER ON NAMUR A satchel charge blows up a torpedo stockpile, and a lot of Marines go up with it	Tolbert, MSgt F. *Leatherneck*	May 44

NAVAL GUNFIRE AT ROI-NAMUR Activities of the Northern Attack Group in support of MajGen Harry Schmidt's 4TH MAR DIV	McMillian, Cdr I., USN *Gazette*	Jul 48	
BATTLE OF ENIWETOK ATOLL	Wilcox, R. *Life*	Mar 13, 1944	**ENIWETOK— 17 FEB 44**
MARINES TAKE ENIWETOK	*Gazette*	Apr 44	
MARINE TANKS AT ENIWETOK	Wilcox, R. *Gazette*	Aug 44	
THE TAKING OF ENIWETOK	Carleton, Capt P. *Gazette*	May 44	
AMPHIBIOUS OPERATIONS: INVASION OF THE MARIANAS	Office of Naval Intelligence, U.S. Navy Department	1944	**MARIANAS— 15 JUN 44**
CAMPAIGN FOR THE MARIANAS Ninety-one page Monograph	Carleton, Capt P., and Capt J. Stockman HQMC	1946	
MARIANAS MERRYMAKER Cartoons by Donovan	Donovan, B. *Leatherneck*	Nov 44	
THE MARIANAS: PLANS AND PRELIMINARIES Part 11: *Marines in the Pacific War*	Pratt, F. *Gazette*	Jul 47	
MARINE AVIATION IN THE MARIANAS Part 5: *Devilbirds*	DeChant, Capt J. *Gazette*	Jun 47	
PRIZE OF THE MARIANAS: GUAM IMPORTANT TO OUR STRATEGY	Pratt, W. *Newsweek*	Jul 24, 1944	
REFERENCES ON THE MARIANAS CAMPAIGN	HQMC	1962	
WHAT THE FIGHTING YANKS SEE	Burnett, W. *Geographic*	Oct 44	
AFTER THE BATTLE	Lucas, Lt J. *American*	Jan 45	**SAIPAN— 15 JUN 44**
ALL HANDS READY TO SAVE LIVES USS Solace, Navy hospital ship, off Saipan	McMillan, TSgt G. *Hygeia*	Mar 45	

BATTALION ON SAIPAN Sherrod is there, as usual	Sherrod, R. *Gazette* Oct 44
BATTLE AT SAIPAN	Morris, F. *Collier's* Aug 12, 1944
BEACHHEAD IN THE MARIANAS: ON SAIPAN	Sherrod, R. *Time* Jul 3, 1944
BLOODY SAIPAN	*Newsweek* Jul 24, 1944
CAVE OF HORROR	Dempsey, Sgt D. *Leatherneck* Sep 44
DEADLIER THAN VOLCANOES: BATTLE FOR SAIPAN	*Newsweek* Jul 10, 1944
FIRES ON SAIPAN	Kinkead, E. *New Yorker* Sep 2, 1944
GONE TO EARTH: HOW THE MARINES WENT ABOUT ONE JOB OF MOPPING-UP SAIPAN'S SNIPERS Good practice for Iwo	Sherrod, R. *Time* Jul 17, 1944
HOW OUR NAVY OUTFOXED THE JAPS AT SAIPAN	Winston, R. *Sat Eve Post* Sep 23, 1944
IS WAR HELL? Rather disjointed autobiography by a Chaplain who served on Saipan. Interesting photos.	Goe, W. Published by the author Los Angeles 1947
LAST CHARGE Japs on Saipan	Sherrod, R. *Time* Jul 24, 1944
MEMORIAL ON SAIPAN	Kalman, Sgt V. *Leatherneck* Oct 44
MOPPING UP SAIPAN	*Life* Jul 24, 1944
OBSERVATIONS ON SAIPAN By an officer who was killed in Vietnam 20 years later	Hockmuth, LtCol B. *Gazette* Jan 45

PRELUDE TO SAIPAN By a Combat Correspondent	Zurlinden, TSgt C. *Proceedings*	May 47
RECORDING THE SAIPAN FIGHT ON WIRE The forerunner of the tape recorder was the wire recorder	Grahame, A. *Popular Science*	Dec 44
SAIPAN AIR-WARNING HORSE After the island was secured, a horse became the main air raid warning device	Merrick, Cpl H. *Leatherneck*	Jun 45
SAIPAN: THE BEGINNING OF THE END Monograph of a most decisive defeat for Japan	Hoffman, Maj C. HQMC	1950
SAIPAN, D-PLUS 200 New camps, PX's and chapels on Saipan after it was secured	*Leatherneck*	Mar 45
SAIPAN: EYEWITNESS TELLS OF ISLAND FIGHT	Sherrod, R. *Life*	Aug 28, 1944
SAIPAN: "HELL IS ON US" Part 13: *Marines in the Pacific War*	Pratt, F. *Gazette*	Sep 47
SAIPAN AND PACIFIC STRATEGY	Schubert, P. *Gazette*	Aug 44
SAIPAN: THE SHOCK AT THE BEACHES Part 12: *Marines in the Pacific War*	Pratt, F. *Gazette*	Aug 47
SAIPAN TANK BATTLE	Donovan, Maj J. *Gazette*	Oct 44
SAIPAN UNDER FIRE 1/24 in the attack on Saipan June 15-July 12, 1944, where the author won the Navy Cross	Stott, Capt F. Published by the author Andover, Mass.	1945
SOUTH FROM SAIPAN	Moore, W. *Geographic*	Apr 45
TACHOVSKY'S TERRORS Scout-Snipers on Saipan	Kalman, Sgt V. *Leatherneck*	Dec 44

THE TAKING OF MT TAPOTCHAU By the author of the Tarawa Monograph	Stockman, Capt J. *Gazette*	Jul 46
30 DAYS IN THE LINE A 4TH MAR DIV Company	Doying, Sgt G. *Leatherneck*	Dec 44
TOMORROW TO LIVE Fiction. Novel about Marine platoon leader which climaxes on Saipan. All the cliches	Herber, W. Coward-McCann Paperback by Bantam Books, Inc.	1957 1960
TRAPPED IN DEAD GULCH Fiction. Marines trapped in a cave on Saipan	Ruder, Sgt E. *Leatherneck*	Oct 44
WAR ON JAPAN'S DOORSTEP: THE BATTLE FOR SAIPAN Chamber's "Raiders" on Saipan	Doying, Sgt G. *Leatherneck*	Sep 44, Jul 72
WATER FOR THE INVASION OF SAIPAN How the Engineers handled the problem	Stearns, Dr. H. *Military Engineer*	Mar 45
WEAPONS COMPANY: A DAY IN COMBAT On Saipan	*Leatherneck*	Dec 44
WHAT IT COST TO TAKE SAIPAN	*Science Digest*	Dec 44
WORTH THE PRICE: STRATEGIC SAIPAN TOUGH ONE FOR U.S. NAVY PUSHING EAST Navy?	*Newsweek*	Jun 26, 1944

SAIPAN MARINES

Gabaldon, PFC Guy

HELL TO ETERNITY Sensationalized novel based on the exploits of 2d Marines Intelligence Clerk Gabaldon, the "Pied Piper of Saipan." He spoke Japanese and talked hundreds of natives and enemy soldiers into surrendering. Movie *In Love and War* based on this book.	Aarons, E. Paperback edition only Gold Medal Books, Greenwich, Conn.	1960

Smith, Gen H. M.			
GENERALS SMITH The famous "Smith vs Smith" controversy wherein Marine Gen Smith relieved Army Gen Smith for dragging his a . .	*Time*	Sep 18, 1944	
SMITH VS. SMITH	Love, E. *Infantry Journal*	Nov 48	
ADVANCE ON OROTE PENINSULA	Walker, Maj A. *Gazette*	Feb 45	**GUAM— 21 JUL 44**
ATTACK ON GUAM	Kaufman, Lt M. *Gazette*	Apr 45	
BANQUET PATROL Guam natives feed Marines patrol	McJennett, Capt J. *Leatherneck*	Dec 44	
THE BATTLE FOR BANZAI RIDGE 21st Marines fight for 3RD MAR DIV beachhead on Guam	Frances, Lt A. *Gazette*	Jun 45	
COORDINATING COMMUNICATIONS AT GUAM	Keller, LtCol A. *Gazette*	May 45	
"CO-PROSPERITY" ON GUAM How the Japs handled the island while we were gone	Fink, PFC S. *Gazette*	Oct 44	
DEATH FOR DIANA Japs execute a Guam teen-aged girl for spying	Purcell, Cpl J. *Leatherneck*	Nov 45	
THE DEFENSE OF GUAM How the Japs defended it	Umezawa, MajGen H. (Japanese Army) and Col L. Metzger *Gazette*	Aug 64	
DUNN ON GUAM Cartoons by Tom Dunn	Dunn, T. *Leatherneck*	Nov 44	
THE FIGHT AT FONTE 2/9 takes Fonte, and today's Commandant is there as a Battalion Commander	Cushman, LtCol R. *Gazette*	Apr 47	
GUAM	Martin, R. *Gazette*	Dec 43	

GUAM	Rowcliff, RAdm G. USN *Proceedings*	Jul 45
GUAM—CAMPAIGN OF MANEUVER Part 14: *Marines in the Pacific War*	Pratt, F. *Gazette*	Oct 47
GUAM, THE CLASSIC AMPHIBIOUS OPERATION	delValle, MajGen P. *Military Review*	Apr 47
GUAM—OUR WESTERN OUTPOST	Nelson, LtCdr F., USN *Proceedings*	Jan 40
GUAM AND TINIAN: PRE-LANDING BOMBARDMENT	*Newsweek*	Jul 31, 1944
THE HANDLING OF SUPPLIES ON GUAM	Klein, Capt E. *Gazette*	Feb 45
I SAW THE MORNING BREAK D-Day at Guam	Smith, Cdr H., USN *Proceedings*	Mar 46
THE JAPANESE SEIZURE OF GUAM	Wilds, T. *Gazette*	Jul 55
LETTER TO BETSEY Letters home from Guam Marine	Touhy, F. *Leatherneck*	May 46
MASSED FIRLS ON GUAM By the artillery expert	delValle, BGen P. *Gazette*	Dec 44
NAVAL GUNFIRE AT GUAM Excellent naval gunfire support given assaulting Marines before and on D-day	McMillian, Cdr I., USN *Gazette*	Sep 48
NOTES FROM GUAM By a Time correspondent	Martin, R. *Gazette*	Oct 44
ONE NIGHT AT ASAN FO's of "E" Batt, 12th Marines, at Guam on night of D-day	Hague, Sgt J. *Leatherneck*	Feb 47, Jul 72
OUTPOST AT FADIAN A 37-day tour on an outpost off Guam	Burnett, B. *Leatherneck*	Apr 45

PRISONER PERSUASION — Hunt, Cpl D.
Guam Japs surrender, for a change — *Leatherneck* Jun 46

THE RECAPTURE OF GUAM — Lodge, Maj O.
Monograph of one of the "cleanest" amphibious operations of WW-2. Everything worked! — HQMC 1954

RECONNAISANCE ON GUAM — Bridgewater, LtCol F.
Cavalry Journal May, Jun 45

REHABILITATION OF GUAM — Larsen, MajGen H.
Gazette Jun 45

RETURN TO GUAM — *Time* Jul 31, 1944

SOME JAPS SURRENDERED — Josephy, MTSgt A.
A good sign, but ones on later islands didn't follow example — *Infantry Journal* Aug 45

TANKS ON GUAM — *Gazette* Oct 44

THIRTY WHO WERE DOOMED — Decker, D.
Because Marines saved a youngster's life on Guam, 30 of them would die later at a party of appreciation — *Leatherneck* Sep 61

TOO MUCH NOISE — Hipple, W.
That describes most battles — *Newsweek* Aug 7, 1944

GUAM MARINES

Flores, Alfred
I PLEDGE ALLEGIANCE — Myers, Sgt R.
Flores is captured on Guam but escapes to resist Japs — *Leatherneck* May 45

Margolis, MGSgt Israel
REQUIEM FOR A HERO — Josephy, SSgt A.
Asks Corpsmen attending him to sing "God Bless America" as he dies from wounds on the beach — From *My Favorite War Story* Wittlesey House 1945

Marvin, GySgt Milton
A MARINE'S MARINE: GUNNER MILTON (SLUG) MARVIN — *Leatherneck* Jul 47
KIA, Guam

	Meyer, Capt Cord, Jr. LETTER HOME To tell his parents he was wounded on Guam	Meyer, Capt C. *Atlantic*	Oct 44
	Perez, Manual Cruz REUNION ON GUAM Marine Perez returns to his family on Guam	*Leatherneck*	Oct 44
TINIAN— 24 JUL 44	BEACHHEAD GOVERNMENT First days at Tinian	Miller, SSgt B. *Gazette*	Nov 44
	THE BUCK ROGERS MEN Marine rocketmen make their appearance for the first time	Doying, G. *Leatherneck*	Apr 45
	40 BOOTS AND A SADDLE Tinian replacements for the 4TH MAR DIV	Cooke, Sgt B. *Leatherneck*	Dec 44
	THE 4TH DIVISION AT TINIAN By the son of the famous Marine author	Thomason, Capt J. *Gazette*	Jan 45
	LANDING ON TINIAN	Bailey, Sgt G. *Leatherneck*	Oct 44
	THE NIGHT ON THE CLIFF 2/8 at Tinian	Hoffman, Maj C. *Gazette*	Feb 47
	THE SEIZURE OF TINIAN— JULY 24 - AUG 1, 1944 Monograph of the "perfect" amphibious operation of WW-2	Hoffman, Maj C. HQMC	1951
	SNAPPING IN ON TINIAN Shooting 19 Japs	Tolbert, Sgt F. *Leatherneck*	Feb 45
	SUPPLYING HELL'S HALF ACRE Marpo Point—Tinian	*Leatherneck*	Jan 45
	THE TALKING JEEP Talking civilians into surrendering	*Leatherneck*	Dec 44
	THEY HIT THE BEACH IN SWIM TRUNKS UDT-Men precede the landing	Say, H. *Sat Eve Post*	Oct 13, 1945

TINIAN: PERFECTION Part 15: *Marines in the Pacific War*	Pratt, F. *Gazette*	 Nov 47
TRICK THAT WON A STEPPING-STONE TO JAPAN	Bishop, J. *Sat Eve Post*	 Dec 23, 1944
WHO DO THEY THINK WE ARE? Masalog Point, where civilians commit suicide rather than risk capture by Marines	Mattie, TSgt G. *New Yorker*	 Dec 30, 1944

PELELIU—15 SEP 44

AMTRACS ASSIGNED THE MOST VARIED TASKS YET IN PELELIU BATTLE	*Chevron*	Oct 14, 1944
THE ASSAULT ON PELELIU Monograph of the most horrible and probably most useless Marine battle of WW-2	Hough, Maj F. HQMC	 1950
BATTLE FOR PELELIU	Schmuck, Maj D. *Gazette*	 Dec 44
THE BATTLE OF SUICIDE RIDGE	*Chevron*	Nov 25, 1944
CAVE FIGHTING ON PELELIU	*Army and Navy Register*	Sep 30, 1944
THE CLOSER THE BETTER About CAS on Peleliu	Walt, LtCol L. *Gazette*	 Sep 46
CORAL COMES HIGH	Hunt, Capt G. Harper and Bros.	 1946

Nobody knows how high better than Hunt, commander of "K" Co., 3/1, assigned the suicide job of right flank protection at Peleliu, Hunt and 21 Marines survived the battle, from a Rifle Company of more than 200.

FIGHTER PLANE STRIKE SCATTERS JAPS	*Chevron*	Dec 16, 1944
FINALE AT PELELIU Japs are still surrendering two years after the war ends.	Polete, Sgt H. *Leatherneck*	 Jul 47
THE FIRST TWO DAYS OF HELL ON PELELIU	*Chevron*	Oct 7, 1944

If there was a tougher battle than this one in *any* war, it has not been reported.

Title	Source	Date
FLAME THROWERS ATTACKING MT UMURBROGOL	*Chevron*	Oct 14, 1944
FOUR GRAVE MEN Vignette from Peleliu combat by two combat correspondents	Wilson, Capt E., and Sgt D. Stick *Leatherneck*	Apr 46
HELL IN THE UMURBROGOL	O'Leary, J. *True*	Oct 45
"INFANTILLERY" ON PELELIU	Evans, LtCol R. *Gazette*	Jan 45
ISLANDS IN THE NEWS Peleliu is bombed before the invasion	*Chevron*	Jul 22, 1944
JAPS STILL HOLDING OUT IN PELELIU Six weeks after the landing	*Chevron*	Oct 28, 1944
MARINE AT WAR First person report of a rifleman in 2/1 from Apr 44 through Feb 46. Includes Peleliu and Okinawa	Davis, R. Little, Brown and Company, Boston Paperback by Scholastic Book Services	1946 1970
MARINE AVIATION AT PELELIU Part 6: *Devilbirds*	DeChant, Capt J. *Gazette*	Jul 47
MARINE AVIATION ON PELELIU	Stauffer, Capt D. *Gazette*	Feb 45
MARINES USE FISTS AND ROCKS IN ALL NIGHT FIGHT FOR HILL	*Chevron*	Dec 2, 1944
PALAU HIT BY MARINES	*Chevron*	Sep 16, 1944
PELELIU Twenty-five year anniversary piece	Williams, SSgt R. *Leatherneck*	Sep 69
PELELIU CLEARED UP BY BATTLING 1ST DIVISION	*Chevron*	Sep 30, 1944
PELELIU: THE HARDEST BATTLE Part 18: *Marines in the Pacific War* And maybe the least needed	Pratt, F. *Gazette*	Feb 48

PELELIU LANDING — Lea, T. — Carl Hertzog Printing, El Paso 1945

This limited edition (only 500 were printed), over-sized book contains the best drawings of combat Marines to come out of WW-2. Lea is an artist and his drawings of battle-weary Marines coming down from the Umurbrogol are unforgettable. Brief commentary accompanies the pictures

PELELIU: TOM LEA PAINTS ISLAND INVASION — *Life* Jun 11, 1945

POINT SECURED — Hunt, Capt G. — *Gazette* Jan 45

By the CO of "K" Co, now an executive with Time/Life, Inc.

75'S MOVE PIECE-BY-PIECE UP CLIFF'S SIDE — *Chevron* Nov 18, 1944

THEY WERE ALL GIANTS AT PELELIU — Blackford, LtCdr C., USN — *Proceedings* Oct 50

TOKYO RADIO CLAIMS JAPS LANDING ON PELELIU — *Chevron* Nov 4, 1944

TOUGH GOING FOR EASY COMPANY — Donahue, Sgt J. — *Leatherneck* May 45

Bloody Nose Ridge

TOUGHEST TERRAIN — *Chevron* Sep 23, 1944

This side of hell

WRITER DESCRIBES BATTLE FOR TOEHOLD ON BEACH — *Chevron* Oct 7, 1944

PHILIP-PINES-2— 21 OCT 44

AMBUSH BAY — Pearl, J. — Paperback edition only, Signet Books 1966

Fiction. A nine-man Marine group lands on an island in the Phillipines to clear the way for MacArthur's return. They are to blow up the mines in the harbor. All are killed, except one, who lives to tell about it.

CLOSE AIR SUPPORT ON LUZON — McCutcheon, LtCol K. — *Gazette* Sep 45

Close Air Support for the Army's 1st Cavalry Division by MAG-24.

	GUNS BEFORE ORMOC Marine artillery on Leyete with the Army	Conner, Sgt J. *Leatherneck*	May 45
	HOW I TOOK MANILA Decker enters Manila with the Army	Decker, Sgt D. *Leatherneck*	Nov 45
	LEYETE LANDING Twenty-seven Marines land with the Army	Conner, Sgt J. *Leatherneck*	Feb 45
	LUZON	Jerome, C. *Gazette*	Nov 65
	MARINE AVIATION IN THE PHILIPPINES The only Monograph for a non-Marine operation.	Boggs, Maj C. HQMC	1951
	MARINE AVIATION IN THE REOCCUPATION OF THE PHILIPPINES Part 7: *Devilbirds*	DeChant, Capt J. *Gazette*	Aug 47
	A PROMISE FULFILLED Second time around with MacArthur in the Philippines	*Gazette*	Nov 65
	THOSE BOGIE BLUES Seagoing Marines hit Luzon with the 3rd Fleet	Tolbert, Sgt F. *Leatherneck*	Jan 45
1945, GENERAL	VJ STATEMENT BY GEN VANDEGRIFT	Vandegrift, Gen A. *Gazette*	Sep 45
	YEAR OF FULFILLMENT	Thacker, J. *Leatherneck*	Nov 45
IWO JIMA—19 FEB 45	ACCOUNT OF THE BATTLE OF IWO Sherrod didn't miss any	Sherrod, R. *Time*	Mar 5, 1945
	AMPHIBIOUS ASSAULT PLANNING: IWO JIMA Neither did Gen Cushman	Cushman, LtCol R. *Infantry Journal*	Dec 48
	AMTRACS ON IWO	Vincent, Sgt J. *Leatherneck*	Jun 45

THE ASSAULT — Matthews, A. Simon and Schuster, Inc. 1947. Paperback by Pocket Books, Inc. 1958

Matthews' 4TH MAR DIV platoon landed on D-Day. On D + 11, he and two others were left. This minute-by-minute account of those 12 terrible days is a microcosm of Iwo Jima. No detail escapes Matthews' trained eye. He was a reporter before stepping up to becoming a rifleman.

BANZAI ON IWO — *Newsweek* Mar 19, 1945

BATTALION ON IWO — Hill, Capt A. *Gazette* Nov 45

BATTLEFIELD OF IWO — *Life* Apr 9, 1945

THE BLOODY BATTLE FOR SURIBACHI — Wheeler, R. Thomas Y. Crowell Company 1965

Story of the Schrier patrol from 3rd platoon, "E" Co., 2/28, the first flag raisers on Suribachi on D + 4. Wheeler was hit and evacuated before the patrol but he pieced the story together from interviews with those few of his buddies who survived. Remarkable photos by Lou Lowery, the photographer from *Leatherneck* who went up Suribachi before Joe Rosenthal, but wasn't quite as lucky.

CRAZY-QUILT OF IWO — Hittle, LtCol J. *Gazette* Mar 46

Sixty thousand troops are scattered over 3.5 miles

D-DAY ON IWO JIMA — Walton, B. *Leatherneck* May 45

THE DECISIVE BATTLE OF THE PACIFIC WAR — Strope, A. *Proceedings* May 46

It sure wasn't this one!

ENGINEER OPERATIONS ON IWO JIMA — Morris, Col D. *Military Engineer* May 48

ENGINEERS ON IWO — Brooks, Lt W. *Gazette* Oct 45

ENTER THE 3D DIVISION — Conner, Sgt J. *Leatherneck* Jul 45

EXPENSIVE, BUT A GOOD INVESTMENT — *Newsweek* Mar 5, 1945
That's what they always say

FIRST JAP PRISONER CAPTURED ON IWO — Lowery, Sgt L. *Leatherneck* Jun 45
Picture story by the intrepid Mr. Lowery

FIRST SIX DAYS ON IWO JIMA — *Gazette* May 45

FIRST THREE DAYS: COURAGEOUS MARINES ATTACK WORLD'S BEST DEFENDED ISLAND — Sherrod, R. *Life* Mar 5, 1945
If reporters wore battle stars, Sherrod wouldn't have enough room!

THE FIRST "29" — Welsh, J. *Leatherneck* Mar 48
The first shot-up B-29 lands on Iwo and the horrible casualties become almost worthwhile.

THE FRIENDLY DEAD — Gallant, T. Doubleday & Company, Inc. 1964; Paperback by Popular Library 1964
Gallant was a sergeant on Iwo but this book is not a narrative of his experiences. It tells the whole story in a semi-objective way. "Carnage," the author's favorite word, seems to characterize this account of the battle. Many undoubtedly realistic but horrible vignettes of the way KIA Marines and Japs looked, and how they got that way

GRIM LESSON — Painton, F. *Collier's* Apr 14, 1945

HELL'S ACRE — *Time* Feb 26, 1945

H-HOUR ON IWO JIMA — *Newsweek* Feb 26, 1945

HISTORY OF U.S. MARINE CORPS OPERATIONS IN WORLD WAR 2: VOLUME 4—WESTERN PACIFIC OPERATIONS — Garand, G., and T. Strobridge HQMC USGPO 1973 (IP)
The official story of Peleliu, Iwo Jima and Philippines.
D 214.13-W89 $10.00

Title	Source
HOT ROCK: THE FIGHT FOR SURIBACHI	Miller, Sgt B. *Leatherneck* May 45, Nov 71
HYAKUTAKE MEETS THE MARINES	Whyte, Capt W. *Gazette* Jul, Aug 45
INEVITABLE ISLAND	*Time* Mar 5, 1945
IWO: BLOODY INCHES	*Newsweek* Mar 12, 1945
IWO—D+180	Jolokai, Sgt J. *Leatherneck* Sep 45
IWO DARK HORSE	Heinl, Maj R. *Gazette* Aug 45
IWO: HOT ROCK "Among the Americans who served on Iwo Jima, uncommon valor was a common virtue."	Lowery, L. *Leatherneck* Feb 70
IWO JIMA	Cates, Gen C. *Gazette* Nov 65
IWO JIMA	*Life* Mar 5, 1971
IWO JIMA Professionally objective account told with 20 years perspective and excellent research into the files from both sides. Even includes the Hearst newspaper editorials bemoaning the high casualties that caused such a furor when they appeared. Jap side constructed from interviews with survivors. Enemy and Marine casualty lists. Best Iwo book.	Newcomb, R. Holt, Rinehart and Winston 1965 Paperback by New American Library 1966
IWO JIMA A collection of Iwo Jima photos by the famous AP photographer	Rosenthal, J. Associated Press, Inc. 1945
IWO JIMA: AMPHIBIOUS EPIC Monograph. Interesting maps. Many little details you don't get anywhere else like insight into the planning of DETACHMENT.	Bartley, LtCol W. HQMC 1954

IWO JIMA BEFORE H-HOUR	Marquand, J. *Harper's* May 20, 1945
IWO JIMA . . . THE LESSON	Dunnagan, C. *Gazette* Feb 65
IWO JIMA: SPRINGBOARD TO FINAL VICTORY Photos and commentary by the Combat Correspondents who were there	Henri, Capt R. U.S. Camera Publishing Corporation 1945
THE IWO JIMA STORY	Hindsman, C. Published by the author Washington 1955
IWO JIMA THEN AND NOW	*Gazette* May 50
IWO JIMA: U.S. MARINES STORM ASHORE ON A TINY ISLAND 600 MILES FROM TOKYO UP correspondent files D-Day story from the beach	Tyree, W. From *Masterpieces of War Reporting* Julian Messner, Inc. 1962
IWO NEVER WAS A PUSHOVER	Clayton, K. *Flying* Jun 45
IWO: THE RED HOT ROCK	Zurlinden, Lt C. *Collier's* Apr 14, 1945
LAST BANZAI ON IWO	Cunningham, Sgt C. *Leatherneck* Jun 45
THE LAST DAYS OF GENERAL KURIBAYASHI About the Japanese Commander by a Jap who was there	Horie, Y. *Gazette* Feb 55
LEFT FLANK AT IWO	Haynes, Maj F. *Gazette* Mar 53
MARINE AVIATION OVER IWO JIMA Part 8: *Devilbirds*	DeChant, J. *Gazette* Sep 47
MARINES ON BLOODY, BARREN SANDS OF IWO	*Life* Mar 12, 1945
MEN AND GUNS AT IWO JIMA	Davenport, W. *Collier's* Mar 31, 1945

THE MORALE BUILDING GOAT A goat survives, believe it or not	Suepp, Capt F. *Leatherneck* Jun 45
MOTOYANIA AIRFIELD NO. 1	*Leatherneck* Jun 45
NARRATIVE OF IWO JIMA	Emmons, MSgt R. *Gazette* Jun 50
ON IWO JIMA: NIGHT IN A FRONT-LINE MARINE HOSPITAL	Sherrod, R. *Time* Mar 19, 1945
OURS, AND PAID FOR	*Newsweek* Mar 26, 1945
POSTSCRIPT TO IWO	Auslander, J. *Gazette* May 46
A REPORTER AT LARGE; D-DAY, IWO JIMA	Lardner, J. *New Yorker* Mar 17, 1945
ROAD TO TOKYO: RED EPIC OF IWO The red is Marine blood	Trumbull, R. *N.Y. Times Magazine* Mar 4, 1945
RODENT EXTERMINATORS Marines who flush Japs from caves	*Time* Mar 19, 1945
SACRIFICE IN A GORGE An incident on Iwo	Vincent, SSgt J. *Leatherneck* Jan 46
SANDS OF IWO JIMA Part 19: *Marines in the Pacific War*	Pratt, F. *Gazette* Mar 48
SELF TRAPPED JAPS OF IWO	Worden, W. *Sat Eve Post* Apr 28, 1945
SOLACE AT IWO There wasn't much of that	Lockridge, P. *Women's Home Companion* May 45
SUICIDE TO THE SNIPER How snipers were handled	Conner, Sgt J. *Leatherneck* Jun 45
TANKS ON IWO	Frothingham, Maj J. *Gazette* May 45

TARGET: IWO Naval gunfire support. Could more of it have reduced the ghastly total of casualties?	Heinl, R. *Proceedings*	Jul 63
TELLING IT TO THE MARINES Editorial about Marine casualties	*Time*	Mar 12, 1945
TEN DAYS ON IWO JIMA	Stott, Capt F. *Leatherneck*	May 45
THEY CALLED IT DEATH VALLEY	Miller, Sgt B. *Leatherneck*	Jun 45
THEY WON A NATION'S GRATITUDE	*Christian Science Weekly*	Nov 10, 1945
THIS IS THE FACE OF WAR	Bolte, C. *Nation*	Mar 3, 1945
THIS IS IWO: STORY OF THE BATTLE For the real story, read Sherrod	Hipple, W., and J. Lardner *Newsweek*	Mar 5, 1945
THOSE WHO FACED US Fiction. Tells the enemy side of Iwo	Miller, Sgt B. *Leatherneck*	May 48
TO THE FINISH—A LETTER FROM IWO JIMA	Jones, E. *Atlantic*	Jun 45
TOWARD THE RIDGE Scout-Snipers at Iwo	Walton, B. *Leatherneck*	Jun 45
THE U.S. MARINES ON IWO JIMA This "succession of simply reported incidents" tells the human interest side of this battle, in a disconnected, jerky way. By the Combat Correspondents. Includes names of more than 5,000 Marine KIA and WIA	Henri, Capt R. Dial Press Infantry Journal Press	 1945 1945
THE UNITED STATES MARINES ON IWO JIMA: THE BATTLE AND THE FLAG RAISING Excellent "Brief History"	Nalty, B. HQMC	1970 (IP)
UP THE ROCK ON IWO THE HARD WAY	Williams, LtCol R. *Gazette*	Aug 45

THE WAR DOGS PAID OFF AT IWO — Decker, Sgt D. *Leatherneck* Jul 45
Saved a lot of Marine lives

WATER ON IWO — Vincent, SSgt J. *Gazette* Oct 45

WHAT MAKES IWO JIMA WORTH THE PRICE — Pratt, W. *Newsweek* Apr 2, 1945
A lot of damaged B-29's

WHAT'S A WOMAN DOING HERE? — Chapelle, D. William Morrow and Company 1962
The Marines' favorite female reporter reports on her adventures on Iwo (and Okinawa)

WING TALK: FIRE BOMBS DROP ON JAP CAVE POSITIONS — Wilson, E. *Collier's* Jun 16, 1945

WITH NOBILITY AND COURAGE — Sherrod, R. *Time* Mar 12, 1945

IWO FLAG RAISINGS

FAMOUS IWO FLAG RAISING — *Life* Mar 26, 1945
The second one

FIRST FLAG RAISING ON IWO JIMA — Wheeler, R. *American Heritage* Jun 64
The Schrier Patrol

HOTTEST FLAG RAISING — Beech, TSgt K. *Leatherneck* May 45
The first one

THE PICTURE THAT WILL LIVE FOREVER — Rosenthal, J., and W. Heinz *Collier's* Jan 18, 1955
Second one

STORY OF A PICTURE: IWO JIMA FLAG-RAISING — *Time* Mar 26, 1945

THE TWO IWO JIMA FLAG RAISINGS — Frank, B. *American History Illustrated* Nov 68
The straight scoop by noted Marine Historian

IWO JIMA MARINES

Cason, Maj Joe Fred
THE PIPER OF IWO — Tolbert, Sgt F. *Leatherneck* Oct 49
Bagpipes at Iwo

	Subject / Title	Author / Source	Date
	Fox, Monroe		
	BLIND ADVENTURE Fox is blinded by explosion at Iwo. This is his story.	Fox, M. J. B. Lippincott Company, Philadelphia	1946
	Gray, Sgt Ross F.		
	FIGHTING PREACHER Gray is killed on Iwo	Hangen, Sgt B. *Leatherneck*	Oct 45
	THE PREACHER'S PERSISTENCE Didn't pay off for him	Hangen, Sgt B. *Leatherneck*	Nov 45
	Hayes, Sgt Ira		
	THE HERO OF IWO JIMA AND OTHER STORIES	Huie, W. Paperback edition only, New American Library	1962
	TAPS FOR IRA HAYES Obit of the Indian hero	Kildare, M. *True West*	Feb 71
	Hughes, Pvt Harry and Cpl Ray Yochim		
	GHOST PLAYERS Two major league ball players are reported killed on Iwo, but they turn up alive	*Leatherneck*	Nov 45
	Jacobson, Cpl Douglas		
	GOLIATH IN GREENS Medal of Honor winner on Iwo. "The greatest living Marine fighting man."	Katz, Cpl K. *Leatherneck*	Jan 47
	Ward, J. F.		
	RADIOMAN TELLS HIS IWO JIMA EXPERIENCE	Ward, J. *Science Newsletter*	Sep 22, 1945
	Wheeler, Keith		
	WE ARE THE WOUNDED Story of Wheeler and how he was WIA at Iwo	Wheeler, K. E. P. Dutton & Co., Inc.	1945
OKINAWA— 1 APR 45	ADMIRAL'S HILL	Myers, Sgt R. *Leatherneck*	Oct 45

AMMO FROM HEAVEN Air drop on Okinawa	Myers, Sgt R. *Leatherneck*	Jan 46
AMPHIBIOUS OPERATIONS—CAPTURE OF OKINAWA, 27 MARCH - 21 JUNE 1945 The official Navy version	Chief of Naval Operations, U.S. Navy Department	1945
THE BATTLE FOR THE MOTOBU PENINSULA By a future Commandant who was there	Shepherd, MajGen L. *Gazette*	Aug 45
BATTLE OF THE WANA DRAW	Mason, Col A. *Gazette*	Oct 45
CAVE WARFARE Wana Ridge	delValle, MajGen P. *Gazette*	Jun 45
THE CONQUEST OF OKINAWA: AN ACCOUNT OF THE 6TH MARINE DIVISION	Carleton, Maj P. HQMC	1946
"DAMNDEST BATTLEFIELD" Comment by Gen Roy Geiger, the Marine aviator who commanded more troops than any Marine in history after Army Gen Buckner was killed	Finian, Sgt J. *Leatherneck*	Jun 45
DRIVE ON NAHA	*Leatherneck*	Aug 45
EYES AND EARS OF G-2 Scouts on Okinawa	Fink, Sgt S. *Leatherneck*	Nov 45
FIGHT IN THE NORTH Early operations before the breakout to the South	Asprey, R. *Gazette*	Apr 55
FIRE POWER IN CAVE WARFARE	delValle, MajGen P. *Gazette*	Sep 45
THE 1ST MARINE DIVISION ON OKINAWA: APRIL 1 - JUNE 30, 1945	Stockman, Capt J. HQMC	1946
HALF A LOAF Sugar Loaf Hill. It looked like just another hill, but it cost the 29th Marines 2600 men on May 12, 1945.	Barrow, MSgt C. *Leatherneck*	Jul 61

HISTORY OF U.S. MARINE CORPS OPERATIONS IN WORLD WAR 2: VOLUME 5—VICTORY AND OCCUPATION This volume includes: Prologue to the End Okinawa The End of the War Occupation of Japan North China Marines Conclusion D214.13—W89/y5 $11.75	Frank B., and H. Shaw HQMC USGPO	1969 (IP)
INCIDENT IN OKINAWA	Fitzpatrick, SSgt R. *Leatherneck*	Aug 45
INTERLUDE ON IHEYA Invasion of the undefended islands of Iheya Jima and Aguni	*Leatherneck*	Nov 45
IT WAS PIE FOR THE PIGEONS Pigeons worked as messengers on Okinawa	Felsen, Sgt H. *Leatherneck*	May 46
JAP TACTICS ON OKINAWA Sophisticated. A preview of what to expect in the invasion of Japan	Williams, LtCol T. *Gazette*	Oct 45
JOE AND SUZI Okinawa natives talk their people into surrendering	Kogan, Sgt H. *Leatherneck*	Aug 45
KEY TO THE CASTLE Shuri Castle	Myers, Sgt R. *Leatherneck*	Dec 45, Apr 72
THE LAST EVENT	Lewis, TSgt M. *Leatherneck*	Sep 45
MARINE AVIATION OVER OKINAWA Part 9: *Devilbirds*	DeChant, Capt J. *Gazette*	Oct 47
NIGHT OPERATIONS AT OKINAWA By Army and Marine units	Stockman, Capt J. *Gazette*	Sep 46
NO ICE CREAM SODAS	Fitzpatrick, SSgt R. *Leatherneck*	Jan 46

OKINAWA: THE COMING OF THE KAMIKAZE Part 20: *Marines in the Pacific War*	Pratt, F. *Gazette*	Apr 48
OKINAWA: CONQUEST OF THE NORTH Part 21: *Marines in the Pacific War*	Pratt, F. *Gazette*	May 48
OKINAWA IN REVIEW	Burton, LtCol T. *Gazette*	Sep 58
OKINAWA: LAST STAND Part 23: *Marines in the Pacific War*	Pratt, F. *Gazette*	Jul 48
OKINAWA: SUGAR LOAF AND SHURI Part 22: *Marines in the Pacific War*	Pratt, F. *Gazette*	Jun 48
OKINAWA: THRESHOLD TO JAPAN Mr. Duncan's usual excellent pictures accompany the story	Duncan, Lt D. *Geographic*	Oct 45
OKINAWA: TOUCHSTONE TO VICTORY Part of the Illustrated History of WW-2 series at your newsstand now for only $1.00	Frank, B. Paperback edition only, Ballantine Books Inc.	1970 (IP)
OKINAWA—25 YEARS AGO	Malcolm, Cpl C. *Leatherneck*	Apr 70
OKINAWA—VICTORY IN THE PACIFIC Monograph of the last multi-division battle (maybe of all time?)	Nichols, Maj C., and H. Shaw HQMC Reprinted by Charles E. Tuttle Co., Publishers, Rutland, Vt.	1955 1965 (IP)
OKINAWA: VICTORY AT THE THRESHOLD	Baldwin, H. *Gazette*	Dec 50, Jan 51
THE OKINAWAN They seemed to like Americans. (After the Japs, they'd like anything!)	Helfer, Sgt H. *Leatherneck*	Jul 45

OLD GLORY ON SHURI 1ST MAR DIV goes out like it came in—A winner.	delValle, MajGen P. *Gazette* Aug 45
1/5 TAKES JICHAKU PLATEAU	Murray, LtCol J. *Gazette* Sep 47
REFERENCES ON THE U.S. MARINES IN THE OKINAWA CAMPAIGN	O'Quinlivan, M., and J. Hilliard HQMC 1964
A REPORTER ON OKINAWA: 1. Suicides and Bushwackers 2. The Tomb Life	Lardner, J. *New Yorker* May 25, 1945
SCHOOL SOLUTIONS ON MOTOBU	Bergren, Maj O. *Gazette* Dec 45
SHOOTING PAINS ON OKINAWA In a Sick Bay there	Felsen, Sgt H. *Leatherneck* May 46
SILENCE ON SUGAR LOAF Bought, and paid for.	Mullahy, Cpl V. *Leatherneck* Nov 45
THE 6TH MARINE DIVISION ON OKINAWA	Stockman, Capt J. HQMC
6TH MAR DIV IN SOUTHERN OKINAWA	Shilin, Lt A. *Gazette* Sep 45
SMOKE SCREEN SURPRISE	Kogan, SSgt H. *Leatherneck* Nov 45
SOUTHWARD FROM SHURI	delValle, MajGen P. *Gazette* Oct 45
SURRENDER—OR DIE Sometimes, the Japs did surrender	Kogan, SSgt H. *Leatherneck* Oct 45
TALES FROM OKINAWA Stories of the Combat Correspondents	*Leatherneck* Sep 45
TANK-ARTILLERY ON OKINAWA	Tomlinson, Maj L. *Gazette* Nov 45
TO YONTAN AND BEYOND	Shilin, Lt A. *Gazette* Jul 45

TYPHOON OF STEEL: THE BATTLE FOR OKINAWA Two former Marines wrote this book—the latest on Okinawa. It is a sort of sensationalized version of a battle that was pretty sensational anyway	Belote, J., and W. Harper & Row Publishers 1970 (IP)
WORD WARFARE Talking the Japs into surrendering on Okinawa	Decker, D., and S. Fink *Leatherneck* Jan 48

OKINAWA MARINES

Atkinson, Lt Fitzgerald and Cpl Robert Boardman	
SNIPER'S BARRICADE They are used by the Japs for target practice on Okinawa	Lucas, Lt J. *Leatherneck* Nov 45
Golar, Cpl Rusty	
GLORY KID Exploits of Golar who rated the Medal of Honor but didn't get it.	Kogan, SSgt H. *Leatherneck* Sep 45
INCREDIBLE REDHEAD Killed on Okinawa	Dempsey, D., and J. Golden *Collier's* Nov 17, 1945
Kennedy, Capt Leo	
INCIDENT IN THE CHINA SEA Kennedy is killed on mission over Okinawa	DeChant, Capt J. *Leatherneck* Jan 46
Mollus, PFC William A.	
A STORY ABOUT WILLIE Killed on Okinawa	Meagher, SSgt E. *Leatherneck* Oct 45
Saracino, PFC Joe E.	
GRENADE PARADE Plays catch with live grenade. Lives to tell it.	Helfer, Sgt H. *Leatherneck* Nov 45
Van Brunt, Lt	
THE FABULOUS TAISHO Fiction. Van Brunt is an actor who plays his biggest role on Okinawa as a Japanese General	Shilin, Lt A. *Leatherneck* Nov 45

WORLD WAR 2, GENERAL

AFTER THE BATTLES	*Gazette*	Feb 44
AMPHIBIOUS ART Photos of paintings of WW-2	*Leatherneck*	Jul 44
AMPHIBIOUS WAR AGAINST JAPAN A preview of future operations published during Guadalcanal	Hart, T. *Sat Eve Post*	Oct 10, 1942
AN ANNOTATED BIBLIOGRAPHY OF THE UNITED STATES MARINE CORPS IN THE SECOND WORLD WAR The best Bibliography published by HQMC. (All 214 items in it are included in *Creating A Legend*)	O'Quinlivan, M., and J. Hilliard HQMC	1965 (IP)
AS SEESE SEES IT Cartoons	Seese, PFC J. *Leatherneck*	Aug 44
ATOLLS: IMPRESSIONS OF KWAJALEIN, TARAWA, MAKIN AND OTHER FAMOUS OCEANIC BATTLEGROUNDS By the famous author	Dos Passos, J. *Life*	Mar 12, 1945
BATTLEGROUND SOUTH PACIFIC Beautiful, oversized book featuring color pictures of Marines' WW-2 battlegrounds. Limited narration accompanies the pictures	Howlett, R. Charles E. Tuttle Co., Rutland, Vt.	1970 (IP)
BEACHHEADS OF WORLD WAR 2	Pratt, F. *Gazette*	Aug 48
BLOODY BEACHES: MARINES DIE HARD Fiction. The title tells you the class in which to put this book (the lower class).	Stagg, D. Paperback edition only, Pocket Books, Inc.	
FOXHOLE ART BY EBY Cartoons by Kerr Eby	Eby, K. *Leatherneck*	Sep 44
GOVERNMENT SHIPMENT "RUSH" That's life on a troop train	*Leatherneck*	Aug 44

HEAR MARINE BATTLES — Official Combat Recordings, Washington — 1948

Actual recording of sounds of Marine battles including Guadalcanal, Saipan, Peleliu, Iwo Jima and Okinawa. (Set the recording industry back thirty years)

HIT THE BEACH: THE STORY OF THE MARINE CORPS IN WORLD WAR 2 — Ageton, Adm H., USN — New American Library — 1961

HIT THE BEACH: YOUR MARINE CORPS IN ACTION, PICTORIAL HISTORY OF THE SECOND WORLD WAR — McCahill, Maj W. — William H. Wise and Co., Inc. — 1948

Volume 8 of the series. This "photographic epic" of 386 pages includes every famous photo, and some infamous ones as well. Brief text is written by the commander of the operation pictured. List of Medal of Honor winners. Brief biographical sketches of the Corps "Top Brass"

HOW AMERICA LIVES IN THE ARMED FORCES — *Ladies Home Journal* — Mar 42

Not as well as you do at home, lady!

THE ISLAND WAR: THE UNITED STATES MARINE CORPS IN THE PACIFIC — Hough, F. — J. B. Lippincott Company, Philadelphia — 1947

Hough admits "It's out of the question for genuine 'history' to be written within such a short time of the events described." Units, not individuals, are featured in a dull, semi-official style. Really an outline which ties the whole war together for the first time

MARINE ARTISTS DEPICT WAR'S GRIMNESS — *Leatherneck* — Mar 44

MARINE BATTLE BROADCASTING SYSTEM — *Gazette* — Apr 44

THE MARINES HAVE LANDED — Parsons, R. — *Atlantic* Mar 43 — *Digest* Jun 43

MARINES IN ACTION: A REVIEW OF THE U.S. MARINE CORPS OPERATIONS IN THE PACIFIC PHASE OF WORLD WAR 2 FROM SAMOA TO PELELIU — Marine Corps Institute, Washington, 1945

THE MARINES IN THE PACIFIC WAR — Pratt, F. — *Gazette* Sep 46-Oct 47

Series preceded book *The Marines War*

MARINES AT WAR — Crane, A. — The Hyperion Press, 1943

Reproductions of paintings and drawings of Marine Combat Artists during the early part of WW-2. Mostly Guadalcanal and the Solomons

THE MARINES' WAR: AN ACCOUNT OF THE STRUGGLE FOR THE PACIFIC FROM BOTH AMERICAN AND JAPANESE SOURCES — Pratt, F. — William Sloane Associates, Inc., 1948

Blend enemy documents with official USMC records. Add interviews with Marine participants. Season with the author's opinion on everything, from the necessity of Peleliu to the fatuous observation that Bougainville "was Guadalcanal with air superiority." The result is the first "objective history" by a professional writer who was not a Marine. After finishing research for this book, Pratt was more Gung-ho than most Marines. So is the book.

"OLD YOUNG MEN" — *Leatherneck* — Jun 43

Letter from Marine in combat to his wife discussing the plight of young kids killing in the war and the effect that it will have on them later.

ON TO WESTWARD — Sherrod, R. — Duell, Sloan & Pearce, Inc., 1945

Personal account of what Sherrod witnessed on Saipan, Iwo and Okinawa. Title of book taken from a verse in a Marine cemetery at Tarawa

OPERATION VICTORY: WINNING THE PACIFIC WAR — Editors of the Navy Times, G. P. Putnam's Sons 1968
Picture book, many of Marines

PACIFIC PROGRESS — *Gazette* Mar 44

PETERS' SKETCHBOOK — Peters, Cpl D. *Leatherneck* Oct 44
Cartoons of Marines in SOPAC

PITCHFORK PENMAN — Jackson, PFC H. *Leatherneck* Aug 44
Cartoons by Jackson

POWER IN THE PACIFIC: OFFICIAL U.S. NAVY, MARINE CORPS AND COAST GUARD PHOTOS — Steichen, Capt E., USNR U.S. Camera Publishing Corporation 1945
The best photos of WW-2 in the Pacific. Many of Marines

PRELUDE TO INVASION — *Leatherneck* Jul 44
Cartoon story of shipboard life

STRONG MEN ARMED; THE UNITED STATES MARINES AGAINST JAPAN — Leckie, R. Random House, Inc. 1962 Paperback by Ballantine Books, Inc. 1970
Narrative history from "The Canal" through Okinawa in the lean, terse style which makes Leckie-writing about Marines the best there is. The time is *now* and you are *there.* He *was* there, as a scout/machine gunner with the 1ST MAR DIV. It shows. His history is alive. You don't get dreary lists of Medal of Honor winners with their fatal asterisks. Instead, the act which earned the Medal is reported in the narrative, where it belongs.

THE U.S. MARINE CORPS — Hawthorne, J. *Public Personnel Review* Jul 43

THE U.S. MARINE CORPS IN WORLD WAR 2 — *Proceedings* Aug 48
Pictorial history

UNITED STATES MARINE CORPS — *Federal Register* Dec 7, 1943

THE UNITED STATES MARINE CORPS IN WORLD WAR 2 — Smith, S. — Random House, Inc. — 1969

"The one-volume history, from Wake to Tsingtao—by the men who fought in the Pacific, and by distinguished Marine experts, authors and newspapermen." This huge (965 pp.) anthology was worth waiting 25 years for. Includes more than 100 narratives by writers like Hersey, Toland and Walter Lord. All of the famous writing is here along with descriptions of the lesser-known episodes. Excellent connecting passages tie the various excerpts together and keep the story moving. Seventy-eight pages of great photos.

WORLD WAR 2 — *Leatherneck* — Nov 50

Complete and valuable chronology of battles and units from Pearl Harbor to the occupation of Japan

YOUR MARINE CORPS IN WORLD WAR 2 — Bergstrom, Capt A., Capt E. Wilson and Sgt F. Sick — Albert Love Enterprises, Inc., Atlanta — 1946

Two hundred page photo history of the Marines in WW-2 with more than 300 photos. Narrative by the Combat Correspondents

AVIATION

GENERAL

AIR MARINES — Fuller, C. — *Flying* — Dec 43

AIRCRAFT INSIGNIA: SPIRIT OF YOUTH — Hubbard, G. — *Geographic* — Jun 43

Color photos of Marine aircraft

BROOD OF NOISY NAN: MARINE AIR FORCE — *Time* — Jan 12, 1944

Noisy Nan was Cunningham's aircraft (first Marine aviator)

DESERT AIRDROME — Mazet, Maj H. — *Gazette* — Mar 44

FLATTOPS FOR LEATHERNECKS — *Time* — Oct 23, 1944

THE FRAMEWORK OF MARINE AVIATION — Graham, Capt G. — *Gazette* — Jan 44

MARINE AVIATION SUPPLY	Butler, Capt E. *Gazette*	Jun 45	
MARINE CORPS AVIATION	*Gazette*	Jun 41	
MARINE CORPS AVIATION, GENERAL, 1940 Pamphlet	Rowell, Maj R. USGPO	1940	
MARINES Review of Marine aviation to date	Mitchell, MajGen R. *Flying*	Feb 43	
SCAT SKETCHES Cartoons	Arlt, Sgt P. *Leatherneck*	Feb 45	
U.S. MARINE CORPS AVIATION This 28 page pamphlet has no date, author or place, but it was published about 1944. Includes black and white photos and two page list of Marine aces			
WING TALK A regular feature in Collier's. These two columns featured Marine aviation	Martin, H. *Collier's*	Jul 28, Aug 18, 1945	
WINGS OF THE MARINE CORPS	Thacker, J. *Gazette*	Aug 43	
THE CORSAIR The best aircraft in Corps history makes its debut	*Leatherneck*	Sep 43	**AIRCRAFT**
FLYING LEATHERNECKS IN WORLD WAR 2 Pictures of aircraft. No narrative	Doll, T. Paperback edition only, Aero Publishers, Inc., Fallbrook, Cal.	1971 (IP)	
REVOLUTION BY RADAR Marine Night Fighters	Phillips, Cpl J. *Leatherneck*	Nov 45	
SEA RESCUE DUMBOS—rescue planes	Miller, SSgt N. *Leatherneck*	Feb 45	
TYPES OF MARINE CORPS PLANES	*Gazette*	Mar 44	
AERIAL SPOTTERS	Watson, Lt T., and Lt F. Calpin *Gazette*	Oct 44	**DUTIES AO'S**

	FLEAS IN THE HAIR OF THE JAPS AO's in Piper Cubs	*Leatherneck*	Jun 44
	NEW VIEWS ON AERIAL OBSERVERS They have guts!	Reese, Capt P. *Gazette*	Feb 45
AERIAL PHOTO	THE AERIAL PHOTO IN AMPHIBIOUS INTELLIGENCE	Colley, LtCol T. *Gazette*	Oct 45
	"AERIAL PHOTOGRAPHY"	Lemly, Maj W. *Leatherneck*	Jul 40
	JAP HUNTING WITH A CAMERA Photo recon	Growden, G. *Leatherneck*	Oct 43
	SKY SPIES	Miller, Sgt B. *Leatherneck*	Jul 44
	TACTICAL AIR PHOTO INTERPRETATION	Utz, Lt J. *Gazette*	Mar 45
	THEY GET THE SCOOP Air Combat Intelligence Officers in the Pacific	Helfer, H. *Leatherneck*	Mar 45
CRASH CREW	CRASH CREW IN ACTION Cherry Point	Burrows, Capt J. *Gazette*	Sep 44
GROUND CREW	MEET YOUR MARINE CORPS—AVIATION GROUND CREW	Murray, PFC B. *Leatherneck*	Feb 44
	THE MEN BEHIND THE PLANES	Goodman, Capt W. *Gazette*	Oct 44
PILOTS	HEROES VS. ZEROS Marine pilots compared to Japs	*Leatherneck*	Sep 43
	MARINE CORPS ACES	*Gazette*	Mar-May 44
	MARINES: NAVY TRAINED AND EQUIPPED, MARINE FLYERS ARE LEADING PACIFIC THRUSTS	*Flying*	Oct 44
	PILOTS, STAND ASIDE	Noble, Capt N. *Gazette*	Jun 44
	PRESIDENT DECORATES ANOTHER MARINE PILOT	*Gazette*	Mar 44
	PSYCHOLOGY PICKS A PILOT	Trawick, Lt M., USNR *Gazette*	Apr 44

THE VANISHING NAP But it took 28 more years for them to completely vanish	Helfer, Sgt H. *Leatherneck*	Dec 44, Jul 72
VICTORY LINE TAG pilots	McElroy, Sgt J. *Leatherneck*	May 45
STORY OF FIVE PILOTS: MARINE PILOTS WHO WON'T BE BACK	Hubler, R. *Flying*	Mar 45

Boyington, Col. Gregory "Pappy"

BAA BAA BLACK SHEEP Boyington tells it like it was scoring six kills with the Flying Tigers and sweating out Marine Corps reinstatement when we got into the war. He finally fought again, with the Black Sheep, in	Boyington, Col G. G. P. Putnam's Sons Paperback by Dell Publishing Co., Inc.	 1958 1959

a Jap prison camp, and later, when the toughest enemy of all became booze. The most honest autobiography ever written by a hero. And one of the best.

"BLACK SHEEP PAPPY"	Hubler, Capt R. *Gazette*	Feb 44
BOYINGTON RECEIVES MEDAL OF HONOR Only he isn't there at the time	*Gazette*	May 44
MAN FROM EVERYWHERE	Phillips, Sgt J. *Leatherneck*	Dec 45
PAPPY BOYINGTON COMES HOME: SKIPPER OF THE MARINE BLACK SHEEP FIGHTER SQUADRON	*Life*	Oct 1, 1945
"YUP, IT HURTS" Author remembers Boyington in prison camp. He was there with him	Tinker, Capt F., USAF *Gazette*	May 70

Brown, Lt Walter F.

RESCUE AT KOROR A DUMBO picks up Brown in the water	Mamer, LtCdr F., USN *Leatherneck*	Jul 45

Clasen, Lt William "Wild Bill"		
WILD BILL	Harvey, Sgt R.	
Fighter-bomber pilot from MSB-232	*Leatherneck*	Feb 45
Foster, Capt John M.	Foster, Capt J.	
HELL IN THE HEAVENS	G. P. Putnam's	
Journal of a Corsair pilot with the "Flying Deuces" of VMF-222. Foster wasn't a hero and his squadron was constantly upstaged by its sister squadron, the famous Black Sheep of VMF-214. VMF-222 still managed to see plenty of combat in the Solomons around Bougainville and over Rabaul. Interesting record of the day-in-and-day-out tedium which predominates over the few seconds of excitement in the life of a fighter pilot.	Sons	1961
Geiger, Gen. Roy		
GEN. GEIGER: 1885-1947	Langille, Cpl V.	
Obit of the Marine aviator who commanded more ground troops than any Marine in history (on Okinawa)	*Leatherneck*	May 47
UNACCUSTOMED TO FEAR: A BIOGRAPHY OF THE LATE GENERAL ROY S. GEIGER	Willock, Col R. Published by the author Princeton, N.J.	1968
Hanson, Capt Robert "Butcher Bob"		
"YOU'D BE SO NICE TO COME HOME TO"	Graham, Capt G.	
But he didn't make it home	*Gazette*	Mar 44
Hawkins, Sgt David H.		
SGT HAWKINS: "MEAT BALL" DESTROYER	*Leatherneck*	Sep 44
Shoots down Japs while AA gunner on the USS Enterprise		
Maas, Gen. Melvin J.		
MELVIN J. MAAS, GALLANT MAN OF ACTION	Zehnpfening, G. T. S. Denison & Co.,	
Biography of a Reserve Marine flyer who went from Curtis Jennys to jets and from Congress to Guadalcanal and Okinawa. Maas, a Congressman from Minnesota, was influential in	Minneapolis	1967

drafting Armed Forces Reserve legislation and was Chairman of the President's Committee on Employment of the Handicapped. He was a Reserve General.

Mix, Pvt John and PFC James Turner
MIX AND TURNER: TWO MEN AGAINST THE SEA — *Leatherneck* — Oct 44
Mix and Turner pull wounded pilot from his ditched plane

Moore, Capt Thomas, Jr.
THE SKY IS MY WITNESS — Moore, Capt T. G. P. Putnam's Sons — 1943
Diary of the short war of Moore, a Marine dive bomber pilot commissioned two days after Pearl Harbor. He saw action at Guadalcanal and was injured when his engine failed after take-off on a mission against Jap transports. He got the Navy Cross and a medical discharge before the end of 1942.

Power, Tyrone
TYRONE POWER: MARINE — Myers, R. *Leatherneck* — Dec 43
Picture story of the movie star turned Marine transport pilot

Segal, Lt Manfred "Murderous Manny"
THINGS ARE BAD ALL OVER — De Chant, J. *Leatherneck* — Feb 45
Shoots down 12 Japs

Sprenger, PFC Ransdell W.
PIN-UPS OVER TOKYO — Ototowsky, S. *Leatherneck* — Apr 45
He paints voluptuous pin-ups on B-29's headed for Tokyo

Stout, Maj Robert F. "Cowboy"
COWBOY PILOT — Nelson, Sgt O. *Leatherneck* — Sep 45
Last flight of 4TH MAW Squadron Commander KIA

Swett, Capt Zeke
SWEATING IT OUT WITH SWETT — DeChant, Lt J. *Leatherneck* — Oct 44
Adventures of another ace

Walter, Lt
SOME COME BACK — Wilson, Capt E. *Leatherneck* — Aug 45
He is shot down, MIA, and returns from jungle

	Wilson, Lt W. A. LOST—A TRUE ADVENTURE OF A MARINE Ditches a crippled plane and finds paradise with natives	Waters, Sgt E. *Leatherneck*	Jan 45
OPERATIONS	ACTION AT LOW ALTITUDE Pilot is killed on bombing mission	Abney, Lt J. *Leatherneck*	Sep 45
	AERIAL EXTERMINATORS Marine torpedo bombers spray DDT on Pacific Islands to kill insects hovering over the estimated 7,000 Jap corpses.	Wilson, E., and J. Kelly *Leatherneck*	Apr 45
	AN AIRFIELD IS PUT IN OPERATION	Gore, BM 2/C W., USN *Gazette*	Jun 45
	AMERICAN HEROES OF THE WAR IN THE AIR Includes all Marine aviation actions from the start until late 1943. List of all decorated Army, Navy and Marine airmen with brief narrative. A valuable book.	Mingos, H. Lanciar Publishers	1943
	AVIATION YEAR Review of 1944	White, SSgt D. *Leatherneck*	Nov 44
	THE BIG, HAIRY DOG FIGHT Corsairs vs. Zeroes	Martin, Lt H. *Flying*	Mar 49
	BOMBER SQUADRON GOES TO WAR	Smathers, Capt G., and MTSgt L. Peever *Leatherneck*	Sep 44
	BOMBS AND BOMBING	*Leatherneck*	Aug 44
	A DAY WITH MARINE BOMBERS	*Leatherneck*	Mar 44
	DAY'S WORK Operations against the Kamikaze	Floyd, Lt C. *Leatherneck*	Feb 45
	DEVILBIRDS: THE STORY OF UNITED STATES MARINE CORPS AVIATION IN WORLD WAR 2 Serialized in the Gazette from Feb-Nov of 1947. Each chapter is listed in the appropriate battle in *Creating A Legend*	DeChant, Capt J. Harper & Bros.	1947

AN EVALUATION OF AIR OPERATIONS AFFECTING THE U.S. MARINE CORPS IN WORLD WAR 2 — MCS, Quantico 1945

Four-part study. Mission of Marine air, development of CAS, influence of air on Marine ground ops and brief summary of air ops during WW-2

FAST FREIGHT TO HELL — Miller, Sgt B.
Marine Combat Air Transport — *Leatherneck* May 44

FIRST FREIGHT INTO SAIPAN — Tolbert, Sgt F.
Col Neil MacIntyre flys MATS into Saipan — *Leatherneck* Oct 44

FIRST THREE AERIAL INNINGS — McVay, I.
Wake, Midway and Guadalcanal — *Leatherneck* Nov 43

FLYING LEATHERNECKS: THE COMPLETE RECORD OF MARINE CORPS AVIATION IN ACTION, 1941-1944 — Hubler, Capt R., and Capt J. DeChant
Doubleday, Doran & Co., Inc., Garden City, N.Y. 1944
Preceded *Devilbirds* by De Chant.

FLYING SERGEANT OVER RABAUL — Allen, Sgt L.
Leatherneck Mar 49

GREATEST FIGHTER MISSIONS OF THE TOP NAVY AND MARINE ACES OF WORLD WAR 2 — Sims, E.
Harper & Bros. 1962
Paperback by Ballantine Books, Inc. 1963
Includes missions of Carl, Smith, Foss, Swett and Walsh

HIDING SPOTTER PLANES UP FRONT — Watson, Capt T.
Gazette Jul 45

HISTORY OF MARINE CORPS AVIATION IN WORLD WAR 2 — Sherrod, R.
Combat Forces Press, Washington 1952
This definitive history was written with the cooperation of HQMC so Sherrod had access to all the records. *Everything* about Marine air in WW-2 is here, from the smallest detail to the "big picture." Too bad that Sherrod's rumored sequel on the ground forces never got off the ground

MARINE ACES RECORDS — *Army & Navy Journal* Feb 19, 1944

MARINE AIR FACILITY	*Army & Navy Journal*	Aug 12, 1944
MARINE AVIATION OBSERVERS IN AFRICA AND EUROPE	DeChant, Capt J. *Gazette*	Jul 46
MARINE FLYERS SHOOT DOWN 21 JAPANESE PLANES IN SOLOMONS	*Gazette*	Nov 42
MARINE FLYERS USE ROCKETS AT RABAUL	*Gazette*	Apr 44
MARINES OFF THE CARRIERS	McJennett, Maj J. *Gazette*	Dec 45
MARINES OVER FORMOSA First Marine strike against Formosa	Goodwin, Lt H. *Leatherneck*	Sep 45
MARKED FOR ANNIHILATION BY AIR	*Gazette*	Apr 45
NAVAL AVIATION'S AIR COMBAT RECORD	*Gazette*	Jun 48
NINE-TO-ONE OVER GUADAL-CANAL It didn't seem to bother Lt. Carl	Carl, Capt M. *Shipmate*	1944
PLANES AND THE PACIFIC	Hubler, Capt R. *Gazette*	Jan 44
PRAISE THE LORD, THE AMMUNITION PASSED US Combat photographer goes on a air strike against the harbor of HaHa Simmo (fiction).	Wilton, R. *Leatherneck*	Apr 45
REDUCTION OF RABAUL Author flew 11 strikes against Rabaul	Goodman, Capt W. *Gazette*	Aug 44
SAIGON STRIKE Marine air raid	Goodwin, Lt H. *Leatherneck*	May 45
"SEEK, STRIKE AND DESTROY"	Maloney, Lt M. *Gazette*	Jan 44
STRIKE ONE! Raid on Tokyo for the first time	Scott, Lt J., USNR *Leatherneck*	Oct 45

TRUCKING TO TRUK USMC bombers	Gordon, SSgt G. *Leatherneck*	Oct 44
TRUK WAS A PHONY Not as powerful a fortress as we believed during WW-2	Cant, G. *Gazette*	Oct 46
WHAT'S LEFT OF RABAUL Not a hell of a lot	Craig, Capt C., and Capt R. Griffin *Gazette*	Apr 46

TRAINING

EAGLE HATCHERIES: CHAIN OF WEST COAST CAMPS	Keen, H. *Flying*	Mar 45
GETTING THE GRAVEL GRINDER'S VIEWPOINT: NEW MARINE AIR CORPS TRAINING PROGRAM	Hailey, F. *Aviation*	Sep 44
HOW MARINE AVIATION PAPER WORK MEN ARE TRAINED	Engel, A. *Ind. Arts & Voc. Ed.*	Jun 44
MAKING OF MARINE PILOT By one of the best of them	Mangrum, LtCol R. *Gazette*	Feb 43
MARINE AVIATION AT CHERRY POINT Sixteen page pamphlet. Illustrated.	Cherry Point, N.C.	1944
MARINE CORPS ADVANCE FLIGHT SCHOOL	*Gazette*	Mar 40
MARINES GROW WINGS AT JACKSONVILLE Is the name of the author familiar?	Holcomb, Capt T. *Gazette*	Sep 43
MARINES HAVE LANDED . . . TRAINING AT LAKEHURST NAVAL AIR STATION	*Scientific American*	Jan 42
SHIP LAUNCHING: SOPAC STYLE Training in proper Ditching Procedure for pilots	*Leatherneck*	Jul 44
SPECIAL DEVICES TRAIN MARINE PILOTS FOR COMBAT	*Gazette*	Mar 45
THEY KEEP 'EM FLYING Jacksonville training for aviation mechs	*Leatherneck*	Sep 43

UNITS MAG-21	... IN THE AIR WITH MAG-21 Early WW-2 memories of CO at the time	Larkin, LtGen C. *Gazette*	Nov 71
VMA-542	**MARINE FIGHTER SQUADRON 542** One of a series of Unit Yearbook-like publications	Army & Navy Publishing Co., Baton Rouge	1946
BLACK JACKS	VULNERABLE SONS OF WILLIAM TELL This Marine squadron of B-26's is used to tow target sleeves	Felsen, Sgt H. *Leatherneck*	Sep 45
BLACK SHEEP—VMF-214	BANQUETS FROM BOYINGTON The Black Sheep raid Japan	Conner, Sgt J. *Leatherneck*	Jul 45
	PAPPY'S BLACKSHEEP: ONE OF THE PACIFIC'S DEADLIEST SQUADRONS And one that sure got the ink!	Littrell, G. *Flying*	Dec 44
HELLHAWKS	"HELLHAWKS" DOWN 102 PLANES	*Gazette*	Jan 44
NIGHTMARES	NIGHTMARES BY THE NUMBERS The "Flying Nightmares" against Rabaul	Bolser, H. *Gazette*	Sep 44
WOLF PACK—VMF-112	A DAY WITH THE WOLF PACK: VMF-112	*Leatherneck*	Jun 44
	WOLF PACK: SQUADRON OF MARINE FIGHTER PILOTS ESTABLISHED A RECORD	Hubler, R. *Flying*	Mar, Apr 44
VMF-221	**HISTORY OF MARINE FIGHTER SQUADRON 221** The author won the Navy Cross and was KIA at Midway	McCarthy, Lt F.	
VMF-422	STAND BY FOR SOMETHING TO POP	Decker, Sgt D., and Sgt S. Fink *Leatherneck*	Jan 46
MSB-234	MILK RUN TO MUNDA From Bougainville	DeChant, Lt J. *Leatherneck*	Jul 44
VTMB-232	THE RED DEVILS History of squadron	Kuhne, Sgt N. *Leatherneck*	Feb 46

TAU Training and duty for the Transport Air Unit	*Leatherneck*	Jul 45	**TAU**
HOTTEST SQUADRON 4TH MAW Medium Bombers	McElroy, Sgt J. *Leatherneck*	May 45	**4TH MAW**
SKY FREIGHTERS SCAT, TAG and CENCAT—MATS groups in SOPAC	Hicks, PFC P. *Leatherneck*	Feb 48	**SCAT**
SCAT South Pacific Combat Air Transport Command	O'Meara, Capt R. *Gazette*	Mar 43	

CASUALTIES

ANGELS HAVE WINGS Navy nurses	*Leatherneck*	Jul 45
ART IN AIEA Rehabilitation for psycho patients at Naval Hospital, Aiea	Doying, Sgt G. *Leatherneck*	Dec 44
FIGHTING PILL ROLLERS Corpsmen	McVay, Sgt I. *Leatherneck*	Jun 44
FLYING OUR WOUNDED VETERANS HOME	Palmer, C. *Geographic*	Sep 45
GRAVES REGISTRATION	*Gazette*	Feb 45
LIFE SAVER + Saving men WIA	Fink, Sgt S. *Leatherneck*	Sep 45
MALARIA: THE SILENT ENEMY	Davis, Pvt T. *Leatherneck*	Feb 44
MARINE CEMETERY	Henri, Maj R. *American Mercury*	Jul 45
MEDICAL AID FOR MARINES	Breard, H. *Hygeia*	Jun 44
THE MEDICAL DEPARTMENT OF THE UNITED STATES NAVY IN WORLD WAR 2 NavMED P 5031, Volume 1	USGPO	1953

	MEDICAL DOPE-OFF Sick Bay commandos	Conner, Sgt J. *Leatherneck*	Jan 45
	MENTAL HEALTH IN MILITARY LIFE	Solomon, LtCdr P. USNR *Gazette*	Nov 45
	MILITARY ASPECTS OF MENTAL DISEASE	Solomon, LtCdr P., USNR *Gazette*	Dec 45, Jan 46
	"MISSING IN ACTION" The dreaded words, but not as dreaded as KIA	*Gazette*	Nov 42
	NAVY CORPSMEN History of their association with the Corps	Irwin, M. *Leatherneck*	May 43
	SICK BAY	Hallman, D. *Hygeia*	Sep 44
	"TAKE IT EASY, SON:" NAVY DOCTOR CARES FOR WOUNDED AND SICK	Sperling, M. *Collier's*	Jul 8, 1944
	THEY TAKE THEIR BEATING STANDING UP Stretcher bearers like Cpl William H. Rolfsen	Donahue, Sgt J. *Leatherneck*	Sep 45
	THREE FOR VICTORY Plasma, Sulfa and Air Lift—the three big ways to help WIA Marines	Davis, T. *Leatherneck*	Jan 44
	TO THE CORPSMAN: COMMENDATION	*Leatherneck*	Jun 47
	U.S. MARINES VS. MALARIA	*Hygeia*	Oct 43

DUTIES

GENERAL	MARINE CORPS AND COAST GUARD JOB FACTS	*Voc. Trends*	May 44
AMPHIB RECON	AMPHIBIOUS RECON PATROLS	Coleman, Col W. *Gazette*	Dec 45, Jan 46
	ADVANCE MAN	Tolbert, Sgt F. *Leatherneck*	Mar 45

AMPHIBIOUS RECONNAISSANCE	Shinn, Lt L. *Gazette*	Apr 45	
THE ARMORER	*Gazette*	Mar 41	**ARMORER**
AND THE BAND FOUGHT ON 1ST MAR DIV Bandsmen on Okinawa	Hawkins, SSgt A. *Leatherneck*	Sep 45	**BAND**
BANDSMEN Cartoons by Rhodes	Rhodes, C. *Leatherneck*	May 45	
DOUBLING IN BRASS Bandsmen in action	McVay, Sgt I. *Leatherneck*	Oct 44	
THE MARINE BAND	*Leatherneck*	Jan 44	
RHAPSODY IN GREEN WM's Band at Lejeune	*Leatherneck*	Feb 44	
BEACH MP'S	Samuelson, LtCol L. *Gazette*	Aug 45	**BEACH GOVT**
LANDING TEAM SGT MAJ	Lyon, SgtMaj H. *Gazette*	Aug 45	
BRINGING THE CHURCH TO THE MARINES	Workman, Capt R., USN *Gazette*	Jan 44	**CHAPLAINS**
DIVINITY IN DUNGAREES Tales of the Chaplain Corps in SOPAC	Helfer, Sgt H. *Leatherneck*	Aug 45	
COMBAT CORRESPONDENTS	Lewis, SSgt M. *Leatherneck*	Oct 44	**COMBAT CORR**
COMBAT CORRESPONDENTS	Epstein, Sgt S. *Leatherneck*	Nov 42	
COMBAT PHOTOGRAPHY	Ohman, Sgt C. *Proceedings*	Oct 44	
COMPACT CORRESPONDENT WM Correspondent Jean Kautenberg	Harwell, Sgt E. *Leatherneck*	Dec 45	
FIGHTIN' AND WRITIN' MARINES How they were trained, what they did	*Leatherneck*	Dec 42	

	MARINES ON RECORD By the first Marine Combat Correspondent on Guadalcanal	Hurlbut, Lt J. *Gazette*	Dec 44
	REFERENCES ON MARINE CORPS COMBAT CORRESPONDENTS AND COMBAT PHOTOGRAPHERS IN WORLD WAR 2	Tyson, C. HQMC	1964
	THE SEMANTICS OF WAR CORRESPONDENTS	Tacitus, Sgt A. *Infantry Journal*	Dec 45
	TELLING IT TO THE MARINES—COMBAT CORRESPONDENTS	*Newsweek*	Aug 10, 1942
	THE WAR OF WORDS IN THE PACIFIC The duties of the Office of War Information	Fields, J. *Leatherneck*	Mar 44
COMMUNI-CATIONS	BE CAREFUL IN THE CLEAR	Browning, Capt M. *Gazette*	Dec 45
	COMMUNICATIONS	*Gazette*	Nov 41
	INDIAN WAR CALL Navaho and other Indian Comm-men in WW-2	Langille, Sgt V. *Leatherneck*	Mar 48
	INTRA-BATTALION COMMUNICATIONS AFTER LANDING	Kerry, Lt T. *Gazette*	May 44
	LEATHERNECKS POUND BRASS: MARINE CORPS IS EQUIPPING ITS FORCES WITH RADIO EQUIPMENT	*Radio News*	May 42
	MEET YOUR MARINE CORPS: FIELD TELEPHONE	Conner, J. *Leatherneck*	Jan 44
	MORE EFFECTIVE MONITORING	Lubin, Capt D. *Gazette*	Nov 45
	NAVAJO CODE TALKERS Indians were used so they could talk in their own tongue and confuse enemy	Marder, MTSgt M. *Gazette*	Sep 45
	"RADIO"	*Leatherneck*	Dec 40

RADIO IN THE MARINE CORPS	Smith, J. *Radio News*	Jan 42	
RADIO IN THE MARINES	Dyer, E. *Radio News*	Jun 43	
TLX—NOT WHAT TO DO, BUT HOW	Twining, Col M. *Gazette*	Jul 45	
DYNAMITE DUTY Ordnance disposal. The ordnance men get more ink than anyone, except the recon boys	Conner, Sgt J. *Leatherneck*	Jun 45	DEMOLITIONS
FIRE IN THE HOLE Demolitions men	*Leatherneck*	Nov 44	
AMPHIBIOUS ENGINEERS	Adams, LtCol H. *Gazette*	Feb 46	ENGINEERS
ENGINEERING PROBLEMS OF MARINE BRIGADES Interesting pre-war examination of the problems to come for the engineers	*Gazette*	Jun 40	
"THE FIRST WAVE" ENGINEERS	*Leatherneck*	Jan 44	
MARINES NOW USING THE BAILEY BRIDGE	*Gazette*	Jun 45	
WATER FOR FIGHTING MEN How engineers provide it. Its almost as important as ammo	Miller, Sgt B. *Leatherneck*	Dec 44	
FOUR ON—SIXTEEN OFF Marines on guard duty around the world	Smith, Sgt J. *Leatherneck*	May 44	GUARD DUTY
HAWAIIAN HORSE MARINES Garrison duty in Hawaii	*Leatherneck*	Feb 43	HORSE MARINES
HORSE MARINES Used to guard Naval Ammo Depots in Pacific	*Leatherneck*	Jul 45	
THE CAMERA IS A WEAPON By the author of *The Big Yankee,* the biography of Evans Carlson	Blankfort, Capt M. *Gazette*	Aug 44	INTELLIGENCE

	COUNTER-INTELLIGENCE	Mullahey, Maj T. *Gazette*	Oct 45
	G-2—A NEW CONCEPT	Coleman, LtCol W. *Gazette*	Jul 45
	HOW THEY MAKE THE MAPS	Walker, C. *Gazette*	Jul 45
	THE MARINE CORPS BATTALION INTELLIGENCE SERVICE	*Gazette*	Nov 41
	OUTGUESSING THE ENEMY	Whyte, Capt W. *Gazette*	Nov 45
	PHOTO LAB TECHNIQUE IN THE FIELD	Bard, Col E. *Gazette*	Apr 45
	RESECTION WITH PRECISION	Curry, LtCol M. *Gazette*	May 45
	WANTED: EYES FOR THE TROOPS	*Gazette*	Mar 41
JOURNALISTS	HARMONY OVER AN UNDER-WOOD Marine Sgt John Davis works on Army newspaper *Stars and Stripes*	Voigt, Cpl R. *Leatherneck*	Aug 46
	THE PIED TYPERS Marine on Pacific *Stars and Stripes* tells it like it was	Davies, J. *Leatherneck*	May 47
LAWYER	FRONT LINE LAW	Helfer, Sgt H. *Leatherneck*	Jul 45
MOTOR TRANSPORT	COMBAT MOTOR TRANSPORT	Long, Maj F. *Gazette*	Jan 46
	MOVE 'EM UP!	Helfer, Sgt H. *Leatherneck*	Jan 45
	THEY KEEP 'EM ROLLING At FMC PAC, Hawaii	Hamilton, Sgt G. *Leatherneck*	Oct 45
	TO KEEP THEM ROLLING	*Gazette*	May 45
PAYMASTER	COMBAT CASH Job of the paymaster	*Leatherneck*	Nov 44
POST OFFICE	MEET YOUR MARINE CORPS—C/O FPO, SAN FRANCISCO, CALIF.	*Leatherneck*	Jun 44

KEEP 'EM Unlauded heroes of the QM Department	*Gazette*	Nov 42	**QUARTER-MASTER**
PROCURING OFFICERS FOR THE EMERGENCY	*Gazette*	Nov 41	**RECRUITING**
THE RECRUITING DRIVE	*Gazette*	Jun 40	
THEY KNOW THE MARINES By the master Marine recruiter of them all	Webb, MSgt P. *Marine Recruiter*	Jul 43	
CARRIER CASUALTY Seagoing Marines are aboard the Princeton when it sinks	Conner, Sgt J. *Leatherneck*	Feb 45	**SEAGOING**
LAST DAYS OF THE USS QUINCY	Baker, Maj W. *Gazette*	Jun 44	
A MARINE ON THE USS HORNET	Gillis, TSgt A. *Gazette*	Jul 44	
SEA DUTY—WAR STYLE	Sutphin, Maj E. *Gazette*	Aug 43	
SOME SEAGOING MARINES Vignettes	Tolbert, Sgt F. *Leatherneck*	Feb 45	
THE COMMANDER AND HIS STAFF	Coffman, LtCol J. *Gazette*	Apr 45	**STAFF**
COMPLETED STAFF WORK	Clement, Col W. *Gazette*	Oct 44	
BABY TRANSPORT Civilians with babies are some-times mixed-in with Marines on Troop Transports	Conner, Sgt J. *Leatherneck*	Dec 44	**TRANSPORT**

ENEMY

BLOCKADES ON THE ROAD TO TOKYO—HOW THE JAPS FORTIFY THEIR CORAL ATOLL OUTPOSTS	*Leatherneck*	Apr 44
DEATH RODE THE DIVINE WIND Kamikazi pilots	Carrison, Cdr D., USNR *Gazette*	Jul 55

DEFENSE OF CHICHI JIMA Island near Iwo that was defended even more heavily. It was not attacked, fortunately for many Marines	Horie, Maj Y., Japanese Army *Gazette*	Jul 53
THE FALL OF JIRO Fiction about pre-war Japan.	Johnansen, Sgt H. *Leatherneck*	Jun 44
JAP TRICKERY Pix story on how the "sneaky, little yellow bast . . . ."operate	*Leatherneck*	Feb 44
JAPANESE BAYONET TECHNIQUE Picture story	*Leatherneck*	Mar 44
JAPANESE JUSTICE Fiction. Their justice is different from ours.	Pipino, Sgt N. *Leatherneck*	Aug 44
THE LAUGHING STOCK OF NINE GENERATIONS How to live with Japs, for postwar Marines in Japan	Lasswell, F. *Leatherneck*	Dec 45
THE LIFE OF 3RD LT HASHIMOTO Fiction. About the nature of the enemy	Denman, P. *Leatherneck*	Feb 43
MEET YAMASHITA Character of the Jap (all bad)	Hays, L. *Leatherneck*	Jan 43
MERCY CRUISE Marines rescue Japs on remote islands after main garrison has surrendered	Burnett, SSgt B. *Leatherneck*	Jan 45
PRISONERS OF THE ENEMY Member of the YMCA Prisoner's Committee tells about Marine and other POW's	Morehouse, Lt C. *Gazette*	Jan 44
THE ROSE OF UCLA Tokyo Rose	Riblett, PFC L. *Leatherneck*	Dec 45
SLEEPLESS FOE	Skinner, LtCdr R., USNR *Gazette*	Sep 44
THESE NIPS ARE NUTS The nature of the enemy	Kogan, TSgt H. *American*	Feb 45

FICTION

From *Leatherneck,* alphabetical by author:

Abney, Lt John
LAST SHOT — Feb 46

Barton, Robert D.
ASSAULT! — Jan 43

Bereny, PFC Sheldon
A DATE WITH PEGGY — Feb 44
Winner of Leatherneck Fiction Award Contest

Brown, PFC Michael D.
PENSEY'S FIGHT — Oct 45

Burks, Major Arthur J.
INVISIBLE GOLIATH — May 44
Gunny Tarr fiction

A MARINE NEVER DIES — Dec 43

ONE-MAN RAIDER — Jan 44

TAYAL TERROR — Mar 44
Tarr is on Formosa

TOJO'S VANISHERS — Sep 44

Cave, Hugh B.
FORGETFUL CHARLIE — Aug 57
Fiction. Marine and Jap alike, but different

Conner, Sgt John
NUTS TO YOU! — Oct 44

Dacus, Cpl Thurman L.
BAD BREAK — Nov 45

DeGrasse, John
NOT THE SAME GUY — Feb 43

Decker, Sgt Duane
EIGHTBALL — Jun 45

FLASH RED—CONDITION YELLOW — Aug 45

HOGAN'S GOAT — Mar 45
A horse-betting Marine puts
$2000 on a nag named "Hogan's Goat"

THE JOINT IS JUMPING	Jul 45
KNOCK IT OFF	Oct 44
STRICTLY A SNOW JOB	Nov 44
Denley, Robert H.	
CENSORED AND HOW!	Nov 43
Felsen, Sgt Henry	
THE EAGLE AND ME	Nov 45
MONKEY BUSINESS	Oct 45
Fink, Sgt Stanley	
10% MC TAVISH	Sep 45
Gherkin, PFC Gunther (Henry Felsen)	
GHERKIN "HEADS" FOR COMBAT	Aug 45
GHERKIN'S WAIKIKI LANDING	Sep 45
NIPPED IN THE BUD	Jan 45
ONION SOUP	Dec 45
REPLACEMENT IS A ROUTINE THING	Oct 45
Gordon, TSgt G. D.	
ROCKBOUND	Sep 45
Helfer, Sgt Harold	
THE AMAZING POWER OF PVT PEEPSIGHT	Jul 45
THE LAST ACT	Apr 44
PARK BENCH HERO	Jan 45
PEEPSIGHT'S PALACE PERFORMANCE	Dec 45
PVT PEEPSIGHT'S STRATEGY	Oct 45
RELUCTANT LADY	Jul 45
THE SERPENT'S TAIL Marines, a good looking gal, and the Japs in Shanghai	Mar 45
TAKE 'EM ALL ON	Feb 45

THE TRIUMPHANT COME-BACK OF PVT PEEPSIGHT — Sep 45

Kalman, Sgt Vic
THE INEVITABLE HOUR — May 45
Hiding in a cave somewhere in SOPAC

Kelly, Capt James A.
SEE A PIN—PICK IT UP — Jan 45

King, J.
SEA STORIES — Apr 64
About wild Marines in Pacific

Knowles, Lt Horace
BATTLE SOUVENIR — Nov 44

Luby, Robert L.
THE MARINE AND THE CO-ED — Mar 47
Another winner in the Fiction Award Contest

MacDonald, Allan W.
THE WHISTLING MARINE — Sep 43

Nohrden, LtCol Maynard M.
RUBBER BOATS — Feb 46

Roberts, TSgt Nolle T.
IT WAS NOBODY'S FAULT — Sep 45

STRICTLY A FRIENDLY GAME — Dec 44

Sanders, Cpl L. A.
BATTLE STATIONS — Feb 45

EAGER BEAVER — Apr 45
A seagoing Marine and his world aboard ship which consists of a gun mount

Saunders, Lt Lawrence A.
MAN FOR MAN — Sep 45

Schuon, Karl
MULLIGAN'S STEW — Mar 47
Mike Mulligan and his leprechaun on Okinawa

Scidmore, Sgt S. B.
POWDER PUFF MARINE — Jan 45

VOLUNTEER — Aug 44
About ASGT Michael McGowan

Suepp, Capt Frank

THE POGIEBAIT MARINE — Jul 44
About Flynn McQueen

Tolbert, Sgt Frank X.

A DATE WITH WAIKIKI — May 45

THE FIRST TEXAS MARINE — Jul 45

THE GOLD MINER FROM GAWGI — Feb 44
About Pvt "Lefty" Hunt, a "China" Marine, now in WW-2

GWENDOLYN — Oct 44
About TSgt Madison LeBlanc

THE MARINE WHO HATED TO GET UP — Aug 43
"Lefty" Hunt

THE MISADVENTURES OF JOHN K — Jun 45

SAKABOO — May 45
"Lefty" Hunt

THE SENIOR PRIVATE USES HIS HEAD — Apr 44
"Lefty" Hunt

SICK INDIAN — Aug 42
Troubles of an Indian Brave in the Corps

THE SOUTHPAW — Jan 43
"Lefty" Hunt

Unsigned

JAW BREAKER — Jul 56
Marines get food from Japs during WW-2

GUNG-HO

THE AMAZING MARINES: THEIR OWN STORY — Holcomb, LtGen T. *United States Navy* Jan 1, 1943

Title	Source	Date
THE BALLAD OF THE LEATHER-NECK CORPS A 78 rpm recording narrated by Tyrone Power, a Marine pilot and written by one of the most famous authors of our time! Priceless propaganda of the early war years.	Wouk, H.	1942
CAUSES AND CONQUEST OF FEAR	Carleton, Capt P. *Gazette*	Mar 44
COMMANDANT DEFINES MARINES	Holcomb, LtGen T. *Leatherneck*	Jun 43
CONQUERING FEAR How "Zeke" Swett, Richard Fleming and George Grady did it	Webb, MTSgt P. *Gazette*	Mar 44
CREDO OF A MARINE	Suddes, T. *Catholic Digest*	Oct 42
CREED OF THE VOLUNTEER	Shalett, S. *N.Y. Times Magazine*	Feb 1, 1942
FIGHTING MARINE: WHY HE'S A FIGHTER	Williamson, S. *N.Y. Times Magazine*	Aug 16, 1942
FIGHTING MARINES	Hailey, F. *N.Y. Times Magazine*	Nov 3, 1943
FIGHTING TRUTHS FOR THE MARINES	*Gazette*	Dec 44
FIRST TO FIGHT	Holcomb, Gen T. *Gazette*	Nov 43
IN THE AIR, AS BY LAND AND SEA, MARINES LIVE UP TO TRADITION	*Scholastic*	Jan 10, 1944
A MARINE EXPLAINS HIS CORPS	*Infantry Journal*	Jun 45
MARINE HEROES FOR WHOM WARSHIPS HAVE BEEN NAMED	Jenkins, J. *Gazette*	Dec 43
A MARINE *IS* DIFFERENT	Wynn, Col C. *Gazette*	May 44

MARINES HAVE LANDED	*Popular Mechanics*	May 42
MARINES IN WAR AND PEACE	Holcomb, LtGen T. *Gazette*	Nov 43
THE MARINES' TASK Speech in New York Oct 27, 1943	Holcomb, LtGen T. *Leatherneck*	Jan 44
MORALE FOR EVERYBODY	Wynn, Col C. *Gazette*	Feb 44
PROFESSIONAL FIGHTERS Digest title is *Marines Have the Situation in Hand*	*Time* *Digest*	Nov 11, 1940 Jan 41
THE RESPONSIBILITY OF THE REGULAR OFFICER	Larson, Col E. *Gazette*	Jun 45
SEA GOING SOLDIERS	*Popular Mechanics*	Feb 41
THE SECRET WEAPON THAT WE DO NOT POSSESS Marines do not want to die for the emperor	Letcher, LtCol J. *Gazette*	Jan 44
SLOUCH AND THE SPRING: A FOOTNOTE ON DISCIPLINE	Heinl, Col R. *Proceedings*	Dec 41
TELL IT TO THE MARINES	Olszuk, L. *Future*	Oct 42
TELL WHAT TO THE MARINES?	Tinsley, F. *Popular Science*	May 44
THE U.S. MARINES IN WORLD WAR 2	Holcomb, LtGen T. *Army & Navy Journal*	Nov 43
WHAT COUNTS: EXCERPTS FROM A LETTER BY MAJOR J.R. TO HIS FATHER	Dobbin, Maj D. *Scholastic*	Jan 18, 1943
WHAT MAKES A MARINE?	*Newsweek*	Aug 24, 1942
WHY BE RAGGEDY MARINES?	Donovan, Maj J. *Gazette*	Dec 44

WHY WARRIORS FIGHT	Edmundson, C. *Gazette*	Sep 44
WILL YOU BE AFRAID IN COMBAT? Yes, unless you're crazy	Cutter, J. *Leatherneck*	Sep 43
YOU AND YOUR TROOPS	Richards, Maj G. *Gazette*	Dec 44
YOUR JOB AS A MARINE OFFICER Talk at Quantico, Sep 22, 1943	Holcomb, LtGen T. *Leatherneck*	Nov 43

LOGISTICS

GENERAL

ADVENTURES IN G.I. CHOW	James, SSgt G. *Leatherneck*	Feb 45
AMMUNITION CONTROL	Wells, Maj W. *Gazette*	Jan 45
ASPIRIN FOR THE QUARTER-MASTER	*Gazette*	Aug 44
BASE DEFENSE LOGISTICS	Rogers, LtCol C. *Gazette*	Apr 45
COMBAT HEADACHE Administrative annex to solve assault supply problems	Hudson, LtCol L. *Gazette*	Jun 45
COMBAT SUPPLIES ON PALLETS	Klein, Capt E. *Gazette*	Jul 45
DEPOT OF SUPPLIES	Muller, Maj W. *Gazette*	Sep 44
EMPTY GAS DRUMS STAY AT WAR	Papurca, Capt J. *Gazette*	Sep 44
THE G-4 IS NOT A QM	Gober, LtCol G. *Gazette*	Oct 45
LUMBER FOR LANDINGS	Otis, Sgt O. *Gazette*	Sep 44
MASTER MENUS All Marines eat the same thing at the same time. Here's how.	Cook, Sgt E. *Leatherneck*	Dec 45

	MOVING COMBAT CARGO	Miller, SSgt B. *Gazette*	Feb 45
	SALVAGING EQUIPMENT	Donovan, Maj J. *Gazette*	Jul 45
	SUPPLY PIPE LINE	Rea, BGen L. *Gazette*	Jul 44
	SUPPORTING THE TROOPS	Hunt, Lt R. *Gazette*	Nov 42
GEAR	THE EXPERIMENTAL PACK	Gordon, Capt R. *Leatherneck*	Oct 40
	HANDY GADGET First balloon life raft	*Leatherneck*	Oct 44
	JURY RIGS FOR RADAR	Beale, Capt C. *Gazette*	Oct 45
	THE MARINE CORPS PACK Description of the pack then in use—M1941	*Leatherneck*	Apr 42
	MARINES HAD RADAR, TOO	Meek, LtCol H. *Gazette*	Oct 45
VEHICLES	THE DUDE Tank Retriever of "C" Co, 3rd Tank Bn, 3RD MAR DIV	Breard, SSgt H. *Leatherneck*	Oct 45
	NEW LANDING CRAFT	Morehouse, C. *Gazette*	Dec 43
	PLASTIC SQUAD ASSAULT BOATS	*Gazette*	Nov 41
	THE WATER BUFFALOES New amphibious tractor	Tolbert, F. *Leatherneck*	Jun 43

MARINES

GENERAL	**AMERICA'S WAR HEROES** Medal of Honor winners including Boyington, Basilone and Foss	Scott, J. Monarch Books, Inc., Derby, Conn.	1960
	BATTLE CRY Fiction. Radio squad of 2/6 from Guadalcanal through Saipan	Uris, L. G. P. Putnam's Sons	1953

THE BIG WAR Fiction. Complicated, wordy novel of Marines in training, home on leave and combat. A big book. Difficult to follow.	Myrer, A. Appleton, Century, Crofts, Inc. 1957 Paperback by Bantam Books, Inc. 1958
CALL HIM MAC A Leatherneck doing his job	Gordon, SSgt D. *Leatherneck* Aug 44
THE CASE FOR THE OVERSEAS MOUSTACHE	Decker, Sgt D. *Leatherneck* Sep 45
CHARACTERS WE HAVE MET AROUND THE PACIFIC Pictures of Marines who are typical of types found in the Corps. (Does the second author sound familiar?	Helfer, Sgt H., and Sgt J. Birch *Leatherneck* Sep 45
THE CRACKER-JACK MARINES Fiction. The battle of Chicago's North Michigan Avenue as fought by Marine PIO men. A really funny book; in a class with *Don't Go Near the Water.*	Masselink, B. Little, Brown and Co., Boston 1959 Paperback by Popular Library 1960
DANGER! MARINES AT WORK! Fiction. About Marine Parachute units tearing up an island in SOPAC while in between battles	Fuller, R. Random House, Inc. 1959 Popular Library 1968
DOPE ON THE CELEBS "Who's who" in the service in 1943. Includes movie stars and sports figures.	Myers, R. *Leatherneck* Feb 43
HANDLEBAR HANKS Mustaches are in fashion.	Helfer, Sgt H. *Leatherneck* Jul 45
HEROES OF THE PACIFIC Many human interest accounts of Marines at Pearl Harbor, Wake, Midway, Solomons, Tarawa	Shane, T. Messner & Co., Inc. 1944
ISLAND INTERLUDE Fiction. Novel about a Marine Barrage Balloon Squadron stationed at Tulagi	Koch, C. Dodd, Mead & Co., Inc. 1951

IT TAKES ALL KINDS TO MAKE THE CORPS "Joe Blow" stories	Gordon, SSgt D. *Leatherneck*	Nov 44
MAGNIFICENT MUTT Canine mascot at Lejeune	Decker, Sgt D. *Leatherneck*	Sep 45
MARINE CORPS GENERAL STAFF Brass of the time	Hittle, LtCol J. *Gazette*	Nov 44
"THE MARINE—I'LL NEVER FORGET HIM" Composite WW-2 Marine	Slocum, SSgt J. *Leatherneck*	Nov 45
A MARINE TO HIS MOTHER Letters tell what he is fighting for—(Her, blueberry pie, and hot dogs).	Josephy, MSgt A. *N.Y. Times Magazine*	Mar 4, 1945
MARINES Fiction. Based on fact. The best fiction about Marines ever written (including Thomason). Short stories based on Leckie's 1ST MAR DIV experiences at Guadalcanal, Cape Gloucester and Peleliu. Nobody can make a Marine story come to life like Leckie	Leckie, R. Paperback edition only, Bantam Books, Inc.	1960
MARINES ARE WHERE YOU FIND THEM	Groenwegen, Capt Q. *Gazette*	Aug 45
MEDALS FOR MARINES Collection of citations which accompanied major medals awarded Marines in WW-2. Some terrible "gung-ho" copy in between. Not a very good book.	Boswell, R. Thomas Y. Crowell Company	1945
NONE BUT THE BRAVE A disabled Marine aircraft lands on a Pacific Island occupied by Japs. At first, they get along without fighting, but then all hell breaks loose. Fiction.	Cameron, L. Paperback edition only Gold Medal Books	1965

OUT IN THE BOONDOCKS: MARINES IN ACTION IN THE PACIFIC — Horan, J., and G. Frank — G. P. Putnam's Sons — 1943

Collection of "hero" stories from the first year of the war. Many about Marine Raiders and Parachute Marines . . . "Those hand-picked, amphibious troops who won the beachhead at Tulagi and Guadalcanal." Written in the dreadful, pulp magazine style of the Combat Correspondents before Denig (or someone) realized that playing it low key in writing makes the deed seem even more important

PLEASURE ISLAND — Maier, W. — Julian Messner, Inc. — 1949

Fiction. Marines land on an island during WW-2. The proprietor of the island has three beautiful and untouched daughters. Will they remain untouched, or won't they?

SEMPER FIDELIS: THE U.S. MARINES IN THE PACIFIC: 1942-1945 — O'Sheel, Capt P. — William Sloane Associates, Inc. — 1947

An excellent anthology of the best stories of Combat Correspondents, carefully selected to "reflect the human side of the entire Pacific experience" as Marines knew it.

THE STUMP JUICE BLUES — Fuller, R. — *Argosy* — Mar 58

Fiction. The 1st Parachute Bn on New Caledonia

WHAT DOES A MARINE LOOK LIKE? — Tolbert, Sgt F. — *Leatherneck* — Jun 45

Various cartoon interpretations

INDIVIDUALS

Bell, MSgt E. R.

DEAN OF MARINE ARTILLERY — Terry, TSgt W. — *Leatherneck* — Nov 44

Biddle, Col Anthony

COL BIDDLE TEACHES 'EM MAYHEM — Myers, R. — *Leatherneck* — Mar 43

The famous hand-to-hand combat instructor

DREXEL BIDDLE, GENTLEMAN TOUGH — McEvoy, J. — *American Mercury* — May 42

FABULOUS FIGHTER — Hicks, Cpl P. *Leatherneck* Sep 48

THE KING OF KILL — Asprey, R. *Gazette* May 67

MY PHILADELPHIA FATHER — Biddle, C., as told to K. Crichton. Doubleday & Co., Inc., Garden City N.Y. 1955

Biography of the man who "knew more ways to kill you with his hands than any man alive." He taught them to Marines in two wars. Biddle entered the Corps as a "Provisional Captain" in 1918. Served in France. Was recalled in 1942 at the age of 67 to teach Marines bayonet, knife fighting and judo. You laughed when you first saw him because he was fat and bald and old. You didn't laugh, after you saw him work.

Bowring, Mrs. Alice

FIRST LADY OF SOPAC — Stewart, AMSgt W. *Leatherneck* Sep 59

The "Canteen Lady" of Noumea, New Caledonia

Brown, Lt David Tucker, Jr.

MARINE FROM VIRGINIA: LETTERS, 1941-45 DAVID TUCKER BROWN, JR., UNITED STATES MARINE CORPS RESERVE, KILLED IN ACTION ON OKINAWA, SHIMA, RYUKU ISLANDS, 9 MAY 1916—14 MAY 1945 — Brown, Lt D. Paperback edition only, U. of North Carolina Press, Chapel Hill, N.C. 1947

Burns, Bob

A MARINES' BEST FRIEND IS HIS BAZOOKA — *Leatherneck* Jun 44

Comedian Burns was a WW-1 Marine. His legacy was the word "bazooka"

Carlson, LtCol Evans F.

THE BIG YANKEE: THE LIFE OF CARLSON OF THE RAIDERS — Blankfort, M. Little, Brown and Co., Boston 1947

This worshipful biography follows Carlson through the Banana Wars as a National Guard officer, in China with the Reds during the 1930's when they were fashionable, and later, as an aide and confidant to

President Roosevelt. Tells how he founded the 2d Raiders and led them through the disaster on Makin and the brilliant patrol on Guadalcanal. Explains his side of why his career went into a tailspin after Guadalcanal. Ends just short of his death of a heart attack in 1947, shortly before he ran for Congress as a Socialist.

CARLSON OF THE RAIDERS — Burke, D. — *Life* — Sep 20, 1943

Cates, General Clifton B., and Gen Franklin A. Hart

IN MEMORIAM: GEN CLIFTON B. CATES AND GEN FRANKLIN A. HART — 4TH MAR DIV Association — 1970

Pamphlet tracing the careers of these two officers who died in 1970

Cheek, Sgt Albert

MARINE TROUBADOR — Tolbert, F. — *Leatherneck* — Apr 45

Cheek was a mortar ace who often put on a one-man minstrel show for Marines in the Pacific

Crowe, Col Henry P. "Jim"

CROWE'S FEATS — *Leatherneck* — Oct 44

HE'S TOUGH ALL OVER — Stiff, Maj H. — *Leatherneck* — Apr 47

MAXIE — Hodgson, D. — *Leatherneck* — Feb 48

Chinese citizen reminisces on all the Marine marksmen he saw in China. Jim Crowe was the best.

Crystal, GySgt William F.

THE UNBREAKABLE CRYSTAL — Tolbert, MTSgt F. — *Leatherneck* — Jun 43

Hand-to-hand combat instructor

Curtis, Gunny

GUNNY CURTIS — Mielke, TSgt A. — *Leatherneck* — Jan 46

Decker, Sgt Duane

MY LIFE AND HARD TIMES IN A CASUAL COMPANY — Decker, Sgt D. — *Leatherneck* — May 45

Diamond, MGSgt Lou

DIAMOND IN THE ROUGH — Tolbert, F.
The legendary mortarman — *Leatherneck* Aug 43

OLD LOU, THE MARINE'S MARINE — Wharton, D. — *Digest* Feb 44

Douglas, Paul

THE FIGHTING PROFESSOR — Anderson, Sgt N.
Went through Parris Island at the age of 50. Twice wounded in combat with Marines. Later, a Senator from Illinois — *Leatherneck* Nov 45

PAUL DOUGLAS — Phillips, Maj C. — *Leatherneck* Sep 51

Edson, LtCol Merritt A. "Red Mike"

EDSON'S STAR — *Time* Dec 27, 1943
It's "General Edson" now

HE KNEW HIS JUNGLES — Thomas, L.
About the Raiders on Guadalcanal — From *These Men Shall Never Die* The John C. Winston Company 1943

RED MIKE — Curtis, TSgt P.
Mostly about Raiders on Guadalcanal — *Leatherneck* Nov 55

"RED MIKE" EDSON — Dieckmann, E.
Biography — *Gazette* Aug 62

RED MIKE AND HIS "DO OR DIE" MEN — Doying, PFC G. — *Leatherneck* Mar 44
Bloody Ridge, Guadalcanal

Edwards, Sgt Phil

"THE GRIPE" — Decker, Sgt D.
Guam DJ — *Leatherneck* Sep 45

Fairbairn, Major

THE DEACON DEALS IN DEATH — Bergman, Sgt H.
Hand-to-hand combat instructor — *Leatherneck* Jun 44

Ferre, E.

TRADE WINDS: ON ACTIVE DUTY WITH THE MARINES IN THE PACIFIC — Ferre, E. *Saturday Review* Jun 2, 1945

Book industry trade column is devoted to Marine duty this time

Fixit, Miss

DEAR MISS FIXIT — Doying, Sgt G. *Leatherneck* Oct 44

Hawaii's version of Ann Landers

Fonte, MGSgt T.

STREET FIGHTER — Tolbert, TSgt F. *Leatherneck* Mar 44

Instructor at Pendleton Raider Training Camp

Francisco & Pedro

PINT SIZE DEVIL DOGS — Geer, A. *Sat Eve Post* June 1, 1946

Francisco and Pedro, Guam natives, are sworn into the Corps. They're kids.

Garite, A. P.

BROTHER LEATHERNECK: THE MONK WHO BECAME A MARINE — Chevigny, H. *Collier's* Sep 8, 1945

Garite, a Carmelite monk, leaves the Order to join the Marines. He is killed on Peleliu.

Geissberger, TSgt O.

CORONET MAN — Helfer, Sgt H. *Leatherneck* Jun 45

Gooker, SSgt Harry R.

A MARINE AT OXFORD — *Leatherneck* Mar 44

Tours England on five-day leave

Graham, Capt Garrett

BANZAI NOEL — Graham, Capt G. Vanguard Press, Inc. 1944

Empty little book (159 pp.) about Graham's experiences aboard a transport en route to SOPAC. Includes his service as a ground officer with the 1ST MAW on Guadalcanal late in 1943. Little action; little of anything else

Subject / Title	Author / Publication	Date
Grell, Capt William F.		
A MARINE WITH THE OSS Experiences with the French Underground	Grell, Capt W. *Gazette*	Dec 45
Hatfields and McCoys		
RECKLESS MOUNTAIN BOYS Descendents of the famous clan are Marine recruiters	*Leatherneck*	Aug 42
Holcomb, Gen Thomas		
FOUR STARS FOR HOLCOMB Retiring Commandant gets fourth star as he gives way to Vandegrift	*Time*	Jan 23, 1944
A VISIT WITH THE COMMANDANT	*Leatherneck*	Jan 44
Holman, Dr. Emile		
SURGEON TO THE LEATHERNECKS	Glass, R. *Gazette*	Nov 67
Hope, Bob		
BOB HOPE VISITS THE MARSHALLS	*Leatherneck*	Nov 44
Kaltenbaugh, Cpl Clark R.		
ACCOUNT CLOSED: C.R.K., MARINE WHO KILLED 17 JAPS He personally revenges ambush of the Goettge patrol on Guadalcanal by killing 17 Japs on Cape Gloucester	Bordages, A. *Sat Eve Post*	May 19, 1945
Kelly, Father Eugene, and Rev George Creitz		
TWINS OF THE 22ND 6TH MAR DIV Chaplains	Decker, Sgt D., and Sgt S. Fink *Leatherneck*	Dec 45
Irwin, Col Ira "Jake"		
THE SPECIAL BREED CO of the 1st Raider Bn from Sep 27, 1942 until Jan 13, 1943	Mainard, TSgt A. *Leatherneck*	Aug 55
LaChapelle, GySgt Al		
MARINE OF THE SEVEN SEAS 24-year career of LaChapelle	Morang, J. *Leatherneck*	Oct 43

Lawford, Roger

BEST THING THAT EVER HAPPENED — Leslie, W. McGraw-Hill, Inc. 1952

Fiction. Rich kid Roger can't hack it in the Corps so he cuts from a place thinly disguised from Parris Island. His adventures while running away form the plot of this rather pointless book. Roger gets his lunch in the end with an accidental shotgun blast in the stomach, proving that Boot Camp would have been a better alternative, after all.

Lucas, Lt Jim

COMBAT CORRESPONDENT — Lucas, Lt J. Reynal & Hitchcock Publishers 1944

Experiences of Lucas starting at Parris Island fresh from his career as a reporter from Tulsa. Departs for Guadalcanal in late 1942. Next, the invasion of the Russells with the Raiders followed by a visit to Camp "Gung-Ho" for a talk with Carlson. At Parachute Marines Camp later, he makes a jump. Then goes on night bombing mission to Bougainville. Hits Dragon's Peninsula in New Georgia with 1st Raider Regiment. There, he kills a Jap. For a finale, he goes in with first waves on Tarawa where he earns a Bronze Star and a Battlefield Commission.

Lyons, Capt Ted

HERO OF THE HURLERS — Myers, SSgt R. *Leatherneck* Mar 44

He is White Sox pitcher, and a great one

Mannion, Father Joseph P.

PADRE OF THE PARAMARINES — Maloof, L. *Leatherneck* Aug 43

6TH MAR DIV Chaplain

Mansfield, Capt Walter R.

MARINE WITH THE CHETNIKS — Mansfield, Capt W. *Gazette* Jan, Feb 46

OSS work in Yugoslavia

Mason, Glen

MASK OF GLORY — Levin, D. McGraw-Hill, Inc. 1949

Fiction. The brief Marine Corps career of Glen Mason, from Boot Camp to advanced training to combat to death. An excellent novel from the anti-war point-of-view

Merillat, Capt Herbert L.
GUADALCANAL TO NORMANDY — Merillat, Capt H. *Gazette* Aug 44
Experiences of the Combat Correspondent who wrote *The Island* about Guadalcanal

Milnitsky, Cpl Ed
RADIO ENTERTAINS A MARINE HERO — *Leatherneck* Feb 44
Navy Cross winner is entertained by radio celebrities in New York

Mitoff, GySgt Simeon
FOREVER MITOFF — Helfer, Sgt H. *Leatherneck* Nov 45
Gunner Mitoff re-ups, to no ones' surprise

Myers, Martin L.
YARDBIRD MYERS, THE FOULED-UP LEATHERNECK — Myers, M. Dorrance & Co., Inc., Philadelphia 1944
Another view of Boot Camp early in WW-2. Myers was always in trouble. Most of the time, he deserved to be in more trouble than he was in. Includes a glossary of Marine slang of the day, much of which is still current.

Ostrum, GySgt Carl
"UNCLE CARL" — *Leatherneck* Jul 44
Carl Otto Ostrum

Plumadore, SgtMaj J. A.
THE SGT HAD ITCHY FEET — Myers, Sgt R. *Leatherneck* Dec 44
First enlisted in 1912

Puller, Col Lewis "Chesty"
"CHESTY" PULLER — Roberts, Sgt N. *Leatherneck* Jun 48

MARINE: LEWIS B. "CHESTY" PULLER, 1898-1971 — O'Leary, Col J. *Gazette* Nov 71
Obituary

MARINE: THE LIFE OF LT. GEN. LEWIS. B. (CHESTY) PULLER, USMC (RET.) — Davis, B. Little, Brown and Co., Boston 1962
Competent, professional biography of *the* professional Marine. Puller's rise

from private to general included tours at Haiti, Peking, Shanghai, Pearl Harbor, Guadalcanal, Cape Gloucester, Peleliu and Korea. How he won the Navy Cross five times is legend. Chesty's comments on everything and the scrapes he got into between combat is more interesting than the legend.

MARINE: THE LIFE OF CHESTY PULLER From the book of the same name	Davis, B. *Gazette* Nov-Dec 62, Feb-Apr 63
TRIBUTE Obit of Chesty Puller	Bartlett, T. *Leatherneck* Dec 71
Ruggles, Charlie RUGGLES' RAUSERS USO Show	 Fink, Sgt S. *Leatherneck* Mar 46
Shoup, Col David TARAWA'S THIRD MEDAL OF HONOR Shoup joins Hawkins and Bonnyman (except that he lived)	 *Time* Oct 30, 1944
Smith, Gen Holland M. **CORAL AND BRASS** Covers the forty-year career of the "founder of USMC amphibious warfare." The narrative is outspoken, like Smith. Includes "Howlin Mad's" verdict on Tarawa . . .	 Smith, Gen H., and P. Finch Charles Scribner's Sons 1949 Paperback by Ace Books 1948

"a mistake." His views on the effectiveness of naval gunfire . . . "seldom effective." His side of the famous Smith vs. Smith" incident on Saipan when he got roasted for relieving a plodding Army general. Ends with the securing of Iwo, after which he retired.

CORAL AND BRASS	Smith, Gen H., and P. Finch *Sat Eve Post* Nov 20, 1948
A MARINE NAMED SMITH Obituary	Martin, B. *Leatherneck* Apr 67
OLD MAN OF THE ATOLLS	*Time* Feb 21, 1944

Smolka, Cpl J.
SMILES BY SMOKEY — Conner, Sgt J. *Leatherneck* Oct 45
Of the 1ST MAR DIV

Sprenger, PFC Ransdell W.
PIN-UPS OVER TOKYO — Ototowsky, S. *Leatherneck* Apr 45
Amateur artist Sprenger decorates B-29's

Summers, TSgt Jack
A MARINE IN TWO WARS — Smith, Sgt E. *Leatherneck* Jun 45

Tower, LtCdr Hansel H., USNR
FIGHTING THE DEVIL WITH THE MARINES — Tower, LtCdr H., USNR Dorrance & Co., Inc., Philadelphia 1945
Another self-published book of experiences and opinions by a chaplain. Tower served with Marine units training at Culebra, Parris Island and New River. He then did occupation duty on an unidentified island in the Pacific.

Underhill, Mrs. J. L.
BETTER KNOWN AS MOTHER — *Leatherneck* Oct 44
Favorite lady of San Diego Marines

Vandegrift, Gen A. A.
BRIG GEN ALEXANDER A. VANDEGRIFT — *Gazette* Jun 40

CHIEF LEATHERNECK — *Newsweek* Dec 13, 1943

GENERAL VANDEGRIFT — Langille, Sgt V. *Leatherneck* Feb 48

MAN WHO LEADS FIGHTING MARINES — Hailey, F. *N.Y. Times Magazine* Dec 19, 1943

ONCE A MARINE: THE MEMOIRS OF GENERAL A. A. VANDEGRIFT, USMC — Vandegrift, Gen A., as told to R. Asprey W. W. Norton & Co., Inc. 1964 Paperback by Ballantine Books, Inc. 1969
Across the Pacific from Guadalcanal through Bougainville to Tarawa, Saipan, Tinian, Guam, Peleliu, Iwo Jima and Okinawa with the most important single Marine of

WW-2. This book gives the inside scoop from the troop commander's point-of-view at Guadalcanal, and then the view from the top as Vandegrift replaces Holcomb. Vandegrift's memory and sense-of-humor and Asprey's writing style make this the best biography of WW-2.

PORTRAIT — *Time* Jan 25, 1943
Cover of *Time* is portrait of Vandy

SUNNY JIM — *Scholastic* Jan 10, 1944
But don't cross him

VANDEGRIFT: THE MAN — Kuhne, Cpl N. *Leatherneck* Feb 44

"VANDEGRIFT OF GUADALCANAL" — Thomas, L. From *These Men Shall Never Die* The John C. Winston Company 1943

VANDEGRIFT OF THE SOLOMONS — Tolbert, F. *Leatherneck* Feb 43
News coverage of his return from Guadalcanal to receive the Medal of Honor

WELL IN HAND: VANDEGRIFT SUCCEEDS HOLCOMB — *Time* Dec 6, 1943

Vanderbreggen, Cornelius

A LEATHERNECK LOOKS AT LIFE — Vanderbreggen, C. Published by the author Lafayette Hill, Pa. 1944
This misleading title has caused more than one Marine to buy this book, start to read it and wish that he had his money back. Author was with 4TH MAR DIV *after* this book ends. This one is about his "wanderings looking for Christ" *before* he became a Leatherneck. He found Him, raspberry lemonade (his favorite drink) and the Corps all at the same time. Book ends on that utopian note

LETTERS OF A LEATHERNECK — Vanderbreggen, C.
Reapers' Fellowship Publications
Rijnsaterwoude, The Netherlands 1948

Story of Vanderbreggen's experiences through OC training at Quantico and combat training at New River. He then served with the 4TH MAR DIV on New Caledonia, Guadalcanal and participated in the Guam operation. As the jacket says, "above all, you will learn how many of them (Marines), even in the midst of much terror, lived unafraid and died victoriously because they had come to know the Lord Jesus Christ."

Yonakor, John

YONAKOR'S GIFT — Harwell, Sgt E.
Leatherneck Dec 45

Ex-Notre Dame All American is a Marine

Willy, Pvt Andrew

THE BARREN BEACHES OF HELL — Cochrell, B.
Henry Holt and Company, 1959
Paperback by Bantam Books, Inc. 1960

Fiction. Thirty months of service in the Corps including Tarawa, Saipan, Tinian, Okinawa and Nagasaki.

Woodward, PFC Luther

NOSE FOR NIPS — Fink, Sgt S.
Leatherneck Aug 45

Black Marine of 4th Ammo Co hunts Japs

OFF-DUTY

From *Leatherneck,* unless otherwise specified:

BIG BUSINESS—PX — Mar 44

COMMAND PERFORMANCE RADIO PROGRAM — Jan 45

DEVILDOG'S LIBRARY IN THE SOUTH SEAS — Tower, H.
Library Apr 1, 1944

HARVEST AT HELL'S HALF ACRE — Doying, Sgt G.
Jun 44

Marines plant Victory Gardens overseas

THE HOURS YOU CAN'T HAVE Two Marines talk nostalgically about their children at home	Wilson, E.	Dec 42
THE LEATHERNECK GOES ON A 10-DAY FURLOUGH Picture story of typical WW-2 leave at home		Dec 43
MR. GOLDWYN, INCLUDE US OUT Lousy movies of WW-2	Decker, Sgt D.	Jun 45
MOMENT MUSICALE Musical movies shown in SOPAC	Felsen, Sgt H.	Oct 45
NEPTUNE'S NONSENSE Ceremonies which take place when you cross the equator for the first time		Dec 44
PACIFIC SLOP CHUTE NCO Clubs in SOPAC	Cochrane, TSgt W.	Jul 45
SHOW STOP USO Tour	Farrell, Cpl B.	Feb 46
THREE MARINES VISIT A NATIVE VILLAGE In the Central Pacific		Dec 44

PERSONNEL

From the *Gazette,* unless specified otherwise:

ADMINISTRATION

ADDITIONAL DUTY CHART	Goldthwaite, 1stSgt K.	Sep 45
CIVIL AFFAIRS	Prud'homme, Capt H.	May 44
MAKE THE MOST OF YOUR PRISONERS		Nov 42
MILITARY VALUE OF WAR DIARIES	Zimmerman, Capt J.	Feb 45
NEW INFORMATION PROGRAM	Ostrander, Capt M.	Oct 45
NEW SCHOOL OF ADMINISTRATION	Felker, Maj R.	Nov 45

	PAY		Nov 41
	PRACTICE WHAT WE PREACH The virtue of being brief in writing	Coleman, Col W.	Aug 45
	STANDARDIZED PROMOTION FOR CORPORALS AND SERGEANTS		Sep 40
	STREAMLINING ADMINISTRATION		Mar 42
	SUGGESTIONS FOR CORPS PERSONNEL AND DEPENDENTS		Sep 42
	WHAT IS SOP?	Rice, Maj H.	Dec 45
CLASSIFI-CATION	CLAMOR IN CLASSIFICATION How classification worked in '45. (Or didn't work)	Conner, J. *Leatherneck*	Apr 45
	CLASSIFICATION—MARINE STYLE	McNicol, Maj P.	Sep 45
	FINDING THEIR PLACES	Hannas, Maj R.	Apr 44
	MARINE CORPS OCCUPATIONAL TECHNICIANS	Hahn, Capt M.	Apr 44
	MEET YOUR MARINE CORPS—THE TALENT PROBERS Classification men	*Leatherneck*	Apr 44
	A SIMPLE APTITUDE EXAMINATION		Mar 42

POSTS/PLACES

From *Leatherneck,* unless otherwise specified:

ALEUTIANS	BAIT FORCE Seagoing Marines there		Sep 44
AUSTRALIA	FRANKSTON PROVING GROUND WW-2 leave in Melbourne tougher than combat	Mielke, A.	Jun 47
BOUGAIN-VILLE	BOUGAINVILLE—1944	Cocklin, R. *Field Artillery Journal*	Jul 44

BOUGAINVILLE; ONE YEAR AFTER	McCarty, M. *Sat Eve Post* Feb 3, 1945	
JUNGLE TO BROADWAY ON BOUGAINVILLE There've been some changes made	Lambert, T. *Christian Science Monthly* May 20, 1944	
SOUTHWARD BY SKY Detachment of Marines leaves for duty in South America right after Pearl Harbor	Conner, Sgt J. Sep 44	**BRAZIL**
AREA REPRODUCTION CENTER, CAMP ELLIOTT	Engel, A. *Ind. Arts & Voc. Ed.* Sep 44	**CAMP ELLIOTT**
CAMP ELLIOTT TRANSFERRED TO NAVY	*Gazette* May 44	
U.S. MARINE CORPS AIR STATION, CAMP KEARNEY, CALIFORNIA Station Yearbook. One of a series published during WW-2.	Army & Navy Publishing Co., Baton Rouge 1942-45	**CAMP KEARNEY**
LEJEUNE LIBERTY Picture story	Aug 45	**CAMP LEJEUNE**
EL TORO	Menken, Maj A. *Gazette* May 44	**EL TORO**
U.S. MARINE CORPS AIR STATION, EL TORO, CALIFORNIA	Army & Navy Publishing Co., Baton Rouge 1942-45	
FANFARE ON FUNAFUTI Field Music Howard Bailing goes underground in air raid on Funafuti	May 44	**FUNAFUTI**
FUNAFUTI: SPRINGBOARD OF THE PACIFIC	Greene, Capt C. Aug 44	
GUADALCANAL REVISITED	Donner, C. *Gazette* Aug 67	**GUADALCANAL**
GUADALCANAL TOURIST BUREAU Changes on "The Canal" since '42	Naylor, N. Aug 43	

	Title	Author	Date
	THERE'VE BEEN SOME CHANGES MADE On Tulagi, Gavutu and Tanambogo	Marston, G.	Apr 45
GUAM	THE BANK OF GUAM Things get back to normal	Miller, Sgt B.	Jul 45
	GUAM GRADUATION George Washington High School's first class since the liberation	Fink, Sgt S.	Oct 45
	GUAM—BEFORE DECEMBER '41	Johnson, Capt L., USN *Proceedings*	Mar 46
	NOBODY CAME FORMAL Party with the Red Cross "girls"	Decker, Sgt D.	May 45
	SOPAC PARTY All they do is party at Guam		Feb 45
	WHY GUAM ALONE IS AMERICAN	Nelson, Lt F., USN *Proceedings*	Aug 36
GUIANA	JUNGLE JAUNT: SCOUTING IN GUIANA Seven-member Marine patrol in British Guiana	O'Leary, J.	Feb 43
HAWAII	GUARDIANS OF THE PEARLY GATES Marine guards at Pearl Harbor		Oct 45
	HOME WAS NEVER LIKE THIS R & R at the Royal Hawaiian		Dec 44
	HONOLULU—PACIFIC LIBERTY PORT		Feb 45
	OVERSEAS REST HAVEN First Marine Convalescent Camp overseas is Kaneohe Bay. It was called Kokokahi	Ruder, E.	Apr 45
	POLICING THE "ROCK" Marine and Army MP's in Honolulu		Mar 45
	SUBSTITUTE HOME R & R for Marine pilots at a plush Waikiki Beach home operated by the Navy		Mar 45

Title	Author/Source	Date	Place
BACKSTAGE IN HOLLYWOOD Two Marines tour the sets		Mar 44	**HOLLYWOOD**
A VISIT TO HOLLYWOOD STADIUM		Apr 44	
BEAUTIFUL BOONDOCKS Marine Barracks in Oregon		Dec 45	**KLAMATH FALLS**
KLAMATH FALLS: A MARINE BASE IN THE MOUNTAINS Reconditioning Base for filariasis victims (that's a tropical disease of the lymph glands)		Nov 44	
PARTY FOR KIDS	Platt, Sgt C.	Aug 45	**MARIANAS**
VICTORY'S PORTRAIT IN THE MARIANAS Excellent pictures accompany the text	Draper, W. *Geographic*	Nov 45	
MIRAMAR MADNESS Camp Miramar Band, 1943	Riblett, L.	Jan 48	**MIRAMAR**
U.S. MARINE CORPS AIR STATION, MOJAVE, CALIFORNIA	Army & Navy Publishing Co., Baton Rouge	1942-45	**MOJAVE**
TWO FEET TO PARADISE Dagura Mission, New Guinea	Richards, G.	Apr 48	**NEW GUINEA**
PALMS AND PLANES IN THE NEW HEBRIDES	Heinl, R. *Geographic*	Aug 44	**NEW HEBRIDES**
NEW RIVER	Breard, Capt H. *Gazette*	Apr 44	**NEW RIVER**
DATE DOWN UNDER The girls of New Zealand		Oct 44	**NEW ZEALAND**
MILITARY GOVERNMENT AT OKINAWA	Jacobs, Ens W., USN *Gazette*	Nov 46	**OKINAWA**
OKINAWA REVISITED	Barrow, MSgt C.	Aug 61	
THEY CALLED IT REST CAMP 1ST MAR DIV in reserve in a place so bad Marines couldn't wait to get out even if it meant combat. (Maybe it was planned that way)	McMillan, G. *Harper's*	Oct 49	**PAVUVU**

Subject	Title	Author	Date
PEARL HARBOR	A DAY AT PEARL HARBOR	Drake, Col C.	Nov 65
PELELIU	PELELIU TODAY	Decker, Sgt D.	Aug 45
PHILADELPHIA	LEATHERNECK VISITS THE DEPOT QUARTERMASTER AT PHILADELPHIA		Dec 43
PHILIPPINES	CROC HUNT Marine pilots take a day off from Zero hunting and switch to crocodiles	Ewin, R.	Apr 45
	RETURN TO THE ROCK Corregidor vet returns after 16 years	Lippard, Capt J.	Nov 58
	TEN YEARS LATER	Burlage, MSgt G.	May 52
QUANTICO	LABORATORY OF LIFE AND DEATH Marine Corps Equipment Board	Conner, Sgt J.	May 44
SAIPAN	FEATHERING THE BONITO Fishing off Saipan	Martin, Lt H.	Nov 45
SAN DIEGO	SAN DIEGO BASE EXPANDED	*Gazette*	Aug 43
	SAN DIEGO! RENDEZVOUS WITH DESTINY	Pepper, J.	Jan 43
	U.S. MARINE CORPS BASE, SAN DIEGO, CALIFORNIA, PARACHUTE SCHOOL (CAMP GILLESPIE)	Army & Navy Publishing Co., Baton Rouge	1942-45
	U.S. MARINE CORPS BASE, SAN DIEGO, CALIFORNIA RECRUIT DEPOT	Army & Navy Publishing Co., Baton Rouge	1942-45
	U.S. MARINE CORPS BASE, SAN DIEGO, CALIFORNIA, RIFLE RANGE (CAMP MATTHEWS)	Army & Navy Publishing Co., Baton Rouge	1942-45
SAN FRANCISCO	JUNIOR OFFICERS' CLUB IN SAN FRANCISCO	*Gazette*	Sep 43
	THE LEATHERNECK VISITS DEPOT OF SUPPLIES—DEPARTMENT OF THE PACIFIC—SAN FRANCISCO		Jan 44

Title	Author / Source	Date	Location
U.S. MARINE CORPS AIR STATION, SANTA BARBARA, CALIFORNIA	Army & Navy Publishing Co., Baton Rouge	1942-45	**SANTA BARBARA**
AMERICAN MICRONESIA	Morehouse, Capt C. *Gazette*	May 44	**SOPAC**
THE BATTLE OF THE ROCKS Duty aboard a "Rock," (a small island) will drive you crazy	Gordon, TSgt G., and TSgt R. Harvey *American Mercury*	Nov 45	
THE MARINE BASE Bases in the South Pacific	*Gazette*	Jun 42	
MARINES' WORLD Where the Marines fought WW-2	Moore, PFC L.	May 46	
NIGHTFALL Cartoons show eerieness of nightfall in SOPAC		Dec 44	
SOPAC REVISITED	Hayes, LtCol R. *Gazette*	Aug 62	
YOU CAN TAKE A MARINE AWAY FROM HOME BUT YOU CAN'T TAKE HOME AWAY FROM A MARINE How Marines live in SOPAC	Palmer, C. *American Home*	Jul 45	
GILBERT ISLANDS IN THE WAKE OF BATTLE	Moore, R. *Geographic*	Feb 45	**TARAWA**
TARAWA AFTERMATH: BETIO SHOWS THE SCARS OF BATTLE	*Life*	Dec 27, 1943	
TARAWA REVISITED	Hipple, W. *Newsweek*	Mar 27, 1944	
TARAWA REVISITED: FOUR MONTHS AFTER HISTORIC BATTLE, ATOLL IS BUSY AND BEAUTIFUL PLACE	*Life*	Apr 17, 1944	
TARAWA TODAY Lewis finds remnants of rusted weapons, coral-encrusted clips of M-1 ammo, etc.	Lewis, J.	Apr 64	

	TARAWA: A YEAR LATER	Tolbert, Sgt F.	Nov 44
	THIS IS TARAWA TODAY	Trefethen, Lt E. *N.Y. Times Magazine* *Gazette*	Mar 19, 1944 Apr 44
WAKE ISLAND	**WAKE: 1568-1946** Pamphlet history of one of most interesting islands in the Pacific	Junghans, Capt E., USN	1946
	WAKE ISLAND TODAY Pictures and story	Stibbens, S.	Sep 64
WARD ISLAND	NATC—WARD ISLAND		Jan 44
WARM SPRINGS	MARINE DETACHMENT, WARM SPRINGS, GEORGIA Protecting President Roosevelt at his favorite vacation retreat		Jan 42
WASHINGTON	POST OF THE CORPS, MARINE BARRACKS, WASHINGTON, D.C. Corps' oldest Post and home of the Commandant since 1806	Langille, V.	Mar 47

POSTWAR

MARINES	"AFTER THE WAR" Marines discuss plans	Rhoads, LtCol C. *Gazette*	Mar 44
	DEMOBILIZATION Point system for discharging Marines at end of WW-2	*Gazette*	Nov 65
	FIGHTER PILOTS PLAN THEIR POST-WAR CAREERS	Palmer, TSgt C. *Leatherneck*	Jun 45
	FIGHTING A NEW ENEMY The boredom waiting for separation	Larson, Col E. *Gazette*	Oct 45
	FUTURE FIXERS MRO—Marine Rehabilitation Officer helps casualties adjust	Decker, PFC D. *Leatherneck*	Dec 44
	GOING HOME Discharge procedure	Wilton, Sgt R. *Leatherneck*	Oct 45

LAST STOP—REHABILITATION	*Gazette*	Sep 45
MARINE CORPS DEMOBILIZATION PLAN At least, it was orderly, unlike the Army's	*Gazette*	Sep 45
MARINES' POSTWAR PLANS	Barr, Sgt F. *Leatherneck*	Aug 44
MUSTERING OUT PAYMENTS	*Gazette*	Mar 44
ONE MARINE VIEWS HIS POST-WAR WORLD It didn't turn out that way	Foss, Sgt M. *Leatherneck*	Mar 44
VETERANS' BENEFITS Review of all available then	*Leatherneck*	Jan 45

MARINE POW'S RETURN

ESCAPE FROM PALAWAN Prison Camp tale	Looman, Sgt R. *Leatherneck*	Aug 45
ESCAPED FROM THE JAPS Sgts Verle Cutter and Onnie Clem escaped from the Japs when their prison ship was torpedoed	Evans, SSgt C. *Leatherneck*	Feb 45
JIMMY JAMES	Camp, W. *Leatherneck*	Dec 47
LAUGHTER IN HELL . . .BEING THE TRUE EXPERIENCES OF LT W. C. GUIREY, USN, AND T/SGT H. C. NIXON, USMC, AND THEIR COMRADES IN THE JAPANESE PRISON CAMPS IN OSAKA AND TSURUGA Fiction based on Marek's experiences. The title tells it all, except that H. C. Nixon is a Marine Sgt captured on Guam in 1942	Marek, S. The Caxton Printers, Ltd, Caldwell, Idaho	1954
MARINES HAD IT TOUGHEST IN PRISON CAMP Japs didn't seem to like them too much. Wonder why?	*Leatherneck*	May 45

NEVER SAY DIE — Hawkins, Col J. Dorrance & Co., Inc., Philadelphia 1961
Hawkins was captured with the 4th Marines on Corregidor. He spent a year and a half in Prison Camps at Davao and Calabatuan in the Philippines and then escaped with five others. He became a guerrilla leader in Mindanao before he was picked up by a submarine. He returned to active duty just in time to participate in Okinawa.

PACIFIC DREAM — Phillips, Sgt J. *Leatherneck* May 46
Sgts Thomas Thompson and James Cavin return home from Prison Camp and "do the town," thanks to *Leatherneck* which picks up the tab.

RESCUED FROM A JAP HELL — Slocum, J. *Leatherneck* Apr 45
Nineteen Marines are released

RETURN TO MITSUSHIMA — Stolley, F. *Leatherneck* Mar 62
Stolley visits his former home, a Jap Prison Camp

REUNION IN FRISCO — Riblett, Cpl L. *Leatherneck* Aug 46
TSgt Raymond Eccles returns from Prison Camp

SOOCHOW, THE MARINE — Owen, R., and P. Lees G. P. Putnam's Sons 1951
The canine mascot of the 4th Marines was captured along with them. He spent the rest of the war in a Prison Camp. This book is his diary (Didn't know that dogs could write, did you?)

SOOCHOW'S DOG DAYS — Langille, Cpl V. *Leatherneck* Dec 46

32 MONTHS A JAP PRISONER — Shimel, WO J. *Leatherneck* May 45
Shimel was captured on Corregidor

$3300 WORTH OF JAP TROUBLE — Helfer, Sgt H. *Leatherneck* Mar 46
Marines in POW Camp

WE STARTED TO LIVE AGAIN — Stolley, F. *Leatherneck* Dec 61
How Marines survived Prison Camp

YANKS DON'T CRY — Boyle, M. Bernard Geis Associates 1963. Paperback by Pocket Books, Inc. 1966

Another scene of Marines in WW-2. Boyle spent the war in Japan, in a Prison Camp. He was captured on Guam. Tells how Marines not only survived. They resisted.

STRATEGY

AMPHIBIOUS STRATEGY — Possony, S. *Gazette* Jun 45

THE GREAT BLUEPRINT — Metcalfe, J. *Gazette* Dec 44
Pacific island-hopping strategy

PACIFIC STRATEGY — Morison, S. *Gazette* Aug, Sep 62
By the famous Navy historian

PEACE AND WAR WITH JAPAN — Metcalf, Col C. *Gazette* Jun 43

SEAWAYS TO TOKYO — Morehouse, Capt C. *Gazette* Jun 44

THE U.S. MARINES AND AMPHIBIOUS WAR: ITS THEORY AND ITS PRACTICE IN THE PACIFIC — Isely, J., and P. Crowl. Princeton University Press, Princeton, N.J. 1951

"Study of the Marine Corps' development of a doctrine of amphibious fighting in the period between the two World Wars and of the application of that doctrine in the Pacific." Surprisingly interesting and easy-to-read for a "scholarly" publication. The events which happened during the amphibious attacks are described but only as they relate to the "master plan." Explains some of the "reasons why" which frequently need explaining. HQMC commissioned this study but did not censor it or interfere with conclusions.

WORLD WAR 2: THE ACID TEST — Hough, Maj F. *Gazette* Nov 50
For amphibious doctrine

SUPPORTING ARMS

From the *Gazette*, unless otherwise specified:

ARTILLERY

ARTILLERY—INFANTRY COORDINATION — Link, TSgt T. Mar 44

	Title	Author / Source	Date
	BIG BERTHA—WORLD WAR 2	Porter, Col F.	Apr 47
	CANNONEERS, POST! History of artillery in SOPAC during WW-2	Conner, Sgt J. *Leatherneck*	Dec 44
	FIELD ARTILLERY FOR THE INFANTRY	Floom, Col M.	Sep 45
	FIRE MISSION: THE WORK OF THE FO	Hague, SSgt J. *Leatherneck*	Aug 44
	ON THE MOBILITY OF BASE DEFENSE ARTILLERY		Sep 41
	SUPER HIGH ANGLE FIRE	Hughes, LtCol T.	Dec 44
	SUPER HIGH ARTY	Smith, Maj I.	Aug 45
	WHY NOT ROCKET ARTILLERY?	Moore, LtCol F.	Dec 46
CLOSE AIR SUPPORT	AIR POWER FOR INFANTRY	McJennett, Capt J.	Aug 45
	AIR SUPPORT OF GROUND UNITS		Oct 43
	CANNONBALL SUPPORT Rocket planes in later stages of WW-2	Braman, Sgt D. *Leatherneck*	Oct 45
	CARRIER AIR SUPPORT	Browning, Capt M.	Dec 44
	CLOSE AIR SUPPORT SOP	McCutcheon, LtCol K.	Aug 45
	IF YOU WANT CLOSE AIR SUPPORT	Pambrun, Lt L.	Mar 45
	IS AIR SUPPORT EFFECTIVE?	McAloney, Capt H.	Nov 45
	ONE JOB—ONE CORPS That's why Marines' CAS works	Goodman, Capt W.	
NAVAL GUNFIRE	THE BATTLESHIP PAID DIVIDENDS In Naval Gunfire support of Marines in WW-2.	Hessler, Lt W. *Proceedings*	Sep 46

FIREPOWER AND THE AMPHIBIOUS ASSAULT — Weller, Col D. — Mar, Apr 52
Author examines glaring weaknesses and poses problems to solve in Naval Gunfire

THE MOST SHOT AT ISLAND IN THE PACIFIC — Heinl, Col R. — *Proceedings* — Apr 47
Kahoolawe, Hawaii. During WW-2, 880 ships used it for target practice

NAVAL GUNFIRE SUPPORT IN COUNTERBATTERY — Nov 41
Problems of effective counterbattery from standpoint of Ship's Control Officers

NAVAL GUNFIRE SUPPORT IN LANDINGS — Heinl, Maj R. — Sep 45
Throughout WW-2

OUR NAVAL GUNFIRE PREPARATION — Oldfield, Maj W. — Jul 45
A staff artillery coordinator advises on the grouping of bombardment ships, shelling times, support and target areas

SALVO—SPLASH! THE DEVELOPMENT OF NAVAL GUNFIRE SUPPORT IN WORLD WAR 2 — Weller, Col D. — *Proceedings* — Sep 54

SHORE FIRE CONTROL PARTIES — Oldfield, LtCol W. — Nov 45
History since Guadalcanal

WHAT THE ARMY SHOULD KNOW ABOUT NAVAL GUNFIRE — Heinl, LtCol R. — *Combat Forces Journal* — Oct 51
Heinl explains differences between naval gunfire and artillery for our friends in the Army who don't know any better

TACTICS

From the *Gazette*, unless otherwise specified:

ACCURACY VERSUS VOLUME IN RIFLE FIRE — Sep 40
Why not both?

PART 3 | WORLD WAR 2

AIRBORNE ATTACK — *Leatherneck* — Apr 42
Gliders and parachute troops. Just the thing for landing in Pacific jungles.

AMPHIBIOUS MIRACLE OF OUR TIME: LANDING TECHNIQUES THAT CANNOT BE STOPPED — Vandegrift, Gen A. *N.Y. Times Magazine* Aug 6, 1944; *Gazette* Oct 44

AN ANALYSIS OF FLANK PROTECTION — Nov 41

BALANCE VS. DISTORTION IN MILITARY THINKING — Irving, Capt E. — Sep 42
Public clamour for the dramatic sometimes leads to distorted thinking

BATTALION LANDING TEAMS IN AMPHIBIOUS OPERATIONS — Cushman, LtCol R. — Jan 45

BUNKER BUSTING — White, Capt R., USA — Jan 44
Lots of practice at Saipan

THE CHEMICAL OFFICER IN BASE-DEFENSE SITUATIONS — Nov 42

COMMAND POST PROCEDURE — Sep 42

DEFENSE OF AIRDROMES AND LANDING FIELDS — Jun 40

DON'T PLAN THESE BATTLES — Sep 41
Play it by ear

A FIVE-PLATOON COMPANY? — Nickerson, Capt N. — May, Jun 43

A FOUR DAY PATROL — Pettus, Sgt F. — Jun 44

THE ILLUMINATION PROBLEM — Sep 40

ISLAND DEFENSE — Mar 41

A JUNGLE AID — Mason, Maj L. — May 44

JUNGLE PATROLLING — Richards, Maj G. — Jan, Feb 45

JUNGLE WARFARE — Jun 44

LIGHTWEIGHT ASSAULT TROOPS — Mar 41

Title	Author / Source	Date
THE MARINE RIFLE COMPANY IN STREET RIOT OPERATIONS		Mar 40
MARINE RIFLE SQUAD IN COMBAT Significant 4-part series		Mar-Jun 45
THE NEW RIFLE SQUAD Pictures of new 13 man squad and how it deploys in combat situations	Bergman, Cpl H. *Leatherneck*	May 44
NIGHT ATTACK 21st Marines did it at Okinawa	Griffith, Col S.	Sep 45
NOTES ON JUNGLE WARFARE Author is Jens Doe (not John Doe)	Doe, BGen J., USA	Feb 44
OBSERVATION VS. THE JAP	Whyte, Capt W., USA	Apr 44
PAPER BULLETS Propaganda leaflets	Helfer, Sgt H. *Leatherneck*	Nov 45
PLANNING PHASE OF AMPHIBIOUS OPERATIONS AS A PRELUDE TO JUNGLE OPERATIONS	Emigh, LtCol J. *Military Review*	Nov 44
A PRACTICAL JUNGLE FORMATION	Mason, LtCol L.	Apr 45
SCOUTS! INFORMATION PLEASE		Mar 40
SEVENTEEN-MAN SQUAD	Chamberlain, Maj W.	Nov 45
SHIP TO SHORE AND INLAND	Stephan, LtCol S.	Jul 45
SHOULD WE EMPLOY TWO FIRST TEAMS Alternate front line troops at frequent intervals	Jenkins, Lt L.	Feb 45
SNIPING AND ANTI-SNIPING	Thompson, SSgt R.	Jun 44
SNIPERS ARE OVERRATED		Jan 45

	Title	Author / Source	Date
	THE SQUAD AUTOMATIC	Johnson, Capt M.	Sep 41
	STREET FIGHTING Emphasis switches to house-to-house fighting as Marines get ready to hit Japan	Holt, Capt M. *Leatherneck*	Mar 45
	TACTICS FOR THE RIFLEMAN	Sager, PFC F.	Jan 45
	TECHNIQUE OF CONTROL IN CLOSE TERRAIN	Simpson, Maj R.	May 45
	THIRTEEN MAN SQUAD: MARINES EXPECT BETTER CONTROL AND BETTER FIRE POWER FROM NEW T/O	*Infantry Journal*	Jul 44
	THROW AWAY THE BOOK?	Whyte, Capt W., USA	Mar 44
	WE'RE ALL INFANTRYMEN 3/10, an artillery unit, gets some ground-pounder action	*Leatherneck*	Jan 45
	THE WHITES OF THEIR EYES		Sep 41

TRAINING

	Title	Author / Source	Date
GENERAL	AMPHIBIOUS TRAINING	Morehouse, Capt C. *Gazette*	Aug 44
	AN EFFECTIVE ORIENTATION PROGRAM	Ostrander, Lt M. *Gazette*	Feb 45
	A BASIC SCHOOL FOR TECHNICIANS	Rose, Capt A. *Gazette*	Mar 46
	A CRITIQUE OF RESERVE TRAINING	*Gazette*	Mar 41
	FIRE CONTROL TRAINING	Conner, Sgt H. *Gazette*	Sep 44
	FIRST CRUISE TRAINING	Heinl, LtCol R. *Gazette*	Dec 45
	GIVE ME THE APA Cruises to Vieques and Little Creek were a lot of laughs	Bristow, V. *Leatherneck*	Sep 54

HOW STAFF OFFICERS ARE TRAINED By a former Raider officer	Currin, LtCol M. *Gazette*	Feb 45
INSTRUCTORS' ORIENTATION	Meyers, Lt L. *Gazette*	Dec 45
MARINE CORPS GROUND TRAINING IN WORLD WAR 2 Pamphlet history of stateside training Sep 18, 1939 to Aug 14, 1945	Condit, K., G. Diamond and E. Turnbladh HQMC	1956
MARINE CORPS HIGH SCHOOL PROGRAM	*Educational Victory*	Jun 1, 1943
A MARINE LEARNS JUDO	*Gazette*	May 45
MILITARY UMPIRES Importance in maneuvers	Levit, Maj M. *Gazette*	Nov 45
NEITHER FISH NOR FOWL Marines should be experts in their fields; not "jacks of all trades"	Fleming, Lt R. *Gazette*	Mar 42
NOTES ON TRAINING FOR COMPANY OFFICERS	*Gazette*	Jun 42
OFFICER EDUCATION	Culhane, LtCol T. *Gazette*	Oct 45
SO YOU'RE GOING TO THE TROPICS A travel guide for Marines	Bergman, H. *Leatherneck*	Oct 43
TOWARD A BETTER LANDING FORCE	*Gazette*	Nov 40
TRAINING JUNIOR OFFICERS	Fitchet, Capt S. *Gazette*	Jun 44
TRAINING THE LANDING FORCE	Heinl, Col R. *Proceedings*	Oct 41
TRAINING THE MARINE	Sandberg, J. *Ind. Arts & Voc. Ed.*	Sep 43
TRAINING OF MARINE INSTRUCTORS	Upshaw, Maj I. *Gazette*	Feb 45

	Title	Author / Source	Date
	TRAINING POLICY FOR PEACETIME	*Gazette*	Oct 45
	TROOP OFFICERS' BATTALION Instruction for instructors	Streit, Maj V. *Gazette*	Dec 45
	UNITED STATES MARINE CORPS AND VOCATIONAL EDUCATION	Fischer, T. *Ind. Arts & Voc. Ed.*	Sep 42
	WHAT TO EXPECT IF YOU ARE CAPTURED BY THE JAPS	Smith, M. *Leatherneck*	Nov 43
	WHY A MARINE IS A SECRET WEAPON How training makes Marines	High, S. *Digest*	Jan 44
EXERCISES	MANEUVERS IN PUERTO RICO	Polivka, D. *Leatherneck*	Sep 41
	MIDWAY MOCK WAR	*Leatherneck*	Jan 45
"HOW TO" ARTICLES	From *Leatherneck*, unless otherwise specified:		
	THE BEST WAY TO USE THE EYES AT NIGHT	*Gazette*	Sep 42
	COVER IS WHERE YOU FIND IT		May 44
	HOW TO COMBAT TRANSPORT BOREDOM	Donovan, Maj J. *Gazette*	Jun 45
	HOW TO LIVE IN A JUNGLE—AND LIKE IT	Johnson, Sgt P.	Aug 44
	HOW TO STOP HEMORRHAGE Useful picture story		Nov 44
	HOW TO TAKE A PILLBOX Without getting a hemorrhage		Jun 44
	HOW TO TREAT A SHELL FIRE WOUND		Aug 44
	"IRON KELLY" Various ways to use the helmet		Mar 44
	THE JUNGLE HAMMOCK	Weindel, SSgt G.	Jun 44
	MANUAL OF THE SWORD	Evans, Sgt E.	Dec 44

THEY MADE IT—COULD YOU? Combat swimming		Apr 44
WAR PAINT How to do camouflage		Jun 44
YOUR FIELD LESSON:		
ASSEMBLING THE PACK		Apr 44
THE BAZOOKA		Jul 44
HOW TO FIELD STRIP THE B.A.R.		Feb 44
HOW TO FIELD STRIP THE CARBINE		Mar 44
HOW TO FIRE THE MORTAR		Jan 44
HOW TO FIELD STRIP THE THOMPSON SUBMACHINE GUN		Jun 44

MARKSMANSHIP

From the *Gazette*, unless otherwise specified:

CAMP PERRY Rifle Matches of 1940	*Leatherneck*	Nov 40
COMBAT RANGE Cartoons	McDermott, Sgt J. *Leatherneck*	Jul 45
KEEP THEM FIRING		Jun 41
MACHINE GUN PRACTICE FOR SMALL COMMANDS		Jun 40
THE MARINE CORPS RIFLE TEAM: 1940		Nov 40
MARINE CORPS NATIONAL MATCH RIFLE AND PISTOL TEAMS: 1940		Sep 40
MARINE CORPS RIFLE TESTS		Jun 41
MARINES OUT-SHOOT USMA CADETS USMA is West Point	*Army & Navy Journal*	Feb 26, 1944
MINIATURE RANGE FOR ANTI-MECHANIZED TRAINING		Mar 42
MOVING TARGET RANGE FIXTURES		Mar 42

A TRADITION OF SKILL — Hamilton, Lt E. *Leatherneck* May 41

TRAINING-SCHOOLS

From *Leatherneck*, unless otherwise specified:

AO

"FLYING SCOUTS;" THE AIRBORNE EYES OF THE BOONDOCKING MARINES — Mattie, Sgt G. — Jul 45
Aerial Observer's school

AMPHIB

MARINES TELL IT TO THE ARMY — Aug 44
Army units trained in amphibious tactics by Marines at Pendleton

ONSLOW BEACH — May 43
Amphib training at Lejeune

QUANTICO—THE MARINE CORPS SCHOOL OF WARFARE — *Gazette* — Nov 41
Amphib strategy and tactics

AA

ZERO BUSTERS — May 44
AA School at Jacksonville

BARRAGE BALLOON

SKY TRAPS — Jan 42
Training at Parris Island

BOOT CAMP

BOOT CAMP — Tolbert, F. — May 42
At Parris Island

BOOT: A MARINE IN THE MAKING — Bailey, Cpl G. The Macmillan Company — 1944
The sounds, smells and feelings of Parris Island are described and the sights are pictured in this little book (130 pp.) by a member of the "Class of '43." From arrival at the forlorn train station at Yemassee through the first encounter with a D.I., the haircut, infirmary visit for shots, clothing issue, Rifle Range; it's all here. Great illustrations. Bailey tells it with a smile

BUILDING UP MARINES AT SAN DIEGO — Budday, Rev C. *America* Apr 11, 1942

REMINISCENCES OF A BOOT — Gallant, T. *Gazette* Nov 69
Sep, 1941 vintage, at Parris Island

Title	Author / Source	Date	Topic
THE SMOOTHEST PRODUCTION LINE PI training	Winn, Col C. *Gazette*	Jul 43	
MAGIC AT QUANTICO	Marie, Col L. *Time*	Mar 3, 1941	**CAMOUFLAGE**
MAGIC MARINES: MARINES CAMOUFLAGE SCHOOL IN HOLLYWOOD	English, R. *Collier's*	Oct 3, 1942	
SEE THE CHAPLAIN Picture story of Chaplain training		Apr 44	**CHAPLAIN**
LIVE OFF THE LAND Training in individual combat at Camp Elliott	Maloney, M. *Gazette*	Nov 43	**COMBAT**
UNIVERSITY OF SURVIVAL 4TH MAR DIV Training Center	Lucas, Lt J.	Feb 45	
GI-DI Training those lovable characters at San Diego	Kuhne, N.	Dec 43	**DI**
DEVIL DOG SCHOOL Training war dogs at New River	Tolbert, F.	May 43	**DOGS**
RATAMACUE AND FLAM PARADIDDLE Field Music School at Parris Island. Title refers to bugle music		May 44	**FIELD MUSIC**
MEET YOUR MARINE CORPS— THREE UP, THREE DOWN FIRST SGTS SCHOOL, PHILADELPHIA		Mar 44	**FIRST SGT**
COW COUNTRY MARINES Eagle Mountain Air Station, Texas. Training for Glider Program	Tolbert, F.	Jul 43	**GLIDERS**
GLIDERS: MARINE CORPS GLIDER TRAINING	Wehle, J. *Flying*	Feb 43	
MARINE COMMANDOES Marines receive guerrilla war training from British Commandos		Dec 43	**GUERRILLA**

LANGUAGE	PARLEY-VOO JAPANESE Language School "somewhere in the Pacific"		Dec 42
OCS	FROM STRIPES TO BARS NCO's become officers at Quantico		Apr 43
	PLATOON COMMANDERS' SCHOOL At Quantico	McWethy, Maj D. *Gazette*	Jun 45
	THEY HAD A WORD FOR IT Selecting recruits has not changed for 1,000 years	Laughlin, Lt P. *Gazette*	Mar 42
	THEY MADE ME A LEATHERNECK "But it wasn't easy," should be the sub-title of this funny little book about an OC Class at Quantico early in WW-2.	Vance, Lt R. W. W. Norton & Company, Inc.	1943

Vance has total recall of the lingo . . .

"I want three volunteers . . . you, you and you!"

"Leave that fly alone. He has to eat, too."

"I am a crudhead. I called my rifle a gun."

He made it through to a commission, largely because of his sense of humor

ORDNANCE	ORDNANCE SCHOOL—MARINE CORPS SCHOOLS At Quantico	*Gazette*	Jun 44
PARACHUTE	MARINE PARACHUTE TRAINING By the CO of the 1st Parachute Battalion later WIA at Tulagi	Williams, Capt R. *Proceedings*	Jul 41
	PARATROOPER TRAINING	Fitzgerald, C. *Gazette*	Jul 43
RAIDER	SCHOOLS FOR KILLERS New River training for Raiders and Parachute Marines		Jul 43
	SPECIALISTS IN SUDDEN DEATH: HOW THEY'RE TRAINED AT THE MARINE BASE AT NEW RIVER	Davenport, S. *Sat Eve Post*	Aug 1, 1942

Title	Author / Source	Date	Category
READY TEAMS EMERGE FROM THIS ACADEMY Scout/Sniper School at Green's Farm north of San Diego	Tolbert, F.	Oct 43	**SCOUT/ SNIPER**
SAN DIEGO'S SEA SCHOOL	Thompson, Sgt R.	Jun 40	**SEA**
SEA SCHOOL, USMC San Diego		Dec 43	
SIGNAL TRAINING AT NEW RIVER	McClelland, Capt F. *Gazette*	Feb 44	**SIGNAL**
TANK TRAINING	Jones, Lt F. *Gazette*	Apr 44	**TANK**
BOOT CAMP FOR WOMEN At Lejeune	Myers, R.	Sep 43	**WR'S**
GIRL MARINES ROLL UP THEIR SLEEVES Lejeune	Myers, R.	Oct 43	
TOUGHENING UP THE WOMEN MARINES	*N.Y. Times Magazine*	Jun 20, 1943	
WOMEN MARINES STUDY RADIO AT UNIVERSITY OF WISCONSIN	*Gazette*	Jan 44	

UNIFORMS/INSIGNIA

Title	Author / Source	Date
BOARD OF AWARDS How decorations are handed out	Myers, Sgt R. *Leatherneck*	Nov 45
BY THEIR STARS, BARS AND STRIPES YOU SHALL KNOW THEM	*Newsweek*	Sep 21, 1942
COMBAT STARS	*Gazette*	Apr 44
A FIGHTING FIT Improving Marine uniforms to get ready for WW-2	Cushman, Capt R. *Gazette*	Nov 41
THE HERALDRY OF HEROISM The 376 approved decorations, medals, service ribbons, badges, and women's insignia	DuBois, A. *Geographic*	Oct 43

	HOW TO TELL THEM: INSIGNIA OF THE ARMED FORCES	Hornaday, M. *Christian Science Monthly* May 29, 1942
	A LETTER TO COLONEL WEARZEM FROM MAJOR MAKESEM	*Gazette* Jun 42
	INSIGNIA OF THE UNITED STATES ARMED FORCES	Grosvenor, G. *Geographic* Jun 43
	MARINE CORPS INSIGNIA	*N.Y. Times Magazine* Mar 1, 1942
	MARINE CORPS SHOULDER INSIGNIA All the Corps, Division and smaller unit patches	*Gazette* May 44
	A NEW TROPICAL UNIFORM	*Gazette* Jun 40
	NINE ARM BADGES RATE MARINE CORPS' ENLISTED MEN	*Popular Science* Mar 41
	RIBBONS—HOW THEY'RE AWARDED	McNicol, Maj P. *Gazette* Jul 45
	UNIFORM REGULATIONS	*Gazette* Apr 44
	WINNING MEDALS AND ALIENATING PEOPLE	Hubler, Capt R. *Gazette* Jan 44

UNITS

FMF	BIRTH OF THE FMF	Shepherd, Sgt R. *Leatherneck* Nov 42
DIVISIONS	**UNCOMMON VALOR: MARINE DIVISIONS IN ACTION** Tell a combat correspondent to write a history of the Division he served with. Naturally, you'll get a history of "the best damn division in the Corps." and why it's the best. That's *Uncommon Valor.* The story of the six best divisions in the Corps. Gung-ho, but exciting. Fun to read	McMillan, G., and Combat Correspondents Infantry Journal Press Washington 1946

Title	Author / Publisher	Date	Unit
1ST MARINE DIVISION, 1941-1945 Mimeograph history of the Division before "The Old Breed" was published as the official history in 1949	Thacker, J. HQMC	1945	**1ST MAR DIV**
THE HISTORY OF THE 1ST DIVISION	Thacker, J. *Leatherneck*	Oct 45	
JAPS REMEMBER THE 1ST MARINES Worden means the 1ST MAR DIV, not the "1ST MARINES"	Worden, W. *Sat Eve Post*	Jan 12, 1946	
THE OLD BREED: A HISTORY OF THE 1ST MARINE DIVISION IN WORLD WAR 2 Official history, and what a history!	McMillan, G. Infantry Journal Press, Washington	1949	
FOLLOW ME! THE STORY OF THE 2D MARINE DIVISION IN WORLD WAR 2	Johnston, R. Random House, Inc.	1948	**2D MAR DIV**
HISTORY OF THE 2D DIVISION	Zimmerman, J. *Leatherneck*	Dec 45	
2D MARINE DIVISION (PRELIMINARY) Pamphlet written before *"Follow Me,"* the official history	Zimmerman, J. HQMC	1945	
HISTORY OF THE 3RD DIVISION	Thacker, J. *Leatherneck*	Feb 46	**3RD MAR DIV**
THE LONG AND THE SHORT AND THE TALL: THE STORY OF A MARINE COMBAT UNIT IN THE PACIFIC Combat Correspondent's report of the 3RD MAR DIV at Guam and Iwo	Josephy, A. Alfred A. Knopf	1946	
3RD MARINE DIVISION	*Saga*	Mar 62	
THE 3RD MARINE DIVISION Official history	Aurthur, Lt R., and Lt K. Cohlmia Infantry Journal Press, Washington	1948	

Division	Title	Author / Publisher	Date
4TH MAR DIV	**THE 4TH MARINE DIVISION IN WORLD WAR 2** Official history in a giant-sized book that won't fit in your bookcase	Proehl, Capt C. Infantry Journal Press, Washington	1945
	THE 4TH MARINE DIVISION IN WORLD WAR 2 Eighty-nine page pamphlet published before the official history	Chapin, Lt J. HQMC	1945
	4TH U.S. MARINE DIVISION, CAMP PENDLETON, OCEANSIDE, CALIFORNIA Cruise-book	Army & Navy Publishing Co., Baton Rouge	1944
	HISTORY OF THE 4TH DIVISION	Chapin, Lt J. *Leatherneck*	Apr 46
	A POCKET HISTORY OF THE 4TH MARINE DIVISION AND THE 4TH MARINE AIR WING IN WORLD WAR 2	HQMC	1965
5TH MAR DIV	THE 5TH DIVISION	Thacker, J. *Leatherneck*	Sep 46
	THE 5TH MARINE DIVISION IN WORLD WAR 2 Twenty-six page pamphlet published before the official history became available	Chapin, Lt J. HQMC	1945
	THE SPEARHEAD: 5TH MARINE DIVISION Three-part history in magazine format	Johnson, E. *Pictorial California,* Los Angeles	1946
	THE SPEARHEAD: THE WORLD WAR 2 HISTORY OF THE 5TH MARINE DIVISION Official history	Connor, Maj H. *Infantry Journal Press,* Washington	1950
6TH MAR DIV	**HISTORY OF THE 6TH MARINE DIVISION** Official history	Cass, Lt B. *Infantry Journal Press,* Washington	1948
	THE 6TH MARINE DIVISION	Stockman, Capt J. HQMC	1946

THE 6TH DIVISION	Stockman, Capt J. *Leatherneck* Oct 46	
		REGIMENTS—
4TH MARINES History of the "new" 4th formed from Parachute Marines	Meagher, SSgt E. *Leatherneck* Oct 45	**4TH MARINES**
THE 9TH MARINES: A BRIEF HISTORY OF THE 9TH MARINE REGIMENT WITH LISTS OF OFFICERS AND MEN WHO SERVED FROM ORGANIZATION TO DISBANDMENT, 1942-45	Burrus, Lt L. Infantry Journal Press, Washington 1946	**9TH MARINES**
SEMPER FI! THE STORY OF THE 9TH MARINES Fiction. An account of the Regiment in WW-2	Hendryx, G. The Pageant Press 1959	
THE 10TH MARINES	Jenkins, J. *Gazette* Apr 43	**10TH MARINES**
14TH REGIMENT (ARTILLERY), 4TH MARINE DIVISION Cruisebook-type publication of which there were many	Army & Navy Publishing Co., Baton Rouge 1942-45	**14TH MARINES**
20TH REGIMENT (ENGINEERS), 4TH MARINE DIVISION	Army & Navy Publishing Co., Baton Rouge 1942-45	**20TH MARINES**
23RD REGIMENT, 4TH MARINE DIVISION	Army & Navy Publishing Co., Baton Rouge 1942-45	**23RD MARINES**
24TH REGIMENT, 4TH MARINE DIVISION	Army & Navy Publishing Co., Baton Rouge 1942-45	**24TH MARINES**
25TH REGIMENT, 4TH MARINE DIVISION	Army & Navy Publishing Co., Baton Rouge 1942-45	**25TH MARINES**
		SPECIAL UNITS—
SERVICE TROOPS, 4TH MARINE DIVISION	Army & Navy Publishing Co., Baton Rouge 1942-45	**SERVICE TROOPS**

SPECIAL TROOPS	**SPECIAL TROOPS, 4TH MARINE DIVISION**	Army & Navy Publishing Co., Baton Rouge 1942-45
	SPECIAL MARINE CORPS UNIT OF WORLD WAR 2 Excellent, much needed history of the Raiders, Parachute Marines, Defense Battalions, Glider Group and Barrage Balloon Squadrons	Updegraph, C. HQMC 1972 (IP)
BARRAGE BALLOONS	BARRAGE BALLOONS	*Gazette* Nov 42
DEFENSE BNS	ACK, ACK, ETC. No one knew what the "etc." was for, so the Defense Bns were disbanded shortly after this article was published	Miller, Sgt B. *Leatherneck* Sep 44
	THE FUTURE OF THE DEFENSE BATTALION As soon as it became apparent that the enemy was in no position to attempt to recapture islands after we took them, Defense Bns had no future	*Gazette* Sep 42
DOGS	ANIMALS WERE ALLIES, TOO	*Geographic* Jan 46
	BATTLE DOGS OF THE DEVIL DOGS	Henderson, C. *American* Aug 44
	DOG HEROES OF THE MARINE CORPS	Goodwin, H. *N.Y. Times Magazine* Oct 8, 1944
GLIDERS	SOARING MARINES Story of Marine Glider Group 71 at Page Field, Parris Island	*Leatherneck* Aug 42
PARACHUTE MARINES	FALLING DYNAMITE	Lord, G. *Popular Mechanics* Jun 43
	JUMPING DEVIL DOGS	*Time* Aug 11, 1941
	PARAMARINES HIT HARD AND HIT OFTEN	Guevara, E. *Travel* Sep 43

Title	Author / Source	Date	Unit
PARATROOPS	Marie, L. *Flying*	Dec 43	
SILKWORM GANG Parachute riggers	Perrin, Lt R., USNR *Leatherneck*		
UNITED STATES MARINE CORPS PARACHUTE UNITS	Johnstone, Maj J. HQMC	1962	
GUERRILLA FIGHTERS OF THE MARINES	Durdin, F. *Science Digest*	Feb 43	**RAIDERS**
MARINE RAIDER? History with conclusion "Bring them back."	Fredericks, H. *Proceedings*	Aug 56	
THE MAGNIFICENT BASTARDS Fiction. "Crockett, L., "is Lucy Crockett," but she sure can write about Marine raiders. This novel is about a tough part-Indian Battalion Commander (William Holden) who makes it tough on his men and tough on Deborah Kerr. She is a typical Red Cross worker in Noumea—the kind of girl you frequently saw. (Movie is *The Proud and the Profane)*	Crockett, L. Farrar, Strauss & Young Paperback by Dell Publishing Co., Inc.	1954 1959	
NO GREATER LOVE: MARINE RAIDERS IN THE SOUTH PACIFIC	Regan, J. *American Digest*	Jun 45 Jul 45	
BLESS 'EM ALL; A CARTOON HISTORY OF THE 1ST MARINE RAIDERS	Hedlinger, C. Titusville Herald, Titusville, Pa.	1943	**1ST RAIDER BN**
COLONEL CARLSON AND HIS GUNG-HO RAIDERS	Hubbard, L. *Digest*	Dec 43	**2D RAIDER BN**
THE RAIDERS Picture story	Tolbert, F. *Leatherneck*	Dec 43	
ROUGHEST AND THE TOUGHEST: CARLSON'S RAIDERS And they also get the most ink	Durdin, F. *N.Y. Times Magazine*	Nov 8, 1942	
THE BOYS FROM ALLIGATOR FLATS 3rd Amtracs of 3RD MAR DIV	Miller, Sgt B. *Leatherneck*	Aug 45	**3D AMTRACS**
FORGOTTEN BATTALION From Tulagi to Guam history	Miller, Sgt B. *Leatherneck*	Feb 45	**2D GUN BN**

8TH GUN BN	**8TH 155MM GUN BATTALION, U.S. MARINES**		1946
12TH BN	**12TH BATTALION, CAMP ELLIOTT, CALIFORNIA**	Army & Navy Publishing Co., Baton Rouge	1942-45
14TH BN	**14TH BATTALION, CAMP ELLIOTT, CALIFORNIA**	Army & Navy Publishing Co., Baton Rouge	1942-45
HDQ BN	**U.S. MARINE CORPS BASE, SAN DIEGO, HEADQUARTERS BATTALION**	Army & Navy Publishing Co., Baton Rouge	1942-45
PIONEER BN	HURRY, HURRY BOYS What the Pioneer Battalion does	Engelman, Cpl C. *Leatherneck*	Jun 44
SIGNAL BN	**U.S. MARINE CORPS BASE, SAN DIEGO, SIGNAL BATTALION**	Army & Navy Publishing Co., Baton Rouge	1942-45

COMPANIES

"C" CO	**U.S. MARINE CORPS INFANTRY TRAINING BATTALIONS, CAMP ELLIOTT, CALIFORNIA, COMPANY "C"**	Army & Navy Publishing Co., Baton Rouge	1942-45
"D" CO	**U.S. MARINE CORPS INFANTRY TRAINING BATTALIONS, CAMP ELLIOTT, CALIFORNIA, COMPANY "D"**	Army & Navy Publishing Co., Baton Rouge	1942-45
"E" CO, 2/7	EASY DOES IT	Decker, Sgt D., and Sgt S. Fink *Leatherneck*	Oct 45
"ORIENTAL" CO	ORIENTAL EXPLOITATION COMPANY	Levin, Sgt D. *Gazette*	Jan 45
RIFLE CO	RIFLE COMPANY	*Gazette*	Jun 44
BLACK MARINES	**A CHOSEN FEW** Fiction. Based on fact. The fantastic story of one of the best kept secrets of WW-2. Black Marines. This novel concentrates on the training at Montford Point near	Rhodes, H. Paperback only, Bantam Books, Inc.	1965

Lejeune and the problems connected with wearing a Marine uniform on leave when no one knew there were Black Marines

COMBAT REPORT: NEGRO MARINES	*Time* Jul 24, 1944	
DUSKY MARINES	*Newsweek* May 17, 1943	
DEVIL DAMES	*Newsweek* Feb 22, 1943	WR'S
HISTORY OF THE MARINE CORPS WOMEN'S RESERVE—A CRITICAL ANALYSIS OF ITS DEVELOPMENT AND OPERATION, 1943-1945	Cheney, Col R., and LtCol K. Towle HQMC 1945	
LADY LEATHERNECKS	Towle, Col K. *Gazette* Feb 46	
A LONG WAY Progress report for Women Marines	Streeter, LtCol R. *Leatherneck* Feb 44	
MARINE CORPS WOMENS' RESERVE IN WORLD WAR 2	Meid, LtCol P. HQMC 1968 (IP)	
MEASURED INTERESTS OF MARINE CORPS WOMEN RESERVISTS	Hahn, M., and C. Williams *Applied Psychology Journal* Jun 45	
OUT-MARINING THE MARINES	Scullin, Lt E. *Gazette* Apr 44	
TELL IT TO THE MARINES	*Independent Woman* Mar 43	
THOSE BRASS-BUTTON QUEENS	Wilson, E. *Time* May 22, 1944	
UNIFORMS FOR WOMEN MARINES	*Gazette* Mar 44	
U.S. MARINE CORPS WOMEN'S RESERVE, CAMP LEJEUNE, NORTH CAROLINA	Army & Navy Publishing Co., Baton Rouge 1942-45	

	WE PLAYED IT COOL IN THE MOTOR POOL WR of WW-2 tells of experiences in Hawaii	Nieuwland, E. *Leatherneck*	Feb 68
	WOMEN MARINES	*Life*	Mar 27, 1944
	WOMEN IN UNIFORM	Bradley, L. *Geographic*	Oct 43

WEAPONS

From the *Gazette,* unless otherwise specified:

GENERAL	STAMPING AND FORMING How weapons are made		Mar 42
	WHY NOT COPY? Innovations in foreign arms	Smith, W.	Jun 45
ABC	ATOMIC BOMB		Sep 45
	MOST DESTRUCTIVE LETHAL WEAPON		May 45
AA	MARINE CORPS ANTIAIRCRAFT	Paige, LtCol H.	Mar 44
BAR	AN ANTIAIRCRAFT MOUNT FOR THE B.A.R.		Sep 42
BAYONET	THE NEW BAYONET Description and pictures	Hart, R. *Leatherneck*	Sep 43
	WEAPON OF LAST RESORT	Stavers, Capt S.	Jun 44
FLAME	FIGHTING WITH FIRE	Crow, PFC M.	Feb 45
	MORE FIRE POWER, SMALLER UNITS	Brooks, LtCol N.	Dec 44
	TACTICAL USE OF FLAME	Myers, Lt L.	Nov 45
KNIFE	A NEW MARINE CORPS KNIFE	Carleton, Capt P.	Jan 44
MACHINE GUNS	LIGHTENING THE HEAVY	McVay, Sgt I.	Dec 44

SHORT BELTS AND SHORT RANGES Machine guns in the jungle	McVay, Sgt I. *Leatherneck*	Aug 44	
THE M-1 RIFLE When it replaced the '03		Mar 41	RIFLE
NOTES ON THE M-1 RIFLE		Jun 40	
ROCKETS	Miller, Sgt B.	Aug 44	ROCKETS
LAST OF THE PACK 75's in the Pacific	Travis, Cpl F. *Leatherneck*	Dec 45	75'S
OUR SUPERIOR MODERNIZED 75'S		Nov 40	
ARMS FOR OFFICERS	Kengla, LtCol W.	Nov 44	SIDEARMS
CARBINE OR PISTOL		Feb 46	
AMPHIBIOUS TANKS IN ACTION		Apr 44	TANKS
ARMORED FORCES AND OUR ARMORED FORCE		Nov 41	
BASIC CONCEPT OF THE TANK FORCE	Browning, Capt M.	Jul 45	
HANDY ANTITANKERS	Kelly, Maj I.	Aug 45	
TANK-INFANTRY TEAM	Lawton, Capt L.	Nov 45	
TANKS Operations of tanks in SOPAC	*Leatherneck*	Sep 44	
TANKS AND TERRAIN	McGill, Lt R.	Jun 41	
TRAINED TANK KILLERS	Kelly, Maj I.	Jul 45	
USING THE TANK PLATOON IN INDIRECT FIRE	Monzani, Maj J., USA	Jun 45	

4.
POSTWAR

The Corps goes from six divisions to less than one in the short five years of peace which ends in June of 1950.

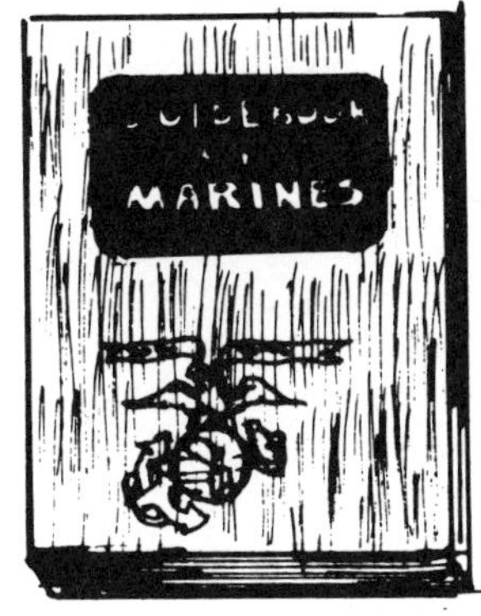

CONTENTS: PART 4

JAPAN

BACK TO JAPAN Big change since VJ Day	Klein, Capt E. *Gazette*	Mar 46	1945
CRAZY BEACHHEAD Invasion of Japan is crazy— no shooting	Decker, Sgt D., and Sgt J. Purcell *Leatherneck*	Dec 45	
D + I ON TOKYO'S GINZA Adventures on the first recorded R & R in Tokyo	Decker, Sgt D., and Sgt J. Purcell *Leatherneck*	Nov 45	
THE FACE OF JAPAN Photo story of Japan rebuilding	Bush, J. *Leatherneck*	Jul 47	
FINALE AT YOKOSUKA 4th Marines hit mainland Japan	Tavis, Cpl F. *Gazette*	Dec 45	
FISH AND FROZEN ORANGES Impressions of Japan soon after VJ Day	Felsen, Sgt H. *Leatherneck*	Feb 46	
FUJIYAMA MEETS THE 4TH 4th Marines "capture" Fujiyama	Aster, Capt S. *Leatherneck*	Apr 46	
IT MAY BE A MASAMUNE Jap swords—how to identify	Ward, D. *Leatherneck*	Apr 47	
KYUSHU DIARY Japs rebuild Japan while Marines watch	Smith, Sgt B. *Leatherneck*	Feb 47	
MARINE AVIATION OVER JAPAN Part 10: *Devilbirds*	DeChant, Capt J. *Gazette*	Nov 47	
NOW THAT IT'S OVER How to live with the "sneaky yellow Jap Bastards."	Roberts, Sgt N., and Cpl B. Davis *Leatherneck*	Nov 45	
OCCUPATION OF KYUSHU Occupation duty for 2D MARDIV	Currin, LtCol M. *Gazette*	Oct 46	
THE OCCUPATION MARINE Set a good example, etc., etc.	Donovan, Maj J. *Gazette*	Apr 46	
OLYMPIC VS KETSU-GO Allied plan for the invasion of Kyushu (Japan) vs. the Jap Defense Plan	Bauer, K. and A. Coox *Gazette*	Aug 65	

PRELUDE AT SHIMONOSEKI Occupation of S. Japan by 3/28, 5TH MAR DIV Oct 45	Cook, Sgt E. *Gazette*	Sep 45
SHOW OF FORCE Flying over wrecked Japan	Griffith, Col S. *Gazette*	Dec 45
TRAIN TO TOKYO Riding the Tokyo Express on VJ +2 Day	Decker, Sgt D., and Sgt J. Purcell *Leatherneck*	Dec 45
THE UNITED STATES MARINES IN THE OCCUPATION OF JAPAN Thirty page pamphlet. How combat Marines became occupation Marines	Shaw, H. HQMC	1970(IP)
VJ HUMOR Cartoons by Rhodes	Rhodes, Sgt F. *Leatherneck*	Nov 45
WHITE KING American Edward Zillig, 82-year-old former Marine, spent the War in a Jap prison	Voigt, PFC R. *Leatherneck*	Apr 46
WINGS OVER FUJIYAMA Marine Air over Japan's most famous landmark	*Gazette*	Mar 46

NORTH CHINA

AMBUSH IN CHINA OSS work with Chinese Communists in 1944	Mansfield, Capt W. *Gazette*	Mar 46
ARSENIC AND OLD CHINA China Marines produce a play	Ewing, P. *Leatherneck*	Mar 48
THE BATTLE OF THE JUNKS Marine Lt Pittman wins a naval battle in North China	Hicks, N., and B. Nalty *Leatherneck*	Nov 63
BUSHWACKERS Chinese Communists vs. USMC	*Time*	Mar 31, 1947
CHINA EXPEDITE MAG-15 takes supplies to Marines in China.	Polete, H. *Leatherneck*	Mar 47

CHINA INCIDENT Graveside ceremony honors Marines killed by Chinese	*Leatherneck*	Dec 46
CHINA POLICE Marines in North China	Polete, Sgt H. *Leatherneck*	Apr 47
CHOREMEN Marines in China hire houseboys to clean, cook, press uniforms.	Polete, Sgt H. *Leatherneck*	Mar 47
THE FIRST CONFRONTATION: U.S. MARINES IN NORTH CHINA, 1945-1947	Palmer, LtCol T. *Gazette*	Apr 70
FUEL FOR THE FIRES OF CHINA Marines guard the Peiping-Mukden Railroad	Moore, Cpl L. *Leatherneck*	Aug 46
HELL DRIVER Off-duty Marines build and race hot rods in China	*Leatherneck*	Aug 46
HOSPITALITY IN TIENTSIN These natives like Marines	*Leatherneck*	Dec 46
HOUSEKEEPERS IN CHINA Marines role in China	*Time*	Nov 19, 1945
HUBBA HUBBA FOR THE HEROES China Duty	Murphy, PFC J. *Leatherneck*	Mar 46
JACFU ON THE RAILROAD: MARINES ON DUTY IN CHINA On Peiping-Mukden line	*Time*	Jan 21, 1946
MARINE CHINESE How China Marines speak Chinese (they don't!)	Moore, Cpl. L. *Leatherneck*	May 47
MARINES IN CHINA	Hersey, J. *Life*	May 27, 1946
THE MARINES IN NORTH CHINA IN PICTURES Photos of the 3D Amphibious Corps, China	Official Photos, Hollywood	1946
MARINES' VITAL ROLE IN CHINA: BARRIER TO FULL SCALE WAR	*U. S. News*	Aug 23, 1946

MEET FOR THE CHINESE Marine track meet in Tientsin	West, PFC B. *Leatherneck*	Jan 47
MEALATHON IN TIENTSIN How Marines got used to Chinese food—(they didn't!)	Chapman, Sgt W. *Leatherneck*	Nov 46
MISSION IN TIENTSIN OSS work with Chinese	Kengla, LtCol W. *Gazette*	Oct 44
"NORTH CHINA MARINE" The old *North China Marine* newspaper is back after the War	Polete, Sgt H. *Leatherneck*	May 47
THE NORTH CHINA OPERATION Excellent 2-part summary	Churley, Maj R. *Gazette*	Oct, Nov 47
NORTH CHINA PATROL Search for Marines captured by Reds in July, 1946	Aplington, LtCol H. *Gazette*	Jun 49
OCCUPATION AT TSING TAO 6TH MAR DIV Occupation Duty	Shilin, Lt A. *Gazette*	Jan 46
ON THE PEIPING-MUKDEN LINE 7th Marines in N. China	Hittle, LtCol J. *Gazette*	Jun 47
RADIO CHINA AFRS (Armed Forces Radio Service) broadcasts	Schuon, Cpl K., and Lt R. Aurthur *Leatherneck*	Nov 46
REDS AND DEATH: RAID ON AMMUNITION DEPOT NEAR TANGKU, NORTH CHINA	*Newsweek*	Apr 14, 1947
$17,596 LIBERTY Leave in Peking with plenty of "funny money"	Harwell, Sgt E. *Leatherneck*	Jan 46
SHANGHAI REVIEWED Where to go and what to see	Johnston, Sgt L. *Leatherneck*	Aug 46
SHANGHAIED IN AN OXCART Seven Marines captured and released by Communists.	Schuon, K. *Leatherneck*	Jan 47
SIGNAL HILL A look at a fortified hill near Tsing Tao. Speculation on how well it was fortified	Evans, PFC H. *Leatherneck*	Apr 46

SITUATION IN NORTH CHINA	Klein, Capt E. *Gazette*	Apr 46
TARGET CEASE FIRE Marines objective in China is a Cease Fire	Moore, Cpl L. *Leatherneck*	Feb 47
TSING TAO OPERATING BASE FOR USMC Hdq for 6TH MAR DIV	*Gazette*	May 47
THE UNITED STATES MARINES IN NORTH CHINA: 1945-1949 Thirty-six pages of Marines vs. Communists	Shaw, H. HQMC	1968 (IP)
VISIT TO THE WALL Great Wall of China—off-duty visit center for Marines	Moore, Cpl L. *Leatherneck*	Oct 46
WAR WITHOUT HEADLINES It goes on in China	Martin, Lt H. *Gazette*	Nov 45

UNIFICATION

ALL FOR ONE Tales of unification of the armed forces	Lasswell, Sgt F. *Leatherneck*	Oct 45
ATTEMPT TO REDUCE MARINE CORPS: ARMY'S DESIRE FOR ITS FUNCTIONS	*U. S. News*	May 21, 1945
THE CASE AGAINST THE CRITICS Hooray for Agnes (. . . Agnes?)	Hirshinger, A. *Gazette*	Jul 46
COMPLETE TEXT OF STATEMENT IN DEFENSE DISPUTE The dispute is unification	Cates, Gen C. *U. S. News*	Oct 28, 1949
THE MARINE CORPS FIGHTS FOR ITS LIFE	Tregaskis, R. *Sat Eve Post*	Feb 20, 1949
MARINE CORPS FIGHTS FOR ITS LIFE	Cates, Gen C. *U. S. News*	Sep 15, 1950

THE MARINE CORPS—HERE TO STAY	Heinl, Col R. *Proceedings*	Oct 50
MARINES STILL HAVE THE SITUATION IN HAND You better believe it!	Bailey, G. *N.Y. Times Magazine*	Jan 16, 1949
NASTY WORDS But it's a nasty business	*Newsweek*	Jan 13, 1947
NEEDED: A MOBILE FORCE —like the USMC	Lawrence, D. *U. S. News*	Sep 15, 1950
RIDDLE OF COMBINED ARMS: 1949 Remarkably accurate forecast of "Limited Wars" to come—why unification won't work	Richards, G. *Proceedings*	Aug 49
THE RIGHT TO FIGHT Review of Postwar attempts to destroy the Corps	Heinl, Col R. *Proceedings*	Sep 62
SHALL WE ABOLISH THE MARINE CORPS? No, says a famous author	Huie, W. *American Mercury*	Sep 48
TELL IT TO THE MARINES Unification position of the Corps	*Newsweek*	May 15, 1947
VANDEGRIFT STATEMENT TO SENATE NAVAL AFFAIRS COMMITTEE, 6 MAY 1946 Against S. 2044 (Unification)	Vandegrift, Gen A. *Gazette*	Jun 46
WELL GUARDED HALLS OF MONTEZUMA Marine Corps has friends	*Nation*	Mar 2, 1946
WHEN CONGRESS CONSIDERED ABOLISHING THE MARINE CORPS	Hyman, H. *Gazette*	Apr 59

EVENTS/JAN 1946-JUN 1950

1946	ANNIVERSARY GREETINGS	Vandegrift, Gen A. *Gazette*	Nov 46

FIRST EXHIBIT CRUISE Floating Marine Corps War Museum	Johnston, Sgt L. *Leatherneck*	Nov 46	
MARINES IN FULL COLOR	Bailey, G. *N. Y. Times Magazine*	Mar 31, 1946	
THE NEW MARINE CORPS Peacetime returns to the USMC	Polete, Sgt H. *Leatherneck*	Nov 46	
OPERATION ALCATRAZ May 46 jail break foiled by Marines and others	Prosser, PFC R. *Leatherneck*	Aug 46	
RETRIBUTION AT WARD ROAD Jap War Crime Trials	Voigt, PFC R. *Leatherneck*	Aug 46	
SAILING OF THE TARAWA Carrier is launched	Tyler, Sgt R. *Leatherneck*	Jun 46	
SO LONG, SWEET SERGEANT WR's leave the Corps	Katz, Cpl K. *Leatherneck*	Apr 46	
VANDEGRIFTS MAKE AN OFFICIAL HOUSE A GRACIOUS HOME: RESIDENCE OF THE COMMANDANT OF THE MARINES	Hart, B. *American Home*	Aug 46	
ANNIVERSARY REVIEW Two years since V-J Day	Langille, Sgt V. *Leatherneck*	Sep 47	**1947**
A CHRONOLOGY OF THE UNITED STATES MARINE CORPS: VOLUME 3, 1947-1964 73-page paper bound pamphlet	Donnelly, R., G. Neufeld, and C. Tyson HQMC	1971 (IP)	
CRAIG OF THE MARINES "Stony" Craig retires. Drawn for *Leatherneck* by F. Rentfrow	*Leatherneck*	May 47	
FAREWELL TO CHARMS Women Marines are phased out	Hart, PFC H. *Leatherneck*	Jun 47	
ISLAND FIRE	*Leatherneck*	Jul 47	
LAST MISSION Marine war dead come home	Linn, Sgt S. *Leatherneck*	Oct 47	
THE LEAGUE'S 23RD Marine Corps League Convention	Allen, Sgt L. *Leatherneck*	Jan 47	

	LOST AND FOUND Butchie Bowers is lost near Barstow. Found by Marines	Riblett, L. *Leatherneck*	Nov 47
	LOWDOWN ON HIGHJUMP Navy and Marine Corps Polar expedition	Langille, Cpl V. *Leatherneck*	Aug 47
	MARINE CORPS ANNIVERSARY	*Army & Navy Register*	Oct 4, 1947
	MARINE CORPS ASSOCIATION —REVISED CONSTITUTION	*Gazette*	Jul 47
	MARINE CORPS MISSION	*Army & Navy Register*	Nov 8, 1947
	THE MARINE CORPS AND THE NATIONAL SECURITY ACT	*Gazette*	Oct 47
	MARINE CORPS: 1947	*Army & Navy Journal*	Jun 47
	MARINE WHO WENT BACK WW-2 battlefield visit	Martin, H. *Sat Eve Post*	Oct 4, 1947
	REMINISCING ON 30 History of *Leatherneck* on its 30th Birthday	Evans, Sgt E. *Leatherneck*	Nov 47
	THE 7TH COMES HOME 7th Marines return to San Diego	Allen, Sgt L. *Leatherneck*	Apr 47
	TOP O'THE CORPS Marine Memorial Club opens in San Francisco	Riblett, L., and Sgt E. Evans *Leatherneck*	Feb 47
1948	THE BAND CELEBRATES 159th anniversary	Evans, Sgt E. *Leatherneck*	Jul 48
	CONVENTION IN MIAMI Marine Corps League Convention	Linn, Sgt S. *Leatherneck*	Jan 48
	ENLISTED CLUB New one at Quantico	Roberts, Sgt N. *Leatherneck*	Aug 48
	4TH DIVISION REUNION	Mellerup, Sgt W. *Leatherneck*	Sep 48

FREEDOM TRAIN Historical exhibit is guarded by Marines	Linn, Sgt S. *Leatherneck*	Jan 48
LAST RITES FOR SOOCHOW POW dog of 4th Marines dies	Ogilvie, G. *Leatherneck*	Oct 48
THE MARINE CORPS IN 1948	Vandegrift, Gen A. *Proceedings*	Feb 48
MARINE MUSEUM It opens at Quantico	*Leatherneck*	Jul 48
MARINES PREPARED FOR PEACE Or War	Jenkins, L. *Scholastic*	Sep 18,1948
MEDITERRANEAN: NEW FOCUS FOR EAST-WEST SHOWDOWN Med Cruise Marines earn pay	*U.S. News*	Jan 16, 1948
MISSION TO RIO Big Mo goes to Rio. Seagoing Marines aboard	Waclawski, Sgt Z. *Leatherneck*	Jul 48
THE NEW COMMANDANT Gen Clifton B. Cates	Polete, Sgt H. *Leatherneck*	Mar 48
THE NEW COMMANDANT	*Gazette*	Jan 48
POLLYWOG TO SHELLBACK USS Missouri crosses the equator with Marines and H. S. Truman aboard	Edgemon, Cpl D. *Leatherneck*	Feb 48
WONDER BARR DE named after PFC Woodrow Wilson Barr—KIA Tulagi	Riblett, L., and K. Hubenthal *Leatherneck*	Jun 48

1949

ANNIVERSARY MESSAGE	Cates, Gen C. *Gazette*	Nov 49
CAPITOL CONCLAVE 4TH MAR DIV Reunion, D.C.	Polete, Sgt H. *Leatherneck*	Sep 49
INAUGURATION DAY Truman sworn in again.	*Leatherneck*	Apr 49
LEAGUE CONFAB Milwaukee Convention	Milhon, Cpl W. *Leatherneck*	Jan 49

	MCROA CONFERENCE IN CHICAGO	McCahill, Maj W. *Leatherneck*	May 49
	MASS ON A VOLCANO In Hawaii	Fisk, J. *Catholic World*	Jan 49
	MICOWE X '49 Amphibious expedition Alaska	Allen, Sgt L. *Leatherneck*	Jun 49
	OPERATION SNOW BOUND Alaska expedition	Sweetser, LtCol W. *Gazette*	May 49
	PUBLISHING THE GAZETTE	*Gazette*	Mar 49
	SOUTH FROM THE SPHINX African trip for three Marines	Houle, Sgt J. *Leatherneck*	Sep 49
	TASK GROUP 44.7 Part of Goodwill Tour to Africa	McDowell, Capt D. *Leatherneck*	May 49
JAN-JUN, 1950	LEAGUE LANDS IN MASS. Marine Corps League Convention	Milhon, Sgt W. *Leatherneck*	Jan 50
	MARINE CORPS HISTORY—REPORT TO THE STOCKHOLDERS How the Historical Branch works	Heinl, LtCol R. *Gazette*	Mar 50

AVIATION

GENERAL	AIRLIFT 1950-A Air in an amphibious assault	Burlage, TSgt G. *Leatherneck*	May 50
	AIR POWER AND AIR BASES Role of aviation	Sturges, BGen S., USA *Gazette*	Jun 49
	AIR TRANSPORTABILITY IN THE MARINE CORPS	Simpson, LtCol O. *Gazette*	Apr, May 49
	ALL-WEATHER FLIGHT	Long, Maj H. *Gazette*	May 50
	THE BLACK SHEEP WIN A NAVY "E"	Helms, Lt J. *Gazette*	Nov 48
	BREAKAWAY COCKPIT	*Gazette*	Apr 50
	DEMON 2 Role of Air in Demon 2	Allen, Sgt L. *Leatherneck*	Feb 49
	FLIGHT SCHOOL On the GI Bill	Allen, Sgt L. *Leatherneck*	May 48

GROUND CONTROL SQUADRON Marine Air Warning Squadron	Gardner, Maj S. *Leatherneck*	May 50
HOW TO BUILD AN AIRPLANE What's involved in building a new Marine Corps fighter	Simmons, Capt E. *Gazette*	Jan 49
INTELLIGENCE FROM THE SKIES	Burns, LtCol R. *Gazette*	Sep 48
JET INFORMATION PLEASE: A MILITARY DIGEST Includes jets on carriers	Brotherton, W. *Gazette*	Jun 47
JET SQUADRON First Jet Squadron in the Corps	Hicks, P. *Leatherneck*	Jan 49
LEATHERNECK AIR FORCE Its' mission and capabilities	Welch, W. *Flying*	Dec 49
LET'S REALLY USE MARINE PHOTOGRAPHY	McDermott, Maj J. *Gazette*	Nov 49
THE LITTLE AIR LIFT Training with Infantry units	Kaltenbeck, CWO R. *Gazette*	Aug 49
MAG-12 MAKES A LANDING	*Gazette*	Feb 49
THE MAG NEEDS REORGANIZING	Johnson, Maj J. *Gazette*	Nov 49
MARINE AVIATION FIRST JET FIGHTER SQUADRON	*Gazette*	Dec 47
MARINE COMBAT AIR OBSERVATION	Lubin, Capt D. *Gazette*	Jun 46
MATS MARINES USMC takes over Pacific when AF, Army, Navy busy in Berlin.	*Leatherneck*	May 50
MCATS Marine Corps Air Technical School, Quantico	Nehf, Maj A. *Gazette*	Feb 50
MR. FUZZY'S LAST CIVILIAN A Marine transport plane named Mr. Fuzzy tells its story	Morris, Sgt W. *Leatherneck*	Dec 48
NAVAL AVIATION IN 1947 Review with training and aircraft summary	*Gazette*	Dec 47

	PORTREX MARINES Marine pilots in training exercise at Vieques	Buttery, PFC G. *Leatherneck*	Jun 50
	RESUPPLY BY AIR	Goldberg, LtCol J. *Gazette*	Aug 49
	THEY TEST THE JETS	Pounds, Maj J. *Gazette*	Jun 48
AIRCRAFT	From the "New Developments" column of the *Gazette:*		
	AD-I SKYRAIDER		Apr 47
	CHANCE-VOUGHT XF 6U-I		Jan 47
	F4U-5: NEW VOUGHT "CORSAIR"		Sep 47
	NEW NAVY PLANES		Feb 48
	NORTH AMERICAN XFJ-I		Jan 47
	RYAN XF 2R-I		Mar 47
	SC-2, CURTISS "SEA-HAWK"		Sep 47
	SNJ "TEXAN"		Oct 47
	XF6UI CHANCE VOUGHT PIRATE		Feb 47
	XF-2 D-1 McDONNELL "BANSHEE"		Sep 47
COPTERS	ACHILLES HEEL OR WHIRLING DERVISH?	Rieder, Maj G. *Gazette*	Dec 47
	EMPLOYMENT OF THE SMALL HELICOPTER	Strieby, Capt R. *Gazette*	Jun 50
	FLYING EGGBEATERS First story on "choppers"	Gould, PFC M. *Leatherneck*	Oct 48
	THE HELICOPTER IN MARINE AVIATION Piasecki Helicopter	Morris, SSgt W. *Leatherneck*	Feb 50
	INDIVIDUAL HELICOPTER	*Gazette*	Jun 47
	THE MARINE CORPS AND THE HELICOPTER	Anderson, Lt R. *Gazette*	Aug 49
	MARINES SHOW HELICOPTER USES	Hotz, R. *Aviation Week*	Dec 27, 1948

THE MILITARY FUTURE OF THE HELICOPTER	Sikorsky, I. *Gazette*	Aug 49	
NAVY ADDS TRANSPORT HELICOPTER	*Army & Navy Journal*	Nov 8, 1947	
OPERATION CROSSROADS Is the copter here to stay?	Marcy, C. *American Helicopter*	Nov 46	
THE TRANSPORT HELICOPTER: NEW TOOL OF SEA POWER	Hittle, LtCol J. *Gazette*	Mar 50	
THE U.S. NAVY'S HELICOPTER PROGRAM	Bunkley, J. *American Helicopter*	Jun 48	
THE VERSATILE WINDMILLS	Cagle, LtCdr M., USN *Proceedings*	Jul 48	
XRP-1; LATEST IN HELICOPTERS	*Gazette*	Jul 47	

DUTIES

UNDER PRESSURE	Goss, Sgt F. *Leatherneck*	Mar 50	**BOMB DISPOSAL**
ROUND PEG, ROUND HOLE	Evans, Sgt E. *Leatherneck*	Dec 47	**CLASSIFI-CATION**
CORPS MOVIE MEN	Allen, Sgt L *Leatherneck*	Jan 49	**COMBAT CAMERAMEN**
COMMUNICATIONS—HOW?	Power, LtCol R. *Gazette*	Jan 49	**COMMUNI-CATIONS**
DO YOU WANT A SMALLER RADIO?	*Gazette*	Mar 49	
THE BAILEY BRIDGE Marine Engineers use it	Thierry, Capt J. *Gazette*	Jun 46	**ENGINEERS**
A HELLUVA ENGINEER	*Gazette*	Feb 49	
THE MARINES AND MILITARY BRIDGING	Mayo, Maj R. *Military Engineer*	Mar 47	
THE WATCH ON THE BRONX UN Guards are Marines	Polete, Sgt H. *Leatherneck*	Jul 46	**GUARD DUTY**

PART 4 | POSTWAR

HISTORIAN	COMBAT HISTORIANS? Who needs them? We do	Heinl, LtCol R. *Gazette*	Sep 47
	COMBAT REPORTS	Setzer, Lt C. *Gazette*	Aug 47
INTELLIGENCE	THE EYES HAVE IT	Kleber, Capt V. *Gazette*	Sep 49
	EYES IN THE NIGHT	Murray, Sgt B. *Gazette*	May 46
	INFORMATION INTO INTELLIGENCE	Whyte, Capt W. *Gazette*	Apr, May 46
MP	TOWN PATROL MP Duties	Allen, Sgt L. *Leatherneck*	Oct 49
NAVAL ATTACHE	MARINE OFFICER-NAVAL ATTACHE	*Gazette*	Oct 49
ORDNANCE	ORDNANCE COURSES AT QUANTICO	Thompson, Sgt J. *Leatherneck*	Mar 50
PUBINFO	THE MARINE CORPS FOURTH ESTATE	Pierce, LtCol P. *Gazette*	Sep 46
	REPORTERS FOR NEWSMEN Who to deal with in PIO work	Lewis, Lt C. *Gazette*	Mar 50
SCOUTS	AMPHIBIOUS SCOUTS AND RAIDERS	Williams, Col R. *Military Affairs*	Fall 49
SEAGOING	SEA SCHOOL AT SAN DIEGO	Allen, Sgt L. *Leatherneck*	Aug 48
	SPRINGBOARD TO THE SEA Enlisted Sea Duty	Milhon, Sgt W., and Sgt J. Thompson *Leatherneck*	Mar 50
	TURKISH DELIGHT Sea-going Marines on the Mighty Mo	Farrell, Cpl B. *Leatherneck*	Sep 46
SPECIAL SERVICES	SMALL DETACHMENTS' SPECIAL SERVICES	*Gazette*	Jun 49
	TROUBLE SHOOTERS Special Services helps the serviceman in trouble	Langille, Cpl V. *Leatherneck*	Jan 47

PIN STRIPE DETAIL	Morris, Sgt W. *Leatherneck*	Oct 49	**STATE DEPT DUTY**
WHY A TQM? Who needs the Transport Quartermaster? You do	Bradley, Maj Q. *Gazette*	Dec 47	**TQM**
THE WEATHER WAR Importance of weather in war	Edgemon, Cpl D. *Leatherneck*	Aug 47	**WEATHER**

FICTION

From *Leatherneck,* alphabetical by author:

Asprey, Capt Robert B.
MONSIEUR SAR-JENT — Mar 50
THE NATURAL TOUCH — Aug 49

Averill, Capt Gerold P.
ACCIDENTAL INTERMISSION — Feb 49
THE BUCK OF TONTOUTA — Jan 49

Barkey, Richard E.
PARTIAL PAYMENT — Mar 48

Carney, Otis
YESTERDAY'S HERO — 1960
Former Marine pilot has trouble adjusting to civilian life. A novel.

Christian, George
RESURRECTION — Dec 47

Church, Robert J.
THE DEVIL AND SPIKE DUDLEY — Apr 48
INSPECTION — Oct 47
A STRING OF PEARLS — Jul 47

Clark, Bob
UNEVENTFUL JOURNEY — Oct 47

Cohen, Lester
COMING HOME — *The Viking Press* 1945
Joe comes home from the Marines to fight corruption in Pittsburgh

Curtis, Sgt Paul
SWEEP AND SWAB — Jul 49

Decker, Sgt Duane	
EIGHTBALL BEHIND THE EIGHTBALL	Aug 47
A HERO FOR KITTY	Aug 46
HOME RUNS DON'T COUNT	Oct 46
De Grasse, J.	
THE WAILING WALL	Feb 49
Donahue, Sgt James A.	
THAT'S ALL, BROTHER	May 47
Farrell, Cpl Bill	
ILLS OF HOME	Aug 46
Finn, Sgt Mickey	
OVER THE FENCE	Apr 49
RESTRICTION	Dec 48
Gabbert, Lt Dean I.	
THE REAL McCOY	Jun 46
SLUG IT PAGE ONE	Apr 47
Gherkin, Gunther (Sgt Henry Felsen)	
CATASTROPHE IN OLD CATHAY	Aug 46
GUNTHER GOES TO A GIRLIE SHOW	Nov 46
GUNTHER RIDES ALONE	Feb 48
GUNTHER SHIPS OVER	Feb 47
IT SHOULDN'T HAPPEN TO A DI	Jun 47
Goldston, Allen M.	
THE MASCOT	Sep 49
Harris, James L., Jr.	
DUAL VIGIL	Nov 47
Helfer, Harold	
BULLY FOR PEEPSIGHT	Nov 47
PEEPSIGHT GOES TO COLLEGE	Jul 47
PEEPSIGHT MET RITA	Jun 47
Hicks, PFC Paul W., Jr.	
THE SHAKEDOWN	Oct 47
Hirschman, Harry	
KAMIKAZE	Sep 47
Jenkins, Leo W.	
GENERAL'S TRICK	Jun 49
Johnson, Ralph	
COURAGE COMES HARD	Oct 49

Owens, Lt Robert A.
SNOW ON THE ROOF — Dec 48

Phillips, Sgt James Atlee
SUCKER PUNCH — Apr 46

Riblett, Leonard
THE HUNCH — Apr 47

Richards, Guy
COFFEE TIME — Jul 48
NO SALE — Nov 47

Roberts, Sgt Nolle T.
THE WATCH — Jul 49

Rooks, Vernon D.
A SAMURAI SWORD — Aug 47

Russ, Martin
WAR MEMORIAL — Atheneum 1967
A terrible novel about an Indian Marine by the author of *The Last Parallel*

Sanders, Lawrence
A PROFESSIONAL SOLDIER — May 47
THE SHIP — Sep 47

Schuon, Karl
BLUE DANUBE — Jan 47
ESCAPE — Jul 47
GOODBYE — Dec 47
THE HEART RETURNED — Feb 47
MULLIGAN'S MATCH — Mar 48
ROOM 32 — Feb 48
SHADOW SILHOUETTE — Nov 46
A SON FOR CHRISTMAS EVE — Dec 46

Sheldon, Lt Allan
OUT OF THIS WORLD — Jun 46

Shilin, Alan
CALIBAN OF THE CORAL SEA — Feb 50
CROOKED FINGERS — Jul 46
GOLDEN BOY — Aug 48
PULL UP THE LADDER — Jun 50

Stamper, Capt W. J.
OLD SALT — Sep 47

Stewart, Ray T.
WITHOUT ORDERS — May 48

Stone, Harold E.
MIEKO'S LITTLE BROTHER — Jun 48

Tackett, Sgt James A.
FEAR IN MIEAZA — Dec 47

Wilson, Earl
A COFFIN FOR TWO — Oct 48

Winslow, Cdr W. G., USN
McGRUDER'S PIES — Jan 49

LEADERSHIP

From the *Gazette,* unless specified otherwise:

THE ABUSE OF HONOR — Sedgwick, PFC M.
Don't be an officer who abuses it — Mar 46

ARE YOU FIT? — Banks, LtCol C.
You lead from ahead — Apr 49

BASE PLATE McGURK, COMPANY OFFICER — McGurk, Baseplate (LtCol W. Jones)
Booklet — Marine Corps Ass'n, Quantico — 1948
(Series in the *Gazette:)*

Good NCO's Are Made, Not Born — Jan 47
Execs are Not Fifth Wheels — Feb 47
Let There Be Light — Apr 47
Appearances Are Deceiving — Jun 47
More on Leadership — Dec 47
Imagination Pays Off — Feb 48
The Defense Rests — Apr 48
Morale, Discipline and Leadership — May 48
Company Office Hours — Jun 48
Counsel on Defense — Aug 48
Esprit de Corps — Sep 48
Our Weapons Are Not One Way — Mar 49

CASUALTY ASSISTANCE CALLS — Klaus, PFC R.
"Corpsman!" — Aug 46

COMMAND TERMINOLOGY, MODERN TOWER OF BABEL — Coleman, Col W. — Feb 49
The language nobody knows

Title	Author	Date
THE CORNER STONE How British maintain discipline	Hargreaves, Maj R.	Oct 49
DISCIPLINE, DEMOCRACY, OR ANARCHY? Which way to go	Wade, Maj J.	Nov 48
DON'T BE A GOOD JOE You don't get paid to be popular	Crumb, MSgt C.	May 49
ESPRIT DE CORPS	Lee, MSgt R.	Jun 49
THE HUMAN FACTOR IN MODIFYING "THE WORD" It never comes out the same	MacNeil, LtCdr H., ChC, USN	Feb 49
KEEP IT CLEAN Be a good example	Aplington, LtCol H.	Apr 49
LEADERSHIP AND FEAR Psychology of combat leaders	Williams, LtCol R., USA	Aug 48
LEADERSHIP AND THE NEW MARINE CORPS You earn respect now	Holt, Sgt J.	Jun 49
LESS STAMMER AND MORE FINESSE Have more than the command presence of a popcorn bag	Blossy, Capt H.	Feb 49
MARINE OFFICER—DISCIPULO DE LENGUAJES Learn languages	Willock, LtCol R.	Jan 50
MUTUAL RESPONSIBILITIES OF THE COMMUNITY, THE ARMED FORCES AND THE SERVICEMAN, U.S. MARINE CORPS	Pollock, D. *Journal of Social Hygiene*	May 49
PANIC, DISCIPLINE AND TRAINING Analysis of panic in battle	Kintner, LtCol W., USA	Sep 47
A PROBLEM IN ORGANIZATION	Baze, Maj G.	Oct 48
PROFESSION OF ARMS	Carleton, Maj P.	May 48
PUBLIC RELATIONS FOR EVERY MARINE		Feb 49

REPLY TO SGT HOLT — Dye, Sgt L. — Aug 49

SPEAKING FOR MYSELF — Kuppenheimer, S. — Dec 49

THE THIN LINE OF TRADITION — Corbin, LtCol. J. — Jul 47, Apr 48
Pleading for a return of the old customs and language

THIN LINE OF TRADITION—III — Heinl, LtCol R. — Jul 49

WHY THE ACCENT ON YOUTH? — Hale, Maj L. — Jul 47
The value of older officers . . . (by an older officer)

WHAT MY GRAMMAR SCHOOL TAUGHT ME — Diehl, Lt E. — Apr 48
To think

LOGISTICS

CHOW

CHANGE IN CHOW — Hart, PFC H. — *Leatherneck* — May 48
Better rations in the new Corps

CHOW HOUNDS — Ruttle, L. — *Leatherneck* — Jan 50
In Heaven with the new chow

WHAT MAKES A MESS — Allen, Sgt L. — *Leatherneck* — Feb 49
Tender, loving care!

GEAR

CASE FOR BETTER GEAR — Carleton, Maj P. — *Gazette* — May 47
How to improve it

DESTINATION ARCTIC — Langille, Cpl V. — *Leatherneck* — Jan 47
Testing of equipment in the Arctic by Marines

EQUIPMENT BOARD — Roberts, Sgt N. — *Leatherneck* — May 48
How it tests gear

MARINE CORPS EQUIPMENT BOARD — Lewis, TSgt R. — *Leatherneck* — Apr 50
USMC "Bureau of Standards"

A "NEW LOOK" FOR INDIVIDUAL EQUIPMENT — Schwaneke, Lt C. — *Gazette* — Dec 48, Jan, Feb 49
A pilot redesigns infantry gear after he serves a tour with the ground-pounders

	"NEW LOOK" WITHOUT EQUIPMENT	Donovan, Maj J. *Gazette*	Apr 49
VEHICLES	AMTRAC REPAIR STATION How to create and man one	Kirkner, PFC P., and Sgt G. Loper *Gazette*	May 48
	THE ARCTIC WEASEL	Ashman, PFC L. *Gazette*	May 49
	THE ARMY AND THE LVT (A)	Collier, LtCol J., USA *Gazette*	Jul 49
	FLEETER MARINE FORCE New landing craft	Evans, Sgt E. *Leatherneck*	Nov 47
	HOW WELL DO YOU KNOW YOUR LANDING CRAFT?	*Gazette*	Mar 48
	THE NEAR FUTURE OF THE LVT	Croizat, Maj V. *Gazette*	Jun 48
	NEW JOBS FOR JEEPS The Jeep's postwar role.	*Leatherneck*	Jul 46
	THE ROLE OF THE LVT (A)	Croizat, Maj V. *Gazette*	Jun 49
	SEAGOING JEEPS	*Gazette*	Jan 47
	SEA-GOING TRUCK Let's build one	Tuban, Capt M. *Gazette*	Oct 46
	THE WEASEL AND ASSAULT SUPPLY	Asprey, Lt R. *Gazette*	Apr 48
	WHY NOT DUKW'S?	Hudson, LtCol L. *Gazette*	Mar 48

MARINES

From the *Know Your Leaders* Series and other articles in *Leatherneck,* alphabetical by the last name of the Marine:

Adams, Hank
- HANK ADAMS CHANGES BEATS — Phillips, Sgt J.
  - California Sheriff back from 1ST MAR DIV — Oct 46

Crosby, Bob
- BACK TO THE BOBCATS — Jolokai, Sgt J.
  - Bing's little brother returns from 5TH MAR DIV — Jul 46

Bailey, Bob
DISC RECRUITER — Allen, Sgt L.
About a Marine Recruiting DJ — Apr 48

Barrett, GySgt Miles T.
HONORABLE DESERTION — Evans, Sgt E.
Deserted from Quantico to get overseas and rejoined in France in World War I — Aug 48

Capodice, SSgt Salvatore A.
PAPPY CAPPY
Marine in World War I loses a leg, enlists again in World War 2 — Feb 48

Carey, MacDonald
MacDONALD CAREY — Riblett, PFC L.
The Soap Opera King was a Marine — May 47

Clement, MajGen Wm T. — Morris, Sgt W.
Jan 49

Deakins, MSgt Hugh F.
40 YEAR MAN — Milhon, Cpl W.
Retirement biography of Deakins — Jan 49

Deeg, Norm
COUNTRY COPPER — Ludwig, V.
Marine POW returns to be sheriff of LaPorte, Indiana — Dec 47

Duncan, David Douglas
LEGENDARY LENSMAN — DeChant, J.
Famous cameraman Marine — Dec 46

Eddy, Col Robert P.
THE INTERNATIONAL EDDY — Allen, Sgt L.
Assistant to Gen Marshall — May 47

Enos, Sgt Tommy
NOTE ON REED — Schuon, K.
Former Sgt Tommy Enos (Now Reed). Band Leader in New Jersey — Aug 47

Erskine, MajGen Graves B. — Hicks, Cpl P.
Nov 48

Fields, Lt Jerry
HORSE OF ANOTHER COLOR — Burns, PFC M.
About FO with Third Corps Artillery — Jan 46

Frye, Kaye
MISS INFORMATION — Riblett, PFC L.
WR on duty at HQMC — May 46

Greenway, Lee
MAKE-UP MARINE — Riblett, PFC L.
Hollywood make-up man is former Marine — Jun 46

Hackett, Bill
THE BUTLER AND HIS MAID — Schuon, K.
Former Marine and his wife become domestics to beat the housing shortage — Jun 47

Hanneken, Herman
BANDIT'S NEMESIS — Hicks, Cpl P.
Retirement biography of the Marine who got the Medal of Honor for killing Charlemagne in Haiti — Oct 48

Harpold, Sgt William Cody
THE REVEREND SERGEANT — McDevitt, Sgt H.
He is a minister in Oxon Hills, Md. — Nov 46

Harris, MajGen Fielding — Evans, Sgt E. — Feb 49

Hart, MajGen Franklin A. — Hicks, Cpl P. — Dec 48

Hermle, MajGen Leo D. — Polete, Sgt H. — Apr 49

Hill, MajGen Wm. P. T. — Goss, Sgt F. — Aug 49

Hoffman, Capt Carl
THE TRUMPETER — Klaus, PFC R.
One of the great jazz trumpeters is a Marine — Aug 46

Howard, MajGen Samuel L. — Goss, Sgt F. — Jun 49

Hunt, LtGen LeRoy Phillip — Thompson, Cpl J. — Oct 49

Hurlbut, Jim
HOT OFF THE WIRE — Katz, Cpl K.
What the first Combat Correspondent on Guadalcanal is doing (News Service in Chicago) — Jul 46

Hyde, Cpl Durwood
SACKRAT SERENADE — Fink, Sgt S.
The famous DJ of Guam — Jan 46

SILENT SACKRAT — Simmons, J.
Guam DJ Hyde again — May 49

Jiggs 4
JIGGS 4 — Klaus, PFC R.
Mascot of the Corps—a Bulldog — Jul 46

Keet, Frank
WAR WAIF — Sep 46
Frank Keet, Orphan

Kidder, PFC William S.
MILLION DOLLAR KIDDER — Farrell, Cpl B.
A PFC almost inherits $1,000,000 (but not quite) — Aug 46

Lees, Paul
PROPOSITION FOR PRESS AGENTS — Allen, Sgt L.
Marine hero blinded in action in movies — Oct 47

Lily, Pete
THE SADDLE SERGEANT — Phillips, Sgt J.
Cowboy returns to Texas from 1ST MAR DIV — Mar 46

McLaughlin, PFC George
BLIND DATE IN JERSEY — Phillips, Sgt J.
Marine blinded in the Pacific marries nurse — Jan 46

Nagazyna, MSgt John J.
OLD NAGY — Allen, Sgt L., and Cpl P. Hicks
Retirement biography — Dec 48

Newcomb, WO Obie
TELEPHONE WEDDING — Woodside, Sgt B.
Freaky telephone wedding—Pearl to San Diego — Dec 46

Noble, MajGen Alfred H. — Polete, Sgt H.
May 49

Pollack, PFC Jim
A MARINE COMES HOME — Phillips, Sgt J.
What former Marine sees when he returns to Tulsa — Feb 46

Rangston, William
PHANTOM MARINE — Phillips, Sgt J.
Impersonation of Arkansas Marine KIA Iwo — May 46

Roach, Lavern
THE NEW FIGHTING MARINE — Gartz, Sgt S.
Middle weight contender is a former Marine — Apr 48

Robertson, Jim
TEXAS JIM — Milhon, Cpl W.
Popular hillbilly singer is a former Marine — Feb 50

Rockey, LtGen Keller E. — Oct 48

Ross, Sgt Austin "Derby"
PROFILE OF SGT AUSTIN "DERBY" ROSS
About horse racing Marine — Tallent, SSgt R. May 50

Sanderson, BGen Lawson McPherson
SANDERSON SAGA — Morris, Sgt W.
Biog of the inventor of dive bombing — Dec 49

Schilt, BGen Christian F.
JET GENERAL — Morris, Sgt W.
Medal of Honor winner Schilt has come a long way from Nicaragua — Jul 49

Shepherd, MajGen Lemuel C., Jr. — Hicks, Cpl P. Mar 49

Silverthorn, MajGen Merwin H. — Thompson, Cpl J. Nov 49

Skoltz, MSgt Sam
PROFILE OF MSGT SAM SKOLTZ — Lewis, TSgt R. Apr 50

Smith, MajGen Oliver P. — Polete, Sgt H. Jun 49

Swanson, LtCol Emmett O.
DEAD-EYE DOC — Feb 50
Twice World champion marksman is practicing dentist

Temple, George
MASTER OF MAYHEM — Riblett, L.
Shirley's brother, former Marine, now pro wrestler — Apr 47

Van Brunt, Lt Tad
RETURN OF THE TAISHO — Allen, Sgt L.
Fiction. He played a general while questioning prisoners on Okinawa. Now goes to Hollywood — Feb 48

Walker, MajGen John T. — Thompson, Sgt J. Dec 49

Wallace, MajGen Wm. J. — Thompson, Cpl J. Sep 49

Watson, LtGen Thomas Eugene — Sep 48

Woods, MajGen Louis F. — Polete, Sgt H. Jan 49

MARINES RETURN

From *Leatherneck,* unless indicated otherwise:

THE COUNTRY'S OPPORTUNITIES — Hoover, J.
How to solve the returning vet problem by the FBI Chief — Jan 46

THE GENERAL'S JOB AND READJUSTMENT — Miller, PFC H. — Jun 46
MajGen Graves B. Erskine heads Retraining and Reemployment

"H" DAY ON THE HOME FRONT — Prosser, PFC B.
Vets look for homes at home — May 46

HOBBY SHOW — Hicks, Cpl P.
American Handicrafts— Company founded by Marines — May 48

HONORABLE DISCHARGE: UPON 21 SURVIVORS OF COMPANY "K", U.S. MARINES, IT BESTOWED 21 VETERANS' PROBLEMS — Hunt, G. — *Fortune* — Sep 47
Peleliu heroes of "K" Co., 3/1.

THE HOT AIR CORPS — Johnston, Sgt L.
War stories are mostly hot air — Oct 46

Title	Author	Date
MANHATTAN GODFATHERS Disabled Marines entertained	Schuon, K.	Jul 47
MURDEROUS MEMENTOS War souvenirs		Mar 46
NORTHWARD, HO! Former Marines like Alaska.	Hicks, PFC P., and A. Mielke	Jul 47
OPERATION MOP-UP Former Marines start business	Gould, PFC M.	Jan 48
RECRUITS FOR RECONVERSION Returning Marines train.	Looman, Sgt R.	Dec 45
RIGHT DRESS U. of Maryland's G.I. students are former Marines	Katz, Cpl K.	Sep 46
THEY'LL DRIVE AGAIN Marine amputees get cars	Katz, Cpl K.	Sep 46
TO THE HALLS OF LEARNING GI Bill; How Marines use it	Farrell, Cpl B.	Jul 46
WAR GOES ON Souvenir guns keep killing	Mann, E.	Oct 48
VETERANS' FRATERNITIES Marine Corps League, Amvets, American Legion, etc.	Allen, Sgt L.	Oct 46

OFF-DUTY

From *Leatherneck:*

Title	Author	Date
AFTERNOON IN THE PHILLIPINES A day off in Manila	Polete, Sgt H.	Jun 47
ANGEL IN THE WARDS Entertaining sick Marines	Milhon, Sgt W.	Jun 49
ANGELS FAIRY TALE Marines search for lost gold off Venezuela	Dieffenbach, K.	Mar 49
BARRELHOUSE IN THE BARRACKS USMC Swing Band led by Cpl Dave Robbins	Klaus, PFC R.	Apr 46

HAMS CAN BE HEROES — Allen, Sgt L.
Radio amateurs become pros — Jul 48

HERE'S HOPE AGAIN — Allen, Sgt L.
Bob Hope, the legend — Jun 47

KODIAK LIBERTY — Massie, LtCol H.
Shooting bear with an M-I — Dec 47

MARINES ON THE AIR — Allen, Sgt L.
Marine Radio Show — Sep 47

MR. WAIKIKI — Sep 48
Marines in weight lifting contest in Hawaii

OPERATION SNOW JOB — Lewis, Lt C.
Marine NCO's Chapter of Toastmasters, Int'l at El Toro — Apr 50

PACIFIC LIBERTY — Dowd, Sgt M.
Marines all over the Far East — Dec 48

PROGRAM FOR HOBBYISTS — Gould, PFC M.
Hobby Shops on bases — May 48

STAND BY FOR MUSIC! — Voigt, PFC R.
Special Services Shows — Aug 46

TIME OF THEIR LIVES — Rosenburg, J.
Marines act at Memorial Theater in San Fran — Nov 48

TRAVELOGUE IN HAWAII — Kutz, Sgt G. — Sep 46

PERSONNEL

From the *Gazette,* unless otherwise indicated:

ADMINISTRATION

AN ADMINISTRATIVE ILLITERATE PROTESTS — Case, Capt J. — Oct 48

BON VOYAGE — Jun 50
Upon retirement

THE BOTTOM OF THE BARREL — McGlashan, LtCol R.
Personnel that don't belong cause problems — Jul 49

CAREER MANAGEMENT FOR ENLISTED MARINES — Godbold, LtCol B., and Maj H. Uphoff — Jan, Feb 49

Title	Author	Date
THE COMPANY PROPERTY BOOK	Shea, Lt W.	Feb 48
COMPETITIVE PROMOTIONS	Banks, LtCol C., and MSgt L. Donahue	Jun 48
CORPS CLASSIFICATION POLICY REVISED	Thurston, Sgt J. *Leatherneck*	Aug 49
THE EFFECTIVE OFFICER	Jenkins, Capt L.	Sep 49
EXHUME THE GUNNERY SERGEANT We officers need him!	Heinl, LtCol R.	Jun 49
FITNESS REPORTS FROM DOWN UNDER Let juniors grade seniors	Vogel, B.	Oct 48
THE GI BILL AND THE REGULAR	McCahill, Maj W.	Feb 48
THE MARINE CORPS' POSITION You had better listen up!		Dec 49
NEW DEAL FOR RATINGS New rank structure and chevrons to match	Evans, Sgt E. *Leatherneck*	Dec 46
THE NEW SERVICE RECORD BOOK The SRB retires after 31 years.	Reardon, Capt J., and P. Pierce	May 48
ORIGIN OF THE NEW PERSONNEL SYSTEM It goes back—way back	Godbold, LtCol B.	Nov 49
PROMOTION EXAMINATIONS	Hayward, LtCol R.	Mar 49
PROPOSED: A NEW TRAINING RECORD CARD	Drake, LtCol E.	Jan 49
REPORT ON FITNESS REPORTS They need help!	Drake, LtCol E.	May 47
RESPECTFULLY SUBMITTED How to write reports	Willock, LtCol R.	Mar 50

RISING TIDE OF ADMINISTRATION It will engulf us all.	Heinl, Maj R.	Jan 48
THE ROAD TO A COMMISSION	*Leatherneck*	Aug 47
SPECIALIST'S TRAINING RECORDS The way to keep them special.	Blyth, Lt C.	Apr 50
TOP GOES OUT ON THIRTY The Top retires	Zimmerman, Capt J.	Jan 48
TOWARD A BETTER UNDERSTANDING That's what reports are for.	Wilbern, Maj J.	Jun 49
WHAT KIND OF FITNESS REPORTS DO WE WANT? How about good ones?	Baze, Maj G.	Apr 48

LEGAL

BEYOND THE COURTS MARTIAL Portsmouth Prison is what's beyond, if you're guilty	Katz, Sgt K.	Nov 46
LEGAL INSANITY	Wilbern, Maj J.	Sep 49
THE MILITARY INVESTIGATOR What he does under UCMJ	Checklou, Lt H.	Nov 49
A NEW COURSE THROUGH ROCKS AND SHOALS New UCMJ	Riblett, Cpl L. *Leatherneck*	Nov 46

POSTS/PLACES

From the "Post of the Corps" series in *Leatherneck*, unless otherwise specified:

BARSTOW Camp Big Bear		Jul 47
BERMUDA	Hicks, PFC P.	Nov 47
BREMERTON	Allen, Sgt L.	Apr 49
BROOKLYN NAVY YARD	Evans, Sgt E.	Aug 49

CAMP LEJEUNE

CAMP LEJEUNE, N.C.		Sep 48
WINDOWS OF THE MARINES		Aug 48

PART 4 | POSTWAR

	CAMP MATTHEWS	Allen, Sgt L.	Mar 49
CAMP PENDLETON	CAMP PENDLETON	Allen, Sgt L.	Oct 48
	COMBAT CAMP Training in Pendleton boondocks	Phillips, Sgt J.	Nov 46
	PENDLETON ROUND-UP	Allen, Sgt L .	Dec 48
	ROUND-UP	Goss, Sgt F.	Dec 49
	CAMP TARAWA POSTWAR Kamuela, Hawaii is deserted now	Beech, K.	Jul 46
	CHARLESTON	Katz, Sgt K.	Sep 47
	CHERRY POINT	Johnston, Sgt L.	Jun 47
	CUBA	Hicks, Cpl P.	Jun 48
	EL TORO	Phillips, Sgt J.	Feb 47
	FORT MIFFLIN	Evans, Sgt E.	May 49
	GREAT LAKES	Evans, Sgt E.	Nov 48
GUAM	BEETLE-BAUM FOR GUAM Snails race on Guam	Milhon, Cpl W.	Dec 48
	TIMES SQUARE OF THE PACIFIC Comment made about Guam by Secretary of Navy Forrestal	Fink, Sgt S.	Mar 46
	KEYPORT, WASHINGTON		May 48
	KODIAK	Allen, Sgt L.	Sep 49
	KWAJALEIN	Polete, Sgt H.	Oct 47
	LITTLE CREEK	Polete, Sgt H.	Feb 49
	MANILA		Mar 48
	MARE ISLAND	Allen, Sgt L.	Mar 48
	NEWFOUNDLAND	Johnston, Sgt L.	Jan 48
	NEW LONDON	Katz, Sgt K.	Apr 47
	NEW RIVER Tent Camp revisited	Miller, PFC H.	May 46
	PANAMA	Hicks, Cpl P.	Aug 48

PEARL HARBOR In 1947	Polete, Sgt H.	Feb 47	
PENSACOLA	Hart, H.	Nov 49	
PHILADELPHIA Depot of Supplies	Polete, Sgt H.	Apr 50	
PUERTO RICO	Hicks, Sgt P.	Jan 49	
FOREST FIRE DEPARTMENT At Marine Corps Schools	Miller, PFC H.	Jul 46	QUANTICO
QUANTICO	Polete, Sgt H.	Jul 48	
ROME, ITALY	Belk, Lt R.	Oct 49	
SAIPAN	Polete, Sgt H.	Feb 48	
NAVAL AIR STATION, SAN DIEGO	Burlage, TSgt G.	May 50	SAN DIEGO
SAN DIEGO	Allen, Sgt L.	May 47	
SAND POINT		Dec 47	SEATTLE
SEATTLE		Dec 48	
SUBIC BAY, PHILLIPINES Marines at Navy Base		Dec 47	
SUN VALLEY Rehab Center for combat-weary Marines	Voigt, R.	Apr 46	
TLYAUTEY, MOROCCO	Burlage, Sgt G.	Jan 50	
TRINIDAD	Hicks, Sgt P.	Apr 48	
VIEQUES Naval Ammo Depot, Puerto Rico	Smith, Sgt J.	Jun 49	
WASHINGTON, D.C. Marine Barracks, Naval Gun Factory	Lewis, Sgt R.	Dec 49	
YOKOSUKA	Polete, Sgt H.	Aug 47	
YORKTOWN Marine Barracks, Naval Mine Depot	Thompson, Sgt J.	Jun 50	

RECRUITING

HERE'S YOUR RECRUIT	Kessler, LtCol W.	Nov 48
MARINES ARE BORN A New York kid honorary member of the Corps	Hicks, PFC P. *Leatherneck*	Apr 47
POSTWAR RECRUITING It's harder than War recruiting	Finucane, Capt F.	Mar 46
RECRUITING—FIRST SERVICE OF THE CORPS Division of Recruiting	Nicholson, Capt D.	Dec 47
SKY HOOKS Marine recruiter Maj A. H. Neff.	*Leatherneck*	Oct 46
SUPERSALESMEN Recruiters are super salesmen	Hart, Cpl H. *Leatherneck*	Nov 47

RESERVE

GENERAL

ESPRIT DE CAMP Reserves get it	Evans, Sgt E. *Leatherneck*	Oct 47
THE I&I MEETS THE CO HALFWAY	Van Stockum, LtCol R. *Gazette*	Sep 49
MAKING OF MORALE (USMCR)	Meyers, Capt L. *Gazette*	Jan 49
MARTCOM AT THE POINT Reserve field training	Morris, Sgt W. *Leatherneck*	Oct 49
THE MCROA CHARTS ITS COURSE	McCahill, Maj W. *Gazette*	Apr 49
MECHANIZED MINUTEMEN Reserve armored units	Allen, Sgt L. *Leatherneck*	Jul 47
THE NEW MARINE CORPS RESERVE	*Gazette*	Mar 47
ORGANIZED RESERVE DUTY IS NO FROLIC	Fleps, LtCol C. *Gazette*	Oct 48
PEACETIME RESERVISTS Mission of USMCR	*Gazette*	Mar 46

THE PEACETIME USMCR	Mielke, A. *Leatherneck*	Nov 46	
RESERVE POWER	Evans, Sgt E. *Leatherneck*	Oct 47	
RESERVE RALLY Philadelphia rally kicks off first Marine Reserve Week	Hicks, Cpl P. *Leatherneck*	Apr 48	
THE RESERVES ARE READY	Polete, Sgt H. *Leatherneck*	Nov 48	
TRAINING OUR NEW RESERVE	Rose, Capt A. *Gazette*	Jan 46	
THE VRO'S GO ON SC-99	*Gazette*	Aug 49	
WHAT ABOUT THE RESERVE OFFICERS?	Lewis Lt C *Gazette*	May 49	
MARINE AIR RESERVE Where we stood then	Thomason, J. *Flying*	Jan 47	**AIR**
THE RESERVES FLY HIGH	Simmons, Capt E. *Gazette*	Sep 48	

From the "With the Reserves" series in the *Gazette:*

Title	Date
FIGHTER SQUADRON 121 NAS Glenview, Illinois	Jul 47
FIGHTER SQUADRON 132 New York	Jun 47
FIGHTER SQUADRON 141 Livermore, California	Aug 47
FIGHTER SQUADRON 215 Olathe, Kansas	Jul 47
FIGHTER SQUADRON 244 Columbus, Ohio	Jun 47
FIGHTER SQUADRON 321 NAS Anacostia, Washington	Aug 47

RESERVE UNITS

11TH ENGINEER BATTALION	*Gazette*	Jul 47	**BALTIMORE**
2D INFANTRY BATTALION	*Gazette*	Jun 47	**BOSTON**

CHARLOTTESVILLE, VA.	EASY COMPANY	Polete, Sgt H. *Leatherneck*	Jul 49
DETROIT	17TH INFANTRY BATTALION	*Gazette*	Jun 47
KANSAS CITY	KANSAS CITY CANNONEERS Summer Training	Polete, Sgt H. *Leatherneck*	Sep 49
PHILADELPHIA	6TH INFANTRY BN	*Gazette*	Jul 47
SAN DIEGO	11TH TANK BATTALION San Diego's Reserves	Allen, Sgt L. *Leatherneck*	Jul 48
	IN RESERVE 11th Tank Battalion	Burlage, TSgt G. *Leatherneck*	Apr 50
SHELBYVILLE, MONTANA	SHELBY'S RESERVES	Goss, TSgt F. *Leatherneck*	Aug 49
TEXARKANA, TEXAS	2D 105MM HOWITZER BN.	*Gazette*	Jun 47
WASHINGTON, D. C.	RESERVES WON'T SINK 1st Infantry Bn. First reserves to include combat swim	Goss, TSgt F. *Leatherneck*	Sep 49
	5TH INFANTRY BATTALION	*Gazette*	Aug 47
	MEDAL DAY 5th Marine Reserve Battalion honored with medals	Polete, Sgt H. *Leatherneck*	Oct 47

SPORTS

GENERAL

All articles in this section are from *Leatherneck:*

AND SO THEY GO Corps' athletes retire	McHenry, Col G.	Sep 49
THE CHISOX LYONIZED Former Marine Ted Lyons manages the Chicago White Sox	Mielke, A.	Aug 46
COLLEGE FOR COACHES At Pendleton	Varlie, MSgt H.	Nov 49
DERBY DATE "Marine Victory" in Derby—Owned by former Marine	Farrell, Cpl B.	Apr 46
IN DEFENSE OF THE JOCKEY *All* sports are competitive	Donahoe, Capt J. *Gazette*	Aug 49

Title	Author	Date
THE FABULOUS FULKS Pro basketball player Joe Fulks, former Marine	Mielke, A.	Aug 47
LEATHERNECK SPORTS Joe Muha, VMI All-American	Harwell, Sgt E.	Mar 46
NEW ACCENT ON SPORTS In the Corps, sports replaces combat	Gartz, Sgt S., and E. Evans	Aug 47
NO. I FAN It's a Marine Master Sergeant	Gartz, Sgt S.	May 49
SCOREBOARD FOR '48 Review of Marine Corps sports	Gartz, Sgt S.	Jan 49
SPORTS ASSORTMENT Marine Corps sports programs	Allen, Sgt L.	Jun 47

BASEBALL

Title	Author	Date
MID-SEASON FORECAST Marine Baseball Teams	Gartz, Sgt S.	Aug 48
ALL-NAVY WORLD SERIES Quantico Marines win	Gartz, Sgt S.	Dec 48
QUANTICO WIND-UP Quantico wins all-Navy	Gartz, Sgt S.	Jan 48
BASEBALL PROSPECTS . . . '49 Outlook for all Marine "nines"	Gartz, Sgt S.	May 49
ROOT THE MAN HOME Marine baseball in Caribbean	Burks, A.	May 49
DIAMOND MASTER Baseball Coach, Quantico	Tallent, SSgt R.	Apr 50

BASKETBALL

Title	Author	Date
CAGE CONSENSUS Basketball season coming up	Gartz, Sgt S.	Mar 48
'48 CAGE FINALS Quantico wins the All-Navy	Gartz, Sgt S.	Jul 48
FIRE HOUSE BASKETBALL 1st Brigade wins Guam title	Gartz, Sgt S.	Apr 49
ALL-NAVY BASKETBALL Marines lose	Tallent, Sgt R.	Dec 49
AT HALF TIME Standing of all Marine teams	Gartz, Sgt S.	Feb 49

	BACK BOARD BULLETIN Marines vie for Navy titles	Tallent, Sgt R.	Jan 50
BOWLING	SET 'EM UP USMC bowling, Quantico	Curtis, SSgt P.	May 50
BOXING	ALL-NAVY BOXING MATCHES Marines role	Gartz, Sgt S.	Aug 48
	ALL-NAVY BOXING '49 Marines win three titles	Gartz, Sgt S.	Aug 49
	BENEFIT BOUTS Marines help Youth Welfare	Gartz, Sgt S.	Apr 49
FOOTBALL	FOOTBALL FOR FUN Touch football	Gartz, Sgt S.	Nov 47
	LEATHERNECK'S 1947 ALL-MARINE FOOTBALL TEAM	Gartz, Sgt S., and L. Allen	Mar 48
	SEVEN ELEVENS Marine football forecast	Gartz, Sgt S.	Oct 48
	LEATHERNECK'S 1948 ALL-MARINE FOOTBALL TEAM	Gartz, Sgt S., and L. Allen	Feb 49
	FOOTBALL FINALS Quantico Marines beat Navy	Gartz, Sgt S.	Mar 49
	FOOTBALL OUTLOOK	Gartz, Sgt S.	Oct 49
	FORGOTTEN FOOTBALLERS Tsing Tao's 1st Marines' team	Gartz, Sgt S.	Apr 49
	PRESS PROMOTERS Marine football at Quantico	Tallent, SSgt R.	Mar 50
GOLF	ALL NAVY GOLF Marines take 4th Place	Borgstede, Sgt A.	Nov 49
	INAUGURATION FOR SPORTS Golf and Tennis Meet	Mielke, A.	Dec 46
SWIMMNG	TANKERS Marine swimmers	Gartz, Sgt S.	Nov 48
TRACK	THE FIRST MEET At Quantico	Gartz, Sgt S.	Nov 48
	CINDER PATH PREDICTIONS Quantico Track and Field Meet	Gartz, Sgt S.	Jun 49

CINDER PATH RESULTS — Gartz, Sgt S.
Track and field meets — Aug 49

WRESTLING

ALL-NAVY MAT MAULERS — Gartz, Sgt S.
Marine wrestling champs — Jun 48

ALL-NAVY WRESTLING — Nierenberg, Sgt E.
Marines win three titles — Jun 49

ALL-NAVY WRESTLING — Tallent, SSgt R.
Includes Marines — Jun 50

SUPPORTING ARMS

From the *Gazette,* unless indicated otherwise:

COORDINATION

COORDINATION OF SUPPORTING ARMS — Oct 46

FIRE SUPPORT COORDINATION IN BASE DEFENSE — Wade, Maj J. — Jul 49

FSCC—ANOTHER EMPIRE? — Reichner, Maj H.
Reduce the Fire Support Coordination Center — Jun 50

GREATER COORDINATION OF SUPPORTING FIRES — Greene, Capt T. — Apr 47
How to do it

ARTILLERY

AMPHIBIOUS ARTILLERY — Rowse, Maj E.
Field Artillery Journal — Mar, Apr 48

AMPHIBIOUS ASSAULT ARTILLERY — Rowse, Maj E. — Dec 48

ARTILLERY ASSAULT FIRE — Feb 47

ARTILLERY PLOTTING BOARD — Jan 47

ARTILLERY REPORT — Evans, Sgt E.
What's new — *Leatherneck* — Feb 49

GOODBYE "LITTLE DYNAMITE" — Hiatt, LtCol R.
Farewell to the "75" — Aug 49

"LITTLE DYNAMITE" — Greene, Capt T. — Mar 49

	THE VT FUSE VS AMPHIBIOUS OPERATIONS It's lucky Japs didn't have it!	Henderson, LtCol F.	May 47
CLOSE AIR SUPPORT	AIR SUPPORT TECHNIQUES World War 2 experiences	McCutcheon, LtCol K.	Apr 46
	CONTROL OF SUPPORTING AIRCRAFT The big question again—how to do it	Megee, BGen V.	Jan 48
	A JOB FOR DIVE AND TORPEDO BOMBER PILOTS Close Air Support	Carr, Capt R.	Sep 49
	MARINE-AIR INFANTRY SCHOOL Close Air Support learning	Ray, Capt J.	Mar 46
	MARINE CORPS AVIATION—AN INFANTRY MAN'S OPINION Mostly about Close Air Support	Rentz, Maj J. *Proceedings*	Nov 49
NAVAL GUNFIRE	CAN NAVAL GUNFIRE BE IMPROVED? Yes, says Parry	Parry, Maj F.	Nov 48
	THE FUTURE OF THE ROCKET IN NAVAL WARFARE Advocating the use of rockets on battleships	Martin, P. *Proceedings*	Aug 45
	GUNFIRE SUPPORT LESSONS LEARNED IN WORLD WAR 2 And learned the hard way!	McMillian, Capt I. USN *Proceedings*	Aug 48
	MAKING THE MOST OF NAVAL GUNFIRE Examples of how cooperation and ingenuity between land and sea forces keynotes effective support fire	McLaurin, Lt J.	Feb 47
	NAVAL GUNFIRE AIR SPOTTER The job	Van Orman, LtCol E.	Aug 47
	NAVAL GUNFIRE: SCOURGE OF THE BEACHES Development, techniques, and doctrines of NGS	Heinl, Col R. *Proceedings*	Nov 45

NAVAL GUNFIRE SUPPORT — Roberty, Maj F., USA
Broad concept of NGS — *Field Artillery Journal* Mar, Apr 49

NAVAL GUNFIRE SUPPORT: A NEW STAFF FUNCTION — Heinl, LtCol R.
The staff side of NGS. — *Combat Forces Journal* Dec 46

TACTICS

From the *Gazette:*

ADVANCE BY FIRE AND MANEUVER — Peatross, Maj O. Nov 48

ATTACK AGAINST A FORTIFIED POSITION — Jan 48

DEFENSE AGAINST AIRBORNE ATTACK — Cushman, LtCol R. Dec 46

DEFENSE IN TOWNS — Williams, LtCol R., USA
How the Army does it — Sep 48

DEVELOPING THE FIRE TEAM — Meyers, Lt L.
Making it a good one — Feb 46

THE EFFECTIVENESS OF PSYCHOLOGICAL WARFARE — Kintner, LtCol W., USA Jan 48

FASTER LANDINGS — Constantine, Lt E.
With faster Amtracs — Jan 50

GETTING ASHORE FASTER — Jones, Maj P.
Before the A-Bomb gets you — Apr 48

HATH MURDERED SLEEP — Henderson, LtCol F. Nov 46

KNOW YOUR SIGNALS — Donovan, Maj J.
Tactical application of pyrotechnic signals in small units — Jun 48

MARINE COMMAND OF THE FUTURE — Haynes, Capt F. Nov 48

ONE EYE ON THE LAST WAR; A MILITARY DIGEST — Milotta, Maj D., USA May 48
Time to plan for new enemies

	Title	Author	Date
	REVERSE SLOPE DEFENSE	Tompkins, LtCol R.	Jul 49
	STRENGTHEN THE BEACH ASSAULT Make it easier to get in	Stuart, LtCol A.	Aug 48
	STORMING FORTIFIED BEACHES	Cushman, LtCol R.	Mar 46
	A SUGGESTED ROLE FOR THE NAVY-MARINE CORPS TEAM Dual purpose striking force	McMillian, Capt I. USN	Oct 49
	SWAN SONG FOR THE INFANTRY? The A-Bomb will replace it.	Williams, LtCol R., USA	Feb 48
	TACTICAL POSSIBILITIES OF AIRBORNE ATTACK Looking for a mission for USMC	del Valle, Maj Gen P.	Dec 47
	TO WAR BY AIR Adopting a Marine Division for airborne use	Tompkins, LtCol R.	Jan 47
	YOU FIGHT BY THE BOOK Even in guerrilla war, you follow the rules	Batterton, Maj R.	Jul 49
	WE MUST LEARN TO STOP TANKS Anti-tank tactics	Stuart, LtCol A.	Oct 47
	WHERE DO WE GO FROM HERE? Tactical and technical problems confronting the FMF	Cushman, LtCol R.	May 48
	WILL THE QUEEN DIE? Infantry is the Queen	Whyte, Capt W.	Jan 46
	From *Leatherneck:*		
FICTIONALIZED TACTICS	AMBUSH What to do when it happens	Tatman, LtCol C.	Dec 48
	THE BRIDGE TO ELBOW ROOM	Hoffman, Maj C.	Feb 49

FIRE, MARINES, FIRE! Use those weapons in combat	Hoffman, Maj C. Feb 50	
NIGHTMARE	Hoffman, Maj C. Jan 49	
OUTPOST ON 603 Combat security duty	Hoffman, Maj C. Mar 49	
SKI'S EIGHT BALL Team spirit separates Marines from the others	Hoffman, Maj C. May 49	

TRAINING

ASSAULT IN MINIATURE Training for Amphibious War	Dahl, Maj N., USA *Gazette* Oct 49	**GENERAL**
BATTLE SOUNDS Have them for real training	Jackson, LtCol W. *Gazette* Sep 49	
BEWARE THE GREEN TRIANGLE	Dean, Lt C. *Gazette* Dec 49	
BREATH OF EXPERIENCE FOR OFFICERS	Ringe, G. *Infantry Journal* Mar 46	
CLOTH TERRAIN MODELS Make your own training aids	Murray, LtCol R. *Gazette* Oct 48	
CRADLE ROCKERS Training requires a "cradle touch"	Owens, Capt R. *Gazette* Nov 49	
EFFICIENCY OF A HIGH SPEED SCREENING PROCEDURE IN DETECTING NEURO-PSYCHIATRICALLY UNFIT AT U. S. MARINE CORPS RECRUIT TRAINING DEPOT	*Journal of Psychology* Feb 46	
FMF TRAINING AFLOAT	Nicholson, Lt D. *Gazette* Mar 46	
THE HILLS, THE WOODS AND JOHN RIFLEMAN Whimsey about training	Cason, Maj A. *Gazette* Jul 48	
INSTRUCTION PROCEDURE New FMF training procedures	*Leatherneck* Jun 48	

INSTRUCTORS EXTRAORDINARY Marines teach Jesuit priests close order drill in New Orleans	Duplantier, C. *Leatherneck*	Apr 47
LET'S HAVE A MANEUVER ENEMY Organize an "aggressor force."	Shuler, LtCol C. *Gazette*	Oct 48
LET'S RETURN TO FUNDA-MENTALS Back to spit and polish	Donovan, Maj J. *Gazette*	Jun 46
MARINE CORPS SCHOOLS STRESS EDUCATIONAL VIEWPOINT	Lejeune, E. *Library Journal*	Nov 15, 1947
MARINE CORPS TRAINING Comprehensive review from Boot to Marine Corps Schools	Zimmerman, J. *Proceedings*	Jul 49
PITY THE POOR PRIVATE Change Bn T/O to make it better for training	Jones, LtCol W. *Gazette*	Aug 46
SECURITY TRAINING Guard duty—How to do it	Prickett, LtCol W. *Gazette*	Nov 49
SO YOU DON'T HAVE TIME TO READ? You better find time, lad!	Taxis, Col S. *Gazette*	Dec 48
THE TARGET GRID SYSTEM And how to teach it	Pounds, Maj J. *Gazette*	Oct 49
TRAINING THE BARRACKS DETACHMENT	Pounds, Maj J. *Gazette*	Dec 48
TRAINING FUTURE MARINE OFFICERS How and where to do it	Donovan, Maj J. *Gazette*	Sep 47
STOP FIGHTING THE JAPS And prepare for a new enemy, whoever he might be	Shinn, Capt L. *Gazette*	Aug 46
WHY NOT A MARINE CORPS ACADEMY?	Reavis, Lt W. *Gazette*	Apr 48
WHY NOT A MARINE CORPS DRILL MANUAL?	Reavis, Lt W. *Gazette*	Jul 48

EXERCISES

AIR LIFT 7th Marines training exercises	Allen, Sgt L. *Leatherneck*	Oct 48
BANANA BORNE LANDING Air/Ground demonstration	Smith, Sgt J. *Leatherneck*	Sep 49
BEACHHEAD AT CULEBRA Caribbean maneuvers	Sewell, Sgt F. *Leatherneck*	Jun 47
CARIBBEAN CALISTHENICS Puerto Rico maneuvers	Polete, Sgt H. *Leatherneck*	Oct 46
CO-OPERATION CAMID Little Creek amphib training for West Point and Annapolis	Polete, Sgt H. *Leatherneck*	Dec 46
INVASION OF VIEQUES Maneuvers of the 2D MAR DIV	Solomon, J. *Leatherneck*	Aug 48
OPERATION PACKARD Amphibious training exercise	Rice, Maj H. *Gazette*	Jul 47
OPERATION PENNEY Amphibious training—Pendleton	Allen, Sgt L. *Leatherneck*	Feb 48
PORTREX PREP Marines TTU trains Army	Goss, Sgt F. *Leatherneck*	Apr 50
PRESS SHOW Maneuvers at Onslow Beach	Polete, Sgt H. *Leatherneck*	Aug 48
THE SECOND CAMID Cadets and Midshipmen in amphibious exercises	Polete, Sgt H. *Leatherneck*	Nov 47
TENJO Guam training exercise	Suhosky, PFC R. *Leatherneck*	Jul 48
TRAINING CRUISE NROTC cruise	Hart, Mid H., USNR *Leatherneck*	Dec 48
VIEQUES AGAIN Amphibious war training	Smith, Sgt J. *Leatherneck*	Jun 49

MARKSMANSHIP

BACKGROUND TO BEAT THE BANZAI USMC marksmanship training paid off in World War 2	Voigt, PFC R. *Leatherneck*	Feb 46
THE BIG SHOOT Rifle matches at Quantico	Gartz, Sgt S. *Leatherneck*	May 47

	FIELD SHOOTING More useful than range shooting	Rodeheffer, LtCol N. *Gazette*	Jul 49
	FOR THE RECORD Quantico matches	Gartz, Sgt S. *Leatherneck*	Jun 48
	THE 1947 RIFLE MATCHES At Quantico	McCluskey, PFC W. *Gazette*	Jul 47
	THE M-I AS A TARGET RIFLE How it stacks up to the '06	Arnold, Capt D. *Gazette*	Aug 46
	THE NEW M-I COURSE	*Gazette*	Apr 49
	OLYMPIC RIFLEMEN Marine Riflemen in Olympics	Gartz, Sgt S. *Leatherneck*	Sep 48
	PISTOLEER Capt Thurman Barrier, World record-holder in pistol	Richardson, Sgt J. *Leatherneck*	Jan 50
	RECORD DAY Marine Corps Matches	Gartz, Sgt S. *Leatherneck*	Sep 47
	REDISK ON THE RANGE Marine Corps Rifle Matches	Allen, Sgt L. *Leatherneck*	Sep 46
	THE RIFLE MATCHES ARE BACK At Quantico again after interruption by war	Klaus, PFC R. *Gazette*	Jul 46
	RIFLE MATCHES . . . '49	Gartz, Sgt S. *Leatherneck*	Sep 49
	WELL IN AT FIVE! Rifle and pistol matches	Gartz, Sgt S. *Leatherneck*	Sep 48

TRAINING—SCHOOLS

GENERAL	SCHOOLS FOR MARINES Complete list of MCS courses available to Marines	*Leatherneck*	Mar 47
AIR OBSERVERS	AIR SCHOOL FOR OBSERVERS At Quantico	Jacobsen, PFC I. *Leatherneck*	May 46
BAND	FROM CONCERT TO COMBAT Training the Bandsmen	Evans, Sgt E. *Leatherneck*	May 48
BASIC SCHOOL	THE BASIC SCHOOL Quantico review	Snedeker, Col E. *Gazette*	Jan 49

AW RUP REEP! Parris Island lingo	Milhon, PFC W. *Leatherneck*	Apr 46	**BOOT CAMP**
DEEP IN THE HEART OF DAGO Texas platoon hits Boot Camp	Riblett, L. *Leatherneck*	Apr 47	
LEATHERHEAD IN BOOK CAMP A hilarious debut for one of the Corps' favorite characters	Packwood, SSgt N. Marine Corps Ass'n, Quantico	1949	
MEN FROM MONTFORD POINT Black Marines are trained	Evans, Sgt E. *Leatherneck*	Nov 47	
NEVER THE TWAIN Which is tougher, PI or Dago?	Polete, Sgt H. *Leatherneck*	Aug 48	
NEW TRAINING FOR OLD HANDS Ex-GI's get special training when they re-enlist.	Allen, Sgt L. *Leatherneck*	Jun 48	
PARRIS ISLAND	Milhon, Sgt W. *Leatherneck*	Jun 49	
THEY MOLD MARINES Recruit Depot DI's	Allen, Sgt L. *Leatherneck*	Apr 49	
CHAPLAIN CORPS How Chaplains are trained—and what they do	Langille, Sgt V., and Sgt S. Linn *Leatherneck*	Apr 48	**CHAPLAINS**
OUR FUTURE DI'S No Marines more important	Heinl, LtCol R. *Gazette*	Mar 46	**DI SCHOOL**
SCHOOL FOR SCRIBES At Great Lakes	Thompson, Sgt J. *Leatherneck*	Jun 50	**JOURNALISTS**
DEHYDRATING THE DIPLOMA	Myers, Sgt R. *Leatherneck*	May 46	**MCI**
THE GLOBE IS THE CAMPUS	Johnston, Sgt L. *Leatherneck*	Feb 47	
NEW EXTENSION COURSES READY From Marine Corps Institute	*Gazette*	Feb 49	
THE STORY OF A DREAM MCI's 30th anniversary	Ruoff, F. *Gazette*	Feb 50	

MCS	MARINE CORPS SCHOOLS How we do it at Quantico	Cates, MajGen C. *Army & Navy Journal*	Oct 46
MOUNTAIN WARFARE	ROPE AND PITON Mountain warfare training	Polete, Sgt H. *Leatherneck*	Jul 49
NROTC	NROTC RESUME	Rouse, Capt J. *Gazette*	May 48
	WHAT ABOUT THE NROTC? Is it a good source of Marine Officers?	Valente, Capt R. *Gazette*	Jul 49
PLC	PLATOON LEADERS CLASS At Quantico	Evans, Sgt E. *Leatherneck*	Nov 48
	PLATOON LEADERS CLASS—POSTWAR PROGRAM	*Gazette*	Apr 47
	THIS YEAR'S PLC	Snedeker, Col E. *Gazette*	Apr 48
	WHAT ABOUT PLATOON LEADERS' CLASS? Does it work?	Lewis, Lt C. *Gazette*	Oct 49
STAFF	LEAVENWORTH AND THE MARINE CORPS Army Command and Staff School	Kintner, LtCol W., USA *Gazette*	Mar 49
WR	HIGH HEELED BOOTS Women Marines training at Parris Island	Milhon, Sgt W. *Leatherneck*	Aug 49

UNIFORMS

BATTLE DECORATIONS Our present award system is very bad, indeed	Cushman, LtCol R. *Gazette*	Jul 48
COLD WEATHER COMBAT CLOTHING We'll need it later (Korea)	Hall, Maj M. *Gazette*	May 48
DRESS RIGHT How to wear uniforms	Evans, Sgt E. *Leatherneck*	Jul 48
LET'S USE OUR DRESS UNIFORMS For Tradition's sake, etc., etc.	Heinl, LtCol R. *Gazette*	Nov 46

THE OFFICERS' NEW DRESS UNIFORM	*Gazette*	Mar 49
OUR UTILITY "UNIFORM"	Hall, Maj M. *Gazette*	Jan 48
THE PROPER WEARING OF RIBBONS	Martin, Lt G. *Gazette*	Apr 46
REBIRTH OF THE BLUES Dress Blues are back	Evans, Sgt E. *Leatherneck*	Sep 46

UNITS

ACTIVATION OF FMF ATLANTIC Fleet Marine Force	*Gazette*	Feb 47
THE DIVISION CONTROL PARTY AND AMPHIBIOUS OPERATIONS	Greene, LtCol F. *Quartermaster Review*	Nov, Dec 47
MINORITY REPORT ON (J) ASCO Joint Assault Signal Co.	Heinl, LtCol R. *Gazette*	Jul 47
THE NEW FMF (J) (P) Series, The Infantry Battalion, the Marine Division, Marine Brigade and Service Command	*Gazette*	May 47
NEW MARINE INFANTRY REGIMENT T/O (J) (P) Series	*Gazette*	Mar 47
THE NEW MORTAR COMPANY	Naylor, Maj J. *Gazette*	Jun 50
THE NEW INFANTRY BATTALION (J) (P) T/O for Rifle Co and H & S Co	*Gazette*	Aug 47
SHORE PARTY REGIMENT (J) (P) Series T/O	*Gazette*	Jul 47
SPECIAL WEAPONS BATTALION	*Gazette*	Feb 47
STAFFING THE PEACETIME MARINE DIVISION	*Gazette*	Oct 47
THE 28TH RETURNS Famous Iwo regiment	Riblett, PFC L. *Leatherneck*	May 46

	WANTED: AN AMMUNITION AND PIONEER PLATOON	Aplington, Maj H. *Gazette*	Jul 48
DOGS	WAR DOGS	Downey, F. *Leatherneck*	Feb 50

WEAPONS

From the *Gazette* unless otherwise indicated:

ABC	AMPHIBIOUS WARFARE AND THE ATOM BOMB It does create a problem!	Brown, Hon J.	Sep 47
	THE ATOM BOMB COMES INTO FOCUS After Bikini tests	Hodgson, Lt R.	Oct 46
	THE ATOMIC BOMB TESTS AND THE MARINE CORPS	Hodgson, Lt D.	Oct 46
	ATOMIC DEFENSE Run like Hell!	Wolfe, LtCol R. USA	Feb 50
	THE BIG BANG AT BIKINI What it means to the Corps		Aug 46
	"NUCLEAR POWER—ITS MILITARY APPLICATION—"	Lapp, Dr. R.	Nov 47
	OUTLAWING WEAPONS BY AGREEMENT It better work!		Jan 48
AUTOMATIC WEAPONS	AUTOMATIC WEAPONS Review of the world's	Evans, Sgt E. *Leatherneck*	Sep 48
	AUTOMATIC WEAPONS FOR THE FUTURE	Johnson, Capt M.	Dec 46
	FOUR TO THE BAR BAR Firepower	Goss, Sgt F. *Leatherneck*	Dec 49
BAYONET	THE OVERRATED BAYONET It's good for opening cans	Meyers, Capt L.	Nov 46
BAZOOKA	THE NEW BAZOOKA M-20 Launchers	Millichap, Maj P. *Leatherneck*	Jul 49
	CONCERNING BAZOOKAS Anti-armored review	Hoffman, Capt C.	Jul 46

Title	Author	Date	Subject
MACHINE GUNS IN THE ATTACK	Sexton, Capt M.	Oct 48	MACHINE GUNS
MACHINE GUNS ARE OFFENSIVE WEAPONS	Van Stockum, LtCol R.	Apr 50	
MINES: AN AMPHIBIOUS THREAT	Carter, LtCol D.	Dec 48	MINES
BUMBLE BEE Guided missile	Lewis, Sgt R. *Leatherneck*	Jan 50	MISSILES
4.5" ROCKET BATTERY		Apr 47	
FRONT SEAT AT THE ROCKET SHOW White Sands rocket testing	Riblett, Cpl L. *Leatherneck*	Oct 46	
GUIDED MISSILES	Walton, Lt R.	Aug 48	
"MIGHTY MOUSE"		Apr 50	
MUGUU Marines in guided missile development	Allen, Sgt L. *Leatherneck*	Mar 49	
MORTARS AND SMOKE	Aplington, LtCol H.	Sep 49	MORTARS
MORTARS: WEAPONS OF OPPORTUNITY	Stoffer, Capt A.	Jun 46	
THE WAR OF WORDS Sticks and stones will break my bones, but . . .	Vogel, B.	Jun 49	PSYCHOLOGY
KICKLESS CANNON 75 mm Recoilless Rifle	Olson, Maj P. *Leatherneck*	Aug 49	RECOILLESS
RIFLE GRENADES How to use them	Goss, Sgt F. *Leatherneck*	Oct 49	RIFLE
STACKING ARMS WITH THE T/O SQUAD	Rogers, Maj L.	Sep 49	
CARBINE OR PISTOL? Why not both?	Nihart, Maj B.	Aug 46	SIDE ARMS
INSPECTION OF SMALL ARMS BARRELS What to look for as you peer in	Voss, MSgt R.	Apr 49	

	WHAT GOOD IS A PISTOL? Makes a fine throwing weapon	Cooper, Maj J.	Sep 46
TANKS	AMPHIBIOUS ARMOR The Armored Force in future beachhead operations	Fraser, Maj A.	Mar 48
	WHAT ABOUT LANDING TANKS? There must be an easier way	Williams, Col R., USA	Aug 49

5.
KOREA

The Official History of *U.S. Marine Operations in Korea* in five volumes, writing about the Inchon Landing, personal experiences and Histories of specific subjects.

CONTENTS: PART 5

EVENTS/JULY 1950-1955

1950, GENERAL

ANNIVERSARY MESSAGE	*Gazette*	Nov 50
BELLEAU WOOD VETERANS PRESENT COLORS TO CORPS	*Gazette*	Jul 50
BIRTHDAY OF THE MARINE CORPS History of forming of the Corps from the Manual	*Leatherneck*	Nov 50
ESPRIT DE CORPS Birthday salutation	*Time*	Nov 13, 1950
HERE COMES THE MARINES	Simpich, F. *Geographic*	Nov 50
MARINE ANNIVERARY: 175TH	*Life*	Nov 27, 1950
MARINE CORPS BAND CELEBRATES ANNIVERSARY	*Gazette*	Jul 50
MARINE CORPS MEMORIAL Iwo statue at Quantico dedicated	*Gazette*	Dec 50
MARINES LAND ON H.S.T. For "police force" remarks	*Newsweek*	Sep 18, 1950
MARINES ON TWO FRONTS: MR. TRUMAN'S LETTER Fighting Truman and Reds	*Ave Maria*	Sep 23, 1950
PRESIDENTIAL VISIT Truman comes to Quantico to patch things up with the Corps	*Gazette*	Aug 50
VINSON JOINS THE MARINES Navy Sec supports Corps	*Newsweek*	Oct 16, 1950
"WHEN I MAKE A MISTAKE" Truman admits he made one about Marines	*Time*	Sep 18, 1950

KOREAN WAR OPENS— 2 AUG 50

FIRST TEAM It's the USMC	*Time*	Aug 14, 1950
GENERAL CATES, GUADALCANAL VETERAN, LEADS MARINES Korea puts Marines in the news	*U. S. News*	Aug 18, 1950

	MARINE LANDING AND A GI BATTLE Marines land in Korea	*Life*	Aug 14, 1950
	MARINE MUSCLE HEADS INTO WAR: IST DIVISION MEN SAIL FOR KOREA	*Life*	Jul 24, 1950
	MARINES GO INTO BATTLE AND REVIVE A COMBAT HISTORY And, what a history!	*Newsweek*	Aug 14, 1950
	NEW BREED: MARINES OF 1ST PROVISIONAL BRIGADE	Conner, J. *Collier's*	Oct 7, 1950
	TO THE SHORES OF KOREA Getting there is half the fun	Slater, L. *Newsweek*	Jul 24, 1950
PUSAN PERIMETER— 6 AUG 50	BRAVE MEN OF NO NAME RIDGE First battle Naktong River	Bell, J. *Life*	Aug 28, 1950
	CHANGALLON VALLEY "B" Co., 1/5, 12 Aug 50	Fenton, Maj F. *Gazette*	Nov 51
	THE EPIC OF BLOODY HILL Battle of early Korea, 17-19 Aug 50	Martin, H. *Sat Eve Post* *Digest*	Oct 14, 1950 Jan 51
	THE FIRST NAKTONG	Murray, MajGen R. *Gazette*	Nov 65
	FLOATING BASES SHOW VALUE Provide Marines with CAS	*U.S. News*	Sep 8, 1950
	HELL RUN OVER KOREA Marine aerial photos over Pusan	Fleming, JO3 K., USN *Leatherneck*	Oct 50
	A HILL NEAR YONGSAN Early Korea operations	Canzona, Capt N. *Gazette*	Jun 55
	MARINE AIR OVER PUSAN CAS strikes help Marines	Giusti, E. *Gazette*	May 52
	THE ORDEAL OF MARINE SQUAD 2 Pusan Perimeter, 17 Aug 50	Martin, H. *Sat Eve Post*	Nov 11, 1950
	THE PUSAN PERIMETER: FIGHT FOR A FOOTHOLD 15 Aug—7 Sep 50	Montross, L. *Gazette*	June 51

PUSAN—A STOP EN ROUTE Early Korea "place" story	Tallent, SSgt R. *Leatherneck* Dec 50	
THE SAGA OF DOG COMPANY, 5TH MARINES Aug-Dec 50	Jones, J. *American Legion* Dec 60	
TANK DUEL—NAKTONG FRONT	Tallent, SSgt R. *Leatherneck* Dec 50	
U.S. MARINE OPERATIONS IN KOREA: 1950-53, VOLUME 1—THE PUSAN PERIMETER Aug-Sep Operations of the 1st Marine Brigade	Montross, L., and Capt N. Canzona HQMC 1954	
CAPTURE OF SEOUL: BATTLE OF THE BARRICADES	Montross, L. *Gazette* Aug 51	**INCHON—SEOUL 15 SEP 50**
DOG COMPANY'S CHARGE Vicious battle of Smith's Ridge, "D" Co., 2/5, 23 Sept 50	Canzona, Capt N. *Proceedings* Nov 56	
FALL OF SEOUL: U.S. MARINES IN STREET FIGHTING	*London News* Oct 7, 1950	
GUNSMOKE REVEILLE 2/1 At Seoul-Inchon Highway	Tallent, SSgt R. *Leatherneck* Jan 51	
HELL OR HIGH WATER: MacARTHUR'S LANDING AT INCHON "Dugout Doug" takes Inchon. Marines go along for the ride. For the real story, get *Victory at High Tide.*	Sheldon, W. The Macmillan Company 1968	
INCHON The nucleous for *Victory at High Tide*	Heinl, R. *Gazette* Sep, Oct 67	
INCHON—ANALYSIS OF A GAMBLE The strategy behind Inchon	Cagle, Cdr M., USN *Proceedings* Jan 54	
INCHON LANDING Historical analysis of one of Corps' finest hours. Emphasis on tank tactics	Halloran, B. *Gazette* Sep 72	

THE INCHON LANDING By the man who led it	Smith, Gen O. *Gazette*	Sep 60
THE INCHON LANDING: PERILOUS GAMBLE OR EXEMPLARY BOLDNESS?	Schnabel, LtCol J., USA *Army*	May 59
INCHON LANDING—VICTORY OVER TIME AND TIDE	Montross, L. *Gazette*	Jul 51
INCHON TO SEOUL The 1ST MAR DIV in action	Tallent, SSgt R. *Leatherneck*	Jan 51
INCHON TO SEOUL	Banks, Col C. *Gazette*	May 51
LARGE SEDENTARY TARGETS ON RED BEACH Beaching of eight LST's at Inchon after initial assault	Montross, L. *Gazette*	Sep 60
MARINE AIR OVER INCHON-SEOUL	Condit, K., and E. Giusti *Gazette*	Jun 52
MATTER OF FACT Combat-Inchon to Seoul	Alsop, J. *Leatherneck*	Dec 50
ROAD JUNCTION "E" Co., 2/1, Seoul, 26 Sep 50	Stanford, Capt N. *Gazette*	Sep 51
STREET FIGHT IN SEOUL 2/1 battles in Seoul	Tallent, SSgt R. *Leatherneck*	Jan 51
THE TRICK THAT WON SEOUL	Worden, W. *Sat Eve Post*	Nov 11, 1950
U.S. MARINE OPERATIONS IN KOREA: 1950-53, VOLUME 2— THE INCHON-SEOUL OPERATION The last great amphibious operation.	Montross, L., and Capt N. Canzona HQMC	1955
VICTORY AT HIGH TIDE: THE INCHON-SEOUL CAMPAIGN Heinl weaves small unit tactics into the "Big Picture" in a fast-moving, interesting way.	Heinl, Col R. J. B. Lippincott Company, Philadelphia	1968
WOLMI-DO: TURNING THE KEY The little island outside Seoul where Inchon started	McMullen, R. and N. Canzona *Proceedings*	Mar 56

CHOSIN RESERVOIR—28 NOV 50

ANABASIS IN NORTHEAST KOREA "Anabasis" is a large-scale military advance. This time it ain't by us!	Dressler, C. *Gazette*	Feb 51
THE BIG HILL Marines fighting South meet relief column fighting North.	Jones, TSgt J. *Leatherneck*	Mar 51
THE BLOODY BREAKOUT 1/7 at Chosin	Davis, Capt W. *Proceedings*	July 53
THE BLOODY TRAIL BACK: EXIT FROM THE CHANGJIN RESERVOIR	Higgins, M. *Sat Eve Post*	Jan 27, 1951
BREAKOUT FROM THE RESERVOIR: MARINE EPIC OF FIRE AND ICE	Montross, L. *Gazette*	Nov 51
CAPTURED CACHE Enemy caves in Hamhung hold explosives and machine tools.	Walden, Cpl J. *Leatherneck*	Apr 51
CARRIER DECK Koto-Ri Airstrip for torpedo planes. They evacuate wounded	*Leatherneck*	Mar 51
CHOSIN RESERVOIR TO HUNGNAM	Shepherd, LtGen L. *Gazette*	Feb 51
THE CHRISTMAS THEY'LL NEVER FORGET Marines get life for Christmas.	Montross, L. *Leatherneck*	Dec 56
THE COLD WAR Cold's effect on equipment, weapons, supplies at Chosin	Banks, Col C. *Gazette*	Sep 51
COMBAT ART Combat artist with 11th Marines at Chosin 28 Nov-2 Dec 50	Gurda, Sgt E. *Leatherneck*	Apr 51
DARKHORSE SETS THE PACE "Darkhorse" is the 5th Marines. They lead the way from Chosin	Taplett, LtCol R., and Maj R. Whipple *Gazette*	Jun, Jul 53
THE DEAD END OF AMBUSH ALLEY 3/1 at Majon-ni	Stiles, Lt C. *Gazette*	Nov 51

THE DOCS Medical personnel at Chosin	Jones, TSgt J. *Leatherneck*	Mar 51
EASY ALLEY CO of Easy Co., 2/5, reviews a night defensive action	Jaskilka, Capt S. *Gazette*	May 51
ENGINEERS IN THE HUNGNAM EVACUATION	Rowny, LtCol E. *Military Engineer*	Sep, Oct 51
ESCAPE Capt E. Stamford, FAC attached to Army's 7th Infantry Division, escapes Red trap west of Chosin	*Leatherneck*	Apr 51
FOX HILL Fox Co., 2/7, at Chosin 27 Nov-4 Dec 50	McCarthy, Capt R. *Gazette*	Mar 53
1ST MARINE DIVISION: NOVEMBER 1-DECEMBER 15, 1950 Small pamphlet on Chosin with great drawings of Marines there	USGPO	1951
HAGARU: PERIMETER OF NECESSITY 3/1, 28 Nov-5 Dec 50	Montross, L. *Gazette*	Dec 58
THE HILL Fox Co defends a thin perimeter near Hagaru-ri	Pierce, P. *Leatherneck*	Apr 62
HUNGNAM EVACUATION AMPHIBIOUS LANDING IN REVERSE	Montross, L. *Gazette*	Dec 51
THE LAST BARRIER Operations of 1/1 at Chosin by the famous Army Historian	Marshall, Gen S. *Gazette*	Jan, Feb 53
LESSONS LEARNED UP NORTH And learned the hard way!	Davis, Capt W. *Gazette*	Apr 52
LOOKING BACK AT CHOSIN By the CO of Marines there	Smith, LtGen O. *Gazette*	Dec 60
MAJON-NI: PERIMETER OF EXPEDIENCY 3/1 defends road junction west of Wonsan 30 Oct—14 Nov 50	Montross, L. *Gazette*	Nov 56

THE MARCH TO GLORY Leckie takes on Chosin. Somehow, you lose. His exciting style isn't needed for an exciting story like Chosin. A little gung-ho for Marines' taste	Leckie, R. The World Publishing Company, Cleveland 1960 Paperback by Bantam Books, Inc. 1961
MARINE AIR AT THE CHOSIN RESERVOIR	Condit, K., and E. Giusti *Gazette* Jul 52
MARINE AIR COVERS THE BREAKOUT	Giusti, E., and K. Condit *Gazette* Aug 52
A MARINE DIVISION IN NIGHTMARE ALLEY A terrible little book which adds nothing to Chosin even though the author was there. (11th Marines). Only 46 pages long. Fortunately.	Campigno, A. Comet Press Books 1958
NEW ENEMY The CCF appears at Chosin	Tallent, SSgt R. *Leatherneck* Feb 51
OUR GUNS NEVER GOT COLD "H" Batt, 3/11 at Hagaru-ri, 25 Nov-8 Dec 50	Read, Capt B. as told to H. Morrow *Sat Eve Post* Apr 51
OUR MEN IN KOREA Task Force Drysdale. British Royal Marines play an important part in the Chosin story.	Linklater, E. H. M. Stationery Office, London 1952
RED CHINA ON THE OFFENSIVE	Montross, L. *Gazette* Jul 53
RIDGERUNNERS OF TAKTONG PASS 1/7, 1-2 Dec 50	Montross, L. *Gazette* May 53
THE ROUGH ROAD TO CHOSIN 7th Marines from Hamhung to Chosin, 29 Oct-15 Nov 50	Sell, Sgt T. *Leatherneck* Feb 51
SNOW AND BLOOD HILL 1/1 assaults Koto-ri	*Leatherneck* Mar 51
THANK GOD, I'M A MARINE Training pays off in combat.	Chandler, Lt. J. *Leatherneck* Jun 51, Aug 72

THERE WAS A CHRISTMAS IN KOREA And the present was your a . . .!	*Life*	Dec 25, 1950
THESE ARE YOUR SONS Good account of the withdrawal from Chosin by a Chaplain	Mulvey, T., USNR McGraw-Hill, Inc.	1953
"TOUGH TEAM" CAS at Chosin	Tallent, SSgt R. *Leatherneck*	Mar 51
TROUBLE IN HELL-FIRE VALLEY 29-30 Nov 50 ambush of Task Force Drysdale	Montross, L. *Gazette*	Mar 57
TRUTH IS STRANGER . . . Cpl James E. Bartles vs. CCF west of Chosin	Mainard, Sgt A. *Leatherneck*	Mar 51
THE 12 INCREDIBLE DAYS OF COL JOHN PAGE (USA) Page is killed directing Marines in rear guard action against CCF	Canzona, Capt N., and J. Hubbell *Digest*	Apr 56
U.S. MARINE OPERATIONS IN KOREA: 1950-53, VOLUME 3—THE CHOSIN RESERVOIR CAMPAIGN From the Wonsan Landing to the Hungnam "Unlanding" and all that happened in between (like being attacked by a new enemy 60,000 strong.)	Montross, L., and Capt N. Canzona HQMC	1957
U.S. MARINES HAVE LANDED AGAIN The dry-foot landing at Wonsan which preceded Chosin	*Newsweek*	*Nov 26, 1951*
THE U.S. MARINES IN THE CHOSIN RESERVOIR OPERATION: A BRIEF BIBLIOGRAPHY	O'Quinlivan, M. HQMC	1955
VERSATILITY Non-combat group in combat	Coon, Cpl G. *Leatherneck*	Mar 51
WE'LL BE HOME FOR CHRISTMAS: A TRUE STORY OF THE UNITED STATES MARINE CORPS IN THE KOREAN WAR Ends with Chosin	Aguirre, E. Greenwich Book Publishers	1959

Title	Author / Source	Date	Section
WONSAN TO THE RESERVOIR: RED CHINA ENTERS FIGHT	Montross, L. *Gazette*	Oct 51	
DIVISION REUNION 1ST MAR DIV, Philadelphia	Tallent, TSgt R. *Leatherneck*	Oct 51	**1951, GENERAL**
FOR EDITORIAL EXCELLENCE Gazette wins Press Awards	*Gazette*	Aug 51	
MARINES AND MARIJUANA Who says it's a new problem?	*Newsweek*	Dec 31, 1951	
MARINES SHOULD HELP PLAN WARS THEY MUST FIGHT Boost for plan to add a Marine to Joint Chiefs	*Sat Eve Post*	Mar 31, 1951	
SPEARHEAD IN MANHATTAN 5TH MAR DIV Reunion	Lewis, TSgt C. *Leatherneck*	Sep 51	
TYPHOON AT KOBE Sept 3, 1950 storm	Griffin, SFC W., USA *Gazette*	Sep 51	
WASHINGTON TRYANNY: ANOTHER CASE STUDY The Fallbrook fight for water rights at Pendleton	*This Week* *Digest*	Oct 7, 1951 Dec 51	
ADVANCE TO THE PUNCHBOWL Operations 22 May-15 July 51	Montross, L. *Gazette*	Aug 53	**EAST-CENTRAL FRONT— 18 JAN 51**
ADVANCE TO THE 38TH PARALLEL: THE MARINES IN OPERATION RIPPER 21 March-5 April 1951	Montross, L. *Gazette*	Mar 52	
AN EARLY AFTERNOON Combat photographer in combat at Hoengsong with 1/7,Feb 51	Tallent, SSgt R. *Leatherneck*	Jun 51	
BUNKER HILL 7th Marines attack hills 749 and 673, 11 Sept 51	Burlage, MSgt G. *Leatherneck*	Dec 51	
BUTTONING UP THE OFFENSIVE: THE MARINES IN OPERATION KILLER Operations, 21 Feb-4 Mar 51	Montross, L. *Gazette*	Feb 52	
THE FMF IN KOREA Marine Corps Birthday celebrated	Donovan, LtCol J. *Leatherneck*	Nov 52	

	HILL 749 Defense against a night attack in the East-Central front	Jobst, Cpl L. *Leatherneck*	Mar 52
	MAO'S STRATEGIC DEFENSIVE Later stages of Korean War	Nihart, LtCol B. *Gazette*	Nov 52
	MARINES COME HOME FROM THE FRONT To find that no one knows about Korea. Or cares	*Life*	Mar 19, 1951
	A NEW KIND OF WAR Trench warfare role for world's finest assault forces	Gray, Lt B. *Leatherneck*	Jul 52
	NOT ENOUGH GLORY HUNTERS But a hell of a lot more than there are now!	*Time*	Jul 23, 1951
	THE POHANG GUERRILLA HUNT: 1600 SQUARE MILES OF TROUBLE 10 Jan-15 Feb 51	Montross, L. *Gazette*	Jan 52
	SUNDAY PUNCH It's the Marines with CAS	*Time*	Nov 24, 1952
	U.S. MARINE OPERATIONS IN KOREA: 1950-53, VOLUME 4—THE EAST-CENTRAL FRONT Marines learn a new tactic, "limited offensive," from 16 Dec 50 through 1 Apr 52	Montross, L., Maj. H. Kuokka and Maj N. Hicks HQMC	1962
	THE VICTORS AT BOOMERANG 1/1 at Hwachin, 23-24 April 51	Reissner, Capt P. *Gazette*	Aug 58
1952, GENERAL	AVIATION BIRTHDAY Background of Marine aviation	Tallent, TSgt R. *Leatherneck*	Jun 52
	CORPS ANNIVERSARY Roundup of 177th events	Morrisey, MSgt R. *Leatherneck*	Nov 52
	THE GOVERNMENT'S BIG GRAB Fallbrook water rights fight at Pendleton	*Sat Eve Post*	Jan 5, 1952
	HERE COME THE LEATHERNECKS	Dempewolff, R. *Popular Mechanics*	Apr 52

OUR HILARIOUS HEROES	Lederer, W. *Coronet* Jan 52	
THE NEW COMMANDANT; GENERAL LEMUEL C. SHEPHERD	Lyons, MSgt R. *Leatherneck* Jan 52	
NEW U.S. WOMEN MARINES' UNIFORMS	*London News* Sep 6, 1952	
REUNION IN EUROPE Gen Shepherd inspects Royal Marines	Lyons, MSgt R. *Leatherneck* Aug 52	
SAVANNAH CONVENTION 28th Annual Convention of Marine Corps League	Lewis, MSgt C. *Leatherneck* Jan 52	
TOYS FOR TOTS	Tallent, TSgt R. *Leatherneck* Dec 52	
HIT AND GIT COMMANDO RAID, NORTH KOREA Marines raid Sorwe Dong near Song Jin, North Korea, April 53	Chambers, F. *Our Navy* Dec 53	**WESTERN FRONT—1952**
THE HOOK Marines take Hook, 26 Oct 52	Jordan, SSgt C. *Leatherneck* Feb 53	
KOREAN VETERANS ROTATE BACKWARDS Second and third tours for Marine volunteers	*Life* Feb 23, 1953	
THE LAST 12 HOURS Fox Company outpost on Molar Hill under fire until cease fire	Heinecke, MSgt R. *Leatherneck* Oct 53	
OPERATION LADY 1/5 sets up pre-fab bunker on 'Lady' Hill under fire	Fugate, MSgt R. *Leatherneck* Mar 53	
OUTPOST WARFARE It's the lonesomest kind	Braestrup, Lt P. *Gazette* Nov 53	
SOMETHING'S GOT TO GIVE IN KOREA	Sherrod, R. *Sat Eve Post* Feb 21, 1953	
UN-GOOK Daylight raid on Un Gook by "A" Co., 1/5	Coleman, TSgt J. *Leatherneck* Jul 53	

	VEGAS, RENO AND CARSON Three hills in Korea	Fugate, MSgt R. *Leatherneck* Jun 53
	U.S. MARINE OPERATIONS IN KOREA: 1950-53, VOLUME 5— OPERATIONS IN WESTERN KOREA Patrols, holding actions and trench warfare	Meid, LtCol P., and Maj J. Yingling HQMC 1972(IP)
1953, GENERAL	THE BAND'S 155TH Marine Band anniversary	Jordan, TSgt C. *Leatherneck* Aug 53
	END OF AN ERA The last Corsair goes to France	McMahon, Capt E. *Leatherneck* Apr 53
	DESERT ROCK Marines in Yucca Flats A-Test	Heinecke, MSgt R. *Leatherneck* Jul 53
	HIGH MAN Marine Col sets speed and altitude records as test pilot	Sarokin, MSgt P. *Leatherneck* Dec 53
	JAMAICAN MATCH Marines-Welsh Fusiliers' Match	Sims, SSgt R. *Leatherneck* Jun 53
	MARINES AROUND THE WORLD 178th anniversary roundup	Marcus, MSgt S. *Leatherneck* Nov 53
	SANTA CLAUS, USMCR "Toys for Tots" campaign	Tallent, MSgt R. *Leatherneck* Dec 53
PANMUNJOM & POW'S— 1953	BIG SWITCH Marine heads command to receive POW's from Reds	Heinecke, MSgt R. *Leatherneck* Nov 53
	FREEDOM VILLAGE Marines build POW processing center near Panmunjom	Fugate, MSgt R. *Leatherneck* Jul 53
	PANMUNJOM Col Murray, only Marine UN Delegate at Peace Conference	Braitsch, MSgt F. *Leatherneck* Mar 52
	P.O.W. Review of treatment given Marine POW's	Jones, GySgt M. *Leatherneck* Aug, Sep 61
	THE PRISONER ISSUE	Murray, Col J. *Gazette* Aug, Sep 55

THE PROBLEMS OF U.S. MARINE CORPS PRISONERS OF WAR IN KOREA — MacDonald, J. MA thesis, Univ. of Md., College Park 1961

1954

ARE THE MARINES REALLY READY TO FIGHT? — *U. S. News* Nov 9, 1954
Try us!

ASSAULT ON A CAKE — *Life* Nov 15, 1954
Usual birthday publicity

BATTLE CRY — Marcus, MSgt S. *Leatherneck* Oct 54
Marines in film *Battle Cry*

DANCE FOR DIMES — Marcus, MSgt S. *Leatherneck* Dec 54
Marines raise $50,000 for polio

DMZ MARINES — Sarokin, MSgt P. *Leatherneck* Oct 54
1ST MAR DIV security force now

DOUBLE ANNIVERSARY — Thacker, J., and M. O'Quinlivan *Gazette* Nov 54
Continental Congress resolution of 10 Nov 1775

FLAGHOIST — Heinecke, MSgt R. *Leatherneck* Aug 54
3RD MAR DIV lands on Iwo again to participate in ceremony

FOUR STAR VISIT — Heinecke, MSgt R. *Leatherneck* Jan 54
Gen Shepherd goes to Korea

FRIENDSHIP DAY — Rodriguez, D. *Leatherneck* Mar 54
St. David's Day greetings to Marines from Welsh Fusiliers, friends since Boxer Rebellion

HOME FOR A HERO — Gross, SSgt J. *Leatherneck* Jul 54
A Marine Medal of Honor winner wins a house

KOREA TODAY — Sarokin, MSgt P. *Leatherneck* Aug 54
Marines find slow progress

MARINE CORPS PRIDE ON TRIAL — *Life* Mar 1, 1954
Col Schwable is tried for conduct as a POW

MARINES DECIDE: COL SCHWABLE CASE — *Time* May 10, 1954

	MISS UNIVERSE Marines secure lush duty	Marcus, MSgt S. *Leatherneck* Oct 54
	OPERATION COMEBACK 4th Marines take Chinese Red POW's to Formosa	Heinecke, MSgt R. *Leatherneck* Apr 54
	SYMBOLS OF TRADITION Smithsonian has big display on Marines	Sarokin, MSgt P. *Leatherneck* Nov 54
	THE WOMAN MARINES 11th ANNIVERSARY	Lyons, R., and MSgt S. Marcus *Leatherneck* Feb 54
1955	CHRISTMAS COMPANY More than 200 separate "Toys for Tots" drives are in action	Tallent, MSgt R. *Leatherneck* Dec 55
	FUJI CLIMB 3RD DIV Marines scale Fuji	Heinecke, MSgt R. *Leatherneck* Jan 55
	GOING HOME 5th Marines return after five years in Korea	Sarokin, MSgt P. *Leatherneck* May 55
	HOME! Heroes' welcome home for 5th	*Leatherneck* May 55
	THE LOU DIAMOND SHOW Marine on TV show	Marcus, MSgt S. *Leatherneck* Feb 55
	MILITARY FIELD MEET Combat shooting competition	Marcus, MSgt S. *Leatherneck* Feb 55
	OKINAWA TODAY 9th Marines transferred to Okinawa from Kobe	Sarokin, MSgt P. *Leatherneck* Oct 55
	OPERATION, FIRE 2d Infantry Training Regiment fights California forest fires	Heinecke, MSgt R. *Leatherneck* Nov 55
	OPERATION, FLOOD 6th Truck Co., Marine reservists, save flood victims in Scranton	Sarokin, MSgt P. *Leatherneck* Nov 55
	ROADEO 2D MAR DIV Truck-Trailer Meet at Camp Lejeune	Suhosky, TSgt R. *Leatherneck* Aug 55

SOUTH AMERICAN VISIT Commandant Shepherd tours	Hawkins, LtCol J. *Leatherneck*	Jun 55
U.S. MARINE CORPS, 1955 Plate No. 124	*Military Collector & Historian*	Fall 56
USMC PLANS ADOPTION OF NEW EQUIPMENT TO GIVE ADDED PUNCH	*Army, Navy, Air Force Journal*	Nov 55
WIZARD FOR THE CORPS Gen Pate, new Commandant	*Time*	Oct 31, 1955

KOREAN WAR

GENERAL

THE ABOMINABLE MARINE Shell shocked victim of Vegas roams the front line areas at night. Fiction (or is it?)	Barrow, MSgt C. *Leatherneck*	Sep 61
AN ANNOTATED BIBLIOGRAPHY OF THE UNITED STATES MARINE CORPS IN THE KOREAN WAR Excellent, 32-page pamphlet which includes more than 285 items about Korea. Subject organized (if only they were all like this!)	O'Quinlivan, M., and J. Santelli HQMC	1970(IP)
C/O FPO SAN FRANCISCO Marine mail zipped to Korea	Braitsch, MSgt F. *Leatherneck*	Apr 53
FIRST TO FIGHT: PICTURE STORY Gung-ho Marine story	*Coronet*	Sep 51
FLEET MARINE FORCE: KOREA Comprehensive review of FMF	Montross, L. *Proceedings*	Aug, Sep 53
G I JACKPOT Korea combat pay	Tallent, MSgt R. *Leatherneck*	Mar 53
KOREA Picture spread	*Leatherneck*	Nov 50
KOREA: LAND OF THE MORNING CALM How the country came back. What it was like in 1962	Barrow, MSgt C. *Leatherneck*	Jan, Feb 62

KOREAN CHRONOLOGY 25 June 50—30 June 51	*Leatherneck*	Nov 51
KOREAN SKETCHES Art of Korea	Packwood, Sgt N. *Gazette*	Feb 52
LETTERS FROM ALMOND Korean interpreter corresponds with 7th Marines' Capt in States	*Leatherneck*	Apr 53
MARINES' REMARKABLE FOREIGN LEGION	Kalischer, P *Collier's*	Oct 25, 1952
THE NEW BREED: THE STORY OF THE U.S. MARINE CORPS IN KOREA Collection of small unit actions. Many, *many* names of junior officers and NCO's. Difficult to read.	Geer, Maj A. Harper and Bros.	1952
OUR FIRST YEAR IN KOREA A collection of articles from the *Gazette*	HQMC	1951
RANDOM NOTES ON KOREA	Batterton, LtCol R. *Gazette*	Nov 55
REFLECTIONS ON KOREA	Canzona, Lt N. *Gazette*	Nov 51
REPLACEMENT Marine replacements take over for Korea combat troops	Tallent, TSgt R. *Leatherneck*	Oct 51
SUHOSKI CINDERELLASAN Marines Korean slang glossary	Woodward, SSgt H. *Leatherneck*	Aug 54
THEY WERE THERE Former Pacific jungle-fighters found two new elements in Korea—mountains and cold	Montross, L., and N. Hicks *Leatherneck*	Dec 60, Jan 61
THIS IS WAR: A PHOTO NARRATIVE IN THREE PARTS Photo review from Pusan through Chosin by the ubiquitous Mr. Duncan	Duncan, D. Harper and Bros. Paperback by Bantam Books, Inc.	1951 1967 (IP)
UN INTERVENTION IN KOREA: MARINES	*Gazette*	Nov 50

WHY WE FOUGHT	Prickett, Col W. *Proceedings*	Jul 54
A YEAR IN KOREA Marines fought everything including the weather	Heinecke, MSgt R. *Leatherneck*	Nov 53

AVIATION

GENERAL

AIR ACADEMY Marines at Pensacola	McCann, SSgt H. *Leatherneck*	Oct 52
AIR INTERDICTION	Folsom, LtCol S. *Gazette*	Jan 54
AIRDALE Training in air emergencies	Burlage, TSgt G. *Leatherneck*	Aug 50
AIR POWER GOES ISOLATIONIST	Reinhardt, Col G., USA *Gazette*	Mar 51
AN AIR PROFICIENCY TROPHY	Steinkraus, LtCol R. *Gazette*	Nov 55
AVIATION INTELLIGENCE	Johnson, Capt J. *Gazette*	Feb 55
AVIATION U Marines learn to be aviation technicians at Pensacola	Suhosky, TSgt R. *Leatherneck*	May 54
AVIATORS SHOULD FLY	Griffits, Capt L. *Gazette*	Feb 51
REPLY TO AVIATORS SHOULD FLY	Saxon, Capt T. *Gazette*	Jun 51
THE BLUE ANGELS Famed jet team gets first Marine aviator	Marcus, MSgt S. *Leatherneck*	Sep 54
CASE FOR THE ENLISTED PILOT	Edwards, LtCol H. *Gazette*	Nov 54
A CLEAN DISH FOR A FAST WALLOP	Hanna, Maj G. *Gazette*	Oct 54
FLYING SERGEANTS Marine enlisted pilots fought for four decades	Sarokin, MSgt P. *Leatherneck*	May 54

FURIES IN THE EAST Marines fly first Fury jets to Japan	Sarokin, MSgt P. *Leatherneck*	May 55
THE FUTURE OF MARINE AVIATION On combat effectiveness	DeChant, J. *Leatherneck*	May 54
GOING UP! Bailing out of Jets is tricky	Marcus, MSgt S. *Leatherneck*	May 54
GRAPEVINE FOR PILOTS Somewhere, you've heard the name of this author!	Glenn, Capt J. *Gazette*	Jul 52
KEEP 'EM FLYING Marine aviation mechanics	Barnum, MSgt E. *Leatherneck*	May 54
THE LAST OF THE CORSAIRS History of U-Bird—1942-53	*Naval Aviation News*	Mar 53
MARINES	*Flying*	Mar 53
MARINES HAVE BARRACKS THAT FLY	*Business Week*	Feb 6, 1954
MESSAGE FROM COMMANDANT OF THE MARINE CORPS	Shepherd, Gen L. *Flying*	Mar 53
THE PILOT FOR THE JOB	Armstrong, Maj W. *Gazette*	Jul 53
THE PLANE FOR THE JOB	Helms, Capt J. *Gazette*	Aug 53
POGO PILOT Marine Colonel flies first vertical takeoff plane	Marcus, MSgt S. *Leatherneck*	Mar 55
ROTATE THE SQUADRON Transplacement for air units	Steinkraus, Maj R. *Gazette*	Jan 55
SECONDARY MISSION	Ewers, Maj N. *Gazette*	Feb 55
THEY HOLD THEIR OWN	Paige, Col H. *Gazette*	Jun 53
THEY'LL GET AROUND Reactivate Navigator's School, Cherry Point	Tallent, TSgt R. *Leatherneck*	Jun 52

THOUGHTS ON ALL WEATHER FIGHTERS	Parnell, Capt R. *Gazette* Mar 54	
TIDDLEDY-DEE Pilotless drones train machine gunner accuracy	Milhon, Sgt W. *Leatherneck* May 51	
60 SECOND MEN Marines save fliers in crash-landings at Cherry Point	Braitsch, MSgt F. *Leatherneck* Mar 51	
WINGED FURY Supersonic Marine jets	Marcus, MSgt S. *Leatherneck* May 54	
ADVICE FOR THE REPLACEMENT PILOT Simpson was KIA two weeks after this article appeared	Simpson, Capt W. *Gazette* Feb 51	**AVIATION, KOREA**
AERIAL SUPPLY IN KOREA	Hospelhorn, Capt C., USA *Combat Forces Journal* May 51	
AIR DELIVERY IN KOREA	Banks, Col C. *Gazette* Nov 51	
CHECKERBOARD SQUADRON Marine pilots aboard Carrier	Braitsch, MSgt F. *Leatherneck* Oct 52	
A CHRONOLOGY OF MARINE CORPS AVIATION IN KOREA	*Leatherneck* Nov 56	
COOK'S TOUR FOR PILOTS	Saxon, Maj T. *Gazette* Nov 53	
EVERYBODY'S ORPHAN	Kuokka, Capt H. *Gazette* Jun 51	
EYES IN THE SKY VMO-6 in Korea	Braitsch, MSgt F. *Leatherneck* Oct 51	
1ST MARINE AIRCRAFT WING By its CO	Harris, MajGen F. *Army, Navy, Air Force Journal* Sep 51	
1ST MAW IN KOREA	Phillips, LtCol C., and Maj H. Kuokka *Gazette* May, Jun 57	

FLYING NIGHTMARES Marine flyers score first night jet kill in aviation history.	Armstrong, TSgt R. *Leatherneck* Aug 53
FLYING SERGEANTS Chevroned Marine pilots, Korea	Braitsch, MSgt F. *Leatherneck* Feb 52
FORCED DOWN Hairy tale of a lucky pilot	Smyth, Maj F. *Leatherneck* Dec 50
JET ACE NO. 1 Marine Maj John Bolt	Heinecke, MSgt R. *Leatherneck* Oct 53
JOURNEY HOME Flight from Korea	Braitsch, MSgt F. *Leatherneck* Jan 52
KOREA—A REFLECTION FROM THE AIR	Folsom, LtCol S. *Proceedings* Jul 56
MARINE AIR WAR Review first two years	Braitsch, MSgt F. *Leatherneck* Nov 51
MARINE AIR WAR 1ST MAW	Braitsch, MSgt F. *Leatherneck* Nov 52
MARINE JETS	Jessup, A. *Aviation Week* Feb 11, 1952
MIG-MAD MARINE	Bartlett, T. *Leatherneck* Jul 72
NAVAL AVIATION IN KOREA	Wheeler, G. *Proceedings* Jul 57
THE NEW LOOK IN KOREA Marines led the way with CAS and Copter ops	Stuart, H. *Air Force* Dec 51
NIGHT INTRUDERS About Marines "Flying Nightmares"	Braitsch, MSgt F. *Leatherneck* Dec 51
PANTHER PACK Tough bunch!	Braitsch, MSgt F. *Leatherneck* Sep 51
PHOTOS BY BANSHEE Marine aerial recon	Braitsch, MSgt F. *Leatherneck* Oct 52
SINUIJU RAID Air raid on the Yalu River	Braitsch, MSgt F. *Leatherneck* Jul 51, May 72

SKY HOOK	Strain, Capt J. *Gazette*	Nov 53	
WIN, PLACE AND SHOW FOR THE JETS No question about their superiority over props in everything	Banks, Col C., and Col J. Cram *Gazette*	Dec 51	
WINGS OF GOLD DON'T RUST Marine and Navy flyers relearn their trade fast when recalled	*Flying*	Nov 51	
ABC'S OF HELICOPTERS	McCutcheon, LtCol K. *Gazette*	Dec 51	**COPTERS**
CAVALRY OF THE AIR	Strain, Capt J., and Lt J. Brannaman *Gazette*	Mar 52	
CAVALRY OF THE SKY: THE STORY OF U.S. MARINE COMBAT HELICOPTERS History of choppers through Korea.	Montross, L. Harper and Bros.	1954	
THE HELICOPTER—AN AIRPLANE, NOT A 6 x 6 Fly it, don't overload it	Hunt, Maj R. *Gazette*	Aug 55	
THE HELICOPTER IN COMBAT	Barker, Lt E. *Proceedings*	Nov 51	
THE HELICOPTER IN MARINE OPERATIONS	Collins, Col W. *Army Information Digest*	Jun 51	
MARINES WANT TO BUY NEW-TYPE HELICOPTERS	*Aviation Week*	Dec 19, 1955	
NOW IT'S A FLYING CUP	Cohn, H. *Collier's*	Nov 26, 1954	
OPPAMA COPTERS Marine choppers save town residents in hurricane	Sarokin, MSgt P. *Leatherneck*	Sep 55	
PEGASUS	Collier, LtCol R. *Gazette*	Jul 51	
THE QUEEN'S COPTERS Copters in British forces	Blore, LtCdr T., RN *Gazette*	Jul 54	

	A REBUTTAL: THE HELICOPTER —A REPLACEMENT FOR THE ARMY MULE	Case, Maj J. *Gazette* Nov 55
	ROTARY AIRCRAFT'S ROLE	Clapp, Maj A. *Gazette* Oct 55
	THEIR MISSION IS MOBILITY	Clapp, Maj A. *Military Review* Aug 53
	THE TRANSFER HELICOPTER	Reavis, Lt W. *Gazette* Jul 52
	USMC SEES HELICOPTERS AS NATION'S BEST SOLUTION TO ATOMIC-AGE ASSAULT	*Army, Navy, Air Force Journal* Dec 54
	WE FLEW THE ATLANTIC IN HELICOPTERS	McGovern, V. *Sat Eve Post* Nov 1, 1952
	WHAT IS THE HELICOPTER?	Wismer, LtCol R. *Gazette* Feb 52
COPTERS, KOREA	COPTER LIFT	Said, Sgt R., and MSgt G. Burlage *Leatherneck* Dec 51
	'COPTERLIFT Daring evac by HMS-161	Braitsch, MSgt F. *Leatherneck* Dec 52
	EQUITATUS CAELI	McCutcheon, Col K. *Gazette* Feb 54
	FLYING WINDMILLS IN KOREA Prelude to their many roles in Vietnam	Montross, L. *Gazette* Sep 53

CASUALTIES

AMBULANCE AIR LINE Marine wounded flown home	Green, MSgt E. *Leatherneck* Mar 52
EASY MED First stop for WIA Marines	Burlage, MSgt G. *Leatherneck* Jan 52
HEY, DOC Marines Medics aided by Korean Labor Force (KSC'S)	Wells, MSgt H. *Leatherneck* May 53

THE JUTLANDER Danish Hospital Ship for Marines	Fugate, MSgt R. *Leatherneck*	Mar 53	
KOREA'S CONTRIBUTION TO MEDICINE Lessons learned the hard way	Ludwig, Capt V. *Gazette*	Jun 55	
PLAN FOR YOUR WOUNDED They are inevitable	Hering, Capt E. *Gazette*	Oct 53	
THEY MAKE MEN WHOLE AGAIN; THE MEDICAL BATTALION AND CHAPLAINS IN KOREA	Montross, L. *Gazette*	Dec 52	
USS CONSOLATION Wounded on hospital ship	Smith, SSgt L. *Leatherneck*	Sep 52	
THE WOUNDED Marines in Pusan Perimeter ops	Waln, N. *Sat Eve Post*	Sep 23, 1950	

DUTIES

THE BAND PLAYS ON USMC Band and Sousa	Lyons, TSgt R. *Leatherneck*	Jul 50	**BAND**
THE MARINE BAND—PRESIDENT'S OWN	Hoffman, Maj C. *Gazette*	Nov 50	
THEY DOUBLE IN BRASS Marine Bandsmen have Security and Machine Gun Drill School	Wells, MSgt H. *Leatherneck*	Jan 53	
YOKOSUKA RAINMAKERS USMC Band and rain go together	Sarokin, MSgt P. *Leatherneck*	Jul 55	
"THE CHAPLAIN CORPS"	Lewis, Lt C. *Leatherneck*	Apr 52	**CHAPLAINS**
THEIR FAITH IS YOURS Navy chaplains	Nicholson, Maj D. *Gazette*	Dec 53	
THE COMMANDER'S VOICE	Singer, Capt F. *Gazette*	Oct 52	**COMMUNICATIONS**
COMMUNICATIONS: OUR SEMI-DILEMMA	Reber, Maj J. *Gazette*	Dec 55	
THE JOB NOBODY WANTS It's stringing telephone lines	Tallent, TSgt R. *Leatherneck*	Aug 51	

Subject	Title	Author / Publication	Date
	LET'S USE WHAT WE HAVE As lousy and old as it is.	Bryant, Capt G. *Gazette*	Dec 51
	LOUD AND CLEAR	Glaeser, Maj R. *Gazette*	Jan 52
	SWITCHBOARDS FOR SOUND WAVES	Jeffcoat, Capt C. *Gazette*	Apr 52
DEMOLITIONS	BLAST MEN Demolitions—high pay.	Willis, MSgt T. *Leatherneck*	Apr 53
EMBASSY	EMBASSY DUTY For Marines around World	Fugate, MSgt R. *Leatherneck*	Jun 54
	LEATHERNECKS AND TOP HATS	Thacker, J. *Gazette*	Jul 50
ENGINEERS	ALL IN A DAY'S WORK: THE ENGINEERS AND SHORE PARTY IN KOREA	Montross, L. *Gazette*	Sep 52
	ENGINEER'S WAR	Jordan, SSgt C. *Leatherneck*	Aug 52
	NEW LOOK FOR THE ENGINEERS	Smith, LtCol R. *Gazette*	Dec 54
	WATER-WATER First Engineers insure fresh water to troops	Fugate, MSgt R. *Leatherneck*	Mar 53
GUARD	HONOR GUARD Marines share Far East Command's Honor Guard	Heinecke, MSgt R. *Leatherneck*	Dec 53
HORSE MARINES	HOSS MARINES Pendleton Color Guard	Stapelton, B. *Collier's*	Oct 20, 1951
I & I	INSPECTOR GENERAL AND HIS TEAMS Troop inspections	Lewis, TSgt C. *Leatherneck*	Aug 51
INTELLIGENCE	DO NOT CONFIRM OR DENY	Head, Maj R. *Gazette*	Feb 54
	THE PRICE OF INTELLIGENCE	Waters, Capt A. *Gazette*	Jul 54
	SECURITY THROUGH CONFUSION	Hiatt, LtCol R. *Gazette*	Aug 51

SEE IT—REPORT IT	Roe, Capt P. *Gazette*	Mar 53	
THE S-2'S CRYSTAL BALL	Watson, LtCol W. *Gazette*	Jun 52	
IF THERE'S A WAY . . . Navy Medical Research Lab has more than 75 Marines.	Suhosky, TSgt R. *Leatherneck*	Sep 53	**MEDICAL RESEARCH**
CAPITOL BEAT Marine tells about D.C. Armed Service Police Beat—MP's	Yeakel, SSgt M., as told to MSgt E. Barnum *Leatherneck*	Jul 54	**MP'S**
ROLL 'EM! Marines at MPPU Diego add Hollywood touch to training	Richardson, MSgt J. *Leatherneck*	Oct 53	**MOTION PICTURE**
43 YEARS OF MOTOR TRANSPORT	Olson, LtCol H. *Gazette*	Dec 52	**MOTOR TRANSPORT**
SADDLE UP	Oppenheimer, LtCol H. *Gazette*	Jul 52	
MISSION FOR RECON	Sexton, Maj M. *Gazette*	Oct 53	**RECON**
SUBMARINE SAFARI Amphib recon from subs	Marcus, MSgt S. *Leatherneck*	Oct 54	
WE STALK THE ENEMY And occasionally we find him.	Martin, Cpl P. *Gazette*	May 53	
SEAGOING MARINES Marines serving aboard ship	Goss, F. *Leatherneck*	Nov 50	**SEAGOING**
TO THE SHORES OF TRIPOLI Med duty	Banks, LtCol C. *Gazette*	Aug 50	
FOX COMPANY Snipers duty in Korea	Jordan, SSgt C. *Leatherneck*	Oct 52	**SNIPERS**
U. N. TOUR	McConnell, Sgt J. *Leatherneck*	Jan 52	**U.N.**
WEATHER BEATERS FORECASTING	Braitsch, MSgt F. *Leatherneck*	Dec 50	**WEATHER**

FICTION

From *Leatherneck,* alphabetical by author, unless otherwise specified:

Albert, Marvin H.

ALL THE YOUNG MEN — Paperback edition only, Pocket Books, Inc. 1960

Novel based on the screenplay by Hal Bartlett. Alan Ladd, Sidney Portier and Mort Sahl act out all the cliche roles of Hollywood Marines

Banks, Taylor

THE DECISION — Jun 52

Picks men for Korean patrol

SNUFFY GOES TO WAR — Jul 52

Press Agent wants civie pay

Bristow, Vance

DEER MAW — Jan 55

Joining USMC through country boy's eyes

Capieu, Charles

TULAGI TREASURE — Sep 55

Marine vet goes back for buried treasure won from his buddy.

Cassidy, James

PRIVATE CRYSTAL BRAIN — Oct 55

Boot becomes psychic wonder

Chalk, Sgt John

CALHOUN'S BRIGADE — Jan 53

USMC Top Kick gets Turks out of Korea trap

Church, Robert J.

ANYTHING FOR SALE! — Jan 52

Marine Reservist sells magazines New Years' Eve

THE GLORY PLATOON — Nov 52

Clelland, Don

THE RIDE — Feb 51

Marines joyride in Cadillac

Coon, Gene L.

MEANWHILE, BACK AT THE FRONT Crown Publishers, Inc. 1961
The only funny book about Korea . . . a thoroughly enjoyable novel about a bunch of screwball Marines.

Crawford, William

GIVE ME TOMORROW G. P. Putnam's Sons 1962
Mexican-American Lt is on last patrol of Korean War—reflects back on futility of war in general and this war in particular

D'Andrea, Tom.

HOLD 'TILL DAWN Aug 62
SSgt John Striker adds new emphasis to word "espirit."

Dunlap, Katherine

THE BELL NEVER TOLD Nov 53
Gunny gets clanger from church bell so old man can sleep later

Dunnagan, Grant

MULDOON'S XMAS PRESENT Dec 54
Borrows new jeep for CP

SAD MULDOON Jul 55
Boot meets General

Frank, Pat

HOLD BACK THE NIGHT J. B. Lippincott Company, Philadelphia 1952 Paperback by Bantam Books, Inc. 1953
"Dog" Co covers the withdrawal from the Reservoir to Hungnam while John Payne treasures his bottle of scotch. Good story.

Frankel, Capt Ernest

BAND OF BROTHERS The Macmillan Company 1958
Rather dull novel of Korea Marines

LIGHT DAY May 53
The kid in the outfit proves himself

Franklin, Edward

IT'S COLD IN PONGO-NI Vanguard Press, Inc. 1965
With a title like this, you don't expect much. That's what you get.

Geer, Andrew
THE BEAT OF THE DRUM — Jun 53
Marine gunner testifies in defense of Marine WW-2 buddy

Green, L.
PROFESSIONAL ATTITUDE — Jun 63

Guilford, James (Karl Schuon)
THE LAMPLIGHTER — Dec 52
THE NOISE-HAPPY GHOST — Oct 60
THREE SECONDS — Oct 52
Former Marine is lion tamer

Haines, SSgt Jonathan R.
THE PIPES OF SCHULTZ — Mar 55
Marine wins kilts at poker

Hodgson, Lt Dick
THE CAPTAIN'S VALENTINE — Feb 52
Comic valentine backfires.
LUIGI'S HARMONICA — Dec 51
Christmas Eve aboard ship

Howe, Charles
VALLEY OF FIRE — Paperback edition only, Dell Publishing Co., Inc. 1964

Johnson, Ralph
11TH HOUR ACE — Aug 51
Pilot shoots one down as WW-2 ends

LaFay, Howard
INCIDENT IN YOKOSUKA — Jul 50
Marine defends Jap troops from protest youths

Lewis, F. J.
SIC SEMPER FIDELIS — Jul 55
USMC Space Age style

Lewis, Jack
CHOSEN TALES OF CHOSIN — Paperback edition only Challenge Books, Inc., Canoga Park, Cal. 1964
Compilation of magazine articles about Marines in Korea
THE SANDTRAP COMMANDOS — Paperback edition only Paperback Library 1970
Sequel to *Tell It To The Marines.* About old men and retreads in Okinawa during an unnamed war

TELL IT TO THE MARINES Paperback edition only
Tales of the drunks Lewis commanded during the Korean War (identified as drunks by Mr. Lewis). Paperback Library 1966

Ludwig, Verle E.
THE BANDITS OF KUMCHON Aug 54
MSgt helps break up Commies.
SPACE DUTY Oct 53
Marines save the day in space world circa 1994

Mahoney, SSgt Patrick J.
GOING HOME Jun 53
It's long wait for Marines

Malliol, William
A SENSE OF DARK Atheneum, Inc. 1968
Brian Locke, only survivor of a London blitz that destroyed his family, becomes a Marine and learns what trouble really is in Korea

Marino, Vic
THE PATHS AND THREE Paperback edition only, Chicago Paperback House, Inc., Chicago 1962
And all three are awful, like this book

Martin, Jack
CHESTER Apr 55
Gunny's secret for bravery is make-believe fox

Martinez, Alfred
HOME BY MORNING Feb 63
Father and son are reunited in Korea
ORDEAL AT OUTPOST HELEN Jun 62
Lone Marine saves the day for "Fox" Co.

McCann, Charles W.
VALLEY OF THE SHADOW Mar 51
Wounded Marine caught between outpost and enemy

McCutcheon, K.
PILOT PICKUP May 54
Whirly Bird rescue of jet pilot

McGraw, J. Phillip
WHITE FEATHER BOY — Apr 51
Proves valor in N. Korea

McKinney, Paul
ANOTHER CAMPAIGN — Dec 50
Pacific vet in Korea
COLOR BLIND — Apr 54
Training Samoan Marine taxes DI

Menard, Wilnon
TAHITI FIREWALK — Jul 53
Marine shows correspondent how to walk on live coals

Newton, SSgt O. D.
LETTER TO LOUISE — Jul 50
5th at Tangara, Solomons

O'Neil, TSgt Francis J.
THE TIP-OFF — Aug 50
Fake MP gives self away

Owen, Lt J. R.
DOUBLE DUTY — Feb 52
Dating 1st Sgt's daughter

Packwood, Norval E., Jr.
THE LAST HILL — Mar 53
For young Marine who had premonition but fought on

Peacock, Jere
VALHALLA — G. P. Putnam's Sons, 1961; Paperback by Dell Publishing Company, Inc. 1967
The story of "Horrible Hog" Company in Japan during and after Korean War. The salty language makes *Naked and the Dead* read like a primer, but the story is confused, and confusing.

Reardon, William R.
GILHOOLEY'S ENTERPRISES — Mar 54
Lottery bootlegging
GILHOOLEY'S REVENGE — Sep 51
Marines mix it up aboard ship

Roberts, Bob
THE GLADHANDER — Nov 51
Marines in Japanese jungle

Robinson, Richard L.
CASE NO. 31643 — Feb 51
Staff Sgt sinks battleship
with tommy gun

Schuon, Karl A.
MULLIGAN'S LAMP — Mar 52
PFC Reservists escapades in Korea
PEANUTS — Feb 54
Big sister of PFC is MSgt of the Marines

Seybold, John Allen and Carl E. Mills
THE SITTING DUCK — Aug 52
Air sortie over Yalu

Sheldon, Walt
LADY KILLER — May 51
Gunny kills lady Col spy
THE RETURN OF THE GREMLINS — Sep 50

Shilin, Alan
CALABAN OF THE CORAL SEA — Feb 50
Horse-trading for cat-eyes
among the Marines and natives.
THE GUNNY WAS WRONG — Oct 50
Ex Film-star has troubles

Shuttlesworth, Jack
THE REGULAR — Jun 55
Guadalcanal vet in Korea.

Smith, Earl E. (Karl Schuon)
CARNIVAL AT CAMP CASEY — May 61

Stolley, MSgt Fred
BROWN VS GREEN — Sep 52
Camouflage colors stir up Branigan
CHIPMUNK'S FIRST TEST — Oct 51
Boot gets first promotion
CHIPMUNK'S PAY — Jun 51
Marine pay habits stretch
everything but money
THE COLONEL — Jun 54

Thornbury, Don

RUN THROUGH THE SUN — Apr 52
The hot Korean Punchbowl

Unsigned

SHIPS DETACHMENT, 1812 — Nov 52
Duel between Constitution and Guerriere

THE WAVING GIRL — Jun 54
Ghost signals ship at Savannah

Wagner, Paul

THE BOP BOOT — Jan 55
Hip musician gets USMC Shape-up

Wiegand, Dennis

SEMPER AND FIDELIS — Sep 52
Recruit named Semper has Sergeant sister named Fidelis

York, Frank Scott

THE BIG RAP — May 54
Top Kick fights heart condition

THE BIGGER THEY COME — Sep 54
Bully kayoed by over-the-hill Major

CHRISTMAS LEAVE — Dec 53
Three Marines battle old jalopy to get to Manhattan

THE DIVE — Aug 53
Guadalcanal buddies fight in ring-windup; bloodied but pals

LEGEND FOR A PILOT — Oct 57
High over the Yalu, the MIG's came swarming

MARCHING THROUGH GEORGIA — Jul 54
Marines stage 4th July parade for Gold Star Mom

OVERRUN — Apr 53

THE RETURN OF CAPTAIN BANNERMAN — Jun 65
About a battle in Korea led by a Captain who died three weeks before.

LEADERSHIP

All articles in this section are from the *Gazette.*

AN OUNCE OF PREVENTION — Jan 53
Be smart at the beginning

Title	Author	Date
AWOL What to do about it	Gardner, C., USN	Oct 55
AYE, AYE SIR	Crumb, MSgt C.	Nov 52
THE BREED APART Leaders are not necessarily popular	Ryan, L.	Nov 55
CALL IT CONDUCT	Prickett, Col W.	Aug 53
CAREER PATTERNS AND MORALE	Greenwood, Capt J.	Oct 55
DEALING WITH OFFENDERS	Mallen, LtCol F.	May 52
DEVELOPMENT AND VALUE OF MORALE	Smith, Lt A.	May 51
DON'T SELL EXPERIENCE SHORT	Long, SSgt J.	Mar 52
ESPRIT DE CORPS		Jan 51
EXCELSIOR Staff NCO must have pride	McPride, MSgt C.	Nov 54
GET WITH THEM	Averill, Maj G.	Nov 53
GRUNTLED	Henderson, Col F.	Apr 55
FROM MERITORIOUS NCO TO SECOND LIEUTENANT	Crumb, MSgt C.	Sep 51
HELP WANTED	Forde, Capt J.	Aug 55
IF YOU WEREN'T SELECTED	Swanson, Maj D.	Feb 52
HOW OLD IS OLD?	Hough, LtCol F.	Apr 55
IDEAS! How ideas can help the Corps perform its mission	Keller, LtCol R.	Sep 55
IMAGINATION FOR LEADERSHIP	Huston, Maj J .,USA	Dec 52
THE IMPORTANCE OF BEING INSPECTED	Stoll, LtCol W.	May 55
ITEMS PECULIAR	Willett, MSgt W.	Nov 51

LOOK BEHIND THE GRIEVANCE	Ofstad, LtCol R.	Sep 53
LOYALTY—HOW FAR?	Wilkinson, Capt J.	Oct 55
A MAN TO LEAD THEM		Nov 54
MORALE	Tobin, Maj J.	Nov 54
NCO'S—A CHALLENGE FROM WITHIN	Heinl, LtCol R.	Nov 54
ON CULTIVATING KERNELS AND COLONELS	Blyth, Lt C.	Mar 51
QUALITIES IN OFFICERS NCO'S EXPECT	Crumb, MSgt C.	Jan 52
READY FOR FEAR	Hudgins, LtCol L.	Apr 55
REALITY	Wilson, Lt W.	Feb 55
THE RIFLE PLATOON COMMANDER	LaFond, Lt P.	Apr 51
"SOME HAVE IT—SOME DON'T" And some are leaders, some are not	Boll, LtCol R.	Mar 52
A STAFF NCO SCHOOL?	Crumb, MSgt C.	Aug 52
YOU CAN'T MAKE THEM DRINK But you *can* lead them	Quirk, Lt B.	Feb 52

LOGISTICS

Articles in this section are from the *Gazette,* unless otherwise specified:

GENERAL

AMPHIBIAN WITH A FUTURE	Croizat, LtCol V.	Feb 53
AND FEED THE TROOPS A HOT MEAL	Jackson, LtCol W.	Apr 50
THE BEST THINGS IN WAR . . . Do's and Don'ts re: supplies	Roose, LtCol A. *Leatherneck*	Apr 52
"BOAR-R-ED" Troop Trains	Banks, LtCol C.	Apr 51
THE CASE AGAINST THE CLOTH BELT	Heinl, Col R.	Jun 55

CONFORMITY AND UNIFORMITY	Curtis, Capt T.	Dec 55
DEVELOPMENT OF OUR BODY ARMOR	Montross, L.	Jun 55
EMBARKATION—THE SECOND PHASE	Wood, Col R.	Jun 55
EQUIPMENT BOARD Mighty Mite Jeep and other equipment tested at Quantico	Sims, SSgt R. *Leatherneck*	May 53
FIELD EXPEDIENTS	Porter, MSgt R.	Oct 55
THE FIELD TRANSPORT PACK	McMillan, D. *Leatherneck*	Sep 55
FOOD TEAM USMC eats $80,000,000 a year	Sarokin, MSgt P. *Leatherneck*	Mar 52
FROM BLUE PRINT TO BATTLE FIELD		Jan 53
FRONTLINE FASHIONS New Marine parka appears	*Leatherneck*	Feb 53
HIGH PRIORITY WOOD	Loughlin, Lt D.	Jul 54
HOT MEALS FOR COMBAT TROOPS	Morgan, Col G.	Jan 52
"INUIT" KNEW HOW How the Eskimo dresses for the cold	Hardwick LtCol G., and Maj V. Boyd	Oct 52
LET'S ADOPT A REALISTIC HOLSTER	McAlister, Capt J.	May 55
LET'S CASH IN ON ENEMY SUPPLIES	Gore, SSgt C.	May 52
MOBILE LOADING IN THE ASSAULT PHASE	Long, LtCol F.	Sep 55
MODERNIZE OUR TENTS	Constantine, Lt E.	Jan 52
MORE POWER WITH GAS TURBINES	Gardner, A.	Sep 54
NEW PRINCIPLE	Greenwood, Capt J.	Jul 54

NO VICTORY WITHOUT ECONOMY	Felps, LtCol C.	Jun 52
ORDNANCE REPAIR	Palmer, MSgt W.	Aug 51
PACK RAT PEGASUS	Johnson, LtCol W.	Aug 54
PACKING IN WINTER OPERATIONS	Roberts, MSgt C.	Dec 54
PRIDE OF UNIFORM	Shaw, Sgt H.	May 55
PROTECTION FOR THE INFANTRYMAN Armor for the gravel cruncher	McGrew, Capt D.	Sep 50
RE-PACK YOUR TROUBLES	Ludwig, Capt V.	Mar 53
RIGGED FOR COMBAT	Wood, LtCol R.	Apr 53
SALVAGE IS EVERYBODY'S JOB	Mallen, LtCol F.	Jan 51
SENSIBLE SUMMER UNIFORMS	Heinl, LtCol R.	Sep 55
TELL 'EM WHAT IT COSTS	Braiser, MSgt R.	Mar 53
WHAT DO YOU KNOW ABOUT SUPPLY?	Benge, LtCol H.	Mar 51
WHY PALLETS?	Long, LtCol F.	Sep 54
YOU HAVE TO TAKE IT WITH Because that's the only way supplies get there	Massie, LtCol H.	Aug 50
YOU'RE MOVING THE WORLD Importance of protecting our sources of supply	Gardner, A. *Gazette*	Sep 53

LOGISTICS, KOREA

KOREAN LIFE LINE Trucks carry everything for War	Tallent, SSgt R. *Leatherneck*	Jul 51
MARINE SUPPLY IN KOREA	Condit, K.	Jan 53

MARINES

From *Leatherneck,* unless otherwise specified:

GENERAL

COLD WAR 1 Former Marines in FBI	Lewis, TSgt R.	Aug 50

Subject	Title / Description	Author / Source	Date
	CORPS LINGO Marine slang censored	Ruttle, L.	Nov 53
	GOLDEN GRIPES Marine laments, like weather, always around	Marcus, MSgt S.	Sep 54
	GUNNY ON THE BEACH Retired Gunny, famous beach-comber in Washington	Marcus, MSgt S.	Jan 55
	HOME REMEDIES FOR MARINES Cures for gripes	Ruttle, L.	Oct 52
	THE LENSMAN LIKED TAMALES Former Marine has tamale factory in Santa Barbara	Heinecke, MSgt R.	Sep 55
	MARINE'S MARINE	*Time*	Aug 24, 1954
	POLICE ACADEMY, L. A. Former Marines train for police	Marcus, MSgt S.	Apr 54
	SEA GOING SALTS How Marines get sea legs	Ruttle, L.	May 52
	THE SEA URCHIN Former Marine owns sloop	Marcus, MSgt S.	Apr 54
	THREE GUNNYS TSgt always will be Gunnery Sgt to Marines	Jones, TSgt J.	Apr 51
	TIGER TALE Flying Tiger Marines	Marcus, MSgt S.	May 54
	UNDER THE GLOBE AND EAGLE Bitching Sgts 30 year men	Johnston, SSgt L.	May 52
	WHO'S GETTING OUT? Buddies get Gunny to sign up for another hitch	Haney, J.	Nov 55
MARINES, KOREA	AN AFTERNOON	McCloskey, Lt D. *Gazette*	Jul 52
	THE CASE OF CORPORAL JAMES Keep your dog tags on!	Berry, Col J.	Apr 51
	THE FEET THAT SHOOK THE CORPS Boot has two left feet, literally!	DeLuna, Sgt F.	Jul 53

IN THE HIGHEST TRADITION . . . HENRY ALFRED COMMISKEY Medal of Honor citation	Marcus, MSgt S.	May 54
IN THE HIGHEST TRADITION . . . ALFRED LEE McLAUGHLIN Medal of Honor citation	Lyons, R.	Feb 54
IN THE HIGHEST TRADITION . . . ARCHIE VAN WINKLE Medal of Honor citation	Marcus, MSgt S.	Jul 54
THE LAST PARALLEL: A MARINE'S WAR JOURNAL Diary of a brash, young rifleman from Nov 1952 thru Truce. Best book written about Korea	Russ, M. Rinehart and Comany, Inc.	1957
LEATHERHEAD IN KOREA The intrepid cartoon character makes a shambles of the 1st MAR DIV in Korea	Packwood, SSgt N. *Gazette*	1952
MARINE TELLS HIS FATHER WHAT KOREA IS REALLY LIKE	Harper, J. *Life*	Dec 3, 1951
THE PRICE OF LIFE How a Marine understands his Korean War role	Von Mann, M.	Sep 52
RECKLESS 1ST MAR DIV horse Reckless comes home.	Geer, A.	May 55
RED CARPET FOR SGT RECKLESS: HORSE OF 1ST MARINE DIV A good short story	Geer, A. *Sat Eve Post*	Oct 22, 1955
RECKLESS: PRIDE OF THE MARINES The good short story becomes a long-winded, padded book	Geer, A. E. P. Dutton & Co., Inc.	1955
TWICE ACROSS THE RAINBOW Experiences while a POW of the Japanese during WW-2 and the Chinese during Korea (They call him "Lucky!")	Harrison, TSgt C. *Proceedings*	May 52

OFF-DUTY

From *Leatherneck*, unless otherwise specified:

GENERAL

Title	Author	Date
"AT EASE" Marine TV from Pendleton	Gartz, MSgt S.	Apr 53
AT HOME IN TOKYO MSgt honeymoon home	Heinecke, MSgt R.	Aug 54
BACK BREAKERS The fish are BIG at Parris Island	Lyons, TSgt R.	Apr 51
BAIT YOUR HOOKS Fishing, Marine style	Carpenter, Maj D.	Apr, May 52
BEAR HUNT Marines bag bears near Kodiak	Heinecke, MSgt R.	Dec 55
CORPS NIMRODS Hunting season	Carpenter, Maj D.	Dec 52
DEAD EYE MSgt has one miss in 200 tries in trap-shooting tourney	Sarokin, MSgt P.	Oct 53
"GOOD HUNTING, MARINE"	Totman, Col C. *Gazette*	Mar 52
GROUND FLYERS Marine's hobby—models	McCollum, C.	Jun 54
HAM HOOKUP Marine hams keep in touch	Jordan, TSgt C.	Dec 53
HOLIDAY IN HONG KONG Marines aboard USS Rochester know all Far East ports-of-call	Heinecke, MSgt R.	Aug 54
L. A. LIBERTY Means girls for Marines, natch	McConnell, SSgt J.	Jun 52
LEJEUNE BLADESMEN Fencing club at Lejeune	Tallent, SSgt R.	Jan 50
MARINES AT THE BOWL GAMES Stateside and Far East	Heinecke, MSgt R.	Feb 54
MOOSE HUNT Marines hunt moose in Argentina, Newfoundland	Suhosky, TSgt R.	Feb 55

NAHA LIBERTY 4th Marines R & R on Okinawa	Heinecke, MSgt R. Mar 54	
NEW ORLEANS LIBERTY Marines prefer French Quarter	Suhosky, TSgt R. Oct 53	
OPEN SEASON Marines hunt moose in Argentina, Newfoundland	Suhosky, TSgt R. Apr 54	
OUTDOOR LIVING HINTS	Carpenter, Maj D. *Gazette* Jul 51	
SHOW DAZE Marines entertain at San Diego	Suhosky, TSgt R. Feb 52	
SHOW MAKERS Enlistees from Show Biz put on USMC production	Suhosky, TSgt R. Sep 53	
SWORDMAKERS Marines collect hand made swords in Japan	Sarokin, MSgt P. Aug 55	
TATOOING Corps emblems popular tatoos	Tallent, TSgt R. Feb 52	
TELECLOWN Ed McMahon is teleclown	McMahon, Capt E. Jun 54	
THEY ROLL THEIR OWN Eleven thousand mobile trailers are home for Marines	Suhosky, TSgt R. Jul 53	
UNDERWATER HUNT Spear fishing	Bolt, Maj J. Apr 54	
VARIETY Twenty-two Marine actors hit the road	Jordan, SSgt C. Nov 51	
WHO'S GOING ASHORE? Marines see the world off-duty	Suhosky, TSgt R. Nov 53	
THE G.I'S AND THE KIDS FROM KOREA: AMERICA'S FIGHTING MEN SHARE THEIR FOOD, CLOTHING AND SHELTER	Mosier, R. *Geographic* May 53	**OFF-DUTY, KOREA**
HOLIDAY IN JAPAN R & R for 1ST MAW	Braitsch, MSgt F. Sep 51	

JAPAN LIBERTY Most Marines live Western style	Heinecke, MSgt R.	Aug 54
ON LIMITS Marines inspect Jap cafes	Heinecke, MSgt R.	Sep 54
OPERATION KID LIFT: KOREAN ORPHANS	Lederer, W. and N. Perry *Ladies Home Journal*	Dec 52
POHANG ORPHANAGE	Barrow, MSgt C.	Jan 62
POHANG ORPHANS Children's home from 1ST MAW	Jordan, SSgt C.	Feb 53
ROAD SHOW Entertainers in Korea.	Heinecke, MSgt R.	Mar 54
SEOUL LIBERTY Three days R & R	Gray, Lt B.	Aug 52

PERSONNEL

All articles in this section are from the *Gazette* unless otherwise specified:

GENERAL

ADMINISTRATIVE FRILLS	Nicholson, Maj D.	May 55
BRVTY AT THE EXPNS OF CLRTY	Howard, Cdr J., USN	Sep 51
CASUALTY? BE SURE!	Cowie, Capt W.	Apr 53
CLASSIFIED	Stallknecht, Capt E.	Jan 55
THE CLERICAL PYRAMID	Sedora, Capt S.	Jun 55
COMPANY RECORDS IN COMBAT	Rich, Lt C.	Jun 52
CONDUCT MARKS IN THE SRB	Welter, MSgt A.	Sep 52
COORDINATION — NOT SUBORDINATION	Stubbs, Maj R.	Sep 54
ECONOMY IN WRITING	Prickett, Col W.	Jul 54
ELIMINATE THE SURPLUS CP	Rich, Lt C.	Jun 54
ENLISTED PROMOTIONS Clarification of procedures	Hunt, Capt R. *Leatherneck*	Mar 51

	READIN', RITIN', AND REGIMENTS	Rudasics, J.	Mar 52
	RETIREMENT AND I	McNiff, Maj J.	Aug, Nov 54
	SKIPPER WITH TWO HATS	Fredericks, Lt H.	Jul 53
	SQUARE-BASHIN' AND TYPEWRITERS	Alsop, S.	May 55
	STAFF EXPERIENCE SPEAKS	Curry, Col M.	May 55
	STANDARIZE THE MARKING SYSTEM	Forde, Capt J.	Sep 54
	A STUDY OF STUDIES		Oct 55
	SURVIVORS' BENEFITS	Smith, Maj R.	Aug 54
	THREE YEARS UNDER THE UCMJ	Bergren, LtCol O.	Sep 54
	TO CLASSIFY OR NOT TO CLASSIFY	Evers, MSgt C.	Feb 54
	"WHADDYA MEAN, NO PAY?"	Petry, MSgt A. *Leatherneck*	Sep 54
DECORATIONS	FOR FOREIGN SERVICE Decorations for Korea	Blakeney, J. *Leatherneck*	Nov 53
	A LOOK AT OUR AWARDS		Nov 54
	YOUR KOREAN DECORATIONS	Blakeney, J.	Mar 54

POSTS/PLACES

From the "Post of the Corps" series in *Leatherneck*, unless otherwise specified:

GENERAL	ANCHORS AROUND THE GLOBE Sun never sets on USMC	Suhosky, TSgt R.	Nov 53
	APARTMENT JACKPOT New housing projects on posts	Thompson, J.	Feb 50
	THE CORPS' EIGHT MAJOR POSTS	*Gazette*	Dec 50
	GOING OVERSEAS?	*Gazette*	May 50

Article	Author	Date	Subject
SLAUGHTER ON THE HIGHWAY Marine auto accidents	Barnum, MSgt E.	Dec 54	
ALAMEDA	Marcus, MSgt S.	Feb 54	
ALBANY, GA	Pugh, MSgt H.	Jan 53	
ARGENTIA, NEWFOUNDLAND	Suhosky, TSgt R.	Sep 54	
ATSUGI, JAPAN	Heinecke, MSgt R.	Dec 54	
BARBER'S POINT, CALIFORNIA	Tallent, SSgt R. and PFC J. Hart	Dec 50	
BARSTOW ANNEX	Suhosky, SSgt R.	Sep 52	
BERMUDA	Marcus, MSgt S.	Mar 53	
BREMERTON, WASHINGTON	Marcus, MSgt S.	Jan 55	
BROOKLYN NAVY YARD	Suhosky, TSgt R.	Mar 55	
CAMP FISHER, KYOTO	Heinecke, MSgt R.	Aug 54	
TENT CAMP TODAY Camp Geiger converts to buildings	Tallent, TSgt R.	Apr 52	**CAMP GEIGER**
CLUB LEJEUNE Expand Staff NCO Club	Tallent, TSgt R.	Mar 52	**CAMP LEJEUNE**
LEJEUNE RECREATION Includes water sports and golf	Suhosky, TSgt R.	Apr 55	
CAMP OTSU	Braitsch, MSgt F.	Nov 51	
CALL OUT THE HOUNDS Canine security	Gartz, MSgt S.	Dec 54	**CAMP PENDLETON**
CAMP PENDLETON	Marcus, MSgt S.	May 55	
COMBAT TOWN Mockup practice at Pendleton	Slockbower, SSgt J.	Mar 51	

	Title	Author	Date
	NEW COMBAT TOWN Complete with Red snipers	Gartz, MSgt S.	Mar 53
	PENDLETON ROUNDUP Marines ride 'em cowboy	Tyler, TSgt C.	Sep 54
	CHARLESTOWN, MASS	Tallent, TSgt R.	Nov 51
	CLEARFIELD, UTAH	Tallent, TSgt R.	Aug 52
	CRANE, INDIANA	Barnum, MSgt E.	Jul 54
	DAHLGREN, VA	Lyons, TSgt R.	Feb 51
	DAMASCUS, SYRIA	Shafranski, MSgt R.	Feb 53
	EARLE, N.J.	McConnell, SSgt J.	Apr 53
	EL TORO	Heinecke, MSgt R.	Oct 55
	GLENVIEW, ILLINOIS	Hart, Lt H.	Jan 52
GUANTANAMO	GUANTANAMO BAY	Tallent, TSgt R.	Apr 52
	MULE MARINES Mules at Gitmo	Tallent, TSgt R.	May 52
	SO LONG, MULES Mules put to pasture at Gitmo	Marcus, MSgt S.	Aug 53
	HAWTHORNE, NEVADA Lake Denmark Ammo Depot	Tallent, SSgt R.	Jul 50
	ITAMI, JAPAN	Heinecke, MSgt R.	May 54
	JACKSONVILLE	McConnell, TSgt J.	Oct 53
	KANEOHE BAY, HAWAII	Morris, TSgt W.	Sep 53
	KEY WEST	Lyons, MSgt R.	May 52
	KODIAK, ALASKA	Heinecke, MSgt R.	Sep 55
	LAKEHURST, NEW JERSEY	Lyons, TSgt R.	Jan 51
	LONDON, ENGLAND	Lyons, MSgt R.	Oct 51

LONG BEACH NAVAL BASE	Mar 51	
MARE ISLAND	Suhosky, SSgt R. Aug 53	
MEMPHIS, TENN	Suhosky, SSgt R. Aug 51	
MIAMI, FLORIDA	McConnell, SSgt J. Jun 53	
WATCHDOGS OF MOROCCO Eighteen Marine War Dogs help guard Port Lyantey	Marcus, MSgt S. Aug 53	
NAPLES, ITALY	Marcus, MSgt S. Jul 53	
NEW DELHI, INDIA	Cooksey, Sgt R. Jul 52	
NATO DETACHMENT, NORFOLK	Barnum, MSgt E. Feb 55	
OAHU	Wilson, TSgt G. Oct 52	
PARIS, FRANCE	Lyons, MSgt R. Dec 51	
PARIS LIBERTY Embassy marines enjoy it	Marcus, MSgt S. Sep 53	
PARRIS ISLAND	Sarokin, MSgt P. Nov 54	
PATUXENT, MARYLAND Marines at Naval Test Center	Morris, Sgt W. Sep 50	
PEARL HARBOR	Tallent, SSgt R. Apr 51	**PEARL HARBOR**
PEARL HARBOR TODAY Marines in charge of security.	Marcus, MSgt S. Dec 55	
MARINE BARRACKS, PHILADELPHIA	Suhosky, TSgt R. Oct 54	**PHILADELPHIA**
PHILADELPHIA DEPOT OF SUPPLIES	Braitsch, MSgt F. Oct 50	
MARINE CORPS SCHOOLS AT QUANTICO	Hart, F. *Army Information Digest* Feb 52	**QUANTICO**
QUANTICO 3	*Army, Navy, Air Force Journal* Jul 55	

	QUANTICO	Suhosky, TSgt R. Jul 55
	QUANTICO'S OTHER SCHOOLS Extension School, Commissioned Officer's School, Ordnance, etc.	Glickert, LtCol R. Oct 54
	QUANTICO RODEO For Marines Relief	Sims, SSgt R. Sep 53
	QUONSET POINT, RHODE ISLAND	Jordan, SSgt C. Feb 52
	ROME	Lyons, MSgt R. Mar 52
SAN DIEGO	SAN DIEGO, CALIFORNIA New boots and old advice	Marcus, MSgt S. Nov 54
	MCRD, SAN DIEGO Boots swarm into base	Burlage, TSgt G. Jan 51
SAN FRANCISCO	100 HARRISON ST.	Suhosky, SSgt R. Dec 52
	MARINE BARRACKS, SAN FRANCISCO	Burlage, MSgt G. Jul 51
	CROSSROADS ON THE COAST Everybody goes to Memorial Club	Suhosky, SSgt R. Jul 53
	SANTA ANA	Burlage, MSgt G. Jun 52
	SEATTLE	Marcus, MSgt S. Jun 55
	TANGIERS, MOROCCO	Bristow, V. Jun 54
	TEXARKANA	Smolkin, Capt W. Jan 53
	TREASURE ISLAND	Marcus, MSgt S. Dec 53
	TRINIDAD	Marcus, MSgt S. May 53
	TWENTY-NINE PALMS, CALIFORNIA	Marcus, MSgt S. Mar 54
SEA DUTY	U.S.S. BON HOMME RICHARD	Burlage, MSgt G. Sep 51
	U.S.S. CORAL SEA	Braitsch, MSgt F. Jun 51

MARINE DET. U.S.S. FORRESTAL AIRCRAFT CARRIER	Suhosky, SSgt R.	Dec 55
MARINE DETACHMENT, U.S.S. NEW JERSEY	McConnell, SSgt J.	Oct 52
8th AND EYE, MARINE BARRACKS	Suhosky, TSgt R.	Nov 55
THIS IS HDQ	Fugate, MSgt R.	
How did I get here?		Jan 54
So you got a promotion		Feb 54
Got a requisition?		Mar 54
Training time		Apr 54
Division of Marine Air		May 54
HENDERSON HALL	Burlage, G.	Feb 50
HQMC	Lewis, R.	
Duties of Marines		Feb 50
MARINE BARRACKS, 8th AND EYE	Porter, J. *Gazette*	Nov 50
MARINE BARRACKS, WASHINGTON, D.C.	Barnum, MSgt E.	Apr 54
YOKOSUKA	Tallent, SSgt R.	May 51

WASHINGTON

RECRUITING

ANSWER THEIR QUESTIONS	Copeland, Lt F. *Gazette*	May 53
BILLBOARD MARINE Reflects pride and tradition. Remains Corps' top recruiter	Tallent, MSgt R. *Leatherneck*	Dec 53
COMPANY OFFICER SHORTAGE	Crumb, MSgt C. *Gazette*	Nov 53
LADY RECRUITER Boosts WR enlistment in N.C.	Braitsch, MSgt F. *Leatherneck*	Oct 53
NOBODY WANTS TO BE A FIGHTING MAN Any more	Ryan, Lt L. *Gazette*	Apr 52
OLD TIMERS Vet pair now recruiting Bowery	Copeland, Lt F. *Leatherneck*	Feb 53

	THE OUTLOOK	Morgan, MSgt J. *Gazette*	Jan 54
	SELECTIVE SERVICE IS THE ANSWER But not for the Corps!	Rankin, LtCol R. *Gazette*	May 52
	SHIP OVER—AND WIN	Bullen, Lt J. *Navy*	Jul 60
	TEN ROADS TO A COMMISSION	Morrison, Capt K. *Gazette*	Apr 53
	$10,000 OVERSIGHT	Bois, MSgt J. *Gazette*	Sep 52
	THAT MONTHLY QUOTA Recruiting fills the bill	Ill, TSgt E. *Leatherneck*	May 51
	THAT WONDERFUL RECRUITING DUTY	Rosoff, Sgt B. *Gazette*	Oct 50
	THEY KNOW THE SCORE New recruits are not naive.	Piehl, Capt R. *Gazette*	Mar 53
	THE TYPICAL MARINE IS GONE	Gore, SSgt C. *Gazette*	Sep 51
	VOLUNTEER RECRUITING IS THE ANSWER	Cereghino, LtCol A. *Gazette*	Aug 52
	WAIT ONE, LIEUTENANT	Bradley, Lt J. *Gazette*	Oct 53

RESERVE

GENERAL	CALL OUT THE RESERVES	*Gazette*	Oct 53
	FROM "ROTSY" TO MARINE	Stockman, Maj J. *Gazette*	Sep 53
	IN CASE OF FIRE Marine Reservists take correspondence courses.	Tallent, SSgt R. *Leatherneck*	Nov 53
	IN RESERVE	Suhosky, TSgt R. *Leatherneck*	Sep 54
	IN RESERVE—WEEK-END WARRIORS	Suhosky, TSgt R. *Leatherneck*	May 54

IN RESERVE The old standby (how it's grown)	Tallent, MSgt R. *Leatherneck*	Nov 54
MARINE RESERVES AND SUMMER CAMP	Kennedy, Maj V. *Gazette*	Aug 55
MCI ART CONTEST	*Leatherneck*	Feb 53
OPERATION INTEGRATION!	Copeland, MSgt F. *Gazette*	Feb 52
RESERVE MEN AT THE POINT Airmen at Cherry Point	Braitsch, MSgt F. *Leatherneck*	Oct 50
THE RESERVES!	Booth, Col A. *Gazette*	Jul 55
RESERVES ABOARD	Ill, SSgt E. *Leatherneck*	Oct 50
THE RESERVES: CITIZEN MARINES	Switzer, Lt L. *Gazette*	Nov 50
RETIREMENT AND I (THE RESERVES)	McNiff, Maj J. *Gazette*	Aug 55

RESERVE UNITS

BALTIMORE RESERVISTS Three units at Fort McHenry	Mainard, TSgt A. *Leatherneck*	Apr 55	
BOSTON PLATOON Women Marines win awards	*Leatherneck*	Feb 54	**BOSTON**
BOSTON RESERVISTS 2d Inf Bn	Mainard, TSgt A. *Leatherneck*	Aug 55	
BROOKLYN RESERVES 1st Inf Bn	Wasserberg, Capt I. *Leatherneck*	Apr 53	
SUNDAY PUNCHERS Reserve Marine pilots at Dallas	Braitsch, MSgt F. *Leatherneck*	Sep 50	
FRISCO'S FIRING SQUAD 12th Amphibian Tractor Bn	Morris, W. *Leatherneck*	Feb 50	
GLENVIEW RESERVISTS Week-end Warriors	Mainard, TSgt A. *Leatherneck*	Jul 55	

HAWAII	DA KIND MARINES All-Hawaii Company Reserve	Harmon, TSgt J. *Leatherneck*	Jan 54
	HONOLULU RESERVISTS 15th Inf Bn	Marcus, MSgt S. *Leatherneck*	Sep 55
	INDIANAPOLIS—WEEK-END WAR	Pambrun, L. *Gazette*	Apr 53
	L.A. RESERVISTS 2d 105 mm Howitzer Bn	Heinecke, MSgt R. *Leatherneck*	Jun 55
	MIAMI RESERVISTS 2d 155 mm Gun Bn	Fugate, MSgt R. *Leatherneck*	May 55
	PHILADELPHIA RESERVISTS 1st 155 mm Howitzer Bn, 2d Depot Supply Bn, WM Supply Plt.	Suhosky, TSgt R. *Leatherneck*	Nov 55
	PORTLAND RESERVISTS 8th Engineers, 2d Eng Field Maintenance Co	Heinecke, MSgt R. *Leatherneck*	Oct 55
	PORTSMOUTH RESERVISTS 75th Special Inf Co	Curtis, TSgt P. *Leatherneck*	Dec 55
RESERVE, KOREA	FIGHTING TEAM Mobilization of reservists at Pendleton and El Toro	Burlage, G. *Leatherneck*	Nov 50
	MARINE RESERVES IN ACTION	Stickney, BGen W. *Military Affairs*	Spring 53
	MINUTE MEN—1950 MODEL; THE RESERVES IN ACTION	Giusti, Capt E. *Gazette*	Sep 51
	MOBILIZATION OF THE MARINE CORPS RESERVE IN THE KOREAN CONFLICT, 1950-51 Sixty page pamphlet with charts and tables. Very factual. Dull.	Giusti, Capt E. HQMC	1953
	NO LONGER YOUNG AND GAY The "Retreads" are called back. Not too happy about it.	Kelley, Capt J., and Lt C. Lewis *Gazette*	Oct 50
	"RECALL" First year of USMCR in Korea	Jones, MSgt J., and TSgt R. Tallent *Leatherneck*	Nov 51

THEY SERVED AND WAITED Reserve call-up for Korea	*Gazette* Nov 65	
UNCLE SAM'S BITTER NEPHEWS The "second-time around" Marines in Korea	Jaffe, S. *Nation* Dec 29, 1951	
WOMEN RESERVES WR's are called back, too.	McConnell, Sgt J. *Leatherneck* Nov 51	

SPORTS

All articles in this section are from *Leatherneck.*

LEATHERNECK SPORTS Series on sports available at USMC bases	Suhosky, SSgt R. Feb-Apr 52	**GENERAL**
RESERVE ATHLETES	Ill, TSgt E., and SSgt R. Suhosky Nov 51	
ALL-MARINE BASKETBALL '51	Suhosky, SSgt R. Jun 51	**BASKETBALL**
ALL-AMERICAN BASKETBALL	Berger, SSgt W. Oct 51	
ALL-MARINE BASKETBALL Quantico wins crown	McCann, Sgt H. Jun 52	
ALL-MARINE BASKETBALL Quantico wins title	Southee, Sgt R. Jun 54	
LEATHERNECK'S ALL-MARINE BASKETBALL STARS	Willis, MSgt T. Jul 53	
CYCLE RACERS Bike champ in 3D DIV, Japan	Frank, TSgt W. Aug 54	**BICYCLE RACING**
MEET THE CHAMP Marines on TV Boxing Show	Suhosky, SSgt R. May 52	**BOXING**
ALL-MARINE BOXING '53	Willis, MSgt T. Jun 53	
ALL-SERVICE BOXING Marines take three titles	Willis, MSgt T. Jul 53	
ALL-MARINE BOXING '55	Suhosky, TSgt R. Jun 55	
BOOT BOWL With DI's at Savannah	Suhosky, TSgt R. Jan 52	**FOOTBALL**

	LEATHERNECK'S '49 ALL-MARINE FOOTBALL TEAM	Tallent, SSgt R., and Sgt S. Gartz	Feb 50
	LEATHERNECK'S '50 ALL-MARINE FOOTBALL TEAM	Ill, SSgt E.	Feb 51
	'51 FOOTBALL FORECAST	Suhosky, TSgt R.	Oct 51
	LEATHERNECK'S '51 ALL-MARINE FOOTBALL TEAM	Suhosky, TSgt R.	Jan 52
	LEATHERNECK'S '52 ALL-MARINE FOOTBALL TEAM	Willis, MSgt T.	Mar 53
	FOOTBALL FORECAST Puts his bet on Quantico	Willis, MSgt T.	Sep 53
	LEATHERNECK'S ALL-MARINE ELEVEN '53	Suhosky, TSgt R.	Mar 54
	LEATHERNECK'S '54 ALL-MARINE FOOTBALL TEAM	Suhosky, TSgt R.	Mar 55
GOLF	TEE SERGEANT San Diego Recruit Depot golfers and TSgt James Frye	Tallent, SSgt R.	Aug 50
HOCKEY	ICEMEN Marine Recruiters' hockey team	Tallent, SSgt R.	Jul 50
TRACK	FIELD MEET '50 Eleven records at Quantico	Tallent, SSgt R.	Sep 50
	TRACK AND FIELD '53 Eleven records at Lejeune	Willis, MSgt T.	Aug 53
	CINDER CIRCUS Set three new records at Track and Field Meets	Suhosky, TSgt R.	Sep 54
	TRACK AND FIELD '55	Suhosky, TSgt R.	Aug 55

STRATEGY

AS THE PRESIDENT MAY DIRECT Mission of Marine Corps	Shepherd, Gen L. *Proceedings*	Nov 51
GEOPOLITICS FOR A MARINE	Brown, Col W. *Gazette*	Oct 50

MARINES AFLOAT: ASSET OR ANACHRONISM?	Reichner, LtCol H. *Proceedings*	Feb 52	
NEWCOMER TO J.C.S.	Johnsen, K. *Aviation Week*	May 26, 1952	
PARA-MILITARY WARFARE	Kintner, LtCol W., USA *Gazette*	Mar 51	
PLANNING FOR ATOMIC WAR	Reber, Maj J. *Gazette*	Jul 55	
SHAPE-UP FOR "A" WAR	Canzona, Capt N. *Gazette*	Feb 54	
TOMORROW'S ATOMIC BATTLEFIELD	Reinhardt, Col G., USA *Gazette*	Mar 54	

SUPPORTING ARMS

AMPHIBIOUS ARTILLERY	Miller, LtCol W. *Gazette*	Aug 52	**ARTILLERY**
ARMS FOR THE ASSAULT	Fletcher, LtCol S. *Gazette*	Jul 54	
ARTILLERY ADVISOR TO THE INFANTRY	Valente, Maj R. *Gazette*	Mar 52	
FAREWELL TO CANNONEERS	Henderson, Col F. *Gazette*	Nov 54	
FDC NEEDS MODERNIZATION	Rowse, LtCol E., and Maj L. Bethards *Gazette*	Apr 55	
FSCC: TWO SCHOOLS OF THOUGHT	Heinl, LtCol R. *Gazette*	Jan 53	
ARTILLERY SUPPORT FOR THE BRIGADE IN KOREA	Wood, LtCol R. *Gazette*	Jun 51	**ARTILLERY, KOREA**
ARTY ROCKETS TO KILL ARMOR	Wade, LtCol J.	May 55	
FIRE MISSION	Standford, Capt J. *Gazette*	Jan 51	
FIRE MISSION Big guns level Red emplacements	Braitsch, MSgt F. *Leatherneck*	Jul 52	

Subject	Title	Author / Source	Date
	MARINE ARTILLERY IN KOREA	Condit, K. *Gazette*	Nov 52
CLOSE AIR SUPPORT	AIR CONTROL GROUP Air support and defense	Braitsch, MSgt F. *Leatherneck*	Jun 51
	AIR—SUPPRESS THAT INCOMING	Wagner, Capt W. *Gazette*	May 55
	CAPTAIN THACH'S PHANTOM CARRIER	Denson, J. *Collier's*	Oct 14, 1950
	CLOSE AIR SUPPORT	*Flying*	Nov 51
	INFANTRY—AIR SUPPORT SINGLE COMMAND Marine better than Army	Standish, Col A., USA *Combat Forces Journal*	Jul 52
	MARINE AVIATION IN SUPPORT OF AMPHIBIOUS TROOPS	Wethe, Maj W. *Gazette*	Jan 51
	TACTICAL AIR SUPPORT OF GROUND FORCES	Megee, MajGen V. *Gazette*	Dec 55
	TRAINED FOR SUPPORT	Keller, LtCol R. *Gazette*	May 54
	THE TRUTH ABOUT AIR SUPPORT	Black, C. *Flying*	Feb 51
CLOSE AIR SUPPORT, KOREA	AERIAL ARTILLERY: THE MARINES FLY CLOSE SUPPORT	Portz, LtCdr M., USNR *Flying*	Dec 50
	AIR POWER IN KOREA—GROUND SUPPORT	*Proceedings*	Feb 52
	AIR STRIKE Air controllers zero in on Chinese Reds	Braitsch, MSgt F. *Leatherneck*	Apr 53
	MAGNIFICENT SUPPORT	*Leatherneck*	Apr 51
	NIGHT FIGHTER SQUADRON CAS at night in Korea	Rineburg, Col J. *Ordnance*	Jan, Feb 65
	NIGHT STRIKE	Packwood, Sgt N. *Gazette*	May 52
	NIGHT SUPPORT: A NEW WEAPON	Smyth, Maj F. *Gazette*	Nov 51

ROUND-THE-CLOCK CLOSE AIR SUPPORT	Matheson, Maj B. *Gazette*	Sep 54
SKY RAIDERS	Braitsch, MSgt F. *Leatherneck*	Apr 52

TACTICS

From the *Gazette,* unless otherwise specified:

GENERAL

AFTER THE FIREFIGHT	Nicholson, Maj D.	Feb 54
ANTI-GUERRILLA WARFARE	Decker, Lt W.	Aug 51
AUSTERITY AND VICTORY	Banks, Col C.	Aug 51
THE BRIDGE	Tompkins, Col R.	Apr, May 51
CANDLEPOWER FOR COMBAT	Pierce, Maj P.	Aug 55
CHECK POINTS	Woessner, LtCol H.	Jun 55
C-O-L-D Cold weather ops		Mar 51
COMMAND POST MINUTE MEN How to combat a surprise guerrilla attack	Bealer, Capt A.	Sep 52
CONSIDER THIS CONCEPT Seaplanes for the assault in amphibious landings	Benge, Col H. *Gazette*	Jun 54
DEFENSE OF THE ARTILLERY POSITION AREA	Smith, Lt K.	Dec 54
DEVELOPMENT OF NIGHT ACTION	Hart, Capt B., British Army	Mar 55
DOUBLE CHECK Being wary avoids ambush	Suhosky, TSgt R. *Leatherneck*	Feb 55
FAIR WEATHER OR FOUL Operations go on with or without air support	Collier, LtCol R.	Jul 55
FIGHTING IN A TACTICAL "T"		Jan 53

FIRST LINE OF OFFENSE It's the USMC	Williams, M.	Jul 50
GIVE THE SIGNAL PISTOL BACK TO THE SIGNAL PLATOON	Barrett, Lt R.	Oct 51
HEALTH TO THE REGIMENT!	Bressoud, M.	Jun 55
HOIST THE REGIMENT!	Vance, Col R.	May 55
HOW FAR IS IT?	Watson, Capt P.	Oct 50
I GOT A MAD ON	Backstrap	Jun 54
LANDING TECHNIQUES—A LOOK TO THE FUTURE	Walt, LtCol L.	Feb 51
LET'S TURN NIGHT INTO DAY Illumination technique	Aldridge, LtCol F.	Apr 51
LET'S USE ARMOR	Piehl, Capt R.	Jul 55
LET'S WORK NIGHTS	Sanders, Capt P.	Feb 53
MAGIC SQUARE	Simmons, Maj E.	Oct 54
MARINE CORPS DEMONSTRATES ATOMIC WAR "VERTICAL ENVELOPMENT" CONCEPT	*Army, Navy, Air Force Journal*	Oct 55
NECESSITY—NOT SENTIMENT	Nihart, LtCol B.	Jun 54
NEW TARGETS	Bacon, LtCol F.	Aug 54
NEW WARFARE—NEW TACTICS	Hart, Capt B., British Army	Oct 55
NIGHT ATTACK How to fight at night	Hoffman, Maj C. *Leatherneck*	Nov 51
NO DINOSAUR HERE Amphibious tactics need review and changes	Aldridge, LtCol F. *Gazette*	Oct 53
THE OLYMPIANS	Hargreaves, Maj R.	Feb 54
ORGANIZATIONS FOR COMBAT ENDURANCE	Roe, Capt P.	Oct 55
ON TRIANGLES AND SQUARES Organization of combat units since 1917	Crown, LtCol J.	Aug 53

POUND FOR POUND—MORE PUNCH	Croizat, LtCol V.	Aug 54
PRINCIPLES OF WAR: CHECKLIST FOR A LANDING	Aldridge, LtCol F.	Jun 53
RE-ESTIMATE THE SITUATION: THE TORTOISE BOAT OF 1950	Richards, Maj G. *Proceedings*	Oct 50
SECONDARY ATTACKS	Martin, LtCol G.	May 55
SMOKE MEANS SURVIVAL	Collier, Maj R.	Feb 51
SOP-NIGHT RAIDS	Nicholson, Maj D.	Mar 55
SPIRIT OF THE OFFENSIVE	Thomas, C. *Naval Review*	Sep 55
SPLITTING THE SECTION	Witkowski, Capt H.	Feb 55
STRONGPOINTS?	Woessner, LtCol H.	Feb 55
TACTICAL RADIO-FAMILY STYLE	Kern, Capt R.	Jul 53
10TH PLATOON, INFANTRY BATTALION	Paradis, Capt E.	Jul 55
THEY CALL THEIR SHOTS	Martin, LtCol G.	Apr 53
TWO MAKE A TEAM	Brooks, LtCol N.	Nov 53
USMC ADOPTS NEW "HIT AND RUN" ANTI-TANK VEHICLE IN SUPPORT OF TROOPS	*Army, Navy, Air Force Journal*	Aug 55
WE CAN BE GUERRILLAS, TOO	Alsop, S., and Col S. Griffith *Sat Eve Post*	Dec 8, 1951
WHEN THE ROADS GIVE OUT	Gilman, CWO K.	Mar 54

TACTICS KOREA

From the *Gazette,* unless otherwise specified:

THE APPROACH MARCH IN KOREA	Bohn, Lt R.	Oct 51

BACK TO THE TRENCHES — Braestrup, Lt P. — Mar 55

CREEPING TACTICS — Nicholson, LtCol D. — Sep 58

LOST ART: 1ST MARINE DIVISION GUERRILLA WAR — *Time* — Feb 12, 1951
We found it again.

NIGHT RAID ON HILL 67 — Nicholson, LtCol D. — Sep 53
Marine unit infiltrates enemy positions at night

THREE UP—NONE BACK — Simmons, Maj E. — May 51
Proposal for four rifle companies per battalion.

THE TIGHT LINE — Suhosky, TSgt R. *Leatherneck* — Jul 55
Trenches again

WHO SAID IMPOSSIBLE? — Reinhardt, Col G. — Jan 55

WHY BUILD A BUNKER? — Witkowski, Lt H. — Apr 52
To save your a--, that's why

TRAINING

From the *Gazette,* unless otherwise specified:

GENERAL

AND STILL "READ RIGHT UP" — Shuler, LtCol C. — Dec 52

BLOW UP YOUR AUDIENCE — Kennon, Lt J. — Apr 55

BLUEPRINT FOR PUBLICATION — Pierce, P. — Apr 55
How to write for military publication

BREAKING THE LANGUAGE BARRIER — Sims, SSgt R. *Leatherneck* — Aug 53
Bilingual DI's for Spanish speaking Boots at P. I.

THE CHANGING OF THE DRILL — Suhosky, TSgt R. *Leatherneck* — Nov 54
Common gripe with Marines

CLOSE COMBAT — Mok, SSgt M. — Oct 55

COLD STEEL — Styers, J. *Leatherneck*
Hand to Hand combat — Jan 52
Knife fighting — Feb 52
The Stick — Mar 52
Knife Throwing — Apr 52

CLOSE FOR THE KILL	Seidler, Prof A., and Maj G. Golleher	Apr 54
DEMOLITIONS—AN INFANTRY WEAPON	De Wease, SSgt A.	Oct 55
DON'T KILL 'EM WITH KINDNESS	Davis, Capt T.	Sep 55
FALL OUT ONE	Donnell, Capt J.	Jun 52
FIND THE GIMMICKS	Barrow, TSgt C.	Dec 51
GOING OVERSEAS?	Donovan, LtCol J.	Apr 51
IF YOU ARE CAPTURED	Johnson, Capt J.	Nov 52
IN THE BOOK Guidebook has everything	Mandeville, S. *Leatherneck*	Dec 53
KEEP 'EM COMBAT READY	Boynton, Lt W.	Dec 52
KNOW THEIR WEAPONS	Marsh, R.	Aug 53
KNOW YOUR ENEMY	Hargreaves, Maj R.	Sep 53
LET'S GO TO COLLEGE	Stiles, Lt C.	Oct 50
THE LITTLE PICTURE	Fortner, SSgt R.	Feb 55
LIVE FIRING EXERCISE	Kennon, Lt J.	Oct 55
THE LONELY ART	Hargreaves, Maj R.	Dec 54
MAKING OF A LEATHERNECK: WITH EXCERPTS FROM LETTER BY M. STITT	Finan, J. *American Mercury*	Apr 51
	Digest	Apr 51
THE "NEW LOOK IN GRIDS"	Barnes, Maj J., USA	Jan 52
NIGHTMARE	Crown, LtCol J., and LtCol W. Bennett	Sep 55
ON LOCATION WITH FEX	Kingsley, Lt J.	Apr 54
ONE HUNDRED BEST BOOKS FOR MILITARY EDUCATION	McRae, LtCol R. USA	Feb 51

PROPS FOR THE "PROF"	Toolin, TSgt L.	Apr 54
REALISM	Sexton, Maj M., and Maj L. Gilson	Jun 52
REPLACEMENTS ARE COMING Pendleton training for Korea	Coggins, LtCol T.	Jun 53
RESERVE TIME FOR TRAINING	Hart, Lt H.	Apr 53
SPEAK THE LANGUAGE	MacDonald, Lt D.	May 53
SQUADS RIGHT		Aug 54
SQUADS RIGHT, PRO . . . CON	Kelly,TSgt D., and MSgt E. Evans	Nov 54
STAGING REGIMENT At Pendleton—for Korea	Gartz, MSgt S. *Leatherneck*	Jan 53
STAND UP AND TALK	Sheppard, Capt G.	Feb 55
STATIC WAR—AGGRESSIVE TRAINING	Nicholson, LtCol D.	May 53
THAT DIRECTION'S NORTH Training for replacement officers	Clapper, Capt P.	Jun 61
T'HELL WITH ROTATION	Lowe, Capt J.	Jun 55
TAKE TEN FOR FEX	Scribner, Capt R.	Dec 55
TAKE TV OUT OF THE BAR—AND PUT IT TO WORK	Collier, Maj R.	Mar 51
TRAINING AIDS DI's have TA libraries	Suhosky, SSgt R. *Leatherneck*	Sep 52
TEACH THE TEACHERS	Pierce, Maj P.	Oct 52
TRAINING GOES ALONG Training can be held anywhere	Marcus, MSgt S. *Leatherneck*	Nov 53
TRAINING—LIFE INSURANCE	Manion, MSgt H.	Aug 54
TRIAL BY ICE Arctic tests	Metzger, LtCol L., LtCol H. Oppenheimer and LtCdr O. Price, USN	Aug 52

TROOP LEADERS' HANDBOOK	Lashington, Lt N.	Jul 51
TUNE-UP FOR TRAINING	Prickett, Col W.	Dec 53
A TURN AT THE WHEEL	Shaw, Sgt H.	Mar 54
USE YOUR EYES	Collier, LtCol R.	Oct 52
USMC TRAINING AND REPLACEMENT COMMAND	Bare, BGen R. *Army, Navy, Air Force Journal*	Jul 52
WHY GO TO COLLEGE?	Persad, M.	Sep 51
THE WORD FOR MARINE WIVES Shape up or else on Marine lore	Stocks, J. *Leatherneck*	Mar 55
YOUR OTHER RIGHT!	Finn, MSgt G.	May 54

EXERCISES

AGGRESSOR Maneuvers at Marshall Air Force Base, Kansas	Ill, TSgt E. *Leatherneck*	Sep 51
AMPHIBIOUS GRADUATION PROBLEM	*Gazette*	Apr 51
ANTIGUERRILLA EXERCISE	Johnson, J. *Gazette*	Dec 55
BIG DELTA	Van Stockum, LtCol R. *Gazette*	Dec 51
DEMON 3 Amphib war training exercise	Burlage, TSgt G. *Leatherneck*	Aug 50
DRY FOOT LANDING Operation Crossover—2D DIV	Braitsch, TSgt F. *Leatherneck*	Jul 50

MARKSMANSHIP

BIG SHOOT USMC Marksmanship Matches	Tallent, SSgt R. *Leatherneck*	Sep 50
THE BLUE VS THE GRAY North-South Rifle Meet	Barnum, MSgt E. *Leatherneck*	Dec 54
CHALLENGE TO OUR PRESTIGE We need to shoot better	Edson, MajGen M. *Gazette*	Mar 55
FIELD MATCHES '51 AT PENDLETON	Gartz, MSgt S. *Leatherneck*	Sep 51
LET 'EM SHOOT	Kelly, TSgt D. *Gazette*	Aug 55

	MARINE CORPS MATCHES At Quantico again	*Gazette*	Aug 50
	MATCH MASTERS '52 Marksmanship Matches	Tallent, TSgt R. *Leatherneck*	Aug 52
	NEW SIGHT PIX New Rifle Coaches	Lyons, MSgt R. *Leatherneck*	May 52
	NATIONAL MATCHES '53 Marines in Rifle Matches	Sarokin, MSgt P. *Leatherneck*	Nov 53
	OUR SHOOTING POSITIONS—UNREALISTIC	Haslam, Capt C. *Gazette*	Dec 55
	PENDLETON SHOOT Pendleton Marines are big winners	Marcus, MSgt S. *Leatherneck*	Mar 55
	PIN-WHEEL PARADE	*Gazette*	Aug 53
	SHOOTERS ARE MADE—MAKE 'EM	*Gazette*	May 54
	SHOOTING STAR Retired CWO Olympic rifle winner instructs Boots	Marcus, MSgt S. *Leatherneck*	Nov 54
	SMALL BORE SHOOTING How to do it	Rodeheffer, LtCol N. *Gazette*	Oct 50
	TARGETS	Fredericks, Capt H. *Gazette*	Mar 54
	TRADITION OF EXPERTS	Crown, LtCol J. *Gazette*	Aug 54
	WELL IN AT PERRY 1955 Rifle and Pistol Matches	Frank, B. *Leatherneck*	Nov 55
	WELL OVER BY FIVE 1950 Rifle Match winners are WO's Remes and De La Hunt	Tallent, SSgt R. *Leatherneck*	Sep 50

TRAINING-SCHOOLS

Articles in this section are from *Leatherneck,* unless otherwise specified:

ACADEMY	ACADEMY MARINES Future Marine officers at Annapolis	Jordan, Sgt C.	Apr 51

Title	Author	Date	Subject
ACADEMY PREP How to get commissioned	Lyons, TSgt R.	Jun 50	
MARINE CORPS BOOT CAMP	*Proceedings*	Aug 53	**BOOT CAMP**
BUGLER'S SCHOOL At Parris Island and San Diego	Marcus, MSgt S.	Jan 54	**BUGLERS**
DISASTER COURSE Civil Defense rescue teams trained by USMC	McConnell, TSgt J.	Jan 55	**CIVIL DEFENSE**
COLD WEATHER TRAINING Simulate Korea weather at Pendleton	Burlage, MSgt G.	Apr 51	**COLD WEATHER**
MOUNTAINEERS Train for Korea hills in Camp Carson	Ill, SSgt E.	May 51	
PICKEL MEADOWS	Wood, Capt R. *Gazette*	Oct 52	
TWIN MEADOWS Marines and British cold weather training in Nevada and Scotland	Suhosky, TSgt R.	Aug 53	
FIELD CORPSMEN Corpsmen training at Pendleton	Marcus, MSgt S.	Jan 55	**CORPSMEN**
DEVIL PUPS Teen voluntary training at Pendleton	Riblett, L.	Oct 54	**DEVIL PUPS**
DI PREP They go to school	Sarokin, MSgt P.	Jun 54	**DI**
ELECTRONICS Guided Missile training	Thompson, Sgt J.	Jul 50	**ELECTRONICS**
ADVANCED TRAINING Post grad courses in combat at Lejeune and Pendleton	Heinecke, MSgt R.	Jun 55	**INFANTRY**
NROTC, U.C.L.A. One-sixth are Marines	Burlage, TSgt G.	Mar 51	**NROTC**
JUMP BOOTS Marine paratroop training	Suhosky, TSgt R.	Dec 54	**PARACHUTE**

RECRUITERS	RECRUITERS' SCHOOL	Lyons, TSgt R. Oct 50
SEA SCHOOL	SEA SCHOOL Marines on Warships tradition since 1775	Suhosky, SSgt R. Aug 52
TTU	LET'S LOOK AT TTU Troop Training Units	Morrisset, Lt M. *Gazette* Sep 50
	TROOP TRAINING TEAM	Fugate, MSgt R. Jun 53
	TTU PAC Marines at Naval Amphib Base, San Diego	Burlage, TSgt G. Jul 50
YEOMAN	YEOMAN SCHOOL Marines train at San Diego	Suhosky, SSgt R. May 53

UNITS

GENERAL	AND NOW THE ANGLICO Background of the Air and Naval Gunfire Liaison Company	Heinl, LtCol R. *Gazette* Jan 51
	COMBAT READY THIRD DIVISION PARADES FOR COMMANDANT	*Pendleton Scout* Dec 12, 1952
	IST PROVISIONAL MARINE AIR-GROUND TASK FORCE, FMF	Batterton, Col B. *Army, Navy, Air Force Journal* Feb 54
	THE FMF TODAY	*Leatherneck* Nov 50
	THE 4TH MARINES History of reactivated regiment	Tallent, MSgt R. *Leatherneck* Feb 53
	THE 4TH MARINES At Kaneohe Bay Air Station	Marcus, MSgt S. *Leatherneck* Oct 55
	MARINE FATHERS USMC Fathers' Ass'n	Lewis, MSgt C. *Leatherneck* May 52
	SERVICE IN ACTION Force Troops	Banks, Col C. *Gazette* May 51
	THE STORY OF THE 3RD MARINE DIVISION IN JAPAN, AUGUST, 1953-AUGUST, 1954	Taylor Publishing Co. Dallas 1954

Title / Description	Author / Source	Date
THE 3RD DIVISION Division reactivated for Korea and ready to go	Gartz, MSgt S. *Leatherneck*	Mar 53
THE 3RD MOVES OUT To Korea from Pendleton	Marcus, MSgt S. *Leatherneck*	Oct 53

WR'S

Title / Description	Author / Source	Date
ALL'S FAIR Women Marines at Lejeune	Klaus, Sgt B. *Leatherneck*	Aug 52
THE NEW CORPS Griping Sarge gets new WR's	Stolley, F. *Leatherneck*	Nov 54
THE TROUBLE WITH IRENE WR overcomes Sgt's prejudices	Scott, A. *Leatherneck*	Apr 53
WOMEN MARINES: THE FEMININE SIDE Historical review	Towle, Col K. *Gazette*	Nov 50
WOMAN MARINES FOR DUTY BEYOND THE SEAS WR's now in Europe and Hawaii	*Leatherneck*	Nov 53
WOTC WR officer training	Bainder, Lt H. *Gazette*	Sep 50
YOUNGEST AND PRETTIEST	*Time*	Mar 9, 1953

UNITS, KOREA

Title / Description	Author / Source	Date
ARMORED ABLE Amtracs and tank fire	Smith, Sgt L. *Leatherneck*	Aug 52
KIMPO PROVISIONAL REGIMENT Marines command UN outfit holding Seoul and Kimpo airfield	Wells, MSgt H. *Leatherneck*	Jul 53
NEW WEAPONS COMPANY IN KOREA	McInteer, Capt J. *Gazette*	Jan 51
SHORE PARTY'S INLAND WAR Aug 50-July 52	Edwards, LtCol H. *Gazette*	Dec 53
THOSE COMMANDOS Marines and British.	Tallent, TSgt R. *Leatherneck*	Jun 52
WONSAN MARINES Marine artillery at Wonsan	Jordan, SSgt C. *Leatherneck*	Jun 52

WEAPONS

From the *Gazette* unless otherwise specified:

GENERAL	HORSE POWER PLUS	Paciulli, Capt O.	Mar 55
	SIGNPOSTS OF THE FUTURE	McCutcheon, LtCol K.	Mar 51
	SUPERCHARGE THE "HARDCHARGERS"	Davis, Lt W.	May 51
	THE SUNDAY PUNCH	Wade, LtCol J.	Oct 52
	WHY NOT USE STAMPINGS?	Loughlin, Lt D.	Dec 53
ABC	AEC'S SHOT 5 Atomic subjects	Hudgins, L.	Aug 53
	THE ATOMIC BOMB IN TACTICAL WARFARE No one should be without one	Canzona, Lt N.	Sep 50
	DON'T WAIT FOR THE H-BOMB	Reinhardt, Col G., USA	Jan 52
	FIRE ONE Marines at Yucca Flats tests	Tallent, TSgt R. *Leatherneck*	Jul 52
	GROUND ZERO	Reinhardt, Col G., USA	Nov 52
ANTITANK	AT REQUIREMENTS—HELIOTROOPS	Brush, LtCol C.	Sep 55
	"H" HOUR—AT GUNS, NOT TANKS!	Aldridge, LtCol F.	Jun 54
	POSSIBILITIES OF THE ANTITANK ROCKET	Gore, Sgt C.	Jul 51
BAR	BAR Rifle worth weight in gold	Averill, Capt G. *Leatherneck*	Jan 51
FLAME	FLAME IN THE LANDING FORCE	Fletcher, LtCol S.	Dec 54
MACHINE GUNS	THE LMG SQUAD	Soley, TSgt M.	Jun 54
MINES	THE BEACH MINEFIELD	Stuart, LtCol A.	Oct 50
	DANGER, MINES	Edwards, LtCol H.	Apr 52

GUIDED MISSILES OVER NEW YORK	Mathieu, Maj C.	Jul 52	MISSLES
THE DEADLY TUBES	Tallent, TSgt R. *Leatherneck*	Feb 52	MORTARS
FIRE FOR EFFECT Mortars are great if they're on your side	Davis, Capt W.	Jul 54	
FOUR-DEUCE IS A WINNER	Kaufer, Capt E.	Dec 52	
MORTAR-HOWITZER	Spring, Lt C.	Sep 55	
NOBODY'S FAVORITE WEAPON	Smith, Capt R.	Oct 54	
"ON TARGET" WITH COMANCHE	Hoffman, MSgt A., and SSgt D. McCarthy	Jun 53	
OF MORTARS AND MEN	Wade, LtCol J.	Jan 54	
RE-ORGANIZED 81 MM MORTAR PLATOON	Paradis, Lt E.	Mar 51	
THE 60 MM MORTARS IN KOREA	Nolan, Lt J.	Jul 52	
75'S UP	DeLong, Lt E.	Aug 52	RECOILLESS RIFLES
ACCURACY OF THE M-1	Mitchell, MSgt T.	Jun 51	RIFLES
THE NEW MILITARY RIFLES	Haslam, Capt C.	Mar 55	
RIFLES FOR MARINES What we need	Walker, Maj A.	Sep 50	
THE STORY OF THE RIFLE	Rankin, R. *Leatherneck*	Jan, Feb 55	
WHY A HEAVY BARRELED RIFLE?	Haslam, Capt C.	Aug 55	
BUNKER BUSTERS Rocket barrages	Braitsch, MSgt F. *Leatherneck*	May 52	ROCKETS
FIRE MISSION ROCKETS	Bailey, Capt E.	Sep 52	

	RIPPLE AND RUN Why the rocket trucks were so unpopular in Korea	Wade, LtCol J.	Mar 53
SMALL ARMS	43 YEARS IN A GI HOLSTER	McAlister, Capt J.	Nov 54
	INTERMEDIATE AUTOMATICS	Marsh, R.	Oct 54
	SAVE WITH SUB CALIBER	Brixley, Capt P.	Nov 53
	YOUR SIDE ARM, SIR!	Curtis, Capt T.	Aug 55
TANKS	MARCH OF THE IRON CAVALRY: MARINE TANKS IN KOREA	Montross, L.	Oct 52
	MECHANIZED FOR MOBILITY	Croizat, LtCol V.	May 52
	SOMETHING TO STOP A TANK	Knox, Cdr D., USN	Apr 51
	THE STRANGE STORY OF THE CDL TANKS	Fuller, MajGen J.	Apr 52
	TANK PATROL Writer goes on Korea sortie	Jordan, SSgt C. *Leatherneck*	Sep 52
	"TANK TEAM"	Chappars, TSgt G., and TSgt J. Jones *Leatherneck*	Aug 51
	TANKMEN Mobile foxholes	Suhosky, TSgt R. *Leatherneck*	Jun 55
	UP WITH THE TANKS Outstanding summary of Marine Tank ops and tactics	Sanders, Capt P.	Feb, Mar 54
	URGENT, LAND THE TANKS	Tompkins, Col R.	Mar 51

6.
PRE-VIETNAM

The Ribbon Creek disaster, John H. Glenn, "The Man Who Rode The Thunder," and the Show-of-Force without a hitch in Lebanon.

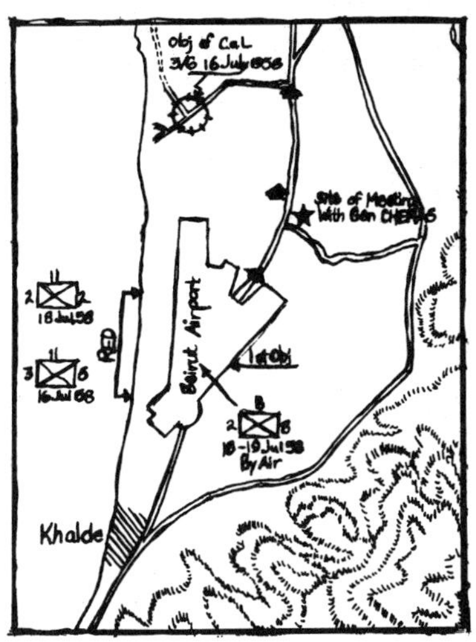

CONTENTS: PART 6

EVENTS/1956-1962

CAREER CONFERENCE Wives and men of Corps tell it like it is to Committee	Mainard, TSgt A. *Leatherneck*	Nov 56	**1956, GENERAL**
MILITARY TOURNEY Contest between Marine Corps Institute and Marine Barracks	Curtis, TSgt P. *Leatherneck*	Feb 56	
PEACEFUL INVADERS: MARINE CORPS IN NEW ZEALAND Reunion of WW-2 Vets	Stone, D. *American Mercury*	Dec 56	
RETURN TO BELLEAU WOOD Marine Generals dedicate monument	Sarokin, MSgt P. *Leatherneck*	Jan 56	
SEMPER FI A. L. McLaughlin, Korea Medal of Honor Marine, Court-Martialed for drunkenness	*Time*	Oct 29, 1956	
TRUMPET IN THE DUST McLaughlin	*Newsweek*	Oct 29, 1956	
DEATH IN RIBBON CREEK	*Time*	Apr 23, 1956	**RIBBON CREEK, 1956**
DEATH MARCH AT PARRIS ISLAND: FROM OFFICIAL RECORD	*U.S. News*	May 11, 1956	
FULL TEXT OF GEN PATE'S LETTER TO SEC NAV ON THE "TRAGEDY OF RIBBON CREEK"	Pate, Gen R. *Army, Navy, Air Force Journal*	May 56	
LIQUOR PLUS BRUTALITY ON TRIAL WITH MARINES	*Christian Century*	Aug 1, 1956	
MAKING OF MARINES	*Newsweek*	Jul 30, 1956	
MAKING TOUGH MARINES	*U.S. News*	Aug 10, 1956	
MARINE CORPS QUANDRY	*Nation*	Aug 11, 1956	
MARINES ON TRIAL	*America*	Aug 4, 1956	
MARINES ON TRIAL (REPLY BY E. CORBETT)	*America*	Oct 4, 1956	

	MARINES STICK TOGETHER	*Newsweek*	Aug 13, 1956
	McKEON CASE: A NATION ON TRIAL, WITH EDITORIAL COMMENT	Petz, W. *America*	Aug 18, 1956
	MISSING PIECES	*Time*	May 14, 1956
	OUR MILITARY TRAINING: HOW FAR IT GOES AND WHY	*Newsweek*	May 14, 1956
	PROPERLY REMORSEFUL Is Sgt McKeon	*Newsweek*	Apr 23, 1956
	RIBBON CREEK, THE MARINE CORPS ON TRIAL Gen McKean, his career ruined by Matthew McKeon, tells what really happened at Ribbon Creek, and afterwards. Not a well written book but a sincere one. Of interest to Marines	McKean, BGen W. Dial Press	1958
	SERGEANT McKEON AND THE CULT OF VIOLENCE	Roche, J. *New Republic*	Aug 27, 1956
	TRAGEDY OF PLATOON SEVENTY-ONE PUTS MARINE TRAINING UNDER FIRE	*Life*	Apr 23, 1956
	TRIAL OF THE CORPS	*Life*	Jul 30, 1956
	TRIAL OF SERGEANT McKEON	*Time*	Jul 30, 1956
	WHERE ARE THEY NOW? M.C. McKEON AND THE 1956 PARRIS ISLAND TRAGEDY He is a civilian in Boston	*Newsweek*	Aug 17, 1970
	WHO WANTS PANTY-WAIST MARINES? A testimonial for Marine training from a fan the Corps could do without (American Nazi Party head who was later assassinated)	Rockwell, G. *American Mercury*	Apr 57
NO-WIVES POLICY, 1956	MARRIED MARINES No wives in Japan	*Ave Maria*	Oct 27, 1956

MARINE WIVES REBUFFED IN HILL APPEAL	*Armed Forces Journal* Feb 8, 1958
MARINES SAY BAN ON FAMILIES IN PACIFIC WILL STICK: HEADQUARTERS OFFICIALS TELL REASONS FOR ORDER	*Army, Navy, Air Force Journal* Oct 56
MARINES WAIL AS WIVES SAIL FROM JAPAN	*Life* Nov 26, 1956
SEC NAV BACKS MARINE CORPS POLICY BARRING WIVES FROM LIVING IN JAPAN	*Army, Navy, Air Force Journal* Oct 56

BERMUDA TATTOO Marines first foreign troops to participate in British Military Tattoo ceremony	Sarokin, MSgt P. *Leatherneck* Aug 57
THE COMMANDANT REPORTS	Pate, Gen R. *Gazette* Oct 57
CORPS SPONSOR Two Hungarian refugees are sponsored by Corps	Johnson, MSgt R. *Leatherneck* Feb 57
THE HELPING HAM San Diego's W6YDK stayed on air three days during search for hikers lost in Mexico	Suhosky, TSgt R. *Leatherneck* Oct 57
LEATHERNECK IS FORTY Apr 1917—*Leatherneck's* first issue	Mainard, TSgt A. *Leatherneck* Nov 57
MAYDAY AT MALIBU For four days, Marines fought Malibu forest fire	Marcus, MSgt S. *Leatherneck* Mar 57
MARINE CORPS TAKES A THUMPING	Price, B. *Nation* Apr 26, 1957
REVOLUTION IN THE MARINE CORPS	*Look* May 28, 1957
SYMPOSIUM 2 Top NCO'S recommend improvements	Sarokin, MSgt P. *Leatherneck* Sep 57

	THEY'RE HAPPY WITH THE BLUES Feb. 13, 1957—14th anniversary of Women Marines.	Suhosky, TSgt R. *Leatherneck*	Feb 57
OPERATION DIABLO, 1957	ATOM ON THE ATTACK In Nevada	*Newsweek*	Jul 15, 1957
	THE BIGGEST STICK After misfire, Diablo proved Marines could be closer to bomb	Suhosky, TSgt R. *Leatherneck*	Sep 57
	MARINES AND A DUD	*Newsweek*	Jul 8, 1957
1958, GENERAL	BRUSSELS VISIT P.I. Band, Drum & Bugle Corps and a Ceremonial Company from D.C., perform at World's Fair	Mosier, TSgt R. *Leatherneck*	Dec 58
	DANGER: LITTLE WARS; BUT U.S. IS READY	Pate, Gen R. *U.S. News*	Jan 10, 1958
	DIVISION REUNIONS	*Gazette*	Aug, Sep 58
	EDINBURGH TATTOO 156 Marines take part in full dress drill in Scotland	Sullivan, Sgt G. *Leatherneck*	Nov 58
	1ST DIVISION REUNIONS	*Gazette*	Oct 58
	MARINE CORPS BRUTALITY	Kennedy, W. *America*	Mar 1, 1958
	MARINE CORPS GENERAL OFFICERS' CONFERENCE	*Gazette*	Sep 58
	MARINE INTEGRATION DEAD-LINE 1 JANUARY	*Armed Forces Journal*	Nov 15, 1958
	MARINE "TOYS FOR TOTS" DRIVE AIDS ONE MILLION KIDS	*Armed Forces Journal*	Mar 1, 1958
	NAVAL REVIEW Marines in Full Dress at British Columbia's 100th Birthday	Johnson, MSgt R. *Leatherneck*	Oct 58
	A SALUTE TO THE MARINE CORPS ON ITS 183D BIRTHDAY	*Armed Forces Journal*	Nov 8, 1958
LEBANON, 1958	THE AMERICAN LANDING IN LEBANON	McClintock, R. *Proceedings*	Oct 62

Title	Source	Date
DATELINE-LEBANON Lejeune Marines in and around Beirut	*Leatherneck*	Oct 58
LEBANON Battle-clad Marines in Beirut	*Leatherneck*	Sep 58
LEBANON	Wade, BGen S. *Gazette*	Nov 65
LEBANON-PROFESSIONALISM AT ITS BEST	Smith, Col L. *Military Review*	Jun 59
LEBANON AND QUEMOY—THE NAVY'S ROLE	Baldridge, Capt E., USN *Proceedings*	Feb 61
MARINES IN LEBANON: 1958 Excellent illustrated pamphlet history of Operation Bluebat	Shulimson, J. HQMC	1966 (IP)
OPERATION BLUEBAT Lebanon 1958	Wade, BGen S. *Gazette*	Jul 59
REFERENCES ON THE U.S. MARINES IN LEBANON	HQMC	1962
SHOW OF FORCE 2D MAR DIV in Lebanon	Pierce, LtCol P. *Leatherneck*	Sep 62
THE UNTOLD STORY OF THE MARINES IN LEBANON	Chapelle, D. *Argosy*	Dec 58
Titled, *The Night War Didn't Come In Lebanon*	*Digest*	Feb 59
WHO'S A REBEL?—THE LESSON LEBANON TAUGHT By CO of unit which landed	Hadd, LtCol H. *Gazette*	Mar 62

1959

Title	Source	Date
COMMANDANT'S BIRTHDAY MESSAGE	*Gazette*	Nov 59
FMF PAC IS INTEGRATED, MOBILE, READY: ABSENCE OF FAMILIES PRAISED AS FACTOR	*Army, Navy, Air Force Journal*	Dec 5, 1959
GEN PATE EXPANDS ON USMC ROLE IN REPLY TO QUESTIONS AT NATIONAL PRESS CLUB	*Army, Navy, Air Force Journal*	Nov 14, 1959

Year	Title	Source	Date
	GENERAL PATE TELLS MARINE PLANS TO CUT UNITS IN REPORT TO SENATE ARMED SERVICES GROUP	*Army, Navy, Air Force Journal*	Nov 14, 1959
	MARINE REUNIONS	*Gazette*	Nov 59
	MARINES MUST CUT 9,000 COMBAT TROOPS; SIX SQUADRONS, UNDER MANPOWER CUTBACK	*Army, Navy, Air Force Journal*	Apr 4, 1959
	MARINES WILL CLAIM "ECONOMY" FORCE	*Army, Navy, Air Force Journal*	Nov 21, 1959
	MCA CONSTITUTION REVISION	*Gazette*	Jul 59
	OPERATION INLAND SEAS Opening of St. Lawrence Seaway. Marines will sail the Great Lakes again	Lyons, R. *Leatherneck*	Jul, Sep 59
	RETIRING COMMANDANT CALLS MANPOWER SHORTAGE "BASIC PROBLEM" OF MARINES Bye, Gen Pate	*Army, Navy, Air Force Journal*	Dec 19, 1959
	STIRRING SPIRIT LIFTED HIGHER	*Life*	Nov 30, 1959
	WHERE DO WE STAND? A PROGRESS REPORT—NOVEMBER 59 Corps ready to fight with new weapons and techniques	Fraser, Col A. *Gazette*	Nov 59
	WHY A MARINE CORPS? By Chairman of House Armed Services Committee	Vinson, C. *Gazette*	Nov 59
1960	ANNIVERSARY PROCLAMATION	*Gazette*	Nov 60
	COMMANDANT'S BIRTHDAY MESSAGE From Gen Shoup	*Gazette*	Nov 60
	THE COMMANDANT'S POLICIES	Shoup, Gen D. *Gazette*	Feb 60
	FMF CONCURRENT REUNIONS All six World War 2 divisions meet in Washington	Jones, AGySgt M. *Leatherneck*	Aug 60

FIRST TO FIGHT: THE UNITED STATES MARINE CORPS STILL HAS ITS FEET ON THE GROUND	*Ordnance*	May, Jun 60
GUNG-HO AT SQUAW PEAK; LEATHERNECKS TAKE ON AN UNUSUAL FOE AT OLYMPICS	*Life*	Feb 15, 1960
HERE'S THE WORD FROM THE NEW COMMANDANT Shoup expounds	*Army, Navy, Air Force Journal*	May 28, 1960
HOUSE CUTS BAR BUILD UP OF MARINES IN FAR EAST: WILL DELAY MODERNIZATION	*Army, Navy, Air Force Journal*	May 28, 1960
INGREDIENTS OF A FIGHTING FORCE Marines have them all	*Navy*	May 60
JCS DIRECTIVE LAUNCHES USMC ON JOINT TRAINING WITH TAC	*Army, Navy, Air Force Journal*	Apr 16, 1960
MARINES: ALL IS WELL	*Armed Forces Independent Journal*	Jan, Feb 60
MARINES SEEK OVERSEAS TOUR CUT	*Army, Navy, Air Force Journal*	Jun 11, 1960
NOW HEAR THIS, YOU PEOPLE, KNOCK IT OFF!	*Newsweek*	Jan 18, 1960
OLYMPIC WINNERS Capt W. McMillan won gold medal. GySgt James Hill won silver medal in Rome	Jones, GySgt M. *Leatherneck*	Nov 60
PARTNER IN THE FLEET, THE MARINES Thanks, Navy!	*Navy*	Oct 60
"SEARCHING INQUIRY" ON MODERNIZATION	*Army, Navy, Air Force Journal*	Jul 2, 1960
WITH THE MARINES	Bullen, G. *Navy*	Jul 60

1961	CAPSULE RECOVERY The Corps may retrieve the first spaceman, John Glenn	Jones, GySgt M. *Leatherneck*	Feb 61
	THE COMMANDANT'S VIEWS, DESIGNS AND POLICIES: GUIDANCE FOR YOU IN 1961	Shoup, Gen D. *Gazette*	Feb 61
	THE FIRST MARINE CORPS HAWK MISSILE BATTALION WILL BE ACTIVATED	*Army, Navy, Air Force Journal*	Mar 5, 1961
	GOLDEN YEAR Nearly 7000 Naval Aviators return to Pensacola June 6-June 11, 1961 for 50th anniversary of Naval Aviation	Kester, SSgt C. *Leatherneck*	Sep 61
	HOW SEMPER FI? Plenty	Shoup, Gen D. *Time*	Feb 24, 1961
	INSIDE STORY ON ARMY-MARINE MANPOWER DECISIONS	*Army, Navy, Air Force Journal*	Jun 61
	NEWER PLANES, SHIPS BOOST MARINE PUNCH	Binney, MajGen A., USA *Army, Navy, Air Force Register*	Jul 29, 1961
	OLD TIMERS Vets of 2D MAR DIV hold 20th Anniversary reunion	Kester, SSgt C. *Leatherneck*	Apr 61
	SEMPER FI: MARINE PVT STOBO C. WEST Inhuman punishment after Courts Martial on Okinawa for black market activities	*Newsweek*	Jul 24, 1961
	TRIBUTE Marines' role in Vets Day, 1960	Schinkel, Cpl P. *Leatherneck*	Jan 61
	VISIT TO POINTE NOIRE 2D MAR DIV paid a Good Will Visit to Pointe Noire, Congo	Foster, Lt T. *Leatherneck*	Apr 61
1962	. . . AND NOW THAILAND May 17, 1962, Thailand asks for help. 3/9 responds. (The end of the pre-Nam era)	*Leatherneck*	Jul 62

CMC BIRTHDAY MESSAGE	Shoup, Gen D. *Gazette* Nov 62
DATELINE: THAILAND 3/9 and VMA-332 in Thailand	Matheson, GySgt M. *Leatherneck* Aug 62
DOLEFUFL DRUMS FOR AN OUTCAST	*Life* Apr 20, 1962
NAVY'S INFANTRY: ALWAYS READY On the way to Thailand	Sexton, M. *Life* Jun 22, 1962
THE MARINE CORPS TODAY	MacDonald, Maj J. *Naval Review* 1963
NO PAPER TIGER: SEATO'S OPERATION TULUNGAN Marines participate just prior to Nam commitment	*Newsweek* Apr 9, 1962

AVIATION

From the *Gazette,* unless otherwise specified:

GENERAL

AGILITY IN FLIGHT	Martz, Capt J.	Jul 56
AIR, SEA AND LAND		Oct 58
AMPHIBIOUS AVIATION	Keller, LtCol R.	Mar 57
AVIATION ALBUM	Gasser, Maj J.	Nov 59
AVIATION GROUND TRAINING FOR DEFENSE	High, GySgt W.	Jun 61
BLOCKBUSTER		Dec 59
COMBAT AIR TRANSPORT SUPPORT	Yeaman, Col R.	May 59
EXECUTING A CARRIER DEPLOYMENT	Jones, LtCol M.	Jun 60
EYES ALOFT	Schimmenti, Maj J.	Sep 61
FMF ORGANIZATION AND COMPOSITION-BOARD REPORT-AVIATION		May 57

A LOOK AT THE FUTURE OF MARINE AVIATION Current goal is to improve its capability to operate in an expeditionary environment	*Leatherneck*	May 60
LOW AND SLOW	Perry, Lt J.	Aug 56
MABS OR MOBS	Maxwell, Maj E.	Sep 62
MARINE AIRCRAFT TODAY		May 57
MARINE AVIATION Around the globe	Evans, SSgt C. *Leatherneck*	Nov 61
MARINE AVIATION COMBAT IN A PACKAGE	*American Aviation*	Oct 20, 1958
MARINE AVIATION GEARED FOR BUILD-UP: PLANS CALL FOR FULL DIVISION AIRLIFT	*Army, Navy, Air Force Journal*	Mar 56
MARINE AVIATION NEEDS MORE COMMAND BILLETS	Ewers, LtCol N.	Sep 61
MARINE AVIATION READY FOR ANY EMERGENCY: AIR-GROUND CONCEPT IS HAILED Review of Marine Air just before Nam committment	Anderson, BGen N. *Army, Navy, Air Force Journal*	Nov 3, 1962
MARINE CORPS AVIATION	Tutton, LtCol M. *Proceedings*	Mar 61
MARINES PRACTICE RADAR UNIT AIRLIFT	*Naval Aviation News*	May 57
NOSE DIVE!	Bailey, Lt F.	Jan 56
OPERATION PINE NEEDLE Eighteen jets set new speed record El Toro to Atsugi	Barrow, MSgt C. *Leatherneck*	May 62
OPERATION TRIDENT British-made jet aircraft	Van Stockum, R.	Sep 62
PAINT 'EM GREEN!	Walsh, R.	Dec 56
PAPER TIGERS	Lynch, Maj M.	Aug 62
PORTABLE TEW LINE FOR MARINES		Jan 58

PRINCETON LANDING	Meyers, Maj B.	Aug 60
RAWIN: OUR ELECTRONIC WEATHER EYE	Carrington, LtCol G.	Oct 62
REALISTIC READINESS	Folsom, LtCol S.	May 56
SINGLE ENGINE TRANPAC	Bolt, LtCol J.	May 61
SPACE AGE CONQUEST	Knocke, Maj J.	May 61
THE STRIKE CELL	Martz, Capt J.	Jul, Aug 60
TACOS	Traynor, Maj W.	Jun 58
TAKE-OFF MONITOR SYSTEM		Dec 58

AIR DEFENSE

ALL-WEATHER AIR DEFENSE	Hunt, Maj R.	Jun 56
THE BEST DEFENSE Is a hell of a good offense, as usual	Martz, Capt J.	May 58
HAVE MISSILES KILLED THE FIGHTER? No	Keller, LtCol R.	Sep 56
HOW TO LASSO A JET With a missile		Jan 59

COPTERS

ACHILLES HEEL OR WHIRLING DERVISH?	Rieder, Maj G.	Jan 58
BIGGER PAYLOADS FOR THE HUS	Nelson, Maj H.	Apr 61
CAN IT BE DONE? ASK HMX-I First Corps copter squadron	*Naval Aviation News*	Oct 59
CANAVERAL DUTY MAG-26 choppers ready to rescue astronauts	O'Brien, C. *Leatherneck*	May 62
CHOPPER PREP Students are briefed to know exactly what to do before taking controls	Blasdell, V. *Leatherneck*	May 59
CHOPPERS AND GRASSHOPPERS Helicopters and Light Observation Planes	Petry, MSgt A.	Feb 56

COPTER CARRIER USS Boxer is now Assault Helicopter Carrier—Amphibious Squadron 10 is aboard	Sarokin, AMSgt P. *Leatherneck*	May 59
DON'T HOBBLE THE HELICOPTERS	Thomas, Capt T.	Apr 57
DUMBO—THE DUNKER The Dunker serves a grim purpose; teaching troops how to escape from copters downed in water	Barrow, MSgt C. *Leatherneck*	Apr 61
FLYING LST Huge Carrier-Based Assault Copters join the Corps	Johnson, MSgt R. *Leatherneck*	May 58
THE HELICOPTER FAMILY	Clapp, Maj A.	Aug 56
HELITACKERS MAG-36 and California forestry officials perfect new firefighting techniques	Jones, GySgt M. *Leatherneck*	Jul 62
HOME FOR THE HAF Marine Helicopter Assault Force on Thetis Bay	Suhosky, TSgt R. *Leatherneck*	Jan 57
LET'S PUT ONE-MAN HELICOPTERS IN THE MARINE DIVISION	Newton, Capt O. *Gazette*	Mar 59
LET'S STREAMLINE OUR HELICOPTER ASSAULT PLANNING PAPERS	Shore, Capt H. *Gazette*	Apr 62
THE MARINES HAVE LANDED Copters take them in	*Naval Aviation News*	May 56
MARINES HAVE OVERCOME "OXCART IDEAS" IN AN ATOMIC AGE Copters are featured	*Army, Navy, Air Force Journal*	Jun 30, 1956
MARINES PUT HR2S IN OPERATIONAL STATUS	Witze, C. *Aviation Week*	Apr 8, 1957

MARINES TEACH COPTER CRAFT	*Naval Aviation News*	Jul 57	
MARINES USING HELICOPTER DITCHING TRAINER	Tully, B. *Aviation Weekly*	Apr 10, 1961	
OUR FRIEND THE HELICOPTER	Cupp, LtCol J.	May 58	
OUR HAUGHTY HELICOPTER	Winecoff, Col J.	Sep 60	
SELF, MOBILITY A REALITY	Canfield, Capt N., and Capt C. Esterline	Sep 60	
SKY CRANE	Dodd, AMSgt J.	Apr 60	
SUSTAINED HELICOPTER FLIGHT	Witwer, Capt R., USN, and Lt C. Metcalf, USN	Mar 57	
TURKEY HOP Helicopters fascinate Turks as Marines land	Mainard, TSgt A. *Leatherneck*	Sep 56	
USMC ADDS PUNCH TO STRIKING FORCE: LEJEUNE GETS FIRST GIANT COPTER SQUADRON	*Army, Navy, Air Force Journal*	Dec 56	
THE WHIRLING DIVERGENCE	Martz, Capt J.	Oct 56	
FLYING HERCULES In-flight refuelers at El Toro	Tyler, GySgt C. *Leatherneck*	Oct 61	**HERCULES**
THE GV-I The Hercules	Armstrong, Maj M.	Mar 62	
WHY MARINE IN-FLIGHT REFUELING? The need behind the Hercules	Bolt, LtCol J.	Mar 61	
AIR-SEA RESCUE El Toro's Air-Sea Rescue teams saved forty Marines from the Pacific	Johnson, MSgt R. *Leatherneck*	Oct 57	**JOBS**
BLUE ANGELS Marine is member of the team	Mainard, TSgt A. *Leatherneck*	May 58	

	CRASH CREW El Toro's crash crews smother fires, salvage planes and keep runways clear	Suhosky, TSgt R. *Leatherneck*	May 57
	EMERGENCY PROCEDURE Controller makes split-second decisions to avoid air collisions	Smith, E. (Karl Schuon) *Leatherneck*	May 58
	ENLISTED PILOTS Some of the most experienced pilots in the Corps are NAP'S	Stewart, AMSgt W. *Leatherneck*	May 59
	EYES AND EARS VMCJ pilots are trained to photograph enemy territory	Johnson, MSgt R. *Leatherneck*	Jun 60
	OVERHAUL AND REPAIR At Cherry Point	Ellis, T. *Leatherneck*	Dec 61
	PILOT TYPES	Kester, SSgt C. *Leatherneck*	May 61
	STANDARD PILOT	Serrin, Maj D.	Jun 62
	VANISHING PEONS Only 56 NAP's left from the more than 400 of WW-2.	Jones, GySgt M. *Leatherneck*	May 62
	WHAT GOES UP El Toro aircraft maintenance	Johnson, AMSgt R. *Leatherneck*	May 60
	WINGS FOR MARINES Former enlistees can train for pilot	Mainard, TSgt A. *Leatherneck*	Feb 56
MOREST	MIRROR LANDING El Toro pilots learn Landing Signal Mirror and Morest pin-point landing techniques	Johnson, MSgt R. *Leatherneck*	May 58
	MOREST Arrest Landing Unit	Sarokin, MSgt P. *Leatherneck*	May 57
SAFETY	HOW MUCH SAFETY SHOULD AVIATION HAVE? That depends on whether you are a pilot or something else	Jones, Maj M.	Oct 58

Title	Author / Source	Date	Subject
IS THE FLIGHT SAFETY PROGRAM HURTING COMBAT READINESS?		Mar 62	
AVIATION SAFETY AND COMBAT READINESS	Fox, Maj J.	Dec 56	
AVIATION SAFETY OR COMBAT READINESS? How about both?	Hiett, Maj C.	Feb 62	
LAUNCH THE RUNWAYS Short Airfield Tactical Support runways	Clapp, Maj A.	Apr 58	SATS/ VTOL
PREFAB AIRSTRIP	Mainard, TSgt A. *Leatherneck*	May 58	
VTOL	Clapp, Maj A.	Jan 57	
ARIO Airborne Radar Intercept Operator School	Evans, SSgt C. *Leatherneck*	May 62	TRAINING
AVIATION BOOT CAMP	Maloney, Maj E.	Mar 56	
AVIATION FUNDAMENTAL SCHOOL	Curtis, TSgt P. *Leatherneck*	May 57	
AVIATION SCHOOLS Marine Air Detachment, Memphis	Ellis, AMSgt T. *Leatherneck*	May 60	
FLIGHT INDOCTRINATION Screening program for pilots set-up at Quantico	Curtis, TSgt P. *Leatherneck*	May 57	
LEVEL READY PILOT TRAINING	McClure, LtCol G.	Mar 61	
LONG HARD CLIMB El Toro's Aviation and Physiological Training Unit helps aviators survive	Barrow, MSgt C. *Leatherneck*	62	
THE MASH IS AIR El Toro class liquifies oxygen for jets	Johnson, AMSgt R. *Leatherneck*	Jan 60	
MISSING LINK Where, oh where, is the Link Trainer?	Clapp, LtCol A.	Dec 61	

	NAVIGATION SCHOOL At Cherry Point	Ellis, T. *Leatherneck*	Dec 61
	SAVE YOUR CHUTE Survival training at El Toro	Suhosky, TSgt R. *Leatherneck*	May 57
	SCHOOL FOR TEST PILOTS	Curtis, TSgt P. *Leatherneck*	Feb 57
	SKYHAWK SQUADRON Cherry Point jets in training exercise BRIGADELEX 11-59 at Puerto Rico	Sarokin, AMSgt P. *Leatherneck*	May 59
	SURVIVE	Johnson, Maj J. *Gazette*	Aug 61
	THEY SHOOT THE STARS	Sarokin, P. *Leatherneck*	Jan 59

DUTIES

From the *Gazette,* unless otherwise specified:

BAND	THE PRESIDENT'S OWN USMC Band has played at every inauguration since 1801	Kester, SSgt C. *Leatherneck*	Dec 62
CHAPLAINS	CHAPLAIN CORPS Combat Marines never forget Chaplains who help the wounded	Jones, GySgt M. *Leatherneck*	Apr 61
COMMANDANT	A DAY WITH THE COMMANDANT From the standpoint of responsibilities, there's nothing like it in the Corps	Lyons, Sgt R. *Leatherneck*	Aug 57
COMMUNI-CATIONS	BATTLEFIELD BRAIN		May 58
	COMMUNICATIONS—A CHALLENGE	Revane, LtCol H.	Feb 57
	COMMUNICATIONS CURSE CURED	Chapman, Capt W.	Feb 56
	CONFESSIONS OF A 2502	Chapman, Capt W.	Apr 57
	THE DEATH OF ABLE BAKER—FROM BOTH SIDES OF THE POND	Murray, Maj J., USA	Jul 56

THE EVOLUTION OF AMPHIBIOUS COMMUNICATIONS	Reber, Maj J. Nov 56	
MICRO-ELECTRONICS FOR THE MODERN DOCTRINE	Newton, Capt O. Jan 60	
MORE ABOUT RADIO RELAY	Green, Capt H., and Lt J. Fullinwider Mar 58	
RADIO RELAY	Bryant, Maj G., and Capt D. Tinius Oct 57	
THE WEAK LINK Sometimes, it's communications	Blyth, Maj C. Mar 59	
THE DI At PI	Suhosky, TSgt R. *Leatherneck* Jun 57	**DI**
DI WIFE They have as much fun as recruits	Cottrell, P. *Leatherneck* Jan 58	
DISTINGUISHED DI'S Commandant honors DI'S of PI and San Diego with trip to HQMC	Tallent, R. *Leatherneck* Jan 58	
I'M A DI What it takes to make Marines from one who knows	McGowan, SSgt A. *Leatherneck* Mar 58	
INSPECTION OF MARINE DRILL INSTRUCTORS Picture story	Phillips, W. *N. Y. Times Magazine* Feb 24, 1957	
LEATHERNECK SALUTES . . . DI'S	Windsor, Sgt L. *Leatherneck* Feb 58	
TODAY'S DI Same problems as always—converting slobs into Marines in 10 weeks	Barrow, AMSgt C. *Leatherneck* Apr 60	
YOU . . . A DI? Toughest duty in the Corps	Curtis, SSgt P. *Leatherneck* Jul 57	
EMBASSY MARINES Marines protect 93 embassies, consulates and legations	Barrow, MSgt C. *Leatherneck* Sep, Oct 60	**EMBASSY**

	USMC MOSCOW Embassy there	Frankel, M. *N. Y. Times Magazine* Nov 8, 1959
	EMBASSY DUTY—TOKYO Eleven Marines guard the Embassy there	Johnson, AMSgt R. *Leatherneck* Oct 59
	EMBASSY MARINES State Department duty requires top clearance, even for Marines	Mainard, TSgt A. *Leatherneck* May 58
ENGINEERS	ENGINEER SUPPORT TO THE FMF	Cooper, LtCol G. Dec 57
	ENGINEER SUPPORT TO MARINE CORPS AVIATION	Brundage, Col. T. May 58
	MEET MR. ENGINEER	Smith, CWO W. Apr 56
GUARD DUTY	PRESIDENTIAL DETAIL Marines guard Ike in Panama	Sarokin, MSgt P. *Leatherneck* Oct 56
HISTORICAL BRANCH	THEY CHRONICLE THE CORPS	Mainard, TSgt A. *Leatherneck* Nov 56
INTELLIGENCE	AERIAL PHOTOGRAPHY FOR GROUND FORCES	Strandberg, Lt C. May 56
	BETTER COMBAT INTELLIGENCE	Perkons, J. Sep 60
	CLOSING THE GAP	Cushman, BGen R. Jul 59
	HOW TO BUILD UP THE "2"	Davis, W. Sep, Oct 60
	MINIMIZING UNCERTAINTY . . . THE THREE-HEADED SPOOK	Masters, BGen J. Jun 58
	MOMENT OF TRUTH	Kelly, Capt T. Oct 60
	"MR. GISH, YOU'RE THE NEW S-2" What do you do then?	Davis, W Mar 61
	RECONAISSANCE—KEY TO THE CONCEPT	Hudson, BGen L. Aug 56
	TAO PLUS YOU	Spiro, M. May 59
	"2"—SECTION TIP	Manion, T. Mar 60
MEDICAL	AIR-MOBILE MEDICAL SUPPORT A concept that was to get a real test in Nam	Wilson, P. Dec 56

CORPSMAN When a Marine needs help, the first thing you hear is . . . "CORPSMAN"	Cushman, GySgt G. *Leatherneck*	Dec 62
FIELD RESEARCH LAB Emergency demands in medical research led to NMFRLS . . . Naval Medical Field Research Laboratory	Ellis, AMSgt T. *Leatherneck*	Jan 60
FIRST AID Atomic style	Hanker, Capt J.	Aug 57
FIT TO FIGHT New medical concepts keep Marines ready to serve	Smith, E. (Karl Schuon) and V. Blasdell *Leatherneck*	Apr 59
THE GUN THAT SAVES LIVES Hypodermic needle to be replaced by a needleless jet gun	Sarokin, MSgt P. *Leatherneck*	Feb 59
PLANNING FUTURE MEDICAL SUPPORT	Johnson, Capt H.	Jul 57
PREVENTIVE MED	Rice, H. *Leatherneck*	Mar 57

MESS DUTY

MESS OFFICER—AN ADDITIONAL DUTY How to handle it when it's your turn	McCarthy, E.	Feb 57

MOTOR TRANSPORT

FORCE MOTOR TRANSPORT	Thompson, Lt T.	Oct 61
WHEELS, TRACK AND OFFICER MECHS Maintenance and repair	Grube, Maj F.	Oct 62

PUBINFO

PERSPECTIVES ON PUBLIC RELATIONS	Lindsay, R.	Jan 56
PUBINFO—A COMMAND FUNCTION Public information	Morrisey, Capt R.	Feb 57

RECON

EYES AND EARS The glamour boys who get more ink than anyone in the Corps	Barrow, MSgt C. *Leatherneck*	Mar 62
FORCE RECON—BY LAND, SEA AND AIR A Corps within the Corps	Nickerson, BGen H.	Feb 59

Subject	Title	Author / Source	Date
	SUBMARINE SAFARI Maneuvers with the Recon forces	Marcus, MSgt S. *Leatherneck*	Oct 56
	SUB-PHIBIOUS SCOUTS	Stewart, TSgt W. *Leatherneck*	Apr 57
	TRIPLE THREAT On land, sea and in the air come the men from Recon	Johnson, AMSgt R. *Leatherneck*	Mar 59
RECRUITING	BOSTON RECRUITERS Beantown sends an average of a platoon a week to PI	Ball, MSgt D. *Leatherneck*	Oct 58
	COOL CAMERA Recruiting films are more numerous than ever	Johnson, AMSgt R. *Leatherneck*	Dec 59
	MINI-MARINES Mannequins used for recruiting look like the real thing	Morehead, ACpl J. *Leatherneck*	Nov 59
	THE NEW APPROACH But we still want men	*Leatherneck*	Jul 56
	RECRUITING DUTY—IS IT FOR YOU?	Zorack, J. *Leatherneck*	Mar 60
	SCARLET AND GOLD PROSPECTOR Recruiting offers many Marines independent duty	Kester, SSgt C. *Leatherneck*	Jan 62
RIOT CONTROL	RIOTS AND MARINES An important duty now	Hutchison, Maj W.	Mar 62
SPECIAL SERVICES	SPECIAL SERVICES Welfare, Morale and Special Service Branch's duties	Ellis, SSgt T. *Leatherneck*	Mar 61
STAFF	THE UNIT STAFF OFFICER How to handle the duty	Donovan, J.	Nov 56
WEATHER	THE BREAKER MEN Four Marines at Pendleton know exactly how many breakers have hit the beach in a specified time. Part of Amphib Warfare study	Jones, GySgt M. *Leatherneck*	Mar 62
	WEATHER PROPHETS El Toro Weathermen map aerial highways for pilots	Johnson, MSgt R. *Leatherneck*	May 58

FICTION

From *Leatherneck,* unless otherwise specified, alphabetical by author:

Austin, William and
James Fraser
MOON SHOT — Mar 59
Colonel disheartened when he read the coded message that blinked steadily from the moon

Blackton, Jim
GLOBE, ANCHOR AND SADDLE — Jul 57
Quick improvisation saved the day for the Horse Marines

JOHN, THE DOG — Mar 57
Thirty years after a stowaway founded a dynasty, his descendant is undisputed King of Guam

Boyd, Ellsworth
'CUDA HUNT — Jan 59
Semi-fiction about Marines on liberty, skin diving with spears for barracuda

Bristow, Vance
ARE YOU A GOOD MARINE? — Sep 60
Questions and answers

THE GREAT BAZOOKANIK — Jan 59
How the Marines launched their own, unofficial missile program

Chase, Eric (Karl Schuon)
THE IMPOSTERS — Oct 62
MSgt Tosselli and SSgt Bonnelli masquerade as "General" and "Diplomat"

THE IRISH PENNANT — Mar 62
A DI has enough problems without having to cope with a platoon of mythical little green men

LOOK LONELY WITH A MAP — Feb 64
Three Marines on liberty use a map to attract local dolls

THE SAGA OF SAM THE BEARD — Mar 61
Fantastic secret of longevity loosed when Sam killed the Scorpion

TO SEE THE DAY — Mar 64
A dying Marine looks into the future

THE VISITOR — Jan 61
Duff was an out-of-this-world Marine, but how far out?

Cook, David D.
SAUCE FOR THE GOOSE — Sep 56
Corporal wins promo by burning gravy

D'Andrea, Tom
GENTLY, GENTLY, GENTLY . . . — May 62
It was scheduled as a routine photo mission, but an aviator's first flight into enemy territory can never be routine

De Chant, Jack
THE BIG YAK — Sep 58
21st Century Marines celebrate landing on Moon

Dieckmann, Edward
HOT ROCK — Aug 56
Marine Sgt uses volcano for ammo

INFERNO ON THE RIVER — Sep 57
Viking Marines

A LONG SHOT PAYS OFF — Mar 56
Top Kick gets Golden Quail's interest

NIGHT ATTACK — Jun 59
A Marine Sgt uses the thunder-weapon of the Gods to defeat the Romans at Ostia

A TIME FOR SERGEANTS — Feb 60
The enemy ships were alive with scimitars

Dubus, Andre
THE LIEUTENANT — Dial Press 1967
Novel about homosexuality in a Marine detachment aboard a carrier in 1960's

Dunnagan, C. Grant
OPERATION-BEAR TRAP — Jun 57

Frankel, Ernest

LIGHT OF DAY — Nov 57
Kid proves himself

Guilford, James (Karl Schuon)

THE BIG SWITCH — Jul 60
Kelly's gag shook up the command, but the Captain was nobody's fool

CHIN — Apr 60
Not even $100,000 could repair Butch's shattered illusions

THE DEVIL TO PAY — Jan 62
One soul in exchange for eight lives was the deal Kelly made

THE FEINT — Jul 61
Cpl Joe Rucci, "The Feint", fights "Wee Willie." The "Feint" faints at the sight of blood

SCHULTZ'S DOPPEL — Feb 61
The entire command was convinced that Cpl Schultz wasn't the rootin, tootin Teuton. Yet, they couldn't explain his presence in two places at one time

TINY KIM — Dec 60
Volunteer patrol on Christmas Eve, looking for excitement, opens door. Finds Tiny Kim

Hammon, Louis (Karl Schuon)

A BIGGER MARINE — Feb 62
New Man is 6'2", 260 lbs of trouble

MERLIN'S FOLLY — Apr 62

THE SWINDLER — Oct 61
If there ever was a heap of nothing, that convertible was it. But the Gunny had an angle

Hassett, Robert L.

ORANGE ONE — Oct 56
Marines eat oranges prized by Captain aboard ship

Jones, Mel
THE LANDLORD — Apr 64
PFC discovers he owns a huge plot of ground in the middle of Lejeune. His enterprises, such as a small race track, cause numerous problems.

Keimel, MSgt Stephen
HAIRY RUN OVER SUAN-YULI — May 60
Korea air adventure

Mainard, MSgt Allen C.
THE ARRIVAL — Jun 59

McCann, Charles W.
THE DIVERSION — May 56
Lieutenant and Corporal wounded

McCarthy, Eugene C.
THE SKIPPER AND SCREAMING WILLIE — Feb 57
Willie has the whole command jumping

McCauley, Thomas J.
PASSING THE WORD — Jan 56
Hearsay can be time wasting

THE TRANSITION — Dec 58
A replacement upset whole company because he couldn't grow a beard

McDowell, Dean N.
RHINO HUNT — Mar 59
Old hands were sure this was not the time of year to hunt rhino. But . . .

Milhon, William
LUNAR OR LATER — Jan 58
Post Office snafus love life of Marine on moon

Moriarty, James F.
HINTS FOR NEW LIEUTENANTS — Mar 59
Notes found among effects of the late Lt Benjamin Iconoclast

Prickett, W. F.
ALIBI ON 24 — Sep 59
Target 24, are you there?

Robinson, Richard L.
TYPHOON — May 59
Storm, lightning, etc., could tear apart aircraft or damage it structurally

Smith, Earl E. (Karl Schuon)
DEAR EDITOR, SIR — Nov 61
Col Brisbane pulled his hair out while the "Supreme Exalted Keepers of the Soap" pulled their usual capers

DEAR YE EDITOR — Jul 59
An eye witness report on the Revolution by *Leatherneck's* Staff

DEAR YE EDITOR — Nov 60
Snodstitch and Trumboli were *Leatherneck's* first headaches

DOWN CHECK — May 61
Sgt Prescot, given a medical discharge for a heart murmur, is given a party.

THE GENEROUS SGT ZIMMERMAN — Dec 57
This 30-year man loves Christmas

RIVER RAID — Mar 58
George Washington had Marines with him crossing the Delaware

SPECIAL PROJECT — Jul 58
NCO'S stage unofficial fireworks

Spotanski, MSgt John H.
NUMBER 19 — May 57
Corporal holds pilot to his promise

Stolley, Fred
BLACKIE WAS A BIRD DOG — Oct 59
Retriever never knew when to quit

BROWN VS. GREEN — Nov 57
Age-old argument

CHIPMUNK'S MAIL — Jun 57
Two Jap WW-2 ex-prisoners meet.

GET THE LEAD OUT! — May 56
Famous phrase began in WW-2

GOZAYAMAS, OHIO — Apr 61

THE HARD WAY — Nov 59
Shortstopping, smokestacking, whistling and barging-in were serious breaches of etiquette in the Old Corps

THE HOMECOMING — Dec 62
Monk had been in the Pacific for eight years, but he was beginning to think his homecoming was a dud.

HOW DOES IT FEEL TO BE RETIRED? — Mar 58
Retirement of Sgt lasts 90 days. Re-ups.

ISLA, MO — Aug 61
When the Old Man tried to close up for the night, the Marines bought him out

THE STREAMLINED MARINES — Dec 56
Boots now have it easy, say vets

YOU ONLY DIE TWICE — Oct 61
One of the hardest things in life is to go on living after you have prepared yourself for death

Styron, William

THE LONG MARCH — Random House, Inc. 1952
One of the two or three best stories ever written about Marines and what makes them tick. Styron was one, and he remembered. Get this book!
Paperback by New American Library 1968. Also in *The World of Modern Fiction,* Simon and Schuster, Inc. 1966

Suhosky, TSgt Robert A.

BIG RED — Jul 56
Three day homecoming for Big Red Platoon

CHABOOM — Apr 56
Finally find and blast bridge

FIND, FIX, FIGHT AND FINISH — Sep 56
Four points help, but so does luck

THE HILL — Aug 58
Boot accidentally clobbers Gunny, first with mud, and then with boulder

Tallent, MSgt Robert W.

THE INCREDIBLE PEEDIES — Oct 58
There's always been a snafued peedie in the USMC, since the first fall overboard near Tun's Tavern

PEEDIE REPORT — Jan 59
The ancestry of Pvt Herkimer Peedie

Unsigned

CHOPPER'S LAST SCRAP — Apr 56
Honor of the Corps gets Marine Pvt into ring and victory

DIALOGUE FOR TWO WARRIORS — May 61

THE HEIGHTS — Oct 58
Vet of WW-2 wins Medal of Honor in Korea

Weiler, Al (Karl Schuon)

THE BIG WIND — Jun 61
The whole command was humming with activity when O'Malley arrived. With reference to his past record, the Top was sure trouble was brewing

CAMEL TROUBLE — Dec 61
Horrible Murphy, Nails Borowski & Company, borrow camels for a Christmas display only to find they can't return them

THE RISK — Sep 62
The survivors of the patrol learned from Monk Flint that they weren't just men. They were Marines

THE SITTER SITTERS — Sep 61
Top brass couldn't recognize need for protective organization until one fateful evening

York, Frank Scott

ACTION . . . CAMERA . . . BEACHHEAD — Apr 59
When Hollywood called upon the Marines to stage a "realistic" landing, the troops went all out

LEADERSHIP

From the *Gazette,* unless specified otherwise:

Title	Author	Date
ARE YOU AN EQUALITARIAN OR AN AUTHORITARIAN?	Simmons, LtCol E.	Feb 57
BATTLE DOCTRINE FOR FRONT LINE LEADERS		Aug-Nov 62
COMBAT LEADERSHIP		Nov 62
THE CARE AND FEEDING OF YOUNG OFFICERS	Metzger, Col L.	Jul 61
BY CHARACTER AND SKILL	Bressoud, M.	Apr 56
CHARACTERISTICS OF LEADERS	Barnes, Col W.	Mar 61
COMMAND PRIMER	Markham, Maj E. *Proceedings*	Sep 60
DECORATIONS AND AWARDS		Sep 57
DEFENSE IN THE SUMMARY COURT	Russell, CWO R.	Nov 60
DELEGATE, SIR	Crumb, MSgt C.	Jun 62
DISCIPLINE HAS NO MOS	Stubbs, Maj R.	Jan 56
DOES THE LEADER MAKE THE DIFFERENCE? Frequently	Crumb, MSgt C.	Aug 60
DON'T EXPECT—INSPECT!	Wilson, Capt P.	Feb 56
ENERGY IN LEADERSHIP	Crumb, MSgt C.	May 56
ESPRIT-DE-MARINE	Gasser, Maj J.	Mar 60
44TH MAN: SECOND LIEUTENANT	Cuneo, Maj E.	Nov 62
THE FUTURE BREED	Thomas, Capt T.	Sep 59
GILDING THE PILL?	Hargreaves, Maj R.	Jun 56
GUIDE POSTS TO LEADERSHIP	Cooper, Cpl G.	Jul 60
THE IG AND THE STAFF NCO'S	Dutton, SgtMaj B.	Nov 61

Title	Author	Date
IMAGINATION	Wilbern, LtCol J.	Jun 59
INITIATIVE	Nicholson, LtCol D.	Nov 57
IS YOUR PRESTIGE SHOWING?	Petry, A.	Feb 59
JACK 'EM UP	Averill, Maj G.	Jan 56
LEST WE FORGET	Johnson, LtCol F.	Jan 60
LETTER TO A STAFF NCO	Berkeley, MajGen J.	May 60
LET'S DELEGATE	Green, Capt F.	Feb 56
LET'S TEACH DISCIPLINE	Howell, Capt D.	Oct 62
MAKE 'EM PROFESSIONAL AND SHIP 'EM OVER	Dye, Sgt L.	Aug 58
MORALE: A STATE OF MIND	Moore, R., USN	Feb 61
NON-JUDICIAL PUNISHMENTS	Stubbs, Maj R.	Sep 56
THE OLD AND THE NEW	Crumb, MSgt C.	Nov 56
THE OLD CORPS	Prickett, Col W.	Jul 56
ONCE A MARINE, ALWAYS A MARINE	Geissinger, Maj R.	Apr 58
PRESTIGE AND YOUR OFFICE	Taylor, AMSgt M.	Oct 59
PROTECTIONISM: MODERN MALADY Dr. Spock started it all	Bethel, Capt W.	May 62
REFLECTIONS ON LEADERSHIP	Williams, LtGen S., USA	Oct 62
THE RETURN OF THE MAN ON HORSEBACK	Henderson, Col F.	Jun 58
SELL YOUR OWN STOCK	Donahoe, LtCol J.	Dec 56
SGT MAJOR OF THE MARINE CORPS		Nov 57
SMALL UNIT LEADERSHIP	Crumb, MSgt C.	Feb 57

SO YOU'RE A CO!	Aldridge, Capt J. Feb 56
SOMEONE INSPECTS YOU EVERY DAY Your wife!	DeCaro, CWO G. Feb 60
SOMETHING TO FIGHT FOR	Tanham, Dr. G. Sep 61
SPECIAL TRUST AND CONFIDENCE	Heinl, R. *Gazette* Nov 56 *Proceedings* May 56
SURVIVAL THROUGH DISCIPLINE	Litzenberg, MajGen H. Jan 59
THE TEN BEST Books for a professional library	Thomas, Gen G. Apr 57 Russell, W. May 57 Hargreaves, Maj R. Jun 57 Marshall, S. Jul 57
A TOCSIN FOR COMMAND	Reichner, LtCol H. Apr 58
A TOUCH OF TRADITION	Magruder, LtCol J. Feb, Jul, Nov 56, Nov 57, Nov 59
UNIFORM: THE WHY AND THE WHEREFORE	Hargreaves, Maj R. Nov 56
WANTED: HAIRY FISTED MARINES	O'Connor, Lt J. Nov 61
WHAT IT MEANS TO BE A MARINE	Crumb, MSgt C. Jan 60
WHAT MAKES FOR ESPRIT-DE-CORPS	*Navy* Oct 59
WHY A MARINE CORPS?	Crown, LtCol J. Nov 58
YOU *CAN* SPEAK IN PUBLIC	Barnes, Col W. Jan 61
YOUR SON CAN BE AN OFFICER	Wilkerson, Capt H. Mar 56

LOGISTICS

From the *Gazette*, unless specified otherwise:

GENERAL

Title	Author	Date
AUTOMATION IN SUPPLY Beginning of supply revolution	Lodge, Maj O.	Apr 59
COMBAT CARGO AIR DELIVERED	Fegley, Maj J.	May 62
COMBAT MAINTENANCE	Donovan, Col J.	Sep 61
COMBAT SUPPLY CLASS I: RATIONS		Jul 61
COMBAT SUPPLY: WATER	Donovan, Col J.	Aug 61
COMBAT SUPPLY CLASS 3: FUEL		Jul 61
COMBAT SUPPLY CLASS 5: AMMUNITION		Jul 61
DIAGNOSIS: THE MALADY OF SERIALIZATION	Long, F.	Jun 59
EMBARKATION VIA MSTS	Long, F.	Jan 61
FMF ORGANIZATION AND COMPOSITION BOARD REPORT-SERVICE ELEMENTS		Jul 57
JET AGE SUPPLY PROCEDURES	Morgan, Col G.	Feb 58
MARINE CORPS SUPPLY SYSTEM COMPLETELY MODERNIZED		Apr 59
MODERN COMBAT LOGISTICS	Donovan, J.	Jul 61
MWSG	Yeaman, Col R.	Apr 56
SECRET WEAPONS FOR SUPPLY	Roose, Col A.	Sep 57
SELF-SERVICE SUPPLY Supply distribution streamlined	Mainard, TSgt A. *Leatherneck*	Dec 57
SHIP TO SHORE	Burton, LtCol T.	Jun 56
SUPPLY AND DEMAND Equipment reaches Marines through Philadelphia's huge inventory control set-up. Comprehensive picture story	Barrow, AMSgt C. *Leatherneck*	Feb 60

SUPPLY AND DEMAND	Snyder, Capt B.	Jan 56
SUPPLY: A FUNCTION OF FIGHTING	Medina, T.	Feb 61
WHY WE NEED SERIALS	Poillon, Maj A.	Nov 59
WIRED FOR SUPPLY Complex electronic "brains" can now furnish fast, accurate picture of Corps' stock-pile	Curtis, AMSgt P. *Leatherneck*	Jun 59

CHOW

FLIGHT RATIONS Flight food for El Toro Marines	Johnson, MSgt R. *Leatherneck*	Jan 67
42,000 MEALS A DAY 4TH MARINES chow at Kaneohe Bay	Marcus, MSgt S. *Leatherneck*	Jan 56
MEAL, 25-IN-ONE, LANDING FORCES The food for the Vertical Envelopment Doctrine	Johnson, MSgt R. *Leatherneck*	Jun 57
REVOLUTION IN RATIONS Better than WW-2 and Korea variety	Jones, GySgt M. *Leatherneck*	Feb 61

GEAR

THE COMBAT LOAD New, lighter packs	Mainard, TSgt A. *Leatherneck*	Jan 57
EQUIPMENT PREVIEW	Mainard, TSgt A. *Leatherneck*	Dec 56
THE MARINES' COMBAT LOAD		Jul 61
NEW BODY ARMOR Redesigning old armor and "782" gear	Ellis, AMSgt T. *Leatherneck*	Dec 59
NEW UTILITY CAP	*Leatherneck*	Dec 59
THE SHORT-SLEEVED SHIRT In June of 1959, the Commandant authorized short-sleeved shirts	*Leatherneck*	Oct 59
USMC ISSUE What the well dressed Marine wore then	Cushman, GySgt G. *Leatherneck*	Nov 61

VEHICLES	BULK FUEL HANDLING	Gunning, Capt T.	Jul 58
	FLYING DUCK		Oct 59
	LVT'S—REMOTE CONTROLLED		Jul 58
	THE MARINE CORPS REVOLUTION IN TRANSPORTATION	Berkeley, MajGen J. *National Defense Transportation Journal*	Nov, Dec 59
	NO PITCH, NO ROLL New Amtrac		Dec 59
	ROLLING FUEL TRANSPORT		Mar 58
	TRANSPORTATION IN THE MARINE CORPS	Paige, MajGen H. *National Defense Transportation Journal*	Jan, Feb 57

MARINES

From *Leatherneck,* unless otherwise specified, alphabetical by the last name of the Marine.

Bartley, MSgt Harry D.
A MARINE RETIRES — McConnell, Sgt J. — Feb 52
Corps' oldest enlisted man retires

Butts, MSgt R.
BUILD YOUR OWN HOUSE . . . — Johnson, MSgt R. — Jan 58
Butts retires and builds house in Lakeside, Cal.

Chance, Will
WILL CHANCE—U. S. MARINE — Stewart, W. — Jan 59
Comic strip character

Clark, 1st Sgt J.
COLOR BREEDER — Johnson, MSgt R. — Aug 58
Clark raises parakeets

Collins, MSgt "Abie"
"ABIE" COLLINS — Lyons, TSgt R. — Jun 51
Mess Sergeant's life in Philadelphia

Collins, Mrs. Alpha
THE DOLL LADY — Johnson, MSgt R. — Dec 57
She makes dolls for needy children in San Mateo, Cal.

Crane, Ichabod
ICHABOD CRANE, LT, USMC — Turnbladh, E. — Nov 59
He was a native of Elizabeth, N.J. Appointed 2d Lt in 1809 and assigned to head a guard detachment aboard ship. Washington Irving must have known him

Esposito, Delmo
JUDO SCHOOL — Wells, G. — Oct 57
This member of the 14th Rifle Co., San Francisco, operates Judo School

Fisher, Major Joe
SALUTE TO THE INFANTRY SKIPPER — Montross, L. — Dec 59
CO of a Rifle Company, his men "love" him

Glenn, LtCol John H., Jr.
SPACEMAN — May 59
Salute to the first spaceman, a Marine

JOHN H. GLENN, ASTRONAUT — Pierce, LtCol P., and K. Schuon — Franklin Watts, Inc. 1962
"Get it out while he's news" biography

Hamblett, Col. A
MEET COLONEL HAMBLETT — Jordan, TSgt C. — May 53
New director of women Marines

Hubenthal, Al
HUBENTHAL: EX-LEATHERNECK — Riblett, L. — May 51
Former Leatherneck cartoonist is now top newspaper artist

Kier, MajGen Avery R.
MAJ GEN AVERY R. KIER, COMMANDING GENERAL OF THE 1ST MARINE AIR WING — Bartruff, D. — *Army, Navy, Air Force Register* April 8, 1961

Kriendler, Bob
THE MAN FROM "21" — Lyons, R. — Feb 57
Owner of New York's famous club is former Marine

Lauryssen, Maj Gaston
LANDLORD TO ROYALTY Barrow, AMSgt C.
One of the World's best-known hosts Sep 59

Lenn, Freddie
FREDDIE LENN Suhosky, SSgt R.
Great fighter and great coach at Quantico Mar 53

Marine, Miss
MISS MARINE Barrow, AMSgt C. Aug 59
Brunette from HQMC is "runner-up" in "Queen of the Armed Forces" contest

McQueen, Steve, John Russell and Jock Mahoney
COLT, MARE'S LEG AND DERRINGER Lewis, J. Jul 60
McQueen plays Josh Randall, Russell is "The Lawman" and Jock Mahoney does the dangerous work for stars as a double. All are former Marines

Megee, LtGen Vernon E.
THE NEW ASSISTANT COMMANDANT Jan 56
Appointment biography

Moulton, "Sarge"
JUNGLE SARGE Barrow, AMSgt C. Nov 59
As a schoolboy, he saw a Marine with "monstrous chevrons". After that, he was hooked on the Corps for life

Mowrey, MSgt J.
PART-TIME SHERIFF Johnson, MSgt R.
Mowrey is volunteer deputy sheriff for Orange County Aug 58

Munn, LtGen John C.
THE NEW ASSISTANT COMMANDANT Barrow, AMSgt C.
Feb 60
Munn's career includes service in Nicaragua's jungles and off the flight deck of the Langley

NO. 9241 Cushman, GySgt G.
Munn flew the F4B-4 during the 1930's May 62

Neil, MSgt Jean "Cheesy"
"CHEESY" NEIL Burlage, TSgt G. Jan 51
Biography of a Marine recruiter

O'Brian, Hugh

THE MARSHAL WAS A MARINE — Suhosky, TSgt R. — Jul 57
TV's Wyatt Earp

Pate, Gen Randolph McCall

THE 21ST COMMANDANT — Suhosky, TSgt R. — Jan 56

Pitman, MSgt Jack

U-BIRD TO WHIRLY BIRD — Suhosky, SSgt R. — Jul 57
Pitman downed five Zeros in four minutes over Bougainville. Now he flies choppers

Puller, LtGen Lewis B.

TOUGHEST MARINE IN THE CORPS — Martin, H. — *Sat Eve Post* — Mar 22, 1952

Rankin, LtCol William H.

THE MAN WHO RODE THE THUNDER — Rankin, LtCol W. — Prentice Hall, Inc. Englewood Cliffs, N.J. 1960 — Paperback by Pyramid Books 1961
Like to free fall seven miles in the grip of a violent thunderstorm without special equipment, live to write about it, and fly again? Rankin did it, and he writes almost as well as he falls. Exciting book about a unique adventure.

NINE MILE PLUNGE — Barrow, AMSgt C. — Nov 59
Magazine version of the fall

Rauber, Sgt Maj F.

CORPS SERGEANT MAJOR — Ellis, ASgt T. — Nov 59
The Commandant gives Rauber his "badge of office" at HQMC

Rentfrow, Frank Hunt

FRANK HUNT RENTFROW — Jones, MSgt W. — Feb 57
Cartoon editor of *Leatherneck* dies one month short of his 30th year

Robinson, MajGen Ray A.

KNOW YOUR LEADERS — Jordan, Sgt C. — Jul 51

Rosenberg, D.

GOOD WILL TUTOR — Smith, E. (Karl Schuon)
Tutors U.S. servicemen on local customs — Jan 61

Shoup, Gen David M.

THE CORPS 22ND COMMANDANT — *Gazette* — Sep 59

MARINE'S MARINE — *Time* — Aug 24, 1959

THE NEW COMMANDANT — Barrow, AMSgt C.
Shoup's friends claim no one has ever been better qualified to be Commandant — Jan 60

SHOUP OF THE MARINES — *Life* — Mar 23, 1962

22ND COMMANDANT OF THE MARINE CORPS — Sep 59
Picture Story of the only Medal of Honor winner to become Commandant. Shoup won it at Tarawa

UNCLE DAVE — *Time* — Feb 23, 1962

Umfleet, SSgt J.

MEMBER OF THE BOARD — Kester, SSgt C.
Full-time Marine and part-time insurance executive — May 62

Voelker, Gordon

BUBBLES, THE WHALE — Johnson, MSgt R.
Baby-sits for 1700 lb whale at Marineland — Jul 58

Woodbury, Woody

PIANO PILOT — Armstrong, TSgt R.
Entertainer was recalled as Marine jet pilot for Korea. Now famous as TV personality — Sep 53

Workman, RAdm Robert D.

LEATHERNECK SALUTES — Suhosky, TSgt R.
New Chief of Chaplains began as a Marine messman — Apr 57

OFF-DUTY

All articles in this section are from *Leatherneck*:

Title	Author	Date
COOL COMBO Radio show at Savannah	Sarokin, MSgt P.	Aug 56
FAMILY CAMP-OUT Cross-country experiences	Crown, J. and S.	May 60
FAR EAST NETWORK Counteracting propaganda and entertaining is mission of Far East Radio Network	Wood, R.	Oct 59
HARD ALEE Sail boats are the most popular form of recreation for Marines (next to girls).	Cornwell, C.	Jul 59
JOE DRAWS A BOAT	Carpenter, D.	Jun 56
OLE'S MARINE Bullfighting Marines	Wilson, E.	Mar 60
PART-TIME PILOTS Marines learn to fly	Suhosky, TSgt R.	Oct 56
PERMANENT PASS The odds in combat are better than those on the highways	Sarokin, MSgt P.	May 56
SHE'LL FLY AGAIN MSgt K. Schoenfeld restores a WW-I Pursuit Trainer	Stewart, AMSgt W.	May 59
SKY DIVER New equipment takes away danger in free fall	Mainard, TSgt A.	May 57
SNOWSHOE DERBY 2/5 Marines stage race at Pendleton on day off	Hart, H.	Apr 58
SOUTH FOR MUSKIES? Some fine fishing holes in the rivers of West Virginia		Aug 59
THETIS BAY, JR. A model ship built by Sgt D. Meisner and MSgt G. Hutchinson at Pendleton	Suhosky, TSgt R.	May 57

	TRANSFER TRAILS Pack a good map when you're driving to your next station	Johnson, MSgt R.	Jun 57
	YELLOW TAIL RUN Fishing off Marine bases	Suhosky, TSgt R.	Oct 56

PERSONNEL

From the *Gazette*, unless otherwise specified:

ADMINISTRATION	CONDITION READY Today's Corps is different	Kester, SSgt C. *Leatherneck*	Nov 61
	ELECTRONIC CASUALTY COUNT		Jun 58
	ENLISTED DETAIL	Drake, LtCol C.	Aug 57
	IS PAPER WORK NECESSARY? Maybe, but not this much	Pickle, LtCol K.	Nov 57
	MACHINE HELP FOR YOUR PAPER WORK	Juett, LtCol J., and LtCol R. MacAskill	Jan 60
	THE MIGHTY MITE! The Corps is going compact, like the cars of the time	Johnson, MSgt R. *Leatherneck*	Aug 60
	MISDIRECTIVES Let's eliminate them for good	Taylor, M.	Apr 61
	THE "NEW LOOK" IN DEFENSE REORGANIZATION	Bergren, Col O.	Dec 58
	PANIC BUTTON Simplified Operational Reading Test given to "D" Co., 2/2	Mainard, TSgt A. *Leatherneck*	Aug 57
	PERSONNEL READINESS	Weller, MajGen D., and Col W. Collins	Dec 58
	RECORD SHOP Records of every Marine are kept in St. Louis	Sarokin, AMSgt P. *Leatherneck*	Apr 59
	REORGANIZATION BETWEEN THE MARGINS	Hudgins, LtCol L.	Jul 58
	R.I.P.	Frank, B.	Jan 60
	STRIKE OFF THOSE ADMINISTRATIVE SHACKLES Arise, all you administrators!	Bacon, LtCol F.	Oct 58

Title	Author / Source	Date	Subject
THERE'S SENSE IN THOSE BILLIONS For national defense		May 58	
THIS IS BUWEPS The Corps Bureau of Personnel, part of HQMC.	Jones, M.	Mar 61	
UNITED STATES MARINE CORPS SLANG	Howard, D. *American Speech*	Oct 56	
WAR ON GOBBLEDYGOOK It never ends	Markham, E.	Jun 60	
WRITE IT RIGHT And you'll eliminate the gobbledygook	Pierce, LtCol P.	Apr 60	
YEMS, YAMS, PG, E3, AND YOU And all that good stuff	Utter, Maj L.	Jul 60	
CLASSIFICATION AND ASSIGNMENT How it works. The test prior to assignment	Johnson, MSgt R. *Leatherneck*	Dec 58	**ASSIGNMENTS**
CHANGE OF STATION	Graham, Maj L.	Jun 56	
INSTANT SAMARITAN Community relations is part of the job	Fairbourn, W.	Jun 62	
"SPECIALISTS"	Hargreaves, Maj R.	May 58	
WHERE WILL YOU SERVE?	Fredericks, H.	Feb 61	
CORPS STRIVES TO BALANCE OFFICER CAREER PATTERNS There are other things besides infantry	Bowser, MajGen A. *Army, Navy, Air Force Register*	Apr 8, 1961	**CAREER PLANNING**
GO FOR THE MAXIMUM	Foster, MSgt W.	Feb 60	
IMPROVEMENT OF USMC JUNIOR OFFICER LINEAL PRECEDENCE	*Proceedings*	Mar 59	
IT ALL COUNTS ON THIRTY Views on reenlistment and retirement	Johnson, MSgt R. *Leatherneck*	Jul 57	

	A LOOK AT THE HUMP As long as there's a war, there's a hump afterwards	Platt, LtCol J.	Jul 56
	MARINE CORPS ISSUES RETIRED HANDBOOK	*Armed Forces Journal*	Feb 8, 1958
	NEW ENLISTED RANK STRUCTURE Here comes the Lance Corporal		Oct 58
	ONCE A MARINE Interviews with retirees	Johnson, MSgt R. *Leatherneck*	Apr 57
	THE OPTION ACT—ELECT OR DECLINE	Lutz, R., USA	Jan 60
	PERSONNEL POLICIES AND YOU	Weller, MajGen D.	Jun 60
	RETIREMENT AND A CIVILIAN CAREER Plan for the career before you retire	Schinkel, LCpl P. *Leatherneck*	Jun 60
	A SECOND FIELD Lejeune Forum		Mar 62
	STAFF NCO SELECTION BOARDS What happens behind those closed doors	Jones, AGySgt M. *Leatherneck*	Apr 60
	THOSE BEST QUALIFIED Promotion is pretty much a "do-it-yourself" deal	Mainard, TSgt A. *Leatherneck*	Apr 56
	WALK BEFORE YOU RUN	Harris, J.	Mar 60
	YOUR CAREER ADVANCEMENT	Collier, Col R.	Jan 60
FITNESS REPORTS	FITNESS REPORTING—SOME ADVERSE REMARKS	Heinl, LtCol R.	Apr 59
	FITNESS REPORTS Commandant Cushman is an author, like most Commandants	Cushman, Col R.	Aug 56
	SRB MARKS—STAFF NCO'S	Galbraith, Capt T.	Jan 56

ALLOTMENT BRANCH More than $17-million is disbursed every month	Ellis, SSgt T. *Leatherneck*	Oct 61	**PAY AND ALLOWANCES**
AN INVESTMENT IN AN INVESTMENT	Cason, LtCol A.	Jun 59	
THE MILITARY PROFESSION: IS PAY THE ANSWER?	Drake, Col C.	Oct 58	
MONEY AND MARINES	Grant, W.	Jan 61	
MUCH ADO ABOUT MONEY	Millichap, LtCol P.	Jan 57	
ROTATE BY BATTALIONS	Sheridan, Capt R.	Apr 57	**TRANSPLACEMENT**
ROTATION BATTALION	Johnson, AMSgt R. *Leatherneck*	Jun 59	
THE SECURITY OF STABILITY	Nicholson, LtCol D.	Apr 59	
STABILITY: IT'S WONDERFUL (IN A TRANSPLACEMENT BATTALION)	Geissinger, Maj R.	Feb 61	
TRANSFER THE UNIT As a whole	Brown, SSgt D.	Jul 57	
TRANSPLACEMENT: OPPORTUNITY AND CHALLENGE	Miller, J.	Feb 61	

POSTS/PLACES

From the "Post of the Corps" series and other articles in *Leatherneck*, unless otherwise specified:

Title	Author	Date	Subject
DUTY IN DIXIE 6th District duty	Tallent, MSgt R.	Aug 56	**GENERAL**
HOSTESS HOUSES		Dec 56	
OUTPOSTS OF THE CORPS Olongapo, La Gonave, Shanghai, Cavite and hundreds of other isolated outposts	Jones, GySgt M.	May 56	
ADAK Most important island in the Andrean group	Johnson, AMSgt R.	Mar 60	**ALASKA**

	Article	Author	Date
	CARIBOU TRANSPLANT Adak Marines raise young animals to start a herd	Newton, Capt O.	Dec 59
	KODIAK Wild weather, high prices and the Kodiak bear	Johnson, AMSgt R.	Feb 60
	ALAMEDA	Kester, SSgt C.	Sep 62
	ALBANY, GEORGIA East Coast Supply Center	Kester, SSgt C.	Apr 61
	ANNAPOLIS Marine Detachment	Curtis, P.	Jan 59
	MARINE BARRACKS, ANNAPOLIS	Evans, SSgt C.	Feb 62
	ARLINGTON NATIONAL CEMETERY Final post for many Marines	Jones, AGySgt M.	May 60
	ATHENS LIBERTY Marines from USS Siboney	Mainard, TSgt A.	Oct 56
	BANGKOK LIBERTY Embassy Marines on holiday	Marcus, MSgt S.	Mar 56
	BANGOR, WASHINGTON	Johnson, MSgt R.	Oct 58
BARSTOW	BARSTOW—THE FIX-IT SHOP Whether it's a torn truck seat or a battered howitzer, Barstow will fix it	Jones, GySgt M.	Apr 62
	ROCK HOUNDS Barstow Marines hunt uranium	Johnson, MSgt R.	Oct 57
BEAUFORT	BEAUFORT Ground Controlled Approach Radar at air station	Kester, SSgt C.	Mar 62
	MCAS, BEAUFORT	Sarokin, MSgt P.	May 58
	BERMUDA No hurry—20 MPH speed limit	Mainard, TSgt A.	Apr 57

BROOKLYN 158 year history of waterfront duty at Navy Yard	Curtis, AMSgt P.	Mar 59	
BRUNSWICK, MAINE	Barrow, C.	Dec 61	
DEDICATION OF LEJEUNE HALL	*Gazette*	Jul 59	
CAMP PENDLETON Every type of combat training takes place at Pendleton	Johnson, SSgt R.	Nov 60	**CAMP PENDLETON**
CAMP PENDLETON, CALIFORNIA	*Proceedings*	Jan 59	
FIREBREAKERS Engineers cut 180 miles of firebreak trails	Suhosky, TSgt. R.	Sep 56	
HORSESHOES AND HISTORY Horse Marines ride again.	Tyler, GySgt C.	Sep 62	
MARINES IN REVIEW Six year history of Pendleton radio show	Suhosky, TSgt R.	Apr 57	
RODEO 15th Annual Pendleton Rodeo	Kester, SSgt C.	Sep 62	
RUGGED IS THE WORD Pendleton terrain	Suhosky, TSgt R.	Nov 56	
WEEK-END RODEO Every Sunday at Pendleton	Johnson, AMSgt R.	Jul 59	
CAROLINA-BOUND Corps bases in Carolinas	Asprey, R. *Gazette*	Jul 62	
CHARLESTON Marines on-duty at "Polarisville"	Jones, GySgt M.	Oct 61	**CHARLESTON**
CHARLESTON Marine Barracks	Stewart, AMSgt W.	Apr 59	
CHARLESTON Marines there since 1801	Jones, MSgt W.	Jul 57	
CHERRY POINT 2D Marine Aircraft Wing	Sarokin, MSgt P.	May 57	**CHERRY POINT**
CHERRY POINT—20TH ANNIVERSARY	Jones, GySgt M.	May 62	

	COUNSELING SERVICE Cherry Point wives help new arrivals	Sarokin, MSgt P. Apr 57
	HOUSEBOAT TSgt E. Lathrop lives on one with his family	Sarokin, MSgt P. Feb 59
	A NEW LOOK FOR NO. 3 Community effort transforms messhall	Jones, AGySgt M. Apr 60
	CHINA LAKE, CALIFORNIA	Johnson, MSgt R. Jan 58
	CONCORD West Coast's largest tide-water ammunition facility	Johnson, MSgt R. Oct 60
	CORONADO Amphibious warfare training in California	Suhosky, TSgt R. Oct 56
	CRANE, INDIANA	Sarokin, MSgt P. Sep 58
	DAHLGREN, VIRGINIA	Jones, MSgt W. Jul 58
EL TORO	DIVING BULLS Skin diving club for Marines	Segel, ASSgt T. Jul 59
	EL TORO BOWMEN Archery for Marine airmen	Suhosky, TSgt R. Jan 57
	EL TORO FISH-OFF All services compete for "Fishing Master" honors	Johnson, MSgt R. Oct 60
	EL TORO RODEO	Suhosky, TSgt R. Aug 56
	FALLBROOK Naval Ammo Depot guard duty	Johnson, MSgt R. Jun 60
	FORT MIFFLIN, PA	Curtis, TSgt P. Nov 56
GREAT LAKES	GREAT LAKES, ILL Duty at Naval Training Center	Sarokin, MSgt P. Feb 57
	GREAT LAKES Marines are primarily concerned with security	Jones, GySgt M. Feb 61

Title	Author	Date	Category
GUANTANAMO BAY Duty at Cuba Naval Station	Curtis, MSgt P.	Jun 58	
AKU MARINES Kaneohe Marines skin dive	Suhosky, TSgt R.	Jul 57	**HAWAII**
CAMP H. M. SMITH	Marcus, MSgt S.	Apr 56	
CAMP H. M. SMITH Headquarters for FMFPac	Moore, M.	Jul 62	
HAWAII BOUND	Johnson, AMSgt R.	Aug 59	
HAWAII LIBERTY Fort DeRussy hub for touring islands	Johnson, AMSgt R.	Aug 59	
HAWAII REVISITED Changes since WW-2		Aug 59	
KANEOHE BAY MCAS	Johnson, AMSgt R.	Aug 59	
MALIHINI OR KAMAAINA Speaking Hawaiian		Aug 59	
CAMP CLOUDBURST Encampment for Marines and families near Bridgeport, Cal.	Lewis, J.	Oct 58	**CAMP CLOUDBURST**
CAMP CLOUDBURST	Martin, J. *Gazette*	Jul 60	
INDIAN HEAD, MARYLAND Marines guard the Navy's only gunpowder factory	Curtis, TSgt P.	Dec 57	
ATSUGI		Mar 58	**JAPAN**
FESTIVAL AT IWAKUNI Marines and Japanese mingle at 7th Annual Good Will Music Festival	Barrow, MSgt C.	Aug 61	
IWAKUNI	Sarokin, MSgt P.	Mar 58	
OPPAMA		Mar 58	
SASEBO Marine Security Guard there	Johnson, AMSgt R.	Dec 59	

	Subject	Author / Date
	TRAINED TO ATTACK Twenty-three sentry dogs help guard Sasebo	Johnson, AMSgt R. Oct 59
	YOKOSUKA	Johnson, AMSgt R. Oct 59
	KEY WEST, FLORIDA	Jones, GySgt M. Dec 62
	LITTLE CREEK Seventy courses in Amphib War	Mainard, MSgt A. Nov 58
	LONDON, ENGLAND "Best duty in the Corps"	Barrow, MSgt C. Sep 60
	MC ALESTER, OKLAHOMA	Suhosky, TSgt R. Aug 56
	MIDWAY With the gooney birds	Marcus, MSgt S. Jan 56
	MIRAMAR NAS in California	Kester, SSgt C. Aug 62
NAPLES	NAPLES	Barrow, MSgt C. Jul 60
	NAPLES, ITALY	Mainard, TSgt A. Sep 56
	NEW LONDON Marines at the Submarine Base	Stewart, AMSgt W. Jun 59
	NEWPORT, R. I. Security duty at Naval Base	Cushman, GySgt G. Apr 62
	NEW RIVER On July 14, 1954, MAG-26 and Air facility there became "Post of the Corps"	Jones, AGySgt M. May 60
NORFOLK	CINCLANT Sharpest Marines in the Corps at FMFLant	Barrow, AMSgt C. Sep 59
	NORFOLK	Jones, GySgt M. Mar 61
PORTSMOUTH	PORTSMOUTH Marines provide guards for Norfolk Naval Shipyard and operate East Coast Sea School	Sarokin, MSgt P. Dec 58

Title	Author / Source / Date	Category
PORTSMOUTH	Ellis, ASSgt T. Apr 60	
NAHA On the East China Sea	Barrow, MSgt C. Jul 61	**OKINAWA**
OKINAWA	Sarokin, MSgt P. Apr 58	
CROSS COUNTRY RECORD Cpls Hartman and Zych hike 100 miles in 24 hours, 58 minutes on Okinawa	McKay, Sgt J. Apr 62	
OKINAWA "Keystone of the Pacific"	Barrow, MSgt C. Jun 61	
OKINAWA LIBERTY When a 3D MAR DIV Marine has liberty, he can tour WW-2 battlefields, visit shrines or relax on beach	Barrow, MSgt C. Apr 62	
RUGGED BACHELORS OF OKINAWA "No wives" policy creates bachelors	Worden, W. *Sat Eve Post* Mar 30, 1957	
"SO YOU'RE GOING TO OKINAWA"	Wickens, J. *Gazette* Sep 62	
RODMAN Canal Zone security provided by Marines	Jones, GySgt M. Jun 62	**PANAMA**
RODMAN, CANAL ZONE	Sarokin, MSgt P. Dec 56	
SAN FRANCISCO, PANAMA Village in Canal Zone	Jones, GySgt M. Oct 62	
PARIS, FRANCE	Mainard, TSgt A. Apr 58	**PARIS**
DATE IN PARIS Lowery photos of Marine and date on liberty	Oct 60	
PARRIS ISLAND	Sarokin, MSgt P. Sep 56	**PARRIS ISLAND**
PI STRONG MEN Weight Lifters	Jones, MSgt W. Jul 57	

	PI TODAY Visit by "Old Breed" Marine	McMillan, G.	Nov 61
	VISITORS' CENTER More than 600 guests a day	Barrow, AMSgt C.	Nov 59
PATUXENT	PATUXENT, MARYLAND Ground was broken for Naval Test Center in 1942	Curtis, TSgt P.	Mar 57
	TEST CENTER	Curtis, TSgt P.	May 57
	PENSACOLA	Mainard, TSgt A.	Feb 56
PUERTO RICO	ROOSEVELT ROADS U.S. Naval Station	Ellis, SSgt T.	Dec 60
	SAN JUAN	Ellis, SSgt T.	Jan 61
	SAN JUAN	Mainard, TSgt A.	Jun 56
	VIEQUES Camp Garcia training for 2D MAR DIV	Ellis, MSgt R.	Dec 60
QUANTICO	QUANTICO Forty-year history	Curtis, TSgt P.	Nov 57
	BATTLE OF U.S. I Quantico Highway Patrol	Petry, MSgt A.	Oct 57
	BEST FISHING BY A DAM SITE Conservation program turns Lunga Reservoir into paradise	Evans, SSgt C.	Jun 62
	EXHIBIT CENTER At MCAS, Quantico	Schneider, MSgt W.	Dec 62
	FROSTBITE REGATTA 10th Annual Sailing Regatta	Evans, Sgt C.	Oct 62
	MARINE CORPS MUSEUM	Jones, GySgt M.	Nov 60
	QUANTICO TOWN "The town that can't grow" because of base	Jones, GySgt M.	Feb 61
	QUONSET POINT Naval Air Station	Stewart, AMSgt W.	Jul 59

Title	Author	Date	Category
The Leatherneck series by Robert C. Hayes:			RETURN TO THE ISLANDS
GUADALCANAL		Jul 60	
KORO		Aug 60	
MELBOURNE		Jun 60	
NEW CALEDONIA		Apr 60	
NEW HEBRIDES		Jan 60	
RABAUL		May 60	
TULAGI-BOUGAINVILLE		Mar 60	
WELLINGTON		Dec 60	
RHODES LIBERTY R & R in Med	Mainard, TSgt A.	Jan 58	
ROTA Spanish-American Naval Base	Barrow, MSgt C.	Aug 60	
SAN DIEGO More than 250,000 have gone through Recruit Depot	Suhosky, TSgt R.	Oct 57	SAN DIEGO
NEW STAFF NCO CLUB The "King of Clubs"	Barrow, MSgt C.	Jun 62	
RECRUIT DEPOT	Barrow, MSgt C.	Mar 61	
HUNTER'S POINT	Kester, SSgt C.	Oct 62	SAN FRANCISCO
MOFFETT FIELD NAS training center for Pacific Fleet Naval Air	Johnson, MSgt R.	Feb 59	
SAN FRANCISCO LIBERTY Stateside, there's none better	Suhosky, TSgt R.	Jan 57	
TERMINAL ISLAND Ups and downs of TI	Suhosky, TSgt R.	Jan 57	
TREASURE ISLAND	Johnson, MSgt R.	Feb 58	
SANGLEY POINT On Luzon in the Philippines	Marcus, MSgt S.	Mar 56	
USS BENNINGTON	Johnson, MSgt R.	Nov 58	SEAGOING

Location	Title	Author	Date
	THE HAVEN USS Haven, floating hospital at Terminal Island	Johnson, AMSgt R.	Jul 59
	USS INDEPENDENCE Twenty-five stories high and quarter mile long	Jones, GySgt M.	May 61
	USS IWO JIMA	Barrow, MSgt C.	May 62
	WEST PAC BOUND Life aboard the USS Lexington	Johnson, AMSgt R.	Sep 59
	USS MACON No. 1 battleship cruiser for U.S. Atomic Fleet	Curtis, TSgt P.	Sep 57
	USS NEWPORT NEWS Cruiser carries Marines	Kester, SSgt C.	Sep 61
	USS OKINAWA	Kester, SSgt C.	Dec 62
	TRIPOLI Tripoli gave the Corps two things—the Marmeluke Sword and a phrase for the Hymn	Maloney, P.	Aug 57
TWENTYNINE PALMS	HELPING HAND Counseling service for Marines and their families	Johnson, MSgt R.	Feb 59
	TWENTYNINE PALMS Huge artillery training base		Jun 57
WASHINGTON	EIGHTH AND EYE Where the big boss lives	Ellis, ASgt T.	Nov 59
	ASSIGNMENT . . . HQMC Where the big boss works	Lang, Cpl D.	Jul 62
	HEADQUARTERS, USMC	Tallent, MSgt R.	Nov 56
	WASHINGTON, D.C. U.S. Naval activities there	Jones, MSgt W.	Jul 56
	WHIDBEY ISLAND State of Washington Navy Base	Johnson, MSgt R.	Aug 58
	YELLOW WATER Florida Naval Magazine	Cushman, GySgt G.	Jun 61

YORKTOWN, VIRGINIA	Ellis, ASSgt T.	Jan 60
YUMA Auxiliary air station acquired from Air Force in 1958	Johnson, AMSgt R.	May 59

RESERVE

From the *Gazette*, unless otherwise specified:

GENERAL

AFT 1962 REPORT	Van Stockum, R.	Nov 62
ANNUAL FIELD TRAINING Five units train at Corpus Christi	Cain, J. *Leatherneck*	Sep 58
BETTER RESERVE TRAINING	Moore, LtCol C.	Apr 60
CASE OF THE VANISHING RESERVE	Fairbourn, W.	Jul 62
DRAGON'S TEETH Reorganization of USMCR into 4TH MAR DIV and MAW provides rapid mobilization	Kester, SSgt C. *Leatherneck*	Jun 62
INACTIVE RESERVES IN KEY ROLES	Van Stockum, R.	Oct 62
LET'S PERK UP OUR RESERVES	Venditto, Capt C.	Aug 60
MARINE AIR RESERVE CHALLENGE	Leek, BGen F.	Jan 60
THE MARINE CORPS RESERVE	Stickney, BGen W.	Oct-Dec 57, Jan 58
MARTCOM REPORT	Moore, LtCol R.	Nov, Dec 60
MARTCOM REPORT	Robertshaw, L.	Jun 61
MCROA Marine Corps Reserve Officers' Association		Jul 58
MERGER TRAINING FOR AIR RESERVISTS	Dantin, M.	May 61
NIGHT OWL RESERVES	Fairbourn, W.	May 62

THE 9TH MCRD	Ball, D. *Leatherneck*	Dec 57
ORGANIZE THE ORGANIZED RESERVE	Sepsis, MSgt J.	Sep 60
ORGANIZED AIR GROUND-RESERVES 1959		Dec 59
PLANNING A COMBINED RESERVE EXERCISE	Godfrey, P.	Aug 61
POWER IN RESERVE		Jun 62
PROGRESS REPORT	Fairbourn, W.	Feb 62
RECALL AND YOU	Venditto, Capt C.	Sep 62
REPORT FROM THE READY FORCES: VOLUNTEER RESERVE	Cooke, Maj M., Capt F. Nelson and Capt J. Everett	Jan 60
REPORT FROM THE READY FORCES: ORGANIZED RESERVE	Owens, Maj T., and Capt J. Everett	Oct 60
RESERVE OBSTACLE COURSE	Liggett, Maj T.	Apr 60
RESERVE READINESS	Fairbourn, W.	Jan 62
RESERVE REGIMENTS	Dure, Capt L.	May 60
RESERVE REORGANIZATION	Van Stockum, R.	Aug 62
RESERVE TRAINING Organized Reserve has 311 units trained and ready-to-go	Daum, MSgt W. *Leatherneck*	Jun 61
RESERVE TRAINING	Fairbourn, W.	Mar 62
RESERVE TRAINING	Singer, Capt I.	Sep 56
RESERVES INFLUENCE CORPS POLICY	Van Stockum, R.	Dec 62
THE THIRD "M" Reserves have been mobilized in 1940 and 1950. They're ready for the "Third M"	Tallent, R. *Leatherneck*	Nov 57
USMCR: AMATEUR OR PROFESSIONAL?	Stickney, MajGen W.	Nov 59

VITALIZING THE VTU	Fairbourn, W.	Jul 60
WHO'S READY?	Fairbourn, W.	Apr 62

RESERVE-EXERCISES

All articles in this section are from *Leatherneck:*

Title	Author	Date	Year
TABMOC West Coast reserve training	Johnson, MSgt R.	Nov 58	**1956**
OPERATION BUSY WEEK Battalion of mixed Reserve units makes amphibious landing at Pendleton	Johnson, MSgt R.	Oct 57	**1957**
NAILIVIC 4th Staff Group, Philadelphia, plans Lejeune Air-Ground exercise	Blair, AMSgt T.	Oct 59	**1959**
OPERATION LITTLE FREEZE 45th Infantry Co., Ogden, Utah	Johnson, AMSgt R.	Apr 59	
OPERATION VIGILANCE Four Reserve units in 5th MCRD in field problem	Barrow, AMSgt C.	Jul 59	
PIROGUE PATROL Louisiana maneuvers	Rudsinske, AMSgt E.	Oct 59	
OPERATION CHARGER Largest peace-time maneuver in history at Twentynine Palms	Johnson, MSgt R.	Nov 60	**1960**
OPERATION FALLING LEAF Marines from Indiana, Ohio and Kentucky participate in five-service "war"	Boyd, Capt C.	Jan 61	
OPERATION WHIPSAW Three-day maneuvers at Lejeune for 2,000 Reserves	O'Brien, C.	Oct 60	
RESMOBEX -60 Reserve Mobilization exercise	Daum, AMSgt B.	Sep 60	
OPERATION DRAGONFLY Three Virginia Reserve units in Blue Ridge mountains	Cushman, GySgt G.	Apr 61	**1961**

	OPERATION INFERNO Reserve maneuver at Twentynine Palms	Tyler, C.	Dec 61
	READY RESERVISTS Operation Inferno	Daum, MSgt W.	Nov 61
1962	THE RESERVISTS HIT VIEQUES Washington, D. C., 13th Infantry Bn trains in Puerto Rico	O'Leary, J.	Sep 62

RESERVE-UNITS

All articles in this section are from the *"Reservist"* Series in *Leatherneck:*

	AKRON 1st Automatic Weapons Battery	Sarokin, MSgt P.	Aug 58
	ALAMEDA MAG-42 flys Skyhawks	Kester, SSgt C.	Dec 62
	ATLANTIC CITY 7th AW Battery	Suhosky, TSgt R.	Dec 56
	AUGUSTA, GEORGIA 2d Truck Co.	Stewart, AMSgt W.	Jun 59
AUGUSTA MAINE	MAINE 105th Rifle Co.	Sarokin, MSgt P.	Dec 58
	MAINE 64th Rifle Co.	Barrow, MSgt C.	Jan 62
	BALTIMORE 4th Pioneer Bn	Cushman, GySgt G.	Jul 62
	BIRMINGHAM City builds USMCR Memorial	Mainard, TSgt A.	Feb 57
	BROOKLYN AIR Five hundred attend training	Mainard, TSgt A.	May 57
	CAMDEN Summer Camp includes history lessons, combat operations and military tactics	Ellis, SSgt T.	Jan 61
	CHARLESTON 53rd Rifle Co.	Barrow, AMSgt C.	Mar 60

Subject	Author / Date	Margin
CHATTANOOGA 1st 105 mm Howitzer Battery	Jones, MSgt W. Mar 58	
CHICAGO 9th and 10th Infantry Bn., and the 2d Comm Support Bn	Jones, GySgt M. Feb 61	**CHICAGO**
CHICAGO Five training centers	Sarokin, MSgt P. Apr 56	
COMPTON 82d Rifle Company	Johnson, MSgt R. Jun 60	
DALLAS AIR From four states	Lewis, J. Apr 58	
DELAWARE 16th Rifle Company	Sarokin, MSgt P. Mar 56	
DENVER Four Marine units there	Mainard, TSgt A. Jan 56	
DETROIT 5th Infantry Bn	Sarokin, MSgt P. Jan 57	
DOVER 7th Rifle Co.	Sarokin, MSgt P. Nov 58	
EL PASO 19th Rifle Co.	Crawford, W. Jun 62	
FLINT 51st Infantry Co.	Sarokin, MSgt P. Jun 58	
FORT SMITH, ARKANSAS 92d Rifle Co., called "Mountain Marines"	Lewis, J. Dec 60	
GROSSE ILE Marine reserves at NAS	Curtis, AMSgt P. May 59	
JACKSON 2d 105 mm Howitzer Bn	Curtis, MSgt P. Feb 59	
JACKSONVILLE AIR VMA-114	Cushman, GySgt G. May 61	**JACKSONVILLE, FLORIDA**
GATOR'S LONG FLIGHT VMA-144 in Puerto Rico	Akey, MSgt C. Oct 62	
KANSAS CITY 2d Weapons Bn	Pearman, R. Sep 59	

	KNOXVILLE 6th Engineer Company	Mainard, TSgt A. Sep 57
	LONG BEACH 5th Communications Co.	Johnson, AMSgt R. Apr 60
	LOS ALAMITOS Air Reserves at Los Angeles	Lewis, J. Jan 58
	LOUISVILLE 7th Special Infantry Co.	Sarokin, MSgt P. Jun 56
	LYNN, MASS 2d Engineer Co.	Cushman, GySgt G. Apr 62
	MADISON 4th Automatic Weapons Battery	Ball, MSgt D. Feb 58
	MEMPHIS Air Reserve Units	Ellis, ASgt T. May 60
	NEW ROCHELLE 2d Rifle Co.	Barrow, AMSgt C. Aug 59
	NEW YORK Manhattan boasts 17 USMCR units and squadrons	Ball, MSgt D. Jul 56
	NORFOLK 3d Service Bn	Jones, AGySgt M. Aug 60
	PASADENA 1st Light Anti-Aircraft Missile Battery	Lewis, J. Aug 61
	PHOENIX 9th Engineer Co.	Suhosky, TSgt R. Jul 57
	PITTSBURGH 12th Infantry Bn	Jones, AGySgt M. Feb 60
	PORTSMOUTH 75th Infantry Co.	Morehead, ACpl J. Dec 59
RALEIGH	RALEIGH 4th 155 mm Howitzer Battery	Sarokin, MSgt P. Apr 57
	RALEIGH 4th 155 mm Howitzer Battery	Kester, SSgt C. Jul 61
	RICHMOND 1st 105 mm Howitzer Battalion	Mainard, MSgt A. Oct 58

Unit	Author	Date	Margin
ROANOKE 5th Engineer Co.	Johnson, MSgt R.	Mar 57	**ROANOKE**
ROANOKE 5th Engineer Co.	Jones, GySgt M.	Mar 51	
ROCHESTER, NEW YORK 3rd Communications Co.	Jones, MSgt W.	Aug 57	
SAN BERNARDINO 32d Infantry Co.	Johnson, MSgt R.	Jul 58	
SAN DIEGO TANKERS 4th Tank Bn trains at Camp Elliott	Kester, SSgt C.	Aug 62	
SAN FRANCISCO 30,000 reserves in the area	Marcus, MSgt S.	May 56	
SAN JOSE 1st Air Delivery Platoon	Johnson, AMSgt R.	Feb 59	
SAVANNAH 5th Rifle Company	Sarokin, MSgt P.	Sep 56	**SAVANNAH**
SAVANNAH "D" Co., 10th Infantry Bn	Barrow, AMSgt C.	Nov 59	
SEAL BEACH 15th Rifle Company	Lewis, J.	Jul 60	
TALLAHASSEE TANKERS 1st Tank Company	Kester, SSgt C.	Sep 61	
TAMPA 1st Amphibious Tractor Bn.	Jones, MSgt W.	Jun 57	
TOLEDO 8th Infantry Bn		Jan 60	
CAPITOL RESERVISTS		Feb 56	**WASHINGTON**
WASHINGTON 13th Infantry Bn	Ellis, SSgt T.	Mar 62	
WASHINGTON AIR Fighter and Air Control squadrons	Sarokin, MSgt P.	May 58	
WASHINGTON AIR VMA-236, VMA-321, MACS-24, VMA-331	O'Leary, J.	May 62	

	WYOMING, PA. 2d Motor Transport Maint. Co.	Jones, GySgt M.	Sep 62

SPORTS

All articles in this section are from *Leathernack*, unless otherwise specified:

BASKETBALL	ALL-MARINE BASKETBALL Quantico Marines win three straight over San Diego	Jones, AMSgt W.	May 59
	BASKETBALL CHAMPIONSHIP San Diego wins All-Marine	Suhosky, TSgt R.	Jun 57
BOWLING	ALL-MARINE BOWLING Competition at Parris Island	Sarokin, MSgt P.	Jun 56
	ALL-MARINE BOWLING 4th Annual Meet at PI	Sarokin, MSgt P.	Jun 58
BOXING	INTER-SERVICE BOXING '56 Marine finalists beaten by Army	Jones, MSgt W.	Dec 56
	ALL-MARINE BOXING Lejeune dominates 5th Annual Tournament		Apr 57
	ALL-MARINE BOXING PREVIEW Lejeune and Pendleton favored	Jones, MSgt W.	Feb 57
	ALL-MARINE BOXING '58 Matches at Quantico	Jones, MSgt W.	Jun 58
	ALL-MARINE BOXING San Diego is host	Jones, MSgt W.	May 59
	ALL-MARINE BOXING Pendleton first, then Okinawa	Olsen, LCpl E.	Jul 61
	CANASTOTA CLOUTER Former Marine Carmen Basilio's career started with Corps in Hawaii	Warner, D.	Jan 58
	PENDER VS. DOWNES Two former Marines meet for middleweight crown	Cushman, GySgt G.	Mar 61
FOOTBALL	ROOKIE RAM Former SSgt is with the Rams	Suhosky, SSgt R.	Dec 52

FOOTBALL FORECAST	Jones, MSgt W.	Sep 56	
LEATHERNECKS' ALL-MARINE FOOTBALL TEAM, '55	Curtis, TSgt P.	Mar 56	
LEATHERNECKS' ALL-MARINE FOOTBALL TEAM, '56 Pendleton best in West—Lejeune and Quantico in East	Jones, MSgt W.	Jan 57	
LEATHERNECKS' ALL-MARINE FOOTBALL TEAM, '57	Jones, MSgt W.	Feb 58	
BOWL TEAMS Marines lose Chattanooga and Galveston Bowl Games	Olund, MSgt R.	Feb 58	
LEATHERNECKS' ALL-MARINE FOOTBALL TEAM, '58 "Big 3" are San Diego, Quantico and Lejeune	Jones, MSgt W.	Feb 59	
BOWL GAME San Diego beats Lejeune 62-22		Feb 59	
LEATHERNECKS' ALL-MARINE TEAMS Quantico and San Diego win two bowl titles in 1959	Ellis, ASgt T.	Mar 60	
LEATHERNECKS' ALL-MARINE TEAM '60	Cushman, GySgt G.	Mar 61	
LEATHERNECKS' ALL-MARINE TEAM '61	Cushman, GySgt G.	Feb 62	
MISSILE BOWL Fort Eustis edges Quantico for service grid title	Cushman, GySgt G.	Feb 62	
ALL-MARINE GOLF '58 4th Annual Meet at El Toro	Barnett, SSgt J., and MSgt W. Jones	Oct 58	**GOLF**
ALL-MARINE HANDBALL '58 Tournament at Pentagon	Jones, MSgt W.	Jul 58	**HANDBALL**
ALL-MARINE JUDO Matches at Parris Island	Curtis, AMSgt P.	Jun 59	**JUDO**

LA CROSSE	LA CROSSE Marines introduce the sport to Hawaiians at Kaneohe	Jones, MSgt W.	May 58
PARACHUTING	PARA MEET Marines are fifth in Armed forces Parachuting Contest	Mainard, MSgt A.	Jul 58
SKY DIVING	SKY DIVER	*Gazette*	Jan 57
SWIMMING	ALL-MARINE SWIMMING AND DIVING '56	Suhosky, TSgt R.	Oct 56
TRACK	QUANTICO RELAYS	Jones, MSgt W.	Jun 56
	TRACK AND FIELD '56	Jones, MSgt W.	Aug 56
	TRACK AND FIELD '57 10th Annual Meet at Pendleton	Martin, SSgt D.	Sep 57
	QUANTICO RELAYS: '58 2d Annual Track Meet	Jones, MSgt W.	Jun 58
	TRACK AND FIELD: '58 11th Annual Meet at Lejeune	Smith, PFC W., and MSgt W. Jones	Aug 58
	PAN AM GAMES Six Corps athletes win medals	Davis, Maj O.	Nov 59
	QUANTICO RELAYS 3d Annual Relays	Morehead, Cpl J.	Jun 59
	ALL-MARINE TRACK AND FIELD '60 Quantico dominated 13th Annual All-Marine Meet	Mingus, Cpl R.	Aug 60
	QUANTICO RELAYS Ten new records set	Ellis, ASgt T.	Jun 60
	QUANTICO RELAYS 14th Annual All-Marine Track and Field	Cushman, GySgt G.	Jun 61
	JOHN UELSES Marine Cpl first in history to pole vault over 16'	Cushman, GySgt G.	Apr 62

STRATEGY

All articles in this section are from the *Gazette,* unless otherwise specified:

LIMITED WAR	Simpson, Col O.	Mar 57
LOOKING AHEAD	Morison, RAdm S., USNR	Sep 62
MARINES AFLOAT	Cryan, Capt W.	Sep 61
THE MARINES HAVE LANDED	LeClaire, LtCol C.	Jul 59
MARINES IN MODERN WAR	Croizat, Col V. *Proceedings*	Aug 59
MARINES AND STRATEGY	Hart, B., British Army	Jan 60
THE NEW DOCTRINE Vertical Assault	Suhosky, TSgt R. *Leatherneck*	Apr 57
OUR CONFUSED CARRIERS They need a mission	Turner, Cdr S., USN	May 63
SINGLE CONCEPT: ROAD TO DISASTER	Eliot, G.	Oct 61
WAR TRENDS Lejeune Forum	Baldwin, H., J. Slessor, S. Griffith and R. Asprey	May 62
WHY NOT COMMANDO SHIPS?	McCain, J.	May 62

SUPPORTING ARMS

From the *Gazette,* unless otherwise specified:

GENERAL

FSCC: WHO'S IN CHARGE? Part 7—*Support by Fire* series	Greene, LtCol T.	Feb 60
GREATER COORDINATION OF SUPPORTING FIRES Better liaison needed between air, NG, artillery and unit being supported	Greene, Capt T.	Apr 59
IS NUKE ANALYSIS NEEDED?	Nethery, D.	Jul 63
TARGET INFORMATION: CARDS FOR HIGH STAKES Part 6—*Support by Fire* series	Greene, LtCol T.	Dec 59

Subject	Title	Author / Source	Date
	TARGETS: THE ETERNAL TRIANGLE Part 8—*Support by Fire* series	Greene, LtCol T.	Feb 60
	TARGET ACQUISITION	Woessner, LtCol H.	Mar 56
ARTILLERY	THE ARTILLERY QUESTIONS—AND SOME ANSWERS Part 2—*Support by Fire* series	Greene, LtCol T.	Aug 59
	AN UNEXPECTED FORCE OF ARTILLERY Artillery tactics	Wilson, Capt P.	Jul 60
	BETTER ARTILLERY SUPPORT NOW	Kramer, Col W.	Sep 60
	CANNONEERS Firing the 155's at Twentynine Palms	Suhosky, TSgt R. *Leatherneck*	Jun 56
	FMF ORGANIZATION AND COMPETITION BOARD REPORT: FIRE SUPPORT		Jun 57
	FORCE ARTILLERY	Anderson, LtCol N.	Oct 61
	A FORWARD LOOK AT THE FORWARD OBSERVER	Davis, W.	Nov 60
	SOMETHING BETTER IN FIRE DIRECTION	Love, Capt J.	Jun 62
CLOSE AIR SUPPORT	BOTTLENECKS IN CLOSE AIR SUPPORT	MacMichael, Capt D.	May 59
	CARRIER CAS IN AFSOUTH	Steinkraus, LtCol R.	Feb 61
	THE CASE FOR JET CAS	Verdi, Capt J.	Jun 61
	CLOSE AIR SUPPORT	Asprey, Capt R. *Army*	Nov 61
	CLOSE AIR SUPPORT	*The Officer*	Jun 57
	CLOSE AIR SUPPORT	Fowler, LtCol D., USA *Military Engineer*	Nov, Dec 60

CLOSE AIR SUPPORT: QUO VADIS? Part 3—*Support by Fire* series	Greene, LtCol T. Sep 59	
GOOD-BYE, ABLE DOG You were one hell of an airplane!	Bolt, LtCol J. Oct 57	
HISTORY AND DEVELOPMENT OF CLOSE AIR SUPPORT	Sullivan, Maj W. Nov 56	
HIT OR MISS	Jones, Maj C. Dec 62	
MARINE AVIATION—A PARTNER With Marine ground forces	Binney, MajGen A. *Army Information Digest* Jul 61	
MARINE TACTICAL AIR SUPPORT	*Armed Forces Journal* Dec 27, 1958	
MOONLIGHTING All-weather CAS	Vincent, Maj H. Jul 62	
NIGHT CAS	Wood, Capt R. Jul 62	
POINT BLANK BOMBING	Bolt, LtCol J. Aug 57	
TAKE COVER IN THE AIR	McClure, LtCol G. Apr 62	
NAVAL GUNFIRE: ADRIFT IN THE HORSE LATITUDES Part 4—*Support by Fire* series	Greene, LtCol T. Oct 59	
NAVAL GUNFIRE AND THE ATOM	Fredericks, Maj H. Sep 58	**NAVAL GUNFIRE**
NGF-FO	Fredericks, Capt H. Feb 56	

TACTICS

From the *Gazette,* unless otherwise specified:

BATTALION AIR MOUNT OUT	Meyers, Maj B. Jan 61	**GENERAL**
A BIGGER BITE FOR INTERDICTION	Johnson, Maj J. May 57	
COLD WEATHER WAR	Van Sant, Capt F. May 62	
THE DASC-NO BOTTLENECK	Ludington, Lt C. Jan 60	

Title	Author	Date
DISPLACE THE COMBAT BASE	Fredericks, Capt H.	Jan 57
DOMAIN OF THE U.S. NAVY: ON THE BEACHHEAD WITH THE MARINES	*Navy*	May 60
END ITEM: TACTICAL CAPABILITY	Collier, LtCol R.	Jun 56
FIGHT THE ENEMY	Prickett, Col W.	Oct 57
FIGHTING FORMATION	Keller, LtCol R.	May 56
FINAL OBJECTIVE	Averill, Maj G.	Aug 56
FIRE POWER AND COMBAT FORMATIONS	Vance, Col R.	May 54
THE FIREX	Elliott, LtCol B.	Jun 60
FOR TO DECEIVE "Faking it" in warfare	Hargreaves, Maj R.	Jan 59
GOLF MINUS TEN	Edwards, LtCol H.	Sep 58
IMPROVISED DEMOLITIONS	Driver, MSgt J.	Mar 59
INFANTRY, DIG!	Kennon, Lt J.	Apr 57
INTO THE ALLIGATOR'S JAWS Amphibious warfare	Marshall, S.	Oct 56
JOHN RIFLEMAN AND FRIENDS Part 1—*Support by Fire* series	Greene, LtCol T.	Jul 59
THE KEY-MOBILITY	Frank, LtCol W.	May 57
LET THERE BE LIGHT Flares at night	DuPras, LtCol E.	Mar 56
LET'S FACE IT	Railsback, LtCol E.	Nov 58
THE MARINES HAVE LANDED Use of pathfinders by Marines	Mickel, Capt L. *Infantry Journal*	Feb, Mar 60
MILITARY OPERATIONS RESEARCH	Mitchell, Dr D.	Feb 57
MISLEAD THE ENEMY	Croizat, Col V.	Oct 59

Title	Author	Date
MISSION FOR MODERN MARINES: THINK!	Greene, LtCol T.	Mar 59
MOBILE DEFENSE FOR MARINES	Wheeler, LtCol E.	Jun 56
MOBILITY FOR BATTALIONS	Frank, LtCol W.	Jul 58
MOVE BY AIR	Donovan, J.	May 61
NO COMPROMISE HERE	O'Keefe, Lt A.	Mar 57
OBJECTIVE: ENEMY BEACH Marines will take all the help they can get on the beach	Jones, AGySgt M. *Leatherneck*	Oct 60
OVER THE HILL	Hicks, Maj N., and T. Strobridge	Nov 62
PENNY-WISE POUND FOOLISH	Sloan, Capt C.	Mar 57
REORGANIZATION FOR THE NEW CONCEPT Rifle Squad	Elliott, AMSgt T.	Mar 59
SEA WALL A-Bomb ended traditional amphibious assault (or did it?)	Mainard, TSgt A. *Leatherneck*	Sep 57
SECURITY: HANDMAIDEN TO SUCCESS	Knocke, Maj J.	Oct 58
SUB LIFT	Johnson, MSgt R. *Leatherneck*	Jun 58
TACTICS OF THE ATOMIC AGE—A STUDY IN PRINCIPLES Commandant writer again	Cushman, Col R.	Feb 57
TWO WAYS TO ORGANIZE A JOINT TASK FORCE	Murray, J.	Feb 58
UNEXPLOITED CONCEPTS	Ogorkiewicz, R.	Apr 61
WAR BY BATTALIONS	Bowser, BGen A.	Oct 56

EMBARKATION

Title	Author	Date
EMBARKATION READY	Cribb, Capt G.	Aug 59
SIGNPOSTS ON THE ROYAL ROAD TO FAILURE OR SUCCESS AT EMBARKATION PLANNING	Long, LtCol F.	Apr 60

GUERRILLA WAR	FIGHTING A NEW KIND OF WAR	Hanker, J.	Oct 60
	GUERRILLA WARFARE	Hanrahan, G.	Mar 56
	HIT BACK HARD That's the way the 1ST MAR DIV fights Guerrillas	Barrow, MSgt C. *Leatherneck*	Jul 62
	HOUND THE ENEMY With dogs. Canine tactics	Clapper, Capt P.	Feb 61
	"NO WHERE—YET, EVERY-WHERE" That's Charlie, or any other kind of Guerrilla	Sollom, Maj A.	Jun 58
NIGHT FIGHTING	NIGHT JUNCTURE	McCrary, Maj N.	Jul 62
	NIGHT OPERATIONS	Hutchinson, J.	Mar 62
	STOP THOSE GUNS AT NIGHT They are keeping me awake!	Reilly, Capt M.	Aug 56
RECON	CASE FOR THE TWO-MAN RECON TEAMS	Knowlton, Capt S.	Apr 57
	EMPLOYMENT OF RECON	Woessner, LtCol H.	Dec 59
	FORCE RECON Training Marines in recon	Meyers, Maj B.	May 61
	RECON FOR REGIMENTS	Pickett, R.	Apr 61
VERTICAL ASSAULT	FAST AMPHIBIOUS FORCE	Stephens, Capt R.	Jan 61
	THE LPH: TEAMWORK IN ACTION	Maxwell, Lt J.	Jan 61
	MARINE CORPS ASSAULT SHIP WILL CARRY 2,000 MAN FORCE, 20 COPTERS, SUPPLIES	*Army, Navy, Air Force Journal*	Mar 57
	MARINE CORPS BARRED FROM BUYING WEAPON THAT WOULD HELP VERTICAL ENVELOPMENT	*Armed Forces Journal*	Feb 15, 1958
	MARINE CORPS STICKS TO SMALLER COPTER: TRIMS DIVISION WEIGHT FOR ENVELOPMENT	*Armed Forces Journal*	Mar 15, 1958

MARINE CORPS TRIMS DOWN FOR VERTICAL ASSAULT	*Armed Forces Journal* Mar 8, 1958
THE MARINES NEW LOOK	Mataxis, Col T. *Military Review* Feb 59
MARINES STUDY VERTICAL ENVELOPMENT SHORT AIR-FIELD: BRINGS CARRIER ASHORE	*Armed Forces Journal* Dec 27, 1958
NAVY AND MARINES TAKE A NEW TACK	*Business Week* Mar 2, 1957
TANKS AND VERTICAL ENVELOPMENT	Forsyth, R., and J. Feb 62
THESE TRICKS WORKED FOR BOXER	Fichter, Capt J. Aug 62
VERTICAL ENVELOPMENT—SUCCESSFUL "IF"	Haslam, Capt C. May 57

TRAINING

All articles in this section are from the *Gazette*, unless otherwise specified:

GENERAL

ADDING REALITY TO LANDING EXERCISES	Hudson, BGen L. Mar 58
ARE YOU A 227 LB. WEAKLING?	Otott, Capt G. Oct 60
BASIC TRAINING	MacMichael, Capt D. Jul 58
BATTLE DRILL	Wisely, Capt W. Oct 56
THE BRAIN PICKERS OF BARRETT HALL Quantico Basic Training School	Nicholson, Maj D. Jul 57
BUILDING THE BATTALION STAFF	Pratt, LtCol H. Oct 59
COMPETITION MAKES MARINES	Fischer, Lt R. Nov 60
DO-IT YOURSELF LINGUIST	Kim, C., and D. Hawkins Mar 61
FOR SALE	Wismer, Col R. Apr 60
FROM THE GROUND UP	Crown, LtCol J. May 60

Title	Author	Date
GIVE THEM PROFESSIONAL KNOWLEDGE	Paradis, Capt E.	Jun 56
"HEEF" THEORY IS WORKABLE TODAY	Wyckoff, LtCol D.	Jul 63
INFANTRY—MARCH AGAIN One of the few articles on infantry in *Creating a Legend.* Why don't writers write about it?	Gross, Maj L.	Feb 56
INSPECTION: INDEX TO READINESS	Hudson, BGen L.	Dec 60
INTRODUCTION TO EOD	Driver, MSgt J.	Nov 60
IS CLOSE ORDER DRILL NECESSARY IN THE ATOMIC AGE?	Williams, Col R.	Feb 56
LET'S TRAIN BY TELEVISION	Lindsay, R.	Jan 59
THE MARINE PROFESSOR	Francis, Maj R.	Jun 60
MARINES LEARN THE "JOINT"	Cushman, Col R.	Jan 57
MORE EFFECTIVE TRAINING	Williams, Col R.	Jul 56
NAVAL TRAINING DEVICE CENTER	Mainard, TSgt A. *Leatherneck*	Feb 58
THE NEW DRILL	Phillips, Lt J.	Jun 56
THE NEW LOOK IN DRILL	McCloskey, Maj D.	Oct 58
ON LAND, SEA, AND AIR		Oct 56
OVER-SHADOWED, UNDER TRAINED	Krider, R.	Mar 60
PEP PILLS FOR TRAINING	Salvo, F.	Jan 60
PREPARE FOR I & I	Davis, Capt T.	Jun 62
PREPARE FOR INSTRUCTION	LaPlant, Maj C.	Jun 56
PREPARE FOR PROMOTION	Erbland, Capt R.	May 56
PROFICIENCY FROM TRAINING	Schulze, Capt R.	Aug 56
RED AND GOLD SCHOOLHOUSE USMC U	Puckett, SSgt H.	May 57

Title	Author	Date
THE SECOND DIMENSION	Prestridge, Lt J.	Feb 59
SHEEPSKIN RUNDOWN	Benn, H. *Leatherneck*	May 59
SYLLABUS TRAINING FOR THE BATTALION	Arsenault, A.	Dec 62
T AND T REGIMENT		Dec 56
TAKE A TACTICAL WALK	Andrews, R.	Nov 60
TEST UNIT ONE It pioneers new battle concepts at Pendleton	Suhosky, TSgt R. *Leatherneck*	Jul 56
TO KILL THE ENEMY	West, Col G., and Capt J. Smith	Oct 60
TOP COMBAT SQUADS Rugged combat course at Quantico	Cushman, GySgt G. *Leatherneck*	Nov 61
TOP SQUAD Nine squads compete	Cushman, GySgt G. *Leatherneck*	Dec 62
TRAINING THE FORCE-IN-READINESS Part 9—*Support by Fire* series	Greene, LtCol T.	Mar 60
TROOP AND STOMP	Grant, W.	Aug 60
TROOP TESTS: SMALL UNIT IDEAS		Mar 61
THE UMPIRE JIC	Wilkes, LtCol W.	Feb 56
WAR GAMES GROUP At Quantico	Lang, Cpl D. *Leatherneck*	Sep 62
THE WAY TO A CHEMICAL PEARL HARBOR Neglect biological warfare	Gratto, D.	Oct 60
WE CAN DOUBLE THE TRAINING WEEK	Greene, LtCol T.	Apr 59
"... WELL WORTH THE EFFORT"	Davis, AGySgt R.	Sep 59
WHAT YOU CAN DO ABOUT DRILL	Rider, Lt J.	Dec 60

WHEN THE GAS TANK'S DRY	Loudoun, J.	Jan 60
YOUR TROOPS WANT BETTER TRAINING They are interested in learning	Rider, ASSgt J.	Mar 60
YOURS FOR THE ASKING	Hess, Maj T.	Aug 57

EXERCISES

All articles in this section are from *Leatherneck*, unless otherwise specified:

ALASKA MANEUVER 2500 Marines test cold weather capacity	Suhosky, TSgt R.	Apr 56
COMMAND PERFORMANCE JFK watches Lejeune Marines		Jun 62
D-DAY IN AMICUS LANTPHIBEX 1-60 was the largest Atlantic Marine/Navy exercise in years	Jones, AGySgt M.	Jun 60
EXERCISE BOB-LO Canadian and U.S. Marines join in training at Grosse Ile.	Lyons, R.	Jan 59
THE FALL OF MARPENSIDE Phiblex 12-59 served as test for Vertical Envelopment	Johnson, AMSgt R.	Apr 59
LAND PHIBEX 1-58 Major NATO exercise for Marines and others	Curtis, MSgt P.	Jun 58
MARINES SIMULATE BRUSH-FIRE WAR	*Aviation Week*	Mar 25, 1957
OPERATION ARBELA 1962	Spark, M. *Gazette*	Jul 61
OPERATION TOTEM POLE 1/9 practices cold and wet weather ops in Alaska	Johnson, AMSgt R.	Feb 60
PACTRAEX 56 1ST MARINES land in Pendleton War Games	Suhosky, TSgt R.	Feb 56
SAND FOR BREAKFAST 1ST MAR DIV in desert training at Twentynine Palms	Jones, GySgt M.	Feb 62

TROOPSHIP TO VIEQUES 6TH MARINES ship out for Puerto Rico	Mainard, TSgt A.	May 56

MARKSMANSHIP

All articles in this section are from *Gazette*, unless otherwise specified:

BERDAN'S SHARPSHOOTERS	Strandberg, Lt C.	Aug 56
COMBAT MARKSMANSHIP COMPETITION	Berckmans, Capt B.	Aug 57
INTRAMURAL SHOOTING	Chinner, Lt J.	Apr 58
LEATHERNECK RIFLE AWARDS	*Leatherneck*	Feb 56
LET'S SHOOT TO WIN	McMillan, W., and R. Woods	Aug 61
M-I MASTERS Training boots at Matthews	Suhosky, TSgt R. *Leatherneck*	Mar 57
MARKSMANSHIP Forty-year history	Sarokin, MSgt P. *Leatherneck*	Nov 57
MARKSMANSHIP TRAINING UNIT HQMC unit seeks to provide better Marine shooting	Jones, MSgt W. *Leatherneck*	Dec 56
MATCH AMMO MAKES A COMEBACK	Gleason, E.	Jun 60
ONE MORE STEP	Krider, R.	Sep 60
PISTOL SHOOTING: EXPERTS IN NAME ONLY The course is too easy	Haslam, Capt C.	Aug 57
RANGE EXPERTS	Curtis, MSgt P.	Feb 58
REALISTIC MARKSMANSHIP More training in combat shooting	Henderson, Col F.	Aug 57
REALISTIC REQUALIFICATION COURSE	White, Lt M.	Aug 56
REQUAL FOR COMBAT	Love, Maj J.	May 62

REQUAL SCORING	McAllister, AGySgt J.	Aug 59
RIFLE TARGETS TELL A STORY	Abel, W.	Jul 62
SHOOT TO HIT! Close counts only in horseshoes and hand grenades	Sanders, Capt P.	May 56
TOP SQUAD IN COMBAT FIRING		Oct 59
WE DON'T NEED TEAM SHOTS	Hickey, GySgt W.	Aug 61

MARKSMANSHIP MATCHES

All articles in this section are from *Leatherneck*, unless otherwise specified:

AND SIX MARINES Marines participate in Matches in Russia	Briggs, SSgt H.	Dec 58
BIG SHOOT 3d Annual Hi-Powered Rifle Matches at Camp Matthews	Briggs, SSgt H.	Feb 58
BIG SHOOT Marines break some records, but Army wins Perry matches	Morrisey, Capt R.	Nov 60
CLEAN SWEEP AT PERRY Marines win all five trophies in World Series of shooting	Jones, MSgt W.	Nov 56
INTERSERVICE MATCH More than 600 regulars and reserves participate in three day matches at Quantico	Cushman, GySgt G.	Oct 61
MARINE CORPS MATCHES	Suhosky, TSgt R.	Aug 57
MARINE CORPS MATCHES	*Gazette*	Aug 58
MID-WINTER PISTOL CHAMPIONSHIPS Marines participate in 26th Annual Pistol Paradise at Tampa, Fla.	Jones, MSgt W.	Jun 57
NATIONAL MATCHES—'58	Pollard, D.	Nov 58
NATIONAL MATCHES: '59	*Gazette*	Aug 59

PERRY MATCHES '61 — Johnson, WO R. — Nov 61

SKY SHOOT — Suhosky, TSgt R. — Jul 56
Aerial Gunnery Meet at Mojave with Marines participating

UNIT COMBAT MARKSMANSHIP COMPETITION—1957 — *Gazette* — Nov 57

WELL IN AT P. I. — Sarokin, MSgt P. — Aug 56
Marine Rifle and Pistol matches at Parris Island

TRAINING-SCHOOLS

All articles in this section are from *Leatherneck,* unless otherwise specified:

API

REALISTIC TRAINING FOR API'S INTELLIGENCE — Ellis, MSgt E. *Gazette* — Jan 57

BASIC SCHOOL

THE E. I. — Barrow, AMSgt C. — Jul 59
Enlisted Instructors teach Marksmanship, Weapons and Tactics to Marine junior officers at Quantico

BOMB DISPOSAL

HANDLE WITH CARE — Curtis, TSgt P. — Jan 58
Explosive Ordnance Disposal School, Indian Head, Md

IT TAKES GUTS — Ellis, SSgt T. — Aug 61

BOOT CAMP

BEATNIK TO BOOTNIK — Bristow, V. — Dec 59
Long-hairs can make good Marines, too

". . . BUILDS MEN" — Kester, SSgt C. — Apr 62
Seven recruits are followed through Boot Camp to note changes

MAKING OF A MARINE — Allen, R. *Ladies Home Journal* — Feb 59
Boot Camp for female readers

NEW APPROACHES TO BASIC TRAINING — Thomas, Capt F. *Proceedings* — Oct 57

Subject	Title	Author / Source	Date
	PARRIS ISLAND EXPOSED Translated from a Russian magazine	*Gazette*	Feb 61
	RECRUIT TRAINING—ALL HANDS EVOLUTION	Venn, LtCol R. *Gazette*	Jan 58
	WITH PLENTY TO SPARE Twelve weeks of conditioning	Curtis, TSgt P.	Aug 57
COLD WEATHER	COLD WEATHER TRAINING	*Gazette*	Feb 59
	ESCAPE, EVADE, SURVIVE! Pickel Meadows training includes course in survival	Lewis, J.	Jan 59
	PICKEL MEADOWS Toughest training in the Corps	Lewis, J.	Aug 58
COMBAT	COMBAT APPRENTICESHIP Vets of WW-2 and Korea train Marines at Lejeune	Mainard, MSgt A.	Jul 58
	COMBAT COURSE	White, Capt M. *Gazette*	Aug 60
	HOW TO WIN AT COMBAT TRAINING	Vance, Col R. *Gazette*	Sep 62
	INDIVIDUAL COMBAT TRAINING 2D ITR at Pendleton	Johnson, MSgt R.	Mar 58
	NEW SYLLABUS AT 1ST INFANTRY TRAINING REGIMENT	Wilkinson, Capt J. *Gazette*	Feb 61
COMMUNICATIONS	COMMUNICATION-ELECTRONICS SCHOOL At San Diego	Jones, MSgt W.	Dec 57
	CAMOUFLAGE: A NEGLECTED ART	DeWitt, B. *Gazette*	Dec 61
COMMAND	COMMAND SCHOOL At Fort Leavenworth, Kansas	Love, Capt J., USA *Gazette*	Jun 58
DEVIL PUPS	DEVIL PUPS More than 1200 teen-agers sample military life at Pendleton	Johnson, AMSgt R.	Dec 59
ENGINEERS	BELVOIR SCHOOLS Marines at Army Engineers Schools, Fort Belvoir, Va.	Cushman, GySgt G.	Apr 61

Title	Author / Source	Date	Subject
BRIDGING THE COLORADO Seventh Engineers practice trade at river site in Colorado		Feb 62	
ENGINEER SCHOOL At Lejeune	Mainard, TSgt A.	Jul 56	
GALLEY CLASSROOM Food Service school at Lejeune	Jones, AGySgt M.	Aug 60	FOOD SERVICE
GENERAL MILITARY SUBJECTS SCHOOL	Pace, MSgt J. *Gazette*	Jul 60	GMS
SET A THIEF . . . Modern training in war against guerrilla	Lang, Cpl D.	Jan 62	GUERRILLA
SPECIAL WARFARE Marines at Army's Fort Bragg	Mainard, TSgt A.	Feb 58	
LANDING FORCE TRAINING UNIT Amphibious training at Little Creek	Ellis, ASSgt T.	Mar 60	LFTU
THREE MONTHS TO TRAIN LFTU regulars train 4021 reservists in one year	Jones, AGySgt M	Sep 60	
MARCADS Marine Cadets train to be pilots at Pensacola	Eastburn, Sgt B.	Oct 59	MARCAD
MCI Marine Corps Institute	Kester, SSgt C.	Aug 62	MCI
MCI/MOS Since 1920, 408,000 Marines have earned MCI diplomas	Mainard, TSgt A.	Jan 57	
ROPE AND PITON Mountain Leadership Course at Pickel Meadows	Wells, MSgt H.	Dec 57	MOUNTAIN WARFARE
IMPROVE THE NCO SCHOOL	Crumb, MSgt C. *Gazette*	Oct 57	NCO SCHOOL
AN NCO SCHOOL IN EVERY COMPANY	Finne, Capt D. *Gazette*	Oct 56	
NIGHT BATTALION	Davis, Maj W. *Gazette*	Dec 58	NIGHT TRAINING

	NIGHT TRAINING FOR MARINES	Simpson, LtCol W. *Gazette*	Dec 56
NROTC	THE NROTC PROGRAM Fifty-two colleges have Marine/Navy candidates	Smith, L.	Oct 56
ORDNANCE	ORDNANCE SCHOOL Training Ordnance men at Quantico	Curtis, MSgt P.	Jul 58
POW TRAINING	"THE FIGHT CONTINUES . . ." If captured, Marines are taught to resist	Jones, GySgt M.	Sep 61
PRE-FLIGHT	CADET DI'S Marines teach basic subjects to future aviators at Pensacola	Kester, GySgt C.	Oct 61
PREP SCHOOL	ACADEMY PREP Navy Preparatory School at Bainbridge, Maryland	Ellis, ASSgt T.	Apr 60
PT	FIT TO FIGHT	Meeker, Capt R. *Gazette*	Nov 57
	KEEP STRONG, KEEP FIGHTING	Weinert, Capt F. *Gazette*	Aug 62
	MUSCLE MARINE GySgt Sam Griffiths puts life into PT programs	Barrow, MSgt C.	Sep 62
	NEW GYM PI has the latest in muscle-building devices	Jones, MSgt W.	Mar 58
	NO PLACE FOR WEAKLINGS	Carey, LtCol R. *Gazette*	Apr 56
	PHYSICAL FITNESS	Drakely, LtCol W. *Gazette*	Sep 56
	PHYSICALLY FIT Today's Marines are best ever physically	Barrow, AMSgt C.	Nov 59
	USE YOUR RIFLE FOR STRENGTH For exercises	Otott, G. *Gazette*	Dec 62

Title	Author / Date	Category
QUARTERMASTER SCHOOL Marines at Army's Supply School, Fort Lee, Virginia	Mainard, TSgt A. Mar 58	QM
RECRUITER PREP At Parris Island	Curtis, MSgt P. Jul 58	RECRUITERS
RECRUITERS' SCHOOL	Cushman, GySgt G. Oct 61	
CAREER COUNSELORS A Navy School which sells vets, not recruits, on a service career	Ellis, SSgt T. Dec 60	RE-UP
RIOT CONTROL WITH CHEMICAL AGENTS Mace training	Miller, W. *Gazette* Mar 61	RIOT CONTROL
SAFETY DETAIL Pendleton School helps civilians solve traffic problems	Suhosky, TSgt R. Mar 56	SAFETY
CAMPUS MARINES Navy's Enlisted Scientific Education Program	Barrow, MSgt C. Jan 61	SCIENTIFIC EDUCATION
J. O. SCHOOL Marines learn how to be Journalists at Great Lakes	Sarokin, MSgt P. Jan 57	SCRIBES
SEA SCHOOL At Portsmouth and San Diego	Curtis, MSgt P. Aug 58	SEA SCHOOL
SIGN OF THE SEAHORSE San Diego	Jones, GySgt W. Mar 62	
SENIOR SCHOOL—THE NEW LOOK Tactics and techniques taught there	Nickerson, Col H. *Gazette* Sep 56	SENIOR SCHOOL
ADVANCED COURSES	Mainard, TSgt A. May 57	TECHNICIANS
TRACKED VEHICLE SCHOOL Tank maintenance taught at Camp Del Mar	Johnson, MSgt R. Apr 58	TRACKED VEHICLES
THE GIRL AT THE DESK	Curtis, MSgt P. Dec 58	WR'S

	HIGH-HEELED BOOTS Men's and women's Boot Camp are a little different	Barrow, MSgt C.	Feb 62

UNITS

From the *Gazette* unless otherwise specified:

FORCE—IN READINESS	FORCE IN READINESS	Zimmerman, LtCol J. *Proceedings*	Feb 57
	FORCE IN READINESS Excellent explanation of new concept	Schuon, K. *Proceedings*	Nov 61
	FORCE IN READINESS—1959	Pierce, LtCol P.	Nov 59
	REPORT FROM THE READY FORCES: FORCE TROOPS, FMF LANT		Oct 61
	REPORT FROM THE READY FORCES: FORCE TROOPS, FMF PAC	Cass, LtCol B., and Maj R. Cunningham	Oct 61
	REPORT FROM THE READY FORCES: FMF PAC		Dec 60
FMF	FAST, MIGHTY, FLEXIBLE	Jones, GySgt M. *Leatherneck*	Jun 61
	FMF 1965 Proposed organization and equipment		Jul-Dec 61
	NEW FLEET MARINE FORCE	Asprey, Capt R. *Proceedings*	Aug 59
	FLEET MARINE FORCE ATLANTIC Organization, Command Lists		Mar 59
	FLEET MARINE FORCE PACIFIC Organization, Command List		May 59
DIVISION	FMF ORGANIZATION AND COMPOSITION BOARD REPORT —THE DIVISION		Apr 57
	REPORT FROM THE READY FORCES: 1ST MAR DIV		Feb 60

Title	Author / Source	Date	Category
REPORT FROM THE READY FORCES: 1ST MAR DIV		Jun 61	
A DIVISION AFLOAT 2D MAR DIV	O'Conner, Lt J.	Feb 60	
REPORT FROM THE READY FORCES: 2D MAR DIV		Apr 60	
REPORT FROM THE READY FORCES: 2D MAR DIV		Mar 61	
REPORT FROM THE READY FORCES: 3D MAR DIV		Aug 60	
THE FIRST MAW Protects 7th Fleet and provides support for 3D MAR DIV	Barrow, MSgt C. *Leatherneck*	Sep 61	**WING**
REPORT FROM THE READY FORCES: 1ST MAW	Malone, Maj C.	Jul 60	
REPORT FROM THE READY FORCES: 1ST MAW	Sullivan, Maj W.	Sep 61	
THE 2D MARINE AIR WING	Lowell, Col A.	Mar 60	
REPORT FROM THE READY FORCES: 2D MAW		Mar 61	
THE 3D MARINE AIR WING	Sullivan, Maj W.	May 60	
THE 1ST MARINE BRIGADE	Suhosky, TSgt R. *Leatherneck*	May 57	**BRIGADE**
1ST MARINE BRIGADE: FMF PACIFIC Cruise Book of this unit training in Hawaii	Miller Publishing Company, Dallas	1956	
REORGANIZE THE MARINE BRIGADE	McLoughlin, Lt H.	May 57	
REPORT FROM THE READY FORCES: 1ST MAR BRIG FMF PAC		Jun 60	
BATTALION OR REGIMENT—ONE HAS TO GO	Sweeney, LtCol J.	Sep 59	**REGIMENT**
CAMP LEJEUNE'S INFANTRY TRAINING REGIMENT	Barrow, MSgt C. *Leatherneck*	Dec 60	

	OVERSEAS STAGING Staging Regiment, Pendleton, and Overseas Drafting Section, El Toro	Johnson, MSgt R. *Leatherneck*	Dec 58
	REORGANIZE THE SERVICE REGIMENT	Warren, LtCol C.	Mar 56
GROUP	MAG-2 MOVE Picture story of move of MAG-2 from Atsugi, Japan to Taiwan	*Leatherneck*	Jan 59
BATTALION	ALERT BATTALION 2D MAR DIV has the most practice for air movement	Donovan, Col J. *Leatherneck*	Nov 61
	ATOMIC BATTALION	Seminoff, Maj N.	Jan 58
	BLT	Jones, GySgt M. *Leatherneck*	Sep 62
	CAPABILITIES OF THE NEW MARINE INFANTRY BATTALION They are fantastic	Wood, LtCol W.	May 58
	GENERAL SHOUP TELLS BLT REACTIVATION PLANS: HAWK MISSILE BATTALION IS PLANNED	*Army, Navy, Air Force Journal*	Jan 30, 1960
	HOW TO ORGANIZE AN NROTC BATTALION	Girard, C.	Dec 60
	MARINES REACTIVATE BATTALION LANDING TEAMS	*Army, Navy, Air Force Journal*	Aug 13, 1960
	PIONEER BATTALION Provides close combat support with engineering	Johnson, MSgt R. *Leatherneck*	Apr 58
	TRANSPLACEMENT BATTALION The ready striking arm of the 7th Fleet	Barrow, MSgt C. *Leatherneck*	Jul 61
PLATOON	AIR DELIVERY PLATOON High morale is their trademark	Barrow, MSgt C. *Leatherneck*	Dec 60
	ATA PLATOON—AN ORPHAN? Wasn't it always?	Kloefkorn, Lt W.	Feb 57
SQUAD	TOP SQUAD Winner in first annual competition is from 8TH MARINES	Jones, MSgt W. *Leatherneck*	Dec 57

WEAPONS

From the *Gazette*, unless specified otherwise:

GENERAL

Title	Author	Date
ALBANY GUNSMITHS When a Marine draws a weapon, it is perfect. Gunsmiths at Albany made it so	Mainard, TSgt A. *Leatherneck*	Oct 57
AN IDEA ON CANNISTER	Driver, TSgt J.	Jul 56
BULLETS, BAYONETS AND GRENADE LAUNCHERS	McDowell, D.	Nov 60
A COMPARISON: MARINE AND RUSSIAN WEAPONS We win some and we lose some	Haslam, Capt C.	Oct 56
EVOLUTION OF FIREARMS	Landers, Maj J.	Dec 62
EXTINCTION OF THE MASTODON	Wisely, W.	Feb 60
A KIND WORD FOR BULL PUP	Dalby, C.	Jan 61
THE LIEUTENANT'S GATLINGS	Dieckmann, E.	Aug 60
THE MAN WITH 5,000 ARMS Former Marine Tom Wallace runs weapons museum at Springfield	Barrow, AMSgt C. *Leatherneck*	Feb 60
THE MONSTER	Cass, Maj B.	Jan 56
NEW DEVELOPMENTS—ORDNANCE	Haslam, Capt C.	Mar 56
NEW FIREPOWER New rifle and machine gun	Stewart, MSgt W. *Leatherneck*	Feb 59
NEW HORIZONS AND WEAPONS	Van Orden, BGen G.	May 60
SMALL ARMS History of Marine weapons	Rankin, Col R. *Leatherneck*	Nov 62
SOLDIER'S WEAPONS	Hargreaves, R.	Aug 59
STILL SHOOTING IT OUT		Jan 60

ABC

Title	Author	Date
THE ABC'S OF WARFARE Gas and what it can do	Barrow, MSgt C. *Leatherneck*	Jun 62

Subject	Title	Author	Date
	ATOMIC FORCES: THE BIG FIRE *Support by Fire* series—Part 5	Greene, LtCol T.	Nov 59
	BIOLOGICAL AGENTS IN FUTURE WAR	Bowmer, E.	Oct 62
	COMBAT UNIFORM—ATOMIC STYLE It's a track suit	Hanker, Capt J.	Apr 58
	THE COMPANY AND THE ATOM	Fredericks, Capt H.	Sep 56
	GAS Tactics and techniques	Fitzgerald, Capt E.	Jun 59
	HAVE TACTICS BEEN INVADED BY THE ATOM	Strawson, LtCol J.	Aug 56
	INDIVIDUAL ATOMIC DEFENSE Use the track suit (run like hell!)	Kritter, Maj E.	May 57
	THE INFANTRY IN ATOMIC WARFARE What Infantry?	Harper, R.	May 57
	MUST OUR CITIES BE BATTLEFIELDS? Only if they are in Vietnam	Parsons, E.	May 57
	NUCLEAR WEAPONS AND TACTICAL OBJECTIVES	Bates, LtCol W.	Apr 62
BAR	HAIL TO THE BAR MAN	Davis, Capt W.	Mar 56
BAYONET	THE BAYONET	Rankin, LtCol R.	Apr 56
	THE PUGEL STICK Bayonet fighting	Curtis, TSgt P. *Leatherneck*	Sep 57
57'S	WHAT HAPPENED TO THE 57? The same thing that happened to the -01	Haffner, Col L.	Dec 56
GRENADE LAUNCHER	THE M-79 Issued to FMF units	Kester, SSgt C. *Leatherneck*	May 61
MACHINE GUNS	GETTING MORE OUT OF OUR M-60'S	Grabowsky, M.	Dec 60
	MADE IN SPRINGFIELD The new M-60 is quite a weapon	Barrow, AMSgt C. *Leatherneck*	Feb 60

M74C MACHINE GUN: A SPECIAL REPORT	Laine, Maj E.	Feb 62	
A REALISTIC APPROACH TO BETTER LMG UTILIZATION	Sheehan, TSgt P.	Sep 56	
YOUR NEW M-60 MACHINE GUN	Edwards, Capt T.	Sep 60	
AGLEX-57G Guided missile platform	Suhosky, TSgt R. *Leatherneck*	Mar 57	**MISSILES**
CHECK-OUT ON MISSILES	Blasdell, V., and E. Smith (Karl Schuon) *Leatherneck*	Jan 58	
GUIDED MISSILES	LaPlant, Maj C.	Apr 56	
MARINES ORDER MISSILE DEVELOPED BY GERMANS If anybody knows how to build one, it's the Germans	*Aviation Week*	Dec 21, 1959	
MISSILES	Cunningham, R.	Oct 61	
MISSILES AGAINST ARMOR	Ogorkiewicz, R.	Jan 59	
MISSILES AREN'T MYSTERIOUS	Dunn, Lt D.	Feb 59	
MISSILES: THE HUMAN FACTOR	Prescott, Capt S.	Jun 62	
SUPERSONIC HAWK Marine missilemen operate the HAWK (Homing-all-the-way killer) program in the Corps.	Jones, M. *Leatherneck*	Dec 61	
SUPERSONIC SIDEARMS	Jones, AGySgt M. *Leatherneck*	Sep 60	
TACTICAL MISSILES AROUND THE WORLD	Geiger, G.	Mar 62	
THE VERTICAL FRONTIER Corps' first missile unit equipped with Terrier	Johnson, MSgt R. *Leatherneck*	Feb 59	
THE VSRBM—HOPE FOR PUSH-BUTTON FIRE SUPPORT	Greene, LtCol T.	Aug 58	
ANOTHER USE FOR THE 3.5 Possibly as a urinal	Dunn, Lt D.	Sep 56	**MORTARS**

	A COMPARISON; OUR OWN AND FOREIGN HEAVY MORTARS We lose	Haslam, Capt C.	Jan 57
	THE MARINE CORPS HAS A MORTAR	Hill, Capt B.	Mar 56
	MORE PUNCH FOR THE 60 MM	Driver, TSgt J.	Apr 56
PSYCHOLOGY	PSYCHWAR: A NEGLECTED WEAPON	Fleming, I.	Nov 60
RIFLES	THE M-14 RIFLE—A COMPARISON	Conroy, Maj J.	Aug 60
	MADE IN SPRINGFIELD Almost all Marine rifles come from Springfield, Mass	Barrow, AMSgt C. *Leatherneck*	Jan 60
	MARINES TEST THE M-14 RIFLE		Aug 58
	THE RIFLE IS FOR BULLETS	Haslam, Capt C.	Sep 60
	ROCKET GRENADE LAUNCHER M-72		Mar 61
75'S	DON'T SCRAP THE 75'S He voted for Goldwater	Ankley, Capt W., USA	Jan 57
	REMEMBER THE 75'S	Vick, MSgt W.	Apr 56
SIDEARMS	SHOULD OUR SIDEARM BE A REVOLVER?	Haslam, Capt C.	Aug 58
TANKS	DESERT TREK M-53's prove themselves at Twentynine Palms	Suhosky, TSgt R. *Leatherneck*	Nov 56
	EMPLOY THE ONTOS	Cooper, Capt C.	Sep 55
	EVOLUTION OF THE AMPHIBIOUS TANK	Ogorkiewicz, R.	Aug 57
	FIRST ONTOS ACCEPTED BY MARINES	*Army, Navy, Air Force Register*	Nov 56
	THE INFANTRY—TANK TEAM Tactics	Norton, Capt R.	Jan 56

MECHANICAL MULE Light weapons carrier drives like a jeep	Johnson, MSgt R. *Leatherneck*	Jul 58
NEW TANK FIRING RANGE At Twentynine Palms		Feb 58
ONTOS	Bale, LtCol E.	Oct 57
TANK KILLER	Mainard, TSgt A. *Leatherneck*	Jul 57
TANKS?	Barrett, Maj W.	Oct 59
TANKS AT NIGHT? They scare you to death.	Graham, Maj C.	Jul 62
TANKS LIGHT THE WAY Night tactics	Hayward, Maj G.	Jul 62
THEY MAN THE ONTOS Crew needs three months training (and prayers)	Mainard, MSgt A. *Leatherneck*	Sep 58
WHY THE ONTOS? Good question	Sexton, LtCol M.	May 58

7.
VIETNAM

Ten years of writing about the war that goes on forever. Units Histories, personal experiences, a protest or two, one Monograph (Khe Sanh) and excellent collections of Marine Corps Combat Art and Combat Correspondents' stories.

CONTENTS: PART 7

EVENTS/1962-1970

Title	Author / Source	Date	Category
COUNTER-INSURGENCY: MARINES AT WORK IN VIETNAM	Sklarewitz, N. *Gazette*	Jan 63	**EARLY OPS 1962-64**
DATELINE: DA NANG	Stibbens, S. *Leatherneck*	Jul 63	
DATELINE: DA NANG	Sklarewitz, N. *Gazette*	Jan 63	
DATELINE: SOC TRANG, VIETNAM	Sklarewitz, N. *Gazette*	Dec 62	
DATELINE: VIETNAM	Croft, A. *Gazette*	Oct 63	
MARINES ALONG THE MEKONG	Crowley, Maj R. *Gazette*	Jan 63	
MARINES' WAR IN VIETNAM	Pickerell, J., and R. Pearman *Gazette*	Dec 64	
THE RAID: MARINES IN VIET NAM	Croft, A. *Gazette*	Apr 63	
THAILAND 3rd Marine Expeditionary Unit, May-Jul 62	Simpson, BGen O. *Gazette*	Nov 65	
MARINE CORPS OPERATIONS IN VIETNAM—1965-1966	Simmons, BGen E. *Naval Review*	1968	**1965, GENERAL**
CHRISTMAS IN VIETNAM Mass by Cardinal Spellman, small Christmas tree, etc. Same as every combat Christmas for Marines	Beardsley, F. *Leatherneck*	Apr 66	
VIET-NAM The first months, Mar-Aug, 65, of heavy Marine involvement	Wheeler, Col E. *Gazette*	Nov 65	
BEACHHEAD: DANANG Landing of the 9th Marine Expeditionary Brigade in Mar 65	*Leatherneck*	Jun 65	**DA NANG—1965**

	DA NANG—RUSSIAN VERSION How the Russians look at the USMC in Nam	Staar, R. *Gazette* Nov 66
	MARINES AND A MESSAGE: GUARDING OF DA NANG AIR BASE	*Newsweek* Mar 22, 1965
	MARINES GET FLOWERS FOR A TOUGH MISSION	Flynn, J. *Life* Mar 19, 1965
	MISSION IS TO KILL: MARINE BRIGADE AT DA NANG AIR BASE	*Newsweek* May 10, 1965
	PROSPECT OF ACTION: U.S. MARINES—THE FIRST COMBAT TROOPS TO ARRIVE IN SOUTH VIETNAM	*Time* Mar 19, 1965
	WAR STEPS UP: WHERE IT'S HEADED It's headed nowhere	Handleman, H. *U.S. News* May 10, 1965
VAN TUONG-CHU LAI—1965	AN AMPHIBIOUS OPERATION IN VIETNAM Van Tuong-Chu Lai	Alexander, J. *Gazette* Jan 66
	APPLICATION OF DOCTRINE: VICTORY AT VAN TUONG VILLAGE	Peatross, BGen O. *Naval Review* 1966-67
	AS THE MARINES SCORED IN VIETNAM	*U.S. News* Aug 30, 1965
	MARINE VICTORY AND OPTIMISM, BATTLE OF VAN TUONG	*Newsweek* Aug 30, 1965
	SEARCH AND CLEAR Typical search-and-clear operation near Chu Lai.	Pearson, G. *Leatherneck* Dec 65
	TANK CREW: CHU LAI Holds defensive perimeter while Seabees build runway	Stibbens, S. *Leatherneck* Sep 65
	THIRD MARINE AMPHIBIOUS FORCE Assault on Van Tuong	Stibbens, SSgt S. *Leatherneck* Nov 65

VICTORY AT CHU LAI More than 600 VC killed in one of the few clear-cut Marine victories in Nam	Bartlett, T. *Leatherneck*	Nov 65	
AMBUSH AT SONG O LAU VC ambush of 2d Bn, Vietnamese Marine Brigade	Campbell, Maj T. *Gazette*	Jan 70	**1966**
BONG SON OPERATION	Leftwich, W. *Gazette*	Jun 66	
BUS TO TRA KHE	Ludwig, V. *Gazette*	Oct 66	
DECISION AT DUC CO	Leftwich, W. *Gazette*	Feb 67	
GENERAL GREENE TELLS THE STORY OF THE VIETNAM WAR	Greene, Gen W. *U.S. News*	Sep 5, 1966	
VIETNAM: PROGRESS AND PROSPECTS	Greene, Gen W. *Digest*	Nov 66	
HARVEST MOON Name of operation near Que Son where Marines fought week-long battle under monsoon conditions	Beardsley, F. *Leatherneck*	Apr 66	
MARINES BLUNT THE INVASION FROM THE NORTH: ACTION IN THE DMZ: REPORT	Parker, M. *Life*	Oct 28, 1966	
OPERATION DOUBLE EAGLE I Amphibious assault on the coast of Central Vietnam. Mostly search-and-clear operation, since Charlie bugged out	Bowen, B. *Leatherneck*	Jun 66	
OPERATION DOUBLE EAGLE I & II 1ST MAR DIV operation, 28 Jan 66	Bowen, Sgt B. *Leatherneck*	Jun 66	
OPERATION UTAH Mar 66	Peatross, O., and W. Johnson *Gazette*	Oct 66	
ROCK PILE Oct 66	*Gazette*	Jan 67	

	ROCKPILE: MARINES CAPTURE THE RAZORBACK AND HILL 400	*Time* Oct 7, 1966
	SMALL, HARD WAR IN THE DELTA	Warner, D. *The Reporter* Dec 15, 1966
	SMALL UNIT ACTION IN VIETNAM, SUMMER, 1966 Interesting account of war the way it was for the "grunt" during that summer.	West, Capt F. HQMC 1967 (IP)
	13/13 VIETNAM: SEARCH AND DESTROY Interesting book about 1966 operations of "I" Co, 3/1	Baxter, G. The World Publishing Company, Cleveland 1967
	VIETNAM BRIEFING	Rogers, L. *Gazette* Jun 66
1967, GENERAL	MARINE CORPS OPERATIONS IN VIETNAM, 1967	Simmons, BGen E. *Naval Review* 1969
	BITTEREST BATTLEFIELD, MARINE CAMPS NEAR DEMILITARIZED ZONE	*Time* Sep 22, 1967
	VIETNAM: THE EYE OF THE STORM: SITUATION IN PROVINCES KNOWN AS EYE CORPS	Sully, F. *New Republic* Jul 15, 1967
	VIETNAM: THE ISSUE AND THE RESPONSE: ADDRESS	Greene, Gen W. *Vital Speeches* Jun 1, 1967
CON THIEN, OCT 1967	BEARING THE BRUNT AT CON THIEN It's the Corps, as usual	Warner, D. *The Reporter* Oct 19, 1967
	BRUTAL BATTLE AT CON THIEN: WHY U.S. MARINES ARE HANGING ON Because they were told to	*U.S. News* Oct 9, 1967
	HIGH VOLTAGE Artillerymen of 12th Marines support the 3RD MAR DIV	Martin, J. *Leatherneck* Aug 68

INDIA SIX
"India 6" is CO of India Co., 26th Marines
Caulfield, Maj M.
Gazette Jul 69

INSIDE THE CONE OF FIRE, CON THIEN
Duncan is there, as usual
Duncan, D.
Life Oct 27, 1967

SIEGE AT CON THIEN
Newsweek Oct 9, 1967

TIME IN THE BARREL
Marines at Con Thien, pounded by Red artillery and mortars and surrounded by 30,000
Martin, B.
Leatherneck Jan 68, Nov 71

1968, GENERAL

MARINE CORPS OPERATIONS IN VIETNAM, 1968
Simmons, BGen E.
Naval Review 1968

ASSAULT AT MUTTER'S RIDGE
Dec 8, 1968
Sexton, Col M., and LtCol J. Hopkins
Gazette Mar 70

BRIDGE AT CAM LE
Aug 68
Davis, Lt C.
Gazette Feb 70

CAM LO: A BATTLE
Part of the Tet Offensive, Feb 1, 1968
Rose, Maj R.
Leatherneck Apr 72

COMBAT JOURNAL
Hammond, J.
Gazette Jul, Aug 68

HOUSE TO HOUSE
Marines fight an Army-type war in the streets of Hue during the Tet Offensive
Martin, B.
Leatherneck May 68

LET'S GO CHARLIE!
"C" Co, 1/1, in Hai Lang forest SW of Quang Tri City
Martin, B.
Leatherneck Feb 68

NOW, A BOMBING HALT? MARINES WITHDRAW FROM THE DMZ
Grant, Z.
New Republic Oct 5, 1968

SECRETARY RUSK COMMENTS, ACTIONS OF MARINE SECURITY GUARDS AT AMERICAN EMBASSY IN SAIGON: REMARKS
Rusk, D.
Dept of State Bulletin Mar 11, 1968

Subject	Title	Author / Source	Date
	SURPRISE FOR THE 803RD Marine ambush, Mar 68	Regal, Maj J. *Gazette*	Apr 70
	TET OFFENSIVE: VICTORY OR DEFEAT Defeat. Perhaps the most significant one of the war for the North	Kraigen, LtCol R. *Gazette*	Dec 68
	WHERE THE OTHER BOYS ARE	*Time*	Mar 15, 1968
KHE SANH, 1968	BATTALION IN THE ATTACK 3/26 attacks Hill 881 on Apr 14, 1968. Last part of the battle for Khe Sanh	Studt, LtCol J. *Gazette*	Jul 70
	THE BATTLE FOR KHE SANH: 1969 Monograph of 26th Marines finest hour since Iwo 203 pp. Cat. No. D/214.13: K 52 S/N0855-0048 $1.75	Shore, Capt M. HQMC, USGPO	1969 (IP)
	BEHIND THE BATTLE FOR KHE SANH	Walt, L. *Digest*	May 70
	CEREMONY AT KHE SANH Memorial services for Marines	Richardson, H. *Leatherneck*	Feb 69
	HELICOPTER OPERATIONS IN KHE SANH	Althoff, LtCol D. *Gazette*	May 69
	HISTORY-BOOK BATTLE: THE RED DEFEAT AT KHE SANH	*U.S. News*	May 6, 1968
	I PROTEST! Black and white photos of Marines at Khe Sanh. Duncan protests fact that Marines can't win this battle, or the war	Duncan, D. Paperback edition only. Signet Books	1968 (IP)
	KEY VICTORY FOR MARINES, BUT WAS THE BATTLE NECESSARY? THREE HILLS OVERLOOKING U.S. BASE AT KHE SANH	*U.S. News*	May 15, 1967
	KHE SANH	Duncan, D. *Life*	Feb 23, 1968

KHE SANH Postmortem on the battle and the situation as Marines dug in for the defense of the area	Martin, J. *Leatherneck* Jul 68	
KHE SANH: READY TO FIGHT	Sider, D. *Time* Feb 16, 1968	
KHE SANH: 6,000 MARINES DUG IN FOR BATTLE	*Life* Feb 9, 1968	
LIVING ON AIR—HOW KHE SANH IS SUSTAINED	*Time* Mar 1, 1968	
STORY OF THE MARINES AT KHE SANH: BATTLEFRONT REPORT	*U.S. News* Feb 19, 1968	
UP HILL 881 WITH THE MARINES	*Life* May 19, 1967	
UP TIGHT AT KHE SANH	Stokes, R. *Newsweek* Feb 12, 1968	
VIET NAM BUILDUP? BATTLE OF THE HILLS NEAR KHE SANH	*Scholastic* May 19, 1967	
WAITING FOR THE THRUST: KHE SANH It never came	*Time* Feb 23, 1968	
WHY U.S. MARINES TOOK WAR TO NORTH VIETNAM'S DOOR-STEP	*U.S. News* May 29, 1967	
MARINE CORPS OPERATIONS IN VIETNAM, 1969	Simmons, BGen E. *Naval Review* 1969	**1969**
BARRIER ISLAND 2d Korean Marine Brigade smashes the enemy enjoying a few days off at Barrier Island	Bowen, SSgt B. *Leatherneck* Jan 70	
DEFEAT OF THE 320TH Summer 69 ops of 3RD MAR DIV	Davis, MajGen R., and Lt H. Brazier *Gazette* Mar 69	
DEWEY CANYON: ALL WEATHER CLASSIC 9th Marines, Jan, Feb 69	Davis, Lt G. *Gazette* Jul 69	

	LANCASTER 2 Northern I Corps operation	*Leatherneck*	Mar 69
	MEADE RIVER Search-and-clear against the VC infrastructure	Richardson, H. *Leatherneck*	Apr 69
	NEW HAPPY HAVEN Moving a Leprosarium that is in the way of operations	Bartlett, GySgt T. *Leatherneck*	Jun 69
	SILENT CHAPELS Of the 3RD MAR DIV in the Quang Tri hills	Howard, Cdr W., CHC, USN *Leatherneck*	Jan 70
	TOO QUIET, TOO LONG Rockets hit Da Nang	Bowen, SSgt B. *Leatherneck*	Dec 69
	YESTERDAY'S COMRADES Ceremony honoring KIA's of 2/1	Davis, Lt C., and GySgt B. Martin *Leatherneck*	Aug 69
1970	MARINE CORPS OPERATIONS IN VIETNAM, 1970	Simmons, BGen E. *Naval Review*	May 70
	HIT HARD, HIT FAST Pacifier ops of 1/5	Elliott, SSgt J. *Leatherneck*	Dec 70
	KILLER FOREST Rung Sat Special Zone, 30 miles south of Saigon	Cowan, Capt W. *Gazette*	Aug 70
	NEXT MARINE BATTLE: MARINES LEAVING VIETNAM	*Time*	Mar 30, 1970
	PARTING SHOT 3rd Shore Party Bn teaches ARVN how to re-supply by copter as farewell gesture	Bartlett, MSgt T. *Leatherneck*	Feb 70
	SIX IN THE OPEN Patrolling around Da Nang	Wolf, Sgt R. *Leatherneck*	Aug 70
	STACK ARMS Ambush is set to prevent Charlie from getting rice	Bartlett, MSgt T. *Leatherneck*	Feb 70
	A WALK IN THE SUN 3/1 patrols Nam-O-Bridge	Wolf, Sgt R. *Leatherneck*	Nov 70

VIETNAM WAR, GENERAL

THE FACE OF WAR Faces of Marines and enemy	Stibbens, S. *Leatherneck*	Nov 65
FIGHTING FRONT It's wherever you are	Bartlett, T. *Leatherneck*	Jul 65
FOR VIETNAM SERVICE Rundown on medals and decorations authorized for Marines by Vietnamese	Martin, B. *Leatherneck*	Apr 67
HE CAN'T COME HOME . . . YET POW's	Noyes, Sgt C. *Leatherneck*	Jan 71
THE INNOCENT Children in Nam	Elliott, C. *Leatherneck*	Jun 72
MARINE CORPS COMBAT ART Eight color prints. Series 3-A Cat. No. D214.16: C/73 no. 3-A S/N 0855-0042 $2.25 Series 3-B. Cat. No. D214.16: C/73 no. 3-B S/N 0855-0043 $2.25	USGPO	1970 (IP)
MARINE CORPS COMBAT LITHOGRAPHS 16 color prints. Cat. No. D214.16:C73/no. 3-A S/N 0855-0044 $2.25	USGPO	1968 (IP)
MARINES ARE MERCENARIES Say the Russians	Staar, R. *Gazette*	Apr 66
THE PROFESSIONALS Marines in Vietnam	O'Rourke, F. Paperback edition only, Avon Books	
SEVENTH FLEET AMPHIBIOUS OPERATIONS, MARCH 1965-DECEMBER 1968	Naval History Division, U.S. Navy	1969
"SORRY 'BOUT THAT . . ." New words in Marine lingo from Nam. They include "Victor Charlie, Charlie Cong, Dinged, ZAP."	Bartlett, T. *Leatherneck*	Jan 66

STRANGE WAR, STRANGE STRATEGY: A GENERAL'S REPORT ON VIETNAM A strange book, by the CO of the 3D Marine Amphibious Corps	Walt, Gen L. Funk & Wagnalls Company, Inc. Paperback edition,	1970 1972 (IP)
TELL THE STORY OF THE WAR: SET UP A SPEAKER'S BUREAU	Como, J. *Gazette*	Mar 67
THE UNITED STATES INTO VIETNAM: A CHRONOLOGY AND A BIBLIOGRAPHY	HQMC	1967
VIETNAM COMBAT ART	Henri, Col R. Cavanagh & Cavanagh	1968
VIETNAM HISTORICAL DATA	Shulimson, J. *Gazette*	Feb 69
VIETNAM SKETCHBOOK: DRAWINGS FROM DELTA TO DMZ	Waterhouse, C. Charles E. Tuttle Co. Rutland, Vt.	1970 (IP)
VIETNAM WAR SKETCHES FROM THE AIR, LAND AND SEA	Waterhouse, C. Charles E. Tuttle Co., Rutland, Vt.	1970 (IP)
WAR WITHOUT HEROES Pictures and commentary through Khe Sanh	Duncan, D. Harper and Row Publishers	1970 (IP)
"WHAT AM I DOIN' HERE?" Attitudes of Marines in Nam. They answer question "Why are you here?"	Bartlett, T. *Leatherneck*	Feb 66
WHO'S FIGHTING THE WAR? The young Marine in Vietnam	Pierce, P. *Leatherneck*	Nov 68
WHY WE ARE IN VIETNAM	Elliott, 1stLt O. *Gazette*	Oct 68
THE WOMEN OF VIETNAM Doing the work of the men	Bowen, SSgt B. *Leatherneck*	Feb 70

AVIATION

GENERAL

AIR DELIVERY PLATOON They deliver by parachute	Thompson, P. *Leatherneck*	Mar 69

THE AIR IS OURS Marines control the air	Bartlett, T. *Leatherneck*	May 66
AIR LIFT What to expect on flight to Nam	Ruhl, R. *Leatherneck*	May 66
BOMB HUMPERS Ordnancemen of VMFA-115 load the bombs on F4B's	Freeman, H. *Leatherneck*	Jan 67
EAGER GOPHERS HMM-263	Bartlett, MSgt T. *Leatherneck*	Mar 70
HUSTLER Featuring Cpl Clevenger, a bomb-humper, with VMA-223. He arms the jets before a mission	Martin, J. *Leatherneck*	Nov 68
INFLIGHT REFUEL VMGR-152	Kernins, Capt A. *Gazette*	Jul 72
MABS' MOB MABS-16	Martin, GySgt B. *Leatherneck*	Jul 69
MARINE AVIATION IN VIETNAM, 1962-70	McCutcheon, LtGen K. *Naval Review*	May 71
MARINE CONTROL OF AIR TESTED IN COMBAT It works!	Plattner, C. *Aviation Week*	Feb 14, 1966
O-1 "CHARLIE" Observation planes	Thompson, P. *Leatherneck*	May 68
ROLLING THUNDER All-weather A-6 "Intruder"	Martin, B. *Leatherneck*	Dec 67
SKYHAWK MAG-12 at Chu Lai	Stibbens, S. *Leatherneck*	Aug 66
TEAMWORK Explosive Ordnance Disposal teams from 1ST MAW	Martin, J. *Leatherneck*	Nov 68
TIGERS IN THE SKY Marine Fighter/Attack Squadron 542 at Chu Lai	Bradshaw, H. *Leatherneck*	May 68
TREBLE TROUBLE MAG-39 supports 3RD MAR DIV from Quang Tri	Martin, J. *Leatherneck*	Sep 68

COPTERS

Title	Author / Publication	Date
CHOPPER COPPERS Marine Heavy Helicopter Squadron 463	Martin, B. *Leatherneck*	Oct 67
CHOPPER PULL-OUT HMM-165 gets a rest	Bowen, SSgt B. *Leatherneck*	Dec 69
CREW CHIEF	Wolf, Sgt R. *Leatherneck*	Feb 71
HELICOPTER WAR IN SOUTH VIET NAM Excellent article about early war for Marines by the Marines' all-time favorite female reporter	Chapelle, D. *Geographic*	Nov 62
HELICOPTERS IN VIETNAM: USE AND MISUSE What the copter was designed to do, and what it did in Nam, were two different things	Rider, J. *Gazette*	Oct 67
HELOS IN VIETNAM	Sabiston, T. *Gazette*	Feb 64
HMM-161 Med-evacs and resupply for ARVN was its mission	Beardsley, F. *Leatherneck*	Feb 66
HUEY COBRA	Thompson, SSgt P. *Leatherneck*	Nov 69
NOWHERE TO GO	Wolf, Sgt R. *Leatherneck*	Oct 70
ONE RIDE WITH YANKEE PAPA: U.S. MARINE HELICOPTER SQUADRON 163 IN VIETNAM Excellent picture story	Burrows, L. *Life*	Apr 16, 1965
PENINSULA ASSAULT Fifteen Marine copters fly Vietnamese Rangers on a combat mission	Robinson, R. *Leatherneck*	May 65
SHU-FLY DIARY Personal experiences of the CO of the first squadron of Marine copters in Nam	Clapp, A. *Proceedings*	Oct 63

CASUALTIES

Title	Source
AMBULANCE VOLANTE	Eiseman, B., USN *Gazette* May 70
AN EXTRA PAIR OF HANDS Nurses	Noyes, Sgt C. *Leatherneck* Oct 70
DAY AT DONG HA: WORK OF DELTA CO., THIRD MEDICAL BATTALION	Stokes, R. *Newsweek* Mar 25, 1968
HEY, DOC! Corpsmen serve Marines in hospitals in Nam	Evans, E. *Leatherneck* Aug 71
MEDCAP Marines and Corpsmen help Vietnamese	*Leatherneck* Mar 69
MED-EVAC How it works to save lives	Freeman, H. *Leatherneck* May 67
MED-EVAC: VIETNAM STYLE	Allgood, F. *Gazette* Aug 68
MILLION DOLLAR FLIGHT Air Force technicians carry litter patients aboard an ambulance bus at Da Nang	Martin, GySgt B. *Leatherneck* Sep 69
RED LION Experiences of a med-evac	Salter, M. *Leatherneck* Apr 69
USS SANCTUARY Hospital ship	Noyes, Sgt C. *Leatherneck* May 70
WHERE THE WAR ENDS At the Naval Support Activity Station Hospital near Da Nang	Martin, GySgt B. *Leatherneck* Sep 69

COMBINED ACTION

Title	Source
AMBASSADORS IN GREEN Good-will Marines try to win over the villagers	Stibbens, S. *Leatherneck* Oct 65
AMBASSADORS IN GREEN Photos and text about Combined Action Marines	Bartlett, T. Paperback edition only, The Leatherneck Association, Washington 1971 (IP)

AS U.S. MARINES LEAVE VIETNAM: A CLOSE-UP OF THE WAR ZONE, COMBINED ACTION PLATOON PROGRAM	Wallace, J. *U.S. News*	Apr 20, 1970
THE BETRAYAL The Pacification War in Nam, and why it is doomed to failure	Corson, LtCol W. W. W. Norton & Company, Inc.	1968
A BRIEFING FOR COMBINED ACTION	Williamson, R. *Gazette*	Mar 68
BUILDING A NATION BEYOND THE KILLING: NEW EMPHASIS ON LAND CONTROL, POPULATION SECURITY AND NATION BUILDING	*Time*	Feb 3, 1967
CAC Combined Action Company Marines fight side-by-side with South Vietnamese Popular Forces	Freeman, H. *Leatherneck*	Apr 67
CIVIC ACTION Role played by Reservists in sending supplies for Vietnamese.	Bowen, B. *Leatherneck*	Dec 65
CIVIC ACTION	*Gazette*	Oct 65
CIVIC ACTION	Holmberg, W. *Gazette*	Jun 66
COMBINED ACTION A unit protecting villages around Phu Bai	Beardsley, F. *Leatherneck*	Apr 66
COMBINED ACTION	Wilson, MSgt G. *Gazette*	Oct 66
DAN SU'VU Medical treatment of civilian children	Bartlett, MSgt T. *Leatherneck*	Mar 70
A DAY WITH MURPHY Ops of Combined Action Platoon	Elliott, SSgt J. *Leatherneck*	Nov 70
FIVE FUNDAMENTALS OF FRIENDSHIP	Gray, D. *Gazette*	Oct 66
FRIENDSHIP: A PRINCIPLE OF WAR	Snyder, K. *Gazette*	Mar 68

GOLDEN FLEECE Golden Fleece is rice. Marines protect it from VC	Bartlett, T. *Leatherneck*	Jan 66
HAND OF FRIENDSHIP How Marines help Viet kids	Bowen, B. *Leatherneck*	Feb 66
A HANDFUL OF MARINES	Wagner, D. *Gazette*	Mar 68
HOA KHANH CHILDREN'S HOSPITAL	Noyes, Sgt C. *Leatherneck*	May 70
HOPE FOR TOMORROW Kids of Quang Tri Province	Bowen, SSgt B. *Leatherneck*	Dec 69
HOW THE MARINES FIGHT THE OTHER WAR: PACIFICATION PROGRAM OF THE COMBINED ACTION COMPANY	Dickerman, S. *The Reporter*	Apr 6, 1967
IT'S MORE THAN A SHOOTING WAR FOR AMERICAN GI'S	Handleman, H. *U.S. News*	Oct 23, 1967
KIM LIEN Civic Action and "Population Control." Efforts to check Charlie	Evans, E. *Leatherneck*	Jul 71
MILITARY CIVIC ACTION History of the effort	Platt, MajGen J. *Gazette*	Sep 70
MOONLIGHTERS Marines of Combined Action Platoon -3, "B" Co, 2d Combined Action Group, set up ambushes	Martin, J. *Leatherneck*	Aug 68
ONE RESPONSE TO PERSONAL RESPONSE	Laws, J. *Gazette*	Mar 68
POPULATION AND RESOURCES CONTROL	Pratt, Maj T. *Gazette*	Sep 70
RICE ROOTS EMPATHY	Martin, GySgt B. *Leatherneck*	Aug 69
SELF HELP Marines share rations with Nam orphans	Bartlett, MSgt T. *Leatherneck*	Mar 70

	SIDE-BY-SIDE "M" Co. 4TH Marines works to win friendship of people	Bartlett, T. *Leatherneck* Nov 66
	THEIR MISSION: DEFEND BEFRIEND: PACIFICATION PROGRAM OF ECHO TWO, COMBINED ACTION PLATOON	Moser, D. *Life* Aug 25, 1967
	U.S. MARINE CORPS CIVIC ACTION EFFORTS IN VIETNAM, MARCH, 1965-MARCH, 1966 When they were at their peak	Stolfi, Capt R. HQMC 1968 (IP)
	U.S. MARINE CORPS CIVIL AFFAIRS IN I CORPS, REPUBLIC OF SOUTH VIETNAM—APRIL 1966 TO APRIL 1967 A review of the means by which Marines attempted to win the hearts and minds of Vietnamese	Parker, Capt W. HQMC 1970 (IP)
	THE U.S. MARINES LEAVE VIETNAM: A CLOSE-UP OF ONE WAR ZONE—COMBINED ACTION PLATOON'S PROGRAM	Wallace, J. *U.S. News* Mar 28, Apr 20, 1970
	USMC CIVIL AFFAIRS IN VIETNAM, A PHILOSOPHICAL HISTORY	Evans, D. *Gazette* Mar 68
	THE VILLAGE A dozen Marines who lived, fought and sometimes died for a Vietnamese village in 1966. The best book yet about Marines in the Vietnamese War	West, Capt F. Harper and Row Publishers 1972 (IP)
	DUTIES	
ADVISORS	THE ADVISORS	Wolf, Sgt R. *Leatherneck* Mar 71
	ADVISORY TEAM 43 Ten Marines who assist the Vietnamese Navy	Rose, R. *Leatherneck* Oct 68
	CAPT. COOL Capt T. Campbell	Bartlett, T. *Leatherneck* Nov 66

Title	Author / Source	Date	Subject
MARINE ADVISOR: VIETNAM	Pickerell, J. *Gazette*	Aug 64	
VIETNAMESE ADVISOR	Tri, N. *Gazette*	Dec 68	
AMGRUNTS Amtrac men provide security or haul combat Marines	Thompson, P. *Leatherneck*	Jun 68	AMTRAC
THE ROAD IS CLEAR "A" Co. 7th Engineers, keeps Highway #5 clear of mines	Bowen, B. *Leatherneck*	Jul 67	ENGINEERS
THE LIEUTENANT Lt R. Sutton, a platoon leader	Stibbens, S. *Leatherneck*	Jul 66	INFANTRY
COMBAT INTELLIGENCE IN VIETNAM	Murtha, J. *Gazette*	Jan 68	INTELLIGENCE
INTELLIGENCE AND VIETNAM	Cohan, L. *Gazette*	Feb 66	
COMBAT HOTLINE	Dalby, Col M. *Gazette*	Apr 69	LOGISTICS
MAINTENANCE PROGRAMS IN RVN	Olf, N. *Gazette*	Apr 67	
MORTAR MAN With "H & S" Co, 3/4	Bartlett, T. *Leatherneck*	Sep 66	MORTARS
A SECRET PLACE Explosive Ordnance Disposal Team at Da Nang.	Bartlett, T. *Leatherneck*	Sep 66	ORDNANCE DISPOSAL
BOAT RIDE Recon patrol waits for air-lift	Richardson, H. *Leatherneck*	Mar 69	RECON
RECON MARINES	Thompson, P. *Leatherneck*	Apr 68	
MEANWHILE, OFFSHORE . . . Marines on the ships off the coast	Martin, GySgt B. *Leatherneck*	Aug 69	SEA DUTY
SNIPER Individual exploits of snipers	Childs, J., and B. Martin *Leatherneck*	Jan 67	SNIPER
HOT LZ: VIETNAM Task Element Marines at Da Nang	Stibbens, S. *Leatherneck*	Jan 65	TASK ELEMENT

TV	CHANNEL 11 Marines involved in first TV station for Americans in Nam	Martin, B. *Leatherneck*	Dec 67

ENEMY

AN UNKNOWN WARRIOR Cong defectors to the ARVN	Clarkson, Maj E. *Gazette*	Aug 70
BAMBOO BRIGADES	Stanford, N. *Gazette*	Mar 66
BLACK PAJAMA INTELLIGENCE	Grier, S. *Gazette*	Apr 67
THE ENEMY	Rogers, L. *Gazette*	Mar 66
THE ENEMY HOLDS SCHOOL How the Reds teach psychology	Savatt, SSgt R. *Leatherneck*	Jan 63
THE GUERRILLA AND REALITY	Krulak, V. *Gazette*	Jul 66
KIT CARSON SCOUTS Training ex-North Vietnamese regulars to be on the other side	Cowan, Capt W. *Gazette*	Oct 69
SAPPER ATTACK The most feared words in Nam	Sexton, Col M. *Gazette*	Sep 69
TERROR! Cong raid on Phu Thanh. One hundred fourteen villagers dead.	Wolf, Sgt R. *Leatherneck*	Nov 70
VIET CONG'S CRUDE WEAPONS Crude, but effective	Neubauer, J. *Gazette*	Oct 63
"WHY THE BRIDGE?" How Cong terror campaign works	Smith, Capt W. *Gazette*	Jun 70

EXPERIENCES

. . . AND A FEW MARINES Personal experiences of a senior advisor to the Vietnamese Marine Corps	Leftwich, W. *Proceedings*	Aug 68

DATELINE: VIETNAM First-hand reports about Marines by the Combat Correspondents	Lewis, J., and Combat Correspondents Challenge Books, Inc., Canoga Park, Cal. 1966
DATELINE: VIETNAM Lucas doesn't forget his Marines as he writes about Nam from Jan 64-May 66	Lucas, J. Award House 1966
FOR FREEDOM A 19-year-old Marine reports on his experiences as a Fire Team Leader	Berkowitz, Cpl H. *Leatherneck* Apr 70
GOIN' HOME After 13 months	Beardsley, F. *Leatherneck* May 66
HAPPY HUNTING GROUND: AN EX-MARINE'S ODYSSEY IN VIETNAM By the author of the best book about the Korean War . . . *The Last Parallel.*	Russ, M. Atheneum, Inc. 1968
THE LEAN AND THE MEAN More stories about Marines by the Combat Correspondents	Lewis, J., and Combat Correspondents Challenge Books, Inc., Canoga Park, Cal. 1970
LETTERS OF PFC RICHARD E. MARKS Letters home by a young Marine KIA	Marks, R. J. B. Lippincott Company, Philadelphia 1966
MARINES COME HOME FROM VIETNAM	Wren, C. *Look* Mar 8, 1966
NINETEEN-YEAR-OLD MARINE IN VIETNAM	Wren, C. *Look* Aug 24, 1965
OF GUTS AND GLORY More Combat Correspondent's stories.	Lewis, J., and Combat Correspondents Challenge Books, Inc., Canoga Park, Cal. 1968
REFLECTIONS OF A COMPANY COMMANDER	Shaver, Maj C. *Gazette* Nov 69

Title / Description	Author / Source	Date
REFLECTIONS OF A MAAG TOUR Advisor to the Royal Thai Marines offers a program	Miller, Maj R. *Gazette*	Mar 72
SEPARATION SECTION How separation works, using Cpl Beck as an example	Thompson, SSgt P. *Leatherneck*	Sep 69
TRIBUTE Cpl Ronald P. Roane and his scout dog "Hobo," KIA in Nam	Brown, LCpl J. *Leatherneck*	Jul 69
VIETNAM AS I LIVED IT Experiences of a Comm-man in the 3RD MAR DIV in 1968. Lots of action.	Larson, L. Vantage Press	1972
VIETNAM DIARY By the author of *Guadalcanal Diary.* But not as good.	Tregaskis, R. Holt, Rinehart and Winston Paperback by Popular Library	1963 1964
YOUNG MAN IN VIETNAM One of the shortest books about Vietnam. One of the longest books ever written in the second person (you). Lt Coe was there. This is his story.	Coe, C. Four Winds Press	1968

MARINES

GENERAL

Title / Description	Author / Source	Date
THE LEADERS Interviews with leaders, from a division commander to a fire team leader	Richardson, H. *Leatherneck*	Feb 69
THE MAGNIFICENT BASTARDS	Cortesi, L. McFadden-Bartell	
THE PROS Vignettes of Marines	Evans, GySgt E. *Leatherneck*	Apr 72
VIETNAM: THE SQUAD "New Breed" squad interviewed	Stibbens, S. *Leatherneck*	Aug 65
THE YOUNG BREED Young Marines' views	Richardson, H. *Leatherneck*	Nov 68

Fall, Bernard		
AN AFTERNOON WITH BERNARD FALL Interview with the famous historian, later killed in Nam	Leftwich, W. *Gazette*	Feb 69
AN INTERVIEW WITH BERNARD FALL	*Gazette*	Apr 67
Gonzalez, Sgt A.		
UP FROM THE RANKS Medal-of-Honor at Quang Tri, 1967	*Gazette*	Nov 70
O'Malley, Sgt Robert		
O'MALLEY'S MEDAL First Marine to win Medal-of-Honor	Ward, W. *Leatherneck*	Feb 67
Zilch		
ZILCH! THE MARINE CORPS MOST GUARDED SECRET Cartoon book	Delgado, R. Paperback edition only, Charles E. Tuttle Co., Rutland, Vt.	1970
MORE ZILCH! THE MARINE CORPS MOST CLOSELY GUARDED SECRET	Delgado, R. Paperback edition only, Charles E. Tuttle Co., Rutland, Vt.	1971 (IP)

OFF-DUTY

CUA VIET R & R	Thompson, SSgt P. *Leatherneck*	Aug 69
DA NANG "500" Marines build go-carts from junk parts. Hold race	Bartlett, T. *Leatherneck*	Aug 66
DA NANG "500" Second running	Martin, B. *Leatherneck*	Sep 67
DA NANG GANG Red Cross girls	Noyes, SSgt C. *Leatherneck*	Apr 71
MISS AMERICA USO SHOW	Elliott, SSgt J. *Leatherneck*	Dec 70

	RECREATION WITH THE MARINES IN VIETNAM	Joyce, D. *Parks & Rec.*	Oct 66
	VOICE OF MORALE American Armed Forces Radio	Bartlett, MSgt T. *Leatherneck*	Apr 70

POSTS/PLACES

GENERAL	JUNK CITY Any village in Vietnam	Bowen, WO B. *Leatherneck*	Apr 71
CAMP REASONER	POST OF THE CORPS: CAMP REASONER Named for Lt F. Reasoner who died while member of 3rd Recon Bn	Bartlett, T. *Leatherneck*	Nov 65
CHU LAI	IT HAPPENED AT CHU LAI "Post of the Corps" story about the "enclave" at Chu Lai	Bartlett, T. *Leatherneck*	Feb 66
DA NANG	THE BRIDGE New 7.5 million dollar bridge near Da Nang	Martin, B. *Leatherneck*	Nov 67
	DA NANG HARBOR ALBUM Picture spread	Bowen, SSgt B. *Leatherneck*	Oct 69
	DA NANG MP'S	Martin, B. *Leatherneck*	Apr 68
	FIVE YEARS UNDER FIRE Photo story of Da Nang Air Base	*Leatherneck*	Jan 70
	HILL 200 1st Recon Bn mans OP near Da Nang	Bowen, SSgt B. *Leatherneck*	Oct 69
	LIBERTY BRIDGE Defense of bridge south of Da Nang	Wolf, Sgt R. *Leatherneck*	Sep 70
	MOUNTAIN MEN Five Marines man OP in mountains near Da Nang	Bowen, B. *Leatherneck*	May 67
DONG HA	DONG HA MOUNTAIN 3/4 defends the mountain in 1969	Bartlett, MSgt T. *Leatherneck*	Jan 70

Title / Description	Author / Publication	Date	Subject
KHE SANH REVISITED Now it's a supply center for the Army. Only Marines there are from 1st Shore Party Bn	Evans, E. *Leatherneck*	Aug 71	**KHE SANH**
KHE SANH: 71 What Shore Party Marines there do in support of the Army	Wold, J. *Leatherneck*	Jul 71	
HUE	Thompson, P. *Leatherneck*	Jul 68	**HUE**
L-Z VANDY Supply base for the "Rockpile"	Thompson, P. *Leatherneck*	Jan 69	**L-Z VANDY**
LEATHERNECK SQUARE 9th Marines defend a piece of terrain near the DMZ	Smith, Col R. *Gazette*	Aug 69	**LEATHERNECK SQUARE**
CROW'S NEST 2/1 mans OP near Da Nang in Marble Mountains	Elliott, Sgt J. *Leatherneck*	Jan 71	**MARBLE MOUNTAINS**
NAN PHONG, THAILAND New home for MAG-15	Coleman, SSgt T. *Leatherneck*	Dec 72	**NAM PHONG, THAILAND**
HILL 510 Marine Fire Support Base	Evans, E. *Leatherneck*	Aug 71	**QUE SON MOUNTAINS**
THE ROCKPILE Ten Marines at 750-ft peak to relay radio messages from patrols	Freeman, H. *Leatherneck*	Mar 67	**ROCKPILE**
MSG SAIGON Marine Security Guard to protect the American Embassy	Martin, SSgt B. *Leatherneck*	Jun 69	**SAIGON**
POST OF THE CORPS: SAIGON Embassy Marines	Bowen, B. *Leatherneck*	Jul 66	
USMC-11 Engineers who built highway to carry supplies to Khe Sanh	Martin, J. *Leatherneck*	Jul 68	**USMC-11**

SUPPORTING ARMS

Title / Description	Author / Publication	Date	Subject
ARTILLERY PLATEAU Eight miles south of DMZ	Freeman, H. *Leatherneck*	Mar 67	**ARTILLERY**
ARTILLERY VS. VIET CONG NO MATCH	Croft, Maj A. *Gazette*	Jan 63	

	BIG MAMA 175-mm SP Gun. The biggest artillery piece ever fielded by the Corps, near Da Nang	Elliott, SSgt J. *Leatherneck*	Feb 71
	GUNS AT DA NANG	Ferguson, G. *Gazette*	Feb 66
	FIRE FOR EFFECT Artillery	*Gazette*	Sep 65
	KILO'S KILLERS M109 155-mm SP howitzers fire into North Vietnam	Martin, B. *Leatherneck*	Nov 67
	RECON'S ARTILLERY Artillery ambushes set-up by Recon patrols	Colby, Maj D., and Maj B. Bittner *Gazette*	Jan 67
	THUNDER AND LIGHTNING And isn't it frightening! 175-mm SP guns	Martin, SSgt B. *Leatherneck*	Jun 69
CLOSE AIR SUPPORT	AIR SUPPORT FOR 3RD MAF	McCutcheon, K. *Gazette*	Aug 67
	CLOSE AIR SUPPORT	Bowen, B. *Leatherneck*	May 67
	I SMOKE . . . YOU LIGHT 01B's drop smoke grenades	Stibbens, S. *Leatherneck*	Sep 65
	NIGHT CAS IN VIETNAM	Lawrence, R. *Gazette*	Mar 63
NAVAL GUNFIRE	THE NAVAL GUN IN VIETNAM	Stewart, W. *Proceedings*	Apr 67
	NAVAL GUNFIRE IN VIETNAM USS New Jersey off Nam	Whitney, Lt C., USN *Ordnance*	May, Jun 69
	NAVY GUNS HELP VIETNAM GROUND WAR Examples of NGF in Nam	Sehlstedt, A. *Proceedings*	Dec 65
	RESURGENCE OF NAVAL GUNS IN THE AGE OF MISSILES	Hessman, J. *Navy*	Jun 69

TACTICS

	AMPHIBIOUS DOCTRINE IN VIETNAM	Hilgartner, P. *Gazette*	Jan 69

ANOTHER ISLAND Marines land by copter and take an island off the coast of Nam. Similar to WW-2 ops	Stibbens, S. *Leatherneck*	Dec 65
ANOTHER LONG WALK Searching for Charlie	Thompson, P. *Leatherneck*	Mar 68
BEHIND THE HEDGEROW Planning an ambush patrol	Findlay, Maj R. *Gazette*	Apr 69
THE BRIDGE: A STUDY IN DEFENSE	Babb, Capt W. *Gazette*	Jun 71
CAM NE (4)	*Gazette*	Oct 65
COMBINED OPERATIONS WITH ARVN	Davis, MajGen R., and Lt S. Bell *Gazette*	Oct 69
DEATH VALLEY Planned ambush turns into sweep-and-clear mission (don't they all?)	Freeman, H. *Leatherneck*	Feb 67
FIRE AND MANEUVER How an area is "prepared" with fire before a patrol goes in	Bowen, B. *Leatherneck*	Jun 66
FIRE SUPPORT BASE DEVELOPMENT	Nicoli, Maj R. *Gazette*	Sep 69
HILL 488; A FIGHT TO REMEMBER	Hubbell, J., and D. Reed *Digest*	May 68
THE HOLE Marines flush VC out of caves like Iwo Jima	Stibbens, S. *Leatherneck*	Sep 66
JUNGLE CANOPY OPERATIONS	Meyers, Col B. *Gazette*	Jul 69
LE MY STUDY IN COUNTERINSURGENCY	Clement, R. *Gazette*	Jul 67
JUNGLE WARFARE THOUGHTS	Wyckoff, D. *Gazette*	Apr 66

MARINES NOT TOO EFFECTIVE Oh, yeah!	Walker, L., and W. Burchett *Gazette*	Apr 67
NO-NAMEVILLE Ops of "G" Co., 2/9, near Da Nang	Stibbens, S. *Leatherneck*	Jul 66
OPERATION INDEPENDENCE Typical sweep-and-clear mission	Bowen, B. *Leatherneck*	Jun 67
THE PATROL Typical search-and-clear mission	Stibbens, S. *Leatherneck*	Aug 65
PLANNING AND EXPLOITATION	Todd, Maj G. *Gazette*	Dec 69
RECON PATROL	Bartlett, T. *Leatherneck*	Nov 65
RETURN TO CONVENTIONAL WARFARE	Warren, Maj G. *Gazette*	Sep 69
REVOLUTIONARY DEVELOPMENT	Kriegel, R. *Gazette*	Mar 67
SILENT VICTORY	Grier, S. *Gazette*	Sep 67
TASK FORCE HOTEL'S INLAND BEACHHEAD	Dalby, M. *Gazette*	Jan 69
THE TRAIL WEST Marines in "six-by's" search for Cong	Richardson, H. *Leatherneck*	Jan 69
WHAT HAPPENS NEXT? Marines assault village of Chau Son	Bartlett, T. *Leatherneck*	Mar 66

UNITS

	REVISED T/E'S FOR UNITS IN RVN	Burns, M. *Gazette*	Feb 67
3RD MAF	3RD AMPHIBIOUS FORCE 1ST and 3RD MAR DIV and 1ST MAW made up the "Force-in-Readiness" that got the first call for duty in Nam	Stibbens, S. *Leatherneck*	Nov 65

1ST MARINE DIVISION IN VIETNAM Oversized book with many color photos. Summarizes each operation of the 1ST MAR DIV. Casualty, awards lists	Hymoff, E. M. W. Lads Publishing Co.	1967	**1ST MAR DIV**
THE 1ST RETURNS Nixon reviews the 1ST at Pendleton	Evans, E. *Leatherneck*	Aug 71	
PRESIDENT NIXON HONORS 1ST MARINE DIVISION	Nixon, R. *Dept of State Bulletin*	May 24, 1971	
THE FIFTH RETURNS The Iwo Jima Division is deactivated at Pendleton on Mar 1, 1966	Lane, GySgt C. *Leatherneck*	Feb 70	**5TH MAR DIV**
FORCE COMM IN VIETNAM	King, Maj B. *Gazette*	Feb 72	**FORCE COMM**
FORCE LOGISTIC COMMAND Headquartered at Da Nang, the FLC provides Marines in Vietnam with 60,000 items of supply	Bowen, B. *Leatherneck*	Aug 67	**FORCE LOGISTIC COMMAND**
SPECIAL LANDING FORCE Seagoing heliborne force capable of launching a surprise attack when needed	Thompson, P. *Leatherneck*	Jun 68	**SPECIAL LANDING FORCE**
THE 9TH MOVES OUT Leaves Vietnam after four years	Bowen, SSgt B. *Leatherneck*	Nov 69	**9TH MARINES**
THE 9TH MOVES IN To Okinawa	Bowen, SSgt B. *Leatherneck*	Nov 69	
RETURN OF THE 27TH First major combat unit to return from Nam	Martin, B. *Leatherneck*	Dec 68	**27TH MARINES**
CONTACT! 1st Recon Bn operations	Evans, GySgt E. *Leatherneck*	Apr 71	**1ST RECON BN**
WHAT WAITS BELOW? Scuba divers of 1st Recon Bn search for mines and booby traps in rivers	Bartlett, MSgt T. *Leatherneck*	Feb 70	

3RD TANKS	STEEL-HORSE MARINES 3rd Tank Bn, 3RD MAR DIV	Thompson, P. *Leatherneck*	Dec 68
11TH MOTOR TRANSPORT	THE ROLLING 11TH Served 1ST MAR DIV	Evans, GySgt E. *Leatherneck*	May 71
2/7	SOLID CONTACT FOR 2/7	Utter, LtCol L. *Gazette*	Apr 66
ANGLICO	BUT NOT FOR THE CORPS . . . What ANGLICO is and what it does	Martin, SSgt B. *Leatherneck*	Jul 69
	"TELL 'EM WE'RE HERE . . ." 1st ANGLICO is last tactical Marine ground unit in Nam	Heim, B. *Leatherneck*	Aug 72
"C" CO., 1/1	TRAUTWEIN'S MARINES "C" Co, 1/1	Bowen, SSgt B. *Leatherneck*	May 69
"F" CO., 2/12	FIRE FOR EFFECT "F" Co, 2/12 provides artillery support on call	Beardsley, F. *Leatherneck*	May 66
EXCHANGE PLATOON	EXCHANGE PLATOON FOR COMBAT MARINES	Fisher, A. *Gazette*	May 67
BAND	MUSIC MEN Marine Bands play for the troops	Martin, J. *Leatherneck*	Jan 69
DOGS	CANINE SCOUTS Scout dogs in action	Bowen, B. *Leatherneck*	Jul 67
	SCOUT DOGS	Martin, B. *Leatherneck*	Jan 69
	TO THE DOGS . . .	Ward, W. *Leatherneck*	Jun 66
WM'S	TO FREE A MAN . . . Fifteen WM's in Saigon	Richardson, H. *Leatherneck*	Apr 69

8.
THE VIETNAM DECADE

The Dominican Republic, probably the last "show-of-force" in history, race riots at LeJeune, prison riots at Pendleton, long hair; all that happened to the Corps outside of Vietnam in "The Vietnam Decade."

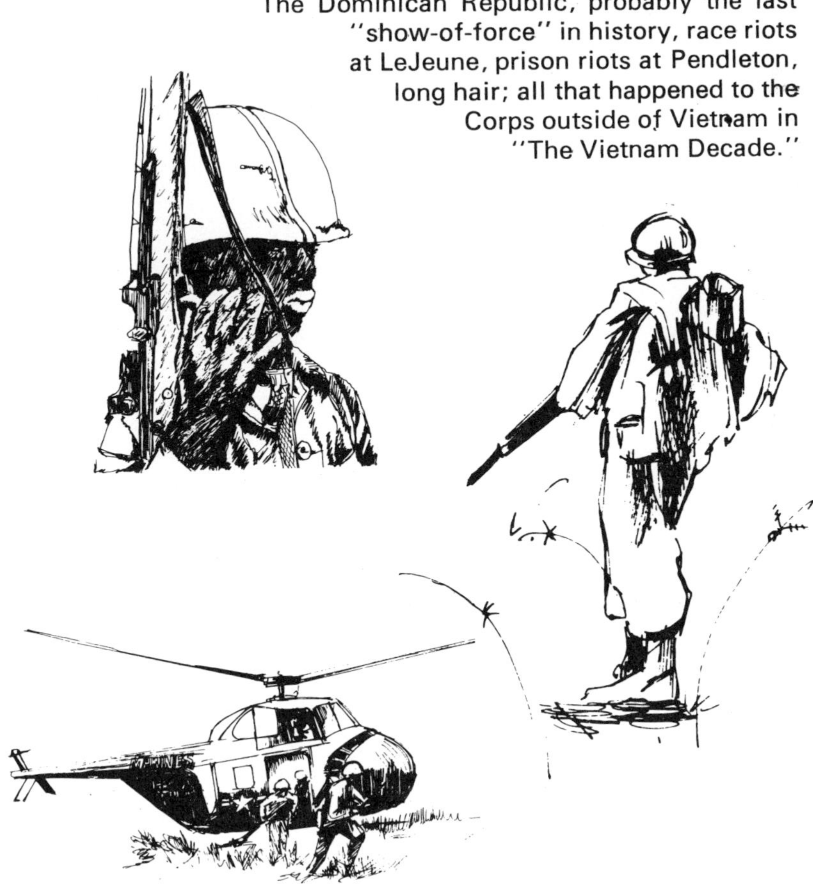

CONTENTS: PART 8

EVENTS/1963-1972

MARINE CORPS PHOTO/LITHOGRAPHS

Set A: 8 color prints per set 16x20.
Cat. No. D214.16/2:A USGPO
S/N 0855-0052 $2.25 1970 (IP)

Includes Skyhawks, Memorial, Good Samaritan, Sunset Parade, Battle Colors, Liberty Call-Japan, Early Mass, Alligator

Set B:
Cat. No. D214.16/2:B
S/N 0855-0053

Includes Marine's Prayer, In Memoriam, Hallmark, Honors, D.I., Hill 170, Sentinel, Logistics.

1963, GENERAL

BEYOND THE WAY-OUT HORIZON — *Time* Oct 4, 1963

BIRTHDAY PARTY — Kester, C. *Leatherneck* Dec 63
Marine Band entertains kids from the Columbia Society for Crippled children

CRISIS REPORT — Jones, GySgt M. *Leatherneck* Apr 63
Marines' role in Hurricane Ella

GUIDANCE FOR THEE IN '63 — Shoup, Gen D. *Gazette* Feb 63
"Now hear this" from the Boss

HAPPY ANNIVERSARY — Hall, Sgt H. *Leatherneck* Feb 63
Women Marines celebrate 20th

THE LIEUTENANT — Jordan, GySgt C. *Leatherneck* Sep 63
TV show stars "Lt Joe Rice"

MARINES — Shoup, Gen D. *Leatherneck* Nov 63
188th Anniversary message from Commandant

MARINES LANDED, TOO: SENTIMENTAL JOURNEY TO NEW ZEALAND — Sherrod, R. *Sat Eve Post* Apr 27, 1963
Sherrod returns with WW-2 Vets of 2D MAR DIV

	Title	Author / Publication	Date
	RED VIEWS CORPS Article in 1963 *Red Star* magazine in which a Red analyzes the Corps	Staar, R. *Gazette*	Jan 64
	REUNION IN KIWI LAND	Jordan, GySgt C. *Leatherneck*	May 63
	ROCKETTE REVUE Musical tribute to Corps from Radio City	*Leatherneck*	Aug 63
	TOP SQUAD Sixth annual Squad Competition at Quantico	Hall, H. *Leatherneck*	Dec 63
	TOP TEEN TEAM Teens from Franklin Lakes, N.J., win physical fitness title	Cushman, SSgt G. *Leatherneck*	Sep 63
	20TH ANNIVERSARY MESSAGE WR'S	Henderson, M. *Gazette*	Feb 63
	USS IWO JIMA: KEEL UP LPH	Howell, Capt D. *Gazette*	Apr 63
CUBA—1963	AUTHOR SAYS HE HAS PLENTY TO YELL ABOUT Col Heinl doesn't like "administrative censure" for Lopez killing	McDermott, J. *Life*	Aug 16, 1963
	CACTUS LINE Guantanamo Marine boundary	Kester, SSgt C. *Leatherneck*	Feb 63
	CAN DO! Seabees help Marines at "Gitmo"	Kester, SSgt C. *Leatherneck*	Feb 63
	INCONSTANT MARINES: CASE OF CAPT JACKSON AND LT SZILI	*New Republic*	May 11, 1963
	JFK'S PEACE CORPS This time it's the Marine Corps	*Newsweek*	Feb 25, 1963
	MARINE JUSTICE: COLONEL HEINL ADMINISTRATIVELY CENSURED IN THE CASE OF THE KILLING AT GUANTANAMO Lopez killing	*New Republic*	Jun 1, 1963

MARINES & CUBA: 145,000 WERE READY	*U. S. News*	Jan 14, 1963	**CUBA**
OCCURRENCE AT GUANTANAMO: SHOOTING OF RUBEN LOPEZ, AN ALLEGED CASTRO SPY	*Nation*	May 13, 1963	
VIOLENCE AND SILENCE: CASE OF RUBEN LOPEZ AT THE U.S. NAVAL BASE: GUANTANAMO BAY	*Newsweek*	May 11, 1963	
ARE THE MARINES REALLY READY TO FIGHT? Try us	*U. S. News*	Nov 9, 1964	**1964**
COMMANDANT'S BIRTHDAY MESSAGE	Greene, Gen W. *Gazette*	Nov 64	
IN GOOD HANDS Unknown soldier from WW-2 returns to US escorted by Marines	Nicholson, D. *Gazette*	Nov 64	
TOP SQUAD 7th Annual Rifle Squad Combat Competition	Bartlett, T. *Leatherneck*	Dec 64	
21ST ANNIVERSARY WR'S on their 21st birthday	Ambrose, J. *Leatherneck*	Feb 64	
A CHRONOLOGY OF THE UNITED STATES MARINE CORPS: 1965-1969	Neufeld, G. HQMC	1971 (IP)	
THE CONGRESSMAN AND THE CORPS Marines and Mendel C. Rivers, Chairman of the House Armed Services Committee	*Gazette*	Feb 65	**1965, GENERAL**
HELICOPTER MARINES AID FLOOD VICTIMS	*Gazette*	Jan 65	
OUR POSTURE IS THE MOST FAVORABLE IN THE HISTORY OF OUR CORPS	Greene, Gen W. *Armed Forces Management*	Nov 65	
BOXER'S FIRST ROUND MMH-264 on the USS Boxer off Santo Domingo	Young, G. *Leatherneck*	Jul 65	**DOMINICAN PUBLIC—1965**

	THE CORRIDOR 3/6 defends corridor in Santo Domingo	Berger, P. *Leatherneck*	Aug 65
	DOMINICAN DIARY	Dare, Capt J., USN *Proceedings*	Dec 65
	DOMINICAN DIARY	Szulc, T. Delacorte Press	1965
	EMBASSY BEACHHEAD Marines protect American Embassy in Santo Domingo	Tucker, P. *Leatherneck*	Aug 65
	MARINES INTO THE DOMINICAN CROSSFIRE	*Life*	May 17, 1965
	PEACE FORCE: ON LINE Marines enter Santo Domingo	Berger, P. *Leatherneck*	Aug 65
	REBELS FIRE FIRST Role of "K" and "L" Co., 1/6, in protecting Embassies	Berger, P. *Leatherneck*	Jul 65
	TROOPS IN DOMINICAN REPUBLIC CONTRIBUTE TO FIRST INTER-AMERICAN PEACE FORCE Show-of-Force by Marines	Tompkins, MajGen R. *Journal of the Armed Forces*	Oct 16, 1965
	TWO GOVERNMENTS, FACE TO FACE	*Time*	May 14, 1965
	UBIQUE Code Name for Dominican Operation, Apr-May, 1965	Tompkins, MajGen R. *Gazette*	Sep 65
	U.S. STEPS INTO ANOTHER HORNET'S NEST: SENDING TROOPS TO SANTO DOMINGO	*Business Week*	May 8, 1965
	WHEN THE MARINES STORMED ASHORE IN SANTO DOMINGO: EXCERPT FROM 30 DAYS IN MAY	Szulc, T. *Sat Eve Post*	Jul 31, 1965
1966	COMMANDANT'S REPORT	Greene, Gen W. *Gazette*	May 66
	MARINE CORPS GAZETTE . . . 50 YEARS History of Gazette	MacDonald, J. *Gazette*	Mar 66

			1966
PROFILE: UNITED STATES MARINE CORPS; 1966	USGPO	1966	
CHANGING THE GUARD: GENERAL WALT APPOINTED MARINE CORPS DIRECTOR OF PERSONNEL Gen Walt returns from Nam	*Newsweek*	May 29, 1967	**1967**
CAMARADERIE BETWEEN FIGHTERS Friendship between USMC and Korea Marine Corps	Kang, K. *Gazette*	Nov 67	
EXPO '67 Marine detachment at Canadian World Exposition	Bowen, B. *Leatherneck*	Sep 67	
FOR NEXT MARINE BOSS: THREE CANDIDATES	*U. S. News*	Sep 18, 1967	
192d BIRTHDAY MESSAGE	Greene, Gen W. *Gazette*	Nov 67	
QUICK AND THE DEAD: CASE OF FIRST SERGEANT CHURCHILL	*Newsweek*	Nov 13, 1967	
TRAVELING THEATRE Corps exhibit travels in portable, balloon-type structure	Paynter, J. *Leatherneck*	Jul 67	
FROM BEAUTY QUEEN TO TEEN MARINE	Bartlett, M. *Seventeen*	Feb 68	**1968**
LADY LEATHERNECK: COURT-MARTIAL ON COUNTS OF DISOBEYING ORDERS	*Newsweek*	Apr 22, 1968	
LEATHERNECK REVOLT Women Marines' trouble	*Time*	Apr 19, 1968	
PEKING MAN AND THE U.S. MARINES Half-million-year-old skeleton disappears enroute to New York museum. It was escorted by Marines	Ludwig, V. *Gazette*	Nov 68	

	PRESIDENT PLEDGES RESISTANCE TO AGGRESSION AS TALKS CONTINUE: REMARKS AT PRESENTATION OF THE PRESIDENTIAL UNIT CITATION TO THE 26TH MARINES	Johnson, L. *Dept. of State Bulletin*	June 10, 1968
	PROFILE: U.S. MARINE CORPS	USGPO	1968
	SAFARI TO SCOTLAND Marines participate in Edinburgh Tattoo	Heinl, R. *Gazette*	Nov 68
	WOMEN MARINES: 25th ANNIVERSARY	Meid, P. *Gazette*	Feb 68
1969, GENERAL	BLAST OFF Marines on Pad at Apollo 10	Bowen, SSgt B. *Leatherneck*	Aug 69
	COMBAT CORRESPONDENTS' REUNION One in Nam and one in U.S.	Noyes, Sgt C. *Leatherneck*	Dec 69
	EIGHTEEN MINUTE VERDICT: MILITARY JUSTICE AND CONSTITUTIONAL RIGHTS; CASE OF W. HARVEY AND G. DANIELS	Polner, M. *Commonwealth*	Mar 28, 1969
	INDIAN ROLL CALL 4TH MAR DIV Reunion Honors Indian Comm-men	Bixby, LtCol W. *Leatherneck*	Jun 69
	LEAGUE CONVENTION 46th Convention of MCL	Evans, GySgt E. *Leatherneck*	Nov 69
	LEATHERNECK BALL Corps Scholarship Foundation Ball in New York	Noyes, Sgt C. *Leatherneck*	Jun 69
	STATE OF THE CORPS—1969 New Commandant	Chapman, Gen L. *Gazette*	May 69
	TWO WALKS Marines' role in space shots	Bowen, SSgt B. *Leatherneck*	Oct 69
	WITH RESPECT AND HONOR St. Louis MCL Convention	Martin, GySgt B. *Leatherneck*	Aug 69

Title	Author / Source	Date	Topic
ANDERSONVILLE-BY-THE-SEA	Sherrill, R. *Nation*	Sep 15, 1969	**PENDLETON BRIG—1969**
IN A MARINE CORPS PRISON: PENDLETON BRIG RATS	Fincher, J. *Life*	Oct 10, 1969	
"WE AIN'T NO DOGS"	Sherrill, R. *Pageant*	Sep 69	
BLACK VS. WHITE: RACIAL TENSION AND DEATH OF CPL BANKSTON AT CAMP LEJEUNE, N.C.	*Newsweek*	Aug 25, 1969	**LEJEUNE RACE CRISIS—1969**
HOW BLACK UPSET THE MARINE CORPS	Morris, S. *Ebony*	Dec 69	
RACE CRISIS AT A MARINE CORPS CAMP	Good, P. *Life*	Sep 25, 1969	
RACIAL TENSION AT LEJEUNE	*America*	Aug 30, 1969	
RUMBLE AT CAMP LEJEUNE	Lewis, F. *Atlantic*	Jan 70	
WHERE MARINES STAND ON AFRO HAIRCUTS	*U. S. News*	Sep 15, 1969	
THE ALL VOLUNTEER FORCE AND ITS IMPACT ON THE MARINE CORPS We're *still* "looking for a few *good* men."	Duggan, Maj P. *Gazette*	Jun 70	**1970**
". . . ALWAYS A FOURTH" 4TH MAR DIV Reunion, Houston	Elliott, SSgt J. *Leatherneck*	Sep 70	
A CONCERNED CONVENTION Montford Point Marine Corps Association Convention of Black Marines	Gnatzig, Sgt B. *Leatherneck*	Dec 70	
CC CONFERENCE Combat Correspondent's Reunion	Bartlett, MSgt T. *Leatherneck*	Dec 70	
FMF FOR THE 70'S: CONCEPT	*Gazette*	Oct 70	

	JOINT REUNION 3D and 5TH MAR DIV Reunion, Washington	Evans, GySgt E. *Leatherneck*	Oct 70
	THE MARINE CORPS LEAGUE—47 YEARS CONVENTION	Noyes, Sgt C. *Leatherneck*	Nov 70
	MERCY MISSION Marine Choppers help earthquake victims in Peru	Pratte, Lt J. *Leatherneck*	Oct 70
	THE OLD BREED REUNION 1ST MAR DIV, Washington	Noyes, Sgt C. *Leatherneck*	Nov 70
	2D MARINE DIVISION ASSOCIATION REUNION	Wolf, Sgt R. *Leatherneck*	Nov 70
	STATE OF THE CORPS	Chapman, Gen L. *Gazette*	Apr 70
	WOMEN MARINES ASSOCIATION CONVENTION	Noyes, Sgt C. *Leatherneck*	Nov 70
1971	CHAPMAN: AN EMPHASIS ON COMBAT READINESS, QUALITY, SPIRIT AND DISCIPLINE So what else is new?	*Armed Forces Journal*	Jan 4, 1971
	A FEW GOOD MEN Start of Marines new recruiting campaign	Bartlett, T. *Leatherneck*	Aug 71
	IN THE WAKE OF JOAN Photo story of typhoon Joan in Philippines. 2/9 is there	*Leatherneck*	Feb 71
	MARINE ASSISTANT COMMANDANT DESIGNATE SERIOUSLY ILL LtGen Keith B. McCutcheon who later died of cancer	*Armed Forces Journal*	Jan 18, 1971
	RETURN TO SOPAC 1ST MAR DIV vet returns to WW-2 battle sites	McMillan, G. *Gazette*	Nov 71
	TUNED IN Recruiting by radio. How it works	Chavez, M. *Leatherneck*	Aug 71
	TOP SQUAD '71 14th annual competition	Weir, LCpl B. *Leatherneck*	Dec 71

YOUTH PHYSICAL FITNESS Corps sponsors Meet at Marine Barracks, D.C.	Weir, PFC B. *Leatherneck*	Sep 71	**1971**
RETURN TO "44 1944 Leatherneck is different from today's	Jaunal, SgtMaj J. *Leatherneck*	Nov 72	**1972**
TOYS FOR TOTS	Vernon, GySgt D. *Leatherneck*	Dec 72	
YOUTH PHYSICAL FITNESS 7th Annual Awards	Young, G. *Leatherneck*	Sep 72	

AVIATION

From the *Gazette*, unless specified otherwise:

AVIATION'S 3-M PROGRAM	McCutcheon, K.	Dec 68	**GENERAL**
BY AIR, ON LAND AND SEA	Berteling, J.	Jun 65	
CMC VIEWS MCA AND CAS Views from the Boss	Greene, Gen W.	Mar 64	
COMMAND OF THE AIR	Mitchell, J.	Dec 67	
COMMAND AND CONTROL	Lapham, Maj T., and Maj R. Lary	May 72	
FOLLOW-ON AIRCRAFT		May 66	
MARINE AVIATION, USA Translation from Russian publication	Staar, R.	Jan 64	
MARINE CORPS AVIATION: AN OVERVIEW	McCutcheon, K.	May 68	
MARINE CORPS AVIATION TODAY Annual Review of Corps aviation	Collins, LtCol G. *Naval Review*	1965	
MARINE TACTICAL DATA SYSTEM DETAILED: EVALUATION OF AIR OPERATIONS CENTRAL	Pay, R. *Missiles & Rockets*	Feb 21, 1966	
MARLOG Marine logistical flights for East Coast Marines to the Caribbean	Kester, C. *Leatherneck*	Jun 64	

	Title	Author	Date
	NEW TEAM CONCEPT Copters and V/STOL from USS Guam	Sneed, Ph1 C. *Leatherneck*	Oct 72
	OPERATION HI-BOY VMA-331 flies Atlantic for NATO exercise	Ward, W. *Leatherneck*	Feb 68
	PILOT RETENTION: THREE VIEWS	Constantino, Maj G., 1stLt J. Nickele and Maj K. Smith	May 68
	PRECISION AIR DELIVERY		Feb 65
	PROGRAMS OR PANIC	Cushman, J.	Apr 66
	RESUPPLY FROM THE SKY	Turley, G.	Oct 65
	SMOKE ALSO RISES	Martz, J.	May 65
	THREE FASTS AND A SLOW	Johnson, W.	Jun 67
	TOUGHEST AIR TROPHY GOES TO NINE SQUADRONS Aviation Safety		Oct 64
	WHO'S IN COMMAND HERE?	Steman, L.	Jan 65
	THE WORD IS ATTACK Mission of Marine Air in 1970	Escalera, Maj D.	May 70
AIRCRAFT	AIRCRAFT INVENTORY—1966		May 66
	AVIATION INVENTORY—1968		May 68
	GO IT ALONE WITH PHANTOM 2	Ohlgren, A.	Oct 63
	HELICOPTER OR FIXED WING? OR BOTH!	New, Col N.	May 71
	IMAGERY MODULE SUPPORTS RF4B		Oct 67
	IMPROVED SKYHAWK BOMBER READIED		Feb 67
	188-E READY FOR PRODUCTION		May 65
	REPORT ON THE TFX		Feb 65
	SPOOKY The AC-46 from WW-2 to Nam	Bowen, SSgt B. *Leatherneck*	Dec 69

WINGS OF THE CORPS Montage of Corps' Aircraft	Hopewell, J. *Leatherneck*	May 72

COPTERS

From the *Gazette*, unless otherwise specified:

ABOVE THE BEST Marine chopper pilots	Cretney, LtCol W., and Lt R. Cooling	Jun 71
CHOPPER SCHOOL MCAF at Santa Ana where Nam vets train pilots	Bowen, B. *Leatherneck*	Feb 67
COBRA OR BRONCO: AN ASSESSMENT OF A MISSION	Rider, Maj J., and Capt W. Buchanan	May 68
COPTER CREW CHIEF	Meskan, Maj D., and Maj R. Marshall	May 72
FLYING CRANE	Locke, F.	Aug 65
HELICOPTER COC	Johnson, W.	Jul 67
HMX-I	Lowe, Capt D.	Jan 68
LET'S PRACTICE WHAT WE PREACH ABOUT HELICOPTER OPERATIONS	Murphy, LtCol D.	Aug 69
LOH: ITS ROLE IN GROUND OPERATIONS Does the Corps need a Light Observation Helicopter?	Graham, LtCol T., USA	Oct 70
MAINTAIN THE BALANCE	Warren, R.	Jan 64
MARINE ASSAULT BY HELICOPTER	Davis, Gen R., and Lt R. Camp	Sep 68
MARINE ONE— HMS-1 flies the President	Bartlett, MSgt T. *Leatherneck*	Jul 70
NIGHT HELICOPTER OPERATIONS Historical summary	Dyer, LtCol R.	Jan 70
RAPPELING OUT OF HELICOPTERS	Walker, R.	Jun 63
SUPER STALLION CH53E New copter for the Corps	Kleppsattel, Col F.	May 72

	TWIN-BOOM BRONCO NEWEST CORPS AIRCRAFT	Houseman, Maj C.	May 68
	TWO OCEANS, FOUR CONTINENTS WITH HMM-365 Mixed copter concept proves itself aboard the USS Guam	Jochims, Lt J., USNR	May 71
	UNSHACKLE THOSE CHOPPERS	Krueger, S.	Jun 63
	WHIRLY BIRDS ON THE GAUGES	Gulling, L.	Jul 63
HARRIER	FIRST HARRIERS DELIVERED TO MARINES British-made V/STOL aircraft	*Armed Forces Journal*	Jan 18, 1971
	FLYING THE HARRIER	Miller, Col T.	May 69
	HARRIER AV-8A	Elliott, SSgt J., and MSgt T. Bartlett *Leatherneck*	May 71
	HARRIER: A NEW DIMENSION IN CLOSE AIR SUPPORT	New, Col N., and LtCol J. Braddon	May 70
	HARRIER PROGRAM SEEKS BROAD VTOL DATA	Brown D. *Aviation Week*	Oct 5, 1971
	MARINES FIT HARRIER TO OWN TACTICS	Brown, D. *Aviation Week*	Oct 18, 1971
	MARINES PLAN FOR HARRIER INTRODUCTION	Hieronymus, W. *Aviation Week*	Sep 14, 1970
	MARINES SEEK APPROVAL FOR HARRIER TEST And get it!	*Aviation Week*	Dec 9, 1968
	PEGASUS JETS FOR MARINE HARRIERS ASSURED DESPITE ROLLS ROYCE TROUBLES	*Armed Forces Journal*	Feb 15, 1971
	WHAT EVERY MARINE SHOULD KNOW ABOUT HARRIER	Braddon, LtCol J.	May 71

AVIATION

JOBS

AIR CONTROL: A TIME FOR CHANGE	Lary, Maj R.		May 70
THE AO AND THE FIELD COMMANDER	Sabia, Capt R.		May 68
ATC: SPECIALIST OR CIVILIAN? Air traffic controller	Robinson, R.		Sep 63
BACKSEAT DRIVERS Airborne Radar Intercept Operators in F4B's	Stibbens, S.	*Leatherneck*	May 65
FLIGHT COMMANDER	Willis, C.		May 64
FLIGHT LINE Photo story of VMA-214 flight line at El Toro	Bowen, WO B.	*Leatherneck*	Mar 71
HOW TO MEASURE A PILOT	Rieder, A.		Feb 63
MARINE AIR OBSERVER Mission of the Div AO	Mulkey, Maj J.		May 69
NAVAL FLIGHT OFFICER	Cummings, Capt J.		May 72
OUR MIS-USED PICTURE TAKERS Better uses for photo recon	Hunter, P.		Nov 63
PATTERN FOR AVIATORS	Braddon, J.		Aug 64
PLANE CAPTAIN Cpl is responsible for Skyhawk Jet	Stibbens, S.	*Leatherneck*	Aug 66
ROUND PEGS IN ROUND HOLES Marine Air finds round pegs for round holes	May, Col D.		May 71
SEARCH AND RESCUE Cherry Point SAR men	Hall, Sgt H.	*Leatherneck*	May 63
WOMEN WITH THE WING	Chavez, Sgt M.	*Leatherneck*	Jul 72

PILOTS

CORPS ANGEL Marine Capt John Kretsinger, a "Blue Angel!"	Jordan, C.	*Leatherneck*	Dec 63

	LEATHERNECK SALUTES CAPT RAYMOND POWELL Aviator of the Year for work on "Snakeye" bomb project	Stibbens, S. *Leatherneck*	May 66
	A TROPHY FOR GLENN Cunningham Award to John H. Glenn, Jr.	Evans, SSgt C. *Leatherneck*	Jan 63
	THE VANISHING NAPS Only two left	Evans, GySgt E. *Leatherneck*	Jul 72
SATS	FIND A NEED AND FILL IT Maybe it's the Short Airfield for Tactical Support	Hill, MajGen H.	May 71
	LANDING PAD WHILE YOU WAIT For the Harrier		Aug 67
	LAND THE SATS	Hartsock, E.	May 65
	SATS	Evans, SSgt C. *Leatherneck*	May 63
	SATS NOW EMPLOYS SOPHISTICATED GEAR	Kinnear, WO J.	Oct 66
	SMALL AIRFIELD FOR TACTICAL SUPPORT Development of SATS, 1953-63	Kinnear, WO J.	Apr 63
	V/STOL TRANSPORT REPORT		May 65
	V/STOL AND THE USMC	Sims, W.	May 65
TRAINING	AVIATION TRAINING AND READINESS	Durnford, Col D., and Maj C. Silard	May, Aug 70
	CAN'T HEAR YOU . . .! El Toro's Audiometric Testing Section	Bartlett, T. *Leatherneck*	Sep 65
	CONTROLLER COLLEGE At NAS Glynco, Georgia	Frye, J. *Leatherneck*	Mar 65
	FLY "LARA" FOR PROFICIENCY	Laning, Maj E.	Jun 64
	MANS WORLD Marine Aerial Navigation School at Pensacola	Elliott, GySgt J. *Leatherneck*	May 72

MTDS Marine Tactical Data System training in air defense and air control	Bowen, B. *Leatherneck*	Feb 67
NAVIGATOR'S WINGS Aerial Navigation Course at Cherry Point	Martin, J. *Leatherneck*	May 68
ONE IN TEN THOUSAND Special contract guarantees aviation	Freeman, H. *Leatherneck*	Oct 67
PRESSURE COOKER Sixteen Marines help train prospective Naval pilots at Pensacola	Elliott, GySgt J. *Leatherneck*	May 72
THE TRAINING WING 2D MAW, Cherry Point	Bowen, B. *Leatherneck*	Sep 66
WING WIPERS Aircraft maintenance training	Thompson, SSgt P. *Leatherneck*	Jan 70
WINGS OF GOLD Marine aviation cadets at Pensacola	Smith, GySgt J. *Leatherneck*	Aug 63

UNITS

ANGELS ON YOUR HELMET Three VMO squadrons	Jones, GySgt M. *Leatherneck*	May 63
BOXCAR SQUADRON Last of the C-119's at Seattle	Evans, GySgt E. *Leatherneck*	Apr 70
EYE IN THE SKY VMCJ-2 at Cherry Point, Electronic Warfare and Aerial Photo Recon	Bowen, B. *Leatherneck*	Oct 66
LAUNCH PEDRO SAR Unit at Cherry Point	Evans, GySgt E. *Leatherneck*	May 72
MAGIS Intelligence is part of their mission	Canton, J.	Feb 69
MOST OUTSTANDING SQUADRON The Black Knights of VMFA-314 win the Robert Hanson Award	Sauer, LCpl R. *Leatherneck*	May 69

	PHANTOM FLYERS VMFA-251 at MCAS, Beaufort, S.C.	Stibbens, S. *Leatherneck*	May 65
	TACRON: WHAT AND WHERE?	Well, J.	Dec 67
	VMCJ Aerial Multisensor Imagery Squadron	Manning, LtCol P.	Oct 72
	WORKING BIRD VMGR-152 hauls more than anybody in its 12 planes	Thompson, SSgt P. *Leatherneck*	Oct 69

DUTIES

From the *Gazette*, unless otherwise specified:

	Title	Author	Date
AIDE-DE-CAMP	AIDE-DE-CAMP They're still around	Leftwich, W.	Aug 65
CHAPLAIN	CHAPLAIN IN THE FMF	Craven, J.	Dec 66
COMMUNI-CATIONS	ARMY UNIT FINDS AN/PRC 25 RADIO IDEAL FOR RECON MISSIONS	Gordon, D.	Mar 67
	COMMUNICATIONS: THE COMMANDER'S DILEMMA	DiCilio, F.	Sep 64
	COMMUNICATIONS IS TOO IMPORTANT	Hammond, C.	Jul 63
	COMMUNICATIONS IS YOUR BUSINESS	Carruthers, R.	May 64
	KNOW THE SYSTEM	Ritts, R.	Oct 66
	A MILITARY DISABILITY	Ripley, G.	Jul 66
	NECESSARY ANTENNA ORIENTATION	Rogers, H.	Oct 67
	OUR SHORT HAUL COMMUNICATIONS GAP	Anderson, R.	Apr 65
	THOSE TINY TRANSISTORIZED TRANSCEIVERS	Chapman, W.	Oct 65
	UNIFORM SIGNAL SYSTEM	Cohan, L.	Jun 66

Title	Author / Source	Date	Subject
JUNIOR DI Profile of one named Dan Clouse	Martin, B. *Leatherneck*	Feb 69	DI
SUPER GRIT School Demonstration Troops at Quantico (A grit is a stateside grunt).	Bartlett, MSgt T. *Leatherneck*	Oct 71	DEMO TROOPS
THE EMBASSY MARINE	Barrett, R. *Proceedings*	Jun 67	EMBASSY
EMBASSY MARINES Duties around the world	Kester, C. *Leatherneck*	May 64	
EMBASSY PREP School for Embassy Marines	Sauer, Cpl R. *Leatherneck*	Jul 69	
MARINE CORPS AND THE FOREIGN SERVICE: A WORKING PARTNERSHIP Address by the Secretary of State	Rusk, D. *Dept. of State Bulletin*	Nov 21, 1964	
COMBAT ENGINEERS	Hall, Sgt H. *Leatherneck*	Jan 63	ENGINEERS
WHAT'S IT LIKE, 1ST SGT?	Evans, GySgt E. *Leatherneck*	Nov 72	FIRST SGT
DEAR DIARY Notes from author of the next article	Gnatzig, Sgt B. *Leatherneck*	May 71	HORSE MARINES
HORSE PATROL Guarding the NAS at Miramar	Gnatzig, Sgt B. *Leatherneck*	May 71	
TRAVELING TEAMS The big teams from HQMC	Hall, H. *Leatherneck*	Apr 64	I & I
A BREED CALLED GRUNT	Bartlett, MSgt T. *Leatherneck*	Apr 71	INFANTRY
PORTRAIT OF A GRUNT The infantry Marine	Hall, Sgt H. *Leatherneck*	Jun 63	
CONFESSIONS OF A BATTALION S-2	Andrews, R.	Sep 64	INTELLIGENCE
COUNTERINSURGENCY INTELLIGENCE	Heilbrunn, O.	Sep 66	

	FRONT-LINE PHOTO DRONE	Charon, L.	Aug 66
	INTEGRATED COMBAT INTELLIGENCE The dream of every commander	Chaplin, D.	Jul 70
	PATROL BRIEFING	Cohan, L.	Dec 66
	TACTICAL IMAGERY PROCESSING	Scott, H.	Sep 66
MED CRUISE	MED CRUISE		Nov 65
MP'S	FAIR SHAKE The "new look" in MP treatment of prisoners	Bartlett, T. *Leatherneck*	Jul 71
	THE MILITARY POLICEMAN'S LOT	Olds, J.	Mar 69
NIGHT DUTY	NIGHT PEOPLE All the Marines who work at night	Bartlett, T. *Leatherneck*	Jul 71
RECON	ALL THE WAY Force Reconners are the glamour boys	Jones, GySgt M. *Leatherneck*	Oct 63
	A DIRECTION FOR DIVISION RECON	Kaye, Maj R.	Apr 70
	FOUR RULES FOR RECON	Colby, D.	Dec 66
	LOCK OUT The glamour boys of Force Recon again	Bowen, SSgt B. *Leatherneck*	Sep 69
	RECON BATTALION: NO! Who needs it?	Wilkinson, J.	Mar 63
	RECON BATTALION: YES! We do!	Carpenter, J.	Mar 63
	RECON OR RAIDER? Why not just plain Marine?	Fable, E.	Oct 68
	RECONNAISSANCE AND SURVEILLANCE PHOTOGRAPHY	Goldhammer, J.	May 66
	SEAT-HIP HELO RAPPELING	Ryan, P.	Sep 66
RECRUITING	THE RECRUITER The duty analyzed	Freeman, H. *Leatherneck*	Aug 68

RECRUITING DUTY — Manion, Sgt Maj H. — Mar 70

SECURITY

CAPITAL SECURITY — Thompson, P.
Security duty around the world — *Leatherneck* Apr 68

CATANIA PATROL — Jones, M.
Shore patrol in Med for Sixth Fleet — *Leatherneck* Mar 64

MONA LISA — Kester, SSgt C.
Guarding the world's most famous painting at the New York World's Fair — *Leatherneck* Mar 63

WORLD'S FAIR 1964 — Jones, M.
Marines on duty there — *Leatherneck* Jul 64

WEATHER

COMBAT WEATHER — Rider, J.
Gazette Sep 64

WR'S

DISTAFF DEXTERITY — Noyes, C.
At Pendleton — *Leatherneck* Sep 68

DISTAFF DUTY — Noyes, Sgt C.
Women Marines at HQMC, Washington — *Leatherneck* Jul 71

GLAMOUR IN THE CORPS — Ward, W.
Pan Am Stewardess' School is open for WR's — *Leatherneck* Sep 67

PENTAGON LADIES — Chavez, Sgt M.
Leatherneck Jun 72

THEY LOOK AT THE SKY — Noyes, C.
El Toro — *Leatherneck* Jun 68

WOMEN MARINES — Noyes, SSgt C.
By one who is one — *Leatherneck* Feb 71

FICTION

From *Leatherneck* alphabetical by author, unless specified otherwise:

Baker, M.
THE BLUFF — Oct 63
Perkins learns that poker is a man's game, especially when your life is at stake

Barrow, C.
THE BELIEVERS Jan 63
A night patrol convinced the gunny that you can learn something from the PIO Sgt

Chase E. (Karl Schuon)
THE BEAVER PATROL Oct 65
An eager beaver wreaks havoc with the peace of his neighbors

DOOLEY'S REVENGE Mar 66
Cpl Dooley's leprechaun masquerades as a full-sized recruit

GILHOOLEY Jun 64
Gilhooley builds a model plane

THE PARADE Mar 65
The leprechaun is back again

REMEMBER ALADDIN May 65
Nails Borowski cons pigeons into buying phony Aladdin Lamps

SPIDER TRAP May 63
Put Spider Webb vs. 1st Sgt Kelly

Fiske, J. H.
STOVEMAN May 66
An eightball makes tent stoves work

Guilford, J. (Karl Schuon)
THE BOWLERS Jan 65
Tailspin McGee, Bunker O'Malley and Horrible Murphy

THE BROTHERHOOD SQUADRON Feb 66
Horrible Murphy and pals again

THE COME-ON Aug 65
Nails Borowski & Company help Korean orphans

CONTINGENCY FUND Feb 67
Ghosts of 1812 return to haunt photographer

COOL IN CORPSVILLE Aug 66
Borowski's kid brother's rock group

DANTE'S VALHALLA Oct 66
Joe Dante dreams of heaven and the activities of the dead Marines there

FAMILY AFFAIR — Jun 66
Borowski and Company vs. 1st Sgt Flint

THE HARD CHARGER — Dec 63
A hard charger supplies the current

THE MARK — Dec 65
Borowski & Company again

THE MASTERMIND — Apr 67
Bareface Brogen moves in on Borowski

MIKE MULLIGAN, JR. — Mar 63
Mulligan's leprechaun haunts him

THE SCIENTIST — Sep 65
A certain Pvt grows rose vines

SERGEANT SANTA CLAUS, ACTING — Dec 64
Nails Borowski gets the Christmas spirit

THE SWORDSMEN — May 64
Borowski & Company organize a fencing team

VALENTINE KNOCKOUT — Feb 65
Horrible Murphy settles his differences with an opponent in a parking lot

Hardman. Ric
THE CHAPLAIN'S RAID — Coward-McCann, 1965
Paperback by Bantam Books, Inc. 1966
Silly novel about a horny Chaplain's aide at Pendleton in the early 1960's

Huter, R.
DOC — Apr 66
Buddies of a KIA corpsman raise money for his kids in a crooked card game

Knox, E. K.
GOMER PYLE, USMC — Paperback edition only, Pocket Books, Inc.
Short novel based on the TV Show

Little, Charles
THE BOLD AND THE LONELY
David McKay Company, Inc. 1966
Paperback by Popular Library 1967
Marine Medal of Honor winner returns from Death Row

McGowan, GySgt A. J.
THE BITTER PILL — Aug 63
MSgt Brand has two pair to open

Schuon, K.
DEAR YE EDITOR — Sep 64
A *Leatherneck* writer-artist team are locked in the Bastille

DIALOGUE FOR TWO WARRIORS — Jul 64
Blinky and Sarge discuss what makes Marines

THE OLD MAN — Sep 64
He was good in combat

Sherwood, D.
DAN FLAGG — Apr 63
Comic strip Marine

Stolley, F.
BIG JIM — Apr 63
New 2d Lt grows old fast

BROWN VS. GREEN — Nov 64
Which side is out?

Unsigned
THE NEW BROOD — Smedley Enterprises, Woodridge, Va., 1965
Cartoons about Marines from the *Navy Times*

Weiler, A. (Karl Schuon)
THE FEUD — Aug 64
A. Smith vs. A. Jones

GHOST STORY — Apr 65
Marine gets shock when he meets man he thought he killed in Korea

York, F. S.
THE LEGACY — Sep 63
Cpl Flood and Lt Trimble have one hope . . . hang on until dark

MAYDAY — Jul 64
A rescue at sea

THE TRANSFER — Mar 67
Cook has too vivid an imagination

LEADERSHIP

From the *Gazette*, unless specified otherwise:

GENERAL

ANYONE FOR TENNIS? Boredom kills morale	Toolin, L.	Apr 64
A BAND OF BROTHERS Marine traditions are both Athenian and Spartan	Harrington, Lt B. *Leatherneck*	Jun 72
THE CHALLENGE OF LEADERSHIP "Where we go from here" statement from the new boss	Cushman, Gen R.	Aug 72
COMPLACENCY: THE ENEMY WITHIN	Christy, H.	Nov 67
"CORPORAL, NOW YOU ARE A NON-COMMISSIONED OFFICER" Act like one!	Manion, SgtMaj H. *Leatherneck*	Sep 70
COURAGE	Nicholson, Col D.	Mar 65
COURAGE	Johnson, R.	Dec 67
THE FIRST LIEUTENANT PROBLEM	Oppenheimer, H.	May 68
4 FORETHOUGHTS	Wyckoff, D.	Dec 68
INSPECTION: THE KEY TO COMMAND	Nelson, H.	Apr 68
LEADERSHIP Officer training the USMC way	Neely, SSgt B. *Leatherneck*	Apr 70
LEADERSHIP AND LOGIC	Dent, J.	Oct 65
MAN OF PEACE Unfortunately, not why LBJ will go in the History books	Johnson, L. B.	Oct 64
N.C.O.	Hargreaves, R.	Jan 68
A NEED FOR PERSONAL RESPONSE We must learn to interact with each other, *and* with civilans	Harig, SSgt R.	Aug 72

Title	Author	Date
"NO PROBLEM, SIR, THE SEABEES ARE SMOKING CIGARS"		Mar 67
THE NON-COMMISSIONED OFFICER	White, H.	Dec 65
ON LEADERSHIP AND HORSE SENSE They go together	Thorn, E.	Feb 64
ON MORAL LEADERSHIP	Diaz-Ugueto, M.	Jul 67
OUR DYING PRIDE	Foote, E.	Jun 63
RULES OF LEADERSHIP	Murray, R.	Jul 65
SEMPER FIDELIS: THE ETHIC OF THE WARRIOR	Cain, S. *Christian Century*	May 14, 1969
SUPERVISION VS. INTERFERENCE A fine line separates the two	Allgood, F.	Jul 67
SYNONYM FOR LEADERSHIP	Love, J.	May 67
THIRTY YEAR MAN	Spring, G.	Sep 63
THOUGHTS OF LEADERSHIP	Erlandson, D.	Feb 66
TOWARDS MORE SERVICE PRIDE	Smith, D.	Dec 63
THE UNITED STATES MARINE CORPS Esprit lives here	Fontana, P.	Nov 66
USS ARIZONA Symbol of what happens when a nation is unprepared	Utter, LtCol L.	Dec 66
WE HIRED ON TO BE TOUGH! The Chapman years for the Corps	Campbell, Col D. *Leatherneck*	Apr 72
"WHY DID YOU JOIN, LIEUTENANT?" You had better have a good answer	Greene, Gen W.	May 67
WO IMAGE	LaTondre, WO R.	Apr 68
A WRONG APPROACH	Allinder, M.	May 67

LeJEUNE FORUM ON OFFICER RETENTION

Title	Author	Date
A BIT OF RIBBON But it does a lot for morale	Hopgood, M.	Oct 68
CLIMBING THE LADDER	Fisher, C.	Apr 68
EXPLODING THE PAY MYTH	Jones, G.	Apr 68
JUST ANOTHER JOB	Allgood, F.	May 67
PERSONAL ATTENTION, A KEY Everyone likes to feel important	Robertson, J.	May 67
POSITIVE MORALE FACTOR	Maxwell, J.	Oct 68
PROGRESS AND PREP FIRES	Allgood, F.	Sep 67
THE REAL PROBLEM	Butchart, E.	May 67
REWARD WITH AWARDS	Burie, J.	Oct 68
SPECIALIST VS. OLD BREED	Hofmann, CWO C.	Apr 68

LOGISTICS

From the *Gazette,* unless specified otherwise:

GENERAL

Title	Author	Date
AMPHIBIAN BRIDGE		Feb 65
CARGO TRANSFER SYSTEM HIGHLINES SHIP TO SHORE		Sep 68
THE CONCEPT OF MODULAR CONSTRUCTION	Revie, R.	May 68
EYE ON SUPPLY Supply management	Ross, J.	Oct 63
F. D. L.	Baldwin, H.	Mar 67
FDL SHIPS: VITAL ELEMENT IN NATIONAL DEFENSE	Sonenshein, RAdm N., and BGen D. Pepke	Dec 67
HOT WATER COMFORT	Blumbey, R.	Dec 68
IN TIMES TO COME New gear being developed by Landing Force Development Center at Quantico	Martin, J. *Leatherneck*	Apr 68
INTERNATIONAL LOGISTICS	DuPre, P.	Oct 66
LIGHTENING THE LOAD Of personal equipment		Apr 65

	Title	Author	Date
	MAINTENANCE MANAGEMENT	Flynn, J.	Apr 67
	MAP OVERLAY REPRODUCTION	Kearney, F.	Jul 68
	MECHANIZED EMBARKATION Automatic data processing	Hyatt, R.	Aug 67
	MOBILE LOGISTICS Supply system must respond to extreme mobility of troops	Lochner, Maj R.	Jul 72
	MOVE OUT	Thomas, Capt W.	Mar 65
	MUMMS AND THE USER Automatic data processing	Fellows, W.	Jun 67
	MUMMS THE WORD	Walling, R.	Jan, Jun 67
	NEW CONCEPTS OF MATERIAL MANAGEMENT		May 65
	ORGANIZE FOR LOGISTIC SUPPORT	Alexander, J.	May 64
	PRIME $ Money is getting tougher to get	Conner, Maj M., and Dr. E. Bump	Feb 72
	PUT LOGIC IN THE SUPPLY SYSTEM	Meeker, E.	Apr 67
	TF61: TF62 How a Bn becomes a BLT for Med Cruise	Jones, M. *Leatherneck*	Mar 64
	WHAT'S NEW? What's being tested at Landing Force Development Center	Bartlett, T. *Leatherneck*	Apr 65
	WHAT'S NEW? New gear being tested at Quantico	Elliott, J. *Leatherneck*	Jun 71
CHOW	BETTER FIELD RATIONS THAN IN OLD CORPS		Jan 68
	"M" PACKET Beats the hell out of a "K" ration	Hall, H. *Leatherneck*	Jul 66
CLOTHING	BACKPACK New one is tested	Callahan, E.	Dec 64

BODY ARMOR Maximum protection for combat Marines	Rankin, Col R. *Leatherneck*	Aug 63
BODY ARMOR OR MOBILITY? You can't have both	Winecoff, Capt D.	Jun 71
TWO UNIFORMS ARE ENOUGH	Driscoll, E.	Aug 64
UNIFORMS OF THE DAY On display in Philadelphia	Wolf, Sgt R. *Leatherneck*	Apr 70

VEHICLES

AIR CUSHION VEHICLES		Dec 66
AIR FREIGHT VIA FOILS		Mar 65
THE CASE FOR THE WHEELED AMPHIBIAN	Shimanoff, M.	Apr 65
GAMA GOAT CLIMBS ROUGH TERRAIN	Swims, E.	Apr 68
LIGHTER AMPHIBIANS		Apr 66
THE LVTP7 AND THE SURFACE ASSAULT New amphibian is not as good a surfer, but better on land	Alexander, Maj J.	Jun 72
OFF THE ROAD IN 1966 Amphibian vehicles		Jan 66
SUPER HOG Corps' new Amtrac	Elliott, GySgt J. *Leatherneck*	Apr 72
TACTICAL MOTOR TRANSPORT	McCollum, R.	Dec 65

MANAGEMENT

From the *Gazette,* unless specified otherwise:

FUNDING AND EQUIPPING FOR LOW INTENSITY WARFARE	Schmid, C.	Dec 66
HOW THE MARINE CORPS BUYS	Stanfield, J.	Jul 64
MANAGEMENT VS. BUREAU	Hewes, J.	Feb 67
MARINE CORPS CONCEPTS OF MANAGEMENT	Metzger, BGen L. *Armed Forces Management*	Feb 65

MARINE CORPS COMMAND AND MANAGEMENT SYSTEMS DEVELOPMENT: AN OVER VIEW — Chapman, Gen L. — Oct 67
From the Commandant

MARINES

From *Leatherneck,* unless otherwise specified, alphabetical by the last name of the Marine

Adams, Eddie
THE GRABBER — Bartlett, GySgt T.
AP photographer specializes in Marines — Aug 69

Anderson, Gen Earl Edward
ASSISTANT COMMANDANT OF THE UNITED STATES MARINE CORPS — Caulkins, MSgt R. — Jul 72

Anderson, SSgt J.
MONEY MAGNET — Bartlett, T.
Anderson's hobby is collecting old money — Aug 72

Barker, MSgt J.
CHUTING STARS — Dartez, Cpl M.
"Chuting Stars" Navy Parachute Team has Barker and SSgt William Shepard as members — Aug 72

Beveridge, Maj Austin
BUSMAN'S HOLIDAY — Dartez, Cpl M.
Beveridge is pilot with Eastern Airlines and member of HMM-68 at Lakehurst weekends — Aug 72

Brennan, MSgt B.
BRENNAN OF THE NORTH — Evans, GySgt E.
MSgt Bob Brennan recruits in Alaska — Jun 70

Canton, LtCol John S.
DIPLOMAT — O'Leary, J. — Jan 65
Decorated for diplomatic services in Morocco

Carlisle, Larry
A LOOK AT LARRY — Gnatzig, Sgt B. — May 71
Defending all-Marine champion middleweight

Caulkins, MSgt R.

THINK	Caulkins, MSgt R.	
Author writes own retirement story		Oct 72

Chaisson, LtGen J.

IN MEMORIAM: LT GEN JOHN R. CHAISSON		Dec 72
PARTING SHOTS: A MARINE WHO COULD HANDLE THE TANK	*Life*	Jul 16, 1971
The late General Chaisson was at home in the Pentagon "Think Tank"		

Chapman, Gen Leonard F., Jr.

CEREBRAL COMMANDANT	*Time*	Dec 17, 1967
MARINES GET A NEW LEADER	*U.S. News*	Dec 18, 1967
MANAGEMENT MARINE: NEW COMMANDANT	*Newsweek*	Dec 18, 1967
THE 24TH COMMANDANT	Bartlett, MSgt T.	Feb 68

Clark, Sgt E.

GUNNY ON CAMPUS	Stibbens, S.	
At U. of Missouri		Sep 64

Cushman, Gen Robert

CMC INTERVIEW	Bartlett, T.	Nov 72
COMMANDANT CUSHMAN	*Newsweek*	Dec 13, 1971
MARINES NEW CHIEF: MAN NIXON NEVER FORGOT	*U.S. News*	Dec 13, 1971
NEW TOP LEATHERNECK: R. E. CUSHMAN	*Time*	Dec 13, 1971
U.S. MARINES: WELL IN HAND	*Newsweek*	Nov 29, 1971

Davis, Gen Raymond G.

GENERAL RAYMOND G. DAVIS, ASSISTANT COMMANDANT, UNITED STATES MARINE CORPS	Bartlett, MSgt T.	
Appointment biography		Apr 71

Donet, SSgt J.

HOPI RECRUITER	Roof, J.	
SSgt J. Dennet is Hopi Indian Marine Recruiter in Arizona		Dec 71

Duncan, David Douglas
YANKEE NOMAD: A PHOTOGRAPHIC ODYSSEY Duncan, D.
Photographic essay including many photos of Marines — Published by the Author 1966

Greene, Gen Wallace M., Jr.
ONCE A MARINE . . . Morrisey, R.
Retirement biography — Mar 68

TOP MARINE WITH SPACE-AGE IDEAS — *U.S. News* Oct 7, 1963

THE TWENTY-THIRD COMMANDANT
Appointment biography — Kester, C. — Jan 64

Haney, Norman and Charlie Connelly
HERMIT HAVEN — Jones, GySgt M.
To escape society, two former Marines occupy a shack overlooking the Caribbean — Apr 63

Hill, MajGen H. S.
MAJ GEN H. S. HILL INTERVIEW — Caulkins, MSgt R. — May 72
Deputy C/S (AIR)

Irish Marines
IRISH MARK ON THE CORPS — Ward, W. — Mar 67
Famous Irish Marines such as Presley O'Bannon, Robert O'Malley, Raymond Murphy, Dan Daly, etc.

Jones, LtGen William K.
AT THE HELM . . . — Elliott, GySgt J.
An interview with Commanding General, Fleet Marine Force, Pacific — Dec 71

Krulak, LtGen Victor and MajGen Lew Walt
PACIFIC COMMAND — Stibbens, S. — Nov 65
Biographies of the commanding general, Fleet Marine Force Pacific and Commander of the 3rd Marine Amphibious Force

Laflin, SgtMaj Corey F.
BANANAS DON'T SQUAWK — Bartlett, MSgt T. — Oct 69
Marine vet recalls "Banana War" experiences

Lenz, MGySgt Robert
A DESKFUL OF $CH_3C_6H_2(NO_2)_3$ — Jones, M. — Aug 64
Lenz is an explosive ordnance expert

Macgruder, John
JOHN MACGRUDER: IN MEMORIAM — Heinl, Col R.
Farewell to Marine historian who died in tragic boating accident — *Gazette* — Nov 72

Otten, SgtMaj Mabel A. R.
WM SGT MAJOR — Chavez, Sgt M.
SgtMaj Mabel A. R. Otten — Sep 71

Pagett, Private
PRIVATE PAGETT, USMC — Williams, BGen D.
The mascot of the Corps was a bulldog—gift from the Royal Marines — *Gazette* — Nov 71

Pusker, Sgt Steve
A RECRUITER'S DAY — Gee, SSgt D.
Sgt Steve Pusker spends his day in Macon, Ga. — Apr 71

Sweet, SgtMaj Herbert J.
CORPS SERGEANT MAJOR — Berger, P. — Jul 65
Announcement article

CORPS SERGEANT MAJOR — Ward, W.
Duties of H. Sweet, Corps' top enlisted man — May 66

Tait, Sgt Glen S.
LEATHERNECK SALUTES — Jones,, MSgt W.
The Corps Color Sergeant — Jan 58

Walt, Gen Lewis W.
FOUR STAR GRUNT — Bowen, SSgt B.
His promotion to four stars — Aug 69

GENERAL WALT — Elliott, SSgt J.
Retirement biography — Feb 71

LEADER FOR ALL REASONS: L. WALT RETURNS TO U.S. — *Time* — Jun 9, 1967

PARTING WORD — Walt, Gen L. — May 71
Farewell statement

THREE STAR GRUNT — Bowen, B. — Apr 67
Walt was then Commander of 3rd Amphibious Force in Nam

TOUGHEST MARINE — Wren, C.
Look — May 5, 1964

TWO WARS OF GENERAL LEW WALT — Leinster, C. — *Life* May 26, 1967

OFF-DUTY

All articles in this section are from *Leatherneck:*

AFTRS — Beardsley, F. — Jul 65
Marines man world's most powerful radio station at Okinawa

CAMP NEWSPAPERS — Cushman, G. — Jan 64
Lejeune Globe, Pendleton Scout

DETOUR FROM TROUBLE — Dartez, LCpl M. — Apr 72
Big Brother Program in D.C.

EAGLE, GLOBE AND ANCHOR — Richardson, H. — Feb 69
Marine TV Show from New Bern

FLYING CIRCUS — Young, G. — Nov 72
Marines and Reserves are among performers near Bealton, Va.

FOR A CAUSE — Bartlett, T. — Jul 72
Marines are suckers for causes, especially if they involve kids

HAMS — Stibbens, S. — Oct 64
Amateur stations in Corps

MARS CALLING — Thompson, P. — Jan 68
Military Affiliate Radio System

NETWORK: THE WORLD — Chavez, Sgt M. — Jul 72
AFRS

NOTHING TO DO? SHOOT! — Bartlett, T. — Jun 72
Photography takes care of idle hours

PERSONNEL

From the *Gazette,* unless specified otherwise:

GENERAL

ARE MEDICAL LOSSES NECESSARY? — White, P. — Mar 67

DOUBLE DUTY MAW — Nov 66
Records and correspondence

Title	Author	Date
THE ECONOMIC FREE HORSE	Smith, K.	Oct 67
FIELD SANITATION: NOW	Duffey, W.	May 63
HOW TO BECOME A U.S. MARINE CORPS OFFICER	MacCloskey, BGen M. *Navy*	Sep 64
JUNIOR OFFICER SYMPOSIUM At Quantico	Smith, Lt G.	Feb 63
LET'S BE FAIR WITH THE FAIR WR'S	Dayton, V.	Feb 63
MANPOWER MANAGEMENT	Armstrong, LtCol P.	Jun 67
MANPOWER: THE PROBLEM ELEMENT Inevitable shortage of manpower post-Nam	Walsh, Maj R.	Jun 70
MANY ARE CALLED	Berry, N., and P. Nelson	Aug 66
MARINE LINGO All Corps slang	Martin, B. *Leatherneck*	Aug 68
MARINE MANPOWER	Davis, R.	Jul 66
MORE THAN QUALIFIED		Jul 72
THE NECESSITY FOR ADMINISTRATIVE SEPARATIONS There will always be eight-balls	Tutterow, Maj H.	Mar 70
NOTRE LANGUE MILITAIRE New military language	Wyckoff, LtCol D.	Oct 63
OFFICE MANAGEMENT Advice from an Admin Chief	Pearsall, SSgt F.	Oct 71
OFFICER RETENTION: REPLACE MYTH WITH THE REALITY	Conaty, Maj D., M. Cooper and P. Duggan	Nov 70
PROTEST AND PROCUREMENT Recruiting the long hairs	Marino, G.	Jan 69
QUESTIONS FACING THE CODE OF CONDUCT Review of the Code reveals how the enemy uses it against us	Marean, LtCol C.	Jul 72

THE RESPONSIBILTY TO WRITE	Hammond, LtCol J.	Jan 70
ROCKS AND SHOALS OF DEPLOYMENT	Broome, N.	Jun 66
SOMETHING OF VALUE Retention and attrition	Clapp, Col A.	Apr 69
TEMPORARY COMMISSIONS	Colassard, B.	Jan 69

AFTER SEPARATION

BRING YOUR OWN DEDICATION Bureau of Narcotics where many former Marines work	Evans, GySgt E. *Leatherneck*	Mar 71
CAMPUS VETS CLUB Ex-servicemen and women band together in college	Chavez, Sgt M. *Leatherneck*	May 72
CAREER OPPORTUNITIES Jobs in Environmental Protection for former Marines	Daniels, D. *Leatherneck*	Jun 72
IT'S UP TO YOU The GI Bill is there to use	Noyes, SSgt C. *Leatherneck*	Apr 71
SIGHTING IN ON A DEGREE Use the GI Bill	Noyes, SSgt C. *Leatherneck*	May 71
WANTED Police Departments across the country favor former-Marines	Martin, B. *Leatherneck*	Dec 68
WHY WE WANT OUT Two Marines who want to be former Marines, and why . . .	Highers, Lt E., and MSgt C. Crawford	Sep 70

ASSIGNMENTS

CAN YOU BE CRITICAL? Classification retraining policies	Jordan, GySgt C. *Leatherneck*	Jan 63
OFFICER ASSIGNMENT POLICIES	Beck, N.	Aug 68
PERSONAL MANAGEMENT	O'Connell, J.	Dec 65
QUO VADIS	Smith, A.	Mar 65
WHO GOES WHERE? How the Corps transfer system works. (You take a set of orders and throw it up to the ceiling . . . if it sticks, etc.)	Berger, P. *Leatherneck*	Feb 64

PART 8 | THE VIETNAM YEARS

Subject	Title	Author/Source	Date
CAREER PLANNING	MARINE GUNNERS GET NEW LIFE		Aug 64
	THE OFFICER INPUT STORY		Apr 64
	SO YOU DON'T MAKE COMMANDANT	Oppenheimer, H.	Apr 63
	SOMEBODY UP THERE CARES About your career	Kemp, Maj G.	Aug 71
	THE VOCATION OF ARMS	Briand, P., and M. Wakin	Apr 64
	YOUR CAREER FORMULA	Lerond, LtCol J.	Apr-Jun 64
FITNESS REPORTS	TOWARD FITNESS REPORT PRECISION	Kennington, C.	Mar 67
	UNSEEN FINESS REPORTS—A SURVEY	Shanahan, T.	Jan 66
MEDALS AND AWARDS	DRESS RIGHT Proper ribbon and medal placement	Wolf, Sgt R., and Cpl B. Gnatzig *Leatherneck*	May 70
	DUMPY DAN, THE MEDAL MAN Rundown of medals and awards from Korea through April, 1965	Bowen, B. *Leatherneck*	Apr 65
PAY AND ALLOWANCES	MILITARY PAY AND ALLOWANCES	Blandford, J.	Jan 65
	NEW MILITARY PAY SCALE		Sep 64
PERSONAL AFFAIRS	A BENEFIT YOU SHOULD KNOW ABOUT	Wagenhoffer, M.	Jun 68
	DRUGS: A ONE-WAY STREET 1. THE DRUG PROBLEM AND HOW IT AFFECTS YOU AS A MARINE 2. BY REASONS OF UNFITNESS 3. THE JURY'S STILL OUT 4. USMC DRUG ABUSE PROGRAMS	Evans, GySgt E., and Sgt C. Noyes	Jul-Oct 70
	FREE: SURVIVAL PLANS FOR OUR RETURNING VETERANS Help when you get out	Harrell, D. *Leatherneck*	Apr 72

HOW TO RETIRE How to retire properly, with all benefits	Martin, J. *Leatherneck*	Mar 69	**PERSONNEL**
"IF THE MARINE CORPS WANTED YOU TO HAVE A WIFE, LIEUTENANT . . ." You'd be issued one	Slough, P.	May 67	
LEGAL ASPECTS OF DRUG ABUSE Close examination of all laws pertaining to drugs on state-by-state basis	Tottenham, Capt T.	Dec 72	
THE MARINE CORPS AND THE SUPREME COURT Legal status of the Corps and individual Marines	McCollum, W.	Sep 67	
PERSONAL AFFAIRS TODAY	Jones, W.	Dec 68	
RETIRED SERVICEMAN'S FAMILY PROTECTION PLAN	Elliott, SSgt J. *Leatherneck*	Apr 70	
YOUR NEXT MOVE Relocation story	Noyes, SSgt C. *Leatherneck*	Jul 71	
"YOU'VE GOT A CASE, MISTER"	Conlin, J.	Jan 64	
HOW PROMOTIONS WORK Promotion system based on supply and demand	Anderberg, D. *Leatherneck*	Feb 69	**PROMOTIONS**
THE NUMBERS GAME	Gray, D.	Feb 65	
YEAR GROUP VS. GRADE		Mar 65	
SUMMARY COURTS MARTIAL	Darley, R.	May 68	**UCMJ**
13 YEARS OF UCMJ Military Justice	Faw, D.	Dec 64	
THE THREE C'S: THE CODE, THE CONVENTION, THE CONFLICT POW behavior standards	Wilson, LtCol P.	Apr 70	

POSTS/PLACES

From the "Post of the Corps" series and other articles in *Leatherneck,* unless otherwise specified:

ALASKA	ALASKA Duty in Adak and Kodiak	O'Neill, E.	Dec 64
	KODIAK Kodiak Island	Evans, GySgt E.	Jun 70
	ALBANY Marine Supply Center in Georgia	Paynter, J.	Feb 68
	MARINES IN THE AMERICAS North, South and Central	Kester, SSgt C.	Nov 63
	MARTD ANDREWS At Andrews Air Force Base, Md	Evans, GySgt E.	Jan 70
	ANNAPOLIS Guard duty at Naval Academy	Bowen, B.	Oct 66
	ARGENTIA Supply activity in Newfoundland	Bowen, B.	Feb 66
	ATHENS Embassy duty in Greece	Woltner, R.	Mar 68
BANGOR	BANGOR Duty in Washington state	Hall, H.	Jan 65
	BANGOR Polaris missile base	Freeman, H.	Sep 67
	BARCELONA CABLE Liberty in Spain	Jones, M.	Mar 64
	BARSTOW Supply Center in California	Hall, H.	Mar 66
BEAUFORT	BEAUFORT MCAS in South Carolina	Richardson, H.	Aug 68
	MCAS BEAUFORT	Wolf, SSgt R.	May 71
	BERMUDA Duty at Naval Air Station	Bowen, B.	Sep 65
	BOSTON NAVY YARD Marine detachment	Martin, B.	Apr 67

MB BREMERTON Marine Barracks	Evans, GySgt E.	Mar 70	**BREMERTON**
BREMERTON	Hall, H.	Jul 64	
BROOKLYN	Berger, P.	Feb 64	**BROOKLYN**
BROOKLYN	Wolf, Cpl R.	Jan 70	
BROOKLYN PARADE Sunset parade at Navy Yard	Wolf, Cpl R.	Dec 69	
CAMP LEJEUNE	Jones, GySgt M.	Oct 63	**CAMP LEJEUNE**
CAMP LEJEUNE	Richardson, H.	Sep 68	
CAMP LEJEUNE	Elliott, GySgt J.	Apr 72	
CYCLE CLUB	Evans, GySgt E.	Nov 72	
LEATHERNECKS AT LEISURE: CAMP LEJEUNE, N.C.	*Recreation*	Jan 63	
A LOOK AT THE FUTURE . . . BARRACKS '68	Richardson, H.	Sep 68	
OVERSEAS AT CAMP LEJEUNE British train there	Hudson, L.	Jan 66	
ACROSS THE BOARD	Cushman, SSgt G.	Sep 63	**CAMP PENDLETON**
BRONCS AND BRAHMAS . . . 23rd Pendleton Rodeo	Gettings, Sgt T.	Oct 70	
BRONCS, BULLS, AND BRUISES 25th Annual Rodeo	Brewster, J.	Oct 72	
CAMP PENDLETON . . . TO MOLD A FINER MARINE Pictorial	Ferguson, G. *Proceedings*	Feb 68	
NEW FACILITY: NEW CONCEPT Pendleton Brig	Elliott, GySgt J.	Oct 72	
PENDLETON A WASTELAND? NEVER!	Gnatzig, Sgt B.	Sep 70	
A TRUE PUBLIC SERVANT Natural Resources Program	Elliott, GySgt J.	Sep 72	

	Title	Author	Date
	SOME REAL FINE DUTY Brunswick, Maine	Bartlett, MSgt T.	Nov 70
	CHARLESTOWN Massachusetts duty	Jordan, C.	Dec 63
CHERRY POINT	BUCK PASSERS Ops Section in action	Bartlett, GySgt T.	Aug 69
	GAME SAVERS Protecting wild life	Kester, C.	Jan 64
	CHERRY POINT		Jun 72
	CHERRY POINT: 2D MAR AIRCRAFT WING	Martin, J.	May 68
	CLARKSVILLE Security watch at Navy base	Ward, W.	Jan 67
	CORPUS CHRISTI Marine Barracks and Marine Aviation Detachment	Ward, W.	Apr 66
	MARTD DALLAS	Elliott, SSgt J.	Jul 70
	EARLE, N. J. Naval Ammunition Depot	Sauer, R.	Feb 69
EL TORO	COMIN' AND GOIN' From Nam and to Nam	Bartlett, MSgt T.	Jul 70
	EL TORO	Kester, SSgt C.	May 63
	EL TORO Marine Air Station	Martin, J.	Jan 69
	EL TORO'S BIG PACKAGE Largest MARTD	Elliott, GySgt J.	Oct 72
	EL TORO TODAY Home of 3RD MAW	Elliott, GySgt J.	Sep 72
	MARINES . . . IN EUROPE	Jordan, GySgt C.	Nov 63
	MARINES . . . IN THE FAR EAST	Hall, Sgt H.	Nov 63
	FORT BRAGG MARINES JFK Center for Military Assistance	Elliott, SSgt J.	Jun 70

FORT HENRY RETREAT Canadian fort visited by Marines	Jones, GySgt M.	Nov 63	
GUARDING OUR NATIONAL SECURITY Marines at Fort Meade, Md.	Evans, GySgt E.	Aug 70	
MARINES . . . IN GREAT BRITAIN	Jones, GySgt M.	Nov 63	
JUNGLE SURVIVAL Jungle Ops School at Fort Sherman	Thompson, SSgt P.	Aug 70	
FRANKFORT Embassy duty in Europe	Hull, D.	Dec 66	
GARDEN CITY First Marine Corps District	Bartlett, T.	May 66	**GARDEN CITY**
GARDEN CITY	Evans, GySgt E.	Feb 71	
GREAT LAKES Duties at Naval Training Center	Paynter, J.	Apr 68	
ARRRUUUGH 2/8 at Guantanamo	Bartlett, T.	May 72	**GUANTANAMO**
GITMO—WE WON'T GET	Bartlett, T.	Jun 72	
GROUND DEFENSE FORCE	Bartlett, GySgt T.	May 69	
GUANTANAMO BAY	Bartlett, GySgt T.	May 69	
MARINE BARRACKS, GUANTANAMO BAY	Kester, SSgt C.	Feb 63	
RENT, 282.19 A MONTH For Guantanamo	Bartlett, T.	Jun 72	
MARINE MILITARY ACADEMY: A DAY IN THE LIFE OF A CADET Rougher than Boot Camp	Bridges, D.	Dec 72	**HARLINGEN**
MMA Marine Military Academy	Thompson, SSgt P.	Mar 70	

	MORE BOOT CAMP THAN CAMPUS: MARINE MILITARY ACADEMY, HARLINGEN, TEX. For High School age boys	*Life*	Oct 22, 1965
	TEGUCIGALPA MARINES Honduras security guard duty	Dilworth, D.	Sep 69
HAWAII	BARBER'S POINT: MCAS		Sep 63
	A BARRACKS AT PEARL	Elliott, GySgt J.	Dec 71
	CAMP GEIGER	Bowen, B.	Aug 67
	HAWAII LIBERTY	Elliott, GSgt J.	Sep 71
	KANEOHE BAY	Kester, SSgt C.	Aug 63
	KANEOHE BAY	Elliott, GSgt J.	Sep 71
	KANEOHE U. Special instruction for Hawaiian Marines	Kester, SSgt C.	Sep 63
	NAMED FOR "HOWLIN MAD" 16th birthday of Camp Smith	Elliott, GSgt J.	Dec 71
	PEARL HARBOR U.S. Naval Base duty	Richardson, H.	Apr 69
HAWTHORNE	HAWTHORNE Naval Ammunition Depot	Bartlett, MSgt T.	Nov 69
	HAWTHORNE	Ward, W.	Sep 66
	ISTANBUL Embassy duty	Woltner, R.	Jan 68
	JACKSONVILLE Naval Air Station	Jones, M.	Apr 65
JAPAN	ATSUGI Naval Air Station	Berger, P.	May 65
	MARINE DOVES AND THE BAFFLED BRASS: AMERICAN SERVICEMEN'S UNION AT IWAKUNI, JAPAN	Smith, C. *Nation*	Sep 14, 1970
	YOKOSUKA Duties and liberty	Berger, P.	Mar 65

Post/Place	Name	Date	
MARINE CORPS FINANCE CENTER "Paymaster" of the Corps	Thompson, P.	Apr 69	KANSAS CITY
KANSAS CITY 9th District Hdq.	Sandbank, R.	Jul 67	
KANSAS CITY	Stibbens, S.	Sep 64	
KEFLAVIK Iceland duty	Berger, P.	Oct 64	
KEY WEST Security duty at Naval Base	Richardson, H.	Jul 68	KEY WEST
KEY WEST	Wolf, Sgt R.	Feb 70	
LAKE MEAD BASE Deactivation	Bartlett, MSgt T.	Oct 69	
LAKEHURST, N.J. Naval Air Station	Berger, P.	Apr 64	LAKEHURST
LAKEHURST	Sauer, R.	Mar 69	
MARINE BARRACKS, LAKEHURST	Weir, LCpl B.	Dec 72	
LAS VEGAS LIBERTY	Bartlett, MSgt T.	Nov 69	
LOS ANGELES Long Beach and LA duty	Bowen, B.	Feb 67	
MARE ISLAND Guard Duty	Freeman, H.	Oct 67	
MC ALESTER Naval Ammunition Depot in Oklahoma	Martin, B.	Nov 68	
MEMPHIS Marines at Naval Air Center	Freeman, H.	Jun 67	
MEXICO CITY Embassy duty	Tyler, GySgt C.	Jan 63	
MARQUETTE UNIVERSITY Milwaukee duty	Coffman, R.	Jan 64	
MOFFET FIELD	Elliott, GySgt J.	Oct 71	

MOLOKAI	MOLOKAI FIVE On remote island in Pacific	Kester, SSgt C.	Jun 63
	THE MOLOKAI FOUR Marine Training Facility	Elliott, GySgt J.	Oct 71
	NAPLES, ITALY Security for Navy facilities	Jones, M.	Mar 64
	NEW LONDON Duty at Navy sub base	Bartlett, T.	Jun 71
	DEDICATION: MC CUTCHEON FIELD MCAS, Helicopter	Evans, GySgt E.	Sep 72
NEW RIVER	NEW RIVER MCAS	Bartlett, MSgt T.	Sep 70
	MCAS NEW RIVER	Freeman, H.	May 67
	NEWPORT, R.I. Naval Base security duty	Bartlett, T.	Jul 71
NORFOLK	HEADQUARTERS FMF LANT		Feb 70
	NORFOLK	Richardson, GySgt H.	Jun 69
OKINAWA	CAMP BUTLER Kawasaki Base for support	Berger, P.	Jun 65
	BEST KEPT SECRET MAG-16 duty at Futema	Berger, P.	Dec 64
	OSLO Embassy duty in Norway	Bartlett, T.	Jun 66
PANAMA	MARINE BARRACKS, PANAMA	Wolf, Sgt R.	May 70
	U.S. EMBASSY, PANAMA	Thompson, SSgt P.	Aug 70
	PARRIS ISLAND	Jones, GySgt M.	Jul 63
	NAVAL AIR TEST CENTER, PATUXENT RIVER Maryland duty for Marines	Elliott, SSgt J.	Apr 71
PHILADELPHIA	NEW HALL Marine Corps Museum	Bowen, B.	Dec 65

Subject	Author	Date	Section
MARINE BARRACKS, PHILADELPHIA Naval Base security duty	Bowen, B.	Dec 65	
PHILADELPHIA	Brooks, LCpl J.	Sep 69	
ROTA Duty in Spain	Hall, H.	Feb 65	
PORT OF SPAIN Trinidad duty	Kester, C.	Jun 64	
PORTSMOUTH Marines at Naval Ship Yard	Thompson, SSgt P.	Dec 69	PORTSMOUTH
HISTORY AND GILLIGAN Cpl J. Gilligan follows 200-year tradition as gate sentry at Portsmouth	Bartlett, T.	Nov 72	
CAMP GARCIA, VIEQUES	Jones, GySgt M.	Apr 63	PUERTO RICO
CAMP GARCIA, VIEQUES	Butchart, Maj E.	Sep 71	
GHOST ON POST Roosevelt Roads tradition	Bartlett, T.	Aug 72	
ROOSEVELT ROADS U.S. Air Station duty	Kester, C.	May 64	
ROOSEVELT ROADS	Paynter, J.	Dec 67	
SAN JUAN	Bartlett, GySgt T.	Aug 69	
SAN JUAN	Hall, H.	Aug 66	
SAN JUAN GETS SHORT Base to close Jun 73	Bartlett, T.	Jul 72	
SAN JUAN LIBERTY	Bartlett, GySgt T.	Jun 69	
MCAS-QUANTICO	Jordan, GySgt C.	Mar 63	QUANTICO
QUANTICO	Jordan, GySgt C.	Jun 63	
QUANTICO	Richardson, H.	Jun 68	

	QUANTICO'S EAGER BEAVERS Conservation program	Bartlett, GySgt T.	Aug 71
	TURNER FIELD Corps' smallest Air Station	Martin, J.	Nov 67
	MB SAN DIEGO	Gnatzig, Sgt B.	Mar 71
	A LIVING MEMORIAL Marine Memorial Club in San Francisco	Bartlett, MSgt T.	Jan 71
SANTA ANA	CLOUDS IN THE HANGERS They are so big	Gnatzig, Sgt B.	Dec 70
	SANTA ANA	Bartlett, T.	Jul 65
SEAGOING	CANOPUS MARINES Submarine Tender duty	Evans, GySgt E.	May 70
	DAY ON . . . STAY ON! USS JFK Marine Detachment	Bartlett, MSgt T.	Oct 70
	USS AMERICA Attack Aircraft Carrier duty	Bowen, B.	Oct 65
	USS NEWPORT NEWS	Woltner, R.	Mar 67
	TWENTYNINE PALMS Artillery training schools	Martin, J.	Dec 68
WASHINGTON	CANDLELIGHT SUPPER Marine Barracks fancy dinner	McGowan, GySgt A.	May 63
	D.C. LIBERTY	Hull, LCpl D.	Sep 63
	FRIENDLY INVASION Marines and Canadians from Ft. Henry have rivalry	Hull, D.	Nov 64
	HENDERSON HALL Permanent residence for HQMC personnel	Sauer, Cpl R.	Jul 69
	HOME OF THE CORPS Marine Barracks history	Bowen, B.	Nov 66
	HQMC	Bartlett, GySgt T.	Jul 69
	MD, NAVAL SECURITY STATION Marines at Security Station	Beardsley, F.	Jan 66

OLDEST POST Eighth and "Eye"	Brown, LCpl J.	Jul 69	
SSMA CLUB Soldiers, Sailors, Marines, Airmen's Club	Ostrander, SSgt D.	Dec 72	
WASHINGTON: THE MONKS AT EIGHTH AND EYE	*Time*	Aug 9, 1971	
WHIDBEY ISLAND Naval Air Station	Evans, GySgt E.	Apr 70	**WHIDBEY ISLAND**
WHIDBEY ISLAND	Hall, H.	Aug 64	
PASSWORD, SECURITY Naval Weapons Station, Yorktown	Berkowitz, Sgt H.	Jan 71	

RESEARCH AND DEVELOPMENT

From the R and D Column of the *Gazette:*

BATTLEFIELD ILLUMINATION	Ogden, B.	Nov 68	**GENERAL**
CARGO TRANSFER SYSTEM HIGH LINES SHIP-TO-SHORE		Aug 68	
COMPUTER-BUILT TEST MODELS		Dec 67	
COMPUTERS IN MAP MAKING	Martz, J.	Jan 67	
CORPS R AND D BUDGET $14 MILLION PLUS		May 67	
DLSC PREVIEWS FUTURE AUTOMATED LOGISTICS PROGRAM		Feb 67	
FY'66 R AND D BUDGET		Jun 65	
HIGH SPEED PICK-UP VIA AERIAL LADDER		Oct 68	
MINIWEIGHT TAC		Aug 67	
"REPRO HELIHUT"	Kearney, F.	Feb 68	
SCIENCE AND THE SOLDIER		Sep 67	
SCOAP: A NEW TECHNIQUE	Alexander, J.	Jun 68	
STILL HOLD SAND, THOUGH		Feb 67	

GEAR	FIL-A-MATIC PRESSURE BLASTER		Aug 68
	FLOATING ARMORED VEST		Oct 68
	WATER-PROOFING FIELD MAPS	Kearney, F.	Dec 67
VEHICLES	AAFS TANK FARMS EXPANDED		Dec 67
	AMBUSH BUSTER PROTECTS CONVOYS	Peterkin, F.	Dec 68
	BRUTE	High, J.	Jul 63
	LVTPX-12 ACCEPTED New Amtrac	Alexander, J.	Nov 67
	LVTPX-12 TEST PROGRAM: A PROGRESS REPORT Testing a new Amtrac	Alexander, J.	Feb 69
	MULTI-FUEL ENGINES From peanut butter oil to gasoline	Kavakich, N.	Mar 64
WEAPONS	BATTLEFIELD MISSILE		Jan 65
	ELECTRONIC KENTUCKY WINDAGE		Feb 65
	GRENADE LAUNCHER FOR RIFLE AND SMG		Oct 68
	LIGHTWEIGHT TANK WOULD SUIT CORPS	Kidwell, B.	Feb 67
	NIGHT SIGHTS	Elsenson, H.	Feb 67
	PORTABLE FLAME THROWER		Oct 65
	REPORT OF STONER-63 Rifle grenade	Weller, J.	Mar 64
	ROCKETS RED GLARE		Jan 65
	STONER-63 RIFLE GRENADE		Feb 66
	30MM GATLING GUN		Aug 67
	VPI SPARES RIFLE ROT		Aug 67

RESERVE

From the *Gazette*, unless otherwise indicated:

GENERAL	ACTIVE INACTIVE RESERVES	Van Stockum, R.	Apr 63

ACTIVE PARTICIPATION IN RESERVE	Stewart, J.	Jul 64
ANNUAL FIELD TRAINING	Van Stockum, R.	Oct 63
APPRAISAL OF DIV/WING TEAM 4TH MAR DIV and 4TH MAW	Van Stockum, R.	Sep 63
CAREPAY	Wright, J.	Sep 68
DIRECTOR CALLS FOR MORE TRAINING	Van Stockum, R.	Feb 63
DIVISION OF RESERVE Where all Reserve planning, projects, programs and procedures originate	Hall, H. *Leatherneck*	Mar 65
FIFTY YEARS READY	Meid, P.	Aug 66
FOURTH MARINE AIR WING	Paynter, J. *Leatherneck*	May 68
I-I: ANOTHER LOOK	Tribe, S.	Sep 64
I-I TRAINING	Hergert, J.	May 65
INSPECTION TRIP OF MIDWEST RESERVES	Van Stockum, R.	Jul 63
LETTER TO A RESERVE UNIT CO	Fennessy, M.	Sep 63
THE MARINE CORPS COMMUNITY TEAM Activities of the enlightened Reserve unit	Weh, Capt A.	Oct 72
MARINE CORPS RESERVE	Stevens, G. *Proceedings*	Nov 65
THE MARINE CORPS RESERVE Joining the Reserve starts at the final reenlistment interview	Pearsall, GySgt F.	Oct 72
MARINES IN AEROSPACE Reserves whose jobs are in Aerospace	O'Brien, C. *Leatherneck*	May 64
MCR TRAINING FACILITIES		Sep 65
MOBILIZATION AND MARINES	Donahoe, J.	Dec 67, Jan, Feb 68

MOBILIZATION AND PERT	Oppenheimer, H., and C. Green	Jun 68
NO ROOM AT TOP FOR EVERYONE There is only one Commandant	Van Stockum, R.	May 63
NO SUCH THING AS EX-MARINE Former Marines, maybe	Van Stockum, R.	Mar 63
PRAISE FOR A FINE PRODUCT		Jul 68
A READY RESERVE FOR THE 70'S	Donald, Maj W.	Oct 65
REPMIS	Drake, C.	Mar 68
RESERVE CENTER Pendleton unit whose job would be handling call-up of Reserve if it were needed. 4TH MAR DIV headquarters nucleus	Bowen, B. *Leatherneck*	Jan 67
RESERVE LIAISON Reserve Liaison Unit prepares schedule for Annual Field Training	Hall, Sgt H. *Leatherneck*	Oct 63
RESERVE REPORT A column which appears every month	Stewart, J.	Jan 65
RESERVE RETENTION VS. READINESS	Ayers, Capt G.	Jun 71
RESERVE TRAINING COURSES	Van Stockum, R.	Dec 63
RESERVES NEED YOUNG BLOOD	Van Stockum, R.	Aug 63
THE RESERVES WEAKEST LINK	Reilly, G.	Jul 68
SUMMER TRAINING	Van Stockum, R.	Jun 63
WE AND THE PEOPLE	Smith, R.	Apr 66
WHY A RESERVIST	Lucey, P.	Nov 66
THE WORD ON RESERVE Interview with BGen Widdecke, Director of Reserve	Bowen, SSgt B. *Leatherneck*	Jul 69

RESERVE-EXERCISES

AIR RESERVE SUMMER TRAINING	Van Stockum, R. *Gazette*	Nov 63	AIR
. . . AND IN THE AIR	Engelman, M. *Gazette*	Aug 66	
OPERATION BEAT TEMPO: AIR Marine reserve exercise, summer '69	Armbruster, Maj R. *Gazette*	Feb 70	
OPERATION COPPERHEAD Training at Twentynine Palms, for East Coast Marines	Kreigel, R. *Gazette*	Sep 64	1964
EAST: COPPERHEAD—WEST: SIROCCO Combined Air/Ground Reserve Training Exercise during summer of 1964	Hall, H. *Leatherneck*	Nov 64	
OPERATION SAND POINT Seattle's 1st Landing Support Co., 4th Service Bn., and 23d Rifle Co., stage land, sea and air operation.	Hall, H. *Leatherneck*	Jun 64	
OPERATION FORTNIGHT Reserve exercise at Lejeune for 4,000 Marines	Freeman, H. *Leatherneck*	Oct 66	1966
OPERATION BELL BANGER Phiblex 2-68 Reserve Training at Pendleton	O'Leary, J. *Leatherneck*	Oct 68	1968
RESMEBLEX '69 Counter-insurgency exercise in North Carolina for 4TH MAR DIV WING	O'Leary, J. *Leatherneck*	Nov 69	1969
OPERATION BEAT TEMPO: GROUND Summer '69 reserve training	Pearman, LtCol W. *Leatherneck*	Jul 70	
BUILDERS IN RESERVE 6th Engineer Bn., Force Troops, FMF, training at Gulfport Seabee Training Center	Gnatzig, Cpl B. *Leatherneck*	Jul 70	1970

	HIGH DESERT '70 reserve training	O'Leary, J. *Leatherneck*	Jan 71
1971	OPERATION BUCKEYE Ohio reservists train near Cadiz, Ohio	Evans, E. *Leatherneck*	Aug 71

RESERVE-UNITS

All Reserve Reports in this section are from *Leatherneck:*

	ATLANTA 4th Maintenance Bn	Jones, GySgt M.	Aug 63
	AUGUSTA 6th Motor Transport Maintenance Co	Frye, J.	Aug 64
	AUSTIN "B" Co., 1/23	Thompson, P.	Dec 68
BALTIMORE	BALTIMORE 4th Engineer Bn	Paynter, J.	Aug 67
	WHERE IT'S AT 4th Engineer Bn	Bartlett, MSgt T.	Apr 71
	BELLINGHAM Training in the cold in northwest Washington state	Hall, H.	Jul 64
	FROST CALL AT BEAR TOOTH 58th Rifle Co., Billings, Mont	Woods, Sgt D.	Dec 71
	BOSTON "H" & "S," "A" Co., 1/25, 2d Staff Group	Martin, B.	Feb 67
	BROOKLYN 4th Communications Bn	Stibbens, S.	Feb 66
	CAMDEN 68th Rifle Co	Berger, P.	May 64
	CHARLOTTE 5th Truck Co	Frye, J.	Dec 64
	CHARLOTTESVILLE Albemarle County unit	Hall, Sgt H.	Apr 63
	CHICAGO 2/24	Hall, Sgt H.	Sep 63

CINCINNATI 4th Communications Co	Noyes, Sgt C.	Sep 69	
COLUMBIA 89th Rifle Co	Frye, J.	Jun 64	
COLUMBUS 3/25	Hall, H.	Nov 66	
BRIDGE RECON Corpus Christi	Elliott, SSgt J.	Aug 70	
CUMBERLAND 43rd Rifle Co. in Maryland	Bradshow, LCpl J.	Mar 63	
DALLAS	Tyler, GySgt C.	Oct 63	DALLAS
DALLAS MAG-41, Naval Air Station	Ward, W.	May 67	
DELAWARE DINGERS "D" Co., 6th Motor Transport Bn., Wilmington	Elliott, J.	Jul 71	
DENVER Marine Air Control Squadron 23	Martin, B.	Jul 68	DENVER
DENVER'S BIG GUNS	Weir, Cpl B.	Jul 72	
DOVER "G" Co., 2/25, New Jersey	Sauer, R.	Feb 69	
EL PASO	Thompson, SSgt P.	Mar 70	
FOLSOM "C" Co., 13th Infantry Bn., FMF, Folsom, Pa.	Bowen, B.	Dec 65	
FORT SCHUYLER New York reservists	Cushman, SSgt G.	Jul 63	
FREEMANSBURG 7th Comm Co., Allentown, Pa	Jones, M.	Oct 64	
READY TO GO . . . "H" & "S" Co., 2/25, Garden City, NY	Evans, GySgt E.	Mar 71	
GARY "A" Co., 6th Engineer Bn.	Martin, J.	Jan 68	
GLENVIEW RESERVISTS	Weir, Cpl B.	May 72	GLENVIEW

HOME OF THE 4TH WING	Weir, Cpl B.	Jun 72
GREENSBORO	Elliott, SSgt J.	May 70
GULFPORT	Bowen, SSgt B.	Jun 69
HOOSIER RESERVISTS Comm Supp Co., 12th Comm Bn., Indianapolis	Martin, J.	Mar 68
ARTILLERY SHOOT 155mm Art Batt, Joliet	Giles, Cpl J.	Dec 69
LAWRENCE 3d Ordnance Field Maintenance Co., Lawrence, Mass.	Bartlett, T.	Jul 66
LEHIGH VALLEY Freemansburg, Pa., Comm Co.	Schuon, M.	Jan 64
LIMA'S LOYAL 6th Ordnance Field Maintenance Co., Lima, Ohio	Bartlett, MSgt T.	Sep 71
LINCOLN Nebraska Reservists	Bartlett, MSgt T.	Oct 69
LITTLE CREEK Supply Battalion, 4th Force Service Regiment. The only Bulk Fuel outfit in the Reserve	Bowen, B.	Sep 66
LONG BEACH 3rd ANGLICO	Bowen, B.	Jan 67
LOS ALAMITOS Aviation units at NAS	Hall, H.	Jan 66
LOS ANGELES	Jones, GySgt M.	Jan 63
LYNCHBURG	Gnatzig, Cpl B.	Jun 70
MEMPHIS 12th Motor Transport Bn	Freeman, H.	Jun 67
MEMPHIS AIR RESERVISTS Five Air Reserve Units train at Memphis NAS	Freeman, H.	Sep 67

MIAMI ANGLICO outfits of Miami (2)	Jones, M.	Feb 65	
MOBILE 3d Force Reconnaissance Co	Stibbens, S.	Jun 65	
MONTGOMERY 38th Rifle Co	Paynter, J.	Feb 68	MONTGOMERY
WHAT'S COOKIN' IN MONTGOMERY? Food Service Operations unit		Dec 72	
NASHVILLE 3d Rifle Co	Ward, W.	Dec 66	
NEW CASTLE Service Co., Hdq Bn	Wolf, R.	Jun 71	
NEW ROCHELLE	Evans, GySgt E.	Feb 71	
NORFOLK VMA-233	Bowen, B.	Oct 65	
OAHU 6th Force Recon Co	Kester, SSgt C.	Jun 63	
OLATHE AIR VMF-113 and VMF-215	Stibbens, S.	Sep 64	
OREGON 12th Engineer Bn., Portland	Freeman, H.	Oct 67	
PHILADELPHIA 3d Bn., 14th Marines	Brown, J.	Apr 69	
PHOENIX 9th Engineer Co	Martin, J.	Nov 68	
PITTSBURGH 4th Military Police Bn	Richardson, H.	Jun 68	
RALEIGH 4th 155mm Howitzer Battery	Sarokin, P.	May 65	
RENO MCAS, Yuma	Bartlett, T.	Aug 65	
RICHMOND 1st and 8th 105mm Howitzer Batteries	Stibbens, S.	Apr 65	

	Title	Author	Date
	ROCHESTER Radio Relay and Construction Co., 12th Comm Bn.	Bartlett, T.	Apr 67
	SAN ANTONIO 4th Recon Bn	Ward, W.	Apr 66
SAN FRANCISCO	HIGH SIERRA Reserves help underprivileged kids	Evans, GySgt E.	Dec 70
	OFF THE STREETS San Fran Reserves help kids	Evans, GySgt E.	Nov 70
	RESERVISTS VTU 1-11 Intelligence unit with parachute capabilities	Bowen, B.	Sep 65
	SANTA MONICA	Lewis, J.	Feb 63
	SAVANNAH 5th Rifle Co.	Frye, J.	Apr 64
	SEATTLE 4th Shore Party Bn	Evans, GySgt E.	Feb 70
	2D BN., 25TH MARINES Reserve units in Battalion	Hall, H.	Feb 64
	SOUTH WEYMOUTH Near Boston Reserves	Jordan, C.	Dec 63
	SPRINGFIELD, MO.	Thompson, SSgt P.	May 69
	SYRACUSE 4th Tank Bn	Berger, P.	Jun 66
	EVERGREEN RESERVISTS 4th Medical Bn, Tacoma	Martin, J.	Apr 68
	FLOAT AND STOMP 4th Amphib Tractor Bn, Tampa	Wolf, R.	Nov 72
	TUCSON 12th Engineer Co	Martin, J.	Jan 69
	TULSA 1st Truck Co	Martin, B.	Aug 68
WASHINGTON	EVERGREEN State of Washington Reserves	McEwen, R.	Jan 65

D.C. RESERVISTS 4th Supply Co., 4th Service Bn	Sauer, R.	May 69	**WASHINGTON D.C.**
WASHINGTON AIR RESERVISTS Summer training at Beaufort, S. C., and Roosevelt Roads	Paynter, J.	Dec 67	
WEST PALM BEACH "C" Co., 4th Amphibian Tractor	Richardson, H.	Sep 68	
WILLOW GROVE Pa.	Jordan, GySgt C.	May 63	**WILLOW GROVE**
WILLOW GROVE Five Marine Air Reserve squadrons at NAS there	Stibbens, S.	May 66	
WILMINGTON "B" Co., 13th Infantry Bn	Martin, B.	Mar 67	
WYOMING, PA. RESERVISTS Wing Equipment Repair Squadron 47-Motor Transport Repair	Bartlett, MSgt T.	Oct 71	
YOUNGSTOWN		Mar 66	

SPORTS

All articles in this section are from *Leatherneck*, unless otherwise specified:

RALLYE Quantico Car Club road events	Grigaliunas, B.	Dec 63	**GENERAL**
TOPS IN SNEAKERS Boxing, basketball, weight lifting	Bartlett, T.	Apr 70	
WHITE DIAMOND Helping Indians in Phoenix	Bartlett, T.	Jul 70	
WORTH THE EFFORT Overview of the Corps' sports program	Gnatzig, Sgt B.	Jan 71	
ALL-MARINE BASKETBALL Quantico wins again	Cushman, GySgt G.	May 63	**BASKETBALL**

	LEATHERNECK'S ALL-MARINE BASKETBALL TEAMS Players from San Diego and Hawaii dominate	Hull, D.	May 64
	ALL-MARINE BASKETBALL Finals at Quantico	Bowen, B.	May 65
	LEATHERNECK ALL-MARINE BASKETBALL SELECTIONS		May 65
BOXING	ALL-MARINE BOXING Pendleton wins title	Cushman, GySgt G.	Jun 63
	CHAMPIONSHIP BOXING Marine boxers stage upset in inter-service bouts	Hull, D.	Aug 64
	INTERSERVICE BOXING	Richardson, H.	Nov 68
FOOTBALL	ALL-MARINE FOOTBALL TEAM	Hull, D.	Feb 64
	LEATHERNECK'S ALL-MARINE FOOTBALL TEAM	Hull, D.	Feb 65
	FOOTBALL-OLE San Diego plays Mexico	Tyler, GySgt C.	Feb 63
	FOOTBALL WRAP-UP Quantico's 1966 team	Bowen, B.	Feb 67
	JR ROTC CHURCHLAND HIGH High School football team visits Marines	Thompson, SSgt P.	Dec 69
HUNTING	PHEASANT HUNT In Korea on R & R	Wisniewski, GySgt D.	Apr 72
	WHEELCHAIR SAFARI Fifteen amputees go hunting	Berkowitz, Sgt H.	Jan 71
SKYDIVING	SKYDIVING Off-duty Marines do it	Weir, PFC B.	Oct 71
TRACK	BOSTON MARATHON Two Marines among the top thirty finishers	Cushman, GySgt G.	Jun 63
	CISM International Armed Forces Track and Field Meets	Cushman, GySgt G.	Mar 63

QUANTICO RELAYS Sixteen records broken	Cushman, SSgt G.	Jul 63
QUANTICO RELAYS Results, records set, etc.	Hull, D.	Jul 64
QUANTICO RELAYS	Bowen, B.	Jul 65
QUANTICO RELAYS	Bowen, B.	Jul 66
QUANTICO RELAYS	Paynter, J.	Aug 67
QUANTICO RELAYS 12th Annual competition	Richardson, H .	Jul 68
THESE LEATHERNECKS HAD FEET TO MATCH Two Marines in Boston marathon	Wallace, R. *Life*	Feb 22, 1963
TOKYO GOLD RUSH Seven Marines in Tokyo Olympics win total of one gold and two bronze medals	Berger, P.	Jan 65

STRATEGY

From the *Gazette,* unless otherwise specified:

AT SEA—WHERE WE BELONG	McFarlane, Maj R. *Proceedings*	Nov 71
BY FORCIBLE ENTRY Amphibious strategy	Soper, Col J.	Aug 72
CHEMICAL WARFARE: A BETTER ALTERNATIVE Its more humane than conventional or nuclear weapons	Peterkin, GySgt F.	Oct 72
ENDS AND MEANS How we allocate our national priorities	Bunnell, Col C.	Aug 72
ESCALATE At that time, it was most fashionable	Clapp, A.	Sep 66
AN EVALUATION OF STRATEGY	Burke, A.	Dec 64
THE FUSION OF MILITARY AND PRACTICAL CONSIDERATIONS: THREAT OF CHALLENGE	Miles, J.	Aug, Sep 68

HAZARDS OF SEABASE	Ludwig, Col V.	Feb 72
LOW LEVEL WARFARE: WHAT RULE FOR THE NAVY?	Reese, H.	Aug 71
THE MALADY OF RESISTANCE TO CHANGE Get the old ideas out of the military	Wolk, Maj C.	Dec 71
MARINE CORPS OF 1973	Saxten, J., and L. Ditta *Proceedings*	Jan 63
MARINE CORPS POLICIES IN COUNTERINSURGENCY	MacDonald, S. *Data*	Dec 64
A MARINE'S VIEW OF THE AMPHIBIOUS ASSAULT FORCES	Soper, LtCol J. *Naval Review*	1966
THE MILITARY-INDUSTRIAL COMPLEX IN PERSPECTIVE	Wolk, Maj C.	Aug 71
MOBILE SEABASE CONCEPT, 1973-1975	Goggin, Col W. and Capt R. Camp	Oct 70
NAVY SEEKS STRATEGIC, LIMITED WAR GAIN Role of Corps in 1972 explained	Brown, D. *Aviation Week*	Jan 31, 1972
THE NEED FOR SEABORNE FORCES	Schofield, B.	Feb 63
THE NEW CONFLICT Nam strategy	Mans, R.	Oct 68
THE NEW WAR Nam strategy by Lejeune Forum		Jan 65
THE PENINSULA OF SOUTHEAST ASIA Counterinsurgency strategy	Croizat, V.	Oct 64
ROLES AND MISSIONS: TIME FOR A CHANGE Amphibious mission is too limiting to the Corps	Webb, Capt J.	Mar 72
ROLES AND MISSIONS: A TRADITIONAL VIEW Wedded to the Navy, the Corps is, of necessity, amphibious	Moore, Col M., and LtCol A. Croft	Jun 72

RUSSIA IN THE MED Expansionist policies of USSR	Gervasi, F.	Dec 71
SEABASE: THE TRUE AMPHIBIOUS OPERATION	Hammond, LtCol J.	Aug 71
SHOOTING SITTING DUCKS	Kipp, G.	Aug 63
A STATEMENT OF DOCTRINE	Anderson, N.	Nov 63
THOUGHTS ON DOCTRINE	Greenwood, J.	Nov 63
TRENDS IN THE USE OF THE SEA	Nitze, P.	Mar 65
U. S. FLOATING DETERRENT		Jul 66

SUPPORTING ARMS

Articles in this section are from the *Gazette* unless otherwise specified:

GENERAL

FIRE SUPPORT COORDINATION FOR INFANTRY BATTALIONS	Solazzo, V.	Apr 68
FSC: COORDINATION, CONTROL OR CONFUSION	Wilson, P.	Dec 67
FSC: TERMS AND TECHNIQUES	Wilson, P.	Jul 68
LAST WORDS IN FIRE COORDINATION	Thomas, W.	Jan 67
LIAISON: THE MISSING LINK	Barnard, W.	Sep 68

ARTILLERY

AMPHIBIAN ARTILLERY ADVANTAGES	Love, Maj J., and Maj J. Rowley	May 63
ARTILLERY AMBUSH	Love, Maj J .	Jul 68
ARTILLERY QUIZ	Wilson, LtCol P.	Dec 66
CIRCLE FIRE SUPPORT	Stewart, J.	Aug 64
FAT CATS	Parry, F.	Jan 64
FIRE THE BARRAGE	Goodson, J.	Mar 64
FIRE FOR EFFECT	Henley, R.	July 65
FIRE MISSION	Stanaro, C.	Sep 64
HERE'S THE HOWTAR The howitzer and mortar marry, but their child is a bastard	Harris, J.	Jun 63

	Title	Author	Date
	LONG RANGE TARGET FIX		Aug 67
	MARINE ARTILLERYMEN SOUND OFF	Love, J.	Feb 67
	RADARS FOR THE ARTILLERYMAN	Schneider, Lt C.	Mar 70
	ROCKET ARTILLERY: A NEW CHALLENGE	Love, J.	Jul 64
	SPEED UP YOUR ARTILLERY	McCaffree, R.	Jul 63
	TO BORESIGHT ARTILLERY	Healy, A.	Sep 63
	WHY NOT AMPHIBIOUS ARTILLERY?	Dawson, C.	Jul 65
CLOSE AIR SUPPORT	AIR/GROUND COORDINATION	Steinkraus, Col R.	May 66
	AIR SUPPORT FOR AMPHIBIOUS OPERATIONS Review of MAW activities including CAS	Gillum, LtCol D., and Maj R. Foster	May 69
	ALL-WEATHER CAS: FACT OR FANCY More fancy than fact now since the A-6A does not perform. It's still a dream	Bateman, Maj K.	Jun 72
	CLOSE AIR SUPPORT	Bowen, Sgt B. *Leatherneck*	May 67
	CLOSE AIR SUPPORT: HOW IT WORKS TODAY	Scholin, LtCol A. ANG *National Guardsman*	Mar 67
	THE HIGH PRICE OF AIR CONTROL Make FAC's enlisted men—not officers	Drago, Maj A.	Mar 64
	LIGHT VMA: A BETTER ANSWER What it takes to make a CAS aircraft	Verdi, Maj J.	Feb 64
	THE L2VMA LIGHT CAS NEEDS BOONDOCKERS	Beckett, Maj W.	Mar 63

MARINE AVIATION—IT PROVIDES AIR SUPPORT FOR THE CORPS GROUND FORCES	*Navy*	Jun 64
OUR GROWING CAS GAP	Beckett, Maj W.	Apr 64
TO IDENTIFY CAS TARGETS	Garcia, C.	Jun 63

NAVAL GUNFIRE

THE GUN GAP AND HOW TO CLOSE IT Use gunfire support ships	Heinl, Col R. *Proceedings*	Sep 65
NAVAL GUNFIRE TODAY AND TOMORROW Need for landing fire support ships	Soper, LtCol J. *Proceedings*	Sep 66
NAVAL WEAPONS TODAY Number of gun barrels available in 1965 compared with 1945	Leunen, Capt P., USN *Naval Review*	1965
NAVY "GUN GAP" WORRIES MARINES Quote from then Commandant Greene	Greene, Gen W. *Proceedings*	Dec 64
PROPOSAL WEIGHED TO BRING BACK IOWA-CLASS BATTLESHIPS For Naval Gunfire Support	*Proceedings*	Feb 63

TACTICS

From the *Gazette,* unless otherwise specified:

AMBUSCADE	Mack, R.	Apr 67
THE ARMORED PITCHFORK	Bess, L.	Jul 67
ATTACK BY NIGHT	Hargreaves, R.	Oct 63
CAN WE DIG IN?	Strandberg, C.	Jun 63
A CASE FOR THE RUSE	Mack, R.	Apr 68
THE CHANGING BATTLEFIELD	Tubley, G.	May 65
COMBAT IN CAVES	Illes, S.	Jul 66
COMBINED OPERATIONS Working with Allies	Anderson, LtCol A.	Oct 71

Title	Author	Date
A COMPREHENSIVE VIEW OF TERRAIN	Mack, R.	Oct 68
COUNTERMEASURES AGAINST MINES AND BOOBYTRAPS	Greene, Maj W.	Dec 69
DEFENDING THE DIVISION REAR	Cooper, Maj M.	Sep 70
DIVISION RECON IN EUROPE Exercise in tactics	MacCaskill, Capt D.	Jul 72
DOES THE FIRE TEAM NEED REORGANIZING?	Morrow, R.	Feb 69
EMPLOYING THE RECON PATROL	Davis, MajGen R., and Lt J. Jones	May 69
THE FINAL PROTECTIVE LINE Machine gun in the defense	Mayer, H.	Dec 71
FIRE SUPPORT IN RIVERINE OPERATIONS	Simpson, LtCol T., and Capt D. LaBoissiere	Aug 69
FROM A COMPANY COMMANDER'S NOTEBOOK	Miller, J.	Aug 66
GAS ATTACK	Olney, H.	May 64
GROUND SURVEILLANCE 3D MAR DIV develops new tactics from Nam	Thompson, SSgt P. *Leatherneck*	Oct 69
INFANTRY BATTALION MEMO	Dean, C.	Mar 67
MARINE CORPS TACTICAL DATA SYSTEM	Vitali, H.	Aug 63
MARINE CORPS TRANSPLACEMENT Experiment of replacement of units as large as a battalion	Dunnagan, C. *Proceedings*	Sept 65
MARINE PATROL	Bendell, L.	Nov 68
MARINE TACTICAL COMMAND AND CONTROL SYSTEM	Owens, R.	Oct 68
MARINE TACTICS 1970	Kyle, BGen W. *Ordnance*	Sept, Oct 65

Title	Author	Date
MARINES AND CRISIS CONTROL Marines as counterinsurgency force in the 1960's	Simmons, Col E. *Proceedings*	Nov 65
MARINES VS. MOBS	Wyatt, R.	Dec 64
NO GAME	Musgrove, E.	Aug 65
ON BRIDGE DEMOLITION	Cassedy, L.	Mar 64
PROGRESS AND PREP FIRES	Allgood, F.	Sep 67
PROPER PATROLLING	Merrill, A.	Jun 68
PROPOSAL	Henderson, D.	Jun 67
RECON'S BIKINI Six month test of Lightweight Battlefield Surveillance System	Martin, B.	Jun 67
THE ROLE OF INFANTRY	Waldrop, LtCol F.	Feb 66
SHADOWS IN THE NIGHT Psychological warfare	Stanford, N.	Feb 63
SMALL UNIT OPERATIONS: FMFM-21 New Field Manual		Feb 63
SMOKE FOR THE LANDING FORCE	Miller, W.	Jun 63
SUPPORT BY THE TON It's important (support), but the guy with the rifle wins the battles	Hall, Sgt H. *Leatherneck*	Mar 63
TACTICAL FLEXIBLITY	Wheeler, Col E.	Apr 66
THE THREAD OF A CONCEPT Tactical Air Medical Evacuation	Brady, Col E.	May 71
TRANSPLACEMENT TREMORS	Sexton, N.	Sep 63
TRIANGULAR AMBUSH	Rogers, L.	Mar 65
UNDERSTANDING EOD Demolitions	Curry, J.	Oct 65
THE UNKNOWN EFFECT Psychological warfare	Whitesell, R.	Feb 64
USE INFANTRY FOR RAIDS Not Raiders		Sep 65

THE VERTICAL ASSAULT: ITS PRESENT AND FUTURE	Cushman, MajGen R. *Naval Review*	1964
WHAT IS A RIVER? A problem, or an opportunity	Zimolzak, F.	Jun 66
WHAT'S NEW . . .? Keep up-to-date and win	Jordan, GySgt C. *Leatherneck*	Sep 63

TRAINING

All articles from the *Gazette,* unless otherwise specified:

GENERAL

AN EDUCATIONAL CRISIS It's time to employ a pragmatic approach to training	Reynolds, MSgt R., and GySgt R. Sorensen	Dec 71
ASSIGNMENT: STUDY	Bell, J., and S. Wilson	Mar 69
THE BEST KIND OF WAR FMF education and training	Green, F.	Nov 64
BLUEPRINT FOR A BATTALION LIBRARY		Sep 66
BOOKS FOR PROFESSIONAL MARINES Lejeune Forum	Krulak, V.	Dec 63
CAMPUS SOCIETY IS CORPS ASSET	Newlin, R.	May 67
THE CASE AGAINST PROFESSIONAL ILLITERACY Marines do read!	Smith, LtCol R.	Jan 70
COLLEGE ASSISTANCE Where to go to college and how to receive assistance	Johnson, D. *Leatherneck*	Mar 70
COMBAT READINESS VS. WASTED TIME	Clarke, B.	Feb 63
CREATIVE THINKING	Donnelly, T.	Jun 65
ESSENTIAL SUBJECTS TRAINING A disregard for human values has led to a negative approach to training	Reynolds, MGySgt R., and GySgt R. Sorensen	Jul 72

GMSP: WHAT'S THAT? General Military Subjects Proficiency testing and scoring	Jacobsen, Maj D.	Oct 72
HEAT CASUALTIES CAN BE PREVENTED Just stay out of the sun		Jun 65
HERE WE COME! Replacements receive 12-day refresher course at Pendleton prior to leaving for Nam	Stibbens, S. *Leatherneck*	May 66
INSTRUCTION IS FOR LEARNING	Gamer, P.	May 63
ITV IN THE MARINE CORPS	Gartrell, C.	Mar 69
LEARN HOW TO READ		Oct 65
MARINES AND MOUNTAINS Need for training in mountain war	Kingsley, N.	Mar 72
THE NEED FOR COMBAT SIMULATION	Loehe, LtCol R. *Leatherneck*	Oct 71
"NO MAN'S GHOST" Training is tough so no ghost comes back to haunt trainer	Schaefer, Capt K.	Jan 70
NO TIME FOR TRAINING	Miille, R.	Aug 64
ON THE JOB TRAINING	Windham, MSgt A.	Jul 66
ORIENTEERING Map-reading and physical training combined	Weir, LCpl B. *Leatherneck*	Dec 71
ORIENTEERING: SPORT FOR MARINES And a sport that pays off in combat	Lundell, LtCol A., Royal Swedish Army	Jun 71
OVERSEAS DUTY How to prepare for overseas	Wason, G. *Leatherneck*	Sep 64
POSTPAID TRAINING	Walters, Capt W.	Aug 66
PREVENTION OF HEAT CASUALTIES	Clarke, B.	Sep 66

Title	Author / Source	Date
A PROFESSIONAL LIBRARY	Laine, E.	Oct 65
PROJECT TRANSITION "Short timers" take advantage of education and training	Anderberg, D. *Leatherneck*	Dec 68
SCHOOLS BATTALION Consolidation of many schools on one "campus" at Pendleton	Bowen, B. *Leatherneck*	Mar 67
SET YOUR SIGHTS ON HIGHER EDUCATION	Bechtold, C.	Feb 68
THE SOLDIER AND THE PRISONER	Spivey, D., J. Keene and J. MacDonald	May 65
SQUARING AWAY THE POW TAG	O'Brien, R.	Aug 66
SOUNDS OF BATTLE	Wyckoff, D.	Mar 64
SPECIALIST TRAINING FOR THE COMPUTER AGE	DiFrank, J.	Aug 67
TEACHING ISN'T EASY	Ferguson, G.	Sep 64
THEORY, THE FORGOTTEN SUBJECT	Colby, D.	Dec 65
3RD MAR DIV COUNTER-GUERRILLA TRAINING: A READINESS REPORT	Edwards, T.	May 63
TRAINING AIDS LIBRARY Photo story on how to use it	Wolf, Sgt B. *Leatherneck*	Feb 71
TRAINING HOME AND APPLICATION ABROAD	Grantham, E.	Mar 69
TRAINING STANDARDS	Tiede, Maj H.	Jun 66
USE HISTORY CORRECTLY	Teisaire, C.	Jan 66
VULNERABLE	Cohan, L.	Apr 67
W.O.S.	LaRiviere, Lt S.	Feb 68
XA VIET THANG #1 Training for Nam	McWilliams, Capt J. *Gazette*	Jul 66

From *Leatherneck,* unless otherwise indicated:

Title	Author/Source	Date
ALKALI CANYON DESFEX 1-72 at Twentynine Palms	Smith, Sgt G.	Dec 72
BAT AN EYE DESLEX 1-71—Twentynine Palms firing exercise for 2D MAR DIV	Bartlett, T.	Dec 71
BLUE AX Dec-Jan Air/Ground exercise of 2D MAR DIV at Lejeune	*Gazette*	May 72
CABLE RUN 3 Recon training in Arizona	Kelly, Cpl M.	May 72
DESLEX 1-71	Bartlett, T.	Nov 71
ESCORT LION 2 Training in Riverine ops	Wolf, Sgt R.	Dec 70
EXOTIC DANCER 3 Training ops at Lejeune	Bartlett, MSgt T.	Sep 70
GAMES BUT GRIM: SILVER LANCE EXERCISE BY MARINES Giant Pendleton maneuvers	*Time*	Mar 12, 1965
GOLDEN SLIPPER Amphibious training at Pendleton	O'Leary, J.	Nov 67
GRASSROOTS Guerrilla training at Army Camp Pickett	Bartlett, T.	Dec 64
HARD NOSE Huge maneuver at Pendleton	Bartlett, T.	Jan 65
LONE EAGLE Exercise on Okinawa	Stibbens, S.	Mar 63
A MATTER OF TASTE Cold weather training with NATO troops in Norway	Bartlett, T.	Jul 66

Title	Author / Source	Date
MEDLAN-DEX 5-63 6th Fleet training in Spain	Jones, M.	Mar 64
OBSERVATIONS: STEEL PIKE AND SILVER LANCE	Soper, LtCol J. *Proceedings*	Nov 65
OPERATION BARFROST 66 NATO training exercise in Norway	Meyer, L.	Jan 67
OPERATION SILVER BLADE Republic of China Marines		Jul 63
QUICK KICK 5 Atlantic Command's Joint Service Task Force training at Lejeune	Berger, P.	Jul 64
SHAMROCK Camp Pickett training exercise for 2d Marines	Martin, B.	Jun 67
SILVER LANCE	Beardsley, F.	Jun 65
SILVER LANCE	Robichaud, C. *Gazette*	Jul 65
SNOWY BEACH 2D MAR DIV hits coast of Maine	Martin, GySgt B.	May 72
STEEL PIKE I Amphibious training ops	Hammond, J. *Gazette*	Jan 65
STEEL PIKE I U.S. and Spanish Marines in amphibious training exercise	Hall, H.	Jan 65
SUREFOOT 2d Recon Bn training near Lejeune	Ellis, T.	Jan 65
SWAMPEX '63 4th Marine Brigade training near Cherry Point	Kester, C.	Jan 64
SWAMP-EX 65 Counterinsurgency exercises near Lejeune	*Gazette*	Dec 65

Title	Author / Source	Date	Subject
SWAMP-EX '65		Jan 66	
TO THE END OF THE EARTH Expedition that preceded Deep Freeze	Jones, M. *Gazette*	Nov 68	
WINTER EXPRESS 3/6 in cold weather exercise in Arctic	Bartlett, T.	Jun 66	
BATTLE TARGETS	Downing, J. *Gazette*	Nov 64	**MARKSMAN-SHIP**
"BEFORE I'M THROUGH WITH YOU . . ." Marksmanship training the Marine Corps way	Wolf, Sgt R.	May 71	
BY THE NUMBERS Training in marksmanship at Parris Island	Stibbens, S.	Sep 65	
CAMP PERRY PROBLEM	Weller, J. *Gazette*	Aug 63	
CHARLIE COURSE Realistic targets simulate enemy bodies in various positions	Martin, B.	Jul 67	
COMBAT RANGE New combat rifle range at Pendleton for Nam training	Tyler, C.	Feb 64	
HOW TO PICK UP PISTOL POINTS	Weller, J. *Gazette*	Aug 64	
IS "C" COURSE THE BEST WE CAN DO?	Rice, W. *Gazette*	Dec 66	
MARKSMANSHIP T.U. Competition In Arms Program permits year-round firing	Hall, H.	Apr 64	
MATCH SCORES	Gleason, E. *Gazette*	Aug 64	
MORE THAN QUALIFIED Current marksmanship practices	Bartlett, T.	Jul 72	
QUICK KILL VS. MARKSMANSHIP Quick kill is Army way	Reusse, Maj E. *Gazette*	Dec 69	

	REALISTIC REQUAL Keeping Marines sharp in marksmanship	Zimmerman, E. *Gazette*	Apr 65
	RESERVE SHOOTERS	Van Stockum, R. *Gazette*	Jan 63
	TEAM SHOTS CAN KILL	Hicks, N. *Gazette*	Dec 63
	WHAT'S WITH THE "X"? Combine marksmanship with combat firing and you have the "X" Course	Bowen, B.	Jun 65
	"YOU MAY FIRE IF READY"	Herron, D. *Gazette*	Nov 64
MARKSMANSHIP MATCHES	ALL READY FOR THE FIRING LINE . . . Marine Corps Matches at Quantico	Gnatzig, Sgt B.	Aug 70
	CAMP PERRY: 1963, SPECIAL REPORT	*Gazette*	Nov 63
	EASTERN DIVISION MATCHES Rifle and Pistol Shoot at Lejeune	Haile, D.	Sep 65
	HI-DESERT RIFLE MATCH High Powered Rifle Match, Twentynine Palms	Berger, P.	Jun 65
	INTERSERVICE MATCHES 70	Groscost, SSgt R.	Nov 70
	INTERSERVICE RIFLE MATCH At Quantico again	Reynolds, A.	Nov 64
	INTERSERVICE RIFLE MATCHES Marines won the distance events at Quantico, but Army shooters dominated	Cushman, SSgt G.	Oct 63
	MARINE CORPS RIFLE MATCHES West Division wins both Rifle and Pistol	Weir, Cpl B.	Sep 72
	NATIONAL MATCHES Camp Perry Rifle and Pistol matches	Bowen, B.	Nov 65

Title	Author / Source	Date	Subject
PISTOL MATCH Reserve-sponsored matches in New York	Thompson, SSgt P.	Jul 70	
READY ON THE LEFT . . . Eastern Division Rifle and Pistol Matches at Quantico	Gnatzig, Sgt B.	Aug 70	
READY ON THE RIGHT . . . Western Division Rifle and Pistol Matches, Pendleton	Lewis, J.	Aug 70	
WELL IN AT FIVE At Camp Perry, Ohio	Hull, D.	Dec 64	

TRAINING-SCHOOLS

From *Leatherneck*, unless otherwise specified:

Title	Author / Source	Date	Subject
1,000 . . . 2,000 . . . 3,000 Parachute training for Recon Marines	Jones, MSgt M.	Jul 63	**AIRBORNE**
2,000 . . . 3,000 . . . 4,000	Martin, B.	Sep 68	
AMPHIBIOUS WARFARE SCHOOL	Moss, R. *Gazette*	Nov 67	**AMPHIB WARFARE**
SCHOOL FOR DOCTRINE Amphibious warfare training	Trainor, LtCol B. *Gazette*	Nov 67	
ARTILLERY SCHOOL	Martin, B.	Jul 68	**ARTILLERY**
BOOBY TRAP SCHOOL	*Gazette*	Feb 66	**BOOBY TRAP**
VC TRAIL At Pendleton	Mason, J. *Gazette*	Apr 69	
BOOT CAMP '66 Parris Island and San Diego	Bartlett, T., and W. Ward	Aug 66	**BOOT CAMP**
CONSCIENTIOUS OBJECTOR AT PARRIS ISLAND Shoot him!	Warner, S. *Atlantic*	Jun 72	
CONVERSATION WITH A BREW Yesterday's Boot Camp was tougher than todays, or was it?	Bartlett, T.	Aug 72	
GOING BACK TO BOOT CAMP Fifteen years later	Aurthur, R. *Esquire*	Sep 65	

	Title	Author / Source	Date
	THE MAKING OF A MARINE	MacDonald, S. *Navy*	Sep 65
	MARINE MACHINE Training Marines	Barry, T. *Look*	Aug 12, 1969
	THE MARINE MACHINE Magnificent photos of Parris Island, 1971. This 144 page book comes to the conclusion that Boot Camp is dehumanizing. (So is getting your ass shot off because you aren't trained right!)	Mares, W. Doubleday and Co., Inc	1971 (IP)
	NEW BOOTS	Evans, GySgt E.	Sep 72
	PARRIS ISLAND	Evans, GySgt E.	Dec 69
	PARRIS ISLAND REVISITED	O'Leary, Col J. *Gazette*	Sep 72
	SEE PARRIS AND DIE: BRUTALITY IN THE U.S. MARINES Two fat, middle-aged "reporters" decided to make some money. Writing about brutality in the Corps seemed like a fast way. From their vantage point as "experts" (never having heard a shot fired in anger), they examined Corps training. This outrageously bad book is the result.	Jeffers, H. and O. Levitan Hawthorne Books, Inc.	1971 (IP)
	TO BECOME MARINES . . . Boot Camp '71 style	Gnatzig, Sgt B.	Mar 71
COMMAND	COMMAND U. At Fort Leavenworth	Stibbens, S.	Oct 64
	COMMAND AND STAFF COLLEGE TODAY Landing Force Operation is still the main course of study	Jaskilka, BGen S. *Gazette*	Jun 72
	EDUCATION FOR LEADERSHIP Command and Staff School	Cole, Maj H., USA *Gazette*	Dec 72
	MARINE CORPS COMMAND AND STAFF COLLEGE	Karch, F. *Gazette*	Jun 67

Title	Author	Date	Category
C-E BN Comm-Electronics School at Twentynine Palms	Gnatzig, Sgt B.	Feb 71	COMMUNI-CATIONS
"TOO DAMMED SMART" Comm-Electronics School at San Diego	Ward, W.	Sep 66	
FMSS Field Medical Service School at Pendleton	Szdlik, F.	Sep 69	CORPSMEN
COUNTER GUERRILLA WARFARE CENTER At Lejeune	Martin, B.	Jun 67	COUNTER-GUERRILLA
VIET VILLAGE—MADE IN USA At Pendleton	Hall, H.	Jan 66	
DATA PROCESSING SCHOOL At Fort Benjamin Harrison, Indiana	Martin, J.	Feb 68	DATA PROCESSING
DI SCHOOL	Jones, GySgt M.	Aug 63	DI
DI SCHOOL	Evans, GySgt E.	Jan 70	
FIRST, GET YOUR HEAD FIXED Final part of three-part series	Bartlett, T.	Oct 72	DISABLED MARINES
JUST AN INCONVENIENCE First part	Bartlett, T.	Aug 72	
REACH OUT AND HANG ON Part two	Bartlett, T.	Sep 72	
THE LOADERS At Little Creek	Richardson, GySgt H.	May 69	EMBARKATION
EMBASSY MARINES: PART I At HQMC	Kester, C.	Apr 64	EMBASSY
ENGINEER'S SCHOOL At Lejeune	Thompson, P.	Mar 69	ENGINEERS
GMS SCHOOL General Military Subjects School at Lejeune	Martin, J.	Jun 68	GMS

Subject	Title	Author / Source	Date
	VIETVILLE Viet Village at Albany, Ga.	Paynter, J.	Dec 67
GUERRILLA	GUERRILLA Training 3RD MAR DIV on Okinawa	Berger, P.	Feb 65
HIGH SCHOOL	HIGH SCHOOL, FMF	Traynor, W. *Gazette*	Jun 63
ITR	ITR: BOOT CAMP POST GRAD Infantry Training Regiment at Camp Geiger	Bartlett, T.	Jun 71
	NEW ITR Innovations in infantry training	Hall, H.	Jan 66
	REPORT ON ITR	Asprey, R. *Gazette*	Sep 63
LFTC	THE LANDING FORCE TRAINING COMMAND PAC	Gartrell, C. *Gazette*	Oct 68
LANGUAGE	LANGUAGE SCHOOL Defense Language Institute at Monterey, Calif.	Hall, H.	Aug 64
LFTU	LFTU Amphibious doctrine training	Tyler, GySgt C.	Jul 63
MADCOP	MADCOP MARINES Marine Corps Associate Degree completion program	Elliott, GySgt J.	Jun 72
MCI	MCI Marine Corps Institute founded in 1920	Anderberg, D.	Apr 69
	MARINE CORPS INSTITUTE 50th anniversary review	Noyes, C.	Feb 70
	MCI MARKS ITS 50TH YEAR	Hokkanen, Lt J. *Gazette*	Feb 70
	MCI—WHAT'S IN IT FOR ME? Benefits of the School	Bartlett, T.	Jan 65
	PROFESSIONALISM: NEW MCI COURSES		Sep 71
MINES	MINE WARFARE TRAINING	Kaasmann, Maj B. *Gazette*	Apr 65

Title	Author/Source	Date	Subject
HAWK SCHOOL Marines attend Army Air Defense School, El Paso	Thompson, SSgt P.	Apr 70	MISSLES
MISSILES IN RESERVE Marine Air Reserve Missile Training Detachment at Twentynine Palms	Freeman, H.	Jul 67	
REDEYE Anti-aircraft missile firing at Twentynine Palms	Freeman, H.	Sep 67	
MWTC Mountain Weather Training Center, Bridgeport, Calif	Bartlett, T.	Jun 65	MOUNTAIN WARFARE
FBI TRAINED How FBI trains MP's at Quantico	Weir, LCpl B.	Dec 72	MP'S
FIELD MUSIC SCHOOL At Parris Island, buglers learn	Evans, GySgt E.	Dec 69	MUSIC
WHILE THE BAND PLAYS ON . . . Marines at Naval School of Music, Little Creek	Chavez, Sgt M.	Oct 71	
NAVAL ACADEMY NEEDS MORE MARINE EDUCATORS	Wagner, D. *Gazette*	Jun 66	NAVAL ACADEMY
NAVAL ACADEMY PROGRAM How an enlisted man can get a commission	Bowen, B.	Jul 65	
NCO LEADERSHIP SCHOOL At Quantico	Sauer, R.	Feb 69	NCO
NCO PREP SCHOOL At Pendleton	Tyler, C.	Feb 64	
NCO TRAINING By Corps' SgtMaj	Manion, SgtMaj H. *Gazette*	Dec 69	
STAFF NCO ACADEMY At Quantico	Elliott, J.	Jul 71	
UNITED STATES MARINE CORPS STAFF NON-COMMISSIONED OFFICERS ACADEMY	*Gazette*	May 71	
OFFICER CANDIDATE COURSE	Bowen, B.	Dec 65	OC

Subject	Title	Author/Source	Date
	OCS Officer "boot camp" at Quantico	Thompson, P.	Feb 69
	OCS	Wickwire, Col P. *Gazette*	Dec 71
ORDNANCE	EXPLOSIVE ORDNANCE DISPOSAL SCHOOL	Gnatzig, Sgt B.	Aug 70
PLC	PLC At Quantico	Berger, P.	Oct 65
PT	CIRCUIT TRAINING	*Gazette*	Sep 64
	FIT FOR THE FUTURE New Physical Fitness Program	Hull, D.	Jun 64
	FIT FOR THE FUTURE PE in the Corps	Shoptaw, Maj R. *Gazette*	Feb 70
	PHYSICAL FITNESS ACADEMY 12 week PT instructor course	Wolf, Cpl R.	Oct 69
	PUSH AND PULL	*Gazette*	Jan 63
	THEY'LL NEVER WALK ALONE Pres. Kennedy's Physical Fitness Program	Jordan, GySgt C.	Apr 63
RADAR	TIPSY-32 Training Marines in new radar		Apr 71
RECON	FAR FROM ROUTINE Recon Indoctrination Program	Evans, E.	Jun 71
RECRUITERS	RECRUITERS' SCHOOL At Parris Island	Wolf, SSgt R.	May 71
RETRAINING	TRANSITION: GOODYEAR STYLE Tire Company sponsors re-training course at Lejeune	Weir, LCpl B.	Apr 72
	LEARNING PLACE Montford Point Supply Schools	Richardson, GySgt H.	Aug 69
	MONTFORD POINT SUPPLY SCHOOLS Food Services, Motor Transport	Hall, H.	Dec 63
SEA SCHOOL	SEA SCHOOL At San Diego	Brey, E.	Oct 68

Title	Author / Source	Date	Subject
SEA SCHOOL	Evans, GySgt E.	Oct 71	
SERE . . . YOU CAN LIVE WITH IT Survive-Escape-Resist-Evade. School at Cherry Point	Bartlett, T.	Jul 71	SERE
ALBANY SCHOOLS Four supply schools at Albany	Gnatzig, B.	Mar 70	SUPPLY
CIRCLE OF SAFETY TRAINING	Wilson, P. *Gazette*	Jul 67	TRAFFIC SAFETY
WARRANT OFFICER PROGRAM	Bowen, WO B.	May 70	WO
GOVERNOR'S PLATOON Fifty women recruits, each from a different state, report to PI	Noyes, C.	Feb 69	WR'S
KEEP IN SHAPE WITH THE MARINES: WOMEN	*McCall's*	Oct 63	
LADY LEADERS NCO School for Women Marines	Ambrose, J.	Jun 64	

UNITS

Title	Author / Source	Date	Subject
A CORPS CRITIQUE FMF organization and equipment	Heiman, L. *Gazette*	Jul 64	FMF
THE FMF: A PROJECTION	Harrison, J. *Gazette*	Feb 67	
FMF LANT: PROFILE OF READINESS	Asprey, R. *Gazette*	Feb 63	
FMF PAC	Kester, SSgt C. *Leatherneck*	Aug 63	
NEW LOOK FOR THE FMF	*Leatherneck*	Mar 63	
THE NEXT STEP	Skaugen, C. *Gazette*	Sep 66	
WHAT'S IN A NAME? FMF organization	Birch, H. *Gazette*	Jan 66	
DIVISION IN MOTION The 3RD on Okinawa	Berger, P. *Leatherneck*	Mar 65	DIVISION

	Title	Author / Source	Date
	REBIRTH OF THE 5TH MARINES: TRAINING AT CAMP PENDLETON	Norman, L. *Newsweek*	Jul 11, 1966
	RETURN OF THE SPEARHEAD	Hallman, S. *Leatherneck*	Apr 66
	1ST MAW Duty at Iwakuni	Berger, P. *Leatherneck*	Apr 65
	SOUND OF FRIENDSHIP 1ST MAW Band at Iwakuni	Berger, P. *Leatherneck*	Feb 65
BRIGADE	THE BRIGADE IS BEAUTIFUL It answers today's problems	Flynn, Lt Col J., and Maj D. Quinlan *Gazette*	Sep 72
	BRIGADE MARINES Headquartered at Kaneohe	Kester, SSgt C. *Leatherneck*	Jun 63
	STAFF THE FIRE BRIGADE NOW Operational readiness	Barlow, G. *Gazette*	Apr 64
BATTALION	AMPHIBIOUS AMBASSADORS Med Cruise of 1/6	Kester, SSgt C. *Leatherneck*	Oct 63
	GATOR'S TALE 2d Amtrac Bn., Lejeune	Hall, Sgt H. *Leatherneck*	Feb 63
COMPANY	HIDE AND SLIDE What's the matter with "H" & "S" units?	Campbell, Capt R. *Gazette*	Mar 72
	MAIL ORDER COMPANY Casual Company. Members scattered over the world	Hall, H. *Leatherneck*	Apr 65
	2D ANGLICO Air and Naval Gunfire Liaison Company at Lejeune	Beardsley, F. *Leatherneck*	Dec 65
	TOPE MARINES 2d Topographic Company at Lejeune makes maps. The only unit of its kind	Gnatzig, Sgt B. *Leatherneck*	May 71
PLATOON	MINE CLEARANCE PLATOON ACTIVATED	*Gazette*	Feb 65
	MORTAR PLATOON	Archer, J. *Gazette*	May 67

Title	Author / Source	Date	Subject
MARINE CORPS HISTORY WRITTEN AND SPOKEN History of the Historical Branch	Frank, B. *Proceedings*	Nov 68	**HISTORICAL BRANCH**
DRUM AND BUGLE TEAM At Puerto Rico's Marine Barracks	Paynter, J. *Leatherneck*	Jan 68	**DRUM & BUGLE TEAM**
DRUMS AND BUGLES The big one from 8th and "Eye"	Evans, GySgt E. *Leatherneck*	Nov 69	
TEXAS HEMISFAIR The big one is there with the Silent Drill Team	Thompson, P. *Leatherneck*	Jul 68	
FRENCH CREEK HILTON Duties of Force Troops at Lejeune	Gnatzig, Sgt B. *Leatherneck*	Jun 71	**FORCE TROOPS**
FORCE TROOPS At Lejeune	Beardsley, F. *Leatherneck*	Dec 65	
POWER BEHIND THE PUNCH At Lejeune	Martin, J. *Leatherneck*	Jun 68	
TEUFELHUND Bring back the War Dogs . . .	Bradshaw, H. *Gazette*	Dec 64	**WAR DOGS**

WEAPONS

From the *Gazette,* unless otherwise specified:

Title	Author / Source	Date	Subject
CALIBER COUNTS	McDowell, D.	Jan 65	**GENERAL**
COLT WEAPONS SYSTEM	Witkowski, H.	Apr 67	
EVOLUTION OF A WEAPONS FAMILY	Brant, R.	Feb 65	
FULL AUTOMATIC FIRE	Weller, J.	May 63	
WEAPONS SYSTEM ANALYSIS	Shuman, P.	Jan 67	
A WEAPONS SYSTEM DEFINED	Cushman, Gen R. *Leatherneck*	Jun 72	
BAYONET Uses of it in the Corps	Hull, D. *Leatherneck*	Dec 63	**BAYONET**
THE MEDIUM MACHINE GUN	Weller, J.	Feb 66	**MACHINE GUN**

MINES	A LOOK AT LAND MINES	Abbott, J. and L. Cassedy	Dec 63
	MINBOTRAP	Mack, R.	Jul 67
	MORE ON CLAYMORE	Murphy, J.	Sep 66
MISSILES	REDEYE If properly controlled, it shoots down enemies, not friendlies	Jackson, Capt M.	May 71
RIFLES	FAST RIFLES	West, F.	Oct 67
	M-14 "BULL-PUP"	Dixon, E.	Apr 64
SMALL ARMS	MILITARY SMALL ARMS SYMPOSIUM	Richardson, H.	Mar 64
	PLASTIC SHOTGUN SHELLS		Jan 68
TANKS	CORPS ARMOR: A CANDID ANALYSIS It is in bad shape	Estes, Lt K.	Dec 72
	LITTLE ORPHAN ONTOS	Lannes, W.	Aug 63
	MARINE CORPS ARMOR	Winter, R. *Proceedings*	Jan 67
	MEN AGAINST TANKS	Love, J.	Oct 63
	PUT TANKS UP FRONT That's better than on top	Wentworth, W.	Sep 64
	TANKS IS TIGHT No outfit in the Corps is "tighter" (esprit-de-corps) than tanks	Evans, GySgt E. *Leatherneck*	Sep 71
	TANK TACTICS FOR UNIT LEADERS	MacLaren, Maj B.	Jul 69
	WASTED TANKS	Coffman, J.	Feb 64

9.
CAREER MARINES

Publications of the Marine Corps Schools, Historical Branch, U.S. Government Printing Office and other publishers of primary interest to career Marine officers and NCO's.

CONTENTS: PART 9

AMPHIBIOUS WARFARE

ADVANCE BASE PROBLEMS	Kelly, F. *Gazette*	Nov 67
AIRBORNE ASSAULT FROM THE SEA	Ashman, Sgt L. *Gazette*	Jun 51
AMPHIBIOUS ARTILLERY OF THE FUTURE	Henderson, Col F. *Gazette*	Dec 55
AMPHIBIOUS ASPECTS OF NORMANDY INVASION	Baldwin, H. *Gazette*	Dec 44
THE AMPHIBIOUS ASSAULT	Bill, Capt D., USN *Proceedings*	Oct 62
AMPHIBIOUS DEVELOPMENT: IN THE BEGINNING Reprinted from "Howlin' Mad's" . . . *Amphibious Tactics* series in the *Gazette* in 1946/47	Smith, Gen H. *Gazette*	Nov 67
AMPHIBIOUS EMBARKATION: FMFM 4-2	USGPO	1961
AMPHIBIOUS INCURSION The author is "Base Plate McGurk" and he knows this subject	Jones, Col W. *Gazette*	Jan 55
AMPHIBIOUS INFILTRATION	Aldridge, LtCol F. *Gazette*	Sep 52
AMPHIBIOUS OBJECTIVES	Aldridge, LtCol F. *Gazette*	Feb 55
AMPHIBIOUS OPERATIONS	Chard, LtCol R. *Military Review*	Oct 43
AMPHIBIOUS OPERATIONS Emphasis mostly on the familiar ones . . . not much on USMC	Whitehouse, A. Doubleday & Company, Inc., Garden City, N.Y.	1963
THE AMPHIBIOUS PATROL Intelligence gathering is its mission	MacMichael, Capt D. *Gazette*	Oct 57

Title	Author / Source	Date
THE AMPHIBIOUS RAID	McGuire, W. *Gazette*	Sep 68
AMPHIBIOUS RECONNAISSANCE: FMFM 2-2 79 pages. Cat. No. D214.9/4: 2-2/2 S/N 0855-0009, $1.25	USGPO	1969 (IP)
AMPHIBIOUS RECONNAISSANCE IN THE U.S. MARINE CORPS: A HISTORICAL BIBLIOGRAPHY All entries about U.S. Marines from this bibliography are included in *Creating A Legend*	HQMC	1956
AMPHIBIOUS SHIPS, LANDING CRAFT, VEHICLES	MCS, Quantico	1971 (IP)
AMPHIBIOUS STRATEGY	Possony, S. *Gazette*	Jun 45
AMPHIBIOUS TRAINING: FMFM 3-2 152 pages. Cat. No. D214.9/4: 3-2/2 S/N 0855-0054, $1.50	USGPO	1970
AMPHIBIOUS TRAINING IS BASIC	Walt, LtCol L. *Gazette*	Jan 49
AMPHIBIOUS VEHICLES: FMFM 9-2 183 pages. Cat. No. D214.9/4: 9-2/2 S/N 0855-0060, $2.00	USGPO	1971 (IP)
AMPHIBIOUS WAR IN THE NUCLEAR AGE Text of a speech Gen Shoup made to this Division's Convention in the 1950's	Shoup, Gen D. 3RD MAR DIV Assn., Washington	
AMPHIBIOUS WARFARE	Baxter, J. *Atlantic*	Oct 46
AMPHIBIOUS WARFARE AND THE ATOM BOMB At that time, Amphib War looked like it didn't have a future.	Brown, J. *Gazette*	Sep 47

Title	Author / Source	Date
AMPHIBIOUS WARFARE: A BIBLIOGRAPHY All entries about U.S. Marines from this excellent bibliography are included in *Creating A Legend*	MCS, Quantico	
AMPHIBIOUS WARFARE DURING THE NEXT DECADE By the Commander of Naval Forces off the coast of Vietnam	McCain, RAdm J. *Proceedings*	Jan 63
AMPHIBIOUS WARFARE: NAVAL WEAPON OF THE FUTURE	Cushman, LtCol R. *Proceedings*	Mar 48
AMPHIBIOUS WARFARE SYMPOSIUM Can this highly specialized art survive the nuclear age? Yes!	Rosoff, AMSgt B. *Leatherneck*	May 60
AMPHIBIOUS WARFARE TOMORROW	Cushman, Col R. *Gazette*	Apr 55
AMPHIBIOUS WARFARE—TWO CONCEPTS	Williams, Col R. *Proceedings*	May 51
AMPHIBIOUS WARFARE YESTERDAY AND TOMORROW	Griffith, Col S. *Proceedings*	Aug 50
AN INTRODUCTION TO THE STUDY OF AMPHIBIOUS WARFARE	Whaley, LtCol L. *Gazette*	Nov 36
AVIATION IN AMPHIBIOUS OPERATIONS	de Saint Marceaux, LtCol B. *Military*	Sep 57
CLOSE AIR SUPPORT IN AMPHIBIOUS OPERATIONS	Pixton, LtCol A., USA *Military Review*	Aug 53
COMBAT HEADACHE	Hudson, LtCol L. *Gazette*	Jun 45
COMMAND RELATIONSHIPS IN AMPHIBIOUS WARFARE How WW-2 problems were solved	Blandy, Adm W., USN *Proceedings*	Jun 51
COMPLETED STAFF WORK The first requisite of successful Amphibious Operations	Clement, Col W. *Gazette*	Dec 44

Title	Source	Date
DEFENSE OF AN ISLAND COASTLINE: G-2 PHASE	*Gazette*	Dec 44
THE DEVELOPMENT OF AMPHIBIOUS TACTICS IN THE U.S. NAVY This 10-part series is *The* history of Amphibious Tactics up to that time.	Smith, LtGen H. *Gazette*	Jun 46-Mar 47
DOCTRINE FOR AMPHIBIOUS OPERATIONS: LFMO-1	USGPO	1967
DOCTRINE FOR LANDING FORCES: LFMO-2	USGPO	1969
EARLY AMPHIBIOUS TRAINING EXERCISES During the 1930's	Hamilton, Capt J., USN *Proceedings*	Jun 48
EVOLUTION OF THE FMF AND MODERN AMPHIBIOUS DOCTRINE	MCS, Quantico	1962
GENERALS AND ADMIRALS: THE STORY OF AMPHIBIOUS COMMAND Concentrates on command relationships in British forces	Creswell, Capt J., RN Longmans, Green, Ltd., London	1952
IS AMPHIBIOUS WARFARE DEAD? No	Canzona, Capt N. *Proceedings*	Sep 55
JOMINI AND AMPHIBIOUS THOUGHT Gen Jomini was a French General and a pioneer in Amphibious War tactics.	Hittle, Col J. *Gazette*	Mar 46
KEEPING UP WITH AMPHIBIOUS WARFARE	Hudson, Maj J. *Gazette*	Dec 46
LANDING PARTY MANUAL The "Bible" for WW-2 ops	USGPO	1935
THE LANDING PLAN	MCS, Quantico	1971 (IP)

LAUNCHING U.S. POWER FROM THE SEA: THE SAGA OF U.S. COMBINED OPERATIONS SINCE 1775 Review of all operations including USMC	Eller, RAdm E., USN *Army Information Digest*	Jul 61
LET'S KICK IT AROUND AGAIN Shore Party operations	Coutts, LtCol L. *Gazette*	Jun 51
MARINE AMPHIBIOUS WARFARE, NEW STYLE Via chopper	*Proceedings*	Aug 50
MECHANIZED LANDING FORCE AND THE BLITZ BEACHHEAD	Stuart, Col A. *Proceedings*	Nov 52
MODERNIZATION OF THE AMPHIBIOUS ATTACK	Stuart, LtCol A. *Gazette*	Jun, Aug 49
THE NAVY BEEFS UP With amphibious ships	*Leatherneck*	Nov 61
PLANNING PHASE OF AMPHIBIOUS OPERATIONS	*Gazette*	Dec 44
PROBLEMS OF THE LANDING ATTACK	Cushman, LtCol R. *Gazette*	Mar 49
THE SEA ECHELON CONCEPT: ECP 3-16	MCS, Quantico	1972 (IP)
SHIP-TO SHORE AND INLAND	Stephan, LtCol S. *Gazette*	Jul 45
SHIP-TO-SHORE STAFF	*Gazette*	Nov 67
SHORE PARTY AND HELICOPTER SUPPORT TEAM OPERATIONS: FMFM 4-3 132 pages. Cat. No. D214.9/4: 4-3/3 S/N 0855-0045 $1.50	USGPO	1970 (IP)
SOME PROBLEMS OF THE AMPHIBIOUS COMMANDER	Powell, RAdm P., USN *Proceedings*	May 50
20TH CENTURY AMPHIBIOUS WARFARE Historical	Hittle, Col J. *Gazette*	Jun 54

Title	Author / Source	Date
THE U.S. MARINE CORPS: AUTHOR OF MODERN AMPHIBIOUS WAR Historical	Heinl, Maj R. *Proceedings*	Nov 47
UNITED STATES AMPHIBIOUS WARFARE CAPABILITY	Tobin, LtCol J., *Royal United Service Institution Journal*	Aug 61

GUERRILLA WARFARE

Title	Author / Source	Date
AN ANNOTATED BIBLIOGRAPHY OF THE UNITED STATES MARINES IN GUERRILLA, ANTI-GUERRILLA AND SMALL WAR ACTIONS All entries about U.S. Marines from this historical bibliography are included in *Creating A Legend*	Johnstone, Maj J. HQMC	1962
ANTI-GUERRILLA ON A SHOESTRING	Beason, R. *Gazette*	Aug 66
ARTILLERY VS. GUERRILLAS	Leach, Capt C., and Capt C. O'Shea *Gazette*	Sep 62
BIBLIOGRAPHY ON GUERRILLA WARFARE	MCS, Quantico	1965
CHEMICALS VS. GUERRILLAS	Miller, LtCol W. *Gazette*	Jul 64
THE COMPANY FIGHTS GUERRILLAS	Wilkinson, Capt J. *Gazette*	Jan 62
COUNTERINSURGENCY OPERATIONS: FMFM 8-2	USGPO	1968
A DOCTRINE FOR COUNTERINSURGENTS	Heilbrunn, Dr. O. *Gazette*	Feb 64
GUERRILLA! Good three-part series	Donovan, Col. J. *Leatherneck*	Jul-Sep 61
GUERRILLA!	Griffith, Col S. *Gazette*	Jul, Aug 50

Title	Author / Source	Date
GUERRILLA AMBUSH: COUNTER-INSURGENCY CASE STUDY By the author of *Sandino and the Marines*	Macaulay, Lt N. *Gazette*	May 63
GUERRILLA AND ANTI-GUERRILLA OPERATIONS	MCS, Quantico	1960
THE GUERRILLA - AND HOW TO FIGHT HIM: SELECTIONS FROM THE MARINE CORPS GAZETTE Published when "our hearts were young and gay" as we went to Nam	Greene, LtCol T. Paperback edition only, Frederick E. Praeger, Inc.	1962
GUERRILLA WAR: A PAPERBACK BIBLIOGRAPHY A book review of this book	Osanka, F. *Gazette*	Feb 62
GUERRILLA WARFARE (Theme of an entire issue) Editorial: The Next Fifty Years	*Gazette*	Jan 63
Intro: The Long, Twilight Struggle	Asprey, Capt R.	
Fighting the Abstract War	Krulak, MajGen V., Col D. Galula and Dr. G. Tanham	
Patience or Panaceas?	Baldwin, H., and Dr. J. Cross	
Problems for Professionals	Griffith, BGen S., and VAdm R. Libby	
Summary: A Realistic Appreciation	Asprey, Capt R.	
GUERRILLAS, SMALL WARS AND MARINES	Spark, Maj M. *Gazette*	Jan 62
JUNGLE COURIER Introduction Why Chi Keng Surrendered An Anti-Communist Agent in Malaya	Clutterbuck, R. *Gazette*	Jun-Aug 64
JUNGLE PATROLLING	Newton, D. *Gazette*	Aug 65
MAP ORIENTATION	Wilder, G. *Gazette*	Feb 65

Title	Author/Source	Date
MARINES AND COMMANDOES IN GUERRILLA WARFARE: A SELECTED BIBLIOGRAPHY	HQMC	1954
OPERATIONS AGAINST GUERRILLA FORCES: FMFM-21	HQMC	1962
REFERENCES ON EMPLOYMENT OF FIELD ARTILLERY IN GUERRILLA OPERATIONS	HQMC	1964
SELECTED BIBLIOGRAPHY ON COUNTERINSURGENCY	HQMC	1962
SMALL WARS—A VANISHING ART? Hardly	Heinl, LtCol R. *Gazette*	Apr 50
UNDER THE CANOPY	Jones, GySgt M. *Leatherneck*	Aug 62
VICTORY IN MALAYA Malaya: 1948-59 The Ambush Jungle Patrolling	Mans, LtCol R. *Gazette*	Jan-Mar 63
VIET CONG Threat to Peace Military Organization Military Training	State Dept. *Gazette*	Apr-Jun 62
VO NGUYEN GIAP ON GUERRILLA WAR Introduction The Viet Minh Army Defeat of the Navarre Plan Fall of Dien Bien Phu Tactics, Soldiers and People	Giap, V. *Gazette*	Apr-Aug 62
WE CAN BE GUERRILLAS, TOO	Alsop, S., and Col S. Griffith *Sat Eve Post*	Dec 2, 1950

HANDBOOKS

Title	Author/Source	Date
BE FIT AS A MARINE By the author of *The Man Who Rode The Thunder* who learned the importance of physical conditioning the hard way	Rankin, LtCol W. McGraw-Hill, Inc. 1962 Paperback by Cornerstone Library	1963

Title	Source
CATALOG Training films, graphic training aids, devices and oral tutoring tape catalog	MCS, Quantico 1972 (IP)
COLD STEEL Explains the use of the knife, bayonet and stick in close combat in 179 pages	Styers, J. The Leatherneck Association, Washington 1952
DICTIONARY OF MILITARY AND NAVAL QUOTATIONS	Heinl, Col R. U.S. Naval Institute, Annapolis 1965 (IP)
FIRST SERGEANT'S HANDBOOK An early WW-2 classic	Hooper, Lt W. Marine Barracks, Navy Yard, Philadelphia 1942
GUIDE TO LIBRARY RESOURCES AND SERVICES All about Quantico's Breckenridge Library	MCS, Quantico 1972
GUIDEBOOK FOR MARINES The classic	The Leatherneck Association, Washington 1972
HANDBOOK Holdings of the Breckenridge Library and Basic School Library	MCS, Quantico 1961
A HANDBOOK OF AMPHIBIOUS SCOUT AND RAIDER TRAINING	Dept. of Personnel, U.S. Navy USGPO 1944
HANDBOOK FOR MARINE NCO'S Priceless guide for the career Marine NCO	Heinl, Col R. Paperback edition only, U.S. Naval Institute, Annapolis 1970 (IP)
HANDBOOK FOR RETIRED MARINES	USGPO 1957
MARINE CORPS DRILL MANUAL	USGPO 1956
THE MARINE CORPS EXERCISE BOOK Illustrated	Otott, Maj G. G. P. Putnam's Sons 1968

Title	Author / Publisher	Year
MARINE CORPS UNIFORM REGULATIONS	USGPO	1968
MARINE CORPS WIFE Too bad it's out-of-print	Jerome, S., and N. Shea Harper and Bros.	1955
MARINES' HANDBOOK Forerunner of the "Guidebook"	Brown, Lt L. Service Typesetting Co., Chicago	1934
THE MARINE OFFICER'S GUIDE Terrific book for new officers. Tells all you'll need to know to make it in the USMC	Thomas, Gen G., Col R. Heinl and RAdm A. Ageton, USN U.S. Naval Institute, Annapolis	1967 (IP)
MARINE TROOP LEADERS' GUIDE: FMFM 1-2 410 pages. Cat. No. D214.9/4: 1-2/2 S/N 0855-0058 $2.25	USGPO	1971 (IP)
MILITARY LAW: A HANDBOOK FOR THE NAVY AND MARINE CORPS	Byrne, LtCdr E., USN U.S. Naval Institute, Annapolis	1970 (IP)
OFF-DUTY EDUCATION MANUAL	USGPO	1957
REGISTER OF COMMISSIONED AND WARRANT OFFICERS OF THE UNITED STATES NAVY AND MARINE CORPS AND RESERVE OFFICERS ON ACTIVE DUTY DEC 31, 1971 Part 2, Marine Corps and Marine Corps Reserve, 1479 pages. Cat. No. D208:12:970-2 S/N 0847-0125, $9.00	USGPO	1971 (IP)
REGISTER OF RETIRED COMMISSIONED AND WARRANT OFFICERS, REGULAR AND RESERVE OF THE UNITED STATES NAVY AND MARINE CORPS, JULY 1, 1968 Part 2, Marine Corps and Marine Corps Reserve, 698 pages. Cat. No. 208.12/3:970 S/N 0847-0119, $5.75	USGPO	1970 (IP)

SMALL WARS MANUAL: UNITED STATES MARINE CORPS,1940	Harrington, Maj S. HQMC 1940		
THE STRATEGY AND TACTICS OF SMALL WARS One of the most significant series in *Gazette* history	Harrington, Maj S. *Gazette* Dec 21-Mar 22		
UNIT LEADERS PERSONAL RESPONSE HANDBOOK 305 pages. Cat. No. 0214.9/2: L46 S/N 0855-0006, $1.00	USGPO	1968 (IP)	
U.S. MARINE PROGRAMS	USGPO	1958	
WRITING HANDBOOK How to write in military style	MCS, Quantico	1964	

OPERATIONS

ABC OPERATIONS IN THE FMF: FMFM 11-1	USGPO		**ABC**
AIR MOVEMENT OF FLEET MARINE FORCE UNITS: FMFM 4-6	USGPO	1968	**AIR**
ANTIAIR WARFARE OPERATIONS: FMFM 7-5	USGPO	1968	
MARINE AIR COMMAND AND CONTROL SYSTEM: FMFM 5-3	USGPO	1969	
ADVANCED NAVAL BASE DEFENSE: FMFM 8-3	USGPO	1967	**DEFENSE**
BASE DEFENSE: FMFM 8-5	USGPO	1969	
ORGANIZATION FOR NATIONAL DEFENSE: ECP 1-6	MCS, Quantico	1967	
MARINE ENGINEER OPERATIONS: FMFM 4-4	USGPO	1968	**ENGINEERS**
HELICOPTER BORNE OPERATIONS: FMFM 3-3	USGPO	1967	**HELICOPTERS**
EFFECTIVE PRESS RELATIONS	Zorthian, Col B. *Gazette*	Jun 70	**PIO**

	JOE BLOW—MORALE BUILDER Defense of the famous WW-2 "Blueberry Pie and Mom is what I miss most" stories	*Gazette*	Dec 49
	ON TIME AND SPACE Broadcast time and print space, and how to get it for the Corps	*Gazette*	Sep 52
	TELLING THE MARINE CORPS STORY	USGPO	1963
	WHAT CAN YOU BELIEVE? About Combat Correspondents	*Combat Forces Journal*	Jan 51
	YOU AND THE PRESS	*Gazette*	Dec 53
RIVERINE	**DOCTRINE FOR RIVERINE OPERATIONS: FMFM 8-4**	USGPO	1967
SPECIAL	**SPECIAL OPERATIONS: FMFM 8-1**	USGPO	1968
TANKS	**ANTI-MECHANIZED OPERATIONS: FMFM 9-3**	USGPO	1967
	TANK EMPLOYMENT 226 pages. Cat No. D 214.9/ 4:9-1/2 S/N 0855-0049, $2.00	USGPO	1970 (IP)
WEATHER	**TACTICAL APPRECIATION OF WEATHER AND TERRAIN: ECP 3-2**	MCS, Quantico	1967

STAFF

	COMMAND AND STAFF ACTION: FMFM 3-1 545 pages. Cat. No. D214.9/4: 3-1/2 S/N 0855-0010, $4.50	USGPO	1970 (IP)
	STAFF BEGINNINGS IN THE U.S. MARINE CORPS	*Gazette*	Nov 42
1—PERSONNEL	**G-1 MANUAL: ECP 1-1**	MCS Quantico	1970
	GUIDE TO ADMINSTRATION: U.S. MARINE CORPS Hard cover classic	Hooper, Lt W. Marine Barracks, Navy Yard, Philadelphia	1943

JOINT MANUAL OF CIVIL AFFAIRS: FMFM 8-6	USGPO	1966	
MARINE CORPS MANUAL It was out-of-date before the ink was dry, but there's never been anything like it	HQMC	1949	
PEER RATING: RELATIONSHIP BETWEEN OFFICER AND PEER-CANDIDATE PREDICTIONS OF EFFECTIVENESS IN A COMPANY-GRADE OFFICER WITH THE U.S. MARINE CORPS	Anderhalter, O., W. Wilkins and M. Rigby Bureau of Medicine and Surgery, Dept of the Navy, St. Louis	1952	
UNIT PERSONNEL AND MATERIAL REFERENCE DATA FOR FLEET MARINE FORCE ORGANIZATONS: ECP 3-9	MCS, Quantico	1963	
BASIC COMBAT INTELLIGENCE FOR GROUND UNITS: ECP 3-14	MCS, Quantico	1968	**2—INTELLIGENCE**
INTELLIGENCE: FMFM 2-1	USGPO	1967	
PRINCIPLES AND TECHNIQUES OF MILITARY INSTRUCTION: ECP 1-2	MCS, Quantico	1966	**3—OPERATIONS AND TRAINING**
THE APPLICATION OF DATA PROCESSING TO LANDING FORCE LOGISTIC PLANNING: ECP 2-13	MCS, Quantico	1966	**4—LOGISTICS**
CASUALTY OVERLOAD: ECP 3-10	MCS, Quantico	1965	
LOGISTICS AND PERSONNEL SUPPORT: FMFM 4-1 233 pages. Cat. No. D214.9/4: 5-1 S/N 0855-0046, $1.50	USGPO	1971 (IP)	
BRIEF DESCRIPTION OF COMMUNICATION-ELECTRONICS EQUIPMENT: TM-2000-15 VOL. 1	MCS, Quantico	1970	**COMMUNICATIONS**
COMMUNICATIONS: FMFM 10-1	USGPO	1965	

Subject	Title	Author/Publisher	Date
MEDICAL	**MEDICAL AND DENTAL SUPPORT: FMFM 4-5**	USGPO	1968
	SUPPORTING ARMS		
	FIRE SUPPORT COORDINATION: FMFM 7-1	USGPO	1967
ARTILLERY	**AN ANNOTATED BIBLIOGRAPHY OF UNITED STATES MARINE CORPS ARTILLERY** All entries about U.S. Marines are included in *Creating A Legend*	Donnelly, R. HQMC	1970 (IP)
	FIELD ARTILLERY SUPPORT: FMFM 7-3 340 pages. Cat. No. D214.9/4: 7-4/2 S/N 0855-0047, $3.00	USGPO	1970 (IP)
CLOSE AIR SUPPORT	**AIR SUPPORT: FMFM 7-3** 230 pages. Cat. No. D214.9/4: 7-3/2 S/N 0855-0029, $2.00	USGPO	1969 (IP)
	AN ANNOTATED BIBLIOGRAPHY OF THE UNITED STATES MARINE CORPS CONCEPT OF CLOSE AIR SUPPORT All entries about U.S. Marines are included in *Creating A Legend*	Santelli, J. HQMC	1968 (IP)
	CLOSE AIR SUPPORT A report from the special sub-committee on Tactical Air Support	House Committee on Armed Services U.S. Congress	1966
	CLOSE AIR SUPPORT Report #3206	Urban, Cdr H., USN Air War College, Maxwell Air Force Base, Ala.	1966
NAVAL GUNFIRE	**AN ANNOTATED BIBLIOGRAPHY OF NAVAL GUNFIRE SUPPORT**	Bivens, LtCol H HQMC	1972 (IP)
	NAVAL GUNFIRE SUPPORT: FMFM 7-2	USGPO	1967

NAVAL GUNFIRE SUPPORT IN COUNTERBATTERY	Hunt, Lt R. *Gazette*	Nov 41	
NAVAL GUNFIRE SUPPORT IN LANDINGS	Heinl, Col R. *Gazette*	Sep 45	
OUR NAVAL GUNFIRE PREPARATION	Oldfield, Maj W. *Gazette*	Jul 45	

TRAINING

DO OR DIE Close combat manual by the officer who taught the Raiders	Biddle, Col A. The Leatherneck Association, Washington	1942	**INDIVIDUAL COMBAT**
GET TOUGH Ju-jitsu manual	Fairbairn, Maj W. The Leatherneck Association, Washington	1943	
HAND-TO-HAND COMBAT: FMFM 1-4	USGPO	1966	
MARINE BAYONET TRAINING: FMFM 1-1	USGPO	1965	
BASIC RIFLE MARKSMANSHIP: FMFM 1-3	USGPO	1968	**MARKSMAN-SHIP**
FIELD FIRING TECHNIQUES: FMFM 1-3A	USGPO	1969	
SNIPING FMFM 1-3B	USGPO	1969	
"TRAINING A MATCH TEAM" By the leader of the 1st Raiders	Edson, Maj M. *Leatherneck*	Aug 40	
U.S. MARINE CORPS SCORE BOOK AND RIFLE MARKSMANSHIP INSTRUCTOR	Harllee, Capt W. International Printing, Philadelphia	1913	

UNITS

ORGANIZATION OF THE U.S. MARINE CORPS: ECP 1-9	MCS, Quantico	1969	**CORPS**
FLEET MARINE FORCE ORGANIZATION-1969: ECP 1-4	MCS, Quantico	1969	**FMF**

	Title	Source	Date
	HISTORICAL OUTLINE OF THE DEVELOPMENT OF THE FLEET MARINE FORCE, PACIFIC, 1941-1950	HQMC	
DIVISION	**MARINE DIVISION: FMFM 6-1** 193 pages. Cat. No. D214.9/4: 6-1/2 S/N 0855-0022, $1.75	USGPO	1969 (IP)
WING	**MARINE AIRCRAFT WING: FMFM 5-1** 117 pages. Cat. No. D214.9/4: 5-1 S/N 0855-0046 $1.50	USGPO	1970 (IP)
REGIMENT	**MARINE INFANTRY REGIMENT: FMFM 6-2** 405 pages. Cat. No. D214.9/4: 6-2/2 S/N 0855-0023, $3.25	USGPO	1969 (IP)
BATTALION	**MARINE INFANTRY BATTALION: FMFM 6-3** 513 pages. Cat. No. D214.9/4: 6-3/2 S/N 0855-0024, $4.00	USGPO	1969 (IP)
COMPANY	**THE COMPANY IN COMBAT**	The Leatherneck Association, Washington	1943
	MARINE RIFLE COMPANY/ PLATOON: FMFM 6-4 419 pages. Cat. No. D214.9/4: 6-4/2 S/N 0855-0025, $3.25	USGPO	1969 (IP)
SQUAD	**MARINE RIFLE SQUAD: FMFM 6-5** 284 pages. Cat. No. D214.9/4: 6-5/4 S/N 0855-0056 $1.75	USGPO	1971
	THE DEVELOPMENT OF THE SQUAD AND THE FIRE TEAM IN THE U.S. MARINE CORPS: A BRIEF BIBLIOGRAPHY	HQMC	1955
FIRE TEAM	**BIRTH OF THE FIRE TEAM**	Holmes, Lt L. *Gazette*	Nov 52

WEAPONS

ARMED FORCES DOCTRINE FOR CHEMICAL AND BIOLOGICAL WEAPONS EMPLOYMENT AND DEFENSE: LFM03	USGPO	1964
EMPLOYMENT OF LIGHT ANTIAIRCRAFT MISSLE BATTALION: FMFM 7-6	USGPO	1970
INDIVIDUAL MOTAR ECP 2-29	MCS, Quantico	1968
INFANTRY WEAPONS: ECP 2-29	MCS, Quantico	1971
JOINT MUNITIONS EFFECTIVENESS: FMFM 5-2	USGPO	1967
M-60 MACHINEGUN: FMFM 6-4-A	USGPO	1970
REDEYE GUIDED MISSLE WEAPON SYSTEM: FMFM 7-7	USGPO	1968
SIGNAL INTELLIGENCE/ ELECTRONIC WARFARE: FMFM 2-3	USGPO	
3.5 INCH AND M72 ROCKET LAUNCHERS, PORTABLE FLAMETHROWER, M3 RIOT DISPENSER, 106 MM RECOILLESS RIFLE: ECP 2-32	MCS, Quantico	1968

10.

MOVIES, PLAYS, POEMS, SHORT STORIES, SONGS AND YOUTH WRITING

Movies, a half-dozen poems and two plays about Marines. *What Price Glory* is the best play; also the best movie. Forty-five books for younger readers. Non-fiction chapter includes all the career books for High School boys. Fiction books are scarce. Almost all are "collector's items."

CONTENTS: PART 10

NOTE: All of the adult novels about Marines (63) are included in the appropriate Part according to their subject matter. For example, the many novels about WW-2 Marine battles are included in the Battle section of Part 3—World War 2.

MOVIES

GENERAL

MOVIE MARINES
Lists all actors who have played Marines in movies up to that time — Wilton, SSgt R. *Leatherneck* Mar 46

SEA SOLDIERS OF THE SCREEN — *Leatherneck* May 35

TITLES

ABROAD WITH TWO YANKS 1944
William Bendix and Dennis O'Keefe are in Australia chasing Helen Walker in between fighting WW-2. Luckily for her, O'Keefe wins. Typical comedy of the time.

ALL THE YOUNG MEN 1960
Alan Ladd (he wore elevator shoes to pass Marine physical) and Sidney Poitier fight each other while Mort Sahl steals this movie about Korea with his sardonic humor.

AMBUSH BAY 1966
Hugh O'Brian (a former Marine) and Marine Mickey Rooney (Mickey Rooney???) help the natives fight Japs in WW-2.

BATTLE CRY 1955
Classic flick of WW-2 training and combat stars Tab Hunter in his best role (maybe his only good role?.) Aldo Ray talks like Aldo Ray and Dorothy Malone pants around chasing Hunter. Based on the book by Uris. Van Heflin is "High Pockets," the Battalion Commander.

BATTLE FLAME 1959
Scott Brady is a wounded Marine Lt who falls for nurse Elaine Edwards in hospital in Korea.

BATTLE ZONE 1952
John Hodiak and Steve McNally are combat cameramen in Korea.

BEACHHEAD 1954
Marine quartet of Tony Curtis, Frank Lovejoy, Edward Franz and Skip Homeier in dangerous mission clearing out mines for beachhead in WW-2. Good action.

THE BOB MATHIAS STORY 1954
Mathias (he was the Olympic Decathlon champion) plays himself in this biographical film. Includes his sports career, Marine duty and family life.

CHINA VENTURE 1953
Barry Sullivan and Edmund O'Brien are out to capture a Jap Naval Commander wanted for interrogation in WW-2. They don't make them like this anymore.

THE COCKEYED WORLD 1929
Sequel to *What Price Glory?* starring Lowe and McLaglen

COME ON, MARINES 1934
Richard Arlen and Ida Lupino in the tropics.

CRAZYLEGS 1953
Fictionalized account of life of Elroy Hirsch, U. of Wisconsin star football player and now Athletic Director there. He was a Marine officer in WW-2. Hirsch plays himself. This movie demonstrates why he decided to stick to football.

DEVIL DOG DAWSON 1921

DEVIL DOGS 1928

DEVIL DOGS OF THE AIR 1935

Stars James Cagney, with Pat O'Brien

THE DI 1957

Jack Webb takes his Dragnet technique to Parris Island where he intimidates recruits as a Senior DI. Webb is a former Marine. He certainly remembered well the fact that DI's never smile.

55 DAYS AT PEKING 1963

Account of the Boxer Rebellion of 1900 stars Charleton Heston, Ava Gardner, David Niven and a "cast of thousands." Good photography. Medium acting. Lousy screenplay.

FIGHTER ATTACK 1953

Sterling Hayden (another former Marine), J. Carroll Naish and Joy Page play in this biographical tale of Hayden's last mission as a Marine in the OSS in Italy in WW-2.

FIGHTING DEVIL DOGS 1943

THE FIGHTING MARINE 1926

Life of Gene Tunney (a WW-1 Marine) in this old Marine flick with screenplay by Mankiewicz.

FIRST TO FIGHT 1967

Chad Everett plays a combination of Mitch Paige and John Basilone in this confusing tale of a Guadalcanal hero who loses his nerve. It's easier to play a doctor than a Marine.

FLIGHT 1929

Marine aero squadron in Nicaragua during the Banana Wars. Jack Holt stars.

FLYING LEATHERNECKS 1951

John Wayne, Robert Ryan, Don Taylor and Janis Carter make this WW-2 film one of the best ever about the Corps. Loosely based on the activities of the "Cactus Air Force."

GREAT MAIL ROBBERY 1927

4th Marine mail guards foil bandits.

GUADALCANAL DIARY 1943

The best Marine movie of WW-2, and it was made right after the battle. Stars Preston Foster, Lloyd Nolan, Anthony Quinn, Richard Conte, and Richard Jaeckel.

GUNG-HO 1943

Randolph Scott plays Evans Carlson in this flick based on adventures of Carlson's Raiders of WW-2. Robert Mitchum gives usual good performance. J. Caroll Naish is Lt LeFrancois. Sam Levine is "Transport" Mahakian.

HALLS OF MONTEZUMA 1950

One of better Marine WW-2 films. Richard Widmark, Robert Wagner and Jack Webb are good. Jack Palance is terrific. Marines are advancing on an island until they are clobbered by secret Jap rockets.

HERE COME THE MARINES 1952

The Bowery Boys (the Dead-End Kids grown up) terrorize the Corps in this low budget but funny movie starring Huntz Hall and Leo Gorcey as the immortal "Spit."

HOLD BACK THE NIGHT 1956

John Payne stars as the Company Commander who takes the brunt of the Chinese attack at Chosin. Fortunately, he has his bottle of scotch. Based on novel by Pat Frank.

IN LOVE AND WAR 1960
The late Jeffrey Hunter in probably his biggest role as Japanese-American Guy Gabaldon, the "Pied Piper" of Saipan.

LADY MARINES 1951

THE LEATHERNECK 1929
William Boyd (Hopalong Cassidy) stars as a Marine stationed near the Manchurian border.

LEATHERNECKING 1930
Nutty saga of carefree Marines at Pearl Harbor. Many stars appeared in "cameo" roles.

THE LEATHERNECKS HAVE LANDED 1936

LET IT RAIN 1927
Douglas McLean stars in this "devil-may-care" adventure of a Marine.

THE MARIENETTES 1918
WW-1 name for Women Marines

MARINE HYMN 1943
Early WW-2 propaganda film from the Department of War Information.

MARINE RAIDERS 1944
Pat O'Brien, Robert Ryan and Ruth Hussey star in this film about the rugged Raider training at Pendleton in early WW-2.

THE MARINES ARE COMING 1934
William Haines gets the girl (Esther Ralston)

THE MARINES ARE HERE 1938

THE MARINES FLY HIGH 1940

MARINES, LET'S GO 1961
Four Marines are on leave in Tokyo. Starring Tom Tryon (maybe this is the movie that made him decide to write rather than act) and some other unknowns.

MARIONETTES 1934

Another spelling for another movie about WW-1 WM's.

MORAN OF THE MARINES 1928

Part of a series about the exploits of Moran as a Mountie, Sailor, etc. Richard Dix stars.

NONE BUT THE BRAVE 1965

Frank Sinatra is a Corpsman who is always smashed, Clint Walker is a Marine pilot and Tommy Sands is the funniest (and most typical) Marine Lt you ever saw in this WW-2 movie. Plot is surprisingly sensitive (Japs are almost human).

THE OUTSIDER 1962

Tony Curtis, looking more like a fat Tony Curtis than Ira Hayes, plays Ira Hayes in this biography of the Indian from Iwo Jima. Could have an impact on you. It doesn't.

THE PEACEMAKERS: AN EDUCATIONAL PICTORIAL SHOWING THE UNITED STATES MARINES IN BARRACKS, AT SEA, AND ON THE FIELD OF BATTLE 1916

PRIDE OF THE MARINES 1945

John Garfield is great as Al Schmid, the Marine hero blinded on Guadalcanal. Dane Clark is his buddy. Based on *Al Schmid, Marine.*

THE PROUD AND THE PROFANE 1956

William Holden and Deborah Kerr wrestle on the beach in the South Pacific where Holden is resting between battles. Kerr works at the Red Cross canteen (Doesn't she look like a typical Red Cross lady?). Based on novel about Marine Raiders, *The Magnificent Bastards.*

RETREAT, HELL 1952

Richard Carlson as a "re-tread" finds the meaning of "patriotism" at Chosin in this dull film about Korea. Also starring Frank Lovejoy and Anita Louise.

Review of the movie *Leatherneck* Apr 52

SALUTE TO THE MARINES 1943

Wallace Beery, who has retired from the Corps, finds himself in the Philippines when war starts. He takes it from there as only he can. Look out, Japs! Featuring Fay Bainter, Marilyn Maxwell and Reginald Owen. Based on the book by Randall White.

SANDS OF IWO JIMA 1943

John Wayne immortalizes "Sgt Striker," who straightens out punk kid John Agar, in one of the best of the WW-2 films. The battle scenes are superb. Forrest Tucker and, of course, Richard Jaeckel, are featured.

SANDS OF IWO — Milhon, Sgt W.
Filming the movie *Leatherneck* Nov 49

THE SINGING MARINE 1937

Dick Powell special, before he began to play the "tough guy" roles. He bursts into song at the least provocation, wearing his dress blues at all times.

SIXTH MARINE DIVISION ON OKINAWA 1950

The official film of this unit in the last great battle of WW-2. By the Navy Department.

SOUTH SEA PARADISE 1953

Burt Lancaster and Virginia Mayo star in this comedy about the 4th Marines in early WW-2

Story about the movie — Heinecke, MSgt R.
Leatherneck Jun 53

STAR SPANGLED BANNER 1916
An Edison Studios (that's Thomas A.) film starring Paul Kelly as a Marine.

STARS AND STRIPES FOREVER 1952
Clifton Webb *is* John Philip Sousa in this fictionalized version of his life with the Marine Band. The music makes you want to re-up.

TARAWA BEACHHEAD .1958
The all-star cast of Kerwin Matthew, Karen Sharpe and Ray Danton gives you a hint as to the quality of this WW-2 film.

TELL IT TO THE MARINES 1927
A Lon Chaney vehicle. He is the tough Top Sgt O'Hara.

A review of the movie *Leatherneck* Jan 27

THE THREE THINGS
A WW-1 recruiting film by the Thomas A. Edison Company.

TILL THE END OF TIME 1946
The Marines' version of "Best Years of Our Lives," about returning WW-2 Marines and their problems adjusting to civilian life. Starring Robert Mitchum, Dorothy McGuire and Guy Madison.

TRIBES 1970
A made-for-TV movie about the arrival of a "hippie" in Boot Camp. He shakes up the Corps like few things have. Excellent drama. Won many awards.

TRIPOLI 1950
Howard deSilva steals the show from John Payne and Maureen O'Hara in this drama about the Marines and the Barbary pirates.

THE UNBELIEVER 1918
WW-1 propaganda film by Edison

UNTIL THEY SAIL 1957

Surprisingly good drama about the impact of Marines on the women of New Zealand. Piper Laurie and Jean Simmons can testify that Paul Newman made some impact.

WAKE ISLAND 1942

Realistic film about Wake Island stars Brian Donlevy, Robert Preston, Macdonald Carey (filmed before he became a Marine) and William Bendix. As exciting as the truth about this battle really is.

WE ARE THE MARINES 1943

A full-length feature using the "March of Time" technique. Westbrook Van Voorhes narrates.

WHAT PRICE GLORY? 1952

Cagney is Flagg and Dan Dailey is Sgt Quirt in this re-make of a WW-1 classic.

Edmund Lowe played Flagg and Victor McLaglen was Quirt in the original. 1925

WITH THE MARINES: CHOSIN TO HUNGNAM 1951

Official Navy Dept films from early in the Korean War.

A YANK IN VIETNAM 1963

Marine chopper pilot, Marshall Thompson, is downed in Vietnam. You know the rest. Screenplay by Jack Lewis. Retitled *Year of the Tiger* for TV use.

YOU CAN'T FOOL A MARINE 1943

Eleanor Powell stars as a sort of female Dick Powell, but she dances rather than sings.

PLAYS

THE BRIG: A PLAY ABOUT THE MARINE CORPS Brown, K. Paperback edition only, Hill & Wang, Inc. 1965

Enjoyed a short run on Broadway.

WHAT PRICE GLORY?
Did more for Marines' image than winning WW-1! — Anderson, M., and L. Stallings

POEMS

THE BALLAD OF TOP-SERGEANT JERRY McDOUGALL McGEE Long saga poem about Marine Sgt and his encounter with Satan	Tooke, A. *Leatherneck*	Oct 42
BODY, BOOTS AND BRITCHES Ballad of the War of 1812 about Jim Bird, a Marine executed for desertion from the Niagara	Thompson, H. J. B. Lippincott Company, Philadelphia	1940
DEATH	Hubler, Capt R. *Atlantic*	Oct 44
DELEGATE AT LARGE Free verse about the UN from a Marine	O'Sheel, Capt P. *New Yorker*	Apr 28, 1945
DEVIL DOG BALLADS The pamphlet that introduced Capt Jimmie Bones	Hitt, N. Baltimore City Printing and Bindery Co., Baltimore	1919
EVERYBODY THINKS	Henri, Maj R. *Sat Eve Post*	Jul 15, 1944
FOXHOLES	Henri, Maj R. *Sat Eve Post*	May 19, 1945
FROM THE GATES OF HELL The most reprinted item in the history of *Leatherneck* is the Jimmie Bones poem by Neil Hitt	Averill, G. *Leatherneck*	Jan 42, Jan 47, May 48, Jul 51, Nov 53, Oct 64
FOREVER NINETEEN About a young Marine who didn't come back from WW-2	Otis, A. Published by the author, Chicago *Leatherneck*	1947 Aug 47

THE LEATHERNECKS AND OTHER POEMS Horrible WW-2 poetry	Hinds, E. Christopher Publishing House, Boston 1944
THE LEATHERNECK SPEAKS Marine poem reprinted from the N.Y. Times	Benet, W. *Leatherneck* Jun 44
MARINES, FALL IN! Rhymes composed and edited by Snedeker	Snedeker, J. D. C. Hardman Co. 1942
NOR ALL MY TEARS About her Marine son KIA in WW-2	Hall, L. Ralph Fletcher Seymour, Chicago 1944
THE PROPHECY Historical poem	Whitten, Sgt L. *Leatherneck* Nov 72
RHYMES OF A MARINE Classic Corps poetry by a giant . . . Percy Webb (the pre-Thomason Kipling of the Corps)	Webb, MTSgt P. Published by the author, Philadelphia 1912
THE SCORNER About the misled doves who scorn the Vietnam War	Church, R. *Leatherneck* Jan 66
SEMPER FIDELIS: (EVER FAITHFUL) A BALLAD OF THE U. S. MARINES Sixty-four pages of Corps' poetry.	Culnan, J. Avondale Press, Chicago 1927
SONG FOR A PILOT	Hubler, Capt R. *Atlantic* Oct 44
A STORY OF THE CORPS Epic poem about Korea	Wilson, Lt P. *Leatherneck* Nov 53
WE'VE MET BEFORE Korea is where you meet WW-2 buddies.	Hodgson, Lt D. *Leatherneck* Nov 51
YOU AND THE STREAM The Corps as "eternity"	Church, R. *Leatherneck* Nov 55

SHORT STORIES

Alphabetical by last name of author:

Burdick, E. REST CAMP ON MAUI 7 AMERICANS, 1 FOREIGNER	From *A Role In Manila,* New American Library 1966
Cassil, R. THE SWIMMERS AT PALLIKULA	From *The Happy Marriage* Purdue University Studies, West Lafayette, Ind. 1966
Cowen, E. TWO YEARS	From *Life in The United States* Charles Scribner's Sons 1933
Fitzpatrick, R. A MARINE AND HIS DOG	From *Stories Boys Like Best* *Appleton, Century, Crofts, Inc.* 1945
Hart, Franklin N. THE AMERICAN	*Copy,* 1925
Ogan, M., and G. TOP SECRET	From *Teen-Age Spy Stories* Lantern Press 1967
Patrick, Q. THE FAT CAT	From *All Cats Go To Heaven* Grosset & Dunlap 1960
Rumaker, M. EXIT 3	From *Gringos and Other Stories* Grove Press 1966
Wilson, M. COME AWAY HOME	O. Henry Award Prize Story of 1945

SONGS

MARINE CORPS SONG BOOK — Hadley, A. U.S. Navy Department 1919

YOUTH WRITING

NON-FICTION

THE BATTLE FOR IWO JIMA — Leckie, R. Random House, Inc. 1967
For boys grades 6-10. Tells the day-by-day story of Iwo in exciting fashion typical of Leckie

DADDY PAT OF THE MARINES: BEING HIS LETTERS FROM FRANCE TO HIS SON TOWNIE — Evans, LtCol F. Frederick A. Stokes 1919
The title tells it all. Interesting commentary on WW-1 as fought by a Marine officer

A DEFINITIVE STUDY OF YOUR FUTURE IN THE MARINE CORPS — Fraser, Col A. Richards Rosen Press, Inc. 1969
Part of an Armed Forces series for High School boys

FIRST TO FIGHT — McCahill, Capt W. David McKay Company, Inc. 1943
Early WW-2 propaganda book for high school age boys. Brief history of the Corps through Guadalcanal

GUADALCANAL — Werstein, I. Thomas Y. Crowell Company 1963
Part of a series for young readers

GUADALCANAL GENERAL: THE STORY OF A. A. VANDEGRIFT — Foster, J. William Morrow and Company 1966
A Morrow Junior (Jr. High School) book concentrates on Vandegrift's Guadalcanal role

HERE COME THE MARINES: THE STORY OF THE DEVIL DOGS FROM TRIPOLI TO WAKE ISLAND — Griffin, A. Howell Soskin, Inc. 1942
Lively stories about Marines from 1798 through early WW-2. For High School age boys

HE'S IN THE MARINE CORPS NOW The routine of becoming a Marine. Chapters include advanced training, weapons, WW-2 history and "slanguage"	Israels, J. Robert M. McBride & Company 1943
A HISTORY OF THE U. S. MARINES For the primary grades.	Trainor, B. Rand McNally, Inc., Chicago
THE ILLUSTRATED STORY OF THE MARINES A comic book	Gilberton World-Wide Publications, Inc. 1959
LEATHERNECK: THE TRAINING, WEAPONS AND EQUIPMENT OF THE UNITED STATES MARINE CORPS Juvenile writing for grades 3-7.	Colby, C. Coward-McCann 1957
LEATHERNECKS: OUR MARINES IN FACT & PICTURE	Boswell, R. Thomas Y. Crowell Co. 1943
THE MARINE CORPS FROM CIVILIAN TO LEATHERNECK Volume 3 in Armed Forces Library series for High School	Hammond, LtCol C. Viking Press 1959
MARINE CORPS IN ACTION History for younger readers (6-12)	Bergaust, E., and W. Foss G. P. Putnam's Sons 1965
THE MARINES IN REVIEW Early WW-2 propaganda book for High School age boys.	Carlisle, N. E. P. Dutton & Co., Inc. 1943
MARINES AND WHAT THEY DO Good summary of the Corps	Smith, E. (Karl Schuon) Franklin Watts, Inc. 1962
MODERN UNITED STATES MARINE CORPS Everything a future Marine would want to know. Brief history followed by job-by-job run-down.	DeChant, Col J. D. VanNostrand, Princeton, N.J. 1966

OKINAWA: THE LAST ORDEAL	Werstein, I. Thomas Y. Crowell Company 1969
OUR MARINES Emotions were running high, and the Japs were "sneaky little yellow bas . . . ." when this was written in early WW-2	Crump, I. Dodd, Mead & Co., Inc. 1944
SEMPER FIDELIS: THE U. S. MARINES IN ACTION Another WW-2 propaganda book aimed at boosting enlistments	Ayling, K. Houghton Mifflin Company, Boston 1943
SEMPER FIDELIS: THE U. S. MARINES IN WORLD WAR 2 Good factual history for high schools	Asprey, R. W. W. Norton & Co., Inc. 1967
THE STORY OF THE U. S. MARINES For grades 4-6	Hunt, G. Random House, Inc. 1951
THE STRUGGLE FOR GUADALCANAL For grades 5-9	Braum, S. G. P. Putnam's Sons 1969 (IP)
TARAWA: A BATTLE REPORT	Werstein, I. Thomas Y. Crowell Company 1965
U. S. MARINES IN ACTION	Elder, A. Whitman Publishing Company, Racine, Wis. 1944
UNCLE SAM'S MARINES—HOW THEY FIGHT Description of Boot Camp, brief history and lots of propaganda. Part of series of books for all the Armed Forces of WW-2	Avison, G. The Macmillan Company 1944
THE UNITED STATES MARINES The best history from 1775 through Korea for High School	Montross, L., and W. Miller Houghton Mifflin Company, Boston 1962

WAKE: THE STORY OF A BATTLE — Werstein, I. — Thomas Y. Crowell Company 1964
One of the four books in Werstein's WW-2 series for young readers

WHAT THE CITIZEN SHOULD KNOW ABOUT THE MARINES — Craige, Capt J. — W. W. Norton & Co., Inc. 1941
Very stuffy Handbook which spells out organization and duties of the Corps in stilted, military terms, like "The Officer."

WRITTEN IN SAND — Case, J. — Houghton Mifflin Company, Boston 1945
The invasion of Tripoli in 1805 by Gen Eaton and O'Bannon

FICTION

AUGUSTUS HELPS THE MARINES — LeGrand (Henderson) — The Bobbs-Merrill Company, Indianapolis 1943
Juvenile fiction, ages 6-10

THE COMSTOCK SERIES — Bishop, Lt Col G. — Penn Publishing Co., Inc., Philadelphia
Richard Comstock is the hero. He is a sort of Dick Armstrong of the Marines

THE MARINES HAVE LANDED 1921
Comstock is an enlisted man in war with Mexico

THE MARINES HAVE ADVANCED 1922
Banana Wars

LIEUTENANT COMSTOCK, U. S. MARINE 1922
WW-1

CAPTAIN COMSTOCK, U.S.M.C. 1923

THE EAGLES OF DEATH — Eliot, Maj G. — Frederick Warne & Co., Inc. 1929
By the famous military author, George Fielding Eliott

THE FEMALE MARINE, OR THE ADVENTURES OF MISS LUCY BREWER — Medlicott, A. — DaCopo Press 1966

GAMBLE OF THE MARINES Gamble is captured by the British but he escapes. Fiction based on fact	Toner, R., and M. Barrett Albert Whitman & Co., Chicago	1963
GRACE HARLOWE WITH THE MARINES AT CHATEAU THIERRY Part of the series for High School girls (what the hell was she doing there?)	Flower, J. Henry Altemus Company, Philadelphia	1920
KNIGHTS OF THE COCKPIT: A ROMANTIC EPIC OF THE FLYING MARINES IN HAITI Marine flyer Rorrie O'Rourke is in Haiti	Franklin, I. Dial Press	1931
LADY LEATHERNECK A Dodd-Mead career book for teen-age girls	White, Lt B. Dodd-Mead & Co., Inc.	1945
MAC OF THE MARINES IN AFRICA Sgt MacLain hunts lions in "darkest, equitorial Africa." A Big-Little book.	Smith, M. Whitman Publishing Company, Racine, Wis.	1936
A MARINE, SIR! The peacetime experiences of Wardy Brown after he enters Corps	Carter, E. Cornhill & Co., Boston	1921
MICAT LEADS HIS MARINES The Yankee invasion of Tripoli in 1805	Hamlin, B. Transcript Press, Inc. Dedham, Mass	1937
RHODES OF THE LEATHERNECKS An Army officer is attached to the Marines in Haiti	Litten, F. Dodd, Mead & Co., Inc.	1935
SOLDIERS OF THE SEA	Waite, Capt J. Cupples and Leon	1943
STEVE FLETCHER, U. S. MARINE Boot Camp at San Diego	Johnson, C. John Winston Co., Philadelphia	1957

THUMBS UP! Marine flyers	Montgomery, R. David McKay Company, Inc.	1942
TO THE SHORES OF TRIPOLI O'Bannon and Eaton. Fiction based on fact.	Briggs, B. John Winston Co., Philadelphia	1955

INDEX OF AUTHORS

Unsigned entries are listed by publisher or magazine.

INDEX OF AUTHORS

INDEX OF AUTHORS

INDEX OF AUTHORS

INDEX OF AUTHORS

INDEX OF AUTHORS

INDEX OF AUTHORS